TROTSKY
IN NORWAY

EXILE, 1935–1937

Oddvar K. Høidal

NIU Press
DeKalb, IL

Library of Congress Cataloging-in-Publication Data

Høidal, Oddvar K.
  Trotsky in Norway : exile, 1935–1937 / Oddvar K. Høidal.
    pages cm
  Includes bibliographical references and index.
  ISBN 978-0-87580-474-3 (cloth : alk. paper) — ISBN 978-1-60909-096-8
  (e-book)
  1. Trotsky, Leon, 1879–1940—Travel—Norway. 2. Trotsky, Leon, 1879–1940—
Influence. 3. Communism—Norway—History. 4. Norway—Politics and
government—1905– I. Title.
  DK254.T6H66 2013
  947.084092—dc22
  [B]
                        2013017702

Dedicated to

Anne & Jon Olav

Contents

Preface

LEV TROTSKY EXPERIENCED EXILE in four different countries after Stalin expelled him from the Soviet Union in 1929. Following stays in Turkey and France, he arrived in Norway on June 18, 1935. Initially welcomed by the socialist Labor government, he was eventually interned and deported to Mexico, where he landed in 1937. Although the shortest of his four exiles, it was by no means an insignificant period in his life. For much of his time in Norway, he was more heavily engaged than ever in his attempt to create a Fourth International, a worldwide movement that he hoped would challenge Stalin's hegemony over world communism. His activity included not only planning political strategy with his followers throughout the globe but also the writing and publication of his last major book, *The Revolution Betrayed*. As its title shows, Trotsky regarded himself as the true heir of the Bolshevik Revolution, while maintaining that Stalin had violated its ideals.

Trotsky's refusal to be quiescent in exile, as Stalin originally believed would happen, had repercussions for his Norwegian stay. Controversial from the start within the country, his asylum assumed international significance with the first of Stalin's major show trials in August 1936, leading to Trotsky's eventual expulsion. As this book shows, Trotsky's experience in Norway indicated, after the beginning of the show trials in which he stood accused of terrorism for having allegedly organized a great variety of crimes against the Soviet state, that it was no longer possible for him to gain asylum in any European country due to Russian pressure.

My interest in him was first aroused when working on my biography of Vidkun Quisling, who gained international notoriety during World War II when he collaborated with Hitler before and during the German occupation of Norway. Quisling's party, National Union, sought to make Trotsky's asylum the central issue in the national election of 1936. Other political parties, however, refused to allow Quisling to monopolize this question, in particular after it became much more explosive when Trotsky's asylum led to apparent complications with the Soviet Union. Consequently, for a time the campaign dispute over why Trotsky had been allowed to enter Norway appeared to threaten the survival of the country's first permanent socialist government. Trotsky's stay therefore significantly impacted Norwegian political history in the 1930s.

This study is not, however, merely a biography of Trotsky's time in Norway. Although he is always its main focus, I have sought to provide the book with a much broader framework. This places Trotsky in a perspective that in particular takes into account his earlier attempts to gain access to Norway from Turkey and France, the political situation that he found himself in when he arrived in the country, his effort from Norway to establish a Fourth International that would rival Stalin's leadership of communism, disagreement within Norwegian political opinion over how the government handled Trotsky, and repercussions from his stay that continued to have an effect in Norway even after his expulsion to Mexico.

That he became the center of a major political controversy should not have been a surprise. Trotsky is the most important historical figure to reside in Norway during its modern history. Yet his exile has received relatively little historiographical and biographical attention. Accounts by foreign writers have been insufficient, due primarily to a lack of language skills, which prevented them from making effective use of Norwegian sources. This has resulted in an absence of detail in their books or factual errors that show an inadequate understanding of Norway's politics and history. And unfortunately, in many instances books by foreign authors have been encumbered by both deficiencies. The main purpose of this volume is therefore to provide a thorough English language account of this period of Trotsky's life. As the reference citations show, much of the book's documentation is based on archival sources.

Norwegian historical writing has also been deficient in its attention to this topic, being largely restricted to Yngvar Ustvedt's single book, published in the early 1970s, plus two well-written theses by history students at the University of Oslo. To fill this gap, my research on Trotsky was first published in Norway.* This book is not, however, a direct translation of the Norwegian edition. It has been revised, with emendations for English language readers. Explanatory text has been added when necessary, while some detail superfluous for a non-Norwegian audience has been removed. The book has also been updated to include new information relevant to the subject that has appeared in recent publications.

It should be noted that, as someone who values democratic government, I do not share Trotsky's Marxist ideology. Every effort has been

---

* Høidal, *Trotskij i Norge. Et sår som aldri gror.*

made to provide a critical analysis of his Norwegian exile. Nevertheless, my research findings did create understanding for his plight, especially his experience during the final months of his residence. Quite plausibly, he regarded his stay in Norway as having been the most difficult of his four exiles (prior to his assassination). Trotsky enjoyed more freedom in all other countries that he lived in during the 1930s than he did during his final days in Norway.

A number of persons have been helpful in making this book possible. My wife, Anne Kløvnes Høidal, not only provided the translation for the Norwegian edition but took part in my research on Trotsky from the very beginning. In particular, her linguistic talents and transcription of documents have been extremely valuable. Without her encouragement and assistance, this project might not have been completed.

Members of the Harald Halvorsen family were very gracious in allowing us to visit Sundby, their villa in Storsand, where Trotsky was interned. Not only have they presented insights into the local society in which Trotsky lived, but the son of the family, Harald Halvorsen d.y., has accumulated an extensive collection of material about Trotsky's internment, which he generously shared with me during the time the manuscript was written.

Another person to whom I am in debt is Dagmar Loe, the daughter of Olav Scheflo. Her father was instrumental in gaining Norwegian asylum for Trotsky. Dagmar Loe provided valuable documentary material, articles, and pictures, and shared her personal recollections from the time that Trotsky resided in Norway. She was also instrumental in introducing me to Sverre Opsal, a former editor of Scheflo's newspaper, *Sørlandet*, with whom I corresponded. He made available his store of knowledge about Scheflo, as well as newspaper articles.

When research for the book was in its beginnings, the head archivist at the Norwegian Foreign Ministry, Erik-Wilhelm Norman, served as my guide when I examined the ministry's diplomatic correspondence in journals from the 1930s. Einhart Lorenz, then associate director (*nestleder*) of the Labor Movement's Archive and Library (Arbeiderbevegelsens arkiv og bibliotek) and later professor of history at the University of Oslo, was most helpful during my research at the archive in providing suggestions about relevant source material, as well as mailing copies of additional documents. Former Labor Party Secretary Haakon Lie invited us, without an introduction, to visit his home, where he kindly shared inside information from his vast fund of personal familiarity about his party in the 1930s.

Georg Apenes, director of the Norwegian Data Control Agency, upon learning of my project, quickly made available family letters and newspaper articles that shed light on Trotsky at the time of his arrival in Mexico. Sven G. Holtsmark, senior researcher at the Institute of Defense Studies in Oslo, sent me documents from Russian collections that pertained to Trotsky in Norway. Professor of history Ole Kristian Grimnes at the University of Oslo has over the years made inquiries on my behalf about pertinent questions that arose while researching and writing the book. He and his wife, Britt Grimnes, also most kindly provided shelter during several research visits. Arnfinn Moland, director of the Norwegian Resistance Museum in Oslo, gave good advice when preparation for the Norwegian edition was in its final phase.

Judith Wilson at the Houghton Library provided valued assistance in obtaining copies of documents from the Exile Papers of Leon Trotsky at Harvard University. Elena Danielson and the staff at the Hoover Institution, Stanford University, were most helpful. Anita Burdman Feferman shared interesting background information about Jean van Heijenoort and Wexhall, where Trotsky resided for most of his stay in Norway. Special thanks to Acquisitions Editor Amy Farranto of the Northern Illinois University Press for her collegial work in bringing the book project to fruition.

Travel grants for research were provided by the Norwegian Foreign Ministry through the Consulate General in New York and by the Norwegian Non-Fiction Writers and Translators Association, which also made available a stipend toward completion of the project. The Labor Movement's Archive and Library generously permitted its illustrations to be used at no cost. Bernt Rougthvedt read an earlier version of the manuscript, resulting in critical, but positive analysis. Professor Emeritus Åsmund Egge of the University of Oslo and independent scholar Lars T. Lih (history of Russia and the Soviet Union) provided trenchant peer reviews. Dagmar Loe read the chapter dealing with Trotsky's visit to the Kristiansand area in southern Norway, while Harald Halvorsen d.y. read segments of the manuscript that pertained to Trotsky's internment at Sundby. Both supplied valuable insights. Any errors in the book, however, are, of course, my responsibility.

—Oddvar K. Høidal
San Diego, California, 2013

TROTSKY
IN NORWAY

Prologue

IN THE LATE AFTERNOON OF SATURDAY, December 19, 1936, a procession of three automobiles left an isolated farm south of Oslo. With its splendid view of the fjord and surrounding landscape, Sundby for the last several months had been the residence of the most famous international figure to guest Norway since Kaiser Wilhelm II cruised the fjords during his summer vacations. But unlike what the former German emperor had experienced, the more recent visitor's stay had not been free of unpleasantness. Since the end of August he had been under police guard. Now, accompanied by his wife, he was leaving the country. The police had made careful preparations. The car that Lev and Natalia Sedova Trotsky entered was equipped with special shades to hide its occupants' identity. Their escorts were not in uniform but in civilian attire. Having traveled the short distance down the hill to the fjord, a special ferry was waiting to transport the three cars alone to the eastern shore. Here the cortege drove north to the small port of Fagerstrand, arriving at 5:25 p.m.

Fifteen minutes later a tanker bearing the prosaic name *Ruth* emerged out of the winter darkness and docked. The middle-aged couple, accompanied by the leader of the police unit, got out of their car and wearily climbed on board their last Norwegian living quarters. The police had succeeded. Their prisoners had not been recognized during the drive. Only a few people on board the tanker knew their identity. At 7:00 p.m. the *Ruth* left the dock and began its journey south along the dark Oslo Fjord, out toward the stormy North Sea.[1]

Neither Lev nor Natalia were looking forward to their voyage. Natalia was so worn out from packing the couple's belongings in box after box that she did not have the strength to write to their son, Lev Sedov, in Paris.[2]

Trotsky feared the effect of the journey on his wife, who suffered severely from seasickness whenever they traveled by ship. As for himself, Trotsky confided to a French friend that his health, as so often during his Norwegian sojourn, was not good.[3]

Both were tired and dispirited as they left Sundby.[4] They had received hardly any time to prepare for their departure. Minister of Justice Trygve Lie, who dealt with Trotsky on behalf of the government, personally informed him on December 18 that he and Natalia had to exit Norway within a time limit of twenty-four hours. Without their participation or approval, the Norwegian government had made all the necessary preparations for them to leave, including the obligatory passport for the Trotskys' entry into Mexico, their next haven.[5]

Their departure was therefore precipitous. Trotsky left complaining that he had only 100 *kroner* in his possession.[6] He was forced to depart without being able to pay his personal physician for services rendered.[7] What mattered most for him, however, was to make certain that his precious books and documents, the source material for his income as an author, accompanied him on his continued exile. He and Natalia had "only a few hours" to pack, which occurred in "an atmosphere of feverish haste." While Lev wrote his last letters from Norway, Natalia began the hard work of packing their belongings. Her work continued during the following day, with Lev joining in the rush to complete the packing of his books. During those long hours, they were helped by their guards, who nailed down each crate as it was filled.[8]

The fact that he was being deported to Mexico did not come as a surprise to Trotsky, only the manner in which it occurred. By December he was anxious to leave Norway in order to escape internment, but under his own terms. Unless this was agreed to, he refused to apply for a Mexican visa.[9] He protested against the government arranging his departure, insisting instead that he be allowed to make his own plans. Specifically, he wanted to discuss the matter with his closest confidants in Norway—Konrad Knudsen, a Labor Party journalist and newly elected member of parliament; Håkon Meyer, a leading Labor Party intellectual; and Walter Held, a German political refugee and Trotsky's most devoted disciple in the country.[10]

Held worked continuously to gain permission for the Trotskys to take the travel route that they wished to follow. In particular, he did everything in his power to avoid direct transport to Mexico. He argued that Natalia's delicate health could not endure a sea voyage of three weeks.[11] He was in daily and fruitless contact with the Ministry of Justice to gain access to Trotsky. Trotsky's supporters wanted him to be allowed to travel out of Europe via Belgium and France.[12] Gerard Rosenthal, his French attorney, was working hard to secure the necessary transit visas from these two countries to permit Lev and Natalia to journey to Mexico via Antwerp and Paris. Rosenthal traveled to Norway in this endeavor, arriving on December 24.[13]

His trip, however, proved to be entirely fruitless. Trygve Lie would not permit any contact between Trotsky and his confidants except in the presence of the police. Trotsky refused categorically to accept this condition. But with the authorities having the upper hand, in the end he was left with no choice. Under protest he resignedly accepted the inevitable outcome. Unlike previous deportations within the Soviet Union and his expulsion to Turkey, when he had physically attempted to resist expulsion, he was forced to accept the government's course of action as his only option.[14]

As he had bitterly experienced so often during his internment, Norwegian officials always had dominant control. Not only did they determine the time and the manner of his departure, they also sought to manipulate news of the event. On Friday, December 18, the day before the *Ruth* was scheduled to lift anchor, the government called a secret press conference. It was represented by none other than the key decision makers who had determined the outcome of Trotsky's exile—Prime Minister Johan Nygaardsvold, Foreign Minister Halvdan Koht, and Justice Minister Lie. Present were a formidable number of media journalists from nearly all the leading establishment newspapers, telegraph bureaus, and Norwegian Radio, NRK. The ministers provided confidential information concerning Trotsky's upcoming journey to Mexico. They urged the assembled newsmen not to publicize the event until the Trotskys were ashore in their new country of exile.[15]

Displaying a solidarity with the government that now is anachronistic among members of the fourth estate, the journalists maintained their silence. Not until Wednesday, December 23, after a Swedish newspaper had broken the story, did the Oslo press print the news of Trotsky's departure for Mexico four days earlier.[16] Only then did his supporters learn that he was already at sea and that assurances to the contrary from the government had been a subterfuge.[17]

The officials had also sought to maintain the illusion that Trotsky was still in the country by having the police guard at Sundby continue its normal routine as if the Trotskys were still present.[18] Similarly, the staff at the house was under strict instructions not to reveal the news of their departure. However, someone obviously failed to keep the secret. When Natalia and Lev were driven away, all the children in the grammar school at Storsand had assembled to watch them leave.[19] Fortunately for the authorities in Oslo, this interesting development remained isolated within the local population.

Although he protested against the way in which he was forced to leave, Trotsky was anxious to depart. Writing to Håkon Meyer on December 16, Trotsky emphasized that the Mexican offer of asylum was an opportunity that had to be taken advantage of immediately lest it be lost.[20] But at the same time he feared for his security. This was his primary motivation when he insisted on being allowed to meet with his friends and supporters in Norway. Because of his distrust of Norwegian officials, he feared the possibility of being lured into a trap. The Soviet Union's network of agents was constantly on his mind. The ship might be stopped at sea, whereupon he and Natalia would be seized by the NKVD. Or the vessel might be torpedoed. Others shared his doubts. His son Lev voiced strong reservations from Paris, and his French attorney, Rosenthal, reminded him of Lord Kitchener's fate.*[21] Trotsky therefore embarked on the voyage in a state of anxiety. He wrote on December 18 to Lev in France that in the event anything happened to him and Natalia, his two sons, Lev and Sergei, were to be his heirs, and that this, his last letter from Norway, should be considered his will.[22] Trotsky gave similar instructions to his French attorney.[23]

His fear of a Soviet plot was shared by Norwegian officials, which motivated their insistence on maintaining the greatest secrecy possible in order to provide for the Trotskys' safety. Not only did they favor moving him out of the country as quickly as possible once his asylum permit expired, but they did not want to assume the onus of having failed to provide him with adequate protection. Specifically, the government feared that if it became known that the couple was traveling on the *Ruth*, the NKVD might succeed in placing an explosive device on board the ship. Trotsky later wrote: "My wife and I could by no means consider the latter fear as unfounded." Therefore, when it became clear that the authorities under no circumstances would allow him to determine his travel plans or even to have a

* Lord Herbert Kitchener, the British secretary of state for war, died in 1916 when his warship struck a German mine.

last meeting with his supporters, he reluctantly accepted the government's arrangements because his safety was a matter of mutual concern. As he put it: "Our own security coincided in this instance with the security of the Norwegian vessel and its crew."[24]

When he left Norway, Trotsky felt only contempt for its socialist government.[25] It had blocked him at every turn during his internment. But his negative feelings did not extend to the country and its people. In one of his final letters, he insisted that he and Natalia were leaving without any bitterness toward Norwegians but instead held great affection for them.[26] His viewpoint did not change once he had left:

> We carried away with us warm remembrances of the marvelous land of forests and fjords, of the snow beneath the January sun, of skis and sleighs, of children with china blue eyes, corn-colored hair, and of the slightly morose and slow-moving but serious and honest people. Norway goodbye.[27]

The anxiety, dejection, and weariness that he felt when he left stood in direct contrast with the mood that he had experienced when he first met the country eighteen months earlier. He and Natalia arrived by boat on a bright sunlit morning in June 1935. Their trip up the Oslo Fjord could not help but impress anyone who experienced it for the first time. The wooded hillsides that extend down to the sea, the blue water of the fjord, and the brightly painted houses that dot the shoreline—a combination of natural and man-made beauty—create a feeling of tranquility and delight. The narrowing fjord suddenly opens up into a large basin at whose end lies Oslo, the city and surrounding islands mirrored in the waters of the harbor. The entrance to Oslo by sea is among the most magnificent approaches to any capital in the world.

Trotsky did not arrive unheralded as he followed Natalia down the gangplank shortly after the ship from Antwerp had docked at 7:00 a.m. on Tuesday, June 18. Although an attempt had been made to keep the news secret, members of the press, undoubtedly having been tipped off, were present to record in word and photos what was regarded as a historic event.[28] The Trotsky party, which also included two male secretaries, was quickly whisked away from the inquiring journalists. His hosts immediately drove him out of the city into the anonymity of the Norwegian countryside. He continued, however, to be impressed by the landscape.

Several times during the drive he insisted that they stop so that he could get out and admire a particularly striking view.[29]

His initial enthusiasm did not diminish. In his first interview, published at the end of July, Lev declared that in the short time he had been in the country, he had become completely captivated by the landscape, the beauty of nature, and the people.[30] By this time he and Natalia were settled down in a villa named Wexhall, located in a small hamlet northwest of Oslo near the little town of Hønefoss. It appeared as if exile in Norway would meet his expectations. He wrote already at the end of June that he was pleased with his housing accommodations. He and Natalia had been received in a warm, comradely manner by his host family, and he was adapting to the country's way of life, which he found to be quite pleasant.[31]

For Trotsky to declare himself satisfied with two rooms in a rented house in isolated Norway, far removed from the mainstream of political events in Europe, indicated the extent to which his political fortunes had declined. Thirty years earlier he had been the firebrand of the Revolution of 1905 in St. Petersburg, denouncing in flamboyant speeches the government of Nicholas II from his position as chairman of the St. Petersburg Soviet. Both before and after the 1905 revolution he had been, from an early age, one of Russia's leading revolutionary exiles, with connections in Western Europe and the United States. With the outbreak of the Russian Revolution, despite previous differences with Lenin, the two entered into a close relationship during the turmoil-laden period that immediately followed the collapse of the Romanov dynasty in March 1917. Trotsky served as Lenin's right-hand man, rising to become once more chairman of the Soviet in the Russian capital. From this key post, in complicity with Lenin, he organized and led the successful Bolshevik overthrow of Alexander Kerensky's Provisional Government. The foundation for the Union of Soviet Socialist Republics had thereupon been created.

The new revolutionary government, however, appeared to be in immediate danger. Forced to sign a disastrous peace with Germany while the First World War was still being fought, the Bolshevik government created both internal and external enemies. To varying degrees, most of its political opponents within Russia backed the loosely united White armies that challenged the Bolsheviks in a bitter civil war. The White cause was supported by the Allied Powers, who not only resented the Lenin government's withdrawal from the war but also detested it for obvious ideological reasons. At this critical time Lenin appointed Trotsky as commissar of war, responsible for managing the military effort against the Whites. He responded brilliantly, creating and molding the new Red Army that successfully defeated the Whites, thereby ensuring the survival of the new communist regime. As Walter Laqueur has written, "The Soviet Union probably owes its survival during the early period of its existence more to Trotsky than to anyone else except Lenin."[32]

Trotsky's position in the government, however, was based largely on Lenin's support. Not having been a member of the Bolsheviks prior to 1917, he was disliked by many of the party's old-time leaders. Although popular with the masses because of his brilliant speaking ability and the dashing figure he cut as head of the Red Army, Trotsky had no political base of his own. Therefore, when Lenin became incapacitated by a series of strokes, dying in 1924, Trotsky stood isolated within the government. He was easily outmaneuvered by his nemesis, Joseph Stalin, who first had Trotsky ousted from his position as commissar of war and then expelled from the governing Politburo.

Unlike other prominent communists who sought to make peace with Stalin after he had defeated them, Trotsky remained defiant and was exiled to Siberia in 1928. But Stalin still regarded him as a threat. He did not dare to execute Trotsky at this time because of the residual popularity that he still enjoyed. Nor did Stalin wish to have him remain in the U.S.S.R. as a potential center of opposition. For Stalin, the solution was to send Trotsky into foreign exile.[33] Thus, beginning in 1929, Trotsky entered upon his wandering travels, first to Turkey, then to France in 1933, and now, in 1935, to Norway.

In exile he could only count upon the limited support of a few dedicated followers, scattered in small groups throughout the world, but predominantly in Western Europe and the United States. They were attracted to Trotsky because of his former renown, because of their opposition to Stalin's transformation of the Soviet Union into a one-man dictatorship, because of their conviction that Trotsky, not Stalin, correctly followed the principles of true Marxism, or because of their natural inclination to side with the underdog. But inside the U.S.S.R. Stalin during the 1930s mercilessly removed from authority within the party all persons who were sympathetic to the deposed former second-in-command.

Trotsky's strengths and failings had been on display during his rapid climb to power—and equally during his meteoric decline. He possessed brilliant speaking and writing ability,[34] and he was regarded after Lenin as one of the most able Marxist theorists within the governing elite. When inspired, he could be a highly effective organizer, as shown by his zeal both in preparing for the Bolshevik takeover of power and in his leadership of the Red Army. Because of his striking presence, he was able to gain considerable popularity among those who heard him speak or who witnessed his dramatic actions.

On a closer, more personal level, however, he was not successful. He did not have many friends, due in part to his personality. He could be haughty and sarcastic toward those whom he considered intellectually inferior, not the best way to inspire backing. He always assumed his position was correct, and he insisted on having his way. But while he was uncompromising when asserting his superiority, after Lenin became crippled by cerebral hemorrhages, Trotsky at critical times failed to take decisive action that could have resulted in successful countermoves against his political opponents. With Lenin incapacitated, Trotsky was left without an anchor. The result was that Stalin had little difficulty in gaining allies who supported him in the political struggle to emasculate Trotsky's power.

For a long time Trotsky underestimated Stalin, believing him to be an undistinguished political hack with little intellectual ability. His misjudgment continued while in exile. Trotsky assumed that Stalin was simply turning the Soviet Union into a state dominated by its bureaucratic elite, rather than a dictatorship based on terror, completely under the power of one man. Trotsky therefore persisted in regarding himself as a true communist and retained his allegiance for the Soviet Union.[35] He hoped to replace Stalin as its leader, but he in no way repudiated the totalitarian nature of the Soviet state.

The man who took up asylum in Norway was physically quite different from the imposing figure who had held world attention as little as a decade earlier, and who had been regarded as a key player in Soviet politics until the late 1920s. Although only 55, the same age as Stalin, his great antagonist, the years had taken their toll on Trotsky. The dramatic, dark-haired man of action had become a grandfatherly figure who had gained weight, and whose hair had largely turned white. Because he had removed his goatee, his fellow passengers on the three-day voyage from Antwerp failed to recognize him. Not only did his years in exile weigh heavily upon him, but so too did the crushing effects of many family tragedies. Both daughters that he had had with his first wife were dead. Nina, the youngest, died of consumption in 1928, while Zina committed suicide in 1933. Their husbands in the Soviet Union were imprisoned. None of the members of his immediate family in the Soviet Union, including his first wife, survived Stalin. Of his two sons with Natalia, only one, Lev Sedov, nicknamed Lyova, lived in relative safety in Paris. The other, Sergei Sedov, had insisted on remaining in Russia in the mistaken belief that his noninvolvement in politics—he was an engineer—would permit him to lead a normal life. He was instead arrested by the NKVD. The last letter that his parents received from him was in December 1934.[36] Although they continued to hope all during their stay in Norway that he could be saved, his fate was sealed. Sergei was executed in 1937.

For Natalia, the plight of Sergei was a constant worry. Still small and petite, her face was ravaged with care, and her hair, like her husband's, was turning gray. The time when she had been a beautiful, rebellious young art student at the Sorbonne while actively participating in the Russian revolutionary movement seemed as if in another lifetime. Lev had met her in Paris in 1902 while in exile and had fallen completely in love, abandoning his first wife and two young daughters. Natalia had thereafter shared his triumphs and tragedies. She had been the director of the theater and arts in the Soviet Union when Trotsky was at the height of his influence. But the days when Lenin played with her children in the halls of the Kremlin were now long past. She had followed her husband into exile, serving as his most loyal supporter, helper, and aide, a role she would continue to play long after his murder.

Despite personal misfortunes that would have crippled a person with less internal strength, Trotsky was determined to persevere. From Norway he intended to continue the struggle, however one-sided, against Stalin. His stay in Norway would therefore be an important chapter in his life. It would also have unexpected effects on the politics of his host country. The physical surroundings, so very different, that marked his arrival and departure stand out because they symbolize the disparity between the cautious optimism he held at the time he came to Norway and the resignation he felt when he left. The sunny June morning when he disembarked in Oslo, causing a media sensation, contrasts sharply with the bleak December evening when his ship moved away from a deserted pier in a small insignificant port, with not a word being printed in the press. But while these two disparate days serve as the parameters of his Norwegian exile, they do not include the totality of his interest in the country: Norway for many years had been a desired place of refuge for Trotsky before he finally gained admission.

1 Early Attempts to Gain Asylum in Scandinavia

> I hope the time is not distant when the working class also can
> welcome those persons it wants as its guests. . . . We must hope that
> Trotsky lives until we obtain a government which overturns the
> resolution adopted by the present government.
> —Olav Scheflo, Storting debate, April 22, 1929

FROM THE TIME HE BEGAN HIS TURKISH EXILE, Trotsky longed to escape. He wished to find a haven in Western Europe that would allow him direct contact with the mainstream of European and world politics. Instead, he was confined to an island in the Sea of Marmara, Prinkipo.* It was here Byzantine emperors used to send princes who were out of favor, frequently after having blinded them.[1] Although Stalin most likely had no knowledge of this morbid historical fact, he would have relished it since his primary purpose for sending Trotsky into exile was to keep him isolated politically.

Contrary to what he had expected, Trotsky was destined to spend four and a half years in Turkey, interrupted by only one brief excursion out of the country. This period of seclusion in a distant corner of Europe was not due to restrictions from his host country. The Turkish government treated him with utmost consideration. What prevented him from obtaining residence in Western Europe in 1929 and during the following years was his notorious reputation. He inspired both fear and loathing among the European bourgeoisie, who felt threatened by the successful communist takeover in Russia, a seizure of power that Trotsky, next to Lenin, had come to symbolize, despite Stalin's best efforts *already* to rewrite history. Even in major Western countries with socialist prime ministers, such as England and Germany, the

---

* Prinkipo is the Greek name for the island. The Turkish name is Buyuk Ada, or Great Island.

antipathy created by Trotsky made it impossible for him to secure political refuge. Both nations rejected Trotsky's application for asylum out of hand.[2] That the British government in particular felt compelled to do so was revealing. As the champion of the right of asylum prior to World War I, England had harbored a wide variety of European radicals, including socialists, anarchists, and nationalists. The war and the ensuing Russian Revolution changed this forever. In the twentieth century European states would adopt a much more restricted and self-serving viewpoint concerning this principle.

It was only after his application had been rejected by the German government that Trotsky considered smaller states, including Norway, as an alternative. He did not apply personally but allowed his supporters to take the initiative. They appealed to the socialist Labor Party (*Arbeiderpartiet*) and the National Federation of Unions (*Landsorganisasjonen*—L.O.), asking them to intercede and obtain a residence permit for Trotsky. However, while he was not personally involved, he followed the effort with considerable interest.[3]

The Labor Party sought at first to approach the government privately because of the delicate nature of this mission. Its vice-chairman, Professor Edvard Bull, discussed the subject on April 4, 1929, with Prime Minister Johan Ludwig Mowinckel, whose Liberal (*Venstre*) minority government was dependent on support from other nonsocialist parties, the Conservatives (*Høire*) and the Agrarian Party (*Bondepartiet*). Mowinckel promised he would bring the matter up for discussion with his cabinet, which he did on the tenth. When Bull phoned the prime minister the following morning to learn of its decision, he received the disappointing news that the ministers had unanimously rejected Trotsky's admission on the grounds that they could not take responsibility for ensuring his safety.[4]

Since his contact with Bull had been confidential, Mowinckel hoped that the matter had been concluded. He discovered, however, that the socialists had no intention of abandoning Trotsky's case. A number of their top figures were favorably disposed, having known him when the party belonged to the Communist International. Furthermore, the Labor Party believed that the act of refusing him asylum might prove embarrassing for the government. Indicating the importance that they attached to the question, the party's chairman, Oscar Torp, and L. O. chairman Halvard Olsen met with the prime minister on April 16. Mowinckel was handed a written request that Trotsky be granted residence. As basis for this formal appeal, the labor movement insisted that this concerned the right of asylum—whether Norway should offer haven to persons who were persecuted for their political beliefs.[5]

The government thereby was forced to take a public stand on this controversial question. Its response came quickly in the form of a press release on the following day. In a brief, one-sentence statement it declared that the cabinet, despite favoring the right of asylum, could not accede to the request because "of the difficulties associated with the necessary maintenance of Trotsky's security."[6]

The refusal set off a bitter polemical debate in both the party press and in the parliament, the Storting. The Labor Party quickly demolished the pretext that Trotsky could not be granted entry because of the expense of providing for his security. Mowinckel himself later admitted that sufficient resources were available to guarantee Trotsky's safety if the cabinet had agreed to allow him asylum. The nonsocialist representatives and their press, however, were by no means on the defensive in the debate but sought to turn the controversy to their advantage. They charged that socialism in general was an evil, as the example of Trotsky clearly showed. Their press emphasized in particular the lack of freedom in the U.S.S.R., the excesses committed by Trotsky during the Russian Revolution and Civil War, and the Labor Party's alleged hypocrisy in championing only political asylum for persons who shared its convictions.[7] Some nonsocialists furthermore pointed out that the issue of Trotsky's asylum was being utilized by the Labor Party not only against its bourgeois opponents but also against the communists.

This observation was quite accurate. The controversy presented the Labor Party with an excellent opportunity to strike a blow against its enemy on the left. Although the Norwegian Communist Party was in decline, it still retained some political influence within the working class, having gained four percent of the popular vote and three parliamentary seats in the 1927 election. Olav Scheflo was the Labor Party's chief advocate in favor of admitting Trotsky. He had earlier been a prominent communist leader when the party was formed but later rejoined the Labor Party. Not surprisingly, the communists bitterly attacked him, charging Scheflo and Sverre Støstad, another Labor representative and former leading communist, with being "renegades" when they spoke in favor of Trotsky during the debate.[8] The Labor Party, however, occupied the best position in this encounter. It drove home the point that the communists, when opposing Trotsky's entry, were allied with the bourgeoisie, or as the Labor Party put it, "with the most reactionary parties."[9]

At the heart of the disagreement, however, was neither the issue of Trotsky's past nor the fact that competing political parties wished to turn the question of his admission to their advantage, although both were important. The nonsocialists were also in opposition because they believed that Trotsky not only could create internal political instability but, even more importantly, because his asylum could have a negative impact on Norway's foreign relations. Although there is no direct evidence indicating Soviet pressure at this time, political leaders, including the prime minister, were fully aware of possible negative repercussions should Stalin's sworn enemy be granted refuge.[10]

The Labor Party, on the other hand, insisted that the principle of the right of political asylum should take precedent over all other considerations. As a result, the Mowinckel administration found itself in an embarrassing predicament because, as a liberal government, it could not openly repudiate the right of asylum. Mowinckel attempted to argue that the issue really did not involve this principle but rather the threat to order and stability that Trotsky's admittance might pose. Scheflo tellingly countered by pointing out that if Mowinckel's definition of granting political asylum was adhered to, only noncontroversial persons would be eligible to receive asylum.[11]

Because the moral advantage rested with the Labor Party, and also because the dispute exacerbated the highly emotional ideological, political, and personal divisions that separated the socialists from their bourgeois and communist opponents, the debate about Trotsky's asylum occurred in a charged atmosphere created by strong, at times intemperate, language that exceeded the norms of even the ordinary level of inflammatory partisan oratory that was standard in the Storting during the 1920s. However, the fiery language, not unexpectedly, failed to persuade almost anyone to deviate from their fixed positions. As expected, when the vote was taken on April 22, the two communist representatives joined sixty-nine nonsocialists in voting against the resolution that the government reconsider its decision. The fifty-one Labor members were joined by only one nonsocialist in favor of the motion.[12]

This outcome made it clear that Trotsky had no chance of finding asylum in Norway as long as a nonsocialist government held office. However, this did not end the matter. The Labor Party's commitment meant that if it ever came to power, the possibility of Trotsky being granted admission was very much a reality. As Scheflo declared in the Storting: "I hope the time is not distant when the working class also can welcome those persons it wants as its guests. . . . We must hope that Trotsky lives until we obtain a government which overturns the resolution adopted by the present government."[13] Scheflo's hope would be realized in 1935, when Trotsky was given admission by a Labor government. But contrary to what the Labor representatives expounded in 1929, their socialist government, when faced with serious problems created by Trotsky's presence, would act in much the same way that Mowinckel's Liberal government had done some seven years earlier.

Despite the disappointments he experienced during his first year at Prinkipo, Trotsky did not abandon hope that he might be able to move. In 1930 he sought to gain admission to a Western European country on the grounds of alleged ill health. A press release from Prinkipo, dated March 19, declared that his physical condition had deteriorated during the last two- or three-month period. In addition to his old maladies, referring to his chronic health problems in the Soviet Union, he now supposedly had developed heart trouble. Added "acute sufferings from gout" made it necessary for him to undergo a cure at a mineral spring, and the press statement indicated that he intended to seek a visa for the summer season.[14]

Showing that the Labor Party had by no means lost interest in his fate, its main Oslo paper, *Arbeiderbladet* (The Labor Paper) editorialized two days later, stressing that he suffered from a lung inflammation. But while it alleged that the need for him to receive medical attention was obvious, *Arbeiderbladet* indicated that he unquestionably would face difficulties. The Soviet government and the communists on one side and the forces of reaction and cowardice in Western Europe on the other, including the Norwegian government, would join together in this case.[15] While this editorial had no more immediate results than had the fruitless effort to help Trotsky get out of Turkey in 1929, it nevertheless had some significance for the future. When he later gained admission to Norway, a major justification provided by the Labor government was that he and Natalia were both ill, needing rest and a period of convalescence.

Furthermore, in 1930 his sympathizers, led by Scheflo, had by no means given up on the idea of getting Trotsky into the country. Having been unsuccessful when attempting to apply the principle of the right of asylum, their next move was to try to arrange a lecture series in Norway for the world-renowned exile, making use of the Norwegian Student Association (*Studentersamfundet*) in their quest.

During much of the 1930s, the Student Association created considerable furor because its board was controlled by a radical socialist group, Mot Dag (Toward Day). Although it lacked a mass following, being restricted almost entirely to persons with an academic background, the organization enjoyed both attention and notoriety because of its influence at the University, a major center of Norwegian culture and political debate.* Earlier, in the 1920s, Mot Dag had been affiliated at different times with both the Labor Party and the communists, but in the early 1930s it adhered to its independent version of looking at the world through a Marxist prism, maintaining that its view represented true communism, in contrast to the deviations of both the Labor Party's increasingly reformist line and the Norwegian communists' slavish conformity to dictates from Moscow.

Karl Evang, later renowned as Norway's health director, wrote to Prinkipo in his capacity as the Student Association's chairman in mid-November 1930 and invited Trotsky to address the organization.[16] Evang included a brief introductory note from Scheflo, informing Trotsky that the Student Association's board of directors consisted of "reliable persons" who had all been members of the Communist International and recommending that he accept an invitation to come to Norway.[17]

Despite the fact that this offered a much wanted opportunity to be exploited for the purpose of leaving Turkey, Trotsky was somewhat guarded in his response, understandably so in the light of previous disappointments. He declared that he was willing to present a lecture, but unlike Evang, who optimistically maintained that no foreign speaker invited by his organization had ever been denied entry,[18] Trotsky expressed doubt about the government's willingness to grant a visa. Nevertheless, he wished the association the best in its attempt to secure a permit for him.[19]

Later events showed that his reservations were justified. The Student Association waited until after the New Year before contacting the Justice Department. The minister of justice, Arne Sunde, himself a member of the association, responded by declaring that he could see no reason for denying the request. But when this became public knowledge on January 5, 1931, another press furor arose over whether Trotsky should be allowed into the country, even if only temporarily to address a public meeting.[20]

This time the nonsocialists were more divided. The more conservative newspapers were hostile as usual.[21] However, the radical wing of the Liberal Party supported the Justice Department's decision.[22] The Labor Party warmly favored admission, while the communists, as expected, responded vehemently and negatively.[23]

* Norway in the 1930s had only one university, in Oslo.

Within the Mowinckel government a number of the ministers did not share Sunde's opinion, and he was criticized for his statement. Nevertheless, his decision was allowed to stand, but the terms by which Trotsky would be admitted were made much more restrictive than Sunde had originally intended.[24] Trotsky would be allowed to stay for only eight days; he could only visit the Oslo area; he had to have a valid passport with return and transit visas valid for two months from the date of his entry; he could only hold one lecture, to be presented to the Student Association; he could not talk about Norwegian politics; and he had to reside at a hotel approved by the police.[25] Clearly, the government intended to discourage his visit by formulating the terms of his entrance permit as narrowly as possible in order to limit his freedom of movement.

His reply showed how desperately he wished to get to Western Europe. He answered immediately that he would accept the government's terms unconditionally, despite their narrow restrictions.[26]

The major stumbling block proved to be difficulties in making travel arrangements. Evang wrote to Trotsky on February 18 that the Student Association's attempt to obtain a transit visa through the German legation in Oslo had been rejected by the German Foreign Ministry on the pretext that Trotsky himself had not made a personal application. Evang had the additional bad news that all Norwegian ships stopping in the harbor of Istanbul carried cargoes from Russian Black Sea ports. No shipping company was therefore willing to provide accommodations for Trotsky unless "difficulties do not arrise [sic] with the owners of the cargo."[27] The possibility that Stalin's government, through its legation in Oslo, might not object to Trotsky's visit, was out of the question, as Evang recognized implicitly.

Trotsky therefore was stymied. He could not travel directly by sea from Turkey to Norway because of the obstacle posed by Soviet influence. Nor could he journey via Germany because of the conservative Brüning government's refusal to issue a transit visa. This ended once and for all any possibility for a trip to Norway in 1931.

In the fall of the following year, however, an opportunity arose that in many ways was similar to the failed visit to Norway. At the University of Copenhagen the leaders of the Social Democratic student organization hit on the happy idea of having Trotsky as a speaker on the fifteenth anniversary of the Bolshevik Revolution. Being somewhat more pragmatic than their Norwegian counterparts, they first secured government approval before extending the invitation.[28]

The group's vice-chairman thereupon wrote to Trotsky, who responded immediately at the end of August. He indicated that he "would be very willing" to hold a lecture on the Russian Revolution and insisted that his presentation would only be of "a purely scientific character." He added the assurance that his stay would be restricted to "a very few days," entirely devoted "to the purpose of the lecture." He suggested that his appearance be scheduled for some time during the second half of November.[29]

Although he had been unsuccessful in securing a transit visa for his proposed visit to Norway in 1931, this time it proved easier. The Radical government of Edouard Herriot agreed to allow Trotsky and his small entourage to travel through France but, as he discovered, under the tightest security. Upon arriving outside of Marseilles, they were whisked across France by car to Dunkirk, with only a one-hour stop in Paris.[30]

Traveling by ship, he arrived in Denmark at the west-coast port of Esbjerg on November 23 and proceeded on to Copenhagen. His presence created a sensation, with a large number of journalists providing coverage, including the international press. For the duration of his stay in Copenhagen, every effort was made to keep his whereabouts secret. He was continuously under police protection.[31]

Publicly, the highlight of his visit came on November 27, 1932, when he spoke to an audience of 2000, which was unusually large for a political lecture in Scandinavia. His two-hour address proved for some to be an anticlimax. Speaking in German with a Russian accent, he was difficult to understand.[32] Also, in accordance with the terms under which he was admitted to Denmark, he took pains to avoid controversy. His analysis of the Russian Revolution, therefore, was presented in a professorial, interpretive tone, not as a personal account by a leading protagonist who had been an active participant during a critical period in history.

Apart from his speech, the last public address that he would ever make before a live audience, Trotsky's appearances were limited. He was interviewed by CBS. Despite what he termed his bad English, he was pleased to have the opportunity of gaining publicity in the United States.[33] He attended a couple of evening get-togethers with prominent Danish journalists and educational personalities, arranged by his student hosts.[34] Much more important from his perspective was his chance to have a hurried meeting with followers from several European countries. This allowed some of the members of his "Left Opposition" to discuss key questions with him as a group, rather than being forced to make long, individual trips to Turkey.[35]

While he enjoyed having contact with supporters in Western Europe, he focused his attention in particular on trying to alter the terms of his temporary visit. Through Danish intermediaries, he appealed to the socialist Stauning administration to grant him a permanent residence permit, but this was immediately rejected.[36]

Undaunted, Trotsky sought to use every avenue possible to extend his sojourn. Even before his arrival in Denmark, he had his main representative in France, Raymond Molinier, resume contact with the Norwegian Student Association about whether it would be willing to have Trotsky come to Oslo to speak.[37] Molinier wrote to the association on November 15, which enthusiastically telegraphed back that its members not only were highly interested in having Trotsky lecture in Norway but that they would also write to Stockholm to help arrange a similar appearance in Sweden.[38]

The political situation in Norway, however, was different from the previous year. Mowinckel's cabinet had been succeeded by a new Agrarian government. The Agrarians in the 1930s were more nationalistic than the Liberals, with some elements of the party, including its minister of defense, Vidkun Quisling, expressing not only strong antisocialist views but also admiration for fascism. Even prior to Trotsky's departure from Denmark, the Justice Department recommended against permitting him to enter the country.[39]

Similarly, Trotsky's attempt to secure a visa for Sweden was turned down. In both Sweden and Denmark, Soviet diplomatic representatives allegedly applied pressure to make certain that his quest would be fruitless.[40] His person was also anathema among dedicated Danish anticommunists. This included even a member of the royal family, Prince Aage, who openly denounced Trotsky.[41]

The controversy concerning his visit to Copenhagen therefore proved to be much more contentious than the Danish government had originally anticipated, ruling out any extension of his temporary visa. During his final hours in Copenhagen, showing how truly desperate he was, he attempted to procrastinate, trying to waste as much time as possible so that he would be unable to reach the ship that was scheduled to carry him out of the country. However, the government intervened resolutely, making certain that he, Natalia, and their foreign entourage were driven by the police to Esbjerg so that they left Denmark even prior to the expiration of Trotsky's permit.[42]

In this manner he was unceremoniously ushered out of the country on December 2. His return journey to Turkey remained as restricted as the trip he had experienced on his way to Denmark. Police guarded his every move in each nation where he disembarked—Belgium, France, and Italy. On December 12 he was back in Turkey.

This time, however, his stay in Turkey did not prove long. Thanks to energetic work on his behalf by advocates in France, the Daladier government agreed to allow him refuge. He landed in France on July 24, 1933. Although the French communists were strongly opposed, he at first avoided notoriety and settled down to an anonymous existence, his places of residence being known only to a limited number of his key lieutenants and French officials.

In Norway the announcement of his arrival in France immediately sparked renewed interest within the Student Association. Only a few days later, its current chairman, doctor Carl Viggo Lange, wrote what by now had become a standard invitation. He informed Trotsky that "the reactionary government" that had refused him entry at the time of the Copenhagen trip no longer held office, having been replaced by a "radical bourgeois government" of Liberals, namely Mowinckel's third government. Since Mowinckel's previous cabinet had granted Trotsky a temporary visa in 1931, the association assumed that he no doubt would be allowed entry if he agreed to come to Oslo, and Lange expressed the hope that Trotsky could address the organization already during the coming fall semester.[43]

The long-expected reply did not come until early October. Trotsky's tone was rather reserved. He explained his delay in answering as due to his move to France and the present negative state of his health. He declared himself willing in principle to hold a lecture in Norway, but the matter would have to be postponed for the next few months because of his physical condition. He therefore asked that the question be put off until the start of the next year.[44]

The Student Association, however, was not willing to wait. Lange's successor, the engineer Kristian Gleditsch, wrote already on December 11, inviting Trotsky to Oslo during the spring semester. Gleditsch was inspired by the Labor Party's strong victory in the national election earlier that fall, in which the socialists gained almost half the seats in the Storting. He declared that this result made it impossible for the current minority Liberal government to deny Trotsky an entry permit. Furthermore, much too confidently, he held out the possibility that the Labor Party might come to power as early as February 1934, forming a government that under no circumstances would refuse an application on Trotsky's behalf.[45]

Not receiving an immediate reply, Gleditsch wrote again at the very end of 1933.[46] To ensure that Trotsky and his followers in France understood that he would receive a friendly reception, Gleditsch stressed that the Student Association continued to be led by "independent communists" belonging to Mot Dag.[47]

This time Trotsky did respond, but he continued to react guardedly, admonishing the association to act discreetly. This would allow for a better chance for success. He nevertheless declared that April would be the best month for him to give a lecture during the spring semester.[48]

Gleditsch replied immediately, assuring Trotsky that the question of his visit would be handled "with the greatest discretion." All preparations would therefore be kept secret until it was absolutely necessary to apply for approval of his permit. But Gleditsch did ask Trotsky to confirm a specific date in April for his presentation and requested that he provide the Student Association with the title of his topic.[49]

Not receiving any response to his letter of January 14, Gleditsch wrote again in early March. The time for applying for a visa on Trotsky's behalf was quickly disappearing.[50] Lev on this occasion did not keep the Student Association waiting. On March 19 he terminated abruptly his correspondence by indicating that he would not come to Norway after all. As justification he maintained, not entirely correctly, that the association's invitation had been based on the assumption that a new Labor Party government would grant him a visa. Since, on the contrary, the socialists had not come to power, he ruled out the possibility of securing an entry permit from the current administration. He would not "under any circumstances" expose himself to the humiliation of having another application rejected.[51]

Trotsky's true motive for turning down the invitation, which he earlier had accepted so enthusiastically in 1931 and 1932, was due to entirely different reasons than those stated in his letter. There was no basis to believe that a Mowinckel government necessarily would have acted differently in 1934 than it had three years earlier, when Trotsky had received an entry permit, if under restrictive terms. What mattered for Trotsky was that his situation had changed from what it had been in 1931. Instead of seeking to escape from distant Turkey, he now enjoyed asylum in France, a center of European and world politics. After a brief sojourn on the Atlantic coast, he moved to Barbizon, where he lived anonymously, only thirty miles southeast of Paris.[52] Here he resumed his literary activity by beginning a biography of Lenin and editing *The Bulletin of the Opposition*, the main international Trotskyite journal. From time to time he traveled incognito to Paris, which allowed him to meet many of the major figures within his nascent worldwide movement. There no longer appeared to be any advantage to be gained from addressing a group of intellectuals in a distant Scandinavian country by going on a trip that would undoubtedly create unwanted attention, perhaps even jeopardizing his stay in France.

His contact with the Student Association thereby ended. In his final letter he declared that the question of addressing the group should be postponed until "better conditions" developed in Norway, meaning an improvement in the political situation. But his satisfaction with life in France did not last long. He had no inkling at this time, but soon afterwards his exile underwent a significant change for the worse. Within a year he would be grateful for the opportunity to leave for Norway, where circumstances seemed to be far better than what he now was experiencing in France.

2 Arrival in Norway

> Now we are living openly and without guard. Even the yard gate is
> wide open day and night. Yesterday two drunken Norwegians dropped
> in to get acquainted. We chatted with them amiably and parted.
> —Lev Trotsky, diary entry, July 13, 1935

SHORTLY AFTER HIS DEPARTURE FOR MEXICO, Trotsky explained
that his motive for seeking admission to Norway had been based on his
hope "to be able peacefully to pursue my literary work in this calm country."[1] Only indirectly did he allude to the real reason he chose to leave
France. It had become anything but "calm" for him and Natalia.

The time he spent at Barbizon proved to be the best of Trotsky's entire
European exile. However, this pleasant interlude came to an end in April
1934, when the public became aware of the location of his residence. Immediately, a tremendous controversy arose. Many Frenchmen had been
led to believe that Trotsky lived isolated in some distant region of their
country, such as on Corsica. Once it was known that he instead resided in
the vicinity of the capital, the popular press, both of the right and the left,
exploded in a barrage of criticism.

The vehemence of the onslaught caused the government to issue an
order for his expulsion. However, since no other country would accept
him—not even a return to Turkey was possible—French authorities had
no choice but to allow him to stay. But the terms of his asylum were made
much more stringent. Forced to move anonymously from place to place,
he eventually settled with Natalia in two rooms in Domène, a small village close to Grenoble, far from Paris. Here, cut off from direct contact
with the outside world, he remained for almost a year—frustrated and un-
productive. Nor did the political situation improve. From the summer of

1934, the French communists were seeking closer ties with the socialists, beginning the process that eventually led to the Popular Front. Internationally, the government of Gaston Doumergue gradually adopted a more cordial attitude toward the Soviet Union. Consequently, France had obviously become an uninviting place to stay. As Trotsky revealed in his diary, he believed the government might even remove him to a distant French colony, "somewhere very remote. . . . That would mean political isolation, immeasurably more complete than Prinkipo. Under these circumstances it is wiser to leave France while there is time."[2]

In several ways, however, his move to Norway was not a desirable choice. Unlike French, the Norwegian language was unfamiliar to him. And being situated in a small country, "off the main track," would make it more difficult for him to communicate with his followers and to keep abreast of the latest international developments. Nevertheless, because of conditions in France, it became his only alternative. As he put it, Norway "is still much better than Madagascar."[3]

The opportunity for him to pursue this option opened on March 20, 1935, when the Labor Party formed a minority government under the leadership of Johan Nygaardsvold. Following events in Norway closely, Trotsky commented two days later in his diary that, while this political development might be of little importance "in the course of European history," it did have meaning "in the course of my life" because now "the question of a *visa* [Trotsky's emphasis] arises."[4] His followers in France and Norway were quickly mobilized. Walter Held reported to Lev Sedov already on March 27 that he had discussed the matter with Olav Scheflo and Erling Falk, the leader of Mot Dag. They had agreed to have Scheflo invite Trotsky to Norway for a vacation at a time when the parliament was in recess, thereby avoiding any major political repercussions. Once Trotsky was in the country, Held optimistically maintained, it would be impossible to expel him "because of the Labor Party's strength." The party, he added, could be depended upon to act more forcefully than its more "decadent" cousins in Denmark and Sweden.[5]

To make more specific arrangements, his attorney and friend, Gerard Rosenthal, traveled to Norway at Easter time, around April 20,[6] to aid Trotsky's quest. Rosenthal maintained that he discussed the matter with Foreign Minister Halvdan Koht and Minister of Justice Trygve Lie. According to Rosenthal, both cabinet members were reserved, referring to the strong objections that were bound to arise from the government's conservative adversaries and, more discreetly, hinting at opposition from the U.S.S.R.[7] Rosenthal had more success when he and Held, who served as Trotsky's main agent in Norway, contacted Scheflo. Although no longer in parliament, this labor movement veteran and newspaper editor still had considerable influence. Not surprising in light of his long-standing support for granting Trotsky asylum, Scheflo promised his assistance. Immediately after Easter he traveled to Oslo to speak with the prime minister. Nygaardsvold, wanting to avoid difficulties, proposed that Trotsky should remain patient until the Storting session was over, after which the government would promptly issue the residence permit.[8] This was fully in accord with the plan that Scheflo had discussed with Held and Falk a month earlier.

Having obtained this assurance, Rosenthal returned to France. Trotsky received the news positively, if somewhat resignedly: "The Norwegian Labor Government seems to have given a firm promise to grant me a visa. It looks as if we should have to take advantage of it. To stay in France would involve greater and greater difficulties."[9]

Trotsky's partisans in Norway, with Held energetically in the lead, resumed their activity shortly before the end of the parliamentary session. Acting on the assumption that preparations were proceeding without difficulties, Trotsky formally telegraphed his application to enter Norway to Minister of Justice Lie on June 7. He asked that he and Natalia be allowed to reside in Kristiansand or in its immediate vicinity "for rest and medical treatment."[10] Their preferred choice was no coincidence. Kristiansand, the major town in southern Norway (Sørlandet), happened to be where Scheflo lived, serving as editor of the local Labor Party paper.

With the formal request having been received, it needed the attention of the entire cabinet. The ministers apparently met on the same day, Friday, June 7.[11] To the satisfaction of the ever alert Held, who followed the proceedings closely, everything seemed to go well. Minister of Defense Fredrik Monsen told Held that matters had now been settled. Trotsky should be informed that he could pick up the desired visa at the Norwegian legation in Paris.[12] Held thereupon telegraphed that Trotsky could expect the visa to be available after the upcoming Pentecost holiday.[13] Jean van Heijenoort, Trotsky's secretary and main helper, brought this seemingly good news with him when he arrived from Paris on June 8.[14]

Lev and Natalia thereupon began to pack on the next day, Sunday. Natalia, aided by van Heijenoort, did most of the work, while Lev concentrated on gathering his precious books and manuscripts.[15] Natalia, already distraught because of no news from their son Sergei, worried about whether some difficulty might arise, in particular since French officials, notified of their departure, had only permitted them a transit stop in Paris of twenty-four hours. Lev, however, was anxious to leave. He had been ill and overworked during the last two months. Although he knew fully well that they were out of funds, which meant they would arrive penniless in Norway, this, he said, "is the least of our worries."[16]

On Monday evening, June 10, they left Grenoble by train for Paris, where they arrived the next morning. But when Trotsky's representative went to the Norwegian legation to obtain the promised visa, Natalia's fears appeared to have been realized. The legation had not received any instructions to issue a visa. Thereafter, Trotsky and his followers experienced a frantic two-day period, with frequent telephone and telegraph exchanges between Paris and Norway. When telephone contact was established with "our comrade in Oslo," Walter Held, he dejectedly reported that the government had begun to have second thoughts, being concerned with the possibility that Trotsky might engage in revolutionary activity while in Norway. In addition, members of the cabinet expressed doubts of being able to guarantee his safety. Making the situation even worse, French authorities believed they had been deceived; that Trotsky had used the pretext of traveling to Norway simply as an excuse to get to Paris. After difficult negotiations officials reluctantly agreed to extend the twenty-four-hour deadline to forty-eight hours but informed Trotsky and Natalia in no uncertain terms that their continued stay, including a return to Domène, was out of the question.[17]

Thereupon every effort was made to exert pressure in Norway. Trotsky personally contacted Scheflo via telephone. He also sent a telegram to Minister of Justice Trygve Lie in which he attempted to counteract reservations that had arisen in the cabinet. He promised that, if granted a residence permit, he would not involve himself in the country's public affairs. Furthermore, he insisted that the authorities would in no way be obliged to provide more protection for him than for any other foreigner. Showing the pressure that he was under, he concluded by respectfully requesting a speedy decision.[18] Trotsky at the same time wrote to Scheflo on the eleventh, urging him to help bring the matter to a speedy and satisfactory resolution. He ended the letter by imploring Scheflo: "Only a positive telegraph message from you can rescue me and my wife from a situation which can without exaggeration be described as desperate."[19]

No such decision was forthcoming on the eleventh, which galvanized Lev to cable Oslo again on the following day, Wednesday. This time, however, the telegram was addressed to the prime minister himself, revealing the seriousness of Trotsky's plight. He declared that, on the basis of a promise from a Norwegian party leader, he had left his residence and obtained a Belgian transit visa. The French government believed "I have deceived them" and was demanding that he leave within twenty-four hours. "I am ill, my wife is ill. The situation is desperate. Am seeking an immediate positive decision."[20] Obviously, he sought to gain Nygaardsvold's sympathy by referring not only to his own predicament but also to Natalia's. This time, however, he did not exaggerate when he emphasized their poor health. Both had been ill while in Domène. His diary entry of May 16 revealed that his wife was running a fever. "She bears all suffering, physical as well as moral, silently, quietly, inside herself. Right now she is more upset about my health than her own." As for himself, he described his condition as "not encouraging. The attacks of illness have become more frequent, the symptoms are more acute, my resistance is obviously getting weaker."[21]

Also in recognition of the seriousness of their predicament, Scheflo flew from Kristiansand to Oslo on June 12 so that he could influence members of the cabinet before they met to make their final decision.[22] For him, this was a most difficult journey since he suffered from chronic arthritis, whose crippling effects had made him an invalid.

When the ministers gathered on the evening of Wednesday, June 12, they had a clear perception that either alternative they might choose could have negative consequences. The admission of Trotsky could create difficulties with nonsocialists in parliament, from whom the government needed support because of its minority status. There was also the threat of a hostile Soviet response. On the other hand, denial of Trotsky's petition could antagonize members of the left wing of the Labor Party, including Scheflo, who would brand the government for having become too "bourgeois" in outlook. But while these political considerations were important, in the end the government's decision in large part was determined by its reaction to Trotsky's plight. His appeal emphasizing the desperateness of his condition made a strong impression, in particular on Prime Minister Nygaardsvold. The cabinet felt that it could not reject a person who was in need. Furthermore, it undoubtedly assumed, hopefully, that its resolution would not create difficulties with the Soviet Union.[23]

The ministers, however, were not unanimous. Two of them, Minister of Social Affairs Kornelius Bergsvik and Church and Education Minister Nils Hjelmtveit, were willing to admit Trotsky only if he had a valid return visa to France.[24] Obviously, this requirement could not be fulfilled since the French government under no circumstances wished to host Trotsky any longer.

These objections notwithstanding, the critical decision had now been reached, to the great relief of his backers. Scheflo and Held sat waiting in the Storting building for the government to conclude its deliberations. When the ministers emerged with the good news, the two proceeded to Hotel Continental for a victory drink and then telephoned Paris. As Held indelicately put it, his message was greeted with "shouts of joy and nigger dancing."[25] Trotsky, reporting on the same event, used more refined language, but he too indicated the tremendous feeling of elation among his followers: "The dejected mood of our young people was transformed into stormy enthusiasm."[26]

One final barrier, however, still needed to be overcome. The Central Passport Office, led by Leif R. Konstad, and the diplomats at the Paris Norwegian legation were in opposition. The consul at the legation announced on Thursday morning that Trotsky and Natalia would have to have a return visa to France. After several telephone conversations with Oslo, however, the matter was settled.[27] The passport office received specific orders to issue the needed visas. It in turn informed the Paris legation that no return visa was required. Thereupon, the necessary documents, valid for two months, were issued to "Mr. Lev Sedoff and Mrs. Nathalye [sic], (alias Trotsky and wife)."[28]

The Central Passport Office similarly telegraphed to Trotsky the terms under which he and Natalia were being admitted. Their residence permit was for six months. Special emphasis was placed on the stipulation that they were not allowed to "carry out any political activity in Norway or any political agitation against a state which is friendly toward Norway." How this clause was later interpreted would have a drastic effect on their stay. Furthermore, Lev and Natalia were to live at a place designated or accepted by the government, which would not guarantee their personal safety beyond that which any foreigner could expect to receive.[29]

Trotsky accepted these conditions without question. What mattered most was that he had been granted entry to Norway. Having at last obtained the long-sought visa, the Trotskys were able to have their Belgian transit visa extended to a new date. After last meetings and fond farewells, they left by train for Belgium just after midnight, in the early morning of June 14.[30] Their destination was Antwerp, where they would board the Norwegian vessel bearing the ironic name *Paris*, a city whose charms Lev would never live to enjoy again. From Antwerp they began the final, and least difficult, leg of the journey that would bring them to their next country of exile, Norway.

Lev and Natalia, after a stay of a day and a half, during which Trotsky met with Belgian sympathizers, went on board the *Paris* at 8:00 p.m., June 15, beginning a voyage of three nights and two days.[31] They were accompanied by two secretaries who also served as bodyguards, Jan Frankel, a Czech, and Jean van Heijenoort, who, despite his surname, was a French national. The result was that the officer in charge of tickets and passports on the ship referred to their group as "a Frenchman, a Czechoslovak, and two Turks" since the Trotskys still carried the passports they had received while in Turkey.[32]

The trip to Norway was uneventful, with the passengers enjoying sunshine and good weather. Lev and Natalia focused on maintaining their anonymity, with great success. They avoided speaking to the other passengers, assuming the characteristics of the "boring French middle class." During meals they concentrated entirely on their plates.[33] To avoid detection, Lev had shaved off his goatee, one of his main trademarks. He ate well and enjoyed being on deck as much as possible.[34]

With their arrival in Oslo harbor, their anonymity was over. Waiting at the pier were not only the expectant journalists but also a delegation from the police, headed by none other than the acting chief of police, to ensure their protection.[35] Once the gangplank was down, the photographers resolutely went to work, seeking their prey. Lev sought to shield his identity behind his walking cane, but with no success. He and Natalia were pictured in the next two days in the Oslo papers both on board the *Paris* and while coming down the gangplank. However, Olav Scheflo soon rescued them from the eager newsmen. He and his daughter, Beret, known to everyone by her nickname, Mosse, were there to take charge of the new arrivals. At first the two were briefly confused, not able to recognize Trotsky immediately because of his absent goatee. But then they met him and his party on the quay. After Lev received a warm hug from Mosse, Scheflo ushered the group into a waiting taxi, and they quickly sped away, leaving the journalists in their wake.[36]

Having thereby given the press the slip, Trotsky regained the anonymity that he always valued. During the next two days the newspapers were full of speculation concerning where he had gone and where he would settle. The first assumption was that he would live somewhere in southern Norway, perhaps close to Kristiansand. Trygve Lie inferred this on the day of Trotsky's arrival, while indicating that the government had not made any decision about his residence.[37] Instead, it appears as if Scheflo had received a free hand to determine this selection.

The latter, it seems, had not made any concrete arrangements for housing accommodations. Instead, he improvised. After disappearing westward from Oslo, he directed the taxi north toward Hønefoss. Here Lev, Natalia, and the two secretaries enjoyed lunch, their first meal in Norway. Scheflo thereafter went to the office of Konrad Knudsen, a local editor who later became Lev and Natalia's host during most of their stay in Norway. The fact that Scheflo sought him out on June 18 seems to indicate that at this time Scheflo already had plans for the Trotskys to reside with Knudsen. However, the editor was not in. Scheflo thereupon had to continue his improvisation. The party drove northeast and spent the afternoon on the shore of a large nearby lake, Randsfjord. That evening Scheflo took them to the village of Jevnaker, at the south end of the lake, where he checked them in at the local hotel.[38] Here, under the pseudonym Sedoff, by now recognizable to anyone who read the press, they spent their first days in the country.

No one interrupted their idyll while they stayed at the Jevnaker Hotel, enjoying the beauty of the lake shore. Lev was pleased to find the peace and quiet that lately had not been possible in France. Writing in his diary on his second day in Norway, he compared his new place of exile with a country that he was more familiar with, Finland, noting their similarities: "Hills, lakes, pines, and firs. Only, the Norwegians are larger than the Finns." The spartan accommodations that he experienced, however, were more primitive than what he was accustomed to in France.[39]

Physically, he had been stimulated by his move from Domène. He had felt better during the trip from France: "Ten days of travel and living in hotels passed well, and I seemed to have revived."[40] News of his refreshed condition, however, was not what the public received. The press presented an entirely different account of his health. Trygve Lie set the tone in an interview, describing both Lev and Natalia as "sick and worn down" when they arrived.[41] *Arbeiderbladet* went even further on the next day, going so far as to maintain that Trotsky suffered from tuberculosis. However, at the moment his major problem, said the paper, was "worn out nerves." It similarly described his wife as being ill from the effects of arthritis and nervousness. Only peace and quiet could restore their health. Scheflo, who had reappeared in Oslo, insisted that Trotsky needed to be left alone, being in no condition to grant press interviews. *Arbeiderbladet* instead rather pathetically described "the sick Trotsky" as having to find refuge in a Norwegian tuberculosis sanitarium, while his "victorious and powerful rival, Stalin," ruled from the Kremlin.[42]

Interestingly, several nonsocialist papers were even more sensational in depicting Trotsky's alleged pitiful physical condition. The liberal *Dagbladet* (The Daily Paper) and the more conservative *Tidens Tegn* (Sign of the Times) both maintained that he was seriously ill with tuberculosis and required special treatment.[43]

As for the Labor Party press, its emphasis on Trotsky's and Natalia's purported serious health problems was clearly for the purpose of gaining them sympathy. Although neither was in good physical shape, their supposedly poor conditions were exaggerated or untruthful, especially allegations that Trotsky suffered from TB. But while Scheflo knew this was incorrect, his primary concern was to eliminate any commotion that might arise due to their presence in the country.

Nevertheless, their sudden and dramatic arrival immediately caused attention to focus on a matter of considerable controversy at the time—the repercussions in the Soviet Union from the December 1934 assassination of Sergei Kirov, the Communist party leader in Leningrad. Although Stalin did not instigate the killing, he used it to greatly extend his power.[44] This led to the Soviet dictator's infamous major purges of the 1930s. Sergei, Lev and Natalia's youngest son, was one of many persons arrested in the aftermath of Kirov's murder. Still a student when his parents were deported, he chose to remain behind to complete his education as an engineer, eventually becoming an instructor at a technical school. He was entirely nonpolitical, and his parents were very careful in their correspondence with him, not only avoiding political questions but making certain that all letters were written by Natalia.[45]

For many months they had led a tortured existence after they lost contact with their son at the end of 1934. Not until the very last days of May

1935 did they receive confirmation of his arrest.[46] In a vain endeavor, Natalia wrote an open letter, hoping that world opinion would be so aroused by Stalin's obvious act of vengeance that this would obtain Sergei's freedom. The letter was released to the French press before their departure and in turn was picked up by newspapers and telegraph bureaus around the world.

On the day they came ashore in Oslo, *Dagbladet* published extracts from the letter under the headline "Stalin revenges himself against our son Sergei." The story stressed that Sergei had not been engaged in politics, that contact between him and his parents had been entirely nonpolitical, and that he had been allowed to concentrate on his professional activity up until the time of Kirov's assassination and the first trial of the Old Bolsheviks, Lev Kamenev and Grigori Zinoviev. Although penned by Natalia, the appeal showed Trotsky's influence by calling for the establishment of an independent truth commission "of the Soviet Union's friends" concerning the murder of Kirov. Stalin had sought to tie the killing to Trotsky, and the open letter pointed out that Sergei's arrest was simply part of this process.[47] *Tidens Tegn* similarly published an account of Natalia's letter.[48]

Both papers made it clear that it had been issued before she came to Norway. *Arbeiderbladet*, as the government's main press organ, was much more cautious. It did not even print an account of the letter's contents but simply quoted Scheflo, who stated that the Trotskys refused comment about "the letter that Mrs. Trotsky has newly made public concerning the treatment of her son, Sergei."[49] The Labor Party clearly wanted to show that the Trotskys were living up to the terms of their admission.

Natalia's appeal proved to be stillborn. If anything, by calling attention to Sergei when they were in the process of moving to Norway, Lev and Natalia heightened Stalin's animosity. They never again received any direct news about their son's fate.[50]

Most Norwegians, including the politically sophisticated, had no concept of Stalin's capacity for evil. One could hardly have expected otherwise. Not even Trotsky, despite his relentless criticism of developments in the Soviet Union, fully recognized at first the major consequences of the great purges, which in the early summer of 1935 were still in the process of being organized. The question of Sergei's fate quickly disappeared from press commentary after a few days. However, there was no immediate calm concerning Trotsky. He continued to dominate the news for the rest of

June. It could scarcely have been otherwise. Lev Trotsky indisputably was the most famous international political figure ever to take up residence in Norway. His presence, with interest stimulated even more by his sudden, unannounced arrival, was bound to create a major sensation.

Considering the political ramifications that resulted from his exile, the question of who was primarily responsible for his admission deserves attention. Two names, Walter Held and Olav Scheflo, stand out. Trygve Lie later wrote guardedly that Scheflo "presumably" urged Trotsky to apply for an entry permit and that Scheflo "probably" acted together with a German political refugee, Walter Held.[51]

As noted earlier, both had been strongly involved in making arrangements for Trotsky. Some writers, however, have maintained that it was the young, energetic Held who acted as the driving force on Trotsky's behalf in May and June 1935, rather than the arthritically crippled Scheflo.[52] One of these commentators, Nils Kåre Dahl, among the few Norwegians who became an active Trotskyite, seems to infer that while both Held and Scheflo worked for Trotsky, Held was most active: "It was really a difficult situation at the beginning of June, and from 1 June to 12 June there was a lot of work for Held in persuading the government to let him [Trotsky] in. The Norwegian state bureaucracy put up every obstacle in Held's way, but finally Trotsky was allowed in."[53]

Held did indeed play a part in getting Trotsky into the country. Like his hero, Held was a political refugee. He had been born Walter Heinz Epe in the Ruhr district on December 26, 1910. While in Germany he preferred to be known as Heinz Epe. He joined the Trotskyite movement as early as 1931 but fled Germany after the Reichstag fire of February 1933. He chose Held as his political pseudonym not simply because it means hero in German but also because it was his mother's maiden name.[54]

He moved first to Prague, where he contributed to one of the movement's major publications, *Unser Wort*. However, in 1934 he attended a meeting of radical leftist youth organizations in Belgium as a representative of the Trotskyite youth group. When the conference decided to establish an international bureau to coordinate the activity of its affiliated revolutionary youth groups, Held was appointed to its secretariat. Although technically headquartered in Stockholm, the secretariat's actual work took place in Oslo at Mot Dag's headquarters. This was conducted by Held, together with Willy Brandt, another German political refugee whose pseudonym became far more famous, and Aake Anker-Ording, a member of Mot Dag.[55]

Held came to Norway in early June 1934. With his youth, vitality, and dark good looks he soon gained entry into leftist political circles, establishing ties with both Mot Dag and the Labor Party. However, as a dedicated Trotskyite, he often became engaged in quarrels, which eventually led to permanent division. He broke first with Mot Dag and later, in August 1935, with Brandt and the International Bureau. He was able to support himself, however, as a language instructor.[56]

Despite the assistance that he provided Trotsky, it was on a different, less significant, level compared with the role of Scheflo. As a radical left socialist, Scheflo had long been an admirer of the Soviet leader, in particular because of the major part he had played in the creation of the U.S.S.R. As shown, Scheflo had since 1929 been a warm advocate favoring Norwegian exile for Trotsky.

When the effort began in earnest in 1935 to get him out of France, time after time Trotsky and his aides turned to Scheflo. Lev's attorney, Rosenthal, getting nowhere with Norwegian officials, contacted Scheflo, and through him it was possible to secure Nygaardsvold's tentative approval. When Trotsky made his first formal application for admission, not surprisingly he indicated southern Norway, where Scheflo lived, as his preferred area of residence. When the government began to have second doubts during the critical days in June, after Trotsky had left Domène, it was Scheflo whom he contacted, asking him to intercede. Scheflo's daughter, Dagmar Loe, vividly remembers hearing her father converse in German with Trotsky by telephone on several occasions prior to his arrival.[57] From every indication it appears that Scheflo's personal intervention had an effect, including the appeal to the government's sympathy concerning Trotsky's alleged poor health, which proved to be decisive in the cabinet's ultimate, somewhat reluctant, decision. Finally, when Trotsky arrived with Natalia and the two secretaries, not only was Scheflo present to meet them but he remained in charge of their movement and their public statements during the next several days.

Held had no part in their activity at this time. During the crisis in June, when Trotsky's move hung in the balance, he worked with Scheflo, but mainly as a conduit to Paris since the latter did not speak French. While Held previously did have some meetings with officials on Trotsky's behalf, he generally was accompanied by a Norwegian. This was only natural. Having only resided briefly in the country, he did not have full command of the language. For example, when he met with Nygaardsvold, then the leader of the Labor Party's parliamentary delegation, in the fall of 1934, Held came with Finn Moe, a journalist for *Arbeiderbladet*. Later, when direct influence had to be brought to bear, Held always contacted Scheflo. Held's work was mainly of a practical nature, which was to be expected. To assume that a young man, twenty-four years old, non-Norwegian to boot, with the status of a political refugee, could exert significant influence on government decision making, is not very likely. It was Scheflo, with his background, authority, and network of contacts, who exerted decisive influence. This has become the standard view within the Labor Party, as confirmed by one of its major figures, former party secretary Haakon Lie.[58]

The Labor Party's effort to preempt condemnation of the government's action by seeking to arouse sympathy for the Trotskys did not succeed. Criticism began immediately in the days after their entry. *Aftenposten* (The Evening Post) led the way with an editorial that later would reflect the position adopted by the Conservatives. The paper declared that Trotsky, in his current condition, posed no danger, and in that sense it had no reservations against permitting him to stay. However, it did not share the government's enthusiasm for having this "earlier mass murderer" as a "guest" in the country, and *Aftenposten* under no circumstances was willing to have him receive greater protection, at the expense of the state, than an ordinary tourist.[59]

The major Conservative paper's negative characterization set off a bitter press polemic. *Arbeiderbladet* replied on the same day in its afternoon edition, editorializing that it was not Trotsky who deserved the characterization "mass murderer," but rather "*Aftenposten*'s friends," the great powers. Not only were they responsible for the mass killings of World War I but they had attempted to destroy the freedom and independence of the "new workers' and farmers' Russia" by encouraging counter-revolution and intervention. *Arbeiderbladet*'s editor, Martin Tranmæl, was very cautious, however, not to support Trotsky in his ongoing feud with Stalin. The paper stated that it lacked the background to determine who was right, going so far as to say that Stalin might possibly have judged conditions in the Soviet Union more realistically than his rival. This did not, however, justify the persecution and deportation of someone of Trotsky's stature, whose name would always stand alongside Lenin in the history of the Russian Revolution. Every democratic people should recognize its proud responsibility to provide him with shelter.[60]

Part of the Agrarian Party's press reacted even more strongly against Trotsky's entry. *Vestopland*, the party's paper in the town of Gjøvik in Oppland province, was harshest in its condemnation, similarly referring to Trotsky as "the executioner." The paper hoped he would be ostracized by all Norwegians and went so far as to hint at encouraging violence against him, if not assassination, by White Russians: "We hope there are so many Russian refugees living in this country that they can make life hot for a man such as Trotsky."[61] *Østlendingen* (The Easterner), the Agrarian Party's major paper in the neighboring province of Hedmark, was slightly more restrained, but it too referred to Trotsky as a mass murderer. The paper further pointed out that no other country in Europe was willing to extend the right of asylum to someone like Trotsky, including socialist governments in Denmark and Sweden. It also referred to the previous unwillingness of the parliament to grant Trotsky residence. *Østlendingen* concluded that Trotsky's admission had been the Labor government's greatest mistake up to the present time.[62]

As indicated, some press response to Trotsky's entry was bitter, even hateful. Tranmæl, in *Arbeiderbladet*, reacted in particular to *Vestopland's* editorial of June 20, describing it as "vulgar" and irresponsible, encouraging "criminal actions." However, he noted that the nonsocialist reaction was not uniform. Although the Conservative press had attacked the government, the Liberal newspapers had either remained passive or responded positively. And while some segments of the Agrarian press, described by Tranmæl as "fascist in character," were strongly negative, the remainder of the party's papers had generally been calm and even-tempered.[63] This was not surprising. Because of the "Crisis Compromise" that had just recently been worked out between the Labor Party and the Agrarians, the latter could hardly afford to jeopardize its agreement to cooperate with the government because of a single issue.

Considering communist opposition in 1929 to whether Trotsky should receive asylum, it proved hardly surprising that the party was even more negative in 1935. He and his supporters were accused in no uncertain terms by the major communist newspaper in Oslo, *Arbeideren* (The Worker), of having "opened the sewer for the most vile attacks" against the Soviet Union. Communist opposition to his presence also involved a strictly domestic component because of the prominence that Scheflo had achieved by being in charge of the Trotskys during their first days in Norway. He continued to be regarded by the communists as a renegade traitor, and *Arbeideren* maintained that the decision to grant residence to Trotsky was part of an organized effort against the U.S.S.R.[64]

Scheflo responded immediately in Trotsky's defense, declaring that the Norwegian working class could be sure that the man who had arrived the previous Tuesday "was no counter-revolutionary," but instead "a revolutionary in the best meaning of the word." Nor was he a broken man, but rather "a comrade-in-arms with an undiminished intelligence and undiminished ethics." Scheflo furthermore, in contrast to Tranmæl's carefully worded neutrality, directly backed Trotsky in his rejection of Stalin's accusations. The current communist campaign in Norway to brand Trotsky, Kamenev, and Zinoviev as "counter-revolutionaries," insisted Scheflo, was nothing more than "lying agitation" conducted in obedience to Moscow.[65]

The communist press had no intention of dropping the matter. It clearly felt the issue could be used in its continuous, if futile, endeavor to outmaneuver the Labor Party in seeking working-class support. The party's paper in Bergen, *Arbeidet* (Work), insisted that the Labor Party had made common cause with the class enemy, the Norwegian bourgeoisie, since they too allegedly favored providing a haven for the traitor Trotsky. Addressing ordinary members of the Labor Party, *Arbeidet* asked if they really wanted to have Trotsky as a comrade?[66]

This attempt to link the Labor government with the bourgeoisie did not prove difficult for the Labor Party to dismiss. It simply turned the issue completely around, pointing out that the communists, when opposing Trotsky's entry, were acting in harmony with not only the conservative bourgeoisie but also with extreme fascists.

The similarity between the communists and elements of the right over the question of Trotsky proved to be an effective argument for the Labor Party. In 1935 National Union (Nasjonal Samling), Vidkun Quisling's party, represented the extreme right in the Norwegian political spectrum. Its highly ambitious leader, Quisling, believed that his recently established party would be the vehicle for him to come to power. Having broken with the Agrarian Party in 1933, he was convinced he could best succeed by imitating dynamic fascist leaders, first Mussolini and then Hitler. By the time Trotsky came to Norway, Quisling increasingly was following in Hitler's footsteps. National Union's opposition to Trotsky was therefore due not merely to typical nonsocialist hostility against his role in the Russian Revolution but also to the party's growing racism in the form of anti-Semitism. Trotsky's Jewish background was constantly stressed, with the party's main publication, *Nasjonal Samling*, referring to him by his Jewish family name as "Leiba Bronstein." Quisling seized on Trotsky's arrival, hoping, like the communists, to exploit it in order to gain popular backing. NS* quickly arranged a rally against the "smuggling of the revolutionary agent, Bronstein-Trotsky, into Norway." This protest, on Friday, June 21, featured Quisling as its main speaker, who talked about the "red politics of world revolution" that Trotsky stood for.[67]

Ordinarily, political opponents of NS, both the Labor Party and the nonsocialist parties, chose largely to ignore Quisling, having adopted this tactic to deprive him of publicity. In this instance, however, the fact that NS and the communists were united in opposition to Trotsky proved to be too opportune for Tranmæl to resist. *Arbeiderbladet* proceeded to lump **all**† of Trotsky's detractors in an unholy alliance, extending from NS and the Fatherland League‡ on the right via prominent antisocialists in the Conservative and Agrarian parties to the communists on the left. This was truly, said *Arbeiderbladet*, a "popular front" of the worst kind.[68]

The debate concerning Trotsky also became an issue in parliament. It was still meeting when the *Paris* docked, contrary to Prime Minister Nygaardsvold's original intent to postpone Trotsky's entry until the Storting's adjournment. This explains to a considerable degree why the government, in the days before it finally approved Trotsky's visa, had begun to have qualms about whether to proceed with an enterprise that could create difficulties with the nonsocialist parties. From the government's perspective, the question had come up prematurely.

Its obvious nervousness was reflected in Minister of Justice Lie's statement on the day Trotsky arrived. Lie insisted that the Labor government followed a consistent policy in applying the right of asylum. All political refugees, he maintained, could expect to receive a residence permit as long as they agreed not to become an economic burden on the state and refrained from participating in political activity. He further sought to

---

* Quisling's party was generally referred to by its initials.

† Unless indicated otherwise, text in bold denotes the author's emphasis (which may also be made explicit for the sake of clarity).

‡ The Fatherland League (Fedrelandslaget) was a right-wing nationalist organization, founded in 1925, that sought to unite all nonsocialists against the perceived threat of revolutionary socialism.

defuse the issue by referring to the alleged precedent established by Mowinckel's government. He pointed out that it had granted Trotsky entry, but
he conveniently failed to mention that the visa had been valid only for a
few days. Even more incorrect was Lie's argument that the Liberal government had never denied asylum to any political refugee.[69]

For a time it seemed as if the Labor government had reason to worry that
there might be repercussions. On the following day, Wednesday, June 19,
several nonsocialist papers reported that the Conservative parliamentary
delegation intended to raise an interpellation. When asked by *Arbeiderbladet* on June 19, however, Storting President Carl J. Hambro indicated
that the Conservatives had not yet made a decision.[70]

Nevertheless, *Arbeiderbladet*'s editorial revealed the party's concern,
emphasizing that the right of asylum had already been established in
Norway. Even "counter-revolutionary Russian emigrants" had received
shelter.[71] But while the Conservatives clearly favored challenging the government with an interpellation, the Agrarian and Liberal parties were by
no means as upset over Trotsky's entry. Although they had not been consulted, they gave every indication of being willing to accept Trotsky's
admission as a fait accompli.[72]

Without support from other nonsocialist parties, Hambro, for clearly
tactical reasons, did not want to see the Conservatives isolated. However,
on Saturday, June 22, he had at least an opportunity to bring the matter up
for discussion. From its annual convention in Stavanger, the Norwegian
Farmers Association (Norges Bondelag) cabled a resolution decrying the
government's issuance of a visa to Trotsky. The petition further demanded
more restrictive and effective immigration control so that "our country
does not become a playground for foreign revolutionary agitators."[73]

Although closely affiliated with the Agrarian Party, the Farmers Association's viewpoint was regarded as more extreme than what the Agrarians
considered realistic. Even Hambro, commenting cautiously, stated that he
did not really wish to have a debate but simply wanted the government
to present a report to the Storting on its policy for issuing entry and
residence permits.[74]

Hambro received only limited support in the person of Gabriel Moseid,
one of the Agrarian Party's leaders. He and Hambro were immediately repudiated by several Labor Party speakers, who defended the government and
impugned Hambro's motives.[75] Although the latter responded sarcastically,
the brief debate ended on this note, with the parliament taking no action.

Arbeiderbladet could therefore triumphantly report on Monday that, while the Farmers Association's telegram had allowed Hambro to make a small "fuss," he did not receive any satisfaction.[76]

There was no sentiment among the nonsocialists to create difficulty over an issue that at the time was regarded as relatively insignificant. The Agrarians, who in earlier times had been even more anticommunist than the Conservatives, were now committed to the "Crisis Compromise" and were therefore muted in their response. The Liberals, whose cabinet had recently been forced from office, also were not ready to challenge the government over Trotsky, in particular since the right of asylum, at least in theory, continued to be part of their party principles. Furthermore, even among the Conservatives there was a shared belief that, at least for the time being, the Labor government, in office for only three months, should be allowed to deal with the problems of the Great Depression since previous administrations had not succeeded in overcoming its difficulties. Therefore, as far as the Storting was concerned, the matter was settled, even though debate still continued in the press for some time. There would be no immediate political repercussions from Trotsky's arrival.

The subject of this controversy had been following it closely in the press.[77] Since he as yet had no understanding of Norwegian, he obviously relied on a native for translations, most likely Scheflo. The latter also eventually got around to finding a permanent dwelling for Lev and Natalia. Their stay at the Jevnaker Hotel lasted through Midsummer Night's Eve, allowing them to experience the bonfires that dotted the shoreline that long summer evening. But on the next day, with the government's approval, they moved to Wexhall in Heradsbygda, the residence of editor Konrad Knudsen.[78]

No official explanation was provided for why the couple ended up in this tiny rural hamlet close to Hønefoss. Originally, as has been seen, most observers assumed the Trotskys would settle in the Kristiansand area, close to Scheflo. It appears, however, that Scheflo had decided otherwise. Kristiansand had obvious disadvantages, both for him and the Trotskys. As a provincial town its location would have limited not only Trotsky's ability to receive information through news sources, but it would also have restricted his opportunities to meet foreign visitors. Hønefoss could be reached from Oslo in about two hours by either car or train. Wexhall's closer proximity to the capital also permitted him and Natalia to have access to superior medical care. For Scheflo personally there was also good reason for not having Trotsky as an immediate neighbor. Politically, the latter remained controversial, and Scheflo, as a major political figure in Kristiansand, concluded it was best to have the "guest" whom he had sponsored housed in the distant district of Ringerike.[79]

Trotsky's move became known by the day after he settled at Wexhall. *Fremtiden* (The Future), the Labor Party's major newspaper in Buskerud province, headquartered in the town of Drammen,* broke the news. This was no coincidence since Trotsky's host, Knudsen, served as the paper's local editor in Hønefoss. *Fremtiden* cited Trotsky as having nothing but positive things to say about Ringerike. The landscape not only was beautiful, but it had a calming influence on his nervous system. The climate appeared to suit him perfectly. And the people whom he had met were nice, straightforward, and pleasant. As an enthusiastic hunter and fisherman, the opportunities that the local area provided were outstanding. His immediate wish was to put his fishing rod over his shoulder so that he could try his luck in the local Sokna River or in the nearby large lake called Tyrifjorden. Knudsen, *Fremtiden*'s source (although not referred to by name), in turn declared that Trotsky was a joy to be together with. He was "the world's most gracious person, good-natured and contented, a highly cultivated and charming individual." His wife was equally "lovely and charming." The paper concluded by stating that "Ringerike is certainly also both enthusiastic and proud to house a world figure of Lev Trotsky's stature."[80]

Evidence suggests that the subject of this flattering article really did have positive sentiments toward Ringerike. Writing to Scheflo two days later, Trotsky voiced pleasure over the reception that he, Natalia, and his secretary, Jan Frankel, had received in "comrade" Knudsen's house. Furthermore, they were adjusting well to the Norwegian way of life. Trotsky hoped that Scheflo had managed to deal with the difficulties that their arrival had caused and, referring to Scheflo's arthritis, that his health condition had improved. He ended by sending best wishes from himself, Natalia, and Frankel to Scheflo and his "dear daughter," Mosse.[81]

Upon moving to Heradsbygda, Trotsky experienced a calm that had been lacking earlier during his exile. In Turkey and in France he had either lived under guard or had furtively attempted to maintain an incognito

---

* Drammen is located approximately twenty-five miles south of Oslo on an arm of the Oslo Fjord.

existence. At Wexhall he needed no protection, although everyone who read a newspaper knew where he lived. He found this most reassuring: "Now we are living openly and without guard. Even the yard gate is wide open day and night. Yesterday two drunken Norwegians dropped in to get acquainted. We chatted with them amiably and parted."[82]

Trotsky had thereupon settled down, beginning the first phase of his Norwegian exile. As in France, he would experience two distinct periods. The first would be the longest, lasting for more than a year. As in France, this initial interlude would be mainly tranquil. But, as in France, it would be followed by a difficult time that would cause him to regret ever coming to Norway. In both periods, however, the conditions he experienced would be determined by political circumstances in the host country. It is therefore important to understand the state of Norwegian politics in the 1930s, how they had been shaped, and, most importantly, how they related to Trotsky.

3 The Norwegian Labor Movement and Its Relationship to Trotsky

Trotsky too, despite his great personality,
stands all alone in the world.
—Jacob Walcher, December 30, 1933

MORE THAN ANY OTHER POLITICAL FIGURE, Trotsky came to regard Martin Tranmæl as his main ideological opponent within the Norwegian socialist movement. He could hardly have chosen a worse adversary. Tranmæl stands out as the leading personality within the Labor Party during the first half of the twentieth century, despite the fact that he never held the office of party chairman (*formann*) or prime minister, and he only served in the Storting once. His primary occupation was journalism, and for most of his career he presided over *Arbeiderbladet* as its editor in chief. Tranmæl's personal influence was based on his total devotion to the labor movement. Worldly possessions were the least of his concerns. When the Gestapo vainly sought to arrest him in 1940, they were amazed to find that Norway's foremost labor leader occupied but a single, small room. Its contents were a bed, a chair, a table, plus books that were stacked from floor to ceiling.[1]

His ascetic way of life and his dedicated work on behalf of the labor movement disguised a basic part of his character—his homosexuality. But Tranmæl successfully suppressed this essential element of his nature. He remained a closet homosexual his entire life.

His main strength was his speaking ability. What made him the most effective orator among Scandinavian socialists was his intensity and the simple message of outrage against unfair social and economic conditions that he expressed to audiences of ordinary people—workers, small farmers, and fishermen.[2] Because of his commitment and selflessness, he had little difficulty in attracting devoted younger followers whom he mentored and who, because of his influence, were placed in higher party positions that he deliberately chose not to hold.

He never became preoccupied with adhering to a specific ideological dogma. What motivated him above all was the need to rebel against established injustice and inequality. Because of his complete dedication, he had little tolerance for independent-minded intellectuals. He especially responded forcefully against ideological criticism of the party. For him, anything that weakened socialist unity had to be dealt with severely, and he used his power to make certain that critically minded opponents of the party leadership were isolated, deprived of influence, or expelled.[3]

During much of the critical period of the 1920s, when the Labor Party emerged as the strongest political force in the country, Tranmæl's most bitter challenger was Olav Scheflo. Both were natives of the region of Trøndelag, with Tranmæl born in the agricultural county (*kommune*) of Melhus in 1879, while Scheflo, three years younger, came originally from the small town of Steinkjer. They were also similar in being proletarianized at an early age. Tranmæl originally was apprenticed as a painter, while Scheflo served as a seaman in the merchant marine. After a couple of years, however, the latter's vocation ended abruptly after a severe fall that resulted in a broken leg. Following a period of employment in the postal service, he began his true career as a journalist. He started as a newspaperman in 1906 by writing for *Ny Tid* (New Times), the socialist paper in Trondheim, the country's third largest city and the center of Trøndelag. Here he met Tranmæl, who also worked for the paper. The two got along very well at first. Tranmæl was then in the process of formulating the views that would make him the most radical opposition figure within the Labor Party. Scheflo firmly shared his convictions and became a member of Tranmæl's faction.[4]

Nevertheless, Scheflo and Tranmæl differed in a number of ways. Scheflo was never wed to the labor movement in the same way as Tranmæl. Scheflo had a more international outlook. Although he too reacted strongly to injustice and inequality, what mattered most for him was his conviction that victory for the proletariat could only be achieved though an international revolutionary process.[5] In contrast, Tranmæl remained focused on the uniquely Norwegian character of the labor movement. Also, unlike Tranmæl, who always sought to have the strongest base of support behind him, Scheflo followed clear ideological lines that he believed were correct.[6] During much of his mature political life, therefore, he was in opposition to the power structure of whatever party he belonged to.

As a person, however, Scheflo was not thin-skinned or quarrelsome. He was humorous, casual, and quick-witted. Even political opponents in parliament were often impressed and charmed by his comments.[7] Unlike the ascetic Tranmæl, who hated the effect of alcohol on the working class and never took a drink, Scheflo enjoyed a glass in good company. He differed also from Tranmæl, the lonely gay bachelor, by having a family life, married with several children.

Their physical conditions similarly were remarkably different. Tranmæl enjoyed hiking in the mountains well into his eighties, while Scheflo already suffered from ill health during his thirties. Whether his disabling fall as a young seaman triggered the disease is impossible to say, but he became crippled with arthritis. At times he was so immobile that he had to be carried to the speaker's platform. During his "last eight to ten years he was either chained to his chair or to his bed."[8] But he never complained and continued to carry out his responsibilities with calm determination.

Of the two, Tranmæl emerged first as a major figure within the labor movement. Already by the end of the first decade of the new century, he had become the spokesman for the left wing of the Labor Party. Having twice been to the United States, whose economic system appalled him, he returned to Norway, influenced to some degree by the Industrial Workers of the World, with whom he had been associated during his second visit. This was shown when he took the lead in organizing a radical faction within the Labor Party known as the Trade Union Opposition of 1911 (*Fagopposisjonen av 1911*). Similar to the IWW, Tranmæl held syndicalist views. He stressed the use of nonparliamentary, revolutionary activity—including strikes, industrial sabotage, and boycotts—as the means for the working class to come to power.

The Labor Party and its closely affiliated National Federation of Unions, L.O., at first were led by moderate reform-minded socialists similar to those who were prominent in other Western European countries. But Norway's late but speedy industrialization, which created social disruption within the rapidly expanding working class, plus the hardships endured by the workers during World War I in contrast to the wealth gained by shipping and business interests, not only increased support for the Labor Party and enlarged union membership but also radicalized the growing ranks of proletarians. The single event, however, that allowed Tranmæl's more radical brand of socialism to break through was the Bolshevik Revolution in Russia under Lenin. Like socialists everywhere, the trend among Norwegians was to regard this dramatic occurrence as the forerunner of the worldwide revolution that would bring the proletariat to power.

Shortly afterwards, in the spring of 1918, the radical left wing of the Labor Party took over at its National Conference (landsmøte). The new leaders were all in their thirties, with Tranmæl, aged thirty-eight, becoming party secretary. Scheflo, closely identified with Tranmæl's faction, now reached the pinnacle of his journalistic career when he was elected editor in chief of Social-Demokraten (The Social Democrat), the party's major paper.* The leadership immediately declared support for the new revolutionary regime in Russia and their allegiance to the principle of world revolution. It was therefore only natural for Labor to join the new Communist International in 1919, thereby abandoning the moderate socialist Second International. This was indeed a unique turn of events. Only in Norway and Italy did unified socialist parties enter the Comintern.[9]

Although Tranmæl at first had no reservations against affiliation with international communism, his concern was soon aroused by the Comintern's insistence on dictating policy to its members. Scheflo, on the other hand, viewed the Comintern as the agent to achieve worldwide victory for the working class. Unknowingly, his enthusiastic championship of the need to maintain solidarity with Moscow would lead to his permanent estrangement from Martin Tranmæl.

For Tranmæl, the prerequisite for the Labor Party to have freedom of action was an absolute necessity because he believed its leaders best understood political conditions in Norway, which might differ considerably from elsewhere. But he faced the dilemma of not being able to reverse his position and expect to have a solid base of support behind him. For the time being, therefore, he remained silent on whether to obey the Comintern. This allowed Scheflo from the columns of Social-Demokraten to attack without reservation those within the party, the moderate wing, who were unwilling to accept the Comintern's commands,

---

* Social-Demokraten changed its name to Arbeiderbladet in 1923.

known as the Twenty-one Conditions (*Moskva-tesene*). Such persons, declared Scheflo, should immediately leave the party.[10]

Thanks to his journalistic skills, Scheflo contributed significantly to the outward acceptance of the Conditions at the party's national conference in 1921.[11] He thereby achieved his goal of driving out the moderate, reform-minded elements within the party. They formed the Social Democratic Party in January 1921, weakening the Labor Party by drawing off electoral support.

Scheflo's apparent victory turned out, however, to be pyrrhic. Tranmæl had no inclination to accept this outcome as permanent. At the national conference he indicated that he would not accept reelection as party secretary but intended instead to return to journalism. He thereby, if indirectly, attacked Scheflo's Achilles' heel. While no one ever disputed the latter's writing skills, his management of *Social-Demokraten* had been disastrous. The paper's strident defense of Moscow, focusing mainly on ideological questions rather than matters closer to home, caused it to lose readership on a massive scale. From having previously been profitable, it quickly descended into serious debt.[12] In part because of this, but also because of the desire to keep Tranmæl in the capital (he had threatened to return to Trøndelag), the national conference elected him editor in chief, thereby ousting Scheflo.

As compensation, the latter became leader of the Labor Party's Storting delegation following the 1921 national election. He was also appointed the party's representative on the Comintern's executive committee. Here he personally became acquainted with Trotsky, who held a leading position on the committee.

Following its national conference in 1921, it was clear that the Labor Party was split into two factions, led by Scheflo and Tranmæl. The latter remained strongly opposed to the Comintern's attempt to micromanage member parties, and he no longer felt the need to avoid voicing his reservations. Scheflo, on the other hand, stayed committed to the ideal of international working-class solidarity, which he firmly believed could only be maintained through the Comintern.[13]

The major problem that Scheflo and like-minded adherents would face was that the organization, despite its name, never truly was international. It was always controlled by the Russian leadership, and its policies changed frequently in order to meet the foreign policy interests of the U.S.S.R., not necessarily those of affiliated national parties. When Lenin in 1921 adopted the New Economic Policy for the Soviet Union, with its partial return to capitalism, this similarly signaled a change in the Comintern's international strategy. Its members were now ordered to adopt a united-front policy, cooperating with socialists and liberal reformists, rather than working avidly for the violent overthrow of capitalism. Trotsky personally introduced this major switch in Comintern planning when he held the inaugural address at its third congress in July.[14]

The Comintern's new approach met with a mixed response in Norway. Scheflo, as parliamentary leader, cooperated fully with the Liberal government, going so far as to declare that the Labor Party was the "legitimate offspring" of the Liberals. Tranmæl, on the other hand, opposed the united-front approach. Not only did it require cooperation with the Social Democrats, which he felt was detrimental, but it also obligated the Labor Party to accept the unpopular measures of the government. By the spring of 1922, the division within the Labor Party factions had been revealed to the public. Scheflo had the bulk of the parliamentary delegation behind him and enjoyed the blessings of the Comintern, while Tranmæl had a majority on the party Central Committee (*sentralstyret*).[15]

Despite a strong effort by the Soviet government in support of Scheflo's faction, which included sending top Russian communists to Oslo in an attempt to influence the choice of party leaders, this failed. In February 1923 delegates to the National Conference voted by a narrow majority to ensure that all top party positions would be held by Tranmæl loyalists. The final break came later in the year at an extraordinary national conference in November, where the delegates by a larger majority repudiated an ultimatum from the Comintern to accept its decisions or face expulsion. This outcome did not come unexpectedly. On the next day, November 4, the Norwegian Communist Party was formed. Its most prominent leader was Scheflo, who assumed the post of editor of the party's major paper, *Norges Kommunistblad* (Norway's Communist Paper).[16]

At the time this breakaway organization was created, it appeared that it would gain the support of perhaps as much as half of the old party. A very large majority of the Labor Party's youth organization joined the new party. Of Labor's twenty-eight Storting representatives, thirteen opted to follow their parliamentary leader, Scheflo, into the communist ranks. A number of Labor Party newspapers also chose to become communist, including the leading daily in Bergen and, ironically, Tranmæl's old paper in Trondheim.[17]

The Labor Party thereby experienced two significant splits during the early 1920s, both concerning its relationship with Moscow. As a result, three socialist political parties coexisted for a time, each maintaining that it best represented the workers' true interests. But for several years afterwards Tranmæl and the majority who remained with him in the Labor Party continued to insist that not only were they true communists, but that the Labor Party was to the **left** of the communists, who sarcastically were referred to as "right communists" or "new communists."[18]

Although he had accepted the break with the Labor Party, Scheflo was too independent minded to remain simply a slavish adherent of Moscow. He therefore came to occupy a position among the communists that, ironically, was analogous to that held by Tranmæl when the Labor Party was affiliated with the Comintern. Scheflo was recognized as the leader of the communist right wing, while the party's left wing uncritically accepted Moscow's dictates and enjoyed the backing of the Comintern.[19]

The first test of electoral strength between the two rival socialist parties, each maintaining it was communist, occurred in the national election of 1924. Scheflo headed the Communist Party list in Oslo. In response, Tranmæl was pressured into opposing him. Scheflo's defeat was total. He gained but 2500 votes, while Tranmæl received more than 45,000 and reluctantly entered parliament. While support for the communists elsewhere in the country was not insignificant, it was nowhere near what many party optimists had expected. They gained 60,000 votes and six parliamentary representatives, as opposed to 85,000 votes and eight representatives for the Social Democrats. But the Labor Party, with its 180,000 votes and twenty-four representatives clearly remained the party of choice for the majority of workers.[20]

The separate position of each of the three parties was shown also in their international affiliations. Whereas the communists of course belonged to the Comintern, and the Social Democrats were members of the socialist Labor and Socialist International, the Labor Party, after its break with the Comintern, for a time remained completely independent. However, in 1925 it joined the International Bureau for Independent Revolutionary Socialist Parties, a loose organization of small political groups in which the Labor Party was clearly the largest member.[21] Although it thereby sought to show its commitment to working class internationalism, in reality this was of minor concern for the party's leaders. Internal politics mattered the most.

After the Labor Party's departure from the Comintern, the road was open for an end to the split with the Social Democrats. With an eye to the upcoming election of 1927, a unity congress was held early in the year. Reunion was agreed on through compromise, with the Social Democrats' more moderate position reflected in the party program. It declared that Labor's primary goal was to gain majority support from the voters for its socialist viewpoint.[22]

The increased strength of the unified Labor Party revealed itself plainly in the 1927 election. It became the country's largest, with fifty-nine representatives, while communist Storting representation was halved, to three. One of these was Olav Scheflo, who made a parliamentary comeback after having earlier resigned as editor of *Norges Kommunistblad*.

Due to its strong parliamentary position, the Labor Party formed its first cabinet in late January 1928. But because of opposition from powerful financial interests, this proved to be the shortest government in Norwegian history, lasting but eighteen days. However, the Labor Party demonstrated not only its willingness to govern but also its acceptance of parliamentary procedure when it left office after losing a vote of no confidence. Clearly, it no longer adhered to the revolutionary slogans it had proclaimed under Tranmæl as recently as just a few years earlier.

The formation of the first Labor government had significance for the communists as well. Scheflo had strongly supported a cabinet made up of workers' representatives. However, only a few days after it had been forced to resign, the official communist position changed 180 degrees. The party press now openly condemned not only the former government but also communists who had backed it, first and foremost Scheflo. This abrupt reversal was, as usual, due to internal developments in the Soviet Union. Having consolidated his position, Stalin in 1928 discarded the New Economic Policy in favor of the first Five-Year Plan, with emphasis on agricultural collectivization and rapid industrialization. Internationally, the Comintern abandoned cooperation with moderate socialists and bourgeois reformers, who once more were targeted as class enemies.[23]

Scheflo immediately resigned on March 3, 1928. He was joined by a number of other leading members, including the entire Mot Dag organization. The Communist Party, only five years after its founding, had lost almost all of its outstanding members. Afterwards, it was led by persons whose only qualification was unquestioned obedience to the Comintern.[24]

Still a member of the Storting, Scheflo asked to join the Labor Party's delegation. Showing bonds that frequently existed even among political opponents in the parliament, Nygaardsvold, the Labor Party's parliamentary leader, did not submit Scheflo's application to the Central Committee, dominated by Tranmæl. Instead, Nygaardsvold gained the delegation's acceptance of Scheflo and then simply informed the Central Committee.[25] This incident also illustrated an important shift within the Labor Party. Since the time that Tranmæl's faction had come to power in 1918, there had been an unwritten rule that the Central Committee, responsible for carrying out the mandates of the party's national conference or the National Committee (*landsstyret*), had the final word. However, with the formation of the first Labor government, the parliamentary delegation gained increased influence in determining policy. This meant that Tranmæl no longer had foremost authority but had to share it with Nygaardsvold.[26] This trend would later have a significant effect on Trotsky. The terms of his stay in Norway would be determined by the government, whose basis of support was in the parliament, not at party headquarters or in the party press.

For Scheflo, his transfer into Labor's parliamentary delegation did not mean that he had been restored to party prominence. Too much past bitterness prevented him from being nominated when the next national election was held in 1930. Deprived of his parliamentary seat, his finances became precarious. He had difficulty supporting his family and had to resort to obtaining private loans from political acquaintances. Consequently, he had no option but to make peace with Tranmæl, asking if he could once more write for *Arbeiderbladet*. Tranmæl rather generously agreed, and Scheflo began to contribute on a freelance basis.[27] Not until 1931, however, when he was appointed editor of *Sørlandet* (Southern Norway), did he finally regain financial stability.

A significant political change had begun by the time Scheflo settled into his editor's chair in Kristiansand. Although its contours were already evident by the end of the 1920s, it was during the first half of the following decade that the Labor Party abandoned the radical ideology it had adopted under Tranmæl in 1918. From being a proclaimed revolutionary "communist" party, within a few years it became a broad populist movement, willing to govern in cooperation with nonsocialists, and strongly defending the democratic principle of majority rule.[28]

Two major international developments influenced this noteworthy transformation—the outbreak of the Great Depression and the growth of fascism. Norway was extremely hard hit by the depression. At its height, in December 1932, forty-two percent of union members were unemployed.[29] This crisis forced the Labor Party to adopt a pragmatic line. If the workers were to maintain confidence in the party and the trade unions, the labor movement had to come up with concrete solutions.[30]

This problem was made all the more urgent by the clear perception of the connection between the economic crisis and the growth of fascism. Hitler's triumphant takeover of Germany and his brutal suppression of the German labor movement came as a shock to Norwegian socialists. If the Labor Party failed to offer remedies, not only might workers be radicalized in the wrong way but so too farmers and fishermen, who with the industrial workers made up the bulk of the population. This had been the case in Germany, where the Nazis garnered votes from large numbers of frustrated citizens who had come to believe in Hitler's promises.

The Labor Party's response was to introduce a new program, based on creating a planned economy. A three-year plan was drawn up that obliged the state to promote employment through investment in various sectors of the economy. Instead of abolishing capitalism, the state would seek to reform it. With its acceptance of majority rule, the program provided no hint of the party's earlier enthusiasm for dictatorship of the proletariat. Tranmæl himself contributed to the implementation of this important change by giving it his full support. He provided space in *Arbeiderbladet* for the new ideas and held the opening speech at the national conference in May 1933, when Labor ratified the program.[31]

The Labor Party thereupon formally renounced its past, which marked an even more significant turn toward the center in politics. And while this change was based on the need to deal with the Depression and the fear of fascism, it also reflected the party's recognition that it would have little chance for greater success if it were to maintain a radical posture, as evidenced in the previous national election of 1930, when its Storting representation declined significantly.[32]

One interesting aspect of this altered course was that internally the party became less tolerant at the very time it externally indicated acceptance of democratic practices. Greater weight was placed on the authority of the central leadership, the need for discipline, and less free expression of independent viewpoints. Party rules were changed to make it easier to suspend or expel dissidents. One interpretation for why this occurred is that the party, because of growing popular support, now had a chance of coming to power permanently and therefore more than ever required unity.[33] Tranmæl, with his authority solidly anchored in the central leadership, naturally favored tightening discipline. Interestingly, had similar regulations been in effect when he began his career, he might never have risen to prominence.

The new party rules also had significance for Lev Trotsky after his arrival in Norway. When the Labor leadership acted against him, the demand for unity made it difficult for his sympathizers within the party to come to his defense.

Considering the major revisions in the new program, it created remarkably little opposition. Some critical voices were raised, however, both prior to and at the national conference. Scheflo maintained the classical Marxist viewpoint that socialism could only be achieved through destruction of the bourgeois state. He decried the new emphasis on majority rule, maintaining it might cause the party to abandon its socialist principles.[34]

Scheflo, when stating such views in 1933, revealed once more an independent perspective. He thereby appeared to be leading a "left" opposition to the party establishment. He was, however, in no position to combat the new course effectively. Not only was he largely isolated, but he was dependent on the Labor Party financially in his editorial post. His crippling arthritic condition also limited action that he might have carried out had he been in better health. Therefore, while he might express reservations about certain aspects of the more moderate policy, once it had been adopted he supported it fully in the election campaign and also later when the party assumed control of government and began to implement reform legislation.[35] This contrasted significantly with his old friend, Erling Falk, who maintained his revolutionary outlook and criticized the Labor Party severely.[36] But despite his acquiescence, Scheflo continued to be regarded somewhat suspiciously as an element of resistance to the party leadership, in large part because of his past. The fact that he maintained personal ties with left-wing critics like Falk further added to this image.

Håkon Meyer, who would provide especially strong support for Trotsky during the latter's internment, also expressed reservations about the party's new direction at the national conference. Because of his reputation as one of the party's leading thinkers, Meyer did so, not surprisingly, for ideological reasons. He insisted that the program revealed that Labor now aimed primarily at gaining command of government, not control of the economy. He further warned against the assumption that socialism could be attained through the ballot box, without recourse to a dictatorship of the proletariat.[37] His criticism voiced sentiments similar to those of Scheflo. But, as opposed to the latter, who at least publicly backed the new line, Meyer continued to speak out against the consensus viewpoint.

He thereby became in many ways the major opposition figure within the party. As a personality, he contrasted strongly with the dedicated young men of working-class background that Tranmæl surrounded himself with. Meyer was not a proletarian. He was well educated, urbane, and widely traveled. He represented exactly the type of intellectual whom Tranmæl disliked and distrusted. Meyer had not, however, become critical of the party leadership at an early date. During the 1920s he fully supported Tranmæl's independent line toward Moscow.[38]

Although not a leader of the top echelon, he nevertheless played a prominent role within the party. Following the split with the communists, he became for a brief time the leader of Labor's new youth group, the Left Communist Youth Organization (*Venstrekommunistisk Ungdomsfylking*). He also served on the party's Central Committee, acted as the party's secretary for international activity from 1922 to 1927, and held the post of editor of one of its major magazines, *The Twentieth Century* (*Det tyvende Aarhundrede*), from 1929 to 1934.[39] He similarly served as paid secretary of the People's Theater Association (*Folketeater-foreningen*) in Oslo. He was actively engaged in politics during the first half of the 1930s, both on the national level and within the capital. He became a member of the board of the Oslo Labor Party in 1933 and served on its nominating committee, which selected candidates for the parliamentary election. In 1934 he was elected as a Labor representative to the Oslo city council. In addition, he was a prolific writer, producing a large number of articles and books on socialist theory and labor history.[40]

His strongest bastion of influence, however, was within the Oslo Workers Association (*Oslo Arbeidersamfund*). Meyer was repeatedly elected as its chairman from 1921 through early 1934. But he gained the active dislike of the party leadership when he began to question the new reformist direction. On two different occasions in 1933, he was refused renomination by the Workers Association's nominating committee. However, his popularity with the rank-and-file membership ensured his reelection.[41] In 1934 party loyalists finally succeeded in ousting him from his post. In

June of that year Labor's leadership similarly retaliated against his critical articles by securing his dismissal as editor of *The Twentieth Century*.[42]

Meyer, however, continued unfazed his oppositional activity. He strongly influenced the left wing of the party's youth organization, now renamed the Workers Youth Association (*Arbeidernes Ungdomsfylking, AUF*). Among those who shared his critical views was the youth section from Kristiansand, whose members included Inge Scheflo, Olav Scheflo's son. Although Meyer and his followers were never powerful enough to dominate the AUF, they definitely made their influence felt, with compromise resolutions frequently having to be worked out at its national meetings in order to satisfy all factions within the organization.[43]

After his expulsion as editor of *The Twentieth Century*, Meyer in the following year played a major role in the creation of an alternative radical cultural group known as the Socialist Cultural Front (*Sosialistisk Kulturfront*). It included individuals from both within the party and outsiders, such as Mot Dag members and communists.[44] From his office in the People's Theater Building, Meyer was also the midpoint in the weekly sessions of the "Thursday Club," whose participants were young left-wing members of the party. This group met regularly from the mid-1930s on, with Meyer as their intellectual leader, helping to orchestrate strategy within the AUF.[45]

Meyer's independent outlook, in particular his antimilitary view, caused him to be labeled a "doctrinaire socialist." By the mid-'30s he no longer exercised significant influence in the party. Nevertheless, he was not unpopular. He was willing to work for Labor as an author and a lecturer. He did not lack bravery, taking significant risks, in Norway and on the continent, to help political refugees escaping fascism. He was able to cooperate well with party chairman Oscar Torp. However, his relationship with Tranmæl was never good. This was due not only to Tranmæl's dislike of independent-minded intellectuals, but also because Meyer did not in any way share Tranmæl's ascetic lifestyle.[46]

Among the small number of prominent persons within the Labor Party who later were strongly critical of the Nygaardsvold government for its treatment of Trotsky, Olav Scheflo and Håkon Meyer were by far the best known. What is important to note is that both had a reputation for being antagonistic to the party's changed policy. As has been seen, Scheflo did not openly attack the new program once it had been approved, but he nevertheless remained critical of some of its features. He also maintained personal contact with individuals who openly opposed Labor's reformist strategy. Furthermore, as leader of the party organization in Kristiansand, he helped to inspire its youth group's radical outlook. In the eyes of Labor leaders in Oslo, Scheflo was therefore not someone who could be regarded as loyal and uncritical. Meyer to an even greater degree was considered an oppositional figure who undisguisedly carried out factional activity. When Meyer and Scheflo, in particular the former, became involved in Trotsky's defense, in the minds of the party leaders this was but one more expression of their obstructionist inclination. It therefore proved to be Trotsky's misfortune to attract support from persons within the Labor Party who already were either in opposition or were regarded as having such tendencies.

Contrary to the warnings of its critics, the new program enjoyed tremendous success. In the national election of 1933 the Labor Party came close to winning a majority, gaining 69 Storting representatives of a total of 150. In contrast, all of the major nonsocialist parties suffered losses, while the communists, as before, did not receive a single mandate.[47] Although still lacking a majority, Labor had a positive program for dealing with the Depression, and it signaled its willingness to cooperate pragmatically with other parties. Consequently, the Agrarian Party negotiated the "Crisis Compromise" under which Labor agreed to concessions to the farmers, in return receiving Agrarian support. This allowed Johan Nygaardsvold to form the second, and more lasting, Labor government in March 1935.[48]

The coming of the Nygaardsvold government served as a turning point in Norwegian history. It marked the beginning of socialist rule, with Labor in control of government for the next thirty years. This change also provided clear evidence of the Labor Party's altered nature. The new prime minister himself specifically indicated this in a radio address the following year, when he declared that the transition to a socialist society could only occur peacefully "through a majority of the people's free will and in consideration of our country's special conditions, the people's temperament, character, and tradition, without interference from other countries."[49] His view was diametrically opposed to Trotsky's vision of how to achieve a socialist society—through revolution on an international level, rather than giving major consideration to an individual country's unique characteristics.

This served to show that when he became a storm center in Norwegian politics, Trotsky's most significant foe was someone whom he initially scarcely recognized—Johan Nygaardsvold. The latter had a solid political background behind him prior to assuming the highest office in the land. First elected to parliament in 1915, he had served as leader of the Labor Party's delegation, and in 1934 he was elected president of the Storting, indicating the respect he also enjoyed among nonsocialists.[50] His background as a seasoned parliamentarian colored his outlook. He was thorough, spoke with authority, and commanded respect, but he also possessed a strong temperament. Although he generally kept his temper under control, at times it got the best of him, resulting in violent outbursts.

While he had participated regularly in the party's national conferences since 1923, Nygaardsvold never played a leading role.[51] He was not interested in ideological questions about socialist theory. What mattered most for him were practical reforms.[52] Once in office he enthusiastically set in motion the party's new program. He received valuable assistance from his cabinet, but it was "the Old Man," (Gubben), as he was popularly known, who set the style and tone. His influence affected all major areas of government decision making except foreign policy.[53]

A significant shift in power therefore occurred within the Labor Party with the coming of Nygaardsvold's government. Rather than the Central Committee under Tranmæl's influence determining policy, decisions now were increasingly made within the government in consultation with the parliamentary delegation. As editor of *Arbeiderbladet*, Tranmæl continued to express his point of view, but the paper's main function was to defend the government's politics.[54] For Trotsky, this meant that the Labor Party's main organ would automatically sustain whatever action the government might take against him.

The cabinet's emphasis on immediate economic improvement similarly had implications for Trotsky. The government's initial weak position was clear. With a minority in parliament, it demanded loyalty and patience from its supporters since the party's more ambitious goals were not attainable. On the other hand, when it did gain success with some of its reforms, the government created renewed confidence among party members.[55] Therefore, even persons critical of the cabinet for being too moderate, such as Scheflo, did not risk voicing criticism for fear that this might weaken it, perhaps even allowing the *borgerlige* (bourgeoisie) to regain power. This explains why even at the height of the government's severe treatment of Trotsky, Scheflo never bluntly stated his dissent.

As a result of the government's energetic actions, optimism began to replace the hopelessness that many had felt during the depth of the

Depression. Unemployment was reduced significantly, a trend that had begun even before Nygaardsvold took office but which was speeded up considerably.[56] Labor union membership grew dramatically, and it became far easier to carry out unionization in all areas of economic activity.[57]

Norway's economic progress mirrored to a considerable extent the general pattern that was taking place in the world economy of capitalist states after 1935. Nevertheless, the Nygaardsvold government's actions undoubtedly speeded up economic recovery and reduced unemployment more markedly than would have been the case had the country followed the policies of previous administrations.[58] Most importantly, Norwegians in general **perceived** the improved conditions as being due to the cabinet's actions and therefore gave it credit.

The government that provided Trotsky with asylum consequently enjoyed broad popular support. Any actions that it might take against him would not generate major opposition. Nygaardsvold's administration furthermore was in the process of carrying out exactly the type of socialism that he abhorred. Rather than attempting to restructure society radically from a Marxist perspective—which would have been impossible—its economic programs and social reforms served to rescue capitalism, introducing greater state involvement in economic activity but remaining far removed from the classical Marxist ideals that Trotsky favored—revolution, dictatorship of the proletariat, elimination of private property, and creation of a classless society.

International relations was the one area of government in which Nygaardsvold did not actively involve himself. He fully agreed with his foreign minister, Halvdan Koht, who received considerable freedom in forming Norwegian foreign policy from 1935 to 1940.[59]

Because of his position, reputation, and strength of character, Koht exercised dominant influence within the government and within the Labor Party when he chose to do so. Intellectually he was without question the cabinet's outstanding personality. Now in his early sixties, he had held the position of professor of history at the University of Oslo since 1910 and had acquired an international reputation as a scholar.

Koht's ideological outlook, favoring integrating the working class into the nation as a whole, coincided with that of the prime minister. Nygaardsvold led a government whose orientation was clearly national, based on overcoming the problems of the Depression by seeking to have the country become as self-sufficient as possible. In foreign relations the government was similarly nationally oriented, striving to avoid complications among increasingly hostile powers by maintaining strict neutrality.[60] Nygaardsvold not only shared Koht's emphasis on neutrality but tended to go even further in wanting to avoid dangerous confrontations in the international arena.[61]

Their viewpoint came under criticism in 1936 prior to the Labor Party's national conference. A key group within the party, including Tranmæl, reacted to the danger from Nazi Germany by favoring collective security under the direction of the League of Nations. Koht attended the conference as acting prime minister as well as foreign minister since Nygaardsvold was ill. Koht faced a unified leadership that was determined to change policy. But when he threatened to resign rather than abandon neutrality, the party leadership immediately gave in, knowing that Nygaardsvold would also resign. It accepted a face-saving compromise that in reality left the government's position completely unchanged.[62]

For Trotsky, Norway's foreign policy, implemented by Koht with Nygaardsvold's backing, would have serious repercussions. The foreign minister's strong desire to avoid difficulties with major powers meant that he would not allow Trotsky to stand in the way of maintaining good relations with the Soviet Union. While Koht adopted a low profile during the controversy surrounding Trotsky in the fall of 1936, there is no question but that someone as strong-willed as he would have intervened had he disagreed with the government's decisions.

The national conference did have to deal with an issue that everyone, including dissidents such as Meyer, could agree on—the party's relationship with the communists. The latter had once more made a change in tactics with the beginning of the Popular Front movement, inaugurated by the Comintern in July 1935. No longer were social democratic parties portrayed as "social fascists," but they were instead invited to cooperate with the communists in defense against fascism. In Norway their changed position was reflected in a positive attitude toward the Nygaardsvold government. They went so far as to propose not only cooperation in the upcoming election campaign but also discussion about possible unification.[63]

The Labor Party chose, however, to keep them at arms length. Even Scheflo, who earlier had favored ending the schism with his former party, was now strongly opposed.[64] In its response the national conference in essence rejected both proposals by insisting on conditions that were unacceptable to the communists.[65]

Despite this rebuff, the latter continued their one-sided love affair with Labor. They did not participate actively in the 1936 election, running a list of candidates only in Bergen. They justified their passivity by maintaining that they did not want to divide the workers' votes.[66] The real reasons were their continuing electoral decline, their obedience to the Comintern's Popular Front tactic, and the hope that they would benefit from supporting the well-liked Labor government. On one issue, however, the communists remained completely unwilling to refrain from criticizing the government. This concerned its decision to provide Trotsky with asylum. Although their negative commentary no longer carried much weight due to the Communist Party's reduced circumstances, Labor strategists like Tranmæl nevertheless took it into account, especially in an election year.

In addition to revising its internal policy, Labor's position within international socialism underwent considerable change following its break with the Comintern. The party at first had no connections with any international socialist organization. However, as noted, this changed when it joined the International Bureau for Independent Revolutionary Socialist Parties, known in short as the Paris Bureau because it initially was headquartered in the French capital. This association reflected the Labor Party's desire to identify itself as a radical socialist party, affiliated neither with the Communist International nor with the Labor and Socialist International, the successor of the Second International.

Labor's move obviously did not have Trotsky's approval at a time when he still backed the Comintern in its clash with Tranmæl. Even afterwards, he maintained that "the Comintern was not completely to blame for the rupture" with the Labor Party.[67] By the early 1930s, however, his attitude had changed, if only briefly. He could hardly disapprove of a party that refused affiliation with the Comintern now that this organization was simply Stalin's rubber stamp.

Although the Labor Party briefly resigned from the Paris Bureau in 1927, when it was in the process of reuniting with the Social Democrats, it rejoined in 1930.[68] The bureau's membership, however, was hardly impressive.

Except for the Norwegian socialists, it consisted of inconsequential factional groups from a variety of European countries.[69]

In an attempt to broaden the basis of its international collaboration, the Labor Party and the British Independent Labour Party took the initiative to establish the International Labor Community of Left Socialist Parties in May 1932, known by its German initials IAG. Headquartered first in Berlin, it had to move following Hitler's takeover. Although its formal name from January 1934 onwards was the International Bureau for Revolutionary Socialist Unity, it most often was referred to simply as the London Bureau.[70] Until 1934 the Labor Party regularly participated in its affairs.[71] The Norwegians enjoyed the distinction of being the largest group within the London Bureau—and also of being its only unified national affiliate. The other members were splinter left socialist parties that adhered to various ideological positions.

There was obvious agreement among the left socialists that both the Comintern and the Labor and Socialist International were failures, in particular because neither had done anything effective to prevent Hitler's destruction of the German labor movement. However, they disagreed concerning the extent to which, if any, the bureau should attempt to replace the two larger internationals. Not surprisingly, the Labor Party became an attractive prize for those who wished to persuade it to adopt a particular ideological and/or organizational perspective. In particular, Trotsky and the exile Socialist Workers Party of Germany (SAP) both hoped to influence the Labor Party.[72]

When he moved to France in July 1933, Trotsky for the first time openly called for a new international. Cooperation thereupon replaced competition between Trotsky and some of the left socialist parties. For a short time he and the leader of the SAP, Jacob Walcher, worked closely together to secure approval for such an international at an upcoming conference of left socialist parties, to be held in Paris at the end of August.[73] Trotsky's followers, who were organized in national sections and known collectively as the International Left Opposition (ILO), were invited to attend.

On August 26, the day before the conference opened, his collaboration with Walcher resulted in the "Declaration of Four," approved by the ILO, the SAP, and two minor Dutch parties. They were in agreement that the condition of world capitalism, the misery of the working class during the Depression, the revolutionary movement of oppressed colonial peoples, the danger posed by fascism, and the possibility of a new cycle of war obligated the "proletarian vanguard" to unite in a **"new (Fourth) International** [emphasis in original] . . . in the shortest possible time."[74]

The other groups at the meeting, however, refused to join the four, providing good evidence of the fractured nature of the left socialist political parties. Because of the Labor Party's prominent position, its repudiation of Trotsky's position was especially noteworthy. Ideologically, it declared that its goal was to work for "international unification based on class struggle."[75] It therefore would not take part in any action that might divide the international labor movement, such as forming a new international organization.

The Norwegian rebuff did not surprise Trotsky. He had already predicted that the Labor Party would not accept the "Declaration of Four." Instead, for the immediate future he placed his hopes in Norway on Mot Dag, insisting it was the proper vehicle for making the country's workers more revolutionary. He afterwards castigated his associate Walcher for having allied with the Labor Party, declaring that this would cause the SAP to lose influence with Mot Dag, which had split with the Labor Party and sought to outcompete it by winning over its left-wing members. Trotsky scoffed at the idea that Walcher, from Paris, might succeed in persuading Tranmæl to move in a more radical direction when Falk, the Mot Dag leader, had not been able to do so from Oslo.[76]

Trotsky's negative assessment was perceptive. Tranmæl's refusal to commit to a new international and his determination to maintain national control over the party was clear. Trotsky furthermore was correct in his analysis that the Labor Party would only be willing to cooperate within the London Bureau as long as this did not involve adopting a radical new policy. But it was extremely irritating for him to recognize that the Labor Party held sway within the bureau. At the Paris conference a majority resolution promoted by the Labor Party was accepted, not the "Declaration of Four." This resolution declared support for international working-class unity but made only vague reference to a future "world congress" that would consider a possible course of action, rather than calling for the immediate founding of a new international.[77]

For Trotsky, this showed conclusively that there was no possibility of influencing the Labor Party as long as Tranmæl remained its leader. Rather than compromise with Tranmæl, Trotsky believed he should be weakened and discredited. Consequently, during the fall of 1933, an increasingly acrimonious debate took place between him and Walcher over how the two signatories of the "Declaration of Four" should treat the Labor Party. Trotsky favored a break in order to demonstrate international socialist displeasure with Labor, headed by Tranmæl. The SAP, while it shared Trotsky's distaste of the party's more moderate position, nevertheless maintained that cooperation was necessary because Labor represented the overwhelming majority of the country's workers. The SAP furthermore believed that through fraternization it might be able to revolutionize the Norwegian comrades, indicating the SAP's complete lack of understanding of conditions in Norway.[78] But while Trotsky comprehended the difficulty involved in winning over the Labor Party, he in turn was deluded when he believed that Mot Dag might outcompete it.[79] His strong distaste for Tranmæl prevented him from assessing the party leader objectively. Instead, Tranmæl became another obsession for him—the embodiment of the kind of right-wing socialist opportunism that Trotsky abhorred. He went so far as to coin the term "Tranmaelism" for this kind of socialism.

The dispute between Trotsky and the SAP also involved the London Bureau. Trotsky predicted that the Labor Party, once it adopted a more moderate position, intended to abandon the bureau at the first opportunity.[80] The bureau's leadership, however, because of Labor's powerful position within the organization, refused to take any action against the Norwegians. Trotsky therefore insisted that his allies who had signed the "Declaration of Four" should resign from the bureau in order to demonstrate to Norwegian workers that internationally Tranmæl no longer enjoyed the company of "honest people" among left-wing socialists.[81]

Walcher completely rejected Trotsky's urgings. By demanding such a radical action, Walcher declared, the International Left Opposition would only succeed in isolating itself from other socialist groups. Rather tellingly, he succinctly summed up Trotsky's position: "Trotsky too, despite his great personality, stands all alone in the world."[82]

Trotsky, however, as the foremost proponent of organizing a new international, insisted on forging ahead, establishing a clear line of division against those who opposed its creation. The SAP, on the other hand, while favoring an international, had as its main priority cooperation with other groups within the London Bureau, which it hoped, unrealistically, to dominate eventually. Such collaboration extended to the Labor Party, no matter how much the SAP leaders might disagree with the trend within Norwegian socialism. As a result, by the end of 1933, the possibility of unity between Trotsky and the other parties that had signed the "Declaration of Four," the SAP being the most important, lay in ruins. In early January 1934, Trotsky appealed to rank and file members of the SAP over the heads of their leaders.[83] In turn, Walcher announced at a party conference in Paris in March 1934 that the alliance made in August should be considered at an end since the Trotskyites had described SAP's membership in the London Bureau as being tantamount to "treason."[84]

By early 1934 the only vestige of what had appeared, in the previous summer, to mark the start of useful collaboration between the Trotskyites and other left socialist parties was a previously scheduled international youth conference, planned for February.[85] Its outcome proved to have significance for Trotsky's movement in general, now having undergone another name change, becoming the International Communist League (ICL) in the fall of 1933. More specifically, the gathering would later also have consequences for his position in Norway. The SAP's main delegate at the February conference, Willy Brandt, had fled Germany at the age of nineteen to become his party's link with the Norwegian labor movement. In Oslo he soon established contacts in the Labor Party, especially within its left wing, joining its youth organization, AUF.[86]

As head of the SAP's youth organization, Brandt at first adopted a more positive attitude toward the Trotskyites than the regular SAP leadership. He felt there was a better possibility for a new youth international than for a Fourth International, and he was not averse to cooperating with ICL youth delegates to accomplish this.[87]

The conference had scarcely opened in Laren, the Netherlands, on February 24, when it was raided by Dutch police under the pretext that its foreign participants had entered the country illegally. Four unfortunate Germans were simply transported to the border and handed over to Nazi authorities. But Finn Moe from the Labor Party and Aake Anker Ording of Mot Dag rescued Brandt, staying with him during the entire episode and advising him to use his Norwegian residence permit for identification. He thereby escaped being deported to Germany.[88]

Instead, the delegates were expelled to Belgium. Four days later they hurriedly assembled a rump session in Brussels.[89] Because of a sincere desire to reach some kind of agreement, the young socialists proved to be more flexible than their elders. This allowed Brandt to work out a resolution that in general terms called for both a new socialist international and a new youth international. More concretely, the delegates agreed to establish an International Bureau of Revolutionary Youth Organizations, with its secretariat in Stockholm. It would be made up of three persons: Willy Brandt, Walter Held from the ICL's youth group, and a representative from the Swedish Socialist Youth League, Karl Kilbom's youth organization.[90]*

From its founding there was little cordiality among the members of the Youth Secretariat. They suspected each other, quite correctly, of only furthering the interests of their respective organizations. The relationship between Held and Brandt was especially filled with controversy. Even before the secretariat had been set up, a dispute arose over exactly what kind of organization it should be. Held insisted on having a centralized office in Stockholm. Brandt and the Swedish representative, Kurt Forslund, objected because it was clear that Held intended to spread pro-Trotskyite propaganda within Kilbom's relatively numerous Swedish youth group. In the end a compromise was worked out whereby the secretariat formally retained Stockholm as its seat (it therefore was sometimes referred to as the Stockholm Youth Secretariat or Bureau), but in reality it was moved to Oslo, with the Swedes transferring their mandate to Mot Dag, represented by Aake Anker Ording.[91]

Held, as Trotsky's youth leader, arrived in Oslo in early June.[92] To a large extent he was financially dependent on Mot Dag, which paid for his living expenses as well as for the secretariat's youth bulletin. Mot Dag also provided office space. The secretariat's start proved to be anything but promising. It was run by two young German exiles whose parent organizations were in the process of distancing themselves completely from each other. Both Held and Brandt were under instruction to carry out factional activity. And the secretariat to a large degree depended on Mot Dag, which also engaged in factional conflict, within Norway and internationally.[93] Because Mot Dag at this time was in rivalry with the Labor Party, the Youth Secretariat quite naturally came to be regarded as simply an extension of Mot Dag. Brandt, although affiliated with the Labor Party through his membership in the AUF, not only belonged to Mot Dag but held a leading post on its board of directors.[94] The Labor Party therefore viewed him with considerable suspicion.[95] The same applied to an even greater degree to the Trotskyite Walter Held.

---

* Kilbom was the leader of the Socialist Party (*Socialistiske partiet*), a splinter group that had earlier split from the communists.

The two rivals, Brandt and Held, were never able to reconcile their differences. For the latter, what mattered most was to achieve a Fourth International and a new youth international as quickly as possible. Brandt, supported by Mot Dag and also the Swedes, insisted that this was premature.[96] With such division, the work of the Youth Secretariat was hardly successful. Not only did constant quarrels between Brandt and Held have a debilitating effect, but the various youth organizations that were formally affiliated with the secretariat, themselves part of small sectarian factions, showed little interest in its work. After a year's existence it was impossible to conceal that it had not made progress toward its goal of outcompeting the youth organizations of the rival internationals, the Comintern and the Labor and Socialist International.[97]

Held's frustrations as the ICL's representative on the secretariat mirrored Trotsky's experiences internationally. He felt himself stymied in his effort to achieve the Fourth International, and he accused the Norwegian Labor Party of playing a major role in blocking international revolutionary unity. "That we must fight for the Fourth International wherever possible is clear. This . . . means an irreconcilable struggle against the treacherous policy of Tranmael and certainly not a brotherhood in arms with him."[98] Trotsky deplored the London Bureau's alleged weakness toward the Labor Party's "reformism," with the organization criticizing Tranmæl only to a limited degree while making certain that its ties with the Labor Party remained unbroken. On the other hand, Trotsky complained, members of the bureau, spearheaded by the SAP, did not hesitate to condemn the Trotskyites severely: "Our highly respectable left centrists become very gruff to [Trotsky's] Bolshevik 'sectarians,' to the Tranmaels they coo like doves."[99]

His aggravation with what he viewed as the bureau's coddling of the Norwegians became so strong that Trotsky insisted on halting all connections with it. When the bureau invited the International Communist League to take part in an international conference it was hosting, he replied with an ultimatum in November 1934. Unless the bureau was willing to discuss issues raised by the ICL, "above all the Norwegian question: namely, what the correct proletarian policy ought to be in Norway," his organization would not participate.[100]

As a result, the ICL was not represented at the bureau's meeting in Paris in February 1935.[101] This did not prevent Trotsky from expressing his opinion about what the conference should discuss. At the head of its agenda, he declared, should be "a merciless condemnation of Tranmaelism and of every policy that flirts with it."[102] But while he rarely failed to offer unsolicited advice, he was not one to accept criticism with equanimity. He followed the gathering closely and became highly agitated when Willy Brandt denounced delegates who favored the early creation of a Fourth International. This caused Trotsky to declare that Brandt's action had created a situation within the Youth Secretariat that was "absolutely intolerable."[103] "Comrade Held is at [sic] Oslo, and the young man of the SAP [Brandt] comes to the Paris conference to attack us."[104] Trotsky ordered all of the ICL's youth sections to denounce Brandt "clearly and mercilessly" and further insisted that the secretariat be reorganized to give the Trotskyites a majority.[105]

For a very brief period, however, Trotsky felt compelled to dampen his negative assessment of Brandt because at the same time that the latter condemned the idea of a Fourth International, he sent the SAP leadership a strong critique of Mot Dag, with which the SAP leadership had enjoyed good ties. Based on his experience in Norway, Brandt emphasized that Mot Dag was an elitist intellectual organization that was doomed to fail because it had not gained significant support from the Norwegian working class. He stressed the need for the SAP to distance itself from Mot Dag, and advised turning toward the Labor Party, in particular to those who might wish to change the party in a more radical direction.[106] By May 1935 Brandt had completed his divorce from Mot Dag, moving the Youth Secretariat out of its offices. In retaliation, Mot Dag withdrew its representative from the secretariat's leadership.[107]

For once, Held agreed with Brandt. The previous positive outlook that Trotsky held toward Mot Dag had changed. The latter increasingly shared the antagonism toward the Trotskyites that was common among left socialist groups affiliated with the London Bureau, of which Mot Dag remained a member. In Norway, this was reflected in Mot Dag's hostile attitude toward Held. Trotsky complained that Mot Dag "refused to allow our delegate [Held] to attend its meetings and to participate in the life of its organization."[108]

Brandt now joined Held in denouncing Mot Dag. This caused Trotsky to believe that developments within the Youth Secretariat had changed in favor of the ICL, and he called on all of its youth groups "to declare that they categorically refuse to collaborate . . . with Mot Dag."[109] For

Trotsky, however, what mattered most was not gaining control of the Youth Secretariat. He stressed that "the future of the [Youth Secretariat] is completely bound up with the development of the Fourth International." Once it had been created, he expected the various left socialist youth organizations to regroup naturally for or against the international.[110]

Following his arrival in Norway, where he could be briefed firsthand by Held, Trotsky, however, became alarmed. The Swedish Socialist Youth League had refused to accept Mot Dag's eviction from the Youth Secretariat. Instead, negotiations between Brandt and the Swedes appeared to be going on behind Held's back. Brandt and Held were deadlocked because neither would accept the other's proposal for radically restructuring the secretariat.[111] These irreconcilable differences, plus Trotsky's attacks against the SAP, made it impossible for the Youth Secretariat to continue in its present form. At a meeting on August 18, Brandt and Forslund, the Swedish representative, combined to oust Held. Brandt thereupon gained effective control over the secretariat for the SAP but had to give in to the Swedes' insistence that Mot Dag be kept informed about its current operations.[112]

With Held's expulsion, the last vestige of cooperation with some of the left socialist groups in the London Bureau, from which Trotsky confidently had anticipated major results in the summer of 1933, came to a dismal conclusion. Differences between them had been irreconcilable, exacerbated by personal animosities, which Trotsky augmented by his biting attacks against all groups that did not accept his viewpoint, especially those that remained affiliated with the bureau.

When condemning the bureau, Trotsky noted with satisfaction that one of his predictions had been proven true. He had always argued that Tranmæl only retained membership in the organization in order to maintain the illusion that the Labor Party was still revolutionary, "thereby allowing the opportunist leadership of the NAP [Norwegian Labor Party] to tame its own left-wing opposition."[113] Labor too was not represented at the bureau's international conference in Paris in February 1935. Trotsky declared that the Labor Party, on "its own initiative brought about the break at the precise moment it chose to do so." Because it had been the only real mass party within the bureau, said Trotsky, the "formlessness of the [bureau] has always been explained and excused particularly by the need of adaptation to the 'great' Norwegian party. Now Tranmael feels he has reached his port, and he says to dear Schwab [Walcher's code name]: the Moor has done his work, the Moor is dismissed."[114]

The Labor Party's refusal to take part in the meeting was not a radical new departure but represented a trend that went back to 1933. At its national conference that year the party had reaffirmed its commitment to "cooperation with the independent parties [of the London Bureau] toward the goal of furthering unification of the working class."[115] However, it also decided to establish closer ties with neighboring socialist parties that belonged to the Labor and Socialist International. As a result, in 1934 and 1935 the Labor Party and the L.O. participated in meetings with representatives from other Scandinavian socialist parties and trade union organizations.[116]

Such collaboration was hardly compatible with the party's professed cooperation with the small left socialist groups within the London Bureau.[117] But not only did the Labor Party refuse to send delegates to Paris, it also withheld paying its dues. The relationship worsened further after Nygaardsvold formed his government in March. In October the bureau declared that considerable criticism had been expressed at its most recent meeting against the new government because the Labor Party "was departing from the revolutionary principles of the Bureau."[118]

As Trotsky's comment showed, the party responded by breaking completely. It insisted that its membership had always been based on the desire to create a unified international labor movement. However, the tendency during the last years had been for the bureau to become a permanent organization, and some of its members were "also working for the building up of a fourth international." The Labor Party formally resigned from the bureau on November 22, 1935.[119] Semantics aside, it chose to end its affiliation because of its desire for closer cooperation with mainstream socialist parties of Western Europe, in particular the Scandinavian parties. Furthermore, having assumed governmental responsibility, Labor wished to make clear internationally, as well as nationally, that it was distancing itself from its revolutionary past, pursuing instead the reformist socialism that Trotsky so bitterly deplored.

He continued his attacks against the Labor Party until just prior to leaving France. In May 1935 he criticized the party in *Unser Wort* for not having acted in a revolutionary manner immediately after its great election victory in 1933. He maintained that the party should have called together a labor congress, supplemented with representatives of the farmers and fishermen, to make demands on the parliament. If the Storting had refused to give in, then the congress should have seized power by dissolving the parliament and deposing the king.[120] Through such bold action, Trotsky declared, the Labor Party could have "transformed Norway into a working class stronghold" capable of instilling "by its example revolutionary courage into the masses of Scandinavia" and becoming "an important factor in the development of Europe."[121]

To a great extent he was suggesting that the Labor Party should have utilized the same tactics that he had employed when the Bolsheviks overthrew the Kerensky government in Russia. His negative commentary toward the Labor Party for adopting reformist policies was therefore very severe. He acknowledged this in his diary, pointing out that "I speak very sharply about the Norwegian Labor Party and its policies while in power" in the *Unser Wort* article. It would therefore not be "surprising if this article should induce the Norwegian government to refuse me a visa at the very last moment." He added fatalistically that this "would be very annoying, but [it was] to be expected."[122]

Considering the vehemence of his assault, especially his hostile characterization of Tranmæl, superficially it might seem surprising that he gained admission to Norway. But while Tranmæl was fully aware of Trotsky's negative opinion of him, he was never one to exercise a grudge; and Nygaardsvold, preoccupied with domestic matters, did not concern himself with questions of international socialism. Also, as has been seen, the decision to allow Trotsky entry was in part based on internal politics, involving first and foremost Scheflo's influence.

Furthermore, while not only Trotsky but also the Labor Party's former collaborators in the London Bureau, such as the SAP and the British Independent Labour Party, might deplore the party's new course, in Norway itself persons who formerly had been critical now generally not only ceased their disparagement, but embraced the party. Members of Mot Dag repudiated their leader, Erling Falk, and ceased their attacks on the Labor Party for allegedly having capitulated to capitalism and thereby preparing the way for fascism. Instead, Mot Dag accepted without hesitation the Nygaardsvold government and soon afterwards moved to join the Labor Party. Its members were admitted in 1936, but only after agreeing to dissolve their organization.[123]

Willy Brandt, representing the SAP, initially adopted a more critical position. He accepted the formation of the Labor government but believed it was necessary to reproach it openly in order to strengthen the party's left wing. He was influenced by what had happened in Germany, where the major socialist party, the Social Democrats, had been moderate reformists, unable to stop the dynamic advance of Hitler's Nazi movement.[124] However, Brandt later concluded that conditions in Norway were different. By adopting a social democratic reform policy, it was possible, Brandt recognized, to better the condition of the working class by alleviating the difficulties of the Depression, thereby helping to eliminate the social and political frustrations that had provided fertile soil for the growth of fascism.[125]

Trotsky, however, lacked both the insight needed to understand Norwegian society and, more importantly, the interest. For him what mattered was furthering proletarian world revolution. This required combat against both Stalin's form of communism, which Trotsky viewed as a betrayal, and democratic reformist socialism, which he regarded as but the precursor to fascism. For him the one true path to socialism lay with the course that he staked out. This meant the creation of a Fourth International, which would outcompete the false versions of socialism represented by the Comintern and the Labor and Socialist International.

After his admission to Norway, he fully understood that he could no longer condemn Norwegian socialism, and he scrupulously abstained from commenting on domestic political issues. His diatribes against Tranmæl were therefore over. But, on the other hand, he continued to attempt to influence international events through his followers who belonged to the Trotskyite sections within the ICL. In the long run, this course of action would have dire consequences for his stay.

4 Life at Wexhall

> Only the victorious revolution can mend the cares, the miseries, and the dislocation of war. . . . Not only will the external foes of the Soviet Union thereby be defeated, but the internal contradictions, which engender the barbarous dictatorship of the Stalin clique, will be overcome. The proletarian dictatorship will unite our dismembered, bled-dry continent . . . will establish the Soviet United States of Europe. . . . All mankind will be brought together into a socialist society and a harmonious culture.
> —Trotsky, *Unser Wort*, early September 1935

FOR SLIGHTLY MORE THAN A YEAR, Lev and Natalia lived in Heradsbygda, a tiny agricultural village close to Hønefoss, whose urban population in 1935 numbered less than 4000.*[1] Despite being relatively near Oslo, the trip to Hønefoss took at least two hours. From the town it took an additional fifteen minutes by car before arriving at Wexhall.[2] Here was where the Norwegian government had agreed the couple could live. As Trotsky later put it, somewhat dramatically: "My wife and I lived in extreme isolation, without thinking of feeling sorry for ourselves."[3] Wexhall† was situated on a slight rise, with views of Tyrifjorden and the rolling ridges of Ringerike. Trotsky loved the vistas from the house.[4] He expressed his admiration of both the natural beauty of Ringerike and the Norwegians whom he met soon after he and Natalia had arrived, declaring that he had

---

* According to the census of 1930, the population of Hønefoss at that time numbered 3193. The adjacent agricultural county (*kommune*) of Norderhov, on the other hand, had 11,468 inhabitants.

† Both Norwegian and foreign writers have misspelled Wexhall in a great variety of different ways. Alternative versions include Wekshall, Vekshall, and Veksal.

become completely captivated by the landscape, the beauty of the nature, and the people in the country. I don't know if the so-called "Aryan" race is descended directly from Norway, but I must say that the tall, strong bodies and faces make a very favorable impression. Nature has the effect—at least in the small part of the country that I have up to now learned to know—of being appealing and calming.[5]

The Trotskys did not dwell alone. They sublet part of the lower floor from Konrad Knudsen, who was in charge of the Hønefoss office of *Fremtiden*. The Trotskys had two rooms completely at their disposal, Lev's workroom and a bedroom. They took their meals with the Knudsen family in the common dining room. Knudsen resided in the other part of the ground floor with his wife Hilda and their two children. Also living with them was the family cook and Trotsky's secretary, Jan Frankel, who had his work station in the dining room, immediately adjacent to Trotsky's study.[6] Adding to the crowded conditions was another tenant family, that of Egil Johansen Wraaman and his wife Gunvor, who lived with their two children on the second floor.[7] Although quite cramped compared with the standards of later, more prosperous times, the housing of multiple families under one roof was by no means uncommon in Norway during the depression-ridden 1930s. Trotsky never complained about his accommodations but on the contrary only had positive things to say about his stay. However, the maximum number of people in the house had apparently been exceeded because when Frankel left Norway in October, his replacement had to be satisfied with accommodations at a neighbor's house.[8]

Natalia and Lev soon established a very close relationship with the Knudsens, as well as with the other residents. The Trotskys were very popular on a personal level, not because of politics.[9] Gunvor Wraamann remembered Lev as a kindly, grandfatherly figure who played with her children and who gave them caramels.[10]

Their hosts, Konrad and Hilda Knudsen became great admirers of Trotsky. While their attitudes were largely personal, there was an element of political empathy involved as well. Knudsen was on the left wing of the Labor Party. Born in 1890, he came from a working-class background. He emigrated to the United States in 1909, where he worked for a number of years as a painter, lumberjack, and manual laborer.[11] Radicalized by his working-class experiences in America, much in the same way as Tranmæl, Knudsen, also like Tranmæl, was associated with the IWW.[12] In 1917 he found his true profession as a journalist, becoming editor of a socialist newspaper in Chicago. However, sentiment in the United States during and immediately following World War I was anything but favorable toward socialism. The Knudsens returned to Norway in 1920. Konrad resumed life as a painter but in 1923 secured his newspaper position in Hønefoss. He was at the same time active in the Labor Party, becoming its salaried secretary in Buskerud. He also held a number of other party positions in the 1920s, including serving on the National Committee in the mid-1920s.[13] In his mid-forties, he was in the prime of his journalistic and political career when he met Trotsky.

The latter commented afterward that the Trotskys' life style at Wexhall could be described as having been "petty bourgeois."[14] For the first time in his exile, he could live openly and feel free. He could go for daily walks, wandering down the slope toward the neighboring old-people's retirement home, running his walking stick along the fence. During his working day he enjoyed long coffee breaks, admiring the landscape from the garden.[15] Once a week he and Natalia accompanied the Knudsens to the movie house in Hønefoss, where they saw two-year-old American films. But the highlight of their day occurred when the local handicapped mailman arrived, by bicycle in summer and by sled in winter, bringing them "heavy packets of papers and letters bearing stamps from every part of the world."[16]

As always, Natalia took care of practical things. When they moved in, she immediately busied herself arranging their living quarters, "hammering nails in by herself, stringing cords, hanging things up and changing them around. . . . She is guided . . . by two considerations: cleanliness and attractiveness."[17]

For Trotsky, what mattered the most was unpacking and setting up his precious books. At Wexhall, as an unfriendly witness, Jonas Lie, would later write, Trotsky "was besieged by books. They lay in piles on the table, on the floor, in opened boxes; they stood in rows like armies on parade in their bookshelves—billions of letters, millions of words."[18]

Although Trotsky had a secretary at his disposal, Frankel did not have command of Russian. This precluded Trotsky from corresponding in his native language. A Russian-speaking typist, Mrs. Elisabeth Dahl, who had been born in Estonia, was thereupon hired to work periodically, but alas, no typewriter with Russian characters was available in Norway. Trotsky was forced to have his own machine sent from France.[19] Once it arrived, with his books in place and with the assistance of his Russian-speaking typist, he could work more and more, providing "my salvation in the literal sense of the word."[20]

While he lived in relative isolation, his whereabouts quickly became known. Media representatives, not surprisingly, wished to have access to this famous and controversial figure. Hollywood agents therefore came calling not long after his arrival.[21] Trotsky at this time, however, had no desire to call special attention to himself and turned down all requests for interviews.

He was therefore allowed to relax during July, with the controversy concerning his unannounced coming gradually dying down. Quisling's National Union did, however, make a few halfhearted attempts to keep the spotlight on him. Knudsen informed Trotsky in early July that the "fascists" were organizing a meeting in Drammen, protesting his presence, but Knudsen did not expect the demonstration to amount to anything.[22] Later in the month National Union's former press chief wrote a diatribe in the party newspaper filled with alleged atrocities committed by Trotsky during the Russian Civil War and deploring the fact that "Mother Norway" had now accepted someone as diabolical as him into "her embrace."[23]

The Trotskys on one occasion did experience closer contact with a hostile critic. In late July a newspaperman from *ABC*, the Fatherland League's weekly paper, crept up on Lev and Natalia as they lay on folding chairs in the garden. The League, while not fascist, was strongly nationalistic and antisocialist. The journalist succeeded in snapping several pictures before being discovered. Lev and Natalia thereupon jumped to their feet, chasing this prototype paparazzo from Wexhall with shouts that they wished to be undisturbed. His pictures were published in the July 25 edition of *ABC*, along with an article denouncing the fact that Norway had given asylum to such a bloody executioner, who allegedly was continuing to indulge in subversive politics. The pictures of Lev and Natalia lying peacefully on chaise longues failed, however, to sustain the sinister figure portrayed in the article.[24]

At this time Trotsky was more interested in the left in Norwegian politics than the extreme right. Although he never spoke out publicly for obvious reasons, his negative attitude toward Scandinavian socialism in general, and Norwegian socialism in particular, remained unchanged. Having been introduced to a number of Labor party editors who were invited to

Wexhall to meet Knudsen's famous tenant, Lev described them as being smug, satisfied, and parochial. They blithely believed they could peacefully introduce socialism by restricting capitalism democratically, having no conception that men such as Marx, Engels, and Lenin had lived, or that the October Revolution and "the upheavals of fascism" had occurred. Decrying the editors' emphasis on piecemeal reforms, Trotsky concluded that for them the future held nothing but "hot and cold showers."[25]

Three far more important guests arrived on July 19, 1935. They were Tranmæl, accompanied by Ole Colbjørnsen, a prominent newsman, and Minister of Justice Trygve Lie, whose department had jurisdiction over foreigners admitted to Norway. Members of the Knudsen family were also present during the visit.[26] Lie did not yet feel fully comfortable in his new position, having held office only four months. His political experience had previously been restricted largely to the local level. He came from a working-class background, raised by a single mother after his father chose to depart for the shores of the United States, prior to his son's birth on July 16, 1896. Young Trygve grew up on the eastern outskirts of Kristiania,* where his mother ran a combined boarding house and café that catered to workers. But despite living in difficult circumstances, he first showed unusual talent as a schoolboy, graduating from the gymnasium and then going on to study law at the University, from which he received his law degree in 1919.

Lie had already become involved in politics as a teenager, taking part in Labor Party campaigns, and he soon rose to party office. He served as chairman of his local county organization in Aker, where he was also elected to county government, and from 1921 onwards he headed the Labor Party in Akershus province, which lay immediately adjacent to Oslo. He became a member of the National Committee in 1926 and earned a reputation within the party for his ambition and decisive character, which gained him both admirers and enemies. He was employed in the Labor Party's main office as a secretary from 1919 to 1922 and then served as the Confederation of Labor's legal advisor (*juridisk konsulent*) until March 1935. He made skillful use of his legal talent to settle a large number of labor disputes on behalf of the Confederation. Lie was chosen to serve as minister of justice primarily because of his professional background in

---

* Norway's capital was renamed Oslo in 1925.

law, then a rather uncommon trait among leading members of the Labor
Party. He entered the cabinet at the age of thirty-eight, well known among
party officers but not nationally within the public at large.

There were several reasons why Lie joined Tranmæl and Colbjørnsen
in making the trip to Wexhall. As leading figures in the Labor Party, they
were interested not only in meeting Trotsky but also curious to see what
condition he was in, physically and intellectually. Lie furthermore later
maintained that he wanted to bring up the subject of the restrictions under
which Trotsky had been admitted in order to avoid future misunderstand-
ings. Finally, with Tranmæl as editor in chief of *Arbeiderbladet* and Colbjørnsen as a journalist at the paper, the opportunity naturally lent itself to
gain a scoop through an interview with the world-famous figure that no
other Oslo newspaper had access to.

Outwardly the encounter went very well. Trotsky made only relatively
brief reference to it in his diary many days later. He noted that they had
"spent the time pleasantly." Lie assured him that the Soviet government
had raised no objections to his settling in Norway, with Trotsky writing
that it was "possible that they [the Russians] considered Norway a lesser
evil than France." Most of the visit, however, was devoted to Colbjørnsen's
interview, with Tranmæl and Lie listening and commenting.[27]

The result was a large, front-page article on July 26.[28] While the paper
was careful not to side directly with Trotsky, the interview nevertheless
was quite positive, declaring that while his actions and viewpoints might
be judged in various ways, few persons "will deny that he is one of world
history's truly great figures." He furthermore was praised as an author,
with his books described as deep and thoughtful and his writing style as
"brilliant." Colbjørnsen expressed the hope that several of Trotsky's books
would soon be published in Norwegian editions by the party's own press,
which was engaged in contract negotiations with his representatives.

The bulk of the interview, however, dealt with Trotsky's comments on
world affairs. Here the article revealed the Labor Party leadership's cautious attitude on how it wished to handle him. First, the article did not
name its author and made no specific reference to Tranmæl and Lie.[29] Instead, it simply stated that "the great former revolutionary tribune" had
been visited by one of the paper's writers, accompanied by "a couple of
other party members." Secondly, it was stressed that Trotsky had restricted
his comments because "he feels himself bound by the terms of [his] entry
permit." Nevertheless, the piece pointed out that Trotsky was free to state

his views in a general way about historical questions or socialism. This was interpreted somewhat liberally because Trotsky, while insisting that the Russian people had experienced some advances as a result of the revolution, voiced cautious, but nevertheless biting, criticism of the current regime. He declared that it consisted of a "new bureaucracy," including "old enemies of the October Revolution." He acidly remarked that the present Soviet ambassador to Great Britain, the former Menshevik Ivan Maiski, had served in the counter-revolutionary White government of Admiral Kolchak during the Russian Civil War. And while Stalin was not referred to specifically, Trotsky did assert that the Soviet Union had retreated from the goal of creating a classless society.[30]

With Trotsky able to state his views to this extent, it is understandable that he did not conclude that the minister of justice had come to Wexhall to reinforce restrictions on his ability to express himself. On the contrary, he regarded the article as an indication of tolerance in enforcing the conditions under which he could make public statements. Although Trygve Lie later insisted that he had made it clear at Wexhall that Trotsky could not comment negatively about any country that maintained friendly relations with Norway, the interview does not support the contention that limits would be strictly implemented.

Trotsky had no intention of restricting his observations abroad about the need to organize a rival international revolutionary movement. Just three days after his interview appeared in *Arbeiderbladet*, he completed a long article, published by *Unser Wort* in early September. Writing openly, he castigated by name prominent politicians and the policies of several European governments. In particular, he voiced his opposition to the popular-front movements that were emerging in countries such as France, Belgium, and Czechoslovakia, whose nonsocialist governments were allied with the Soviet Union against Hitler. Not unexpectedly, the "Soviet bureaucracy" was equally the target of his invective. The only path that true socialists could follow, he insisted, was to work for the success of the great international proletarian revolution. This would result not only in the defeat of imperialism and fascism but also in the overthrow of the "barbarous dictatorship of the Stalin clique."[31]

Within Norway, communist reaction to *Arbeiderbladet*'s interview showed that they believed he had expressed himself to a far greater extent than should have been permitted. *Arbeideren* protested in its August 2 edition that Ole Colbjørnsen had allowed Trotsky to discuss current political issues, in direct violation of his residence permit.[32] The mention of Colbjørnsen revealed, not surprisingly, that within the small circle of Norwegian journalists the attempt to disguise his authorship had not succeeded.

Not surprisingly, communist arguments failed to generate outside support. The nonsocialist parties could not be expected to back communist concerns about an article that was critical of the Soviet leadership. But while the issue therefore died down during the fall of 1935, Quisling's major paper, *Nasjonal Samling*, could not later resist printing an article that insinuated the existence of a sinister connection between Trotsky and Colbjørnsen, the Labor Party's leading advocate of government-regulated economic planning. The latter was described as speaking out of both sides of his mouth, telling working-class audiences that the Labor Party was introducing socialism, while reassuring nonsocialists that the party had no intention of radically restructuring society. There were many indices, the paper insisted, that showed how Colbjørnsen's devious approach had been "concocted by fellow party member Bronstein-Trotsky, the master of revolutionary tactics."[33]

The master tactician depicted by National Union was actually forced to restrict his activity significantly in the late summer and early fall of 1935. Although he had felt fine during his voyage from Antwerp and the first hectic days in Norway, after his move to Wexhall he was struck down by the mysterious, debilitating illness that had plagued him since the early 1920s, a malady that no doctor had been able to diagnose: "weakness, temperature, perspiration, inner physical emptiness. It's an affliction, there is no other word for it."[34] He could not work and lay prone "for days at a time." If the weather permitted, Natalia prepared a chaise longue for him outside in the fresh air.[35] Here he spent his time reading radical writings, including books by Emma Goldman and Mother Jones.[36] By mid-July he continued to rest, but the arrival of foreign correspondence and newspapers stimulated him so that he could dictate letters to Frankel.[37] When Tranmæl, Trygve Lie, and Colbjørnsen arrived on July 19, they found him "still quite weak," having had a relapse during the previous week. Nevertheless, he was described as having remarkable vitality for someone who had experienced what he had gone through. Expected to arrive from Paris within a few weeks, his personal doctor, it was hoped, would prescribe treatment to restore his health.[38]

The physician, Dr. Franz Breth, turned out to be Czech, not French. He was definitely a follower, described by Trotsky as one of "ours." He subjected Trotsky to tests, with the patient being required to walk vigorously, which worsened his "condition . . . right away." Moreover, the good doctor was no more successful in coming up with a diagnosis than any of his predecessors. Following his departure, Lev resumed his "recumbent mode . . . and soon recovered."[39] He described the ensuing period of renewed energy that he experienced in August as one in which "I could work quite busily and productively, without resulting in any inconvenience." However, this fruitful time came to an end when he went on a brief vacation to what he described as "a wooded area."[40]

At the end of August, Konrad Knudsen asked Nils Kåre Dahl, one of Trotsky's few active Norwegian followers, whether he could find an out-of-the-way site where Lev and Natalia could spend time without being recognized. Dahl knew just the place—the resort of Andorsrud in Skoger, an isolated, forested community located some ninety kilometers south of Oslo, well inland from the coast. Although they were not aware of the visitors' identities until after they had left, longtime residents of Skoger still recalled in the 1990s that the Trotskys had been guests at Andorsrud during the 1930s.[41] The property consisted of a large main house, plus a number of smaller buildings, all surrounded by an extensive stand of forest.[42]

The Trotskys planned to stay a week, as did also Nils Kåre Dahl. The interlude passed pleasantly, with Trotsky enjoying the freedom of being on vacation. Dahl spoke German well and could converse easily with Lev. However, Dahl's ability to communicate in French was limited, but this was compensated for by his wife, who had been in France and who therefore got on quite well with Natalia. Discussions around the fireplace were therefore memorable. But one thing that Dahl had planned ended in fiasco. He had brought lobster and wine for their enjoyment, expensive gourmet items, especially during the Depression. But to his great disappointment he discovered that Trotsky was a teetotaler.[43]

Much of Trotsky's time was devoted to outings in the woods. He always enjoyed physical activity, but on this occasion he overexerted himself by going on "a walk of more than two hours." Consequently, his illness recurred with a vengeance. This relapse occurred shortly before he once more was to be examined for his mysterious malady, and he hoped its return might make it easier for the doctors to come up with a correct diagnosis.[44]

The extensive period of hospitalization that he now underwent, from September 19 to October 20, 1935, was carried out under the direction of Dr. Carl Müller, whom Trotsky retained as his primary physician during his stay in Norway, and whom he trusted explicitly.[45] Müller wrote to Knudsen on August 23, informing him that his "guest" could be admitted to Ward 8 of Ullevål Hospital after September 17. Müller assured Knudsen that he would arrange for Trotsky to have a room for himself, a luxury in the 1930s. The doctor could not guarantee that the admission could be kept secret, but he promised to do everything possible to ensure that the hospital maintained "discretion."[46]

Initially, Trotsky's stay took place uneventfully. While he underwent tests, he had plenty of time for himself. He was able to read extensively, in particular newspapers. Also, he received daily visits from Frankel, who moved to Oslo so that Trotsky could maintain his international correspondence.[47] He was free to walk the grounds of the large hospital complex.[48] In the Norwegian edition of his autobiography, whose preface he wrote while at Ullevål, he had nothing but praise for the personnel. Everyone had met him with "consideration, sympathy, straightforward and genuine humaneness."[49]

The staff maintained complete confidentiality. However, his cover was blown by a visitor who came outside normal visiting hours. He recognized Trotsky immediately, despite the fact that Lev had once again allowed his beard to grow. The anonymous visitor noted how strange it had felt for him to observe a person who at one time had been one of the world's "most powerful and feared persons standing only a few meters from me, watching with interest some patients who are playing croquet." The informer immediately passed the news on to *Dagbladet*,[50] and Trotsky's admission to the hospital under a false name thereby became grist for the journalists' mill.

As usual, any public mention of this controversial figure resulted in a series of press articles. National Union's main paper, describing Trotsky as "the Marxist government's guest and the county of Oslo's free patient at Ullevål," proceeded to publish a lurid, provocative, and highly fictional account that accused Trotsky of having been in charge of the "socialization" of young girls in Russia while leading the Red Army during the Civil War, describing in detail how his alleged policy had resulted in the rape of innocent young daughters of the bourgeoisie, after which many were subjected to bestial acts of torture and murder.[51] *Aftenposten*, on the other hand, ran a series of articles in which Trotsky was charged with having been admitted anonymously to the hospital under false pretenses, displacing Norwegian citizens while receiving free medical care. The controversy became so sensitive that Dr. Müller felt obliged to write an open letter to *Aftenposten*'s editor in which he strongly rebutted the accusations, declaring that he was responsible for having Trotsky admitted because the latter required urgent medical attention.[52]

Arbeiderbladet, in its counterattack against Trotsky's detractors, made Dr. Müller's letter its centerpiece. The Labor Party's main organ also interviewed administrators at the hospital, who insisted that Trotsky's admission had not violated regular procedures. He had paid the full price required of foreigners, and Dr. Müller had acted in an entirely professional manner.[53]

Despite his respect for Müller's competence, the patient did not, however, gain the recovery he hoped for. On the contrary, he emerged from the hospital in worse condition than when he entered it. With only some exaggeration, Trotsky later described December 1935, as "the worst month of my life. I was all the time in bed."[54] Almost as an act of desperation, he allowed himself to be persuaded by the Knudsens to move to their cabin, hoping that the change of air would have a beneficial effect.[55]

Considering the fact that this occurred in ice-cold and snowy midwinter, the risky nature of this venture was clear. The Knudsen cabin lay on Ringkollen, a peak directly east of Hønefoss, jutting more than 2100 feet above the surrounding low-lying countryside. The Trotskys set off at about noon on Friday, December 20, accompanied by Knudsen's son, fourteen-year-old Borgar; Astrid, the family cook; and Lev's ever-present secretary. Konrad drove them the first part of the way, but at the foot of the mountain, the party had to switch to a rented sleigh. At the top they reached the cabin with some difficulty because of deep snow.

During their stay, the secretary and Borgar were active, chopping wood and skiing through the forest to Øyangen, a nearby lake.[56] But for the Trotskys there was really nothing to do. Natalia, much later in Paris, would nostalgically remember winter in Norway as having "a pure beauty, with its clear skies, glittering snow and the dark snow-clad firs. At nightfall, flames of crimson spread over the white expanse and the sky blaze[d] up for a few moments." She and Lev were "spellbound by the austere magic of the winter cold."[57] However, as foreigners in a country where almost everyone knew how to ski, they were out of sync with the population. Trotsky, more prosaic than Natalia, described their experience as imprisonment. They could not take the smallest walk because the cabin was surrounded by four and a half feet of snow, and the cold was so intense that the iron stove had to be fed continuously so they would "not . . . freeze to death."[58] Their sense of isolation was reinforced by incessant snowfall. They remained at the cabin for three days until, in desperation, on the twenty-second they made a dash through the deep snow to a nearby tourist hotel, Ringkollstua, on the summit of the mountain. From here they were transported back to Wexhall in time for Christmas. But while they joined the Knudsen family for the traditional celebration, Lev resisted all pressure to join in singing carols around the Christmas tree.[59]

Considering the state of his health and his strenuous exertion at Ring-kollen, he rather remarkably emerged with no serious physical consequences. Although he maintained that this "attempt to escape from the illness" had been unsuccessful,[60] within a relatively short period he began to stage a surprising recovery, to the amazement of the physicians who had earlier examined him. During the spring of 1936, he was able to work long hours at full speed.[61] His illness appeared to have been shed completely.

He needed to work. His financial situation was precarious. To a great degree it was the income he earned from his pen that allowed him to survive. He had earlier complained from his hospital room, in a letter asking an American follower for financial support, that the cost of his stay at Ullevål had almost depleted his resources.[62] However, in March 1936 he was well off enough to pay Dr. Müller the outstanding sum of 100 kroner ($605; 3385 kroner—2012 value).[63]

The secretary who had intrepidly followed Lev and Natalia to Ringkol-len was not Jan Frankel but rather Erwin Wolf. During his exile in Norway, Trotsky had a succession of secretaries, but Wolf stayed by far the longest. The Trotskys had originally brought two secretaries with them to Norway, Jean van Heijenoort as well as Frankel. However, because of the limited space at Wexhall, Trotsky had to be satisfied with a reduced secretariat of one. Van Heijenoort returned to France on June 25, having been in the country for only one week.[64]

Frankel contacted Ringerike police headquarters on August 13 and submitted an application for a residence permit. His passport, however, had been forged to remove an expulsion order from France, where he had earlier taken part in leftist demonstrations.[65] He used this passport when he accompanied the Trotskys to Oslo, and he also submitted it as personal identification when he applied for residency.[66] But when the police decided to examine his application more closely, Trotsky recognized the potential for scandal. The decision was therefore made to have Jan leave at the end of October.[67]

Back in Prague, he worked hard to find a replacement. His choice was a fellow Czech Trotskyite, Wolf.[68] The latter came from a wealthy bourgeois family in the Sudetenland. He had studied in Berlin, where he joined the Trotskyite movement in 1932. Following Hitler's takeover, he lived in both France and Czechoslovakia, where he held prominent positions within the International Communist League.[69] Wolf arrived in Norway on November 16, 1935, and two days later submitted his application for a residence permit. A young radical activist like his predecessors, he too was regarded suspiciously, but police investigations only showed that he had been in "close personal contact" with the International Communist League, whose purported leader was Trotsky. This was not considered incriminating enough to deny him residence.[70]

Young Erwin had no difficulty adapting to Heradsbygda. Not only was he quite intelligent, but he had a lively personality and possessed considerable charm. For Lev and Natalia, he was welcome company. The well-traveled young European was even more appealing to Hjørdis Knudsen, Konrad Knudsen's beautiful twenty-one-year-old daughter, with whom he soon developed a full-blown romantic liaison. This inevitably bound the Trotskys and the Knudsens even closer together with ties of mutual affection.[71]

As Trotsky's right hand, Wolf lacked the secretarial expertise of his predecessor, Frankel. Nevertheless, Wolf did as well in his position as could be expected. He not only took dictation and carried out much of Trotsky's correspondence, but he had to handle all inquiries concerning his employer.[72] His workload was not made easier by being relegated to an area of the dining room that was used for other purposes as well. Most significantly, when judging his performance, had Trotsky been dissatisfied with Wolf, his displeasure would not have remained unspoken.

Because the exile's economic well-being depended in large part on his writings, it was not surprising that plans were underway to publish his autobiography, *My Life*, in a Norwegian edition only a week after his arrival. The publisher was Tiden norsk Forlag (Times Norwegian Publishers), the

Labor Party's publishing house. The book was to be based on a translation of its French edition. Tiden offered an advance of 500 kroner, a considerable sum for that time.[73]

Trotsky agreed immediately.[74] But he did indicate some concern later about the choice of My Life's translator. He had warmly recommended Held and his companion, Synnøve Rosendahl-Jensen, for this task. However, Tiden had reservations about giving such a key assignment to two inexperienced translators[75] and chose instead Helge Krog, a major cultural personality, well known as a playwright, a literary reviewer, a political and social critic, as well as a solid translator.[76] While Trotsky accepted, he pointed out that since he was not familiar with "herr Krogh's [sic] translations," he was forced to depend entirely on the publisher.[77] The choice, however, proved to be fortunate. Not only was Krog highly competent, but he became one of Trotsky's most partisan supporters. This was not, however, entirely coincidental since Krog happened to be Håkon Meyer's brother-in-law.[78]

As many an author has experienced, Trotsky's relationship with his publisher was not entirely problem free. His inability to read Norwegian prevented proofreading of the translation,[79] and the late arrival of the royalty advance, if only by a few days, created frustration.[80] The small number of free copies that Tiden provided—only ten—also caused a problem. Trotsky had his list of lucky recipients drawn up even before the books arrived. Held and his Synnøve, in part as compensation for not being given the translation, had to receive a copy.[81] He had also promised copies to Dr. Müller and the director of Ullevål Hospital, and the Knudsen family were to be remembered, which meant that his remaining quantity had to be rationed carefully.

Since the Norwegian edition was simply a translation of a previously published book,[82] only the foreword contained new material.[83] It is therefore an important original source because it best reflected his outlook at the time the book appeared, in November 1935. His viewpoint was definitely colored by his Norwegian exile. Whereas he was very negative toward Stalin in the main part of the book, which covered Trotsky's life up to the time of his expulsion from the Soviet Union in 1929, in the foreword references to Stalin were more circumspect. He was not criticized by name, although there was no mistaking to whom Trotsky alluded.

In the foreword, Trotsky's attitude toward Soviet society remained ambivalent. He maintained that in a period of counter-revolution, exemplified by the rise of fascism, the Soviet Union symbolized hope for the future because it was continuing to develop "on the foundation which the October Revolution created." However, this positive advance was threatened by "the bureaucracy," a new class that had secured "unlimited power" and appointed one of its own as "an absolute and infallible leader."[84] Not unexpectedly, Trotsky explained Stalin's rise to power in Marxist terms—as the product of a particular class that sought to protect its special privileges—not as the result of Stalin's ability as a skilled intriguer, able to manipulate the political system that Lenin and Trotsky had helped create. Trotsky concluded that further progress in the Soviet Union was impossible unless society's "socialist foundation is liberated from its bourgeois-bureaucratic and Bonapartist super structure."[85] In other words, he called for a mass overthrow of the Stalin regime.

Did this constitute a violation of the terms of his asylum? One Conservative newspaper, *Adresseavisen* (The Address Newspaper) in Trondheim, felt that the autobiography clearly provided evidence of this. *My Life*, the paper observed, revealed how Trotsky, while in exile in Russia and Turkey, had stubbornly refused to cease his political activity. There was no reason to believe that he was doing anything different in Norway.[86]

The government, however, obviously did not share this opinion. The ground rules established when Trygve Lie visited Wexhall were still in effect. Trotsky was allowed considerable latitude in his criticism of the current Russian government. The fact that his autobiography was published by the labor movement's own publishing house simply reinforced this conclusion. And when the book appeared in print, it received, on the whole, a positive review in Tranmæl's *Arbeiderbladet*, written by none other than its foreign editor, Finn Moe.

Moe defended Trotsky against the "meanness and repulsiveness" of communist attacks, including those from the Norwegian party. This did not mean, however, that the editor was uncritical. He pointed out that the book was subjective. Stalin, Moe stated, might be "ruthless and brutal," but he was not, as Trotsky maintained, a "mediocrity." The reviewer furthermore stressed major weaknesses in Trotsky's personal character. He tellingly pointed to Trotsky's egocentricity and individualism, shown by his stubborn insistence that only he was right. While Trotsky's Marxist program for achieving a classless society might be correct in the long run, he lacked a sense of reality by wanting to achieve it immediately, as shown by his insistence on founding a new fourth international, side by side with already existing internationals. Despite these criticisms, Moe concluded by stating that this was a compelling book, written by a personality who was supremely intelligent. His style, which sparkled, provided time after time revealing insights.[87]

As could be expected, communist papers reacted otherwise.[88] On the whole, however, the publication created little negative controversy outside the communist press. This was shown by the fact that at the time the autobiography came out, Tiden was seriously considering having other works by Trotsky published in Scandinavia.[89] He responded eagerly to Tiden's inquiry, suggesting that his large book, *The History of the Russian Revolution*, be considered.[90] Tiden reacted positively, and Trotsky duly forwarded a large number of reviews for distribution to Danish and Swedish publishers.[91]

The reviews failed to have the desired result. On April 22, 1936, Tiden's editor-in-chief, Kolbjørn Fjeld, had to express regret that his efforts to secure publication of a joint Scandinavian edition of *The History of the Russian Revolution* "had failed." Publishers elsewhere in Scandinavia must have concluded that there was less public interest about Trotsky in their countries, where he did not reside, than in Norway. Swedish and Danish publishers were similarly unwilling to issue *My Life*.[92]

Fjeld's letter did show, however, Tiden's "greatest interest" in Trotsky's long-anticipated biography of Lenin.[93] Its initial volume, the only one he completed, covered Lenin's youth up through the age of twenty-three. Trotsky had begun the biography while in France.[94] At the most, he may have proofread the final manuscript of the first volume while at Wexhall. When the book was published in March 1936, it received attention in Norway. Interviewed by *Arbeiderbladet*, which challenged a false claim by *Aftenposten* that Trotsky planned to leave Norway, Konrad Knudsen stated that since *My Life* had sold so well in France, there was every reason to believe that this new book would similarly be published in Norwegian.[95]

It was no coincidence that *Arbeiderbladet* at the same time printed a review of the French edition of Trotsky's Lenin biography by none other than Walter Held. Although the latter frequently complained about not being allowed to express his views in *Arbeiderbladet*, in this instance it had no objection. Appearing in the March 20 edition, Held, as fitting of a true disciple, praised the author for his "solid, reliable, and conscientious coverage of the historical material," resulting in a significant biography based on "the historical-dialectical method."[96]

Trotsky therefore remained hopeful that at least in Norway he could expect to have new editions of his books published. However, because of events that summer, the possibility that Tiden would ever again bring out a work by Lev Trotsky was brutally ended. Similarly, a planned book project by Held on Trotsky's writings during his years in exile, 1929–1935, never materialized.[97]

Writing to Fjeld in June 1936, Trotsky referred to another volume that was nearing completion, *The Revolution Betrayed*.[98] It was written entirely in Norway during the first half of 1936. Considering the poor state of his health at the end of 1935, Trotsky's ability to finish a book within such a short time indicated a significant change for the better, undoubtedly stimulated by his effort to reveal how, in his view, Stalin was destroying the ideals of the Bolshevik Revolution.

Assessment of *The Revolution Betrayed* has varied considerably. Isaac Deutscher judged it to be "one of the seminal books of this [the twentieth] century," in which the author assumed no fewer than three distinct poses: as a "detached and objective thinker," as the leader of the defeated opposition movement in the U.S.S.R., and as a "passionate . . . polemicist."[99] Dmitry Volkogonov, on the other hand, dismissed it as being poorly written and badly organized, having been hurriedly thrown together.[100] These two contrasting opinions simply reflect the differences between a time when the Soviet Union was still a major force in world affairs, having discarded some of the worst excesses of the Stalin regime, which was true when Deutscher wrote in the 1960s; whereas in the early 1990s when Volkogonov gained international attention as a major Russian critic of Soviet communism, the system that Trotsky championed had come to be regarded as a discredited failure.

Examined from the perspective of when it was written, *The Revolution Betrayed* reflected Trotsky's critical opinion of the Soviet Union in the first half of 1936. In this context, as Ian D. Thatcher has pointed out, the book "has much to recommend it."[101] Trotsky's condemnation would later become far more severe with the start of the Moscow show trials, which occurred only a few days after he had finished the final draft of his manuscript. *The Revolution Betrayed* also contained his ideal view. His account was therefore both a polemic and a program for world revolution.

In greater depth than in the foreword of his autobiography, he used the book to attack the bureaucracy that he maintained had usurped the Revolution. It had, said Trotsky, not only defeated the Left Opposition that he headed during the 1920s, it had "conquered the Bolshevik party."[102] Like many other writers, including prominent historians who wrote much later, he frequently compared revolutionary developments in the Soviet Union with the different stages of the French Revolution. He regarded the current period as a "Soviet Thermidor" in which there had occurred "a triumph of the bureaucracy over the masses."[103] As leader of this elite group, Stalin received the epithet of having become a new kind of Bonaparte.[104]

With this being the current condition of historical development, as he saw it, Trotsky raised the question: "Will the bureaucrat devour the workers' state, or will the working class clean up the bureaucrat?"[105] For Trotsky there could be but one answer: "the inevitability of a new revolution."[106] And he would be in its forefront, as he had been in 1905 and again in 1917. This meant that he, having been expelled from the Soviet Union, would now lead the revolution from the outside. This was what he clearly inferred in *The Revolution Betrayed*.

Trotsky was not the only one who was conscious of the role he intended to play. When he sent a copy of the manuscript to his son Lyova at ICL headquarters, a Stalinist agent who had infiltrated the Trotskyite group in Paris immediately succeeded in getting his hands on the text. As a result, Stalin was aware of the book's contents even before its publication.[107] Trotsky's call for revolution therefore most likely heightened Stalin's paranoid determination to crush all potential opposition to his dictatorial control. Having himself risen to power as a result of the opportunities created by the chaos of the Russian Revolution and Civil War, and having watched closely Trotsky's activity during this time, it is understandable that someone with Stalin's suspicious nature would regard a movement headed by Trotsky as a potential threat, no matter how weak his challenger might be. However, *The Revolution Betrayed* did not trigger the mass purges of the 1930s. They had already been set in motion immediately after Kirov's murder.

Trotsky was blissfully unaware of the storm that would soon break. Having as usual written the foreword last, he was looking ahead to relaxing peacefully when he mailed the manuscript to his French and American publishers on August 5, 1936. He thereafter left with Natalia and the Knudsens for a vacation on the sunny south coast of Norway.[108] Little could he know that by the time his final book appeared in print, in May 1937,[109] not only his stay at Wexhall but his sojourn in the country would have ended months previously.

A major reason for Trotsky's vulnerability when he later became the center of controversy was his isolation. During his stay he did not establish close ties with anyone in government circles. Furthermore, his contacts with other Norwegians were also limited. In part this was due to his remote rural location, as well as his aloof, independent nature, but there were other factors as well. His attention was focused externally, toward the Soviet Union and the ICL sections in Western Europe and the United States. Not only did he regard Norway as rather insignificant, but more importantly, he did not wish to jeopardize his asylum. As he put it: "I had almost no contact with the radicals, in order to avoid even the appearance of mixing in local politics."[110]

The Labor Party's attitude, as expressed in *Arbeiderbladet*, augmented his isolation. It maintained a position as reserved as his, not willing to take a stand in his conflict with Stalin. Held complained in early 1936 that the "the reformists" and "the Stalinists"—his terms for the Labor Party and the communists respectively—had established a "non-aggression pact."[111] While no such compact had formally been made, the communists did largely refrain from attacking Labor in the election year of 1936. Held, moreover, had a personal reason to feel aggrieved. As they had for his fellow political refugee, Willy Brandt, the Labor Party had initially provided Walter with limited financial support. But undoubtedly because of Labor's cool attitude toward the Trotskyites, it informed him that he would no longer receive its 40-kroner monthly subsidy in 1936. Consequently, he complained about "unforeseeable economic difficulties" in the coming year.[112]

Trotsky's main source of support among Norwegians continued to be Olav Scheflo. The latter, following Trotsky's arrival, became an even stronger admirer, adopting many of the same foreign policy positions as Trotsky. The contrast between Scheflo's uncritical approval of Trotsky's international viewpoint and his acceptance of the Labor government's piecemeal reforms, in collaboration with nonsocialists, has been described by one writer as "schizophrenic."[113] This insight is quite perceptive. Scheflo had always been a romantic socialist, never a consistent theorist.

He used the columns of *Sørlandet* to provide protection for Trotsky whenever he came under attack. But while Scheflo's enthusiasm for debating controversial questions remained as spirited as ever, his body was increasingly fighting a losing battle. Shortly after Lev and Natalia had moved to Wexhall, Scheflo in early July expressed his regret for not being able to work due to his crippling arthritis.[114] On a number of occasions during the late summer and fall, attempts were made to arrange meetings between him and the Trotskys, but they had to be cancelled due to his ill health.[115] On January 7, 1936, his assistant editor and right-hand man, Sverre Opsal, sadly reported that Scheflo had been quite sick for some time, and on that particular day he was so ill that he could neither write nor dictate. Once again it would be necessary for him to be hospitalized in Oslo at the National Hospital, Rikshospitalet.[116]

His disability would have sidelined someone with less willpower. Trotsky admired Scheflo and obviously wished to retain strong ties with him. But Trotsky typically maintained a superior attitude toward his defender. He described Scheflo privately as "a serious and honest member of the Labor Party," but added that many such "honest friends" could often be "very politically naive."[117] It is fair to conclude that Trotsky, while maintaining friendship and respect for Scheflo, nevertheless regarded him as an inferior thinker and strategist. But he was extremely useful.

In the fall and early winter of 1935, the fate of Sergei, Lev and Natalia's youngest son, once again became an issue of concern for the Trotskys. Although Scheflo was peripherally involved, Held was responsible for first raising the question. His dentist in Oslo, a communist (a rather risky choice for a young Trotskyite to make), informed Held that he had ascertained through his sources that Sergei allegedly was not under arrest in the Soviet Union, although he was described as being under surveillance, with his mail censored.[118]

Held immediately reported this to Trotsky in September. In response, Trotsky displayed an unsentimental objectivity that can only be described as admirable, considering the pain, frustration, and loss that he felt over his son's disappearance. The dentist's news, said Lev, was simply a cover story, manufactured by the Kremlin to soothe the consciences of foreign communists. The account was untrue because (1) there was overwhelming evidence that Sergei had been arrested, and (2) he had no opportunity to correspond with anyone, so talk of his mail being censored was sheer myth. Sergei undoubtedly was languishing in a "sorry prison."[119]

Nevertheless, the Trotskys had not entirely given up hope of reestablishing contact with Sergei's family. For three months they attempted to forward money to his wife in Moscow, with the funds formally sent by Natalia. But their efforts only had the same discouraging outcome. The recipient could not be located.[120]

Scheflo was of course fully aware of the anxiety that Lev and Natalia felt for their son. He proposed on December 10 that they should meet with him to discuss various possibilities to lessen Sergei's plight.[121] Trotsky thanked Scheflo heartily for his suggestion. However, the Trotskys rejected this idea, based on their experience that attempts to apply pressure from the outside only caused Soviet authorities to increase their reprisals. A previous endeavor, said Lev, had resulted in "the imprisonment of our daughter-in-law." He insisted that only "*in the last instance*" (Trotsky's emphasis) could a press campaign have any hope of gaining a "practical result."[122]

Trotsky nevertheless resorted to just such an effort in late 1935, but wanting to avoid problems, he launched it in neighboring Sweden. Two letters concerning the arrest of Sergei and his wife, again in Natalia's name, were published in radical newspapers, Kilbom's *Folkets Dagblad* (The People's Daily) and the syndicalist daily, *Arbetaren* (The Worker). This led to a polemic between the two and the communist *Ny Dag* (New Day), which insisted that this venture was simply the start of Trotsky's major campaign against the Soviet Union, financed by the "huge sums" he was earning from bourgeois publishers and the Social Democratic press. *Arbetaren* and *Folkets Dagblad* were described as dupes for printing anti-Soviet propaganda. *Arbetaren* responded by denouncing *Ny Dag's* "sordid methods," pointing out that while it did not share Trotsky's views, it had chosen to involve itself for "purely humanitarian demands." Natalia's facts could not be refuted, and anyone who possessed "decency and fairness" could be expected to react against the mistreatment of Sergei and his family.[123]

Despite the Swedish communists' obvious bias, there was an element of truth to their charge that Trotsky was intent on organizing an effort to discredit the Stalin regime. This involved two fortunate ex-prisoners who had managed to get out of the Soviet Union. He planned to publicize their firsthand accounts of Stalin's camps and in this way win the backing of "true" friends of the Soviet Union, the country he idealized and wished to lead.

The first was Arben Tarov, an Armenian who had escaped imprisonment in Soviet Central Asia.[124] Following his arrival in Turkey, he experienced considerable hardship. Since Trotsky was "entirely without money," he asked Held on September 2, 1935, to contact Labor Party officials for aid. Reflecting the positive atmosphere that existed between Trotsky and the party after top members had met with him at Wexhall, Trotsky urged Held to call Tarov's plight to the attention of "comrade Tranmæl" himself.[125]

Tarov did manage to reach France safely, and the *Bulletin of the Opposition* subsequently published several of his articles. This was enhanced by Trotsky, who in an unsigned article described how Tarov had witnessed "a horrible scene of persecutions and reprisals . . . [against] devoted, unselfish, and self-sacrificing revolutionists."[126] Proclaiming the need to assist these maltreated victims of Stalin's terror, he clearly hoped to place himself at the head of a mass protest against the Soviet leadership. However, his attempt, through Held, to marshal support in Norway failed utterly. Tranmæl refused to involve the Labor Party in such a campaign and thereby risk being associated with the Trotskyites.[127]

Use of Tarov, however, was just the start of Trotsky's drive. His plan was further stimulated by Anton Ciliga, a Yugoslav communist who had resided in Russia since 1925. As a member of the Left Opposition, he had been arrested in 1930. Most uniquely, rather than dying in one of Stalin's camps, he was deported in 1935.[128] In late December Trotsky stressed that Ciliga would be a key player in the ICL's effort to build up "a broad-based organization to help revolutionaries imprisoned in the U.S.S.R."[129] Trotsky wrote to Scheflo on December 24, informing him that "Comrade Ciliga . . . has written his first letter about the crimes of Stalin's bureaucracy."[130]

Scheflo responded positively, suggesting that a protest be sent to the Soviet government. But he insisted it should be worded carefully to make it clear that its signers were true friends of the Soviet Union. The letter should therefore be drawn up by a committee and presented to the Labor Party's affiliated political and union organizations for support, removing suspicion that it came from persons hostile to the labor movement.[131] He intended to contact key people in Oslo to join such a committee.[132]

Quite naturally, Trotsky proclaimed himself to be in full agreement.[133] But it was not until January 16 that Scheflo had a chance to see a translated copy of Ciliga's letter when he met with Held at the National Hospital.[134] Five days later Held could further report that he had succeeded in publishing an article in *Arbeiderbladet* that was critical of the Soviet system, announcing proudly that his condemnation would help "prepare the ground for the [protest] committee's activity, because as long as the Norwegian working class believes that everything in the Soviet Union is all right, then the committee will be in a difficult position."[135]

By early 1936 the campaign was well under way, with Trotsky making his usual contribution internationally. In an article in the American Trotskyite paper, the *New Militant* on February 1, he declared that "letters and documents recently published by Comrades Tarov and Ciliga" had stimulated great interest in the repression of "revolutionary fighters" by the "Soviet bureaucracy."[136]

As is unfortunately true for all periods of history, those who provide accurate information are not necessarily successful in their effort to reveal the truth. Trotsky and his sympathizers suffered from several limitations when they sought to report on the horrible treatment experienced by suspected dissidents at the hands of Stalin's regime. In contrast to the far better-organized followers of the Kremlin, the Trotskyites were small in number and relatively ineffective politically. Furthermore, the Soviet Union still enjoyed considerable goodwill within a wide range of leftist opinion that extended into the ranks of liberal members of the bourgeoisie. Finally, the communists were not caught off guard. As early as December 18, 1935, just a few days after the ICL had established contact with Ciliga, the French communist press revealed that Trotsky was about to launch "a large campaign . . . against the Soviet Union."[137] When news reached Wexhall, Trotsky and Wolf could only wonder how the communists had learned of this so soon.[138]

Trotsky personally followed at close range the difficulties of the operation in Norway, where Held served as his representative. The latter discounted even the possibility of arranging a lecture for Ciliga. The Labor Party had already indicated its refusal to be a sponsor, and Mot Dag was also ruled out due to its breach with Held.[139]

Even the endeavor to create a committee of prominent persons to protest the treatment of Russian political prisoners experienced serious obstacles. Scheflo vetoed the participation of Dr. Johan Scharffenberg, a well-known radical cultural personality. On the other hand, Scheflo approved the memberships of Håkon Meyer and Karl Evang. But Scheflo disagreed with Meyer over who should serve as head of the committee—in reality a front man. Adding to their dilemma was Scheflo's physical condition. He remained incapacitated.[140]

Despite such disappointments, plans moved ahead. Held appears to have allowed Meyer to assume the lead in founding the committee, most likely due to Scheflo's health problems. In late March Meyer took the initiative to call together a preliminary planning session, consisting only of himself, Trotsky, Kjell Ottesen,* and Evang. Since Evang and Ottesen belonged to Mot Dag, the purpose of the gathering was to see whether Mot Dag might take part in investigating and condemning the imprisonment of opposition figures in the U.S.S.R. The meeting revealed, however, strong disagreement, causing Trotsky and Meyer to voice resentment against Mot Dag. Consequently, Dr. Evang dropped any thought of joining the committee. Furthermore, Ottesen received an ultimatum to cease his association with a factional group such as the Trotskyites. If not, he was expected to leave Mot Dag.[141]

As this incident showed, it appears highly unlikely that the committee could have attracted significant support in Norway. However, it never saw the light of day because of Trotsky's sectarianism. He was determined that only he should head a protest effort on behalf of Stalin's victims. He therefore became concerned when he learned that Ciliga, after having a number of his articles published in Trotskyite periodicals, was establishing ties with persons whom Trotsky regarded as enemies. Trotsky issued the final ban in June, when he openly denounced Ciliga for having considered it possible "to collaborate with the Mensheviks. . . . We are obliged therefore to cease publication of Comrade Ciliga's articles."[142] The outcome illustrated once again how Trotsky regarded himself as the only true leader of the "world working class," and his unwillingness to compromise. Only he and those who remained committed to his leadership were the true heirs of Marx and Lenin.

This stillborn endeavor was one of the few made on Trotsky's behalf in Norway before his internment. His attention remained fixed primarily on external developments. He maintained contact with the various sections of the International Communist League. Its International Secretariat in Paris, where Lev Sedov was the leading figure, faced the daunting task of coordinating the fractious sections, often torn by internal bickering. Trotsky continued also to write prolifically for Trotskyite publications. However, in order not to call too much attention to himself, he frequently published anonymously, "Crux" being his most common pen name.

---

* As a past secretary for Erling Falk, Ottesen no doubt served as a liaison between Trotsky and Mot Dag's former leader. A student, Ottesen also helped Trotsky by providing a variety of services, in particular driving him between Hønefoss and Oslo.

His main priority continued to be his attempt to create the Fourth International.[143] In early August 1935 he cosigned as "Crux" an open letter in *Unser Wort* entitled "For the Fourth International." It declared that the two existing internationals were absolute failures. The Labor and Socialist International had sold out to bourgeois capitalists, while the "uncontrolled bureaucracy" of Stalin's "conservative absolutism" was destroying the Comintern. Only a Fourth International could "continuously and uncompromisingly" carry out the class struggle needed to win the support of the masses.[144] But while he could clearly proclaim his goal, the means of achieving it remained elusive.

Trotsky's correspondence further revealed the extent to which he sought to micromanage his movement, despite his out-of-the-way location. His primary means of communicating with his followers was restricted largely to use of the mail, with only occasional foreign visitors coming to Hønefoss. The large volume of dispatches to and from Wexhall was handled by Wolf, who in January 1936 complained of being overworked.[145]

Trotsky sent detailed instructions to the International Secretariat about what he considered to be the right course for the sections to take. Despite the relatively small total of adherents that he had, this involved a significant number of countries. He in particular engaged himself in his sections' relations with socialist parties or factions, which they either merged with or broke away from in repeated disputes.[146]

In addition to his ongoing combat with the communists, Trotsky concentrated his attention on the German exile SAP party, now also regarded as a major enemy. In July 1935 he expressed concern that the SAP might have successfully infiltrated his organization, and he cautioned his followers to be extra careful in their contact with SAP members.[147]

The growing threat of fascism similarly preoccupied him. As early as July 1935 he advised the International Secretariat that although it might not be necessary for the time being to move *Unser Wort*'s editorial staff from Paris, nevertheless one needed to prepare to transfer the paper's operations to Copenhagen "in case it must leave France."[148]

The foreboding that he felt was due not only to the increased strength of fascism but also to the apparent success of the Soviet effort to end Russia's international isolation. The "popular front" movement in Europe coincided with his Norwegian exile. With socialists drawing closer to the communists in a number of countries, the opportunity for Trotsky's followers to cooperate with the socialists increasingly became more difficult.[149]

His sections at times annoyed him, especially due to their frequent internal strife. Each side would naturally appeal to the head of the movement, in far-off Norway, for support. This was in particular standard practice for groups within the French section. In a letter that he wrote to Paris at the end of December 1935, Trotsky strongly insisted that he needed to have "at least four weeks' 'leave,'" during which he should not be bothered by letters from various sections.[150] He did not, however, obtain peace, repeatedly complaining to Lyova during the spring of 1936 about the "silly intrigues" of the "French cliques."[151]

Another source of interruption was the arrival of foreign visitors, whose numbers were far fewer than those he had been able to meet in France.[152] They included Czechs, German refugees, Frenchmen, Englishmen, Americans, and Canadians.[153] They never came unannounced. Following their journey from Oslo, they usually went to Hjørdis Knudsen's small bookstore in Hønefoss. She would thereupon notify her father, whose office was in the same building. After an interval Konrad would drive them to Wexhall, or they would be transported by a local taxi.[154] During their stay they were housed either at a hotel in Hønefoss or closer, in the homes of neighbors in Heradsbygda.[155]

With the exception of Fred Zeller, the most important foreign visitors came in the summer of 1936. The purpose for their journey generally concerned deep divisions within Trotsky's movement. Raymond Molinier, one of the founders of the French section, arrived in mid-July. He had originally been highly regarded by Trotsky, who described him at the time of their first meeting on Prinkipo as being "one of the most obliging, practical, and energetic men that one can imagine."[156] Not even Lev Sedov's seduction of Molinier's wife, who abandoned her husband in favor of Trotsky's son, could end Molinier's devotion to the cause.[157]

There had always, however, been disagreement between Molinier and his rival, Pierre Naville, each of whom headed a faction. Their differences were more personal than ideological. During the early 1930s Molinier's group enjoyed Trotsky's favor.[158] This led to a split in 1934, when Trotsky advised the section to join the Socialist Party for tactical reasons. Molinier agreed, with the result that most French Trotskyites entered the party. Naville, however, at first refused,[159] but later his faction also joined. This led to reconciliation between the two groups when the socialist leadership expelled them both in the fall of 1935. Naville thereupon became the head of the section, which later was reorganized as the Internationalist Workers Party (Parti Ouvrier Internationaliste). Molinier, however, ranked among its top members.[160]

Not unexpectedly, it did not take long for him to become discontented, and at the beginning of December, he broke away to publish his own newspaper, *La Commune*. But despite appeals from Molinier's faction, Trotsky sided unmistakably with the majority headed by Naville. To a visitor in 1936, Trotsky is quoted as having said: "It is the same story for *seven years now* (emphasis part of text), Turmoil in the French group and M[olinier] at the center of it. He is like the cow who gives a lot of milk, but every time kicks the pail over when it is filled."[161]

When the "cow" arrived in Norway, he could scarcely expect a cordial welcome. During the course of two meetings, on July 15 and July 16, Trotsky coldly made it clear that he supported the French leadership, and he refused to discuss internal affairs with someone who had been expelled.[162]

Considering the prominent position that Molinier had held within the movement, Trotsky's abrupt dismissal was not well considered. The reasons that Trotsky cited for the rift were largely personal and did not reflect ideological differences. Even the compliant Lev Sedov was critical, declaring that a compromise should have been worked out. In an unmailed letter to Natalia of April 16, 1936, Lyova temperamentally declared: "I think that all of [father's] deficiencies have not diminished as he grew older, but under the influence of his isolation . . . [have] gotten worse. His lack of tolerance, hot temper, inconsistency, even rudeness, his desire to humiliate, offend, and even destroy have increased."[163]

The grounds Trotsky used to justify the expulsion were not particularly convincing. He was well acquainted with Molinier's propensity to take bold action, as he had demonstrated many times in the past. The argument defending his ouster because of his refusal to abandon business dealings was equally flimsy since Trotsky had known of Molinier's commercial activity from the start of their relationship. Despite the fractious nature of French Trotskyites, the outcome of this episode leaves the impression that it could have been handled better if Trotsky had not committed himself to Naville's group in such a rigid, partisan way. The estrangement between Molinier and the French leadership remained in force for many years. Reconciliation did not occur until the middle of World War II, which Trotsky did not live to experience.[164]

He acted entirely differently in his relationship with the American section, then known as the Workers Party of the United States. He had good reason for doing so. The U.S. section was decidedly the largest within his movement. A permanent split would therefore have been a serious setback.

This possibility appeared to be very real. The Workers Party had been formed in 1934 as a result of a merger between a dedicated core of Trotsky supporters led by James Cannon and Max Shachtman, former leading members of the American Communist Party, and a group headed by Abraham John Muste, a left-wing radical and former pastor who enjoyed a certain amount of influence among American socialists due to his outspoken and sincere idealism. Cooperation between the two factions did not last long because of personal differences, with Muste, who served as the party's national secretary,[165] suddenly refusing to have any contact with Cannon and Shachtman.[166]

Trotsky, however, responded to Muste's action in a very pacifying manner.[167] Thanks to his patient conciliation, Trotsky succeeded in creating outward unity once more. Shortly thereafter, Muste left for Europe in order to get a personal impression of the international Trotskyite movement, in whose affairs he intended to play a major role.[168] He began by going to Norway to meet with the leader himself.

The greeting he received stood in marked contrast with what Molinier would experience just a few days later. The new American leader was accorded no less than a week of the master's time, from June 28 to July 5.[169] Trotsky went out of his way to flatter Muste, discussing in detail the movement's internal affairs. Trotsky's appeal to his visitor's ego paid off. Muste gained the impression that Trotsky "made it clear that he counted heavily on my help in European situations."[170]

When Shachtman arrived later in the month, it seemed as if all differences had been swept aside. He informed the International Secretariat that he and Muste were in full agreement concerning an upcoming ICL conference to be held in Paris at the end of July.[171] Trotsky therefore appeared to have good reason to believe that by his charm and diplomatic skills, he had effectively eliminated sectarianism within the American group. But while Muste did participate in the Paris conference, only a short time later, in September 1936, he repudiated not only the Trotskyite movement but Marxism in general: "I had come to reject the dogmatic

Marxism-Leninism for which . . . the Trotskyites stood."[172] Trotsky's efforts
to make Muste, the quixotic idealist, a permanent part of his cause ended
in failure.

While individuals such as Muste and Shachtman ranked high within
the movement, or, like Molinier, had formerly done so, their stay created
little notice outside of Hønefoss. This was not the case, however, with a
young Frenchman with a very non-French name, Fred Zeller. A former
secretary of the Socialist Party's youth organization in the Seine district, he
fell into disfavor with the party leadership, in part due to his collaboration
with young Trotskyites. The socialists expelled both his faction and Trotsky's
followers at the end of July 1935. He and his supporters thereupon joined
the French section, forming a new youth group.[173] The acquisition of Zeller's
membership was regarded as a triumph. Trotsky boasted optimistically that
Zeller had 3,000 followers and that his publication reached 12,000 readers.[174]

The latter in turn was eager to meet the leader of the cause that he now
had dedicated himself to,[175] but he had to postpone his visit until early
November because of Trotsky's hospitalization. Although Lev's condition
remained poor after his release from Ullevål Hospital, Zeller's visit was
given highest priority. His stay lasted no less than ten days, during which
he enjoyed long talks with Trotsky.[176]

Exhilarated by his encounter, Zeller sent a postcard to a friend in Paris, a
communist.[177] Written in a teasing manner, he described Trotsky as "the
one and only true interpreter of Lenin's ideas and the real organizer of
the October Revolution." Zeller maintained that sooner or later Trotsky
would triumph, and he closed with the mocking salutation "death to
Stalin" ("*mort a Stalin*").[178]

Inevitably, the postcard came to the attention of the French Communist Party's Central Committee, who used it to start a campaign against
Trotsky. Thousands of copies were made, with the communists ominously
maintaining that the postcard revealed evidence of a plot to murder Stalin.
The Norwegian communists joined the attack, with *Arbeideren* headlining
on December 13 that "Trotsky's Assistant, Fred Seller [sic], Is Encouraging
Stalin's Murder." The paper asked rhetorically how long Norwegian workers would be willing to allow Trotsky to remain in the country.[179]

Newspapers representing the majority of Norwegian workers responded quickly. As could be expected, the first reply came from Olav

Scheflo's *Sørlandet*. In a sarcastic article the paper stated that while workers might not know that "death to" in French could also mean "down with," they easily understood that neither Trotsky nor his so-called "rabble," if they really intended to kill Stalin, would plan a murder on a postcard.[180]

Arbeiderbladet devoted less space and less indignation to the affair, but it too labeled the communist attack as a "New Slander against Trotsky." The paper doubted that a single worker would pay attention to this "smear campaign."[181] The charges also did not arouse special interest among nonsocialists. *Tidens Tegn* commented coolly that the postcard was "hardly so sensational" as the communists maintained.[182]

The incident faded away as the Christmas holidays approached. Trotsky, however, believed it had long-term implications. When he thanked Scheflo for his support against the communists, he pointed out that the purpose of their assault had been to "slander me, to make a scandal, to frighten the bourgeois parties and to make my stay in Norway difficult."[183] He insisted that his followers ought not to be content merely to allow the episode to end in the belief that the very foolishness of the charges discredited the communists. Instead, they must make known to the world the nature of Stalin's repression.[184]

Trotsky was correct when he assumed that the controversy over Zeller's postcard was more than an isolated occurrence. While it did not have any immediate results, some six months later similar accusations of alleged terrorist conspiracy against the Soviet leadership would be revived, but at this time with such tremendous force and on such a broad, worldwide scale that Trotsky's efforts to respond, as well as those of his defenders, would simply be overwhelmed.

The polemics concerning the Zeller postcard occurred shortly before Trotsky's residence permit was due to expire. It had gone into effect on the day that he and Natalia arrived and was valid for only six months.[185] But in reality their stay was indefinite, as those who opposed their exile recognized. Already on August 28, 1935, *Aftenposten* headlined the question: "Will Trotsky Remain in Norway Permanently?" The paper noted that he had been admitted for six months so that he could recover his health. But after this time had elapsed, where would he go? He did not have a return visa to France or Turkey. *Aftenposten* drew the unwelcome conclusion that "there is not the slightest reason to believe that any other country . . . is willing to grant him a residence permit."[186]

Those hostile to his stay sought to apply a strict interpretation to the terms of his admission—that he literally could not engage in any political activity against a country with which Norway maintained friendly relations. Consequently, not just the communists argued that he had violated this restriction. On November 29, 1935, *Adresseavisen* cited as evidence the recently published edition of *My Life*. The paper referred not only to his point-blank refusal to refrain from political activity during his internal exile in Russia but also to how it had been impossible to isolate him from his followers while in Turkey. If Trotsky had collaborated in revolutionary politics at that time, *Adresseavisen* argued, could there be any "possibility that he will refrain from all political activity here . . . in this country?" The paper pointedly noted that his residence permit expired on December 18. Quite clearly, *Adresseavisen* did not favor its renewal.[187]

The target of this criticism obviously felt differently. On December 11 Lev addressed a letter to Minister of Justice Lie, politely requesting that his permit be extended.[188] At this time there was no reason for the Labor government to deny his application. Despite attempts by his enemies, especially the communists, to create controversy about his asylum, they had failed to make it a significant political issue. As anticipated, the permit was renewed unchanged on December 18. Furthermore, Wolf shortly afterwards received his extension, also for another six months.[189]

With renewals taking place almost automatically, there appeared to be no reason but to assume that Trotsky could reside in Norway as long as he wished. The Nygaardsvold government did not then reveal a negative attitude. Although Lie later maintained that police officials in Ringerike had carried out investigations about possible violations each time Trotsky received an extension, this was simply an attempt to show that Lie's department had been more vigilant, and critical, about Trotsky's exile than was really true. It was transparently clear that he was in contact with his followers, not only by mail but at times also directly. The arrival of foreigners in the small town of Hønefoss was a most unusual occurrence and was not only noticed but commented on. There is no reason to believe that leaders of the Labor Party were unaware of this activity. But as long as there were no repercussions, they benignly chose not to object.

Trotsky himself continued to assume that the government regarded his exile with sympathy. His main concern was hostility from the political extremes on the left and right. Two days before his residence permit again was renewed, in the summer of 1936, he wrote to Trygve Lie, enclosing two threatening letters from "fascists" who objected to his being allowed to remain in Norway. Trotsky asked whether in the future the length of the renewal might not be revealed ahead of time because the "fascists" were "well informed" concerning the dates of the extension.[190]

The question of whether or not he adhered to the terms of his residence permit remained a topic in ongoing attacks by Norwegian communists. Early in 1936 they made issue of an article that his disciple, Held, published in *Arbeiderbladet* on January 20. In it he condemned the Stakhanov movement, which was part of Stalin's ambitious drive to modernize the Soviet Union through rapid industrialization. Held argued that this system, which rewarded workers by how much they could produce above established quotas, really reduced the wages of the average worker and therefore violated true Marxist principles.[191]

As could be expected, criticism of the Soviet Union had immediate repercussions. While *ABC*, the Fatherland League's weekly, printed excerpts of Held's arguments, the communists' *Arbeideren* attacked Trotsky, maintaining that **he** was the article's real author, while denouncing *Arbeiderbladet* for having published it.[192] The Labor daily most likely had some doubts about whether to print the article, as shown by foreign editor Finn Moe's decision to shorten it considerably.[193] But *Arbeiderbladet* did not back down. It stated unequivocally that Held was the author, and it defended Trotsky, insisting that he "has conducted himself entirely correctly in this country."[194]

Arbeideren felt compelled to accept Held as the author of the anti-Stakhanov article, "although we have difficulty believing it."[195] The paper's somewhat defensive tone in early 1936 was undoubtedly due to yet another communist accusation that similarly proved to be untrue and which occurred at almost exactly the same time. In the United States the Hearst newspapers printed a highly critical anti-Soviet exposé on January 19. Trotsky was alleged to have written it. In reality, however, its author was Arben Tarov, whose criticism of conditions in the U.S.S.R. had originally been published in the United States by the Trotskyite *New Militant* during the previous fall.[196] But the major communist publication in the United States, the *Sunday Worker*, immediately charged that the article in the Hearst press provided proof that Trotsky had sold out and become an agent of American capitalism.[197]

The communist accusation that Trotsky earned income from the capitalist enemy reverberated worldwide and was repeated in Norway. On

January 30 Trotsky wrote to Scheflo that *Arbeideren* had just published the assertion that "Trotsky is waging a war against the Soviet Union in an alliance with Hearst," whom Trotsky described as "a world-famous thug, and an ally of Hitler." The purpose of the communist attack, he insisted, was to divert attention away from revelations by Tarov and Ciliga about persecutions of his sympathizers in the Soviet Union. Since Moscow was in no position to deny this, it was attempting to smear him. It first had done so by trying to implicate him in the murder of Kirov. Then the communists sought to use the Zeller postcard issue. When neither endeavor succeeded, they were now resorting to trying to connect him with Hearst.[198]

Trotsky responded vigorously. He recommended that his U.S. followers consider suing Hearst: "It would be good if we could use the judicial process to extract a tidy sum from Mr. Hearst for the benefit of the Fourth International."[199] Trotsky also released a statement to the Associated Press in which, citing "authentic sources" such as Tarov and Ciliga, he stressed the terrible treatment accorded political prisoners in the Soviet Union.[200]

In Norway, *Sørlandet* strongly rejected the idea that Trotsky was writing for the Hearst press. In an editorial Scheflo's conclusion was damning: "When it concerns Trotsky, it has become a good communist tactic to lie as often and as grossly as possible."[201]

The firm insistence by the Labor Party press that Trotsky was being falsely accused diminished for a time the vehemence of communist opposition in Norway. However, Labor's protective attitude toward Trotsky showed a tendency to change by the summer of 1936. On July 3 *Arbeiderbladet* published a long anti-Trotskyite article that caused indignation and concern among Trotsky's backers. Held referred to its author, Halvard Bojer, as the "son of a stupid bourgeois novel writer."*[202] The offensive article directed biting criticism against Trotsky's American followers in the Workers Party, who, Bojer insisted, were doing everything in their power to sabotage the creation of a broad-based American labor party. Instead, they were constantly agitating for a Fourth International. And while they were in the process of joining the American Socialist Party, like their French compatriots, they were only doing so in order to create advantages for themselves, intending to leave at the first favorable opportunity.[203]

Held quite realistically recognized that *Arbeiderbladet's* willingness to print Bojer's article was a clear indication of "how the wind is now blowing

---

* Held's description of Johan Bojer, Halvard Bojer's father, as "stupid" is hardly fair. Although literary experts agree that Bojer's production was of uneven quality, nevertheless several of his books are considered classics.

here." Not only did it show that the "Mot Dag rabble" (Bojer belonged to Mot Dag), who naturally hated the Trotskyites, had been granted a special opportunity, but it revealed that the group's activists would be allowed to "carry out a campaign against [Trotsky] in the Labor Party" itself.[204] This negative assessment of the party's attitude toward Trotsky's movement was to a considerable degree based on the Labor leadership's awareness that the Trotskyites were aggressively attempting to challenge the communists both in Western Europe and in the United States. As earlier, the Labor Party refused to provide any support, despite Trotsky's residence in Norway. That he actively sought to dictate policy to his followers no doubt caused added concern.

The caution displayed by Norwegian socialists was due especially to developments in France. In the spring of 1936, the coalition of socialists, Radical Republicans, and communists won a major electoral triumph, leading to the formation of Leon Blum's Popular Front government. This victory created great expectations among the French workers, who believed the time had come to realize their long-suppressed ambitions. Beginning on May 14, before Blum had formally assumed office, there broke out what Joel Colton has called "the greatest strike movement in the history of the Third Republic."[205] Throughout France workers not only halted production but staged sit-down strikes, seizing control of the factories. The country appeared to be in the initial stage of a great revolutionary uprising, similar to those earlier in its history.[206]

The pleas of Popular Front leaders for the workers to cease their strikes fell largely on deaf ears. The Blum government thereupon resorted to a traditional French political tactic—to blame unrest on sinister conspiratorial forces. It accused antidemocratic groups such as the "rightist" Croix de Feu and the "leftist" Trotskyites of "fanning discontent for their own purposes."[207]

The accusations against the Trotskyites, although greatly exaggerated, were nevertheless accurate. They were doing their best to take advantage of the unrest, even though their role was quite restricted. When the strike movement was at its maximum, the reorganized Internationalist Workers Party called on the workers to organize armed militia groups, which immediately brought to mind the chaotic conditions in Russia prior to the Bolshevik takeover. Blum, wishing to demonstrate that his government was one of "order" and not of "anarchy," ordered troops to take action if necessary. Among the government's targets was the Trotskyite newspaper, *La Lutte Ouvrier* (The Struggling Worker), which was shut down and its issues confiscated.[208]

In the end, however, votes in the French parliament proved to be primarily responsible for ending the strike movement. Frightened by the workers' militancy and the potential for revolution, the legislature proceeded rapidly to pass Blum's reform legislation.[209] By June 26 the number of strikers had decreased significantly, and the movement dissipated shortly afterwards, bringing the June crisis to an end.[210]

From Wexhall Trotsky listened with growing excitement to broadcasts of the unfolding events in France. He wrote: "Never did the radio seem so precious as during these days. From a distant village in Norway one can follow the pulse beats of the French revolution."[211] Inspired, he immediately wrote an article bearing the inflammatory title "The French Revolution Has Begun," intended for immediate publication. The strikes in France, he maintained, formed only the first wave of revolution, which agents of the "counter-revolutionaries [the Popular Front]" were intent on defeating. But even if it failed, there would come a "second wave," he predicted, which would be far less good natured. His movement would then assume leadership of the struggling masses who had been betrayed by their old leaders, the trade unions, the socialists, and the communists. It would be a revolution from below, with "industries and factories" electing their own deputies. Harking back to his Russian background, which would always form the core of his outlook, the name of the new organization was clear: "the Soviet of Workers' Deputies."[212]

Because of the suppression of *La Lutte Ouvrier*, the article did not appear in France during the disturbances but was printed later in the United States in the *Nation*, which would eventually cause difficulties for its author. While Trotsky provided a general course of action for his French section, most of the article consisted of analysis of what he believed was happening, presented within the framework of his revolutionary outlook. In this sense his commentary, except for its explicit focus on France, differed little from views he had expressed previously, such as those in an article written almost exactly one year earlier, in July 1935, subsequently published under his name in *Unser Wort* in September.[213] Here he had insisted that "Labor's vanguard" should denounce the collaboration among socialists, communists, and bourgeois nationalists in the name of opposing Hitler—in other words, the united-front strategy. Even if a war involving Hitler ensued, only a victorious revolution can mend the cares, the miseries, and the dislocations of war. Not only fascism but imperialism will thus receive its death blow. Not only will the external foes of the Soviet Union thereby be defeated, but the internal contradictions, which engender the barbarous dictatorship of the Stalin clique, will be overcome.[214]

The main difference, however, between the impact of the two articles was not so much their content but rather the changed circumstances under which Trotsky's views would be reacted to. By the summer of 1936, the condition of Europe was becoming uncertain. Mussolini had successfully repudiated the League of Nations and annexed Ethiopia; Hitler had remilitarized the Rhineland; France was unstable because of political and economic turmoil; and the Spanish Civil War would soon break out, in July. The Nygaardsvold government now began to exhibit disquiet about the controversial figure it had granted asylum to, in particular because of the negative commentary he received in the French press during the strikes of May and June. Trygve Lie's Justice Department therefore requested the police to investigate the extent to which he had been associated with the actions of the French Trotskyites.[215]

Accordingly, the powerful Oslo police chief who also controlled the security service,[216] Kristian Welhaven, wrote to his "dear colleague" in Paris, Pierre Mondanel, the controller general of the Criminal Police, on June 27. Welhaven enclosed the translation of an article that had appeared on June 24 in *Fritt Folk* (Free People), the new main organ of National Union, accusing Trotsky of having been actively involved in the French disturbances. Because Trotsky had been allowed to enter Norway, wrote the chief of police, under the condition that "he refrained from all political propaganda," it was "of great importance for me to gain accurate information whether the article's content is based on facts."[217]

That an inquiry concerning Trotsky's alleged activity in France would be launched by Norwegian officials on the basis of such a dubious source as *Fritt Folk*, which was noted for printing fabricated stories about its political enemies, in particular the Labor Party, was a clear indication of the nervousness with which the cabinet was beginning to view his stay. With a national election coming up, and with the Labor Party in control of the administration for only a year, its first priority was to keep the government in office. This might be jeopardized by controversy over Trotsky's asylum.

The *Fritt Folk* article proved to be completely bogus. Allegedly written by a "private" source in Paris, it combined fact and fiction to arrive at a completely absurd conspiratorial conclusion about Trotskyite involvement in the strike movement. Supposedly, reconciliation had occurred between Stalin and Trotsky and their Third and "Fourth" Internationals, whereby Moscow agreed to finance revolutionary activity by the ICL in Western Europe. This secret funding had allegedly allowed the French Trotskyites to operate on a large scale during May and June, thereby explaining why the strikes had had such a destabilizing effect.[218]

Any attempt by the French police to ascertain Trotsky's connection with the strike movement on the basis of such a flimsy account was bound to fail, as Lie later admitted indirectly in a report to the Storting, when he stated that the investigation in Paris had not "for the time being led to any positive result."[219] But despite the renewal of Trotsky's residence permit on June 18, the government was becoming uneasy about his continued stay.

The subject of this increased scrutiny was entirely unaware of what was taking place. Instead, when midsummer arrived he was in an optimistic frame of mind. With his health restored, he looked optimistically toward the future. He was inspired by the French disorders and by the earlier creation of the Spanish republic. To his American follower, A. J. Muste, he confided that events in France had been "tremendously encouraging." New leaders had led the revolts, not the Socialist Party and the "trade union bureaucrats." These true proletarian leaders were bound to join his movement: "We are small, as the Bolshevik forces were in 1914, but we too have the possibility of victory." Muste reported that "T[rotsky]'s confidence and faith are unshaken and magnificent—the attribute of a man who sees the road ahead."[220]

Encouraged by international upheavals, Trotsky believed the time was now at hand for creating the Fourth International—not that he had lost his zeal at any time while in Norway. Already in July 1935, less than a month after he arrived, he wrote to the ICL Secretariat, urging that a council of representatives from the national sections be established for "preparation for the 4th International."[221] Internal divisions within the Trotskyite groups, as well as his serious health problems, prevented him from pursuing this ambition more actively. However, in April 1936 he returned to arranging the groundwork for the Fourth International. He proposed a conference be held some time in the fall, perhaps in Luxembourg.[222]

In Oslo he delegated responsibility to young Walter Held for drawing up a preliminary program for the gathering.[223] This was but one indication of Trotsky's intent to handcraft how its proceedings were carried out. He planned first to hold a "preconference" for a limited number of top representatives at a location where he could be present, which obviously had to be Oslo (codenamed Berne), thereby allowing him to influence the agenda of the main conference. He scheduled the preconference for early July, while the main meeting was changed to take place in Paris (codenamed "Geneva") at the end of the month.[224]

Preparations, however, did not go smoothly. As he experienced over and over again, he faced obstacles from his individualistic followers, who, in many instances had equally dogmatic opinions about how to achieve a socialist triumph. At this time the Dutch section of the ICL presented him with many difficulties. Under the lead of the strong-willed Henricus Sneevliet, the Dutch had earlier been designated by Trotsky to be in charge of the "secretariat" for the Fourth International. They received responsibility for planning the practical details of the conference. But instead, to Trotsky's great frustration, Sneevliet and his cohorts deliberately sabotaged his effort. They often failed to respond to his letters, despite repeated requests. Consequently, the hard work that he, Held, Wolf, and the ICL Secretariat in Paris carried out in preparation for the meeting was placed in jeopardy. Sneevliet refused point blank to come to the preconference, and thanks to his obstruction, it had to be cancelled.[225] Trotsky had to be content to meet at Wexhall with the two Americans, Muste and Max Shachtman, who were expected to have leading roles at the main conference.

The negative attitude of the Dutch leaders was due to their opposition to holding **any** gathering. They had serious reservations about the Fourth International. Instead, much to Trotsky's chagrin, they still maintained contact with the London Bureau, even though he had formally broken with it. They similarly had ties with the British Independent Labour Party, which belonged to the Bureau.[226] The Dutch obviously regarded themselves as go-betweens, hoping to bring about conciliation between the Bureau and the ICL and not create added division among socialists. In addition, the Dutch also opposed Trotsky's tactic of having his sections join socialist parties—the so-called "French turn," employed first in France and Belgium, then later in the United States. Sneevliet clearly felt that this practice would damage Trotskyite unity.[227] The Dutch consequently let it be known that they would attend the Paris meeting only if their objections would be taken into account and open to discussion.

Trotsky, however, responded directly to this challenge. While the pre-conference could not be salvaged, he would not under any circumstances accept reconciliation with the London Bureau.[228] Although he wrote diplomatically to the Dutch, he clearly let it be known, directly and indirectly, that if Sneevliet and his backers obstinately continued their association with political groups that he had broken with, especially the London Bureau, then he would insist that the Dutch section be expelled.[229]

Faced with this possibility, the two main leaders, Sneevliet and Peter Schmidt, gave in and agreed to be represented at the conference. It was held in Paris on July 29–31, 1936. But Trotsky could only watch from the sidelines, expressing his "regret that I cannot meet with you in Geneva."[230] He had reason to feel this way. Contrary to what he had hoped, the delegates chose to postpone founding the international. They instead established what they called the "Movement for the Fourth International."[231] They were not yet ready to follow his lead and create a fully independent organization. The Dutch Trotskyites, to a great degree, had prevailed.

The summer of 1936 proved to be demanding for both Lev and Natalia. Not only were foreign visitors arriving in Ringerike more frequently, but Trotsky was also engaged in writing proposed resolutions for the Paris conference and completing the final draft of *The Revolution Betrayed*. In a letter to Shachtman in early July, he stated the need for "a period of complete rest after the tiring work of the month of [July]."[232]

The weather did nothing to make his work easier, although the season had begun pleasantly enough. In mid-June Håkon Meyer expressed the hope that Lev and Natalia were enjoying "the beautiful summer" and indicated that he and his wife Ingerid would very much like to visit on one of the upcoming weekends.[233] Lev graciously replied that he and Natalia, as well as the Knudsen family, extended a warm welcome to Meyer and his "dear wife."[234] But unfortunately, their daughter Karin had to be hospitalized. The trip was therefore first extended and then postponed indefinitely.[235] Little did he know it, but his change of plans meant that Meyer lost his opportunity for a final face-to-face meeting with Trotsky.

By the time Meyer was putting off his visit, the weather in eastern Norway had become downright hot. Held voiced concern in late June, asking whether Trotsky wasn't "suffering on account of the heat." He suggested that Trotsky "move to the mountains for a couple of weeks."[236] Busy as he was, Lev had no time for excursions in July. But he was looking forward to getting away as soon as possible and decided to vacation near Kristiansand, close to where his patron, Scheflo, lived. Trotsky sent him a letter, posted on July 28, in which he inquired about spending "two weeks in the area of Christiansand [sic]." He wished to live as isolated as possible. Above all, he wanted to enjoy the "sea, fishing, and nature."[237]

Scheflo responded immediately that he could provide a "lonesome cabin near the sea where he [Trotsky] can be quite by himself." A cook-cleaning woman would be found to serve as housekeeper. And Trotsky could have a small motorboat for fishing near land. But he would also have a chance to brave the North Sea for fishing further out should he desire.[238]

The necessary plans had thereby been completed for the couple to get away for their first vacation since their stay at Andorsrud the previous fall. However, as they set off for Kristiansand in anticipation not only of a needed rest but also a reunion with their major political benefactor, an attack had already been set in motion that would have a significant impact on the rest of their exile. With the election approaching in the fall, Quisling's NS had been making careful preparations for gaining the victory that had eluded the party three years earlier, when it had plunged into an election campaign only a few months after its founding. As part of its strategy, NS placed great emphasis on its national newspaper, *Fritt Folk*, whose first issue appeared at the end of March. Party members believed the new daily would significantly improve their chance for success.[239]

Whereas NS had been an extreme right-wing nationalist party, strongly antisocialist, when it first came into being, by 1936 Quisling had become a direct imitator of Hitler. Quisling now rejected Norway's parliamentary system, with its tradition of democracy, and adopted the posture of a fervent anti-Semite.[240] Since Norway had fewer than two thousand Jewish citizens, plus a small number of Jewish refugees who had fled persecution in Germany, Quisling, like Hitler, gave his anti-Semitic attacks a global scope by portraying the Jews as being responsible for both international communism and capitalist exploitation.[241] In this context Trotsky was a natural target, and while NS had earlier made isolated attacks against him, with the appearance of *Fritt Folk* it became quite obvious that Quisling was using Trotsky's asylum as a major campaign issue.

From the spring of 1936 onwards, the newspaper carried a series of articles with vicious commentary. It not only constantly hammered home the argument that Trotsky was using Norway as a base to plot revolution, but it repeated the charge that he was acting in secret concert with the Soviet Union, despite his outward hostility toward Moscow, which was simply a facade. The paper referred to him, literally, in animal terms, insisting that this "wild beast" had to be expelled.[242] As the time drew near for the renewal of his residence permit, *Fritt Folk* echoed the communist demand (although this was never acknowledged) that it not be extended, maintaining that the Labor government intended to grant him an indefinite stay that would allow him to become a Norwegian citizen.[243] Another repeated theme was the assertion that Trotsky supposedly had received favorable treatment while hospitalized the previous fall. The paper presented a maudlin account of how Norwegian taxpayers were supposedly kept waiting for many months before being admitted to a hospital, where they were housed in rooms holding six to seven patients, while Trotsky received immediate admission and was given a single room, from which he could conduct revolutionary activity, attended by two [sic] secretaries.[244] However, Quisling's paper always returned to its main accusation that Trotsky was involved in a huge international conspiracy and that the Labor Party aided this process by allowing him to remain.[245]

Trotsky's defenders made no effort to rebut these accusations. Held informed Trotsky on June 25 that the Norwegian "Nazi paper" was agitating against him daily. But Held felt that issuing denials might cause some people to assume that what "the fascists" were writing was true.[246] As the press campaign heated up, however, events would show that NS members were not satisfied with merely demanding Trotsky's expulsion. Activists among them would instead take direct action in order to secure this outcome.

5 From Vacation to House Arrest

> I, Lev Trotsky, declare that I, my wife, and my secretaries shall not engage in political activity in Norway or carry out political agitation or activity against any state that is friendly toward Norway. . . .
>
> I declare that I, my wife, and my secretaries shall not in any way . . . participate or involve ourselves in current political questions abroad. I declare that my activity as an author will be limited to historical writings and general theoretical reflections that are not directed toward any country.
>
> I declare that I accept having my . . . outgoing mail and all telegrams controlled by the authorities.
>
> I declare that I shall not be interviewed by Norwegian or foreign journalists.
> —"Declaration" submitted to Lev Trotsky by the Norwegian Justice Department, August 26, 1936

WITH THE MANUSCRIPT OF *THE REVOLUTION BETRAYED* mailed, Trotsky set off on his long-anticipated vacation. He and Natalia were joined by Konrad and Hilda Knudsen. Also in their company was a shadowy figure named Erich Löffler, who had arrived at Wexhall at the end of July.[1] An element of mystery has surrounded him.[2] He was a personal friend of Erwin, serving as the latter's replacement as secretary since Wolf was now in England.[3] But Löffler's stay was cut short, possibly because something in his past might have been embarrassing at a time when public attention once more was riveted on Trotsky. Löffler apparently exited the country, as unheralded in his departure as he had been on his arrival.[4]

The quintet left Hønefoss on Wednesday, August 5, setting off on what they believed would be a pleasant two-day drive on the dusty and narrow, but nevertheless scenic and uncrowded, roads of southern Norway. Rather than driving directly down the coast, Knudsen first chose to show the Trotskys the natural beauty of southeastern Norway, traveling through central Telemark to the picturesque village of Seljord, where they stayed overnight.[5]

It was here that they realized the trip would not be as uneventful as they had expected. They were being shadowed by NS members who were intent on following Trotsky's every move to make him feel uncomfortable. Having tapped the telephone at Wexhall, the plot leader, engineer Thomas Neumann, knew Knudsen's travel route and drove to Seljord. As National Union's propaganda chief in Akershus province, he was closely associated with Johan B. Hjort, the party's number two man. Neumann was accompanied by Harald Franklin Knudsen, who later served briefly as Quisling's secretary in April 1940, at the time of the German invasion.[6]

When Konrad Knudsen and his passengers left Seljord the next morning, the NS members were in close pursuit. They followed Knudsen's car all the way to Kristiansand, despite several attempts to throw them off.[7] Furthermore, on the same day that the travel party had left Wexhall, a group of NS members, also part of Neumann's plot, broke into the house in search of incriminating documentation. It seemed, however, as if the burglary had been foiled, with the police having caught the perpetrators and learned their identities.[8]

The Trotskys therefore at first paid little attention to the break-in. They arrived at Scheflo's home in Kristiansand that evening, where they were warmly welcomed, with Scheflo's wife, Dagmar, serving coffee to the celebrated guests.[9] Then it was time to set off for the island where the Trotskys hoped to remain undisturbed for the next two weeks. But first it was necessary to get rid of their persistent trackers, who had been joined by two other NS members.[10] Konrad Knudsen left his car in Kristiansand, hiring instead a taxi to drive east along the coast, with the NS contingent right behind. But when they reached a ferry crossing, Konrad confronted their pursuers, temperamentally informing them that he would report them to the authorities, and he insisted that under no circumstances should they be allowed on the vessel.[11] He received strong backing from the skipper, and they had no recourse except to accept defeat.[12] They turned around and set up guard outside *Sørlandet*'s office in Kristiansand, believing Trotsky might soon come back.[13] Having thereby given them the slip, the couple at last seemed to have found the solitude that they had been looking forward to. They spent the next ten days in what Lev described as a "solitary fisherman's cottage built on the rocks of [a] tiny island."[14]

The island was called Stangnesholmen and lay in Randesund, an arm of Kvåsefjord, due east of Kristiansand. The cottage where the Trotskys stayed had indeed once been a "fisherman's home," but now the entire island was owned by a "non-political" secondary school teacher (*lektor*), Per Johnsen, an acquaintance of Scheflo, who had agreed to rent the cottage.[15] Scheflo also arranged to have a friend of the family, Kathinka Zahl, serve as housekeeper. Extroverted and fun loving, with the nickname Thinka, she got along well with the Trotskys. Even though she did not speak foreign languages, she was able to communicate with them in simple Norwegian.[16]

In this vacationer's paradise, Lev, a passionate angler, could indulge himself to the utmost because fishing was much better than later in the century. Since his favorite food was fish, Thinka Zahl kept busy, cooking the large catches that he brought ashore.[17] He had at his disposal Scheflo's boat, which the editor had specially fitted out with a chair in the stern, allowing him to go on outings despite his crippled condition.[18] Trotsky had no difficulty in obtaining others to join him. Two of Scheflo's children, Inge and Dagmar, were among the many who took part. Dagmar, Scheflo's youngest daughter, who was named after her mother, recalls Lev as a kindly, grandfatherly type whom she enjoyed speaking with in English.[19]

Lev, accompanied by Natalia, Thinka, and friends of the Scheflo family, also went on pleasant sailing excursions along the coast. There was time for Trotsky to receive visitors at Stangnesholmen that included acquaintances of Scheflo, such as the controversial poet Arnulf Øverland.[20] Especially memorable were island gatherings that included the Trotskys, the Knudsens, Scheflo's family members, Thinka, and assorted individuals from the wide circle of Scheflo's connections. Here, close to the fjord, they picnicked, enjoying each other's company over coffee, pastries, and other delicacies.[21]

Their stay was not, however, entirely tranquil. Natalia's overriding anxiety continued to be Sergei, whose fate remained unknown. She gave the impression of being weak and sickly and was generally quiet and withdrawn.[22] Providing security for the Trotskys was also a concern. Knudsen had charged the NS members who pursued Trotsky with harassment, but the police chief in Kristiansand chose not to prosecute them, stating that they had simply indulged in a youthful prank. Scheflo reacted by writing editorially that the police chief not only was pro-fascist but also suffered from "stupidity and incompetence."[23] The nonsocialist press in the area in turn did not mirror Scheflo's favorable attitude toward the famous vacationer. The Conservative Party's *Christiansands Tidende* (Christiansand's News) went so far as to accuse *Sørlandet*'s journalists of plotting revolutionary strategy with Trotsky.[24]

Due to press coverage, including sensational news reports about the burglary at Wexhall, it proved impossible to keep Trotsky's location secret very long. Fearing a possible assassination attempt, he always had his pistol ready. On one occasion Thinka Zahl is said to have playfully pointed it at him. He reacted furiously, ordering her never to do so again. It took a while for him to regain confidence that she did not pose a danger.[25]

Natalia was noticeably anxious about their security. Aware of Stalin's methods and what was happening in Russia, she slept badly. To have added protection, Trotsky asked Inge Scheflo and his friend, Bjørn Hilt, to maintain guard outside the cabin at night, entrusting them with the pistol. They set up a tent, taking turns doing guard duty. However, on the only occasion when prompt action was needed, they failed dismally. A motorboat full of rowdy young people appeared late one night and began to shout insults at the former leader of the Russian Revolution. But Inge and Bjørn were sound asleep. Together with Thinka, Trotsky himself had to chase the intruders away.[26]

While this incident had comic overtones, it showed that the country's mood toward Trotsky was changing significantly. Previously, after the sensation of his arrival had died down, he had been the subject of only periodic attention, but now he became the constant focus of media interest, due in particular to the NS action at Wexhall. Lev and Natalia were able to remain largely undisturbed for only seven days. Then, on August 14, none other than Reidar Sveen, the chief of investigations (*opdagelseschef*) of the Oslo police department's Investigative Police Unit (*opdagelsespoliti*), arrived by air in Kristiansand.[27] His assignment was to question Trotsky concerning the NS break-in. This burglary had set in motion a series of developments that would forever alter the conditions under which Trotsky lived and operated in Norway.

Planning for the break-in originated when a group of NS militants decided that the party's anti-Trotsky campaign needed concrete evidence to prove that he was engaged in revolutionary activity. Although Neumann technically led the operation, Johan B. Hjort not only was aware of it and provided encouragement but most likely instigated it as the NS provincial leader (*fylkesfører*) in Akershus.

As a preliminary move NS members had established base in a tent by a bridge over the Sokna River, about fifteen minutes' walking distance from Wexhall, as early as June 28–29, pretending to be on a camping trip.[28] From here they conducted espionage, noting who came on visits to Trotsky. Using Neumann's technical expertise, they also tapped Knudsen's telephone.[29] They furthermore had access to the house itself, which was for sale. Pretending to be would-be buyers, NS members visited Wexhall several times.[30] On one such trip Neumann, accompanied by his subordinate, Didrik Rye Heyerdahl, inspected the villa from basement to attic, but they showed special interest in Trotsky's workroom.[31] During unguarded moments they were able to steal a few papers from his desk.[32]

Not satisfied with limited results, they proceeded to take direct action. In the afternoon of August 5, young Borgar Knudsen answered the telephone. During his conversation with one of the plotters, who gave a false pretext for calling, Borgar mentioned that he was home alone.[33] Acting on this information, a gang of six NS members arrived shortly before midnight, expecting to have to deal only with a fifteen-year-old boy. Leaving the driver outside, the group burst into the house when Borgar answered the door. They pretended to be police officers who were conducting an investigation. Heyerdahl nervously read a fictitious Justice Department warrant that authorized them to search Trotsky's rooms. Displaying phony police insignia, they maintained that their late arrival and civilian attire was because they did not wish to arouse attention in the neighborhood.[34]

Heyerdahl discovered, however, that the situation at Wexhall was quite different from what he had anticipated. Following a teenager's natural inclination to take advantage of his parents' absence, Borgar had stayed up late with two friends, playing *ludo*, a popular Norwegian board game. Furthermore, his sister Hjørdis was also at home, together with a female friend from the bookstore.[35] Hjørdis at once became suspicious and insisted that Heyerdahl read the "warrant" several times. His obvious nervousness increased her conviction that this was not a genuine operation. She demanded that the local sheriff (*lensmann*) verify Heyerdahl's credentials. The latter dutifully placed a telephone call and pretended to have a conversation that confirmed his authority. But he refused to allow Hjørdis to

speak with the "sheriff" on the other end of the line. She remained uncon-
vinced and protested loudly when the "police" began to examine papers
on her father's desk. She next placed herself directly in front of the door
to Trotsky's workroom and refused point-blank to allow anyone to enter.
When the "police" threatened to remove her by force, she ordered Borgar
to get insurance inspector Egil Wraaman, the tenant on the second floor,
to come down. Upon his arrival, Wraaman also insisted that the local police should be there when Trotsky's rooms were searched.[36]

At this point, with so many witnesses present, Heyerdahl and his gang
gave up. Insisting they would return with local police backing, they sped
off in a car with altered license plates—but not before Borgar succeeded
in jotting down its license number.[37] The sheriff, Johan Hansen Kiær,[38] was
contacted immediately and arrived soon. Determining that a criminal
break-in had occurred, he phoned the police chief of Ringerike, Robert
A. Urbye,[39] in Hønefoss. The two began a search of the area and then wid-
ened their hunt. Not until considerably later, at approximately 3:30 a.m.,
did they come across the suspects on their way to Oslo. The NS members sought to escape, but the police eventually forced them to stop. After
briefly maintaining their innocence, they soon confessed to having been
at Wexhall.[40]

One might thereupon have concluded that this was an open-and-shut
case—that the perpetrators of a criminal act involving the impersonation
of police officers, the use of bogus government documents and official
symbols, and the use of force to gain entry to a residence under false pretenses would immediately be brought to justice. But the incident immediately took on a unique character. First, the group that was stopped by
Sheriff Kiær and Police Chief Urbye consisted of five, not six. The missing
participant had earlier left the automobile not far from Wexhall. Per Imerslund, who in World War II would symbolize the ideal pro-Germanic NS
volunteer fighting against the Russians, made his way back to the house,
found an open window, and climbed in. Not daring to turn on any lights,
he snatched up all loose papers he could get his hands on.[41] Thereafter
he slipped away into the darkness, made his way to Hønefoss, and in the
morning caught a train out of town.

Secondly, although the accomplices in the break-in admitted their
complicity; maintained they were justified in their action because Norway, in their opinion, did not have a "legal government"; and asked to be
represented by J. B. Hjort; they nevertheless were permitted by Urbye to

go home on their own recognizance after having given their names and addresses.[42] This caused the Labor Party press to react, with Scheflo describing the police chief's decision as "scandalous," in particular since the crimes that the suspects admitted to were punishable by up to three years in jail.[43] The Labor Party clearly felt that Urbye was motivated by political considerations that were anything but friendly toward the government.[44]

His superiors similarly viewed Urbye with suspicion. Minister of Justice Trygve Lie promised that the case would be investigated thoroughly,[45] while Attorney General (*Riksadvokat*) Haakon Sund described the crime as "very serious." And although Urbye for the time being remained in charge on the local level, Sund announced that the state attorney (*statsadvokaten*) for Buskerud and Oppland provinces, Sverre Riisnæs, had been instructed to keep a close eye on how Urbye carried out his assignment.*[46] Consequently, it did not take long before the NS suspects had to answer for their actions. By August 8 they were in Oslo for police interrogation and the start of a preliminary hearing to determine what charges would be brought against them.[47]

In order to divert attention, the energetic NS second in command, Hjort, had already swung into action. Indicating his belief that the best defense was to go on the offensive, his carefully planned response to the break-in further showed that he must have known about the operation before it was executed and quite likely was its brain. On the day following the burglary, he personally contacted Urbye.[48]

Hjort filed a formal charge (*anmeldelse*), published the next day in *Fritt Folk*, demanding that legal action be initiated against Trotsky. Hjort accused "Leo Bronstein Trotsky" of having violated Norway's criminal law, as well as the terms of his residence permit, which, according to Hjort, required Trotsky "to abstain from any type of political activity." Specifically, Hjort charged Trotsky with (1) intending to have Norway become part of a foreign power, (2) seeking to create war, (3) carrying out plans to achieve both of the above, and (4) having violated Norway's constitution.

However, Hjort revealed that proof of such alleged duplicity was quite thin when he insisted that Wexhall be searched immediately to prevent

---

* State Attorney Sverre Riisnæs gained a negative reputation among NS members because of his initially stringent prosecution of the six accused of the burglary at Wexhall. Interestingly, Riisnæs joined NS during World War II and became infamous as minister of justice under Quisling. He feigned insanity at the end of the war and escaped receiving a severe sentence, most likely the death penalty.

relevant evidence from disappearing. The blatant political, rather than legal, nature of this maneuver was also exposed by his assertion that since there was every reason to believe that Trotsky's supposed subversive activity had been conducted with approval of the government, Urbye was advised not to discuss the case with the Justice Department until verification of Hjort's complaint had been obtained. *Fritt Folk* similarly made it plain that Minister of Justice Lie should be ineligible to take part in the process.[49]

Labor responded with scorn. Typically, Scheflo referred to the move as being "insolent," denouncing Hjort's accusations as false. The entire case, Scheflo stated, should serve to establish a clear warning for "Norwegian fascists." "They need to realize that we have not yet come so far as in Germany, where fascist bandits can do exactly what they wish."[50]

This acrimony was but part of a great public debate that erupted immediately after the police detained the five suspects. Still preoccupied with catching whiting in Randesund, Trotsky was featured in newspaper headlines as never before. More press commentary was written about him in the next thirty days than at any other time during his Norwegian exile.

Fritt Folk naturally led the way, maintaining that the NS members had succeeded in obtaining proof that Trotsky had violated his asylum and further accusing the Labor government of being aware of his revolutionary activity.[51] Although the "evidence" it presented initially was weak, restricted to a "report" by Heyerdahl on so-called revolutionary talk he had overheard at Wexhall, on August 8 the NS paper presented more damning material, namely excerpts from Trotsky's manuscript of "The French Revolution Has Begun." This, *Fritt Folk* maintained, provided confirmation that he was behind preparations for establishing soviets in France.[52]

NS also accused Trotsky of being responsible for "Bolshevik orgies in Madrid and Barcelona," citing the *London Times* as its source.[53] With the Spanish Civil War having recently broken out, NS, along with the more conservative nonsocialist parties, naturally sympathized with the Nationalists. On August 10 the NS paper presented more of what it considered to be convincing proof in the form of a letter by Trotsky commenting on internal developments within his movement. This included the expulsion of Molinier and the evaluation of candidates to serve on the Fourth International's secretariat. This showed, said *Fritt Folk*, how Trotsky was in charge of a "world encompassing conspiracy."[54]

The Labor Party responded by seeking to turn the controversy to its advantage. *Arbeiderbladet* specifically accused the entire nonsocialist press except *Tidens Tegn*—representing the Independent People's Party—of siding with the "NS gangsters."[55] The contrived nature of the situation, Labor papers insisted, was shown by the fact that while the nonsocialists had a majority in parliament, they nevertheless had remained largely silent, not only when Trotsky arrived but also when his residence permit had been renewed on two separate occasions. Only now, with an election approaching, did the nonsocialists try to use his asylum to attack the government.[56]

As for NS, the Labor Party insisted that its involvement in the break-in was not restricted just to the five "gangsters." Not only was J. B. Hjort fully implicated, but *Arbeiderbladet* insinuated that Quisling himself must have had knowledge of what was planned.[57] Labor's focus on "Nazi leaders" was concentrated, however, primarily on Hjort. Not only was he closely associated with those who took part in the burglary but his family lineage made him an inviting target. His mother was the daughter of an aristocratic German general, and Labor linked Hjort directly to Hitler, accusing him of wanting to introduce Nazi conditions in Norway. It was especially despicable, said Scheflo in *Sørlandet*, that a large part of the nonsocialist press chose either to defend or to cover up Hjort's role.[58]

The Labor Party also sought to tie the dispute to political differences concerning the Spanish Civil War. Therefore, when the party arranged a large outdoor rally in Oslo, supporting the Spanish people against the "traitorous military clique" that was attempting to crush "the country's legally elected government," a resolution was also passed condemning the "criminal activity" of NS.[59]

Viewed against the entirely different position it would adopt shortly afterwards, the initial reaction of the Norwegian Communist Party was noteworthy but logical. It sought to play the popular-front role prescribed for stronger communist movements elsewhere in Europe and accordingly supported the Labor government. The communist response to the break-in was therefore at first even stronger than the Labor Party's. Even before the incident the communists had described NS agitation against Trotsky as "senseless and stupid," based on lies. Commenting on the episode itself, they too referred to the group that carried out the burglary as "gangsters."[60]

Communist motivation was entirely political, as shown when the party accused nonsocialist papers, especially *Aftenposten*, of exploiting fallout from the burglary because the bourgeois parties did not really have other issues in the election campaign. *Arbeideren* demanded not only that the five accused NS members should be brought to trial but Quisling as well, while National Union should be outlawed. The communists furthermore urged Trygve Lie to eliminate all "fascist forces" within the police—not just those involved with the break-in like Urbye, but officers on a higher level who had recently been promoted.[61]

Nonsocialist reaction to the burglary was actually more nuanced. The bourgeois papers, equally preoccupied with the election, were fearful of anything that might divide the *borgerlige* anti-Labor campaign. They therefore assumed at least in part a critical attitude toward NS because Quisling had decreed in 1936 that NS was opposed to **all** other political parties, not merely the socialists. Consequently, his party did not take part in any electoral cooperation, while the major nonsocialist parties worked together.

It was *Nationen*, the organ for the Farmers Association, that most strongly expressed understanding for what the five NS members had done, although the paper did point out that their action was illegal. It demanded that Trotsky immediately be expelled and went so far as to insinuate that the "people's will" might be carried out if the government failed to act.[62] *Nationen's* strong hostility toward Trotsky and the Labor Party reflected, however, more the personal views of its editor, Thorvald Aadahl, than the Agrarian Party leadership.

Aftenposten, despite being singled out as the staunchest backer of the NS operation, was in fact more moderate, initially describing the break-in as a failure.[63] Such actions, the paper argued, created conditions that could lead to civil war. Trotsky would be the one to benefit because he had traditionally taken advantage of social unrest. So while *Aftenposten* strongly advocated Trotsky's expulsion, it rejected the methods that NS employed.[64]

The Liberal Party's *Dagbladet* was even more negative. It immediately criticized NS as a party that did not hesitate to use illegal means to gain its goals. Not only should the NS members be punished severely, but their leaders should simultaneously be prosecuted because they had openly voiced approval of the burglary.[65]

Two papers that under different circumstances might have been more conciliatory because ideologically they were closest to National Union, having earlier supported Quisling, came out in opposition. *Tidens Tegn* assumed a hostile attitude from the beginning, maintaining that the type of activity carried out by the five NS members served only to create conditions that could lead to civil war and dictatorship.[66] *ABC*, the Fatherland League's weekly, sarcastically insisted that the NS operation had been stupid, having failed completely to obtain new information about Trotsky.[67]

Despite the degrees of difference expressed in the nonsocialist papers, they had, however, one thing in common. Although they disagreed on whether Trotsky should be expelled, they favored a full inquiry to see whether he had violated his asylum. While none would admit it, this meant that the nonsocialist press, including papers strongly hostile to NS, affirmed that Hjort's activists had succeeded in forcing the authorities to pay attention to their accusation that Trotsky had failed to abide by the terms of his residence permit.[68]

Although this had not been their original intent, officials were already conducting an investigation that would eventually have serious repercussions. It grew out of the inquiry into the actions of the five NS "gangsters," as they were repeatedly called in the Labor press, which began immediately after their apprehension. It was quickly taken out of the hands of the local police, thereby removing Urbye from the scene. The attorney general decreed that the Oslo police department's Investigative Police Unit should conduct the investigation, while prosecution was assigned to State Attorney Riisnæs.[69]

Initially the case seemed to be quite straightforward. There was no possibility of holding the NS leadership accountable, with Quisling as well as Hjort denying foreknowledge of the burglary. This meant that those directly involved would face the charges alone. Although three of the five at first refused to answer questions at Oslo police headquarters when examined on August 8, they soon changed their minds after Riisnæs took the unusual step of beginning a preliminary hearing (*forhørsrett*) that same afternoon, on a Saturday. While the NS members pleaded not guilty, they readily admitted that the prosecution's facts were true.[70] Similarly, although he at first was unwilling to hand over all papers stolen from Wexhall, Heyerdahl, as the leader of the group, quickly adopted a different stance when threatened with spending the remainder of the weekend in jail. After he received the requested material, which had been sequestered in *Fritt Folk*'s office, Riisnæs concluded that there was no longer reason to hold the defendants since the case "must be considered solved."[71]

It was not settled in such an open-and-shut manner, however. First, the defendants still had some explaining to do. Secondly, the preliminary hearing had to consider Hjort's accusation that Trotsky had violated

his residence permit. Because he was a party to the case, Hjort was dis-
qualified from serving as counsel for the defense. Another NS attorney,
Albert Wiesener, replaced him.[72]

Although Hjort was a skilled attorney, qualified to argue before the Supreme Court (*høyesterettsadvokat*), he had meager evidence because of
the limited items that NS had been able to pilfer from Wexhall, consisting mainly of material previously published in *Fritt Folk*: Trotsky's article
on the disturbances in France, his letter about Molinier and candidate selection for the Fourth International's secretariat, and two envelopes with
names on them. As added proof, Hjort stressed that Trotsky had conspired
with dangerous communist revolutionaries who visited him.[73] Except for
Fritt Folk, the press did not find this convincing. Hjort was sarcastically
repudiated because his accusations were untrue, which was the position of
the Labor Party, or because they did not add anything new to the obvious
fact that Trotsky had violated his asylum, which was the view expressed by
Aftenposten, *Tidens Tegn*, and *ABC*.[74]

Hjort also had some difficulty explaining a startling and embarrassing
statement made by Heyerdahl during the initial meeting of the preliminary
hearing. He shocked his interrogators by declaring offhandedly that a list of
names and addresses of persons living in Germany, on an envelope stolen
from Wexhall, had been sent to the Gestapo. This created a sensation because
it appeared to show direct ties between NS and Hitler's Nazi regime.[75] Adding fuel to such speculation was the arrival of two mysterious Germans in
Hønefoss shortly after the list had allegedly been turned over to the Gestapo.
Furthermore, none other than Heyerdahl had paid their hotel bill.[76]

Hjort, in a letter to *Tidens Tegn*—which had gleefully reported Heyerdahl's indiscretion—categorically denied NS cooperation with the already
dreaded German secret police. He insisted that no list found at Wexhall
had been forwarded to Germany and that the two alleged Gestapo agents
were only vacationing schoolboys whom Heyerdahl had taken pity on because they had lost their travel money. Finally, Hjort described Heyerdahl's
original boast at the preliminary hearing as having been made flippantly
in jest.[77] Heyerdahl himself later corroborated this explanation in court.[78]

The question of whether the NS members had shared information
with the Gestapo was never confirmed, and most likely it was a figment

of Heyerdahl's imagination. It did, however, reinforce the image that the party was inspired by National Socialism.* With questioning of the defendants out of the way, along with the submission of Hjort's charges, the preliminary hearing recessed for the time being at 12:15 p.m. on Thursday, August 13.[79] It did not appear that the NS accusations had been particularly persuasive. *Arbeiderbladet* described the stolen material that NS had acquired from Wexhall as "worthless papers."[80] In refutation, the paper also published an interview with Walter Held (whose last name was misspelled Helt), in which he point by point denied the allegations. He insisted that "The French Revolution Has Begun" was not a call for violent upheaval but simply Trotsky's analysis of the situation in France, which had first been published in the *Nation* and then reprinted in various European publications. Trotsky's letter to France about Molinier and potential candidates for positions in the Fourth International was described as a reflection of Trotsky's personal viewpoint, nothing more. Held further explained deceptively that foreign visitors to Hønefoss were primarily representatives of European and American publishers. As for Trotsky's alleged involvement in the Spanish Civil War, Held more truthfully pointed out that the Trotskyites no longer had an organization in Spain.[81]

Trygve Lie also publicly repudiated National Union, and he castigated bourgeois papers such as *Nationen* and *Aftenposten* for allegedly excusing the implicated NS members. But, as head of the Justice Department, he could not just simply dismiss out of hand the validity of the NS charges. Choosing his words carefully in a campaign speech, he did indicate that "the authorities of course will investigate if Trotsky has violated the terms of his residence permit."[82] This statement proved ominous. On August 14, the day after the preliminary hearing recessed, Lie sent Chief of Investigations Sveen to Kristiansand to question Trotsky.[83]

Upon landing outside of town, Sveen made his way to Stangnesholmen, accompanied by an investigator and a female stenographer. He arrived to find Trotsky at sea, fishing as usual, leaving the chief to contemplate the beauty of the island until Lev came ashore. There followed a three-hour interview in the cottage, while Konrad Knudsen was simultaneously questioned by Sveen's subordinate about the break-in.[84] Trotsky insisted that

---

* Although National Union by 1936 was clearly influenced by National Socialism, with Quisling closely imitating Hitler in a failed effort to garner political success, the NS leader had not yet established direct ties with the Germans.

under no circumstances had he violated his asylum. During his stay in Norway he had been an author, nothing more, and his writings had been confined to analysis and commentary, not agitation. This was true, said Trotsky, of "The French Revolution Has Begun," which had first appeared in a "democratic" American weekly and then had been translated and published in a number of countries. He denied any involvement in Spain.

When asked about his contact with followers abroad, Trotsky was not equally forthcoming. He obviously needed to downplay the influence that he exerted within the ICL. He stated that there were groups in France and other countries who agreed with what he expressed in his writings. Some members of these groups wrote to him from time to time to obtain his opinions about various questions. However, he only answered a small number of such inquiries, and his responses represented only his personal viewpoint. He never, he asserted, gave orders. The letter concerning Molinier should be regarded, he maintained, in this light. As for the subject of the Fourth International, which Sveen also brought up, Trotsky, for once correctly, referred to it as an emerging movement rather than a hard-and-fast organization. Furthermore, it did not, he claimed, have a general secretariat.[85] He made no mention, however, of the International Communist League with its secretariat in Paris, headed by his own son.

On the surface, the interview appeared to have been concluded satisfactorily. The chief of investigations, back in Oslo on the following day, told journalists that his meeting with Trotsky had gone very well. He therefore was of the opinion that his investigation was finished, and he intended to send all of his material to State Attorney Riisnæs. But Sveen indicated that he would also consult with the Justice Department, which meant first and foremost Trygve Lie. Sveen also stated that it might be necessary at some future date to "call in both Trotsky and editor Knudsen for a court investigation."[86] While this sounded innocent enough at the time, the outcome of this inquiry would prove to be anything but agreeable for Trotsky.

Initially, the latter was fully content with what he believed had been a cordial and complete meeting with Sveen. Trotsky received a copy of their interview, as well as a notice on behalf of State Attorney Riisnæs, dated August 18, indicating that Hjort's charges had been dismissed.[87] As a result, Trotsky had every reason to believe that the case had been resolved in his favor. He failed to take into account, however, that the question of whether he had violated the terms of his residence permit was not included in the notice from the police.

By this time, moreover, he was fully preoccupied with a problem that he considered far more important than the burglary, although as the future would show, the two issues were interrelated. On August 13 Martin Bolstad, the chargé d'affaires at the Norwegian legation in Moscow, reported to the Foreign Ministry that Russian newspapers, led by *Pravda*, had during the last few days been full of inflammatory articles about a conspiracy purportedly organized by Trotsky, Zinoviev, and Kamenev. Allegedly, this plot had now developed to the point that the "conspirators" had made common cause with "German fascism" against the Soviet leadership. Since Zinoviev and Kamenev were imprisoned, Trotsky was assigned primary responsibility. Bolstad noted skeptically that the charges were "to a certain degree imaginary." Nevertheless, he observed that because these accusations were made by a great power, they "could create difficulties" for continuing Trotsky's right of asylum and maintaining his personal protection.[88]

On the next day, Friday, August 14, the news bureau TASS officially declared that sixteen defendants, headed by Zinoviev and Kamenev, would be brought to trial on the following Wednesday. They were accused of a variety of crimes, including personal responsibility for the murder of Kirov. Furthermore, Trotsky and Zinoviev had since 1932 reputedly headed an anti-Soviet bloc to which Kamenev also belonged. Trotsky was responsible for allegedly sending would-be assassins "from abroad in order to carry out terrorist actions against leading men within the Soviet Union's Communist Party and the Soviet state."[89] This announcement marked the beginning of Stalin's infamous major show trials of the 1930s.

The accused prisoners were not Stalin's main objective. As Dmitry Volkogonov has pointed out, "the chief target was Trotsky."[90] He alone of former top leaders who had served under Lenin was out of reach, attempting from Norway to organize an international organization challenging Stalin's control of the communist movement. Trotsky and his son Lev were therefore also on trial "**in absentia**—Trotsky as the arch conspirator."[91] This was not the first time that Stalin or his agents had accused Trotsky of organizing murder plots against Soviet leaders. The ridiculous episode concerning Fred Zeller's postcard was but one of many attempts to smear him with this charge.[92]

Having earlier that day been interviewed by Sveen, Trotsky was completely taken aback by the vilification hurled against him from Moscow. Furthermore, he at first did not fully comprehend what was taking place. Isolated Stangnesholmen, perfect for fishing, was hardly the place for maintaining an up-to-date understanding of foreign affairs. Because the cottage lacked electricity, the only source of information was Knudsen's battery-driven travel radio. Unfortunately, it did not work well that evening, being able to pick up only fragmentary news about the upcoming trial.[93] Not until the following morning did Per Monsen, the son of Minister of Defense Fredrik Monsen who worked as a journalist for Scheflo, arrive with a complete set of notes on the TASS statement.*[94]

In reaction to the grave nature of the denunciations, Trotsky immediately sought to refute the charges. Even before having seen the original text, he issued a statement, printed in *Sørlandet*, condemning the announcement as "one of the largest pieces of falsehood in all political history." There was not "a shadow of truth" in the charge that he was leading a terrorist conspiracy. On the contrary, he had been an "uncompromising opponent" of individual acts of terror ever since joining the revolutionary movement in 1897.[95]

He went on to proclaim that the only way to test the truth was to have a "competent governmental commission" investigate the indictment's documentation. He was prepared to provide a day-by-day, hour-by-hour account of his activity in Norway. An objective report from such a commission, he maintained, would utterly destroy the false charges.[96] In the next several days, as the show trial ran its course, he continued to call for an impartial examination. He now insisted, however, that an "independent Norwegian court" would be the best forum in which to test the accuracy of the Russian accusations. He similarly demanded that socialist leaders worldwide should send a commission to the Soviet Union to investigate the trial.[97]

Trotsky's attempt to involve an official Norwegian commission or court in an inquiry proved, however, to be a major error. His asylum thereby assumed an entirely different character. Since the break-in at Wexhall, the dispute had been an internal matter that involved NS illegality as much, if not more, than the issue of whether he had respected the obligations of his asylum. Now, however, he threatened to become the center of a controversy that could create difficulties for Norway's relations with a nearby major power. This was recognized immediately. A number of newspapers that earlier had expressed varying degrees of criticism about the NS burglary now changed their focus. While *Aftenposten, Tidens Tegn, Nationen*, and *ABC* all cast doubt on the truthfulness of the Kremlin's accusations,

---

* Per Monsen later married Scheflo's older daughter, Mosse.

this did not hinder them from vigorously insisting that Trotsky be expelled because his presence was detrimental to Norwegian interests.[98]

Within the nonsocialist press in Oslo, *Dagbladet* went furthest in rejecting the Russian charges. It declared that the entire legal process was reminiscent of what had occurred in Germany two years earlier, when Hitler killed Ernst Röhm, the head of the S.A., and his lieutenants. *Dagbladet* asserted that not only was it highly unlikely that Trotsky had been allied with Himmler and other Nazi leaders but that none of the court's charges against him could be believed.[99]

Among the nonsocialist parties (although he maintained that his party was no longer bourgeois), Quisling's anti-Semitic, anticommunist, and pro-German National Union ironically enough accepted most uncritically the show trial's accusations. In his stubborn effort to make Trotsky the major election issue, Quisling uncritically accepted almost all of the negative Soviet attacks, no matter how illogical. *Fritt Folk*, for example, published on its front page on August 14 a headline accusing Trotsky of inciting rebellion in the Soviet Union from Hønefoss, while another headline on the same page proclaimed that Trotsky and Stalin were cooperating together to create a soviet republic in Spain by taking advantage of the chaos resulting from the civil war.[100] During the show trial *Fritt Folk* continued enthusiastically to publish a great variety of crimes that Trotsky supposedly had been involved in. The one exception was a studious avoidance of any mention of his alleged cooperation with Himmler's Gestapo.[101]

National Union's inconsistency did not escape notice. *Dagbladet*, in a sarcastic commentary entitled "The Devil at Hønefoss," pointed out how *Fritt Folk* maintained that "Trotsky had already practically murdered Stalin and was the driving force in a conspiracy to break down the Soviet Union," while at the same time reporting that "Stalin and Trotsky in full understanding had arranged the outbreak of the Spanish Civil War." *Dagbladet* facetiously went on to hold Trotsky responsible for all existing ills in Norway, including the unusually heavy rainfall in Oslo in August.[102]

Not surprisingly, Norway's Communist Party equaled NS in accepting unquestioningly the indictment against Trotsky, but obviously for different reasons. However, the communists had some difficulty reconciling their renewed hostility toward him with their previous denunciation of the NS break-in. Furthermore, they had earlier largely ceased their objections to his asylum because of their need to maintain good relations with the Labor Party. But now, due to Moscow's accusations, they quickly reversed their position.

With the start of the show trial, they abandoned any tendency to treat Trotsky mildly. Not only did their press demand an end to his asylum but also that he should be sent to Moscow to stand alongside Zinoviev, Kamenev, and "the other terrorists" and share their fate.[103] It proved awkward, however, to explain why they now echoed National Union, even to the point of urging Trotsky's deportation.[104] The communists dealt with this by arguing that while the "fascists" were attacking Trotsky, this was really done in order to damage the Norwegian labor movement. The "reactionary bourgeoisie" and the "fascists" still "rage against Trotsky" because they had not forgotten or forgiven him for having stood together "for a short time" with Lenin, Stalin, and the Bolshevik Party. But now, argued the communists, the "fascists" failed to comprehend that when attacking Trotsky, in reality they were striking out against one of their closest allies. National Union and Trotsky belonged to the same camp. Both were the enemies of the labor movement and would therefore have to be neutralized.[105]

Political expediency similarly explained why the communists were somewhat less critical of the Labor Party's immediate negative reaction to the show trial's accusations. The party and its government were described by the communists as being ignorant when they assumed that Trotsky still maintained a positive attitude toward the Soviet Union, instead of being a criminal conspirator.[106]

The Labor Party's press, on the other hand, showed little inclination to spare communist feelings. *Arbeiderbladet*'s initial response was to quote Scheflo, who branded the charges as "sheer lies."[107] The first Moscow show trial marked yet another turning point for him. Despite his break with the Communist Party, he had maintained a positive attitude toward the Soviet Union because of its experiment in seeking to create the world's first classless society. This favorable viewpoint began to change following the Kirov murder. Thereafter he published editorials that criticized as well as praised the U.S.S.R. However, from the start of the show trial, with its grave accusations against Trotsky, Scheflo consistently condemned the Soviet Union as a repressive dictatorship.[108]

Tranmæl was initially more cautious editorially, but he made it clear that the Labor Party regarded the upcoming trial in Moscow as a reflection of factional divisions within the Soviet Communist Party, rather than a criminal matter.[109] But Konrad Knudsen's paper, *Fremtiden*, showed no inclination toward restraint. It stated pointedly that Stalin personally bore responsibility for providing Norwegian fascists with backing in their campaign against Trotsky.[110]

If anything, the Labor press at first defended Trotsky even more strongly as the start of the show trial drew near. Although Trotsky had carefully adhered to the terms of his residence permit, insisted *Arbeiderbladet*, a campaign of persecution had been started against him that was part of the strategy for the upcoming election led by "fascists," while the "half-fascists" followed after. They had earlier argued that Trotsky and Stalin were secretly cooperating to bring Norway under the Russian yoke. Now, however, after Soviet authorities accused Trotsky of terrorist activity, the "reactionary press" had reversed itself and completely accepted the Russian indictment.[111]

On the trial's first day, August 19, Tranmæl voiced even stronger condemnation of the Russian government. The charges, said Tranmæl, were clearly in violation of the judicial practices that a workers' state ought to follow. He then went on to attack the Norwegian communists for their blind acceptance of everything emanating from the Comintern.[112] In a brief but direct editorial the next day, *Arbeiderbladet* presented the strongest condemnation yet of the show trial. It concluded that in the name of humanity and above all in the name of the working class, protest must be made against the "crime that the Russian Communist Party's leadership is now in the process of carrying out."[113]

Such a powerful denunciation, echoed by other Labor Party papers, created a reaction. *Tidens Tegn* asked whether Labor was now serving Trotsky's cause. This put Tranmæl on the defensive. He insisted that *Arbeiderbladet*, whenever necessary, had always been in the forefront of defending the Soviet Union against hateful attacks in the "anti-worker, reactionary press." But while it was understandable that a dictatorship had developed in Russia because of its past history, Tranmæl repeated that Stalin's system had obvious weaknesses that should be avoided by all democratic nations.[114]

Trotsky immediately abandoned any thought of continuing his vacation when TASS publicized the upcoming show trial. He returned to Wexhall early in the week, most likely on Tuesday, August 18.[115] Fully engaged in challenging Stalin's lies, he worked tirelessly. When the trial opened, he told the *New York Times* that it "puts the Dreyfus scandal and the Reichstag fire trial in the shadow." The entire process was "fraudulent," with the defendants' confessions having been "forced by the GPU." But he declared his determination to prove the accusations false: "I will make the accusers the accused."[116]

He sent a letter on the same day to Chief of Investigations Sveen, while simultaneously releasing it to the press.[117] The missive was therefore both a public defense of his right of asylum and a rebuttal of Moscow's charges. He insisted that he was only required to refrain from involvement in Norwegian politics and to avoid "illegal, secret, or conspiratorial activity against countries that maintain a friendly relationship with Norway." This did not mean, he declared, that he was obligated to cease writing about economic, social, and political matters. He had never disguised his point of view, as shown by his contributions to the world press long before his arrival in Norway, as well as his writings in periodicals that now "have associated themselves with the Fourth International." He also maintained that his visitors included individuals who were simply curious to see him, others who wanted his opinions on what they regarded as important matters, as well as journalists, publishers, and so forth. To require him not to meet such people would mean that he did not enjoy "the democratic right of asylum," but rather imprisonment.[118]

As for the Soviet accusations, he stated that if they contained even "a kernel of truth," this would naturally show that he had violated his asylum. But he hoped to prove that if a crime had occurred, it was not one that he had committed but rather a crime against him by the GPU and those who had inspired the secret police to act against him.[119]

Trotsky undoubtedly received help from Konrad Knudsen, an experienced journalist, when formulating the communiqué. His open letter implied that two cabinet ministers supported his view that he was respecting his exile. Foreign Minister Halvdan Koht was quoted as saying that the government knew when Trotsky was admitted that he would continue to write about world affairs. Reference was also made to Trygve Lie's contention that Trotsky's political outlook differed from that of the Labor Party—which implied that Trotsky was not in any way involved in Labor's politics. Similarly, to legitimize his writings, he pointed out that not only had his autobiography, containing his revolutionary views, been published by the Labor Party's main publishing house, but that Tiden just the day before had contacted him to discuss issuing his Lenin biography.[120]

On the next day, August 20, the press was full of accounts of the Moscow trial, with emphasis, naturally enough, on the sensational denunciations made by the accused against Trotsky. Of the sixteen defendants, it later became known that no fewer than seven were acting on behalf of the secret police, the NKVD.[121] They provided lurid testimony concerning not only how Trotsky, together with Zinoviev and his supporters, supposedly had been behind the murder of Kirov but also how he had, with the connivance of the Gestapo, allegedly been responsible for sending would-be assassins into the U.S.S.R. to kill Stalin and other top leaders.[122]

Trotsky knew few of the shadowy figures who hurled such accusations against him. He stressed this on August 20 at a well-attended press conference that he held at Wexhall. Appearing fit and tanned from his vacation, he provided his listeners with a detailed discourse about his past, as well as the issue at hand. He insisted that until now he had only wished to live in peace, not wanting to call attention to himself. But, as a result of the trial, all his reservations had disappeared. At stake were the lives of many persons in Russia, as well as his own reputation as a politician. The charges against him were lies, based on "gross forgeries." And while such falsehoods might remain unchallenged in the Soviet Union, this was not the case in Norway. He concluded with a challenge: "Here we have the opportunity to raise criticism, and I, gentlemen, intend to criticize."[123]

The planted NKVD witnesses made the most concrete indictments against Trotsky—that they allegedly had been associated either with him, with his son Lev, or with both in plotting the murder of Stalin and his cohorts. In the days afterwards, Trotsky frantically sought information about his mysterious detractors. He received aid from Walter Held, who came to Wexhall for that purpose. Held sent out a circular letter, entitled "*Very important*," that called on all Trotskyites to help refute the charges, in particular to supply information about the unknown "accusers." What were their true names?[124] Writing to Czech followers on August 23, Trotsky revealed that five of the witnesses were unknown, while several others were minor political figures with whom he had had but limited contact.[125] He did refute forcefully, however, allegations that he had met with the would-be assassins, first in Copenhagen and later in Oslo. When he came to Copenhagen to hold his lecture in 1932, he stressed in a press statement on August 23, he had always been surrounded by bodyguards. None of his supposed coconspirators could therefore have visited him secretly. In Norway he had received no visits from Russians whatsoever.

Here he was making reference to one of the NKVD agents, K. B. Berman-Yurin, who testified that he had met Trotsky in Oslo. During the course of their discussions, Berman-Yurin maintained that he had received detailed instructions from Trotsky on how to kill Stalin. However, *Dagbladet* contacted the Oslo police department's foreign office (*fremmedkontor*), with which all visitors from abroad had to register. A careful examination of the records failed to show that Berman-Yurin had ever been in Oslo.[126] This would not be the last time that the NKVD's manufactured "evidence" failed to stand up to scrutiny.

As for his son's purported involvement in the alleged conspiracy, Trotsky pointed out that when he had held his lecture in Copenhagen, Lyova was tending to his studies in Berlin, and he continued his education at the Sorbonne after moving to Paris. To accuse a young student of being the center of a plot to murder top Soviet leaders, said Trotsky, was completely ridiculous. The only reason the secret police resorted to this fabrication was because it was easier for the GPU's "spies" to maintain that they had contact with a student in major cities such as Berlin or Paris, rather than with Trotsky, in remote Norway.[127]

He further declared in his August 23 statement that all the information that he had provided was only preliminary. He was currently reworking his evidence into a major brochure that would provide broad political and legal analysis. He also restated his desire to have all charges against him brought before "an independent Norwegian court."[128]

Trotsky predicted that Stalin wished to end the trial as quickly as possible, thereby preventing its errors and contradictions from becoming obvious.[129] His assertion proved true. The proceedings were already finished by Sunday, August 23, with the prosecution demanding the death penalty for **all** the unfortunate defendants, Old Bolsheviks and NKVD witnesses alike. The one exception remained, of course, the resident of Wexhall, safely outside the court's grasp.[130]

In reaction, *Arbeiderbladet* issued its strongest condemnation yet. No event since the October Revolution, Tranmæl avowed, had been more "disheartening" and damaging to the reputation of the Soviet Union than this "witch hunt." The accusations and the defendants' "confessions" had been "completely fantastic and unreasonable." To save their lives, they "in particular have been good at accusing the absent Trotsky of being the mastermind and the great seducer."[131]

Tranmæl stated that his criticism did not include progress that had been made in Soviet society but was solely directed against Stalin's brutal treatment of political opponents. The editor was very careful, moreover, to keep his distance from Trotsky, already possessing information that the government intended to silence the tempest surrounding its highly controversial exile. *Arbeiderbladet* therefore insisted that it did not share Trotsky's opinions, although Tranmæl added that "we recognize his accomplishments during the Russian Revolution and our responsibility to maintain the right of asylum."[132]

Tranmæl's worst fears were realized. No more than twenty-four hours elapsed from the issuance of the verdicts to the executions. The defendants, both Stalin's former adversaries and the planted secret-police witnesses, believed until almost the last minute that their sentences would be commuted, which they had been promised if they cooperated. They failed, like so many others, to understand the depth of Stalin's ruthlessness. Like a good Mafia boss who eliminates his hit men, he made certain that there would be no living witnesses to his perfidy. Trotsky understood this. When informed of the executions, he commented: "Now both those who have accused themselves and those who have operated as spies are brought to eternal silence."[133]

However, since he had been charged with plotting terrorism while in Denmark, France, and Norway, which was illegal, he argued that he had the right to have these allegations tried in court. *Dagbladet*, in response, commented rather acidly about his intent to use "a free and liberal country's courts," whose concept of law he detested and which he had never permitted Russians to benefit from when he was in power.[134] The paper might not have been so smug had it been clairvoyant enough to foresee that Trotsky in no way would be allowed to disprove Stalin's lies and distortions in Norway's "free and liberal courts."

Speaking for the Conservatives, *Aftenposten* was even more negative, as well as inconsistent. Whereas it earlier had reservations about the accuracy of the show trial's indictments, it now maintained that the victims deserved their fate. Since there was no possibility within the Soviet Union to express political disagreement, the paper argued, the sole alternative was to conspire against its government, including resort to political murder. As for Trotsky's insistence that "a Norwegian court should whitewash him," the paper stated that Norway's judicial system

should not become involved because such a spectacle would only enhance his status. It would "be simpler and less expensive simply to send
Mr. Trotsky out of the country."[135]

As the press debate revealed, vilification from Moscow could very well
adversely affect the status of Trotsky's asylum. He and his adherents were
aware of this. They immediately set in motion a campaign to counteract
the show trial's indictment. The International Secretariat in Paris sent out a
notice for all Trotskyites to do their utmost on his behalf.[136] As part of this
effort, Held and three other signatories mailed a form letter dated Oslo,
August 16, in which they appealed to their "comrades." It declared that
Trotsky's exile was threatened by the combined pressure of the "Soviet bureaucracy, the German Nazis, the Norwegian fascists, and the conservative
bourgeoisie." Recipients were asked to cable appeals defending Trotsky's
right of asylum to the Nygaardsvold government and the Labor Party.[137]

The struggle to influence opinion proved to be extremely unequal.
Upon returning to Wexhall, Trotsky only intermittently had Knudsen's assistance, as well as that of his "young friend," Walter Held.*[138] For the first
time in Norway, he lacked a secretary when he most needed help. Trotsky's
followers recognized his plight, however, and took steps to provide him
with two secretaries. Erwin Wolf, who had been in England, arrived first,
on about August 23.[139] Jean van Heijenoort came from Paris via Antwerp
two days later. They immediately began to assist with the myriad of press
inquiries concerning the Moscow trial.[140]

They did not have the satisfaction of aiding their chief for very long.
As van Heijenoort noted, by the time he reached Wexhall, the government "was taking a harsher and harsher attitude toward him [Trotsky]."[141]
Held similarly experienced this. While he helped Trotsky with his papers,
Held's companion, Synnøve, removed periodicals and other written material to Oslo, where they were stored in the basement of the building where
her parents lived. Unfortunately, some "fascists," as Held described them,

---

* Although Trotsky sometimes referred to his young secretaries with the same term, in
this instance he undoubtedly meant Held. The "young friend" discovered several letters
for Trotsky to use as early as August 20. This precluded Wolf, since he did not arrive at
Wexhall until August 23 at the earliest. Furthermore, as shown earlier, Held's presence at
Wexhall before August 23 is documented.

resided at the same site. They discovered the incriminating writings with references to Trotsky, whose name was widely recognized due to extensive press coverage. The "fascists" immediately called the police, who confiscated the material and ransacked the apartment of Synnøve's parents on August 24.[142] This incident illustrated how the police now regarded Trotsky and his associates as being inimical to Norwegian interests.

In the fall of 1936, the primary concern of the government was to win the upcoming election. It intended to eliminate its dependence on nonsocialist support, as the party's Oslo office succinctly made clear: "The Norwegian Labor Party this year is firmly determined to win a majority in the Norwegian Storting."[143]

Except for the communists, the remaining parties were equally resolved to block this ambition. Again with one exception, National Union, the major nonsocialist parties cooperated to keep the Labor Party short of an absolute majority in order to prevent the government from gaining a free hand to enact socialist legislation. But with the country experiencing improved economic conditions, the nonsocialists had difficulty finding issues to influence the voters. The controversy over whether Trotsky had violated his asylum therefore appeared to provide them with an effective weapon, in particular after it became clear that he also had the potential to harm relations with the U.S.S.R.

What had therefore been an issue largely identified with National Union became a controversy in which all of the nonsocialist parties joined in attacking the government. Rather than Quisling being identified as the foremost opponent of Trotsky's stay, it was the Liberal leader, Johan Ludwig Mowinckel, who, as the election campaign evolved, increasingly occupied the spotlight in condemning the government.[144] Dagbladet's sarcastic commentary of August 25 concerning Trotsky's wish to use the court system reflected the beginning of this change in Liberal strategy.[145]

The Conservative Aftenposten found itself in a position fairly similar to that of National Union, if not quite as extreme. Even if one chose to regard Trotsky in the mildest possible manner and not accept all the terrible accusations of his Soviet detractors, the paper maintained that by his own admission he had conducted incitement while in Norway, which provided grounds for expulsion.[146]

As the election drew nearer, Labor therefore became isolated as the only party that defended the government's decision to grant Trotsky a haven.

Indeed, *Arbeiderbladet* early theorized that the nonsocialists intended to make this the central issue in the campaign.[147] As noted, Labor newspapers, spearheaded by *Arbeiderbladet*, defended the right of asylum as a democratic principle that was under attack by those who favored dictatorship. But with the coming of the Moscow show trial, a curious dichotomy developed between Labor's newspapers and the government over what position to take toward Trotsky, as the question assumed greater and greater significance.

Government unease about Trotsky's asylum becoming a campaign issue extended back to June 1936, well before the show trial, when, as noted, the Justice Department inquired about his possible involvement in France's unrest. Although no direct link was found, after the NS burglary and the subsequent newspaper debate, the government's concern became more pronounced. While the criminal charges that NS levied against Trotsky were dismissed, Trygve Lie stipulated as early as August 11 that his department would investigate whether Trotsky had respected the terms of his asylum.[148] Lie would not have taken this step without approval from the prime minister. As Haakon Lie has noted, these two, Trygve Lie and Nygaardsvold, "both had a strong desire to be free from the problem child Lev Trotsky."[149]

Before the show trial, however, Lie had not ruled out exonerating Trotsky. When the chief of investigations returned from questioning Trotsky, *Arbeiderbladet*, in an article overwhelmingly positive toward Trotsky, simply reported that Sveen intended to forward his findings to the appropriate authorities, State Attorney Riisnæs and Attorney General Haakon Sund.[150]

Contrary to what Sveen stated, his report was sent to neither. With the TASS notice about the pending show trial, the government's position changed significantly. Trygve Lie announced instead on August 18 that the Central Passport Office and the Justice Department had assumed jurisdiction over the case, with the final decision to be made by the government. Rather portentously, he added that the investigation would be based on documents, articles, and other material that originally had been obtained as a result of charges brought by NS, plus the results of Sveen's inquiry.[151] Acting on Lie's instructions, Sveen sent this information to the Central Passport Office on the same day.[152]

Although facts in its own pages revealed the government to be positioning itself to crack down on Trotsky, *Arbeiderbladet* continued to provide him space to refute Soviet allegations. The paper also downplayed the inquiry by the Central Passport Office. On August 19 the paper stressed instead that the ongoing case against the five "Nazi gangsters" captured following the break-in might include additional indictments. *Arbeiderbladet* made only brief reference to the fact that the Central Passport Office was now in charge of examining the "question about Trotsky's residence permit and the conditions attached to it."[153] *Tidens Tegn* was far more prophetic the next day. It believed that the government was considering tightening the terms of Trotsky's residence permit and that he would be required to sign a new statement to this effect.[154]

On August 24, in a terse front page notice, *Arbeiderbladet* made known that the long-awaited report, with its recommendation, would be forwarded by the Central Passport Office to the Justice Department "in a couple of days."[155] This appeared on the same page on which Trotsky had the opportunity to denounce the death sentences issued in Moscow and the suicide of Mikhail Tomski, one of the few major victims of Stalin who escaped being purged by taking his own life.

The head of the Central Passport Office, Leif Ragnvald Konstad, was a controversial figure because of his right-wing sympathies. Trygve Lie knew full well that any ruling by Konstad would receive widespread criticism from, among others, members of his own party. This most likely explains why Johannes Halvorsen, the acting director of the Passport Office, instead received the assignment to draw up the report. There was little chance, however, for him to reach a conclusion that Lie might object to, considering Halvorsen's subordinate position as secretary in the Justice Department.[156]

Halvorsen exceeded *Arbeiderbladet*'s expectations by submitting his report by August 25. It is immediately striking, when examining its rationale, that he based his findings in large part on documentation provided previously by National Union. This was the very "evidence" that the government's major press organ had earlier characterized as being "worthless papers."[157] These included the few items that the NS "gangsters" had managed to grab during the burglary. In addition, Halvorsen relied on reports and testimony from Didrik Rye Heyerdahl, the leader of this foray, plus Hjort's testimony. Also included was Trotsky's article, "The French Revolution Has Begun," from which *Fritt Folk* had published excerpts. Trotsky, however, had never denied authorship of the article, having forwarded an English language version to Sveen on August 19. Finally, Halvorsen made use of Sveen's report of his interview with Trotsky, plus Trotsky's open letter to Sveen of August 19.

The conclusion was foregone: Trotsky had violated his entry permit. Specifically, Halvorsen declared that Trotsky's writings had not merely been theoretical and analytical but had advocated specific actions, such as the establishment of soviets in France. Halvorsen also maintained that Trotsky was guilty of advising his followers in various countries about concrete political issues.[158]

Considering the weak if not questionable documentation that he used, Halvorsen's case was not impressive. But while the terms under which Trotsky had been admitted were open to differing interpretations, a rigid literal reading of the text of his asylum permit inevitably led to the same conclusion. Even though he did his best to downplay this, Trotsky had provided his adherents with advice about what actions to take, including negative conduct against governments with which Norway maintained friendly relations. Furthermore, he was a professional revolutionary, which he did not disguise. When he was first admitted, the government, in view of the then-current political situation, had adopted a liberal attitude toward him because it believed that his activity was largely ineffective or harmless. But by the fall of 1936, the government faced conditions that were very different. Internally it was in an election campaign in which he had become a major issue, while in its conduct of foreign policy, it had to deal with a Soviet regime whose judiciary accused Trotsky of masterminding horrendous crimes. Moreover, international relations between the great powers were becoming more tense. The Spanish Civil War had just broken out, a war in which the communists would increasingly become more dominant politically on the Republican side. In France the socialist premier, Leon Blum, headed a Popular Front government with communist backing. In the League of Nations and elsewhere the Soviet Union presented itself as a bulwark against the threat from a Nazi Germany that was rapidly rearming. Trotsky had expressed strong anti-Stalinist views on all these questions, but he was in particular adamant in defending himself against the crude, baseless accusations from Moscow. This made him the focus of world attention, as well as a center of controversy within Norway. Based on self-interest, the Nygaardsvold government refused to allow this state of affairs to continue.

Its decision to take forceful measures had clearly been made in anticipation of the Central Passport Office's conclusion. As evidence, a carefully orchestrated series of steps unfolded. On the same day that Halvorsen forwarded his finding, Trygve Lie reacted by immediately ordering the Passport Office to make the terms of Trotsky's residence far more restrictive.

Consequently, Halvorsen traveled to Wexhall the next morning, August 26, accompanied by Carl Bernhard Askvig, the head of the State Police (*Statspolitiet*), Norway's national police. Halvorsen presented Trotsky with a copy, in German translation,* of the Justice Department's order, plus a more detailed declaration of the new restrictions on his residence permit.[159] The provisions were quite draconian. The declaration required Trotsky to swear that neither he, his wife, nor his secretaries would engage in "political agitation or activity" against any state that had friendly relations with Norway. Indicating that he might soon be forced to move, the declaration further stated that he would take up residence at a location determined by the government. Going into more detail, the document stated that Trotsky was to agree on behalf of himself, Natalia, and his secretaries that they would not—directly or indirectly, in written form or orally—involve themselves in current events taking place abroad. He would be required to restrict his writings to historical subjects or to theoretical reflections that were not "directed toward any country." He further had to accept that all outgoing correspondence and telegrams—his own, Natalia's, and the secretaries'—"be controlled by the authorities." Finally, he had to cease granting interviews to journalists.[160]

Essentially, these new requirements meant that Trotsky would become a ward of the state. Trygve Lie, however, sought to lessen the impression that the government wished to make him a quasi-prisoner. The Justice Department's press release, issued on the same day, therefore, did not mention that Trotsky's correspondence would be censored or that journalists would be prohibited from interviewing him.[161]

Halvorsen demanded that Trotsky sign on the spot. The latter must initially have assumed that he was dealing with Konstad, since Trotsky, writing to Scheflo the next day, described the official who confronted him as being "completely reactionary, coarse, and unfair."[162] Trotsky's anger was fueled by the transparent purpose of the declaration. Not only would it restrict him from writing critical commentaries about foreign events, most noteworthy in the Soviet Union, as well as limit his ability to stay in touch with the emerging Fourth International, but from his immediate perspective, more importantly, it would prohibit him from counteracting Moscow's untruthful, terrible accusations.

For a man of his character, fearless and defiant in the face of adversity, the thought of signing this document was abominable. His reaction

---

* German was Trotsky's foreign language of choice.

did not catch officials by surprise. Eight constables from the State Police had accompanied Halvorsen and Askvig to Wexhall. While their chief returned to Oslo with Halvorsen following Trotsky's refusal, the constables remained. Lev and Natalia, as well as Wolf and van Heijenoort, were henceforth under police guard. Two constables were assigned to patrol Wexhall, while the remaining six, when not on duty, were lodged in the neighboring old-people's home.[163]

On the same day that Trotsky was placed under house arrest, *Arbeiderbladet* ceased refuting accusations that he had violated his residence permit. Tranmæl now agreed with the Central Passport Office's conclusion. This especially was true, said Tranmæl, due to Trotsky's involvement in political disturbances in France.[164] Thereupon the dichotomy between the government and its main press outlet was over. *Arbeiderbladet* from now on loyally adhered to the government position. Among Labor Party editors, only Scheflo responded with criticism. Very much up to date about what was happening in Oslo and at Wexhall, he voiced his disagreement in frustration. Without mentioning the government directly, he insisted that Trotsky had not written anything illegal about the disturbances in France. He had authored comparable articles earlier, which similarly had contained "open criticism." By being compelled to write only historical and theoretical works, said Scheflo, Trotsky was placed in a unique position, bound by rules that did not apply to any other refugee who enjoyed asylum. But Trotsky, Scheflo concluded sarcastically, had now been placed under the protection of "the fascist Askvig," and Norwegians could "therefore feel safe from this dangerous man."[165]

When he and Natalia retired to bed that evening, Lev could hear the crunch of gravel under the boots of patrolling guards. He was of course used to being watched over, at times by his own protectors, as well as by agents of hostile regimes. But on this occasion the apparent sudden change in the government's position took him by surprise. He did not yet fully understand how seriously his situation had deteriorated. Those who enjoy the advantage of viewing historical events with hindsight, however, recognize the full significance of what had occurred. His French biographer has entitled the final period of Trotsky's stay in Norway as "The Descent into Hell."[166] By the evening of August 26, however, he had only entered the First Circle.

Arrival: Natalia Sedova Trotsky (at left), Lev Trotsky, and Jean van Heijenoort disembark in Oslo, June 18, 1936 (the woman in front of Trotsky is unknown). Scanpix, Oslo.

Trotsky and Martin Tranmæl at Ringkollen in 1936. This was before *Arbeiderbladet's* editor had begun to criticize Trotsky's alleged violation of his asylum. Courtesy of the Labor Movement's Archive and Library, Oslo.

Håkon Meyer in the
1920s. Courtesy of
the Labor Move-
ment's Archive and
Library, Oslo.

Olav Scheflo at the
time he became
editor of *Sørlandet*.
Courtesy of the Labor
Movement's Archive
and Library, Oslo.

Erwin Wolf, who was Trotsky's longest-serving secretary in Norway, together with Lev at the pretrial inquiry (*forhørsretten*), Møllergaten 19, August 26, 1936, the day on which Trotsky was interned and Wolf arrested. Scanpix, Oslo.

Picnic with friends on Stangnesholmen: includes clockwise, Olav Scheflo (with his back turned), Konrad Knudsen, Lev and Natalia Trotsky, Hilda Knudsen, Mosse Scheflo (leaning forward), and Thinka Zahl (shading her eyes). Courtesy of Dagmar Loe, Oslo.

The Nygaardsvold government, from positive host to hostile enemy. Front row from left, Defense Minister Fredrik Monsen, Foreign Minister Halvdan Koht, Prime Minister Johan Nygaardsvold, Finance Minister Adolf Indrebø, and Agriculture Minister Hans Ystgaard. Back row, Social Minister Kornelius Bergsvik, Trade Minister Alfred Madsen, Church and Education Minister Nils Hjelmtveit, and Justice Minister Trygve Lie. Courtesy of the Labor Movement's Archive and Library, Oslo.

State Police guards at Sundby, together with Aagot Sæthre (at left) and Karoline Robert. The foreman of the guard (*vaktsjef*) is in civilian attire. Courtesy of Harald Halvorsen d.y., Oslo.

Adios: Lev and Natalia Sedova Trotsky disembark from the Norwegian oil tanker *Ruth* in Tampico, accompanied by Frida Kahlo. Scanpix, Oslo.

They experienced a tragic fate. Walter Held (Heinz Epe) and his companion, Synnøve Rosendahl-Jensen. Courtesy of the Labor Movement's Archive and Library, Oslo.

6 The End of Asylum

> To refrain from bringing me to trial . . . and at the same time to rob
> me of the opportunity to appeal to public opinion on a question that
> concerns myself, my son, my whole political past, and my honor,
> would mean to transform the right of asylum into a trap and to allow
> free passage to the executioners and slanderers of the GPU.
> —Lev Trotsky to Trygve Lie, August 26, 1936

Although Trotsky's status had changed significantly when he was
placed under house arrest, the extent of the transformation did not immediately become apparent. To a considerable degree life at Wexhall
went on as before. *Tidens Tegn*, hoping to capitalize on the controversy,
sent both a reporter and a photographer to Wexhall on August 27.[1] They
discovered that Heradsbygda was as quiet and sleepy as ever, with the
residents enjoying the warmth of a late-August day. Hjørdis and Borgar
Knudsen were sunning themselves on the porch at Wexhall. Hjørdis, a
personality in her own right thanks to extensive news coverage of her
resolute defense against the NS "gangsters," had no objection to being
photographed. She and Borgar were joined by Gunvor Wraaman, whose
two small daughters and their playmates were using the swing in the
courtyard. A single constable from the State Police, in civilian attire,
oversaw this tranquil scene.

The guard had no objection to talking with the inquisitive journalist. Nor
did he prevent Erwin Wolf, described later in print as "a small person with
a Semitic appearance," from speaking with the newsman. Erwin refused his
request for an interview with Trotsky. The photographer, however, would
not be denied. He snuck up to the window behind which Trotsky was
working and managed to click off a shot. But the curtain was drawn, and

Wolf reappeared to chase away the photographer. Trotsky was nowhere to be seen while this was happening.[2]

Assisted by his secretaries, the latter was conducting a two-front operation, against his Soviet adversaries and the Norwegian authorities who restricted his freedom. He clearly considered the threat from Moscow more important. In a letter to Scheflo, he concentrated almost entirely on refuting the "evidence" introduced in the show trial.[3] And even in his brief analysis of his Norwegian difficulties, he was off the mark. He concluded that the government's action was due to pressure from the "fascists and Stalinists," which had forced the minister of justice to give in to demands from the Central Passport Office.[4]

While internal opposition and foreign policy concerns did influence the government, Trotsky was completely incorrect when he assumed that Lie had yielded to pressure from Konstad. On the contrary, the Central Passport Office was acting on the orders of the justice minister. Trotsky, moreover, wrongly imagined that the restrictions he had rejected were still open to negotiation. Immediately after refusing to sign the declaration submitted by Johannes Halvorsen, Trotsky wrote to Lie on August 26, insisting that he had always sought to comply with the conditions governing his stay in Norway, "at least as I understand them." He did indicate that he was prepared to accept a clarification of his residence terms if he received assurance that "this new interpretation could be reconciled with my dignity as a human being and as a writer." But he objected to having Konstad, "in a democratic country," determine whether his writings were "only scientific or also politically topical."[5]

Comparing himself to Karl Marx when he wrote *Das Kapital* in Great Britain, Trotsky argued that his article, "The French Revolution Has Begun," was equally "scientific in character" when it maintained that the "struggle in France" could only have as its outcome "a victory for military reaction or the building of soviets." As for the demand that he cease meeting journalists, Trotsky ironically reminded Lie that until the last few days, he had only given a single interview in Norway, to *Arbeiderbladet*, "and this, sir, in your presence, and even with you kindly taking part."[6] But now, Trotsky asserted, the situation had changed, with his being unjustly accused of organizing "terrorist acts." If Norwegian officials believed it likely that the charges were true, then he expected to be arrested immediately and brought to trial. He desired nothing more than to disprove "this monstrous crime of the GPU and the powers behind it." But if the government found it impossible to intervene, then it at least should have "the elementary duty" to allow him "to tell the truth to the whole world." To prevent him from bringing his case before a court, while being denied "the opportunity to appeal to public opinion on a question that concerns myself, my son, my whole political past, and my political honor, would be to transform the right of asylum into a trap and to allow free passage to the executioners and slanderers of the GPU." It was therefore impossible for him to sign the declaration that the head of the Central Passport Office had presented.[7]

Trotsky enclosed a copy of this message in his letter to Scheflo. Trotsky confided that he might later make his communication to Lie public but for the time being it should be considered confidential.[8] Clearly, he felt that this was not the time to risk a breach with the minister of justice. He had, it seemed, reason for being cautious. Lie phoned Wexhall once he learned that Trotsky would not accept the more severe restrictions. When informed of Trotsky's letter explaining his refusal, Lie agreed to have Wolf come to Oslo to deliver it personally. Upon reading it, Lie immediately requested that it not be made public, holding out the possibility that the Justice Department would later issue a statement favorable to Trotsky's position.[9]

Trotsky and his secretaries were therefore shocked when newspapers later the same day, August 26, published the Central Passport Office's conclusion, with no indication that the government intended to revise this finding. Although highly irritated, Trotsky nevertheless remained careful. In response to inquiries from foreign journalists, van Heijenoort simply stated that Trotsky, in agreement with Norwegian authorities, would make no comment until the matter had been settled.[10]

For the Norwegian press, however, Trotsky did issue a brief statement, insisting that the Passport Office's report was untrue. He contended that political conditions might have changed, causing government officials now to accuse him of violating provisions that had only become relevant the previous day, which was unfair. He emphatically denied that he had violated the stipulations he had accepted when he came to Norway.[11]

The battle was thereupon joined. It revolved around whether or not Trotsky's activity contravened the terms under which he had entered the country. These were open to a wide range of interpretation. While he insisted that he had in no way deviated from the original agreement, only his supporters agreed.

He at this time had to face the full force of the Labor Party's opposition. Although Tranmæl printed Trotsky's statement to the press on August 27,

Arbeiderbladet appended its own commentary wherein it made plain that his "special pleading" was not worthy of consideration. The Central Passport Office, said *Arbeiderbladet*, had ascertained that he had contravened his asylum terms, which was easily proven simply by comparing what they said with the activity he had engaged in. Furthermore, he had been aware of these requirements from the time he entered Norway.[12]

Arbeiderbladet also contained a long statement from the minister of justice. Although headlined as his response to Trotsky's "special pleading," the piece interestingly enough was mainly a reaction to the **letter** that Trotsky had sent Lie the previous day, which had not yet been published. Readers must therefore have been somewhat puzzled because Lie focused overwhelmingly on explaining why he had visited Trotsky on July 19, 1935, a meeting that Trotsky had not even alluded to publicly.

Lie stressed that he had gone to Wexhall to make certain no misunderstanding should arise concerning Trotsky's asylum. According to Lie, Trotsky and his wife had agreed to refrain from carrying out political activity in Norway or from conducting political agitation or undertakings against any state with which Norway maintained cordial relations. And while he had been allowed to write historical and biographical works, as well as articles for the foreign press about social, economic, and political matters, these could not contain pointed attacks against the government of a country with which Norway had good ties. Lie declared that he had left feeling confident that Trotsky fully understood this and that there would not occur any differences concerning "the terms of his residence permit in Norway."

Lie concluded by insisting that the Justice Department's revised stipulations for Trotsky's continued stay were not really new except for two provisions.[13] He conveniently failed to mention that these (1) required censorship of Trotsky's correspondence and (2) prevented him from granting press interviews.[14] Lie similarly refrained from letting readers know that the major result of the visit to Wexhall the previous summer had been *Arbeiderbladet*'s interview with Trotsky in which **nothing** was said about Trotsky's asylum terms. The piece similarly had not even mentioned that Lie, Tranmæl, and Ole Colbjørnsen were present. And while the tone of Colbjørnsen's interview had been cautious, it did contain Trotsky's criticism of the Soviet government.[15]

In support of Lie, Colbjørnsen also provided a statement in *Arbeiderbladet*. He maintained that his sole reason for accompanying Lie had been to serve as interpreter, thanks to his knowledge of Russian. Colbjørnsen similarly made no reference to his interview, nor did he refer to Tranmæl. Uncritical readers again were told that the sole purpose for the visit had been to make certain that Trotsky fully understood the limitations of his terms of asylum.[16]

Lie therefore had good reason to obfuscate the interview, and he did everything in his power to suppress Trotsky's letter. Not only did it fail to appear in print during the critical days leading up to Trotsky's internment, but Lie sought to confiscate all copies. However, he did not succeed. Wolf managed to get one back when, during an unguarded moment, he snatched it up from a desk at police headquarters in Hønefoss.[17] Thanks to his quick action, the letter later was published abroad, in the *Nation*, on October 10, 1936.[18] But contrary to what Wolf believed, this was not the only duplicate that survived. *Dagbladet* had previously made the letter public on September 9. This allowed *Fremtiden* to quote it extensively without comment.[19] Although *Dagbladet* never revealed its source, it most likely was Scheflo.

Trotsky's main argument—that he was being treated unfairly—was objectively correct. Even a Dutch newspaper commented shortly afterwards, in early September, that "competent" persons in Oslo had undoubtedly been aware of Trotsky's involvement in other countries' politics and yet had chosen to ignore his actions until just a few weeks earlier.[20] But now, after Trotsky had become a major issue in the election and threatened to create complications with the Soviet Union, the government had adopted a narrow literal interpretation of his asylum terms and accused him of having violated them.

Despite having been placed under police guard, Trotsky had not yet been fully blocked from getting his views to the public. In addition to his press statement of August 27, he was able to provide an interview to a cable news service, Myres Pressebyrå, by telephone. No longer attempting in any way to be diplomatic, he blasted Stalin as the leader of a new ruling class, while the mass of the Russian people lived in "the greatest misery." He further interpreted the execution of Zinoviev and Kamenev to mean that from now on everyone who opposed Stalin and was labeled a Trotskyite would receive the death sentence. Trotsky again predicted, accurately, that the just-completed trial was but the first of its kind. The bureaucracy was now free to do what it wished. The result would be growing conflict with the people, leading to terrible future developments.[21]

The interview was published in a regional newspaper, *Tønsbergs Blad* (Tønsberg's Paper) on September 1. As a supporter of the Conservatives and a rival of *Fremtiden*, the paper succeeded in embarrassing the government. The Justice Department immediately investigated how Myres Pressebyrå had been able to contact Trotsky. It concluded that while the State Police patrolled Wexhall, accompanied Trotsky on walks, and had orders not to allow the press into the house, prior to August 28 his mail and his telephone conversations had not been censored.[22] The interview therefore undoubtedly took place on August 27. Even before it appeared in print, however, officials began to make certain that he would never again be able to state his views publicly in Norway.

The means that the authorities chose to use was the ongoing preliminary hearing of the NS members who had broken in at Wexhall. The court resumed its questioning on August 20, after having been in recess for a week.[23] On August 26, as *Arbeiderbladet* headlined "Trotsky's Articles on Current Political Questions Are in Violation of [His] Residence Permit," the probe reached a high point when the two Knudsen siblings, Hjørdis and Borgar, told the court about the suspense-filled evening when the intruders had burst through the door of their home.[24] Their father followed them to the witness stand on the next day. But whereas his children had been examined in detail about what occurred on the night of August 5, Konrad Knudsen experienced a rather different line of questioning, with the judge focusing his queries more on Trotsky than the defendants. When Knudsen asked if the inquiry was not to deal with the break-in and the theft of items, Judge Darring replied that while this was true, there were "so many [additional] elements that could be of significance" and the court therefore needed to obtain "the most complete picture of the entire event." He proceeded to ask about Trotsky's stay at Wexhall, including who his visitors had been. Darring's line of questioning was augmented by the NS defense attorney, Albert Wiesener, who obviously wished to implicate the Labor Party with having ties to Trotsky. Although he failed to discover any contact between Trotsky and the government except for Trygve Lie's sole visit, the defense attorney was successful in soliciting information from another witness, Mrs. Hilda Knudsen, that Tranmæl had also been at the now-famous meeting—a revelation that *Arbeiderbladet* tried to bury as inconspicuously as possible.[25]

The Oslo newspapers had for days been anticipating the testimony of the most famous witness, Lev Trotsky himself. He arrived under heavy police escort on the morning of August 28. He was driven into the back-yard of police headquarters at Møllergaten 19* in downtown Oslo, from which he went up to the second floor, where preliminary hearing court rooms were located. His secretary, Wolf, who also expected to testify, accompanied him.[26] The government displayed great concern for security, with guards posted at all entrances. Anyone who wished to enter had to have proper credentials, and the courtroom not only had two uniformed policemen on duty but also several members of the Investigative Police Unit in civilian attire.[27] A large contingent of press photographers was on hand, to whom Trotsky reacted with well-accustomed ease. Photos of him and Wolf in court graced the front pages of the major Oslo papers that same day. Trotsky appeared vital, with a fresh summer complexion, and his distinctive goatee had once more assumed its well-known contours. *Aftenposten* went so far as to declare that only his grizzled hair gave him a different appearance from when he was "at the height of [his] power in Russia during and after the revolution."[28]

The proceedings began promptly at 9:30 a.m., with Trotsky in the witness chair. He appeared relaxed, leaning back while answering Judge Darring's questions. Identifying himself as "Lev Sedov, called Trotsky," the fifty-six-year-old declared himself to be a stateless person, a writer by profession, who resided at Wexhall, Hønefoss.[29] In the next three-quarters of an hour he recounted his experience during the trip to southern Norway, pursued by four NS members headed by Neumann, as well as what he could tell about the break-in. He stated that he had lost only a limited amount of material, including part of a letter, plus possibly a manuscript in English. He added that some additional miscellaneous papers might have been stolen that he was unaware of.[30]

Judge Darring thereupon began the most critical part of his examination, described as "several more general questions." From these it was clear that the judge, as he had done with Knudsen previously, pursued a line of inquiry that served the interests of the government, in particular the Justice Department. It concerned "first and foremost Trotsky's arrival [in Norway] and [his] residence requirements." Trotsky confirmed that the

---

* Møllergaten 19 was a large building complex that included not only police headquarters but also courtrooms and a prison. It gained even greater notoriety during World War II when the Germans used it to incarcerate Norwegians suspected of engaging in resistance activity.

conditions of his residence permit were identical to those made public by the Central Passport Office. However, he insisted that his understanding of the terms was correct. He therefore did not hesitate to answer in the affirmative when asked if he had corresponded with members of groups, factions, or party organizations that accepted his ideas. He further stated that he had responded to inquiries about current political issues, advising his followers how they should react to specific political developments. He did add the caveat that in most instances, nine out of ten, his reply had come after the question had been settled. Darring, however, was not interested in the qualification and demanded that Trotsky give a clear answer, yes or no, as to whether or not he had provided political advice. After thinking this over carefully, during which time the judge repeated his query, Trotsky reconfirmed that he did counsel his followers.[31]

He similarly did not appear reluctant to furnish information about his correspondence with contacts abroad. The initials C. K., he explained, stood for the Central Committee, while "section" referred to a national group working for the creation of the Fourth International. He also identified the initials I.S. as standing for the Trotskyite International Secretariat in Paris, although he understandably did not reveal that "Durand" was the code name for his son, Lev, who headed the secretariat. Trotsky stated that "Durand" was merely an ordinary French name, one that he did not recognize as belonging to any of his acquaintances.[32]

He did not try to disguise the authority he held among his supporters. When Raymond Molinier's trip to Wexhall was brought up, Trotsky revealed that he had refused to give the visitor his "moral support," which meant that Molinier's expulsion from the French section was irreversible.[33]

As he had done before, Trotsky also verified that he had written articles for Trotskyite publications, but he took issue with the judge's assertion that his writings contained attacks against states with which Norway had good relations. He maintained that while he might have criticized political parties that had power in certain countries, such as that of "Herr Hitler," he had not disparaged a people as a whole. He further declared that none of his commentaries had ever been prosecuted, nor had they violated press laws. "My writings have been issued also by bourgeois, even conservative, publishers, despite their revolutionary tendency."[34]

By this time Trotsky had been testifying for some two and a half hours, and he was visibly becoming tired. He therefore welcomed the judge's decision to break for lunch before defense attorney Wiesener and police attorney (*politifullmektig*) Berg would be permitted to examine the witness.[35]

After the recess Trotsky had far less difficulty dealing with these two questioners. He parried quite nicely Berg's attempts to get him to identify the names on envelopes stolen by the NS "gangsters" and now presented as evidence by the Justice Department. Wiesener on the other hand continued to try to link him to the Labor Party. In response, Trotsky did note that Trygve Lie had explained the terms of his asylum to him shortly after he had entered Norway[36] and also mentioned that Lie had been accompanied to Wexhall by both Tranmæl and Colbjørnsen,[37] which most newspapers now chose not to pass on to their readers.

The judge, however, conveniently cut Wiesener off when he continued his effort to ascertain "the extent to which Trotsky had contact with the Norwegian Labor Party." The latter, however, dealt with the same question indirectly at the end of his testimony when he stated categorically that "his political outlook" differed greatly from "that of the . . . Labor Party." He similarly did not satisfy Wiesener when he curtly replied that the Norwegian edition of his autobiography, *My Life*, in no way had violated his asylum. The defense attorney, however, did present a more challenging set of questions when he asked Trotsky to explain his relationship with *Bulletin Oppozitsii* (Bulletin of the Opposition), published in Russian by his followers in Paris. Trotsky responded that he had nothing to do with editing the *Bulletin*, but he had been a major contributor for the last eight years, showing that his association with the periodical had preceded his arrival in Norway by quite some time. Wiesener went on to raise the even more significant issue of whether the *Bulletin* was smuggled into Russia. Trotsky evasively declared that he did not know and that in any event he certainly did not do so. The attorney next asked if the publication contained material that agitated against the Russian government, to which Trotsky truthfully replied that the *Bulletin* provided "criticism, often strong criticism." But when Wiesener wanted to know whether the publication's staff was "now conspiring against Stalin's government in Russia," the judge again intervened, declaring that this line of inquiry was a waste of the court's time.[38]

Trotsky easily dealt with Wiesener's remaining points. He emphasized that he had never concerned himself with Norwegian politics, not even in private conversations. He furthermore maintained that he had no Norwegian followers. When Wiesener inquired if Trotsky would object to a police search of his residence, the latter simply stated that he would not reply since this question was "irreconcilable with my personal honor." In response to whether he wanted the indicted NS members to be punished, he again took the high road, declaring that this was a matter "for the Norwegian state" to decide. Wiesener also asked whether there was any reason for why Trotsky had chosen to come to Norway, to which the latter answered, not quite accurately, that he could have remained in France, but that he had decided to move to "peaceful Norway" because of "the growing fascist danger" in France. There were, he added more truthfully, no other alternatives.[39]

With defense questioning concluded, Trotsky's long stay on the witness stand finally was over, in the late afternoon. He felt that he had acquitted himself well, having presented a reasonable explanation for why he in no way had violated his asylum. What he failed to recognize, however, was that he had supplied the government with new ammunition to restrict his freedom. Previously, criticism that he had allegedly disregarded his obligations had focused on statements and writings that were hostile to Stalin's regime or that favored revolutionary action. During the preliminary hearing, however, Trotsky also admitted involvement with his emerging Fourth International movement. He did so on the assumption that the government already knew about his contact with foreign supporters. Furthermore, since Norwegian authorities had not objected to this previously, he believed his activity was permissible as long as he maintained a low profile. However, because of the changed political situation that both he and the government now faced, his testimony was extremely damaging, as court observers immediately recognized. On the very day he appeared as a witness Dagbladet and Aftenposten came out with almost identical headlines, respectively proclaiming, "Trotsky admits to involvement in contemporary politics" and "Trotsky admits he has carried out political activity."[40]

On August 28 the afternoon editions of the Oslo newspapers carried yet another disclosure—that Trotsky could expect immediate dire consequences. Directly below the papers' coverage of the court proceedings appeared a brief press notice, issued by Trygve Lie's office to the Norwegian Telegram Bureau (NTB), that Trotsky would be "requested" to attend a conference in the Justice Department once he had completed his "explanation" in court. The announcement further stated that not

only Lie and Justice Department officials would be present but also Leif Konstad of the Central Passport Office and State Police Chief Bernhard Askvig.[41] Several of the papers speculated, correctly, that the purpose of the meeting was to force Trotsky to sign the government's more severe residence restrictions.[42]

Although not mentioned in the news release or subsequent official reports, Konrad Knudsen also attended the gathering, to which Trotsky was escorted by guards as soon as he and Wolf left the courtroom.[43] The presence of Trotsky's host was obviously intended to convince him that he had no choice but to sign the new restrictive requirements. Olav Scheflo had earlier, prior to Trotsky's trip to Oslo, made a similar effort to persuade him that this was his only alternative.[44] The declaration that Lie now asked Trotsky to approve contained, with some modifications, the same terms as the one he had refused to sign on August 26. But the restrictions were even more limiting. Not only would all his outgoing mail be censored but incoming correspondence as well. Use of the telephone by Trotsky, Natalia, and the secretaries was also added to the means of communications that were to be under the control of the authorities. And while the more severe limitations of August 28 did not specifically outlaw interviews, any press contact, along with written articles, could not be directed "against the government of any foreign state," not merely, as earlier, nations that had friendly relations with Norway. In essence, Trotsky's ability to express himself about current events would be blocked, with his writing limited strictly to "historical works, biographies, and memoirs."[45]

Lev understandably became highly agitated by these demands and expressed himself angrily in no uncertain terms. As *Dagbladet* unsympathetically stated: "He is said to be filled by an intense rage toward the government's actions, which in one day [sic!] has changed him from an honored and deeply grateful guest into a prisoner snorting with anger."[46] His wrath was heightened by Lie's duplicity, in not refuting in any way the Central Passport Office's report. Not unexpectedly, Lev began to "polemicize," as Lie put it, against the government for having attacked him when he was most vulnerable. Although Lie maintained that he promised Trotsky that the restrictions would not prevent him from defending himself against Soviet accusations, the latter realistically placed no faith in such assurances since the document said exactly the opposite. Trotsky therefore remained determined not to sign the statement, in particular since the government had already made him a prisoner.[47] Expressing his deep distrust of the justice minister, he specifically declared that he preferred arrest to being subjected to Lie's "equivocation—or a trap."[48]

This did not come as a surprise. For Trotsky to accept limits on his political activism was as unthinkable now as it had been when Stalin first deported him. As Trotsky then wrote: "To demand that I renounce all political activity is to demand that I abandon the struggle for the cause of the international proletariat, a struggle I have supported ceaselessly . . . from the very beginning of my conscious life."[49] His break with the Norwegian government was therefore total. Once this was clear, Lie icily asked when Trotsky could leave Norway. He replied that the minister of justice, by accusing him of violating his residence permit, had made it impossible to obtain a visa to any other country.[50]

While expressing sympathy for the difficulties that Trotsky faced, Lie later pointed out that the government also had been confronted with a thorny situation. Based on information that resulted from the NS break-in and, most significantly, Trotsky's court statements during the preliminary hearing, the government's attitude was clear. As Lie put it: "We had admitted him because he was sick and persecuted—not in order to give him opportunity to continue his feverish conspiracy with followers throughout the entire world."[51] Furthermore, Trotsky stubbornly refused to halt his political activity, insisting that he was not required to do so under the terms by which he originally had been allowed to enter Norway. Prime Minister Nygaardsvold consequently expressed his frustration with Trotsky on August 28, when he was quoted as having said in a cabinet meeting: "If he does not sign, we will send him to Siberia."[52]

After half an hour of fruitless discussion, it became obvious that Trotsky would indeed be treated more severely. He was ushered out from Lie's office under strict guard, being physically separated from Wolf, waiting in the anteroom, who up to then had been allowed to accompany him. Moreover, Trotsky was not permitted to ride back to Wexhall with Knudsen. The two were required to travel separately in cars driven by the State Police.[53]

Even as Trotsky was under way, Lie's office issued a press release concerning the meeting. It succinctly spelled out exactly what awaited Trotsky upon his return, declaring that since he had refused to accept the changed terms for his asylum, the Justice Department had decided "that Trotsky and his wife shall immediately be interned." Furthermore, until arrangements had been made to provide them with a new place to stay, "Trotsky and his wife will be isolated in their present residence."[54]

Lev and Natalia from then on were confined to their bedroom, whose door was always kept ajar. They were separated completely from the Knudsen family. Hilda, always accompanied by two policemen, brought them their meals.[55] They were indeed prisoners in every sense of the word.

Even as they were placed in strict custody, Trotsky's secretaries were in the process of being expelled. Lie had informed Trotsky that Wolf and van Heijenoort could remain only if he signed the declaration of August 28. He reacted by declaring this to be "scandalous." Neither he nor his secretaries had done anything to warrant such treatment.[56]

However, once he rejected the ultimatum, the Justice Department proceeded to take equally forceful measures against the secretaries. While Trotsky was in Lie's office, Wolf waited outside, still believing that the government might honor Lie's inferred promise to distance itself from the Central Passport Office's report. This assumption was rudely shattered when the State Police chief, Askvig, personally prevented Wolf from joining Trotsky.[57]

The State Police instead drove Wolf to the Hønefoss police station. In the meantime, two members of the police unit at Wexhall suddenly entered the house unannounced. One proceeded to dismantle the telephone while the other seized the unfortunate van Heijenoort, who was immediately dispatched to the police station. Here Wolf joined him when he arrived from Oslo, but the two were confined separately. After some two hours had elapsed, they were brought back to Wexhall and ordered to pack their belongings. With difficulty, Wolf received permission to talk briefly with the Trotskys through the almost closed door in order to deal with some last minute practical matters, but only in the presence of the guards. Thereafter, Wolf and van Heijenoort were driven back to the police station, where they remained incarcerated.[58] Attempting to put the most positive spin on their treatment, *Arbeiderbladet* mendaciously reported the next day that the two secretaries had "voluntarily left Wexhall."[59]

Police Chief Urbye was responsible for sending Wolf and van Heijenoort, under guard, to Oslo on the morning of August 29, where they were handed over to the Investigative Police at Møllergaten 19.[60] Here they were asked to sign a declaration that they were leaving Norway "voluntarily."[61] They refused, pointing out that they had not violated any Norwegian laws. In addition, Wolf had a valid residence permit that did not expire until December 18, the same date as Trotsky's.[62] Reidar Sveen thereupon handed the two recalcitrants over to Konstad, who immediately ordered their formal arrest.[63] Relishing his authority over the leftist radicals, he threatened to deport them on the next ship to Hamburg. Not wanting to fall into the clutches of the Gestapo, Wolf and van Heijenoort protested energetically and managed to establish contact with Finn Moe at *Arbeiderbladet*. Thanks to his intervention, Konstad's threat was not carried out. After all, as both Wolf and van Heijenoort stressed, they carried valid passports and had broken no laws.[64]

This did not, however, prevent their deportation. The Central Passport Office simply cancelled Wolf's residence permit.[65] Konstad thereafter informed the press that the secretaries would be placed on the next train leaving the country later that day.[66] Van Heijenoort and Wolf thereupon found themselves bound for Sweden on the evening of the 29th. Making certain that their expulsion occurred exactly as intended, an escort of two policemen accompanied Trotsky's secretaries as they departed Norway for the last time.[67]

As proof that inter-Scandinavian police cooperation functioned well in the '30s, once they reached the border, the nationality of their guardians changed. The same occurred when they crossed into Denmark. No fewer than six policemen traveled with their train to the central railroad station in Copenhagen. Expecting to be taken to a hotel, they once more found themselves housed in a jail cell.[68]

After they left Norway, Wolf and van Heijenoort most urgently wanted to get their story out about how Trotsky was being treated by Norwegian officials. In Denmark they drew up a joint statement denouncing the actions against Trotsky, which the two attempted to send to the major Copenhagen daily, *Politiken* (Politics). They failed.[69] Instead, they were unceremoniously transported to the harbor and placed on board what van Heijenoort described as a "very small, old boat," the *Algarve*, ironically flying the Norwegian flag.[70]

It immediately left for Morocco to pick up a cargo of copra. However, underway it was scheduled to stop in Antwerp, allowing the secretaries to disembark and thereby avoid falling into German hands.[71] However, when they arrived at the port on September 2, the press must have been alerted. Van Heijenoort and Wolf were photographed as they departed the ship.[72] Most importantly, they at last had the opportunity to reach public opinion. They were interviewed by the Antwerp paper *La Metropole*, a conservative Catholic daily, on September 5.[73]

The two did not, however, enjoy a significant triumph. Although it printed their story, *La Metropole* was by no means positive, voicing disapproval of Trotskyite views.[74] Furthermore, Wolf and van Heijenoort were none too pleased when the freedom they had enjoyed on the *Algarve* came to an end, as they traveled by train across Belgium to France. Once more they were securely under police supervision. But just before they reached France, the Belgian constables mysteriously disappeared. Quite clearly, they did not want to alert their cross-border colleagues about the secretaries' Trotskyite connections, afraid that the French would force Wolf, a Czech, back into Belgium.[75]

Therefore, it was only after they arrived in France that Wolf and van Heijenoort were completely free to express themselves, at last allowed to present the declaration they had drawn up in Copenhagen. In their statement they maintained that the show trial had been conducted entirely for the purpose of compromising Trotsky morally and politically. But when he attempted to defend himself against Moscow's false accusations, the minister of justice had gagged him. "The trial against the fascists [NS members who burglarized Wexhall] under the Norwegian justice system was turned into a process against Trotsky. . . . He was denied all contact with the outside world." The secretaries went on to deny that Trotsky in any way had violated his asylum. Instead, they insisted that world opinion would condemn the minister of justice for having greatly damaged Norway's democratic reputation.[76]

Deprived of his secretaries, Trotsky appealed to Attorney General Haakon Sund in a handwritten letter dated August 29. Since he was under guard, he must have received assistance from someone at Wexhall to smuggle it out. He raised two main protests. First, he stated, indirectly, that he was being treated inhumanely. He was under house arrest, with his secretaries arrested and deported. He and Natalia had no opportunity to communicate with anyone. He maintained that this "punishment" was being inflicted for the sole reason that he had published "legal articles" that he had signed *"under full name"* (Trotsky's emphasis). Furthermore, there had never previously been any complaints about his activity. On the contrary, *Arbeiderbladet*, the government's leading paper, had always described his behavior as being loyal. *"Only after the fascists broke into my house"* (Trotsky's emphasis) had he—as well as his wife—been declared criminals and treated as such.

Secondly, he pointed out that Sund was obviously aware of the extraordinary accusations that Russian authorities had made against him, unheard of in modern history. Since he was on Norwegian soil and under the protection of Norwegian law, he was certain that no modern country's laws permitted the use of administrative measures to prevent someone who was wrongly accused and deeply offended from defending himself.[77]

Any prospects of gaining redress from the attorney general, however, were dashed immediately. In a tersely worded response, Sund washed his hands of the entire matter. He asserted that drawing up asylum terms for residence in Norway was not under his authority and he therefore could not comment about Trotsky's treatment. Instead, he stated that he would forward the complaint to the department that had jurisdiction.[78] This meant, of course, that there was no possibility of escaping the clutches of the Justice Department. Lev continued to remain under the control of the person whom he increasingly regarded as his nemesis, Minister of Justice Lie.

The cabinet members who determined how Trotsky was handled had kept their eyes directed abroad as well as at home as the show trial unfolded, being kept updated by the Norwegian legation in Moscow, which carefully monitored the court proceedings. Minister Andreas Urbye was extremely skeptical about their validity in general, and specifically about the charges made against Trotsky and his son Lev.* They of course were found guilty in absentia and could expect to be brought before the Soviet Union's highest military tribunal should they ever be taken captive on Russian soil. But Urbye reported to Oslo that Trotsky's place of asylum had not been mentioned at all in the courtroom, while major Soviet newspapers had only briefly alluded to Norway during the trial.[79]

This relative calm ended on August 28, the same day that Trotsky was interned. Both *Pravda* and *Izvestia* launched violent diatribes against Norway for having granted asylum to "the rabid fascist dog Trotsky."[80]

Izvestia was the most mendacious, alleging that a broad popular protest had arisen among the Norwegian people once news of Trotsky's terrorist activity had been revealed in Moscow. Mass demonstrations against him were alleged to be growing in size, to the extent that he had been forced to flee into "the interior of the country."[81] *Pravda*, on the other hand, launched a somewhat more sophisticated "exposé" in which the "fascist" break-in was depicted as really having been arranged by the Gestapo to

---

* Urbye, an experienced politician as well as diplomat, had, among other posts, served as minister of justice in 1916–1917.

give the world the impression that Trotsky was still a "revolutionary" and a "Bolshevik," engaged in anticapitalist activity. *Pravda* insisted, however, that he was the "leader of the Gestapo's band of agents and the organizer of counter-revolutionary murders." Furthermore, the Labor Party's leaders were held responsible for having provided a safe place for his "criminal terrorist activity." *Arbeiderbladet* in particular received strong condemnation for its defense of Trotsky both before and during the show trial.[82]

Despite the violent language employed initially in the Soviet press, its criticism was carefully directed toward the Labor Party and its leaders, not the Norwegian government. However, as the *New York Times* noted perceptively, the "violent attacks against the Labor Party" in *Pravda* and *Izvestia* were most likely an indication that Stalin's government intended to make a formal complaint to Norway for having granted Trotsky asylum, "on the grounds that he has violated his pledge not to engage in political activity."[83]

The anticipated protest came on the following day, Saturday, August 29, delivered by the Russian minister to Norway, Ignatiev S. Jakoubowitch. On Friday he had received a directive from Moscow to hold discussions with Norwegian officials about depriving Trotsky of his asylum. The envoy immediately arranged to meet with Trygve Lie, who served as acting foreign minister while Koht was on vacation.[84] During their meeting Jakoubowitch received assurance that the Soviet initiative would be presented to the government without delay. The acting foreign minister was quite forthcoming, obviously currying Russian favor. He resentfully attacked Scheflo for being responsible for Trotsky's coming to Norway, and according to Jakoubowitch, declared that the Labor Party was considering Scheflo's expulsion.*[85] The diplomat similarly reported that Lie had harshly denounced Trotsky, going so far as to read excerpts from the letter of August 26, in which Trotsky sardonically reminded Lie of his visit to Wexhall in 1935.[86]

Because of the obvious importance of the matter, Lie did not feel comfortable acting on his own. He therefore asked the diplomat to present his message to Koht, even though the latter was officially still on leave.[87] Both with Lie and during his subsequent meeting with Koht, however, Jakoubowitch only relayed the Soviet request orally. Koht made a note of its contents, but when the Foreign Ministry asked for a written version, the

---

* Although it is likely that Lie mentioned the possibility of Scheflo being expelled from the Labor Party, this, of course, did not occur. With the upcoming election less than two months away, the Labor Party would not have risked taking such a divisive step, no matter how annoyed some party leaders might have been with Scheflo at that moment.

Russian legation replied that the message was intended for oral transmission only.[88] Nevertheless, the wording of the Russian *démarche* did not remain unknown. The Soviet press published it in its entirety already on August 30,[89] and it was quickly picked up by the international press, including Norwegian papers.[90] This tactic—on the one hand refusing to provide Norwegian officials with a written copy, while on the other immediately releasing it to the press—clearly was intended to put added pressure on the cabinet.

Specifically, the Soviet initiative declared that Trotsky had been found guilty of leading the terrorist organization that had assassinated Kirov and was planning the murder of other top Russian officials. To allow Trotsky to continue to enjoy asylum might consequently "harm the friendly relations existing between the USSR and Norway" and would be in conflict with "modern conceptions . . . of international law." The Soviet government therefore assumed that the government would "not fail to take appropriate measures to deprive Trotsky of the further right of asylum on Norwegian territory."[91]

The government was not taken aback by the Russian move. As early as August 13, on the eve of the show trial, the Norwegian legation in Moscow, as noted, had warned about future difficulties concerning Trotsky's asylum. Minister Jakoubowitch commented later that "our initiative clearly did not come as a surprise for the Norwegian government."[92] On August 28, the day **before** Jakoubowitch met with Lie and Koht, Frede Castberg, the Foreign Ministry's leading consultant on international law, drafted a memorandum in which he concluded that the Soviet Union had no legal basis under international law to request Trotsky's extradition. On the other hand, the government, under Norwegian law, had the authority to deport Trotsky, should this be desirable.[93] The Russians could therefore not expect to achieve the expulsion of Trotsky to the Soviet Union, something that Jakoubowitch, a professional diplomat, clearly understood. He reported to his superiors that on the basis of his discussion with Lie, he had concluded that while the Norwegian government undoubtedly would be happy to be rid of Trotsky, "difficulties would arise" if a deportation process were to begin.[94] In his conversation with Koht, the latter had been even more direct, declaring that Norway had no treaty obligations with the Soviet Union concerning "the question under discussion." However, he ended their meeting with a statement that proved to be extremely meaningful. The only part of the Russian *démarche* that he would take into account, said Koht, concerned maintaining "friendly relations between the two countries," and this, he added, was something to which he attached "great weight."⁹⁵ Jakoubowitch, in his report to the Russian Foreign Ministry that day, stated that this consideration would undoubtedly prove decisive in determining the Norwegian position.⁹⁶

Initially, however, it seemed as if Koht would reject the Russian request. During a campaign speech in Trondheim on August 30, the foreign minister declared that the government continued to adhere to the principle that Norway, as a free country, would provide asylum for political refugees, no matter what their nationality or political convictions might be. The Nygaardsvold government, he contended, would not allow itself to be "bullied."⁹⁷ This apparently principled stand gained favorable reaction abroad. The *Washington Post* voiced its approval of Norway for having "refused to comply with the Russian demand that Leon Trotzky be expelled from the little Scandinavian country. Here is a gratifying reminder that the right of asylum is not yet wholly destroyed in a world where so many nations are forgetting even the ordinary amenities of civilized intercourse."⁹⁸

Koht's ostensible strong stance was in reality, however, a smokescreen. The foreign minister proceeded deliberately to distance himself almost entirely from the controversy with the Russians. He preferred to have Trygve Lie assume the responsibility of handling Trotsky—a task that the ambitious Lie did not shy away from. At this critical moment Koht departed on a campaign tour of North Norway that kept him away from Oslo during the entire period when discussions with the Russians continued to be held. Koht left Lie in charge as acting foreign minister. The political opposition did not fail to note this move. *Dagbladet* commented sarcastically: "One usually does not accuse foreign minister Koht of undervaluing his importance. But it is most noticeably modest for him to dare to allow the country to be without a foreign minister at such a serious time, and quite cold-bloodedly embark on a lecture tour of North Norway."⁹⁹

Within the Foreign Ministry the delivery of the Russian message on August 29 resulted in hurried reaction. By the following Monday, August 31, Frede Castberg had drawn up a memorandum regarding the Soviet request to deprive Trotsky of asylum. He noted that the Russian *démarche* did not constitute a formal demand for extradition. However, it must be interpreted as a motion "that the Norwegian state should *expel* Trotsky from Norway" (Castberg's emphasis). But Norway did not,

Castberg asserted, have any obligation to do so under international law because there did not exist any treaty that could serve as a legal basis.[100]

The professor of jurisprudence insisted that the government's only option was to affirm its intent to adhere to the "principles of the right of asylum." However, his final conclusion in no way upheld Trotsky's rights. Castberg declared that since Trotsky had violated the stipulations under which he had been admitted to Norway, the government **prior** to the Russian inquiry had already "placed Trotzky under such control that it will be impossible in the future for him to take any action that could strike or threaten Russian state interests."[101]

The government, however, was prepared to go even further than simply relying on this memorandum. At a hurriedly assembled conference, the cabinet on August 31 received for its consideration a special provisional decree (*provisorisk anordning*) drawn up by the Justice Department. Except for the absent Koht, who contended he opposed the action that sanctioned Trotsky's internment but who made no effort to stop it,* the cabinet approved the edict in a session at the Royal Palace. King Haakon signed the decree, which was countersigned by the prime minister. Consisting of simply a long sentence, it stated that when a foreigner whose stay or activity was in conflict with the state's interests either would not or could not leave the country, the Justice Department could restrict his freedom of movement and contact with other persons to the extent that the department desired.[102]

Judicially as well as physically, the terms of Trotsky's internment were thereupon settled. He would remain under confinement for the remainder of his stay. But although the conditions under which he and his wife lived had been altered radically, the Labor Party continued to insist that Nygaardsvold's administration had not changed policy. On the same day that the provisional decree was enacted, *Arbeiderbladet* editorialized: "Norway is a free country and will uphold the principle of the right of asylum." Trotsky had been provided refuge even though he earlier had violently attacked the Labor Party. However, said Tranmæl, those who enjoyed asylum must also understand that the government did not intend

---

* Koht's attempt to distance himself most likely was based, at least in part, on his desire to maintain his international credentials as an idealistic peace advocate. He served on the Nobel Peace Prize Committee from 1918 until 1936, when he resigned because it had become obvious that his position as foreign minister was incompatible with membership on the committee.

to allow Norway to become involved in conflict with other countries, least of all the Russian workers' state, because of the activity of those who had been granted exile. "If they do not voluntarily understand this, then the government must do what is necessary, as it has done in the Trotsky case." The cabinet, Tranmæl argued, had "acted wisely and correctly." It had maintained the principle of the right of asylum, and would continue to do so, while at the same time it "has looked after the country's interests and prevented those complications that could have occurred."[103] But no matter how he and other Labor leaders tried to disguise this, the opinion that Tranmæl enunciated was in reality the tried and true practice of having national interest take precedence over all other considerations, including the values of free speech and protection under the law.

Trotsky was taken aback when he realized that he would not be allowed such rights. But true to his nature, he would not give up. He would use legal maneuvers to try to circumvent the restrictions imposed upon him almost to the very end of his exile in Norway.

After careful editing, which involved several different drafts,[104] the government presented its response to the Soviet Union on September 3. With Koht away, Lie did the honors of formally delivering the document to Jakoubowitch.[105] The government's *aide-mémoire* carefully stated that even if Trotsky had been involved in planning the assassination of Kirov, this could not have occurred on Norwegian soil since he was murdered in December 1934, whereas Trotsky did not arrive until June 1935. Furthermore, the government rejected completely the allegation that it had been negligent in preventing its territory from being used as a base for threatening another state's security. It had previously not had any reason to suspect Trotsky of carrying out political activity against foreign states, nor had Norwegian officials, prior to his internment, received any message that he was conducting "political agitation" that was harmful to other countries. However, as a consequence of the police investigation resulting from the break-in at Trotsky's residence, it had been determined that he had not adhered to the conditions under which he had been allowed to enter Norway. In addition, his court testimony had revealed even more starkly that he had "violated the terms of his residence." Consequently, the "conditional right of asylum" that Trotsky and his wife had received when they came to Norway was "restricted" on August 25, when he was placed under house arrest, and eliminated entirely on August 28, following his court appearance, when he was interned. With these steps having been taken, Trotsky was under such control that it must be considered impossible for him to execute any action that could strike at or threaten Russian interests.[106]

While it was clearly intended to address Soviet concerns, the note also took special pains to emphasize that the measures against Trotsky had been carried out **before** the government received the Soviet inquiry.[107] Obviously, the Nygaardsvold administration was concerned about public opinion, especially in an election year, wanting to avoid the impression of having caved in to foreign pressure. The official reply therefore assumed an assertive tone when it expressed regret that the Soviet government had chosen a "form for its communication that does not appear to be entirely in congruence with the friendly relations that exist between Norway and Soviet Russia."[108]

As could be expected, the Russians were not willing to allow such criticism to remain unanswered. Jakoubowitch declared that the reply was "not completely satisfactory." The critique of the Soviet government was misdirected. It was the Norwegians who, by allowing Trotsky to remain in the country, were permitting a situation to continue that could be regarded as a reward for organizing "the killing of Soviet politicians."

Again Lie made it clear that he wished to maintain good relations with the Soviets. The critical formulation toward the Soviet Union, he stated, had been inserted at the insistence of Koht.[109] If Lie's inference were true, then the only way the absent Koht could have added his input must have been by telephone to the Foreign Ministry. Lie went on to assure Jakoubowitch that his government had decided to deny Trotsky renewal of his residence permit once it expired in December. Nor would the government pay attention to any requests by Trotsky to lessen the restrictions of his confinement in return for agreeing to a new set of residence terms. Finally, Lie confidentially informed Jakoubowitch that he intended to sabotage all attempts by Trotsky to bring cases before Norwegian courts[110] (a promise that Lie would resolutely keep). As his assurances indicated, the acting foreign minister did everything in his power to satisfy the Soviet diplomat and thereby get the issue out of the way.

Initially, however, the Russians were not content. Minister Urbye reported to Oslo on September 5 that the Soviet press contained major articles castigating foreign criticism of the Kamenev-Zinoviev trial. *Arbeiderbladet* had specifically come under attack in *Pravda* for its defense of Trotsky's right of asylum. This, said the Communist Party's main organ, meant that in reality his right to conduct terrorist activity against the U.S.S.R. would continue.[111]

Urbye several days later had a meeting in the Russian Commissariat of Foreign Affairs, from which he gained the impression that Soviet authorities would have been quite pleased if Trotsky had simply been handed over to them. In reply, the minister made it clear that this would have involved extradition, which the Russians had not requested. Nevertheless, Urbye felt that Moscow originally had believed that the Norwegian government might respond to the Soviet inquiry by declaring it could not expel Trotsky because no country would admit him, thereby allowing the Russians to declare that **they** were quite willing to accept him. In reality this meant that the *démarche* of August 29 had as its goal the delivery of Trotsky to the tender mercies of Stalin's henchmen. This caused Urbye to caution that his message should be treated as "*strictly confidential*" (Urbye's emphasis).[112]

But while Soviet newspapers continued to chastise the Labor Party, Urbye noted that the official Norwegian response of September 3 had not been mentioned with one word.[113] Not until a week later did Jakoubowitch appear in the Foreign Ministry with the Soviet Union's formal written reaction. The reply was very brief. It stated that the Russian government unfortunately could not consider the Norwegian *aide-mémoire* to be satisfactory and in conformity with the friendly relations that existed between the two countries. It added that the Norwegian government must therefore assume full responsibility for the steps it had taken, as well as for Trotsky's continued stay in Norway.[114]

Despite the somewhat hostile tone of this note, the Russians made no further diplomatic moves. Stalin unquestionably would have preferred to have Trotsky dispatched to Moscow so that he could become the next featured victim of the show trials. However, seasoned diplomats knew from the start that there was no chance that the Norwegians would permit his expulsion on the basis of a diplomatic inquiry that was presented only orally. Nor was the Soviet government willing to make a formal request for extradition because this quite likely could have resulted in a hearing before a Norwegian court, allowing Trotsky the opportunity he longed for—to refute Russian charges. The next best outcome for Stalin was therefore to have him silenced, denying him access to the press. Furthermore, while interned, his ability to influence his followers would be limited.

The Russians appeared satisfied with this. Minister Urbye forwarded the news on September 16 that, except for an initial TASS report, the Soviet press had not made any comment about the latest diplomatic exchange. He concluded that, from the Russian point of view, "the matter temporarily is regarded as finished."[115] Diplomatic contact on a higher level appeared to bear this out. When Foreign Minister Koht conferred with the Soviet foreign minister, Maxim Litvinov, at a meeting of the League of Nation's General Assembly in Geneva on September 25, the latter inquired if anything new had occurred in the Trotsky case. Koht replied no, and added that his government did not intend to answer the latest Soviet comment. Litvinov assured him that the Soviet Union did not expect a response. Koht reported: "Between us we thereupon agreed that the matter was decided and concluded." The two diplomats next looked forward to having a good meal together.[116]

It needs to be emphasized that Norwegian leaders never accepted the exaggerated and untruthful Soviet charges that Trotsky was a terrorist. Martin Tranmæl's rejection of the show trial has already been noted. From Moscow, Minister Urbye not only forwarded the assessment that the trial was unfair but showed no hesitation in expressing his attitude to fellow diplomats. The U.S. chargé d'affaires, Loy W. Henderson, reported to Secretary of State Cordell Hull that Urbye "has informed me . . . he considers the trial to be a farce and that . . . the charges that Trotski had participated in a plot to kill Soviet leaders [are not] substantiated."[117]

However, while the Norwegian government, through diplomatic channels, was accurately informed about the true character of the trial, nevertheless there had for some time existed disquiet among its envoys concerning Trotsky's activity, a mood that preceded the trial and even the break-in at Wexhall. Diplomats, in particular in France, Belgium, and the Soviet Union, had sent information to Oslo concerning Trotsky's activity as leader of the emerging Fourth International. From its attention to this subject, it is plain that the Nygaardsvold government feared potential repercussions before they actually occurred.[118]

There furthermore existed broad consensus within the government that maintaining good relations with the U.S.S.R. was of major importance, taking precedence over consideration for Trotsky. The latter fully recognized this but in true Marxist fashion assumed that Norwegian priorities were based on economic motives, maintaining that Stalin's government had "threatened Norwegian commerce with a boycott. . . . *That* was the reason for my arrest" (Trotsky's emphasis).[119] His biographers have frequently accepted this viewpoint.[120] However, the person who exercised dominant influence over foreign policy, Foreign Minister Koht, never regarded the threat of a Soviet economic boycott as a major concern. At the time that the diplomatic exchange took place, he declared that he did not fear that the Trotsky affair would lead to a break in trade relations, pointing out that commerce with Russia had already declined significantly.[121] Had he regarded this as a major problem, he would have involved himself much more directly in the handling of Trotsky than he did. Moreover, the foreign minister did not allow the government to act without first being fully briefed. Upon returning from North Norway, he made a point of informing the public that he had been in contact with acting Foreign Minister Lie so that everything that was said in the exchange of notes with the Soviet Union "occurred in consultation with me."[122]

Security considerations were much more important in determining policy toward the Soviet Union. The Norwegian government became adamant in its determination to block Trotsky from speaking out once it was apparent that his activity threatened to undermine relations with the Russians. As one of the Labor Party's official historians and the biographer of Trygve Lie has openly stated, the purpose for the action against Trotsky was to prevent him from replying to Stalin's accusations.[123] The Labor cabinet took this step, fully recognizing that it could expect to be criticized from both political and legal perspectives.[124]

Ultimate accountability for the decision to intern Trotsky, however, lay with Prime Minister Johan Nygaardsvold. This conclusion is contrary to the popular notion, widely prevalent inside and outside Norway, that Trygve Lie bore primary responsibility. Trotsky and his followers focused their hostility on Lie in large part because his department had foremost authority for dealing with exiles and because the government's Police Department, as part of the Justice Department, directly supervised Trotsky's internment.[125] But Lie simply carried out the prime minister's policy and did not act independently. As the youngest member of the cabinet, Lie in 1936 did not enjoy the prestige and influence that he later acquired as foreign minister and the first secretary general of the United Nations. He instead curried Nygaardsvold's favor. The two met regularly for lunch. During these get-togethers, Lie served as a major source of information about internal matters within the Labor Party since Nygaardsvold lacked the personal insight into the party bureaucracy that Lie possessed.[126]

Superficially, however, it is possible to question whether Nygaardsvold was fully in charge when Trotsky was interned. The prime minister suffered from rheumatic fever, causing him to be bedridden during much of 1936. He missed the Labor Party's annual meeting in May, and he also did not regularly take part in the fall election campaign.[127] However, he appears to have made at least a temporary recovery in late August 1936, presiding at the cabinet meeting that approved the provisional decree that legalized Trotsky's internment. Furthermore, when Koht left for North Norway, he observed that "Prime Minister Nygaardsvold was functioning again."[128]

When the government moved to place Trotsky under house arrest, it did not consult the Labor leadership. The question of Trotsky's residence permit was never submitted to the party's Central Committee, either when he was offered asylum or when it was withdrawn.[129] This explains why the change in the party press was so sudden, quickly reversing itself from defending Trotsky to attacking him, with no smooth transition. Tranmæl later described how *Arbeiderbladet* "found itself in the situation that we had to *explain* what had happened, something that definitely was not so easy!" (Tranmæl's emphasis).[130]

At the time that the cabinet changed its treatment of Trotsky, it did not, however, face significant opposition from within the party. A major reason was that, despite its disaffiliation from the Comintern and later adoption of more moderate socialist policies, it still harbored widespread sympathy for the Soviet Union during the mid-1930s. The U.S.S.R.'s attempt to establish a true "workers' and farmers' state" was regarded positively. While specific Soviet actions might be criticized, overall sympathy for the communist experiment remained constant. The government therefore did not risk arousing widespread disapproval from its own party members when it sought to reach a favorable accommodation with the Russians concerning Trotsky.

Trygve Lie, always sensitive to political opinion, actually believed that the diplomatic exchange with the Soviet Union, which occurred during the 1936 election campaign, had resulted in a positive outcome for the party. The sharp tone of the Russian inquiry, Lie felt, made it more difficult for critics to accuse the government of being too friendly toward Moscow. On the contrary, it was now the bourgeoisie that were concerned "because the relationship with the Soviet Union had become cooler."[131]

Such worries did not mean that the nonsocialist parties had suddenly assumed a more positive attitude toward Russia. Instead, it was but one more indication of how "the Trotsky affair" remained a major election issue, with all parties seeking to turn different aspects of the controversy to their advantage. Press coverage remained as sensational as earlier in the summer, with extensive space devoted to Trotsky when he first was placed under house arrest, followed by his court appearance, and concluding with his arrest and internment.

As before, the Labor Party defended itself from attacks extending from National Union on the extreme right to the communists on the left. *Arbeiderbladet* reminded its readers that the Conservatives had not put the issue of Trotsky's asylum to a vote in the Storting, knowing that they would be defeated. For once, if only indirectly, indicating a slight amount of guilt concerning Trotsky, the paper pointed out that "limitation" of the right of asylum had unfortunately occurred in most countries during and after World War I. Nevertheless, extending this right was one of Norway's "democratic responsibilities," making it available to refugees of radically different political persuasions. It was therefore in everyone's interest, maintained Tranmæl, to be calmer and maintain a sense of balance.[132]

To expect calm and balance on a political issue as divisive as the Trotsky affair was, of course, impossible. The communists again trotted out the Fred Zeller postcard incident as evidence of Trotsky's terrorist complicity and bitterly derided both the bourgeois press and the Labor Party papers for having allowed Trotsky to denounce the Moscow trial.[133]

Fritt Folk, under a massive headline, proclaimed "Total Victory for NS in the Trotsky Affair."[134] The feeling that NS had triumphed and that the Labor Party had suffered a significant setback was not, however, limited just to Quisling's party. Writing in *Fremtiden* on August 29, Konrad Knudsen ironically declared that Trotsky's internment showed that "our Norwegian Nazis" had got their way after all. Knudsen did concede that Trotsky might have violated his residence terms to a certain degree, but this was at best a matter of interpretation. The fact that Trotsky chose imprisonment rather than accept restrictions, said Knudsen, showed that Trotsky had acted in good faith. It was not worthy, Knudsen continued, to silence Trotsky when he needed to defend himself from opponents in both Moscow and Berlin.[135]

His strong words could not go unanswered in a Labor Party newspaper. *Fremtiden*'s editor in chief, in an addendum, maintained it was not "Nazi provocations" that had caused Trotsky's internment but rather his violation of his residence permit. Nevertheless, the editor regretted the affair's outcome, declaring that a different procedure should instead have been followed to avoid the "drastic measures" now being employed against Trotsky.[136]

Knudsen's attitude, of course, was shared by Olav Scheflo, who published without comment Knudsen's article in *Sørlandet*, taking care, however, also to include *Fremtiden*'s editorial comment.[137] Some union members similarly viewed Trotsky's internment with disfavor. At a meeting of local unions in Oslo on September 11, a resolution was passed that strongly "protested against the government's capitulation for Nazi gangster rule in the Trotsky affair."[138]

As critical voices within the labor movement indicated, its members were not entirely unanimous in their reaction, a divide that the party's opponents sought to exploit. *Tidens Tegn* quoted extensively from Knudsen's criticism, citing it as proof of division even within Labor's top leadership.[139] However, with the election rapidly approaching, the party had to be unified. As Haakon Lie* has put it: "The loyalty we felt toward our own government was so root bound that we remained quiet concerning the infringement [of Trotsky's rights]. We bore our shame in silence."[140]

The party steadfastly insisted that its government had done only what was proper. It had upheld the right of asylum by admitting Trotsky. On the other hand, it had made certain he would not be able to carry out "hostile activity against the Soviet Union" from Norway. *Arbeiderbladet* concluded that the Nygaardsvold administration deserved praise for having defended Norwegian interests and farsightedly eliminating future complications.[141]

No other party, however, was willing to allow such a self-serving claim to stand unchallenged. The left wing of the Liberal Party might be closest to the Labor Party ideologically among the nonsocialists, but *Dagbladet* did not hesitate to portray the government's action negatively. While agreeing with the right of asylum in principle, the paper argued that if

---

* Haakon Lie later became renowned as the Labor Party's strong-willed party secretary from 1945 to 1969, when he was the architect of a number of election victories for the socialists.

Trotsky's activity had been restricted from the time he was first admitted, the current dilemma that Norway faced with the U.S.S.R. might never
have materialized. At the same time the paper scornfully rejected National
Union's boast that it had been victorious in the Trotsky affair. *Dagbladet's*
editorial writer pointed out that it was the Moscow trial that had made the
dispute about Trotsky's asylum significant. NS's bragging was compared to
that of a fly riding on the back of a truck on a dirt road, shouting, "See how
much dust I am stirring up."[142]

When the Soviet Union protested Trotsky's residence in Norway, *Aftenposten* helpfully pointed out its solution to the dilemma. Since the Russians
and the entire bourgeois press in Norway wanted to get rid of Trotsky, as
did no doubt the government itself and "the great majority" of its party,
then Trotsky should simply be deported.[143]

This absurd recommendation was but another demagogic contribution
to the campaign debate. *Dagbladet* on August 31 prominently featured
a large article by former foreign minister Arnold Ræstad that provided
a more realistic assessment. He indicated that Trotsky could neither be
handed over to the Soviet Union nor expelled capriciously. He had to be
accorded the legal protections of the Norwegian constitution. However,
the constitution did permit the king in a special situation to intern persons
who had not been tried, in expectation that the parliament later would give
its sanction.[144] Ræstad, with his high-level connections, simply anticipated
the inevitable. His views were published on the very day that King Haakon
signed the provisional decree that legalized Trotsky's internment.

Even after the government action had acquired a sheen of legality, the
debate continued. *Nationen* remained entirely negative. Editor Thorvald
Aadahl maintained that, although Trotsky was now a "prisoner," this did
not mean that Stalin necessarily was satisfied. Aadahl hinted gloomily that
the Soviet Union, in order to have its way, might actually launch a military
attack against Norway.[145] National Union similarly continued to remind
voters that it was the only party to have strongly opposed Trotsky's admission. Bourgeois politicians were condemned for not having listened
to Quisling's warnings, having instead handed over the government to a
party that they themselves had previously branded as treasonous. Support
for NS in the struggle against the international Marxist conspiracy was
therefore "a question of life or death for our people."[146]

The Labor Party clearly was irritated by the continuation of the partisan debate, which it had hoped Trotsky's internment would end. Tranmæl

accused the bourgeois parties of hypocrisy. Their leaders were faulted for speaking positively about basic democratic principles, like the right of asylum, while violating those ideals once it was necessary to apply them concretely. Former prime minister Mowinckel boasted how he and his government earlier had denied asylum to Trotsky, while Hambro stressed how he had attempted to question whether Trotsky should be allowed to stay in Norway. Hambro in particular was strongly attacked because he had maintained that the Labor Party and its unions had solicited Trotsky to come to Norway as part of their propaganda strategy. This accusation, which was repeated by the Conservative Party's press office, said Tranmæl, showed how the Conservatives lacked respect for telling the truth.[147]

The Conservatives not unexpectedly disagreed with the Labor Party view that the issue should be eliminated from the election campaign. It was very relevant, *Aftenposten* insisted, because the main decision facing the voters was whether they favored or opposed Norway becoming socialist. Trotsky had helped to create the Soviet social order, which was based on terror. The Conservatives would therefore not forget to remind the voters that the "chapter on Trotsky" clearly showed the dangers of adopting socialism.[148]

To the Labor Party's relief, however, by the end of the first week of September 1936, with Trotsky no longer able to express himself publicly, interest inevitably began to wane, although the newspapers would again focus extensively on him, especially in the weeks before the election. But *Arbeiderbladet* on September 3 editorialized that "the hysterical and demagogical" manner in which the "fascist or semi-fascist" press had conducted itself in the Trotsky affair was in the process of culminating. Commenting on the more "suitable" residence that Trotsky had been moved to, Tranmæl, seeking to appear solicitous, maintained that it was an ideal location for him to continue his work. In addition, internment would provide better security, something that he needed, as shown by the break-in of the "Nazi bandits," as well as by threats in the communist press from both Moscow and "here at home."[149]

Minister Jakoubowitch, reporting to the Russian capital on September 9, similarly observed that much less was being written about Trotsky. The Norwegian press had also "calmed down" in its discussion of the Moscow trial "against the terrorists." Jakoubowitch stated with satisfaction that this in part was due to the U.S.S.R.'s translation of a full transcript of the trial, which had led to positive results. *Tidens Tegn*, not particularly procommunist, had published excerpts in a large article, covering several columns in its September 9 edition.[150]

By mid-September both the Labor Party and Soviet officials therefore had reason to feel satisfied that news coverage about the show trial, Trotsky's reaction to it, and the controversy over the terms and manner of his stay in Norway—resulting in divisive debate that had gone on since the evening of August 6 when NS activists confronted Hjørdis and Borgar Knudsen—was now coming to an end.

Having been sealed off completely on August 28, Lev and Natalia lived under more severe limitations than would have been true if Trotsky had accepted the restrictions offered by Lie. The Justice Department issued special instructions to the Central Passport Office on September 1 that "Lev Trotsky and his wife shall be isolated and under constant guard." They were prohibited from carrying out political activity in Norway and prevented from conducting "political agitation" against any nation with which Norway maintained friendly relations. They could not have visitors without permission from the Central Passport Office. Nor could they use a telephone. All correspondence mailed to them had to be first examined by the Passport Office. Similarly, all outgoing letters had to be censored. Their receipt of newspapers was dependent on permission from Konstad's office, as was the decision of whether or not they could have a radio.[151]

They were cut off from their friends and sympathizers. One of them, Håkon Meyer, complained bitterly, declaring that a jailed prisoner enjoyed more rights. He was correct. During their entire internment, except for their attorneys, the only visitor they officially were allowed to receive was Olav Scheflo. He succeeded early during their internment in persuading Kornelius Bergsvik, the minister of social affairs, who served as acting justice minister while Lie was on vacation, to grant Scheflo a brief visit, despite Konstad's opposition. However, parts of the press severely criticized this decision.[152] This no doubt contributed to Trygve Lie's determination not to allow any subsequent visits.

Strict as the restrictions were, Trotsky nevertheless accepted them initially, having experienced worse imprisonments during his lifetime. He informed the State Police chief that neither he nor his wife would "create any practical difficulties" as long as the authorities honored "our most elementary interests and rights." But he warned that if their treatment became more severe, they would employ "passive resistance" and, if necessary, resort to a "hunger strike." He was able to smuggle out this threat in a note to a Labor Party member (most likely Knudsen or Scheflo), declaring that it would also be beneficial for "party circles" to heed his warning.[153]

He did not have to resort to either expedient. The government, at least for the time being, was satisfied with isolating him, thereby eliminating his criticism of Stalin and the show trial. He was stymied, prevented from completing his main project since the time of the trial. This, as earlier mentioned, was namely a "major publication" to expose "the greatest falsification in political history." Trotsky indicated that he was working on this large brochure when he was still free to grant interviews. It had been van Heijenoort and Wolf's responsibility to help him, but with their ouster this was impossible.[154] This too was something the government was fully aware of when it deported the two secretaries. Although Tranmæl hinted in *Arbeiderbladet* in early September that Trotsky might be allowed technical assistance,[155] officials consistently refused him secretarial help. He had to carry out all correspondence by himself, aided only by Natalia.

Trotsky and his followers quickly perceived that under these circumstances a different tactic would have to be employed to achieve the same objective—to provide him the means of refuting the show trial in general, and specifically the charges levied against him and Lyova. Unable to reach the public directly, the alternative would be to project his message from the courtroom. Within two days after his internment began, on Sunday, August 30, Walter Held contacted an attorney after having consulted Scheflo. In a letter to Trotsky, Held insisted he was certain that if any attorney could be of help, then Michael Puntervold was the right choice. He added: "Scheflo is of the same opinion." The young Trotskyite described Puntervold as "one of the best known attorneys in the entire country."[156]

The latter accepted the challenge on the spot, which was most surprising. To serve Trotsky under the prevailing circumstances, with his client decidedly persona non grata in Norwegian society, was an undertaking that more career-minded attorneys would have avoided. But Puntervold did not hesitate. On Monday, August 31, he telegraphed Wexhall that he had agreed to Held's proposal to use his legal expertise in order "to protect your interests in Norway." He added, unquestionably to Trotsky's satisfaction, that the press would immediately be informed. He further stated that he had already been in contact with the proper officials, and the road was clear for him to meet with Trotsky on the following day. Indicating Scheflo's influence in his hiring, the attorney forwarded greetings from *Sørlandet*'s editor and his family to Lev and Natalia.[157]

Puntervold most likely was the last visitor that Trotsky received at Wexhall. Justice Department officials were determined to remove him to a place where he could be kept better isolated than his cramped but friendly quarters in the middle of Heradsbygda. The police had therefore been on the lookout for a more suitable site, and by the end of August they reported success. Their choice was a two-story villa on a farm called Sundby, located south of Oslo in Hurum County in Buskerud, lying adjacent to the Oslo Fjord. Lie signaled his approval on September 1, with a rental agreement having been signed that allowed for cancellation after December 1.[158]

The move followed almost immediately afterwards. Trotsky only received very hazy information about his pending transfer. State Police Chief Bernhard Askvig notified him that he and Natalia would be relocated to a remote house in a wooded area. In a note that he managed to smuggle out from Wexhall, most likely through Hjørdis Knudsen, Trotsky urged his followers to exert influence to make certain that the residence would be comfortable, with an electric kitchen, bath, and a heated toilet. It also needed to be close to Oslo so that he could have access to good medical attention.[159]

On September 2 the Justice Department issued a brief press release, stating that Lev Trotsky had been transferred earlier in the day to Hurum, "where a house has been made available for him and his wife, plus the police."[160] For the Trotskys, the trip took place with no prior notice. Gunvor Wraaman recalled how she attempted at the last minute to give Natalia a bouquet of sweet peas as they were being escorted out the gate. The police, however, confiscated the flowers.[161]

The latter had made careful preparation for the journey, which began shortly after noon, with Askvig personally in charge. In addition to six police cars, the motorcade included "a large gray truck," which carried the Trotskys' baggage. They traveled first from Hønefoss to Drammen, and then south to the village of Storsand in Hurum.[162] Here the Trotskys would remain at Sundby for the greater part of the next four months.

Initially Lev's followers greeted the change with some relief, pleased that the impasse at Wexhall had come to an end. Held reported to the ICL that Trotsky was receiving better treatment from the police, almost like an "honored prisoner." Furthermore, the accommodations were superior to what Lev and Natalia had formerly experienced. Now they had the second floor of the villa at their disposal, which, Held enthused, had all indoor amenities, "bath, etc." Trotsky also was allowed to receive his longed-for publications, such as books and periodicals from abroad. While his mail remained under censorship, Held made the erroneous assumption that the authorities would be somewhat lenient in permitting visitors. He did stress, correctly, that Trotsky enjoyed far better protection at Sundby "than we at any time would have been able to provide." His adherents clearly were concerned about his safety, which, as later events would show, they had every reason to be.

Held therefore looked forward to the coming months. Puntervold had visited Trotsky and received full authorization to act as his attorney. Thereupon, the legal campaign was already beginning to take shape. Held declared that "future propaganda" should be directed primarily against the Soviet government, not the Norwegian, because the latter was under constant pressure from Moscow. He further pointed out that Trotsky would require considerable financial support because of his legal expenses, and Held called on all of Trotsky's followers and sympathizers to begin a fundraising drive. For that purpose Held had already instructed his companion, Synnøve, to open a special bank account where deposits from abroad could be made.[163]

The young Trotskyite's initial impression about Trotsky's new internment site proved to be far too optimistic. For Lev and Natalia life at Sundby assumed a completely different character from what they previously had been accustomed to. While their living quarters at Wexhall had been restricted, they nevertheless had enjoyed a feeling of freedom that now was gone. No longer could they experience close companionship with the Knudsen family, contact with the other residents at Wexhall, and visits from the Knudsens' circle of friends and acquaintances. Gunvor Wraaman, their second-floor neighbor, fondly remembered, for example, the happy celebration when Lev turned fifty-six, and the birthday cake bore the inscription "Long live the world revolution."[164] Nor could Lev and Natalia any longer accompany friends to the local movie theater in Hønefoss. They could not look forward to the arrival of the postman with much anticipated mail from abroad, nor could Trotsky immediately dispatch his messages to trusted, or rebellious, followers with the valuable aid of his secretary. Finally, he could not, as discreetly as possible, receive visitors, who came to receive inspiration from the leader himself. For Lev and Natalia, looking back on what they previously had enjoyed, their days at Wexhall assumed the character of a lost paradise, and their attitude toward Norway, especially its government and the Labor Party's leaders, became a feeling of lost innocence and trust.

7 Internment at Sundby

Lev Trotsky and his wife are from now on to be held under strict police supervision. Their walks, restricted to one hour each morning and one hour each afternoon, are always to be under police escort. Their isolation indoors is also total. . . . Not one word about regulations and conditions [at Sundby] may be communicated to journalists or other persons. . . . Members of the State Police carry out their duties in their standard dark uniform with cap. They carry a bandolier and loaded pistol with a filled magazine. They are in addition equipped with a rubber truncheon, lantern, and handcuffs. The guardroom contains a machine gun and three carbines with filled magazines. Also a searchlight.

—Guard instructions, Sundby, September 4, 1936

THE TROTSKYS' NEW RESIDENCE, Sundby, had several advantages compared with Wexhall. The setting was even more beautiful. Situated above the Oslo Fjord, the main building had a panoramic vista over the water and the surrounding countryside. Directly across the fjord was the picturesque village of Drøbak, which had ferry connection three times daily with Storsand. And looming in the middle of the fjord was the fortress of Oscarsborg, which—unbeknown to everyone at Sundby—would be the site of a major naval action four years later.*

Sundby was the largest farm in the area, consisting of approximately 135 *mål* (34 acres) of cultivated land and more than 2500 *mål* (618 acres) of outlying fields and forest. In addition to the two-storied main house,

---

* On April 9, 1940, the heavy cruiser *Blücher* was sunk by the guns and torpedo batteries at Oscarsborg, thereby delaying the German capture of Oslo. This allowed the government and royal family to escape capture.

with its twenty-two rooms, the property consisted of a tenant's house (*for-pakterbolig*), a barn, two chicken coops, a garage, a smithy, and a store house (*stabbur*).[1]

Despite its size and proud heritage (the farm dated from the Middle Ages), it was chosen as a place of internment for a more prosaic reason. Sundby was one of the few places in Hurum that had an indoor bathroom, having gained the distinction of being the first as early as 1920. It was also a good choice because it lay close to Oslo but at the same time was secluded. Open fields surrounded the farm, and the main house was enclosed by high fences and a stone wall, making it easy to guard.[2]

Unlike their limited space at Wexhall, the Trotskys occupied, besides the bathroom, a large bedroom, a living room where they took their meals, and a drawing room. Lev used what had formerly been a child's bedroom as his study. The Trotskys also had at their disposal an enclosed veranda from which they could view the fjord. Here Lev would spend a considerable amount of time, especially when his health failed, wrapped in blankets against the autumn cold on the unheated and uninsulated veranda.[3] His archive of more than forty boxes, minus his most important books and papers, which had been moved into the house, was placed in the store house.[4]

However, in contrast with Wexhall, their landlord was not pleased to have them as tenants. Harald Halvorsen, a successful shipping agent (*speditør*), had purchased Sundby in 1905.[5] During the 1930s his family did not reside permanently at the farm, only in the summer. For the rest of the year they lived in Oslo but spent time at Sundby on weekends and holidays. The family had a deep love for their farm.[6]

During the summer of 1936 the Halvorsens' idyllic vacation came to an abrupt and unexpected end. State Police Chief Askvig insisted that the property be rented out to house Trotsky.[7] Harald Halvorsen protested, but to no avail. In the 1930s the government exercised a degree of power that today would be unthinkable. Under the requisition law of 1933, it had the authority to take over, in return for paying compensation, all property that the police needed "to maintain peace and order." Halvorsen had to accept the inevitable.[8]

He and the other members of the family were forced to move immediately to a small house located nearby.[9] The government agreed on a rental fee of 250 kroner per month for the villa, half paid by the state, half by Trotsky. In addition, the Trotskys were charged 11 kroner per day for their meals. Five rooms were closed off on the first floor, allowing the Halvorsen family to store their best furnishings in two of these.[10] However, they received only limited reimbursement for damage, including dents in the parquet floor from the guards' heavy boots.[11]

Lev and Natalia were not alone at Sundby. The property continued to be farmed by its tenant and his staff of four. But it was anything but an ordinary farm when the Trotskys lived there. Its regular workers had hardly any contact with the main building. Thirteen members of the State Police kept watch twenty-four hours a day, with a changing of the guard every three hours. In addition to occupying the first floor, they had four bedrooms on the second floor, in the north wing, separate from the Trotskys. Assistant police chief (*statspolitifullmektig*) Jonas Lie* had responsibility for security. He did not stay at Sundby but visited regularly. He used the library as his office, insisting that he be served his meals there, rather than dining with his subordinates in the kitchen. Askvig visited periodically to make certain that everything was in order. At key times Trygve Lie came to confer with Trotsky. Lie always stayed overnight on the neighboring farm.[12]

Because the tenant and his employees performed no work for the Trotskys or the guards, extra staff had to be hired from the local community. Karoline Robert was in charge of the household. She spoke French and could therefore communicate with the two internees, in particular Natalia. Aagot Sæthre was assigned as chambermaid.[13] With a total of eighteen people in the house, including at times Jonas Lie, the tasks of the two women, cooking and cleaning, were heavy and demanding.[14]

Everyone, police and staff, were under orders not to communicate with outsiders. Strict confidentiality had to be maintained. Furthermore, no one was allowed to take pictures, in particular not of Lev and Natalia.[15] There was no contact with the local community. Even neighbors who wanted to purchase milk had to have a special permit to enter. Trotsky was not popular in the village. Because of his presence, Storsand suddenly gained notoriety, which did not please its residents. He was regarded as a "dangerous man."[16] Several would have preferred to have him interned at Oscarsborg, where his security would be guaranteed, and from which it would be impossible to escape.[17]

The area immediately surrounding the house, including the garden, was fenced in, with barbed wire at the top. The fence furthermore was electrified.

---

* Jonas Lie became notorious during World War II, regarded as the Norwegian equivalent of Himmler, when he served as the head of Quisling's police department.

A bell would ring whenever anyone or anything came in contact with it.[18] Sundby was sarcastically described by persons who opposed the internment as "the first Norwegian concentration camp."[19] This characterization conformed fully with Trotsky's view. He consistently referred to it as "Sundby Prison."[20]

When Lev and Natalia ventured out of doors, the police always accompanied them. Natalia restricted her activity to the courtyard.[21] Lev, on the other hand, wanted more exercise, which at first was allowed. He took walks along the road, with one policeman in front and two behind him. He was permitted to go as far as Lower Sundby Pond, which lay some distance from the house. But when the police encountered a suspicious person in the vicinity, whom the local population quickly concluded must have been a Russian with evil intentions,* the guards immediately prevented Trotsky from going outside the fence. From then on he had to be content with walks in the garden. Local residents recalled that by the time he left, his pacing had worn rings in the grass around several large pear trees.[22]

He quickly settled into a routine that remained largely unchanged until his departure. He immersed himself in newspaper articles and books, including Norwegian papers. He complained that while he could receive bourgeois papers such as *Aftenposten* and *Dagbladet* regularly, he obtained foreign newspapers and *Arbeiderbladet* only once or twice a week.[23] He often listened to the radio, which was capable of receiving broadcasts from all over Europe. In one sense, however, it made life even less endurable because he now had to hear as well as read constant propaganda directed against him from Moscow, without being able to respond.[24]

Only when he had appointments in Oslo with his doctor or his dentist could he leave Sundby. He would be accompanied by his usual complement of guards, now in civilian attire. Jonas Lie was always present.[25] On one occasion, however, the police were outsmarted. Lyova asked Held to send flowers to Trotsky for his fifty-seventh birthday, on November 7. Having learned of his upcoming dental visit in early November, Held ordered a "huge" bouquet of roses, which was delivered to the dentist's office. The dentist's wife unpacked the flowers and presented them, along with a card which informed Trotsky that his friends were all well. The police reacted with consternation, but after consultation with Konstad's office they allowed Trotsky to keep the roses.[26]

---

* Most likely this individual, whom the police failed to apprehend, was a snooping journalist, but the possibility that he was a Russian agent cannot be ruled out entirely.

He visited his doctor due to the mysterious malady that had plagued him all his adult life. Although he informed his supporters when first interned that he was feeling well,[27] this did not last. Writing to his son in early October, Lev declared that his health had declined, with a significant change for the worse during the last two weeks.[28] But he never found a cure, or even a diagnosis, for this ever-recurring ailment.[29]

The atmosphere at Sundby no doubt influenced his condition. When he and Natalia first arrived, their stay "seemed like a rest cure" after the nervous exhaustion brought on by the Moscow trial and the hectic activity of their final days at Wexhall. Knudsen and his family were pleased that Lev and Natalia "under the circumstances are not living so badly."[30] It was good for them to be by themselves, without having to deal with constantly changing news, mail, telegrams, and telephone calls. However, with the arrival of the first newspapers, internment "became a torture."[31]

There was no way that Trotsky could respond to the bias directed against him. In a letter to Knudsen, he declared that the worst thing was the lack of assistance. Without a secretary and a typist, he found it impossible to work.[32] According to Held, both Trotsky and Puntervold appealed numerous times for permission to hire a typist. But all requests went unanswered.[33]

The weather during the fall did not improve the mood of the internees. It turned foggy and rainy, making them feel even more enclosed and isolated. Lev described the atmosphere in "the wooden house" as "half . . . occupied by slow-moving, heavy policemen who smoked pipes, played cards, and at noon brought us newspapers overflowing with slander."[34] Adding to their loneliness was their fear and uncertainty about the fate of their son, Sergei. The guards often heard Natalia wandering about in the dining room late at night, crying, and the maid, Aagot Sæthre, recalled that Trotsky's face one morning was red and swollen.*[35] He did not take out his frustration, however, on those around him. He maintained a cordial relationship with the guards and the staff. Sæthre remembered him as being calm, objective, and very correct, as well as friendly.[36]

His equanimity did not extend to the government. Testifying to the Dewey Commission in Mexico, he described Sundby as having been "a

---

* Aagot Sæthre, in later interviews, confused Sergei with his brother in Paris, believing that the Trotskys were grieving for Lyova. His death under mysterious circumstances did not occur, however, until February 1938, after the Trotskys had left Norway.

prison in every respect. We could not leave the house and the courtyard. We could not correspond, and we could not have visitors. It was worse than the Tsarist prison because in the Tsarist prison we had visits from friends and from my relatives. Here I had no visits at all. All correspondence passed through the police."[37]

This description, while on the whole correct, did contain certain exaggerations, omissions, and even inaccuracies. Trotsky dramatized to some extent the limitation he experienced at Sundby. Compared with the standards of a tsarist prison, he and Natalia certainly enjoyed greater comfort. Furthermore, he was not entirely isolated. He had regular visits from his Norwegian attorney, Puntervold. Trotsky's French legal counsel, Gerard Rosenthal, also was allowed to meet his client. After a period of waiting, he visited Sundby in early October.[38] And on one occasion even Walter Held managed to penetrate the government cordon when, in the guise of being a translator, he accompanied Puntervold to a meeting with Trotsky. However, Held's subsequent requests to return in the same capacity were brusquely denied.[39] Finally, as mentioned previously, Olav Scheflo on one occasion did receive permission to visit.

Similarly, Trotsky was not completely cut off from his supporters. He wrote shortly after the start of internment that it was incorrect for his "friends" to assume that they could not exchange letters with him. They could correspond "about everything," with the Moscow trial being the major exception. He stressed that "*control* does not mean *blockade*" (Trotsky's emphasis) and that censorship restrictions had been imposed solely for the purpose of preventing "*my* involvement in active politics" (Trotsky's emphasis).[40] Whereas he could not send out "political" letters, he had permission to receive all correspondence mailed to him. Furthermore, he could communicate with persons outside Norway. After having been censored by the Central Passport Office, his letters were forwarded to Puntervold, who mailed the originals after making copies that were kept in his office.[41]

As Trotsky perceived, censorship was primarily to prevent him from issuing **political** statements. This meant that anything in Russian was especially subject to scrutiny, which became apparent when he submitted three manuscripts of *The Revolution Betrayed* that he wanted to send to foreign publishers.[42] Since neither the Justice Department nor the Foreign Ministry had a translator/censor available, Foreign Minister Koht eventually suggested that Konstad employ an outside specialist.[43] Professor Olaf Broch thereupon received the assignment. He concluded that Trotsky had written nothing that could be considered illegal if the author had been Norwegian, nor was there anything in the text that had not previously appeared in print by detractors of Stalin. Although Broch did not express a personal opinion, nevertheless his tone showed that he did not believe the manuscripts should be suppressed.[44] Having also been advised that the book had already been published in other foreign languages, the Justice Department released the manuscripts in early November.[45] Trotsky, however, had not been told about this lengthy evaluation process. He assumed that the Passport Office was simply holding the manuscripts to frustrate him. He complained bitterly to Puntervold at the end of October that they had been detained for almost two months even though the book had been finished three months earlier, with English and French translations having been sent out of the country before his internment.[46]

Despite instances of major annoyance, he nevertheless recognized the need to cooperate with the authorities. His followers were advised to write always in a major European language, preferably German, so that mail might not be needlessly held up.[47] However, although he corresponded either in German or in French, most often with Lyova in Paris, this did not necessarily ensure smooth passage. The government remained vigilant to prevent the spread of controversial viewpoints. Trotsky complained indignantly that there were no hard and fast rules concerning censorship.[48] He sent out several appeals for international support through Puntervold and Rosenthal,[49] but they were regularly returned with the message that the Central Passport Office was unable to forward them.[50]

Trotsky personally held Konstad responsible for blocking his mailings and developed a strong grudge against him, like that he held for Trygve Lie. Lev regularly referred to Konstad as a "fascist,"[51] a term used also by the official's other detractors during the 1930s. But while Konstad during World War II belonged to National Union and served on Quisling's Nazified Supreme Court, during Trotsky's internment he outwardly maintained the pose of a nonpartisan civil servant. Furthermore, as has been seen, it was the Justice Department, not Konstad, that had ultimate authority over censoring Trotsky's mail.

The department also used its power to prevent him from having contact with outsiders who might relay information detrimental to Norwegian interests. This was shown in the incident involving a well-known

Canadian-American writer, Charles Yale Harrison. He arrived in Oslo in mid-September to gather material "for an impressionistic book on Leon Trotsky."[52] Although Koht, whom Harrison initially contacted, recommended that he be allowed to interview Trotsky with certain restrictions,[53] the Justice Department disagreed. Minister of Social Affairs Kornelius Bergsvik, who served briefly as acting minister of justice during Trygve Lie's absence, already on the next day, September 21, rejected Harrison's application "in consideration of the consequences."[54]

Harrison took the denial very hard, going so far as to complain to *Arbeiderbladet*. But he directed his grievance toward the head of the Central Passport Office. Bergsvik apparently had first referred Harrison to Konstad, and the latter refused access to Trotsky. According to the author, Konstad had also said that, in the Trotsky affair, "I am a fascist" who derived pleasure from censoring Trotsky's correspondence, newspapers, and books.[55] Konstad in turn maintained that Harrison's accusations were "gross lies." *Arbeiderbladet*, which regarded the former with distaste, nevertheless felt compelled in this instance to concede grudgingly that Konstad had not expressed himself as Harrison alleged.[56]

The government's determination to limit access to Trotsky similarly served as a barrier against all who sought to obtain his release, or who simply wanted to milden the restrictions against him. His backers in turn made an effort to marshal pressure against the government. Young Walter Held as usual threw himself energetically into the fray, urging well-known personalities, workers' organizations, and other prominent groups from abroad to protest against "the scandalous course of action" followed by the Norwegian officials. In Norway, Held maintained, sympathizers such as Olav Scheflo would publicize these protests.[57]

As a result of both organized campaigns by Trotsky's followers and independent, spontaneous reactions, the government received numerous letters and telegrams from outside the country during the fall of 1936, opposing the treatment of Trotsky.[58] To cite but one example, a protest meeting in Paris at the beginning of September succeeded in gaining "significant attendance," according to a note from the Norwegian legation.[59]

Håkon Meyer similarly engaged himself fully in attempting to mobilize opinion. Through his international contacts, he arranged for the publication of two critical articles by major leaders of the Labor and Socialist

International: Friedrich Adler, its president, and Louis de Brouckere, its secretary. Adler maintained that Moscow's charges amounted to a "witch trial" conducted in order to deprive Trotsky of his asylum. Brouckere strongly decried how the denial of rights for political refugees had become general in Europe.[60] These views appeared in *Kamp og kultur* (Struggle and Culture), a new socialist monthly devoted to literature and politics that had been founded in Oslo in 1935. Meyer exercised significant influence on the journal's contents while serving on its editorial board.[61]

He, along with Scheflo and Knudsen, also wrote negative commentaries concerning the internment of Trotsky.[62] Another active member of the small band of supporters who rallied behind him was Jeanette Olsen, formerly prominent in both the Labor and Communist parties. She published in the fall an appeal that called for Trotsky's release and for him to be granted full rights to defend himself.[63] But such efforts by Trotsky's limited number of sympathizers within Norway bore no fruit. As for the protests from abroad, they were largely ignored. *Arbeiderbladet* concluded that members of the Norwegian labor movement had no interest in them.[64] It similarly refused to make space available for Held, who wrote numerous articles in the vain hope of arousing sympathy for Trotsky within the party.[65] He also tried to get around *Arbeiderbladet*'s blockade by urging foreign backers to send protests to other media outlets, such as the Norwegian Telegraph Bureau and *Dagbladet*, as well as to newspapers that were friendly toward Trotsky, like Scheflo's *Sørlandet*.[66] But there is no evidence that these endeavors had any success.

Efforts were also made by Norwegian sympathizers to appeal directly to the government. Håkon Meyer was especially active. He had been out of the country from August 1 to September 7, when the entire Trotsky controversy in the summer of 1936 had run its course, from the NS break-in to internment. Back home, Meyer immediately sent a request to acting Minister of Justice Bergsvik on September 9, asking to visit the Trotskys. At the time this did not seem entirely unrealistic since Scheflo had just recently been allowed to pay such a call.

Bergsvik, however, urged Meyer to drop the matter. The latter wrote instead to the prime minister, asking him to intercede. Meyer did not pull any punches. Although he pointed out that he disagreed with Trotsky politically and that he was aware of the disruptive role the latter played in international socialist politics, Meyer insisted that Trotsky inspired the labor movement in Europe and America with revolutionary fervor. Meyer reminded Nygaardsvold that Trotsky's internment had created "a storm of indignation" within the international labor movement's "more radical circles." When he now wished to visit the "concentration camp" housing Trotsky and his wife, it was not to pay a social call but rather to place himself at Trotsky's disposal. Meyer also made it clear that he wanted to go to Sundby frequently, not just once.[67]

Considering its tone, it is little wonder that his demand was rejected. Nygaardsvold wrote a personal reply in which he held Trotsky responsible for forcing the government to act. The prime minister emotionally declared that Trotsky could have avoided internment if he had only kept his word and not involved himself in politics. Instead, he had sought to make fools of the government, which had made the prime minister "furious." And since Trotsky had refused to sign the government's new restrictions, then he deserved nothing better. But despite Nygaardsvold's rejection, he did not want to break personally with Meyer and invited him to supper in the next week.[68]

Konrad Knudsen followed a more circumspect approach. On Saturday, September 12, he went to Storsand, having first phoned the Central Passport Office and Bergsvik, who agreed to relay his request to the prime minister.[69] Knudsen actually got as far as the courtyard before being stopped. He was only allowed to hand over flowers for the Trotskys, which the police promised to deliver.[70]

Despite Nygaardsvold's attempt to dissuade him, Meyer continued to pursue the issue aggressively. He next joined Scheflo in drawing up a letter to the Labor Party's Central Committee that contained significant criticism of the internment,[71] and he had no difficulty in also persuading Knudsen to attach his signature.[72] Their joint letter was forwarded on September 30. The trio pointed out that the government's treatment of Trotsky had created "horror within the international labor movement." To alleviate this, they referred to a number of ways that his situation could be improved. Specifically, they asked that Trotsky be allowed to receive uncensored reading material; that control of his correspondence be made less rigorous and that Konstad be removed in favor of someone "better suited"; that the number of guards under the "reactionary" Jonas Lie be reduced; that the Trotskys be allowed visits; and that he be permitted assistance with his writings. The Central Committee was requested to "maintain the party's best traditions" by using its influence to obtain needed changes in Trotsky's internment.

Although worded far more diplomatically than Meyer's previous communications, the endeavor failed. Party leaders had no interest in challenging the government's authority.[73] But the issue would not die. The attempt by Trotsky's small band of Norwegian sympathizers to alleviate his plight became a crusade. Because of the standing that he still enjoyed within the Labor Party, although considerably reduced, Meyer in particular was the driving force in this endeavor. Two weeks after his previous request was denied, Meyer again sought to visit Sundby, sending his application to Trygve Lie, now back in charge of the Justice Department. Indicating the importance he attached to his request, Meyer sent a copy to Nygaardsvold.[74]

He enjoyed no more success than previously. But during the fall he and Trotsky were in close written communication. The latter understandably was grateful for Meyer's efforts and sent him the new American edition of his *History of the Russian Revolution*. In the accompanying letter of October 17, Lev commented on how he had reason to feel grateful that he had finished his book while in "backward Turkey" because had he been in "a modern democratic country . . . ruled by a socialist party [Norway]," this would have been impossible. He also compared his isolation at Sundby with "the good old days" before 1914 when he could receive many visitors while imprisoned, unlike what he was experiencing now in a "modern democracy, which is too delicate to allow internees to have visitors."

He went on to ask whether Meyer could send him a "*German* translation" (Trotsky's emphasis) of Ibsen, declaring that the playwright had been "one of my greatest literary loves" when he was young.[75] Meyer immediately forwarded the desired volume. Considering Trotsky's current predicament, it was no coincidence that the first play to catch his attention was *Pillars of Society*.* He appreciated the irony, writing to Meyer on October 22: "We should study and study again the best way to shore up society." He also expressed interest in an article by Meyer in *Kamp og kultur* and asked for a copy. Lev stated that while he was making "some efforts" to learn Norwegian, he found his results "still hopeless."[76] Nevertheless, he had no difficulty in deciphering most of the newspapers that he perused daily.[77]

Meyer in the interim energetically continued his quest. He now shifted tactics, writing to Oscar Torp, chairman of the Labor Party, pointing out

---

* Henrik Ibsen's 1877 play deals with moral decay within the top level of society in a small Norwegian coastal town.

that Trotsky wished to contact several international socialist organizations about establishing a commission to look into the validity of the Moscow trial. Meyer requested as a member of the party's International Committee that a written communication be sent to the organizations in question, informing them of Trotsky's desire.[78]

In spite of the generally good relations he enjoyed with Torp, Meyer received the negative response that he invariably was greeted with.[79] He was not surprised, being aware of the party's wish to play down the issue during the election campaign, as shown on October 20 when he wrote to Trotsky, suggesting that a visit might be possible now that the election was over.[80]

Meyer wrote again to Sundby four days later, indicating that he intended to seek to present a program about Trotsky on the radio.[81] But he had reason to feel pessimistic concerning his chances. He had earlier, in September, failed to have the controversy over Trotsky debated in the Oslo Workers Association.[82] Nevertheless, he sent his proposal to NRK, the Norwegian Broadcasting System. He very carefully stayed away from any direct mention of the internment. But while he worded his application tactfully, he could not resist observing ironically that he had earlier given a radio lecture on Stalin that had not created "difficulties."[83] The topic of Trotsky, however, had nothing to do with objectivity and everything to do with politics. The head of NRK replied personally to Meyer, expressing regret that the radio service* did not "have the possibility of making room for the lecture."[84]

In addition to such attempts to rally internal and foreign opinion, to improve the conditions under which Trotsky lived, and to gain access to him, his supporters, as well as he himself, initially placed major emphasis on using the legal system to regain attention, allowing him to repudiate the charges from the show trial. In this effort, a great deal depended on Michael Puntervold.

The attorney was at the end of a long and at times controversial career when he became Trotsky's legal counselor. Born in 1879, he grew up in Horten, the site of Norway's major naval base, where his father was a career naval officer. Puntervold, however, early abandoned a military career in favor of teaching, journalism, and eventually the law, having

---

* NRK at the time had a monopoly on broadcasting radio programs.

been attracted to socialism at the beginning of the twentieth century. He gained a reputation as a radical firebrand within the labor movement, in particular for his antimilitary viewpoint. Having been employed by *Social Demokraten*, he abandoned journalism in 1910, opening his own law practice.[85] Both before and afterwards, he served as attorney for a number of unions as well as the National Federation of Unions, L.O. When handling cases for L.O., he at times worked with another lawyer, seventeen years younger, the ambitious Trygve Lie, who acted as L. O.'s legal consultant.[86]

As the Labor Party increasingly became radicalized under Tranmæl, Puntervold belonged to the right wing of the party. When it split in 1921, he was one of the leaders of the new Social Democratic Party, becoming its vice-chairman. However, in the years afterward he gradually abandoned politics.[87]

Although he at one time had sympathized with the Russian revolutionary movement, he felt no ideological empathy with Trotsky. Monetary gain was the sole reason why he agreed to serve. Held complained that Puntervold had requested a sum of 15,000 kroner for the entire case, which Trotsky's young disciple correctly said was "hair-raising," based on the standard Norwegian fee structure of the 1930s.[88] Held did depict Puntervold as having been "one of the best attorneys in the country five—six years ago." This was an accurate assessment. Puntervold had acted as Roald Amundsen's attorney at the time of the great explorer's death in 1928. His financial affairs were in a sorry mess, leaving behind an estate that in reality was bankrupt. But Puntervold within a year succeeded in "eliminating the bankruptcy while providing full compensation to all creditors."[89]

His status had changed significantly, however, by the fall of 1936. Although he originally had recommended Puntervold, Scheflo informed Held early in September that the attorney was an alcoholic. But, unable to suggest a replacement, Scheflo added that he did not doubt Puntervold's ability.[90] Trotsky's backers, however, became increasingly more critical. Held later wrote directly to Sundby, declaring that he had been informed by "respectable citizens" that Puntervold had developed a drinking problem, causing him to neglect his practice.[91] Other sources would similarly warn of his failings, including Erling Falk, who described Puntervold as "an old conservative social-democrat, and I imagine that he is rather objectionable in some other respects also."[92]

Trotsky's case nevertheless seemed at first to get off to a positive start. As promised, Puntervold in early September provided the press with legal justification for why he had advised his client to sue the editors of communist and N.S. newspapers for libel. Puntervold argued that since the U.S.S.R. had not formally requested Trotsky's extradition, then his only alternative was to initiate legal action to prove the Soviet accusations invalid.[93] In an interview with *Arbeiderbladet* on September 3, Puntervold similarly insisted that Trotsky must have the right to defend himself against attacks within Norway. Puntervold declared his intent to have a formal complaint ready within the next few days, to be presented at the required preliminary hearing.[94]

Arbeiderbladet came to the not surprising conclusion that such a hearing would create significant notoriety and asked Attorney General Sund to comment. He carefully replied that while "under ordinary circumstances" a foreigner had exactly the same right as a citizen to initiate a libel case, in this instance it would be up to the government to determine whether or not Trotsky's action would violate "rules and obligations" that had previously been established.[95]

The latter at first did not anticipate any obstacles. He wrote to Lyova, asking him to collect evidence for Puntervold's use. Trotsky advised against a parallel lawsuit in France to refute Moscow's charges that Lyova had been involved in terrorist activity along with his father. Instead, Trotsky urged his son to appear as a witness in Oslo, because, as Lev naively put it, one could expect "more objectivity from a Norwegian court than from a French [court]."[96] Lyova fully agreed. He wrote on September 12 that he had been in touch with Gerard Rosenthal, who had already left for Oslo in order to coordinate the effort to an even greater degree.[97] He intended to establish contact with both Puntervold and Trotsky while in Norway.

In preparation for the trial, father and son exchanged information, pointing out the inconsistencies and inaccuracies in witness testimony, as well as in the prosecutor's arguments, during the show trial. Both Trotsky and Lyova eagerly anticipated refuting these slanders.[98] Puntervold informed Trotsky of his readiness to accept all data that foreign "friends" could supply. The attorney's office thereupon became a clearinghouse both for material sent to Norway, as well as for requests sent to Trotsky's supporters abroad for specific information for the trial.[99] When Rosenthal arrived from Paris, he and Puntervold held strategy discussions about the upcoming legal process.[100]

Although Puntervold thereby became fully engaged, nevertheless his relationship with Trotsky and his backers began to sour. Recriminations were made by both sides, resulting in a decidedly negative atmosphere.

Part of this was due to personality conflicts and philosophical differences, coupled with quarrels over money, but of major importance was the growing realization by everyone concerned that their hopes of having a courtroom trial had been misplaced.

The initial setback that Trotsky experienced occurred when he sent Puntervold on September 15 a detailed typewritten commentary on the exchange of diplomatic notes between the Soviet and Norwegian governments. Considering the effort that he put into it, he obviously believed that making the statement public would constitute a major success. In his account he concluded that the Soviet government had not demanded his extradition because it lacked proof to support its infamous charges. The accusations against Lyova, Trotsky argued, were equally false. If they were true, why had not the Soviet government also protested to France (where his son lived)? The answer was that France, as opposed to Norway, was a strong country that could not be bullied diplomatically. Trotsky further emphasized that his internment was not due to alleged "'terroristic' activity," but because he as "an author is writing *in the spirit of the Fourth International*" (Trotsky's emphasis), being true to his ideological convictions.[101]

The Central Passport Office, however, refused to permit Puntervold to publicize the commentary, and when the attorney appealed, the government upheld the denial. He could therefore only report this negative outcome in a letter to Trotsky on October 6, along with news that the statement also could not be sent to Lyova—who would have publicized it in France.[102] Trotsky's attempt to reach world opinion had thereby been effectively thwarted.

Puntervold also informed Sundby about how he had repeatedly inquired with the Central Passport Office concerning the fate of Trotsky's manuscripts, having emphasized to Konstad how "economically important" it was to have them forwarded to publishers in Prague and Paris. Puntervold had good reason for wanting to increase Trotsky's earning power. The attorney clearly had concluded that he was not benefiting financially from his legal assignment. He complained that he had not received the retainer Trotsky had promised during their initial conference, having only been paid a smaller amount in several installments. He further deplored being forced to neglect other clients while engaged with Trotsky's case.

He also insisted he had ably looked after Trotsky's interests as much as time allowed. In his letter of October 6, he pointed out that he had just delivered his complaint (*forliksklage*) to the Conciliation Board. He defended the delay in filing legal papers on the grounds that the editor of *Arbeideren* had only now returned to Oslo, and Puntervold wanted to include both him as well as the editor of *Fritt Folk* in the preliminary complaint. In the conclusion of his message, Puntervold added sardonically that he was tired of being advised about how to proceed because in the end he was the one to decide what legal action to follow.[103]

Held especially showered Puntervold with unwanted advice. Relations between the radical young Trotskyite and the middle-aged social-democratic attorney were at times contentious. Held drew up a list of complaints on October 7, stating that Puntervold had deliberately neglected the case because he had not received an anticipated retainer of 5,000 kroner. But Held was quick to point out that Puntervold had personally obtained 1000 kroner from Trotsky directly and that the attorney could expect additional payments.[104] Trotsky's defender Håkon Meyer would later similarly levy a standard accusation by Trotsky's backers—that Puntervold had delayed taking initial action in the case for six weeks, while pressing Trotsky to pay "large advances" amounting to approximately 2000 kroner.[105] Held consulted Meyer and Scheflo, and they agreed that "continued cooperation with *herr* Puntervold" would be a large monetary drain.[106]

Held, however, failed to find a replacement. This forced him to refrain from mailing his devastating critique of Puntervold to Sundby.[107] Nevertheless, two days later Held did send a letter in which he, somewhat more moderately, fully informed Trotsky of Puntervold's inadequacies, including his drinking problem.[108] This critical assessment did nothing to improve Trotsky's attitude. Not only had Puntervold failed to provide much positive news in his letters to Sundby, but he visited Trotsky only infrequently. Scheduled appointments were repeatedly postponed, and Trotsky therefore concluded that the Central Passport Office was preventing Puntervold from meeting his client. This caused Puntervold to send an assurance on October 17, explaining that other legal obligations had prevented him from coming that week. But he held out the possibility of soon having more time for Trotsky's "previously begun case," and he promised a visit on Wednesday, October 21.[109]

For once the meeting took place on time, but it was hardly successful. Trotsky was not assuaged by Puntervold's insistence that he had not been hindered by the police. Trotsky was frustrated over how his internment was progressing, with far greater limitations having been imposed than he had anticipated, and he resented how Puntervold accepted with little opposition the restrictive rules and regulations of the Justice Department and the Central Passport Office. Trotsky gave full expression to his anger, accusing Puntervold of acting as "Konstad's and Trygve Lie's attorney."[110]

Not only did he make this wounding remark directly, but he repeated it in writing on the same day. But what could very well have led to an open break was negated by the fact that Puntervold was in considerable financial straits. He needed Trotsky as much as the latter needed him.[111] Trotsky's legal representation therefore remained unchanged.

In addition to being concerned about the slow progress of his legal case, Trotsky was engaged in other matters as well during the first two months of his internment. One of his main priorities was to stay in touch with his international followers, whom he had assigned a crucial role in his anticipated showdown with "the Stalinists." Being firmly convinced that Stalin had made a major error in conducting the show trial, Trotsky from the beginning of his internment planned to have his movement assist in compiling documents that could be used to refute Moscow's accusations, even though he might be "removed from political life for an indefinite period."[112]

He was convinced that the most effective way to disprove the allegations was to show the numerous errors that had been made in the trial. He therefore sent a list of facts to Lyova on October 12, asking him to provide each point with supporting evidence.[113] The list dealt specifically with Trotsky's visit to Copenhagen in 1932, which was not surprising because, according to Moscow, this was when he and his son had conspired to murder Stalin in meetings with a large number of conspirators, including several of the NKVD "witnesses" planted in the trial.[114] Not only did Trotsky intend to show that the alleged discussions had not occurred but that Lyova had not come to Copenhagen at all.[115] Disproving such allegations by the incompetent NKVD officials who had scripted the trial would later prove to be not too difficult. The absurdity of many of the claims was obvious—except for those who were blinded by pro-Stalinist or anti-Trotsky feelings. For example, one of the accused in the trial, E. S. Holtzman, testified to having conspired with Lev Sedov at a Copenhagen hotel that had been torn down fifteen years earlier.[116]

Although, as shown, Trotsky initially believed that Moscow's accusations could best be disproved in a Norwegian court, by the beginning of October he had clearly begun to reconsider. In a letter to Lyova, he declared that it might indeed be a good idea to start legal action in Prague because in Norway "things are going *very* slowly" (Trotsky's emphasis).[117]

In sympathy with his plight, his followers exerted themselves. Legal procedures were initiated in Czechoslovakia and Switzerland.[118] And in Paris, as could be expected, Lyova and Rosenthal took the lead, forming a Committee for the Investigation of the Moscow Trial. This was simply an extension of their earlier campaign to call attention to the treatment of political prisoners in the U.S.S.R. In addition to consisting of a core of dedicated Trotskyites, this coterie also attracted some noncommunist leftist intellectuals, including André Breton and Victor Serge. Beyond Paris similar work was carried out on a much more limited basis in certain major French cities.[119]

Denmark's small group of Trotskyites was also quite active. Its members helped organize a petition, presented to the Russian embassy, that called for an international committee to investigate the Moscow trial. It gained the signatures of approximately thirty intellectuals and union members.[120] Although the Danish Trotskyites did not have a newspaper, they were nevertheless successful in publicizing counterarguments to disprove communist charges. It was through their efforts, for example, that the socialist *Social-Demokraten* quickly informed readers that the Hotel Bristol, where Lev Sedov allegedly had plotted against Stalin, had been torn down in 1917. Not until after five months of silence did the Danish communists unconvincingly try to show that Lyova had been in Copenhagen after all but had supposedly stayed at a hotel that lay immediately adjacent to a café that bore the incriminating name "Bristol."[121]

Across the Atlantic an effort was also made in Trotsky's support. Trotskyites within the Socialist Party organized a committee for his defense.[122] Sharing a widespread American trait, they were adept at fund raising, sending some $1,250.00 to Paris for their leader's legal defense. Their British cousins, in comparison, managed to collect only £50.[123]

At the same time, Trotsky also exerted himself in favor of an investigatory commission. Although his direct appeals had been blocked, there was nothing to prevent his attorneys from doing so. Consequently, Puntervold sent letters to the Administrative Committee of the International Federation of Trade Unions in Amsterdam, the Secretariat of the Labor and Socialist International in Geneva, and the Secretariat of the International Bureau of Revolutionary Socialist Parties in London.[124] Trotsky similarly directed Gerard Rosenthal to send letters to these socialist organizations, urging an inquiry.[125] None of the groups, however, agreed to take action.

Not until 1937, during his stay in Mexico, did Trotsky succeed in having a commission investigate Moscow's accusations. Although headed by John Dewey, the distinguished American philosopher and educator, it did not enjoy the official backing of any leading international organization.

Trotsky sought any public forum that might allow light to be shed on the falsity of Moscow's charges. Puntervold therefore forwarded an appeal to the League of Nations. He argued that since the League was considering setting up a permanent tribunal against terrorists, it was "self-evident" that it should also protect persons who had "false accusations of terrorism" brought against them "for purely political reasons."[126] The League secretariat eventually sent a polite acknowledgement, which Puntervold released to the press.[127] Although Trotsky would later, in 1938, address a similar request to Geneva, he again experienced no better success.[128]

Despite gaining no noteworthy victories, committed Trotskyites maintained the optimistic viewpoint that they would eventually prevail. Their devotion was admirable. With his father interned, his thirty-year-old son ambitiously attempted to exercise control over Trotsky's scattered movement to an even greater degree than before as head of the ICL Secretariat. But Lyova complained in early September that this effort lacked coordination. He only haphazardly received delayed news from "friends" about what was transpiring in their countries.[129]

But at the same time, of necessity, he became even more focused on developments in France. Lyova, as noted, worked closely with Rosenthal in trying to form a legal strategy in support of Trotsky. In the first instance this involved a special commission established by the French League for the Rights of Man to investigate the charges from the Moscow trial.

The commission began its proceedings by receiving a report from its judicial committee, written by its head, Raymond Rosenmark, who uncritically accepted the Russian court's premises, placing emphasis on the fact that all the defendants had confessed their crimes.[130] This implied that the prosecution's denunciations of Trotsky must have been equally valid. The commission tentatively accepted Rosenmark's view, causing Lyova to complain that it was entirely "in the hands of the Stalinists." Nevertheless, the investigation had not yet reached a definitive conclusion, and he hoped somewhat inconsistently to be able to influence its outcome.[131]

During October, however, he and his small group of helpers within the secretariat were primarily preoccupied with the publication of his personal repudiation of Moscow's indictments. Written initially in Russian, it was published as a lengthy article in the *Bulletin of the Opposition*. Subsequently Lyova and his assistants translated it, in the form of a large brochure, into French and German.[132] The French edition, entitled the *Red Book on the Moscow Trial* (Livre rouge sur le procès de Moscou) received considerable attention. Rosenthal later described it as the "most important refutation of the lies from Moscow."[133] It clearly rebuked the accusation that Lyova had conspired in Copenhagen. Not only did the Hotel Bristol not exist, but his passport showed that he had never visited Denmark, and his university records indicated that he had been taking an examination in Berlin at the time he allegedly had been in the Danish capital.[134]

Upon the *Red Book*'s completion, Lyova proudly announced that he had become an "author" like his father, and he frequently used the term about himself in their correspondence. Work on the translation, however, required a great effort. Consequently, Lyova and his "friends" neglected compiling the information that Trotsky wished to utilize in the great investigatory commission on which he pinned his hopes. In reaction, while generally approving his son's article,[135] he did not hesitate to complain that far more important work was being ignored.[136]

The "author" admitted that, while it was true that information gathering in Paris was proceeding "very slowly," he nevertheless justified the secretariat's work on the article and its translations. His organization had been under great pressure to publish a brochure refuting Moscow's accusations, in particular since the French communists had taunted the Trotskyites that, by not replying, they simply confirmed the validity of the charges. However, Lyova promised that once the secretariat finished the translation, they would resume their investigative work with "full energy."[137]

This pledge proved to have little significance. With the advantage of hindsight, it is clear that the limited resources, both human and monetary, that Trotsky and his followers had made it difficult, if not impossible, for them to gain more than transitory triumphs. Even if Lyova and the French Trotskyites had concentrated all of their efforts on gathering evidence, the results would scarcely have been more successful. The defense of Trotsky was drowned out by Soviet propaganda, which was repeated not only by communist parties throughout the world but spread still further by their many front organizations—the "friends of the Soviet Union" that existed in various guises.[138]

Communist pressure hobbled Trotskyite endeavors in other ways as well. In Switzerland and Czechoslovakia, Stalin's adherents used pressure and intimidation to frighten away several prominent attorneys who originally had agreed to serve Trotsky.[139] In the nerve center of Trotskyite activity—France—it also proved impossible to obtain legal support beyond that provided by dedicated followers such as Rosenthal. Although several leading attorneys were initially sympathetically inclined toward Trotsky, the political situation in France during the Popular Front period made it simply impossible for top legal practitioners to take up the cause of the unpopular exile. They were even unwilling to present arguments before the League for the Rights of Man's commission.[140]

Although activity on behalf of Trotsky continued unabated in the next months, by the end of October 1936 it had already become clear that this effort would not achieve the results that had been hoped for immediately after the show trial. Internationally his followers had to deal with not merely the hostility of communists and their sympathizers, but with a significant number of noncommunist leftists—socialists and radical liberals—who were friendly toward the Soviet Union. Some of these had become so alienated by previous Trotskyite tactics that they found it difficult to reject, at least initially, the trial's preposterous accusations. With more conservative nonsocialists, Trotsky's person remained anathema. A breakthrough for his cause therefore continued to be out of reach. And in Norway his situation did not improve.

Trotsky was still of some concern for Koht's foreign policy. The need to maintain friendly relations with the Soviet Union remained paramount. News from Moscow was therefore positive, from the Foreign Ministry's perspective, when Minister Urbye reported that he had received an extremely friendly welcome from the new head of the department for Scandinavian affairs in the Soviet foreign ministry. Urbye noted the latter had displayed no trace of "ill will concerning the Trotsky matter." Urbye had therefore been able to say, without fear of contradiction during their meeting, that the Trotsky issue "now was finished."[141]

Even though Trotsky was confined behind barbed wire, to the Kremlin's satisfaction, the Norwegian government still continued its vigorous search for news about his former political activity. It exchanged information with other governments, who were equally interested in gaining confidential intelligence about what Trotsky and his followers had been planning. For example, the Justice Department allowed the French minister to view documents "concerning Leon Trotsky's activity"—papers that undoubtedly pertained more to Paris than to Oslo. The diplomat was grateful, expressing thanks "for having had the opportunity of becoming acquainted" with the documents' contents.[142]

During his internment, however, the greatest notoriety created as a result of Trotsky's alleged revolutionary activity concerned France's immediate neighbor, Belgium. Because of deteriorating economic conditions during the Great Depression, resulting in significant unemployment, the country experienced strikes and political unrest simultaneously with the labor disturbances across the border that reached their peak when the Popular Front government swept into office. In the uneasy atmosphere created by such disorder, conspiracy theories were bound to flourish, as shown in newspaper headlines when Belgian authorities on September 19 raided the domiciles of a number of persons with ties to Trotsky. These included Georges Vereecken, who had been involved in strike activity, and Walter Dauge, another leading Belgian Trotskyite. Trotsky had corresponded with the two both before and during his exile in Norway. Consequently, newspapers in Belgium accused him not only of advising his Belgian followers but also of recommending the formation of armed insurrectionary groups.[143]

Although press reports and Norwegian diplomatic representatives in the Low Countries alerted the Foreign Ministry,[144] there was no reaction in Oslo until October 7, when Attorney General Sund recommended that the Justice Department should consider obtaining intelligence, including copies of incriminating correspondence, through diplomatic contacts. Trygve Lie agreed, and on October 13 he forwarded Sund's request to the Foreign Ministry.[145] Koht in turn sent this on to his minister in Brussels.[146]

Diplomatic bureaucracy worked slowly during the 1930s, in particular since the Belgians did not give the request high priority. In the meantime the question of Trotsky's alleged revolutionary agitation had already been thoroughly aired in the Norwegian press. In a headline on September 23, *Tidens Tegn* accused Trotsky of personally having "stimulated the revolutionary movement in Belgium" by ordering it to establish "special armed groups." A careful reading of the article, however, simply showed that Trotsky had mainly corresponded with Vereecken and Dauge about establishing a new political party. Although *Tidens Tegn* portrayed this as being "Machiavellian in character," it was hardly the type of revolutionary activity proclaimed in the headline.[147]

Furthermore, Trotsky for once was not silenced. He succeeded in having Puntervold issue a press release in which the charges were effectively refuted. Trotsky pointed out that he had discussed with Belgian socialists the need to create unity within their labor movement long before he came to Norway. He also tellingly observed that Dauge had written to him by addressing letters via the Central Passport Office. Was this an effective procedure to follow, Trotsky asked, if he and Dauge were really plotting "a secret uprising against the Belgian government?"[148]

When the Belgian foreign ministry finally, in early November, supplied Norwegian officials with the desired intelligence, it simply confirmed in large part Trotsky's previous denial. Although Vereecken and Dauge, as members of the "revolutionary group" Action Socialiste Revolutionaire, had "exchanged a number of letters with Trotsky," these had not been incriminating, as shown by the fact that they were not confiscated.[149] While this outcome proved disappointing to the Justice Department, the incident illustrated that the government would continue to monitor Trotsky in the hope of finding evidence to justify its policy against him.

At Sundby, Lev faced still another difficulty. During a time when he could work least effectively, he was more than ever in need of funds. Not merely were his personal expenses greater than what he and Natalia had earlier spent at Wexhall, but more importantly, the legal process that he had set in motion was costing him a significant sum of money.[150] With no secretary and typist, and with writing being his major source of income, he found himself in the weak position of having to negotiate new contracts for books he had already completed.

One such possibility involved publishing his autobiography in Sweden. In the fall Kolbjørn Fjeld discovered a potential publisher in Stockholm, Natur och Kultur. However, it offered quite a small royalty.[151] Trotsky initially asked Tiden to obtain a higher percentage, but the Swedish publisher refused to increase its bid.[152] Faced with not earning anything from Sweden, there was no realistic alternative. Trotsky approved the contract in December, and Natur och Kultur published the book some months later.[153]

When it came to publications in the United States and Great Britain, Trotsky employed the services of his son—yet another responsibility for the overburdened Lyova. Trotsky instructed him on September 5 to conclude agreements with American and English publishers "as soon as possible."[154]

Relations with publishing houses in the United States and England, however, were rather strained at the time, brought on in part by Trotsky's use of different firms, no doubt based on an ill-disguised capitalist desire to receive the highest possible royalties. Consequently, in the United States his autobiography had been published by C. Scribner's Sons (1930), his *History of the Russian Revolution* bore the imprimatur of Simon and Schuster (1st ed., 1932), and he had received an advance from Doubleday, Doran and Co. to write the biography of Lenin. However, while in Norway he had dropped all work on the biography in order to write his strong critique of Stalin, *The Revolution Betrayed*. This naturally created resentment within the offices of Doubleday, which expected Trotsky to fulfill his contract.[155]

Compounding his difficulties was his relationship with his translator, Max Eastman, a prominent writer and journalist in leftist New York circles. Eastman had originally been a dedicated Trotskyite, serving for a time as Trotsky's biographer and literary agent as well as translator, but he became disillusioned with Trotsky in the early 1930s.[156] By 1936 Eastman had earned approximately $4000.00 from Trotsky—rather good pay for a humble translator, but he was by no means humble.[157]

By focusing all his attention on *The Revolution Betrayed*, Trotsky jeopardized his contract for the Lenin biography, which he desperately sought to avoid. Furthermore, Eastman had earlier written to Doubleday, insisting that there was no hope that Trotsky would ever finish the biography. When he learned of this betrayal, Trotsky asked whether Eastman was seeking "to appease his ill feeling toward me."[158]

Despite Eastman's negative, but accurate, assessment, Doubleday agreed to publish *The Revolution Betrayed*, with none other than Eastman as translator. Lev Sedov received instructions from Sundby at the end of September that rights to the book had been transferred to Trotsky's editor at Doubleday. Furthermore, another edition was scheduled to appear in England.[159] Sedov had refrained from signing a contract because of uncertainty over who would pay for the translation. But once Trotsky insisted that the English publisher should have "free hands" to decide whether or not to use Eastman's translation, then Lyova obediently signed the contract.[160]

The publication of this edition did not, however, proceed smoothly. Trotsky had great difficulty collecting royalties from London, which he rather unfairly held Lyova responsible for, considering how he had urged his son to sign the contract as soon as possible.[161] Furthermore, because of his literary reputation and excellent style, Max Eastman enjoyed a near monopoly in translating Trotsky's works from Russian to English. But Eastman carried out his work when and how he pleased. This prevented serialization of *The Revolution Betrayed*, which deprived Trotsky of added income.[162] Someone should tell Eastman, Trotsky later wrote, "that his elementary duty is to [set] me free."[163] His wish was not fulfilled. Long after the assassination in 1940, Eastman remained Trotsky's translator.*

Not all financial matters, however, proved negative for Lev during the fall of 1936. His loyal agent in the United States, Sara Weber, forwarded $1900.00 in October,[164] which was a significant sum of money. However, as the future would show, he would have more than enough expenses during the remainder of his stay in Norway, seriously depleting his resources.

One related issue began to become an item of concern at the very time he received his royalty payment. Norderhov County's tax office made an initial inquiry concerning his earnings and the amount of tax he had paid when he lived at Wexhall. Puntervold attempted to postpone this issue, while assuring Trotsky that it was a trifling matter.[165] The latter would learn, however, that when it came to paying income tax in Norway, the question was anything but trivial.

More immediate than this future problem was Trotsky's reemergence as a controversial subject as the election campaign of 1936 drew to a close. For a brief time after his internment had been thoroughly digested, the press, as noted, paid limited attention to him during the first half of September. Even *Arbeiderbladet* felt secure enough to publish an article by Johan Scharffenberg on September 4 that strongly championed the right of asylum holders to have freedom of speech, which he proclaimed was the lifeblood of democracy. While Scharffenberg did not directly appeal for Trotsky's release, this could be implied.[166]

But as the election drew nearer, blatant partisanship again became the order of the day. The bourgeois parties used every possible issue against the Labor Party in the final phase of campaigning, among which Trotsky's continued presence in Norway featured prominently. From the second half of September through the day of the election, October 19, his name

---

* *The Young Lenin*, with Max Eastman as its translator, was published by Doubleday after Trotsky's death, in 1972. Later editions and reprints of a number of Trotsky's books similarly list Eastman as their translator.

repeatedly graced the headlines of the nonsocialist press. When news of his connection with Trotskyites in Belgium became known, *Tidens Tegn* immediately declared that Trotsky had encouraged his followers to organize revolutionary strikes, form Red guards, and seek to take advantage of any disorder that might occur.[167] The paper left no doubt that he was a danger who should remain under strict confinement.[168] Emphasis on the need to keep him securely locked up became an issue because Olav Scheflo's recent meeting with Trotsky had become known. The nonsocialist press maintained that the visit had violated the rules of internment because all persons allowed access to Sundby had to have the approval of Konstad, which Scheflo had not sought.[169] Konstad subtly supported the *borgerlig* viewpoint.[170]

Each nonsocialist party made a special effort to show how Trotsky represented a particular threat to its core voters. *Nationen* therefore emphasized that Trotsky was the enemy of the Russian peasants, responsible for collectivizing agriculture and thereby turning the Soviet Union into a "hopeless communist desert ruin."[171] The paper conveniently failed to note that forced collectivization had occurred under Stalin, after Trotsky was exiled. *Tidens Tegn*, whose readers were always conscious of Norway's international relations, contained an article with sensational allegations that Stalin would shortly carry out another show trial against prominent communists, including Karl Radek and Grigori Sokolnikov.[172] The inference was that Norway's relations with the Soviet Union were bound to deteriorate since Stalin's victims would be identified with Trotsky. While the persons mentioned were later tried and condemned, this did not occur until January 1937, after Trotsky had left. *Tidens Tegn* similarly kept Norwegian diplomats and police officials busy disproving an article by Waldemar Brøgger, a prominent conservative cultural personality, who repeated the NS accusation that government officials had time after time ignored complaints from concerned citizens about Trotsky's alleged violation of his residence permit.[173] Attorney General Sund determined that there was no basis for this claim but concluded that Brøgger had made his accusation in good faith.[174]

Another bone of contention concerned the expense of keeping Trotsky interned (Natalia's expenses, for obvious propaganda reasons, were ignored). *Nationen*[175] and *Aftenposten* were especially critical. Eleven days before the election, *Aftenposten* exaggerated grossly when it reported that the annual cost of Trotsky's internment would be close to 200,000 kroner.*[176] Furthermore, the paper warned that he might remain in Norway for the rest of his life.[177]

Trotsky's attempt to conduct a legal strategy through the judiciary was also denounced. *Tidens Tegn*, to cite but one example, editorialized that no court action could succeed in disproving any of the charges made during the Moscow show trial because all of the Soviet evidence would have to be presented in Norway, and this was simply impossible. Trotsky should therefore keep quiet. He had violated his asylum and had to accept the consequences.[178]

In response to this barrage of criticism, *Arbeiderbladet* consistently maintained that Trotsky's continued stay demonstrated the Labor Party's determination to uphold the right of asylum as "an important democratic principle," a right that the "Nazi and bourgeois parties" wanted to violate.[179] Nevertheless, its adversaries' repeated use of Trotsky as an election issue caused the Labor Party to make explicit its disapproval of him. *Arbeiderbladet* went to the extreme of maintaining that, despite his earlier historical importance, there was no political figure whose aims were now more different from the party's than Trotsky's.[180]

While there was a whole myriad of accusations and countercharges concerning Trotsky immediately prior to the election, two controversies in particular stood out. The first was entirely manufactured. *Tidens Tegn* sent one of its journalists, Jonas Schanche Jonasen, to Paris to dig up incriminating material about Trotsky's connections with his French followers. As a result the paper published a series of articles, beginning on October 8, that graced its pages almost to the very end of the campaign. Schanche Jonasen's first story bore a giant headline that warned that if Trotsky were not freed, Minister of Justice Lie would soon become a corpse.

This dramatic opening was followed by a detailed account of the author's visit to the French Trotskyites' headquarters. He luridly depicted its location in a stinking little Parisian passageway, its rooms filled with revolutionary posters and manned by fanatical young people. But not only did Schanche Jonasen freely gain admittance to this nest of revolutionary vipers, he supposedly also was accorded an interview with Pierre Naville himself, described as a "skinny, pale, swarthy gentleman with

---

* The actual cost for keeping Trotsky interned was considerably less, to put it mildly, amounting to 23,311.40 kroner.

a pronounced Semitic appearance." The latter, if the journalist's account was to be believed, spoke freely about his group's intentions. They were engaged in carrying out Trotsky's ambition of world revolution. Their two immediate goals were to gain freedom for Trotsky and to have the Moscow show trial investigated by an international commission. Naville was quoted as saying that if Soviet agents succeeded in killing or kidnapping Trotsky, Trygve Lie would immediately experience the same fate. Naville was also alleged to have said that a Norwegian cabinet member had promised the release of Trotsky after the election so that he could continue his work for his Fourth International.[181]

Schanche Jonasen concluded his "scoop" by maintaining that he had been able to discover conclusively that Trotsky during his stay in Norway had presided over an international revolutionary organization that had cells in "almost every country on earth." Norway was no exception since Trotsky's disciples had successfully infiltrated the Labor Party. These alleged revelations were exactly what Norwegian antisocialist newspapers had been waiting for, and they received widespread coverage.[182] The Conservative *Morgenbladet* (Morning Paper) went even further than Schanche Jonasen, directly accusing Trygve Lie of promising to free Trotsky once the election was over. The paper similarly accepted the charge that there existed a "partially disguised" Trotskyite opposition "within the Labor Party," including one individual who had visited Trotsky at Sundby. While Schanche Jonasen did not name him, *Morgenbladet* did not hesitate to conclude that it was Scheflo.[183]

Arbeiderbladet immediately declared *Tidens Tegn* guilty of conducting "cock and bull journalism."[184] However, Trotsky's defenders reacted with concern to Schanche Jonasen's purported Paris interview. Walter Held complained that Naville had committed a major folly. His greatest stupidity, said Held, was to reveal that a cabinet member had promised improved treatment for Trotsky after the election. This had resulted in a "categorical denial by the government," which it would be bound to respect. Furthermore, the minister who had made the promise, whom Held did not name, had now "broken his connection with us."[185] The identity of this shadowy well-wisher was never disclosed. It is quite likely that Held interpreted a vague statement of sympathy by a government minister to imply much more than intended.

Tidens Tegn's star journalist, however, was not allowed to have the field to himself. In a telegram to Puntervold on October 10, Naville "denied categorically *Tidens Tegn*'s false interview."[186] Puntervold immediately drew up a press release in which he quoted Naville's denial.[187] Interestingly, however, it was the Justice Department's police office, not Trotsky's attorney, that released the statement to the Norwegian Telegraph Bureau on October 12.

Schanche Jonasen responded by maintaining that a "Consul Werring," who had accompanied the journalist to Trotskyite headquarters on October 2, could confirm his account. But Werring, a vice consul in the Norwegian Consulate General, refused to corroborate Schanche Jonasen's story because it contained details that he was unfamiliar with. Werring informed the Foreign Ministry that he had gone with Schanche Jonasen only because he had felt obliged to assist a countryman.[188]

Unlike the Justice Department, the Foreign Ministry stayed out of the fray and did not publicize the vice consul's denial.[189] Nevertheless, faced with Naville's vehement rebuttal, Schanche Jonasen began to backtrack. Although he upheld the accuracy of his reports, he now stated that he had only been told when leaving Trotskyite headquarters that the person whom he had interviewed was named Naville. *Tidens Tegn* chose instead to emphasize on October 13 yet another of Schanche Jonasen's revelations. The paper quoted extensively from a Trotskyite Paris publication, which supposedly disclosed that the Norwegian government had known of Trotsky's effort to create a Fourth International at the time he was admitted and yet had freely granted him entry.[190] The paper continued its onslaught the next day with yet another major front-page article, thanks to the exertions of Schanche Jonasen, which maintained that the government had stood idly by while Trotsky was allowed to work for world revolution from Hønefoss.[191]

Tidens Tegn and *Nationen*, in addition to *Fritt Folk*, remained in the forefront of the thrust by nonsocialist papers in Oslo to exploit Trotsky as an issue in the days just before the election. *Nationen* contributed its own front-page article on October 14 with a different slant. Citing an article by state archivist Jakob Friis, a bitter opponent of Trotsky in the Labor Party, the newspaper maintained that Trotsky had called for a socialist seizure of power in Norway after the Labor Party's major victory in 1933, including removal of the king and abolition of parliament. This alone should have alerted the government to the type of person he was. *Nationen* thereupon shifted its attention to another subject, declaring that Trotsky's "Norwegian attorney," a member of the Labor Party, was serving as the messenger for Trotsky's international intrigues.[192] *Tidens Tegn* followed *Nationen*'s example and also focused its attention on Puntervold. On October 15 the paper published yet another front-page article, complete with a strongly anti-Semitic cartoon of Trotsky and his followers, which contended that through Puntervold Trotsky was able to send uncensored letters to his French attorney, giving him "uncontrolled connections" outside of Norway.[193]

The accusations were quickly rejected not only by Trotsky's attorney but also by Konstad's office, which declared that Puntervold conscientiously and loyally adhered to an agreement that allowed his correspondence with Trotsky to be censored by the Central Passport Office. *Arbeiderbladet* was pleased to publish the denials of Puntervold and the Central Passport Office.[194] *Tidens Tegn*, however, continued to insist that Puntervold's visits to Sundby constituted a danger because the Russians could regard his uncontrolled admittance to Trotsky's residence as a violation of the internment restrictions.[195]

The Labor Party, encouraged by Schanche Jonasen's weakened credibility, sought to eliminate any influence that *Tidens Tegn*'s attacks might have. *Arbeiderbladet* interviewed none other than the prime minister, who declared that the journalist's adventures in Paris were largely fictitious, while the allegation that a cabinet member had promised to assist Trotsky amounted to "baloney and nonsense." No member of the government, said Nygaardsvold, had met with Trotsky after he had been interned; no minister had given him a promise of any kind; and no one would do so in the future.[196] Although this had not been its original intent, what the Nygaardsvold interview made clear was that *Tidens Tegn* had ensured that Trotsky's treatment would not improve following the election.

Moreover, concerned that the Trotsky affair might continue to create difficulties for the government, the Labor Party did not end its effort to discredit Schanche Jonasen after the election. On the next day, *Arbeiderbladet* published a detailed article insinuating that his purported Naville interview had been plagiarized from Trotskyite publications. For his part, Schanche Jonasen reaffirmed the credibility of his information and again cited Vice Consul Werring as a witness. *Arbeiderbladet* responded by pointing out that Naville had never disputed Schanche Jonasen's presence in the Trotskyites' office. Naville had not even denied speaking with the journalist. What he rejected, said *Arbeiderbladet*, was ever having granted Schanche Jonasen an interview. Furthermore, said the paper, the journalist now had nothing whatsoever to say about Naville's denial of having threatened to turn Trygve Lie into a corpse if Trotsky's situation did not improve.[197]

Although Schanche Jonasen reiterated on October 24 what he had said earlier, this was vehemently rejected by Naville, who threatened legal action. The journalist did not respond.[198] *Fremtiden* maintained that his silence was caused by recent public knowledge that Consul Werring had notified his superiors of his unwillingness to substantiate Schanche Jonasen's alleged interview.* *Fremtiden* declared that this explained why the Foreign Ministry had not engaged itself in the press debate. If, as Schanche Jonasen alleged, a threat to murder Trygve Lie had actually been made, then Werring would unquestionably have warned Oslo. *Fremtiden* concluded that Schanche Jonasen was a blot on the reputation of Norwegian journalism.[199] But this repudiation did not injure his career. He was later promoted to editor in chief of *Tidens Tegn*.

Trotsky's alleged negative impact on Norway's international trade constituted the second major election controversy that revolved around him. As a consequence of having allowed him into the country, the nonsocialists held the Labor Party responsible not only for causing diplomatic complications with the U.S.S.R. but also for supposedly damaging Norway's foreign trade with its communist neighbor. The nonsocialists thereby criticized the government for injuring commercial relations with the Soviets, while simultaneously attacking the Labor Party for allegedly being a dangerous threat to capitalism.

Demonstrably revealing that politics are frequently irrational, the economic issue received steadily increased coverage as the election approached, although it never assumed the hysterical tone of press accounts about Trotsky's supposed revolutionary threat. The controversy largely involved two different trade interests: fishing and hunting operations from harbors on the west coast and North Norway and freight bids for influential merchant shipping firms. Interest groups involved in both fields insisted that Trotsky was having a disastrous impact on their ability to conduct business with the Soviet Union.

The Gratangen Skippers Association on September 23, 1936, forwarded to the Foreign Ministry a unanimous resolution calling for the expulsion of the "alleged agitator Lev Trotsky." The skippers, situated in Troms province

---

* The Labor Party press thereafter stopped referring to Werring as a "half fascist."

in North Norway, emphasized the need to maintain a friendly relationship with the Soviet Union, in particular due to the "understanding and good will" shown by the Russians toward Norwegian seal hunters in the White Sea region.[200] Shortly afterwards, Johan Ludwig Mowinckel, the Liberal Party chairman, held an election speech in Trondheim in which he emphasized how the Trotsky affair jeopardized trade with the Soviet Union, declaring that he knew personally of a "large herring sale" that Norway had lost.[201]

The Norwegian Shipowners Association (Norges Rederforbund) next weighed in at a meeting at the Foreign Ministry on September 30, stressing that brokers representing the group's shipping firms had not been allowed access to Russian bid lists, whereas Danish and apparently also Swedish brokers had been permitted to place bids.[202] Although the association's president and administrative director provided this information "in all friendliness," in the ensuing discussion it became evident that they felt the apparent boycott was due to the current situation involving Trotsky.[203]

Since the association's members largely supported the Conservatives, the shipowners' unhappiness soon leaked to the press. This, combined with Mowinckel's comment about the alleged Russian refusal to buy Norwegian herring, set in motion a united campaign by the nonsocialists, including N.S. *Fritt Folk* commiserated about the country's poor fishermen, who were forced to pay the price for Trotsky's asylum. The Conservatives issued an election appeal that declared that his presence threatened Norway's relationship with "Europe's greatest power" and most certainly had already led to serious losses in trade and shipping.[204]

The controversy over the economic issue intensified in particular immediately before the election. *Aftenposten* had several front-page articles condemning the government for having given Trotsky shelter, thereby allegedly damaging the country's economic interests.[205] On election day *Morgenbladet* editorialized on the same theme, asking the voters to give the government the fate it deserved.[206]

In addition to facing press attacks, the Labor government continued to be pressured by the Shipowners Association, both before and after the election. At a meeting with Koht at the Foreign Ministry on October 16, the association's vice president and its administrative director repeated their contention that the Soviet Union was deliberately refusing to allow Norwegian ships to carry Russian cargo. When Koht asked whether they wanted the Foreign Ministry to expel Trotsky, William Dahl-Hansen, the vice president, declared that, while he personally did not wish to see Trotsky handed over to the Soviet Union, there undoubtedly existed "one or another Negro republic that would accept him [Trotsky]."[207]

Responding to their request that he discuss this issue with the Russians, Koht met with Jakoubowitch already on the following day, Saturday, October 17. The Foreign Minister asked directly whether "the Soviet government will punish Norway economically because we have not been willing to expel Trotsky." The Russian envoy, according to Koht, "immediately" denied that this was true. During their discussion Jakoubowitch stressed repeatedly that his government did not "discriminate against Norwegian ships."[208] This assurance did not, however, satisfy the Shipowners Association, although its president, Fr. Odfjell, was more diplomatic in a message sent to the Foreign Ministry on December 14. The organization's latest finding remained the same—no vessel had obtained a Russian contract since mid September.[209]

Whether Stalin's government, because of Trotsky, deliberately discriminated against Norwegian shipping specifically, and adopted a negative trade policy toward Norway generally, cannot be answered with absolute certainty. Norway's Central Bureau of Statistics (Statistisk Sentralbyrå) has no figures concerning freight cargoes carried by the merchant marine from Russian harbors during the 1930s.[210] It is doubtful, however, that the Shipowners Association would deliberately have misled the government concerning this question. But whether Soviet leaders had intentionally instituted a discriminatory policy, or whether lower-level bureaucrats were simply playing it safe, knowing that Norway housed Trotsky, remains to be determined. Koht, however, chose to accept Russian assurances at face value for two major reasons. First, he did not wish to jeopardize Norway's relationship with the Soviet Union by becoming engaged in a dispute over alleged discrimination of Norwegian economic interests. Secondly, he had to take into consideration internal politics. Not only was the question of Trotsky's asylum a matter of controversy during the election, but it remained potentially explosive afterwards. With the Nygaardsvold ministry continuing as a minority government, an admission that Trotsky's presence had damaged relations with the Soviet Union could have been a serious liability.

As for the more general claim that Norway's total trade with Russia was injured due to Trotsky, here the evidence is somewhat clearer. Although trade statistics indicate that exports to the Soviet Union declined significantly during the time that Trotsky resided in Norway, they do not provide incontrovertible evidence that the decrease was primarily due to him. There had been a pronounced reduction in the export of goods to Russia **before** Trotsky gained asylum—from commodities worth 20.4 million kroner in 1933 to 8.4 million in 1934. In the two years that he resided in Norway, sales continued to decline—to 4.8 million kroner in 1935 and 2.0 million kroner in 1936. However, the reduction in exports persisted in 1937—reaching a low point of 1.7 million kroner, even though Trotsky had been expelled from the country. And while there was a pronounced increase in sales in 1938, to 9.6 million kroner, exports again sank in the final year of the 1930s, to 3.6 million kroner, which was lower than in 1935 when Trotsky was living at Wexhall.[211] These figures lead to the conclusion that there is no direct evidence that Trotsky's presence necessarily affected the country's ability to sell products to the Soviet Union. Claims to the contrary by the Labor Party's political adversaries, although sincere in some instances, must on the whole be viewed as being mainly motivated by the subjective desire to gain as many votes as possible.

Trotsky's former host, Konrad Knudsen, was heavily engaged in the election campaign as it neared its climax. As fifth on the Labor Party's list of candidates in Buskerud, his election was by no means assured. He was therefore constantly on the campaign trail, accompanied by young Borgar, who, despite his age, served as his father's driver. In September Knudsen set off on a three-week speechmaking tour that, ironically, began in Hurum. In a letter to the Trotskys, he bemoaned the fact that he was not able to pay a visit, but he assured them that the bourgeois "United Front," formed against him because of his friendship with Trotsky, would not succeed. On the contrary, he insisted that the Trotskys enjoyed broad sympathy among thousands of Norwegians.[212]

His view was disputed strongly by those who sought to benefit from the Trotsky controversy. National Union had by no means abandoned its claim to having sole ownership of this issue. It spread flyers in Buskerud, declaring that "the Jew Lev Bronstein Trotsky" was the world's greatest murderer of proletarians, allegedly having ordered the execution of "1,860,000 persons" alone during the first year of the Russian Revolution, with no fewer than one million described as "workers and peasants." Labor Party leaders stood accused of licking the boots of this "mass murderer." The voters were reminded that if they wanted Trotsky and his gang of criminal supporters "out of the country," then the only choice was "National Union."[213]

The Labor Party no longer had to face criticism from the communists. While their press continued to attack Trotsky, they were nevertheless satisfied with his internment and supported the government as the campaign proceeded.[214] With the bourgeois parties, however, there was no possible accommodation. The nonsocialist press continued to emphasize the Trotsky issue up until the last minutes of the campaign. On Saturday, October 17, two days before the election, *Nationen* published a large front-page cartoon that showed not only Nygaardsvold and Tranmæl being swept away by a violent "election wind," but also Trotsky and Scheflo, with a subcaption that read, "Let the Trotsky supporters feel in what direction the wind is blowing."[215] And *Aftenposten* on election day called on its readers to vote Conservative and thereby oust the Labor government, which stood accused not only of favoring stone throwing against political opponents,* high taxes, compulsory government regulations, and pro-Russian activity, but also of being "Trotsky's friends."[216]

The outcome did not result in the "sweeping" change that the bourgeois parties had hoped for. Instead, Labor consolidated its position, increasing its popular vote from 40.1 to 42.5 percent, gaining more than 100,000 additional votes. Clearly, a large percentage of the voters indicated approval of the government's reform efforts. As for Labor's opposition, only the Conservatives enjoyed a limited advance, with their voter support increasing from 20.2 to 21.3 percent. The percentage for other parties that had used Trotsky as an issue declined absolutely. To the great relief of almost everyone, Quisling's NS failed to gain a single seat in the Storting. Soon afterwards the party imploded, becoming a politically insignificant sect, with only a small remnant of true believers remaining loyal to Quisling. The Independent People's Party, represented nationally by *Tidens Tegn*, similarly was unsuccessful in electing candidates to parliament. On the opposite political extreme the communists, who, as has been noted, ran only a token campaign, remained without representation.

While the election resulted in a clear victory for the Labor Party, it did not, however, prove decisive. Because of very effective electoral cooperation among the major opposition parties—the Conservatives, Liberals,

---

* Throwing rocks against political opponents refers in particular to a sensational episode during the election campaign, when Labor Party supporters broke up an NS rally in Gjøvik by pelting Quisling's followers with stones.

and Agrarians—the Labor Party, despite its significant gain in votes, only improved its Storting representation by one, from 69 to 70, out of a total of 150. Johan Nygaardsvold therefore remained head of a minority government that on any major issue still needed the support of at least one nonsocialist party.

Because of the solid advance made by the Labor Party in votes, statistics initially give the impression that concern about Trotsky did not prove noteworthy in determining the outcome. And unquestionably, economic issues having to do with increased employment, social reforms, and a higher standard of living were far more important. For most voters Trotsky's asylum and its consequences were peripheral matters. But this was not true in all parts of the country. Haakon Lie has pointed out that in certain provinces where the sale of fish products was important economically—Rogaland, Møre og Romsdal, and Troms—the Labor Party received **fewer** votes in 1936 than in 1933. Lie therefore concluded that the nonsocialist parties had succeeded in gaining votes in these provinces at the expense of Labor by claiming that Trotsky's asylum damaged fish exports.[217]

This trend, however, did not affect every province where fishing was a vital economic sector. In Sogn og Fjordane, Nord Trøndelag, Nordland, and Finnmark, the Labor Party **strengthened** its position. For the nation as a whole, it can therefore be concluded that the Trotsky controversy did not prove crucial in determining the election. It did detract somewhat from the Labor Party's victory but not enough to make a significant difference.

In a post-election letter to Sundby, which he signed as "Tamada," Trotsky's nickname for him, Knudsen was more upbeat. He regarded the outcome in Buskerud as a personal triumph. He admitted that he had feared losing when the bourgeois parties united against him for being a friend of "the bandit Trotsky." But "Tamada won overwhelmingly" and was now a member of parliament. An additional "most happy result of the election," said Knudsen, was the crushing defeat of the "Nazis" (NS). They had flooded the entire country, with their "flyers and slogans seen everywhere," but they had received only "ca. 10,000 [sic!]" votes out of a total of ca. 1,400,000 [sic]" cast.*[218]

Trotsky wrote to Wexhall on the same day, October 23, declaring that he and Natalia were greatly pleased by their friend's victory. They had been anxious that "Tamada" might have been injured politically because of his

---

* National Union received 26,577 votes out of a nationwide total of 1,741,905.

hospitality and friendliness toward them. Fortunately, said Trotsky, the Norwegian people had not been influenced by the "libels" against Knudsen. More dubiously, he claimed that the people "do not believe the libels that are directed toward me."

While he was gladdened by "Tamada"'s success, Lev did not share his friend's joyful outlook. The atmosphere at Sundby continued to deteriorate. He complained that the house was not adequately insulated for the coldest period of the year. His outdoor walks were now restricted to the grounds immediately adjacent to the villa. Konstad's office confiscated the majority of important letters that he wrote for his legal actions. But most significantly, he deplored his inability to work effectively. Nevertheless, he remained defiant. Trotsky remarked that while many undoubtedly hoped he would surrender and abstain from politics, Knudsen could inform colleagues in the newly elected Storting that he would never agree to cease his involvement in international political activity that was within legal bounds.[219]

Revolutionary politics were his lifeblood, and they continued to be so to his very end. Writing three days later, he instructed Puntervold to make public a petition from French sympathizers, whose signatories included "important personalities," many having just previously belonged to the "Stalinist camp." The fact that they now had changed opinion, said Trotsky, showed that the truth would win out, as it had in the Dreyfus Affair.[220] But shortly after he wrote these words, action was taken to make certain that the truth, as he viewed it, would remain suppressed to an even greater degree than before, thanks to the main enemy he had been battling since the end of August. This was not the revengeful, diabolical dictator in the distant Kremlin but rather the socialist cabinet of Prime Minister Nygaardsvold.

As events would show, the legal maneuvers that Trotsky and his backers planned when he was moved to Sundby did not prove successful in getting around the internment restrictions. *Arbeiderbladet*, revealing the government's reaction, described Puntervold's September 3 announcement of his intent to bring suit against the editors of *Arbeideren* and *Fritt Folk* as a "foolish scheme." The newspaper maintained that the "Nazi and the communist press" lacked credibility with the Norwegian people and the lawsuit could therefore hardly be expected to amount to more than "an empty blow."[221]

Furthermore, doubts began to arise shortly afterwards as to whether the case would be allowed to proceed. A prominent attorney, Annæus Schjødt,* wrote an opinion piece in *Dagbladet* on September 10 in which he initially argued that a trial of this kind had foreign-policy implications. A foreign state or its rulers could regard it, whether correctly or incorrectly, as an insult. The rest of Schjødt's article, however, focused on his main thesis—that the libel case represented a serious threat to freedom of expression. Someone such as Trotsky, because of his international notoriety, would inevitably be attacked by political opponents on a different level, and in far harsher terms, than an ordinary person. Furthermore, Schjødt pointed out that there was precedence in Norwegian jurisprudence concerning press attacks against politically prominent individuals in which the court had determined that protection of freedom of speech was more important than insults against a politician's character. What Trotsky was attempting to do, Schjødt concluded, constituted a misuse "of Norwegian courts for political purposes."[222]

Although he did not hold an official position, his views reflected sentiments that were being discussed on the highest level in legal circles. In a letter that Puntervold wrote to Trotsky on October 10, the attorney reported on a conversation he had had with a well-known Supreme Court justice on the previous day. The latter had informed him, said Puntervold, that he believed it likely that the government was planning to issue a new provisional decree prohibiting an interned person from bringing a case to court. And while he sought to reassure Trotsky, the attorney admitted being alarmed. His talk with the justice, wrote Puntervold, had given him the impression that legal experts seriously believed that a provisional decree was in the offing, and he referred specifically to Schjødt's newspaper article as evidence.[223]

Trotsky reacted realistically, and pessimistically, to this information. He wrote later in the month to Lyova, advising him now to initiate legal action in Paris since it appeared unlikely that a court case would be permitted in Norway. Trotsky added caustically that "reactionary newspapers" were already calling for cancellation of the trial, and in Norway the reactionaries were "in command!"[224]

Within the government "drawn out secret negotiations" had been taking place concerning a provisional decree,[225] and as generally happens under such circumstances, news leaked out, allowing Puntervold to alert

---

* Schjødt later served as state prosecutor during Quisling's postwar treason trial.

Trotsky. According to Trygve Lie, the cabinet had been in agreement that Trotsky could not be allowed to carry out a "counter trial" against Stalin in the Norwegian court system.[226]

Despite these signals Puntervold nevertheless went through the motions of proceeding with the lawsuit. As noted previously, he formally submitted his preliminary complaint to the Conciliation Board on October 6. If the parties could not be reconciled, then the dispute would go to trial. In his complaint Puntervold had little difficulty in documenting how the editors of the two papers in question, Henry W. Kristiansen of *Arbeideren* and Herlof Harstad of *Fritt Folk*, had both published defamatory articles. The attorney simply quoted the accusations from the Moscow trial, repeated in the papers, which stated that Trotsky was the organizer of terrorist activity against leaders of the Soviet Union. In support of his contention that this constituted libel, Puntervold cited relevant paragraphs in the Norwegian criminal code (*straffelov*) concerning compensation for slander and the right for a plaintiff to have false statements declared null and void. Furthermore, Puntervold intended to have the court find the defendants responsible for all legal expenses incurred in the case.[227]

The groundwork for the lawsuit had thereupon finally been completed. On Monday, October 26, exactly twenty days after Puntervold filed his preliminary complaint, the issue came before the Conciliation Board. As fully expected, the parties in the lawsuit failed to reach agreement. Trotsky's attorney thereupon immediately filed charges with the Oslo municipal court (*byrett*).[228] Three days later the government intervened, issuing its second provisional decree against the troublesome exile. Under its terms a foreigner who has been interned as a result of the provisional decree of August 31, 1936, could not, as a plaintiff, bring a case before a Norwegian court without the consent of the Justice Department. Such permission would not be granted if it negatively affected Norway's relations with another state. Trygve Lie simultaneously informed the chief judge (*justitiarius*) of the municipal court that the Justice Department would not allow "Lev Trotsky's lawsuit against the editors of *Arbeideren* and *Fritt Folk*" to proceed.[229]

This was a brutal setback for Trotsky, exacerbating his resentment toward the government. It deprived him of the main strategy he had hoped to employ, following his internment, to counteract Stalinist charges. His mood was not enhanced by the near unanimous approval that greeted the action. *Arbeiderbladet*, in a brief editorial, stated that the government's resolution "will be received with satisfaction by the general public." The paper went on to say that while it previously had expressed "very sharp" opinions about the Moscow trial, nevertheless its decision had been upheld by the Soviet Union's supreme court and should therefore be accepted. Norwegian courts lacked the means to try objectively a case like the one Trotsky had proposed. Norway's relationship "with a friendly state" also had to be taken into account, a state that would undoubtedly have been insulted if the case had been allowed to proceed. *Arbeiderbladet* concluded that it would instead be best to have the controversy investigated by an international commission that could present its results as objectively and impartially as possible.[230] This changed outlook by the Labor Party's leading newspaper about the outcome of the show trial lasted until Trotsky's departure from Norway.[231]

Nonsocialist newspapers were generally in accord. As *Aftenposten* correctly headlined, "foreign policy considerations" served as the reason to deny Trotsky the use of Norwegian courts.[232] The bourgeois reaction showed that, with the general election over, the Trotsky affair was not for the time being a source of major dispute. The most urgent necessity facing the government when it issued the second provisional decree had unquestionably been to head off a negative Soviet reaction—something that undoubtedly would have occurred if the trial had been allowed to proceed. This focus on foreign affairs did not mean, however, that Trotsky's stay in Norway had become irrelevant. Once the new parliament met at the beginning of 1937, the prime minister had reason to believe that the nonsocialists would again go on the offensive.[233] Nygaardsvold therefore was motivated to have the matter settled permanently, preferably with Trotsky no longer in the country. The issuance of the provisional decree of October 29 should also be viewed in this light.

The fact that the cabinet had stymied Trotsky's legal effort did not mean he accepted this outcome fatalistically. On the contrary, he continued to pursue legal action during the rest of his stay. Puntervold indeed gave every impression of intending to follow an aggressive approach. He declared to the press on October 29 his resolve to challenge the provisional decree's legality. Maintaining that he had anticipated the decision, he insisted that not only did the government lack constitutional authority to issue the decree but that it was in direct conflict with paragraph 97 of the constitution, which specifically prohibited a law from having "retroactive effect."[234]

Walter Held endorsed this challenge, declaring defiantly, "We are not capitulating." He personally had no intention of giving in. The large amount of correspondence he conducted with Lev Sedov and others revealed the major effort he made during Trotsky's internment.[235] But Held also sought to take credit for the legal work being done for Trotsky, stressing the many hours he was putting in every day at Puntervold's office. Held, however, was clearly exaggerating his importance to comrades in Paris. While he no doubt handled much of the foreign correspondence, he lacked knowledge of Norwegian law. Although Puntervold's capacity to work may have been reduced, the veteran attorney, both in his comments to the press and in his legal briefs, demonstrated that he still had the ability to present strong, effective judicial arguments.

More objectively, Held admitted that at present the situation did not look good.[236] By the end of October, the future seemed more uncertain and bleak for Trotsky than at any time in Norway. While his followers and sympathizers made futile attempts on his behalf, the restrictive nature of his internment had become more locked in than ever. During the most difficult and frustrating autumn in his life, the days continued to grow shorter and darker at Sundby.

8 Adios Noruega

Never, anywhere, in the course of my entire life . . . was I persecuted with as much miserable cynicism as I was by the Norwegian "Socialist" government. For four months these ministers, dripping with democratic hypocrisy, gripped me in a stranglehold to prevent me from protesting the greatest crime history may ever know.
—Lev Trotsky, December 1936

I have most likely never met a person with greater knowledge and greater intelligence than Lev Trotsky. But he was to a high degree arrogant and egocentric, which great men often tend to become as they grow older.
—Trygve Lie, *Oslo-Moskva-London*

LEV TROTSKY TURNED FIFTY-SEVEN on Saturday, November 7, 1936, in a setting that he could not have imagined a year earlier. At Wexhall he had celebrated his previous birthday with friends in an atmosphere of warmth and conviviality. But at Sundby he was isolated except for the faithful Natalia, with little hope of improvement, a reality that he and his supporters now had been forced to admit. Trotsky had to be satisfied with birthday greetings from Håkon Meyer, signed also by his wife and two daughters, who hailed "the living as well as the historical person."[1]

From Paris, on a more positive note, came news from Lyova that Lev and Natalia's young grandson, Vsevolod Volkov, known familiarly as Seva, was adapting well. He was making good progress in school and, most importantly, learning to speak French without an accent. Lyova also reassured them that Seva had been outfitted with warm clothing to withstand the rigors of a Parisian winter. But while he was pleased with his nephew's progress in a new country, Lyova was worried about his parents, in particular "Papa's health."[2]

Trotsky wrote at the end of November that he had been suffering from his mysterious illness during "the last few weeks." Convinced that it was psychosomatic, brought on by his dismal situation, he maintained that any possibility for recovery was "outside the realm of medicine."[3] However, with Dr. Müller monitoring his progress, by early December, Trotsky, cautiously optimistic, revealed that he had felt better during the last four or five days.[4]

During his final weeks in Norway, he and his defenders pressed on to improve his position. The establishment of an international socialist investigatory commission still remained a major objective. Lev Sedov contacted Friedrich Adler on November 8, urging the Labor and Socialist International to support such an effort. What was at stake, Lyova maintained, was nothing less than the entire "moral atmosphere in the [international] labor movement" if Moscow's accusations were not examined impartially. He further added that there was good reason to assume that the Soviet Union was on the eve of a new "witch trial." The only way to rescue additional victims was to discredit the previous trial.[5]

Apparent corroboration of this prediction occurred just a few days later during a regional court trial in Novosibirsk, whose defendants stood accused of sabotaging Stalin's industrialization plan. Their forced confessions were especially ominous because they were linked with Yuri Pyatakov, a prominent Old Bolshevik. He had been part of Trotsky's Left Opposition in the 1920s but recanted and was allowed to reenter the party in 1928. Pyatakov received a prominent position within the industrialization program but was arrested in the fall of 1936, prior to the Novosibirsk trial.[6]

There was, therefore, good reason to assume this to be the preliminary step for another major show trial.[7] Such a trial, Lyova insisted, would also inevitably be an indictment against him and his father because part of the "evidence" presented in Novosibirsk dealt with an alleged conspiratorial meeting between himself, Pyatakov, and Smirnov* in Germany in 1931.[8]

While obviously no such conspiracy ever took place, Lyova nevertheless had in fact accidentally run into Pyatakov at that time in Berlin, allowing Trotsky's son the opportunity to hurl a contemptuous remark after the

---

* Ivan Smirnov, also a prominent Old Bolshevik, was executed together with Zinoviev and Kamenev as a result of the first Moscow show trial.

turncoat.[9] Lyova was now concerned that this fleeting encounter could be used as "evidence" by the NKVD in the anticipated trial. He and Trotsky thereupon began immediately to gather information to refute such a charge.[10]

The Trotskyites, in their ongoing battle with Stalin's minions, had reason to fear the secret police. As proof that the NKVD stopped at nothing, Sedov pointed out to Adler, Soviet agents just a few days previously had stolen documents from a Paris depository where fifteen bundles of Trotsky's correspondence were stored. The burglary's purpose, said Lyova, was clear: to obtain information that could compromise Trotsky in upcoming trials.[11] Although the depository contained many valuable documents, only Trotsky's papers were taken.[12]

He found the theft of even part of his papers to be extremely upsetting.[13] While it was obvious that NKVD agents had been behind the break-in, it proved impossible for the police to obtain leads. In Norway Trotsky, not surprisingly feeling paranoid, immediately concluded that a direct connection existed between the Paris burglary and the NS break-in at Wexhall. Both, he felt, had been conducted to allow the NKVD to gain control of his correspondence. Soviet operatives, he contended, had simply hired the "Norwegian Nazis."[14] In the conspiratorial world of agents and double agents of the 1930s, it is not at all surprising that he could firmly believe in such collusion, even though his assumption was the mirror image of Stalin's accusation that Trotsky was cooperating with the Gestapo against the Soviet government.[15]

His belief that the NKVD would use the pilfered material in upcoming trials did not turn out to be accurate. Although he continued to be depicted as a Gestapo agent in the second Moscow show trial in early 1937, the prosecution relied entirely on the defendants' "confessions." While the reason for the break-in remains an open question, one hypothesis that appears logical is that the NKVD wanted to secure letters between Trotsky and Andres Nin, the Catalan POUM leader whom they barbarically eliminated during the Spanish Civil War. Of his voluminous correspondence with Trotsky, fewer than thirty letters are known to exist.[16]

Adding to Trotsky's frustration during his last weeks in Norway were on-going difficulties with publishing *The Revolution Betrayed*. His book was one of the few weapons he could deploy, and he desperately wished to have it disseminated broadly. But he was largely dependent on his son to arrange for its publication. Trotsky at times expressed the feeling that Lyova was not up to the task.[17] His English publishing house, John Lane, had at one time been one of the country's most renowned, but by 1936 it was bankrupt.[18] Lyova sought compensation from the company's trustees and a formal termination of the contract, while simultaneously searching for a new publisher.[19] Trotsky grew ever more impatient, demanding that Lyova act decisively rather than depending on his "dilettante friends."[20] But despite inevitable delays due to the involvement of lawyers, the final outcome proved satisfactory for both Trotsky and his son. A "good and solid" British publisher, Faber and Faber, issued the English edition of *The Revolution Betrayed* in 1937.

When it came to the publication of his book in Russian, here Trotsky and Sedov did not have a choice. There was only one publisher outside of the Soviet Union, Petropolis, that brought out books in Trotsky's native language.[21] But although the firm was housed in Paris, Lyova had great difficulty in reaching an agreement.[22] By mid-December, however, he believed he had reached his goal: "Finally."[23] But his youthful exaltation proved misplaced. Whether Petropolis deliberately kept him on a string or had originally intended to publish, only to reach an opposite conclusion, is difficult to say. But the company undoubtedly recognized that there were too many liabilities involved in issuing a book by someone as controversial as Trotsky. Potential critics included not only socialists with various outlooks but also White Russian refugees who were by no means disposed toward Trotsky in a friendly manner. The hoped-for Russian edition of *The Revolution Betrayed* therefore never appeared.

Despite having been thwarted repeatedly, Trotsky and his backers remained determined to pursue court action. From Paris, Rosenthal reported on November 6 that, in accordance with Trotsky's orders, he was coordinating contact with attorneys in various countries.[24]

Trotsky had to be circumspect when writing about legal and political strategy from Sundby, knowing that every word was being censored. Walter Held, on the other hand, was not affected. In a letter to Sedov on the tenth, he urged that legal proceedings against local communists begin in Switzerland as soon as possible.[25] Trotsky himself placed major importance on this lawsuit. He believed, quite correctly, that press laws in Switzerland concerning libel were the most favorable in Europe.[26] He would eventually prevail, being awarded a sum of 10,000 Swiss francs in damages.[27]

In early November, Held, working in tandem with Puntervold, was also thinking offensively about legal proceedings in Norway. Held informed Sedov that the government's use of provisional decrees was being appealed: "We are going to the Supreme Court." In addition, Trotsky intended to broaden his attempted use of the courts to include his son. Acting on Trotsky's instruction, Held informed Lyova that he should authorize Puntervold to initiate a libel action against the editors of *Fritt Folk* and *Arbeideren*,[28] similar to the lawsuit that Puntervold had begun for his father.

The legal offensive stranded at this point, however. The Justice Department was, of course, fully informed concerning Trotsky's stratagems, and Trygve Lie intervened once again to stifle Trotsky, adhering to his policy of reducing public notice of Trotsky as much as possible. Lie therefore blocked **all** cases that Trotsky might initiate. On November 11 Lie informed Trotsky in writing, through Puntervold, that the Justice Department would prevent any legal actions by Trotsky in foreign courts. If he wished to pursue them, it would have to be done after he had left the country.

Lie's ultimatum did not restrict itself just to legal matters, however. Trotsky was bluntly told that he needed to apply for a residence permit in another country as soon as possible. Moreover, censorship of his correspondence became more restricted. He no longer was allowed to discuss strategy. From now on he could only write about factual details. Lie's letter concluded with an ominous warning. Since Trotsky's housing was a major cost, he should be prepared to move in the "not distant future" to new housing that would "reduce expenses significantly."[29]

The veiled threat gave him considerable alarm. Writing to Rosenthal on November 22, he wondered whether this might even mean expulsion to the Soviet Union? He added that, while he theoretically could seek asylum anywhere in the world, he had no illusion that it could easily be achieved. Furthermore, the government's treatment of him had undoubtedly provided other countries the excuse to deny him exile on the assumption that he must have been guilty of the charges that caused him to be interned. It was incredible, he declared, to be confined because he only wished (1) to publicize books and articles within the bounds of legality and (2) to defend himself against the "most slanderous defamations imaginable."

He was also concerned about Natalia. Lie made no mention of her in his letter. Did this mean, Lev wondered, that they might be separated, with his being moved to an unknown location while she would have to remain "in this frightful place," Sundby?[30] Natalia was equally alarmed, causing her to write to Rosenthal for the first time. She added that the uncertainty they were experiencing was made worse by Trotsky's recurring illness, which weakened him greatly. He needed a period of rest at a sanatorium or under a doctor's supervision. Instead, he was threatened with being moved to a new place of internment. "You can imagine [our] anxieties under these conditions."[31]

While Trotsky was effectively stymied, Lie's move stimulated Puntervold to greater activity. Two days later he presented a petition to the Oslo Municipal Court in which he argued forcefully that the provisional decree of October 29 was invalid. He maintained that provisional decrees could not be in violation of either the constitution or of laws passed by parliament. Under the Criminal Code's paragraph 253, a libeled plaintiff had the right to have a court declare false accusations "null and void" if no evidence had been presented to the contrary. Furthermore, said Puntervold, the Justice Department's application of the provisional decree violated the constitution's prohibition against laws being applied retroactively.[32] He presented additional arguments one week later in support of his contention that a provisional decree could not violate principles on which the constitution was founded. The constitution, he maintained, did permit a foreigner to present his case in a Norwegian court without hindrance.[33]

The Justice Department's reaction did not come until December 7, when Trygve Lie wrote to the Oslo Municipal Court. In his rejoinder he at times applied rather dubious legal arguments. He maintained that the provisional decree of October 29 had not been applied retroactively because it dealt with a court case that had already been initiated. As for the argument that the decree violated current statutes,[34] he claimed that no law existed that allowed everyone free access to Norwegian courts. The Minister of Justice appeared to be on firmer ground when he pointed out that the government had the right to issue provisional decrees because the cabinet operated continuously, while the Storting only met part of the year. Therefore, if an unexpected situation arose while parliament was not in session, the king [i.e., the government] had the authority to issue needed regulations. As precedent, Lie cited previous provisional decrees that had been upheld by the Supreme Court.[35]

As opposed to Puntervold's detailed arguments, Lie's defense was brief, consisting of three double-spaced pages. However, by the time he sent his response, he had no reason for going into detail. It was already known that Trotsky's stay was coming to an end. In less than two weeks he and Natalia would be on the Atlantic. There was no chance that Puntervold's appeal would be heard by the Oslo Municipal Court, much less the Supreme Court.

Although Trotsky's internment quite clearly decreased the amount of attention that he received, as the government intended, foreign observers nevertheless made their opinions felt during the fall of 1936. The Norwegian government received numerous protest letters and telegrams, asking that he be released from internment and that his right of asylum be respected. In light of his later experience, one such message that stands out was a telegram signed by Diego Rivera on behalf of all Mexican workers in the International Proletarian Front, who demanded that Trotsky be freed.[36] Norman Thomas, an equally well-known figure (for his politics rather than his art), added his voice to those seeking liberty for Trotsky. Having just completed the second of five presidential campaigns as the American Socialist Party's candidate, he urged that Trotsky be allowed to continue his asylum in Norway after December 18. Thomas maintained that it was quite possible for the government to protect itself against "the danger of Trotsky hatching plots" while still providing him the rights that "political exiles have always enjoyed in free countries."[37]

As for Trotsky himself, not until early December did he become reconciled to leaving Norway. Prior to then he continued his embattled posture of seeking to go on the offensive. From Paris, Lyova and Rosenthal maintained contact with him, despite obstacles from Konstad's Passport Office. The League for the Rights of Man remained a primary concern. It would mean a great deal for the Trotskyites if this prestigious human-rights organization could conclude that Stalin's charges in the Moscow trial had been false. Lyova reported in early November that the situation seemed somewhat improved. The League apparently had decided not to make public Rosenmark's uncritical report until after witnesses had been heard. Lyova believed that both he and Victor Serge, and possibly others, would be able to present their damning indictments of the trial's falsehoods, causing the League to adopt a different conclusion.[38]

Other news from France was also encouraging. André Gide, having returned disillusioned from a visit to the Soviet Union, had written a highly critical book. Despite having earlier been closely associated with the French communists, he refused their pleas not to publish. Furthermore, the Trotskyites succeeded in establishing contact with the eminent author, who indicated his willingness to serve on a commission to investigate the Moscow trial.[39] In addition, he showed personal concern for Trotsky's plight.[40]

To the delight of Trotsky's supporters in France, Gide's criticism created a great deal of controversy. Not only did the French communist press react indignantly but bourgeois publications took notice of his changed outlook, some going so far as to declare that he had now become a "Trotskyite." Sedov, who happened to meet the author by coincidence, was delighted to report that Gide accepted being called a "Trotskyite" with good humor.[41]

Trotsky was also "very pleased" with yet another leading writer, Jules Romains, who had signed the Trotskyites' protest against the show trial. Once he learned of this, Sedov immediately sent Romains a copy of his *Livre rouge* and revealed that he would soon try to establish closer ties with the author.[42] The support that Trotsky received from major literary figures such as Gide and Romains had special meaning for him due to his love of French literature. One of his major concerns during his stay in Norway was always to have on hand a good supply of French novels.

The proceedings of the League for the Rights of Man did not, however, develop in the manner that the Trotskyites had hoped. The organization set up a special commission to look into the Moscow trial's accusations, headed by its renowned president, Professor Victor Basch, whose civil-rights credentials dated back to the late nineteenth century when he had strongly championed Dreyfus.[43]

Indicating the importance he attached to this investigation, Trotsky wrote personally to Basch on December 3, stating that it was "absolutely impossible" for the commission to render a decision without first having interviewed him since he was the only one fully familiar with the Soviet Union's judicial "machinations."[44] Basch did make an attempt to secure Trotsky's views, asking the Norwegian legation in Paris for a copy of Trotsky's memorandum that repudiated Moscow's allegations.[45] However, the Norwegian government refused to comply. Responsibility for presenting Trotsky's case to the League fell thereupon on Puntervold, who sent Basch a letter, asking his commission to refrain from issuing its finding until Trotsky's attorney had an opportunity to reply to Rosenmark's draft report.[46]

The Basch commission, however, was too strongly influenced by French politics to permit an impartial inquiry. Victor Serge was never allowed to present his firsthand account of his experience as a Soviet prisoner, while Sedov's testimony was repeatedly delayed. After five postponements, he at last was scheduled to appear on December 22.[47]

By that time the question had been settled. The commission accepted Rosenmark's report as the official conclusion of the League for the Rights of Man. Trotsky angrily repudiated the League, instructing Rosenthal to inform Basch that Trotsky's correspondence with him should be regarded as "null and void." Already looking forward to wielding his pen without restraint once he was free, Trotsky vowed that he then would "give all these gentlemen the reply they deserve."[48]

During November and December Håkon Meyer continued to try to improve Trotsky's position. But because of his devotion to orthodox socialist principles, augmented by his outspoken criticism of how Trotsky was being treated, his influence in the Labor Party increasingly became marginal. Meyer attempted to compensate by emphasizing his strong contacts with foreign socialists, who, he argued, were opposed to Trotsky's internment. In early November Meyer sought to persuade the Oslo Workers Association to allow him to present a lecture on the labor movement's "international problems" that would include "the right of asylum and the treatment of Trotsky," matters that he had discussed with Friedrich Adler and A. Fenner Brockway, the head of the London Bureau, at an international conference in Brussels.[49] The association's board of directors decided on November 7, however, to table Meyer's proposal "for the time being."

He simultaneously sought to bring international pressure to bear on the government. He wrote to Brockway on November 7, referring to a previous proposal to Adler, and recommended that the London Bureau send "a strong protest against the treatment of Trotsky" to Prime Minister Johan Nygaardsvold, Minister of Justice Trygve Lie, Chairman of the Norwegian Labor Party Oscar Torp, and the Norwegian Telegraph Bureau. Meyer added that the complaint should be followed by a letter to the Labor Party's Central Committee, stating that the bureau was aware that the party [on paper] favored having an international investigation of the show trial, and that the bureau was willing to work with the Labor Party toward the formation of such a commission.[50] He clearly hoped to drive a wedge between the Nygaardsvold government and the Central Committee.

Brockway followed Meyer's suggestion. Writing to Torp, Brockway welcomed the Labor Party's decision favoring an "International Commission of Investigation" and promised his organization's cooperation. He sent a separate letter to Nygaardsvold, with copies to Lie and the NTB, "protesting against the restrictive condition applied to Trotsky" and urging that he be allowed to have a trial. Brockway also suggested to the political groups within the London Bureau that they send similar appeals to Norway.[51] His letter to Nygaardsvold, dated November 23, was on behalf of the Independent Labour Party, the British member of the bureau. Brockway decried the fact that Trotsky was "virtually a prisoner," and he urged the Nygaardsvold government to permit "an impartial investigation" of the charges against Trotsky by a commission of "working class representatives."[52]

Meyer sought to influence the government even before the protests he had instigated arrived. Writing to Lie on November 9, he maintained that socialists abroad felt that the government's restrictions on Trotsky undermined the principles of the right of asylum and worker democracy. He was furthermore convinced that Adler and Brockway were ready to work for the creation of an international investigative commission, something that the Labor Party, Meyer argued, also favored. He therefore requested permission to visit Sundby to serve as a liaison between Trotsky and Adler and Brockway. Copies were also sent to Nygaardsvold and Torp.[53]

Meyer received a strong answer. The prime minister wrote personally, using the blunt language he was noted for. Declaring that it was useless to ask Meyer to allow the matter "to rest in peace," Nygaardsvold insisted that nothing would change his mind, no matter how many protests he received. If Trotsky did not leave Norway as soon as possible, the prime minister would find him another residence. Making no attempt to disguise his intentions, he threatened to have Trotsky incarcerated, "*either in a fortress or in a prison*" (Nygaardsvold's emphasis). Almost as an afterthought he added that no visit to Sundby would be allowed. His letter was originally written on November 13, but after having postponed sending it "for several days," he concluded that he would not change a word.[54]

Nygaardsvold's strong rejection demonstrated once more how he was the final arbiter of Trotsky's fate. Meyer was fully aware of this. He had earlier described the prime minister as having been a friend for ten years. Meyer portrayed Nygaardsvold as a man of character who had performed great services for his party. As a result he had gradually gained respect, love, and support. But in the Trotsky affair, about which they so bitterly disagreed, Meyer held Nygaardsvold responsible for being "the driving force" against Trotsky. While he could not exactly explain why this had occurred, Meyer believed that Trotsky's "arrogant manner" had greatly upset the prime minister. Nygaardsvold's "strong temperament" had gradually become "agitated" and "furious" toward Trotsky. Meyer maintained that while some cabinet members at first had been of a different opinion, the prime minister had energetically prevailed.[55]

Nygaardsvold's intemperate message of November 13 made it clear that outside pressure would not have any salutary result. But while he definitely had developed an antipathy toward Trotsky, it was based not so much on the latter's arrogance toward the government—which Nygaardsvold did react to—as it was his conviction that Trotsky posed a serious impediment to his government's success, in foreign relations as well as in domestic politics.

Meyer in turn remained equally obstinate, knowing full well that his determination to aid Trotsky would weaken the left opposition within the Labor Party. His motivation was based primarily on principle. He felt so strongly about Trotsky's unfair treatment that he refused to back down. Insisting again that he was not a Trotskyite, Meyer enumerated seven specific points to explain to Nygaardsvold why he would not abandon his quest: (1) Trotsky was innocent of the accusations "raining down on him"; (2) there was no single person in contemporary history who had made a greater contribution to "revolutionary socialism" than he; (3) Trotsky was one of the most important literary figures within the international socialist movement; (4) he had no means of protecting himself against the false defamations hurled against him; (5) the restrictions imposed on him were affecting him physically and psychologically, preventing him from achieving his fullest potential through work and contact with others; (6) the restrictions furthermore resulted in the repression of socialist rights that the labor movement and Meyer had personally battled for; (7) the actions against Trotsky could lead to legislation that would have wide-ranging negative effects for socialist refugees in Norway and in other countries.

He therefore asked whether Nygaardsvold might not accept a compromise. Trotsky would be willing, said Meyer, to abandon his legal efforts if an international investigation could take place. He offered to act as

an intermediary between the Norwegian labor movement and those segments of international socialism that favored an inquiry: "social democratic, socialist, and Trotskyite."[56]

Meyer succeeded only in making Nygaardsvold more irritated.[57] The
fact that he could not cease his effort, knowing that he angered his former
friend, again indicates the principled stand that Meyer took. Furthermore,
the revelation that he and other Trotsky sympathizers intended to pursue
their campaign meant that they in turn could expect attacks from the Labor Party. Walter Held reported to Sedov in mid-November that a negative
campaign had already begun within the party press, with threats being
made to oust Scheflo as editor of *Sørlandet*.[58]

Despite the danger that this posed for the crippled Scheflo, who faced
the prospect of not being able to support his family, he remained sympathetic toward Trotsky, although he could not openly defy the party leadership. Nevertheless, on December 14 he published without comment
Meyer's letter to Trygve Lie in support of an international investigation.[59]
Others among Trotsky's small band of sympathizers were also doing their
best. Erling Falk, himself an outcast now that most members of Mot Dag
were firmly in the embrace of the Labor Party, worked to provide evidence
disproving communist charges about the nature of Trotsky's visit to Copenhagen.[60] Another former prominent radical on the left wing of the labor movement, Jeanette Olsen, signaled her total commitment to Trotsky.
In her brochure, *Trotsky: Enemy of the Labor Movement?*, published in November, she portrayed Trotsky heroically as someone who had refused to
give up his battle for the final victory of the proletariat over the bourgeoisie, resulting in his imprisonment by the Labor government. "We have arrived at the strange situation that we have a prisoner . . . who has not been
judged by any court and who is denied having his case tried by the court."
Urging workers to protest, Olsen reminded them that it was the right of
asylum that had allowed Marx to write his historic work, *Das Kapital*, and
that permitted Lenin, Trotsky, and other revolutionaries to plan the Bolshevik victory.[61]

In an undated letter, most likely written in November, Held reported to
Trotsky that his backers were carrying out additional activity. Helge Krog
(better known as a playwright than as a translator) was writing a series of
uncompromising articles that most likely would appear in *Dagbladet*. Held
also revealed that he and Meyer had worked hard to create a committee
to protect Trotsky's "right of asylum in Norway." In addition to Meyer, it

included two famous authors who previously had revealed sympathies for Trotsky, Arnulf Øverland and Sigurd Hoel, as well as loyal backers like Konrad Knudsen, Nils Kåre Dahl, and Kjell Ottesen. Due to his vulnerable position, Scheflo was not a member, but Trotsky received assurance that the editor remained willing to work for the cause.[62]

Trotsky's supporters actually went on the offensive in November by launching a polemical newspaper debate, brought on by the realization that his position was becoming more precarious. Even before Trygve Lie sent his intimidating letter of November 11, evidence of the government's intent to pressure Trotsky to leave by threatening to worsen his confinement had become plain. At the Labor Party's national conference on the weekend of November 7–8, Scheflo demanded immediate suspension of internment. But Nygaardsvold responded harshly, declaring that Trotsky's treatment if anything would become stricter in the future. Walter Held, upon being informed of this menacing comment, stated the need to condemn the cabinet's threat in the press.[63]

Unlike preelection squabbles in which nonsocialists were highly involved, the exchanges in November were largely between Trotsky's limited backers and members of the Labor Party. The first volley came from an independent-minded socialist intellectual, Trygve Braatøy, whose scathing article appeared in *Dagbladet* on November 7. Braatøy, a medical doctor and psychiatrist with close ties to prominent literary figures earlier associated with Mot Dag such as Hoel and Øverland,[64] insisted that the cabinet had known when it admitted Trotsky that it was impossible to distinguish between his active involvement in politics and his historical, analytical scholarship. Therefore, to maintain that he had abused his asylum was hypocritical, and Braatøy attacked the Nygaardsvold administration for violating democratic principles. With limitations having been imposed on freedom of speech and the right of asylum, Braatøy commented caustically that the government and its press should not use terms such as "democracy and freedom" as being representative of Norwegian society.[65]

Martin Tranmæl, with his well-known antipathy toward intellectuals, responded with a vehement denunciation on November 10. He condemned Braatøy for having written in a Liberal paper. During the last election, Tranmæl pointed out, the Liberals had falsely used the issue of Trotsky's asylum against the Labor Party. But the "loudmouth" Braatøy had not protested. With his "foolishness and snobbery," he was declared guilty of preparing the way for "reaction and fascism."[66] Tranmæl clearly wanted to show that the doctor, a well-educated "parlor radical," was alien to the working class.

Arbeiderbladet's counterattack continued the next day with Jakob Friis, Trotsky's most hostile critic among leading party members. Although Friis and Scheflo formerly had been good friends, they parted bitterly because of differing perceptions of Trotsky.[67] Friis attacked Trotsky on several fronts. He was declared incompetent as a socialist theorist. Friis denounced Trotsky even more strongly because of his opposition to the Popular Front government in France, based entirely on his hostility toward Stalin. Friis's major charge, however, was to portray Trotsky as not a true socialist, being much more akin to Bakunin than to Marx. Friis thereby sought to discredit Trotsky by comparing him to the anarchist firebrand of the nineteenth century.[68]

Håkon Meyer was permitted to respond on November 17. He criticized Friis's assertion that the cabinet's internment of Trotsky protected the working class from his dangerous influence. Trotsky, wrote Meyer, had never attempted to organize in Norway, and those who defended him were not his adherents. Meyer went on to stress the negative impact that Trotsky's treatment was having on international socialism. Democratic governments, he argued, should not allow themselves to be used as tools by dictatorial regimes.[69]

He also had strong words against Dr. Scharffenberg, who no longer was in the good graces of Trotsky's sympathizers. The doctor, despite his earlier defense of the right of asylum, vacillated when it came to signing a petition on behalf of Trotsky[70] and resisted pressure to join the newly established Trotskyite front organization, the "Friends of the Right of Asylum." Meyer criticized Scharffenberg in particular for repeating his naive argument that Trotsky ought to return to the Soviet Union in order to clear his name, which Meyer correctly declared would only result in Trotsky's murder. A far better solution, maintained Meyer, was for the Trotsky affair to be examined by an international body that enjoyed the confidence of European socialists.[71]

Held was also allowed access to *Arbeiderbladet*'s columns in November but at first only to respond to *Dagbladet*, which had gone so far as to hint at a possible link between Trotsky and the Nazis because of their common opposition to Stalin. Held pointed out that Trotskyites had been persecuted in Nazi Germany and that they were fighting against Franco's German-supported rebellion in Spain. He also described in detail Trotsky's anti-fascist credentials. At the end of his article, however, Held succeeded in criticizing the Labor Party subtly by quoting Finn Moe's favorable review of Trotsky's autobiography in *Arbeiderbladet* in December 1935, which expressed "loathing and disgust" for Trotsky's detractors.[72] Held thereby slyly showed how the party had changed its position about the legitimacy of Trotsky's political activity.

The Labor establishment's annoyance with Trotsky's defenders was shown by yet another anti-Trotsky editorial in *Arbeiderbladet* on November 21. Tranmæl defensively tried to shift blame for the enactment of the provisional decree of October 29 by arguing that it could have been avoided if Trotsky and his attorney had not "*forced*" (*Arbeiderbladet*'s emphasis) the government to act due to their alleged "misuse" of the court system. Tranmæl repeated the argument that lack of evidence would have prevented holding a libel trial of this kind. Alluding indirectly, and very briefly, to foreign policy constraints, he admitted that consideration of a "friendly minded state" also had to be taken into account. And for once referring to international disapproval of Trotsky's treatment, Tranmæl declared that it was incorrect for "foreign circles" to protest against the provisional decree. Such complaints should instead be addressed to "*Trotsky and his attorney*" (*Arbeiderbladet*'s emphasis).[73]

Although he had earlier presented himself as the defender of the right of asylum, Scharffenberg openly displayed his fundamental loyalty to the Labor Party by taking issue with Meyer on November 23. Arguing that asylum was not a right but rather a privilege granted by the state, Scharffenberg pointed out that Trotsky's freedom had also been restricted in Turkey and in France. In Norway he had been interned for conducting illegal political activity, including "secret propaganda" against the Soviet Union, and there were additional unknown "compelling reasons" to justify the government's action. Referring specifically to Meyer, Scharffenberg stated that he would not join the "Friends of the Right of Asylum" because a protest from this "young and weak organization" would not help Trotsky but might damage the possibility of providing aid for other "poor refugees."[74]

Even though largely sidelined because he could not openly oppose the party's position, Scheflo succeeded in entering the fray thanks to Tranmæl's editorial of November 21. Since the government encouraged the ending of Puntervold's legal activity, Scheflo asserted that Trotsky would be willing to do so but he should then be allowed to defend himself. In this context Scheflo noted the latest accusation from Russia—that Trotsky had instructed Soviet engineers to poison mine workers. Scheflo cunningly suggested that the government ought to investigate whether someone charged with such serious criminal conduct should be extradited. But if the Soviet Union did not request extradition, then the government needed to take "new considerations" into account.[75] Scheflo obviously alluded to the end of internment.

Walter Held met head-on the attempt to cast aspersion on Trotsky's Marxist credentials with an onslaught against Jakob Friis in *Arbeiderbladet* on November 24. Held maintained that Friis was falsifying history in his negative account of Trotskyite involvement in the Spanish Civil War and Trotsky's activity during the Russian Revolution. While both exaggerated the role of the Trotskyites in Spain, Held effectively demolished Friis's attempt to belittle Trotsky's importance in gaining victory for the Bolsheviks. Held similarly repudiated convincingly the notion that Trotsky was similar to Bakunin by emphasizing that Trotsky, like Marx, rejected acts of individual terror but not revolutionary violence on behalf of the working class.[76]

In a final response four days later, Friis maintained that Marx would never have encouraged arming the lowest-paid French workers to do battle against a government led by socialists. Similarly, he declared that Marx would not have criticized the Soviet government. This type of behavior, Friis reiterated, was more like Bakunin than Marx.[77]

Arbeiderbladet printed Meyer's repudiation immediately below Friis's reply. In reaction to Friis's accusation that he was a Trotskyite because he favored withdrawal from the League of Nations, Meyer countered that the Labor Party had been opposed to Norway's membership in the League as recently as the previous year. That he continued to uphold this view could by no means be regarded as proof of Trotskyite tendencies. In a strongly worded conclusion, Meyer stated directly that Friis lacked integrity, indicating even more the press debate's intensely negative tone.[78]

With temperatures running high on both sides, Trotsky's partisans were primed for action when the Oslo Workers Association announced that Scharffenberg would lecture on "The Right of Asylum" on Saturday, November 28, followed by discussion. This proved to be a highlight in the conflict over Trotsky because it occurred in the full light of public debate, involving the active participation of prominent persons within the Labor Party. The gathering also showed how explosive the Trotsky affair had become in the conflict over public opinion. Both Minister of Justice Lie and Foreign Minister Koht received special invitations to the meeting.[79] Koht was absent, but Lie was very much in attendance, which caused Walter Held to arrive early, eagerly looking forward to posing embarrassing questions to the justice minister. As a preliminary step Walter had joined the Workers Association and thereby also automatically became a member of the Labor Party. However, he had made enemies as a result of the newspaper polemic he had just taken part in. When he noticed that Held was present, Lie let it be known in no uncertain terms that he would leave unless the young Trotskyite was expelled. The latter's affiliation with the Labor Party thereby ended abruptly. His membership book was taken away, and he was unceremoniously ousted from the gathering.[80]

Held naturally resented being expelled from an association that prided itself as "the country's freest" debating society. He protested his exclusion, which the Workers Association justified by his membership in a "foreign organization," thereby disqualifying him from joining the Labor Party. He argued cogently, but to no avail, that his affiliation with the German Trotskyite group did not make him any more ineligible than it did for other German refugees, including Social Democrats, SAP members, and communists.[81]

Despite his absence there were plenty of fireworks during the discussion. To the enjoyment of the audience, a heated exchange occurred between Lie and Håkon Meyer. Lie excitedly denounced Trotsky for having acted in an "arrogant and superior" manner toward him, in particular at the conference in the justice minister's office just prior to Trotsky's internment. Lie went so far as to say that he had been so angered by Trotsky's insolence that he might not have been able to restrain himself if he had had a pistol. The audience applauded this macho statement, but Lie in turn was reprimanded by Meyer, who strongly defended Trotsky and condemned the justice minister's inflammatory statement. Meyer too harvested his share of applause but only from a minority of the listeners.[82]

Following this dramatic exchange the controversy briefly came to a halt, although, as will be seen, headlines about Trotsky continued to grace the newspapers, but they concerned other aspects of his stay in Norway. However, in mid-December the dispute over his internment resumed with a vengeance. On December 14 Trotsky's sympathizers fired a double salvo at the government. First, Scheflo proceeded to publish Meyer's letter to Trygve Lie of November 9. Although Scheflo did not provide any additional commentary, the headline "Allow Trotsky's Case to be Investigated by an International Commission" clearly expressed the veteran editor's sentiments.[83]

The loudest shot, however, came from Helge Krog. Even though he suffered from heart problems that left him bedridden at times, he had been strongly "agitated" by the government's handling of Trotsky. Encouraged by Held, who with "almost childish enthusiasm" provided him with material and unsolicited advice, and also making use of documents from Meyer,[84] Krog completed a highly critical essay, published as no fewer than two articles in separate issues of *Dagbladet*. What made his exposé unique, however, was its scope. Unlike earlier articles limited to specific arguments in support of Trotsky, Krog's powerful denunciation covered chronologically the entire period extending from the NS burglary at Wexhall up to the time the articles were printed, followed by detailed criticism of the Labor Party's justifications, as well as a broad examination of the right of asylum, which Krog accused the Labor Party of trampling on. But what gave the piece special zest was its sardonic humor, which Krog used effectively to flay the government and its spokesmen, in particular Tranmæl.

Krog began by denouncing the government for its reaction to the break-in. Instead of simply returning stolen documents to their rightful owner, the Justice Department had used them to start an investigation, and Trygve Lie thereby had made himself an accessory to a crime. Furthermore, the cabinet as a whole had "indirectly approved of burglary and theft as acceptable methods in political campaigns." This initial lapse in judgment began a process in which the authorities launched "more and more brutal assaults against Trotsky." However, while NS members had set in motion this chain of events, Krog emphasized that Trotsky would not have experienced the limitations imposed upon him if it had not been for Stalin's influence. Specifically, Krog pointed out that the Labor Party changed its attitude toward Trotsky in the days between August 17 and August 26, 1936, as revealed in *Arbeiderbladet*. As for the argument that Trotsky deserved to be interned because he had violated his asylum, Krog pointed out that Trotsky while in Turkey and France had "stubbornly and tirelessly" conducted his campaign against Stalin's regime, which the Nygaardsvold government had been fully aware of. Furthermore, said Krog, the government's own main organ had published on July 26, 1935, Trotsky's negative opinion of the Soviet Union. And who had conducted

the interview for this article? None other than the unholy "trinity" of Tranmæl, Trygve Lie, and Ole Colbjørnson. But now, after having interned
Trotsky due to Soviet pressure, the government prevented him from defending himself, first denying him access to Norwegian courts and then halting
him from taking legal action abroad. So if Trotsky wanted to have his case
tried, Krog commented sarcastically, "it would have to be on the moon."

He thereupon denounced the Labor Party's press for being hypocritical
by continuing to profess support for the right of asylum. He documented
his accusation by quoting effectively from *Arbeiderbladet*, showing how its
idealistic statements were contradicted by the stringent measures imposed
upon Trotsky. This revealed the government's hypocrisy in "full flower."
What Krog found especially damaging was how the government and its
press carried out a "grotesque swindle" by their use of "words such as the
right of asylum, freedom of speech, and democratic rights," thereby "un-
dermining" the true meaning of these terms. It might have been shameful
but nevertheless better, he maintained, if the government had simply admitted to giving in to outside influence.

He then went on to show how the right of asylum historically had been
important for those who loved liberty, from Voltaire to Thomas Mann. But
as a radical socialist, what mattered most for Krog was how Marx and Lenin
had benefited from this right. Now, however, ministers such as Nygaardsvold, Lie, and Koht would no doubt have hindered Marx and Lenin from
fulfilling their "historical mission" if they had sought refuge in Norway.

In his conclusion Krog revealed the influence of his in-law, Håkon
Meyer. Krog argued that the government, by not allowing Trotsky to present evidence to an international commission, was in opposition to the
Labor Party's stated position favoring such an investigation. The Nygaardsvold administration, by creating Norway's *"first concentration camp"*
(Krog's emphasis), was guilty of establishing an ominous precedent. The
playwright asked whether the only Western European government made
up of working-class representatives would respect the appeals of international socialism while there was still time. If not, then the Trotsky affair
would become "a monument of shame" for the Labor government in Norwegian history and in the history of the international labor movement.[85]

Krog's exposition not surprisingly created consternation. But Trygve
Lie admitted that only a few of its points could be factually refuted, and
he recommended that Krog be ignored. His views, said Lie, would soon be
forgotten with Christmas approaching.[86]

Contrary to Lie's advice, Krog's polemic proved impossible to disregard, having been duly noted in all political circles. One of the first to respond was J. L. Mowinckel, Jr., the son of the Liberal leader, whose commentary was published in *Dagbladet* on December 17. He expressed wonderment that someone as intelligent as Krog had failed to understand that humans act more according to feelings than reason. It was quite common for people to abandon their principles under difficult circumstances but only natural for them to deny that they had violated them. This, said Mowinckel, Jr., was what had happened in the Trotsky affair. In a backhanded compliment, the writer declared himself pleased that "our dear Labor government" had shown itself capable of acting realistically on the country's behalf during this difficult episode.[87]

Considering the beating that it took from Krog, *Arbeiderbladet* could hardly be expected to be as philosophical. Tranmæl, also on December 17, denounced the playwright as he previously had done Braatøy, belittling Krog for acting in a "shallow, superficial, and irresponsible" manner. But, as Lie had feared, this attack only provided Krog with more ammunition. Since he was persona non grata in the Labor Party, his reply came in the "bourgeois" *Dagbladet* on December 22. *Arbeiderbladet*'s reaction, said Krog, was simply to repeat arguments that he had shown to be false. If workers really wanted to know what was true, he declared, they should read Jeanette Olsen's brochure about Trotsky. Only she, Braatøy, and Meyer (Krog omitted mentioning Scheflo for obvious reasons) had denounced the government for its persecution of Trotsky. Using language almost like an Old Testament prophet, Krog proclaimed that what was catastrophic in this case was that a socialist government had committed treason against democratic and socialist principles, had stabbed international socialism in the back, and was doing its best to disarm everyone who was fighting against reaction, fascism, and Nazism.[88]

In a short editorial the next day Tranmæl provided proof of Krog's reference to the Labor Party's unwillingness to discuss specifics. As before, the editor repeated what was by now a cliché—Trotsky had been interned because he would not accept the government's restrictions of his illegal activity. As for Krog, he and his "henchmen" stood accused of failing to recognize that when it came to the right of asylum, times were different from what they had been before World War I. At the same time, however, using vague language, *Arbeiderbladet* sought to assure its readers that Soviet pressure was not responsible for how Trotsky was being handled.[89]

As these exchanges show, Krog and Tranmæl detested each other. Each believed the other to possess the worst qualities that a socialist could have. On one occasion Krog referred to his opponent as "Martin Pontius Pilatus Tranmæl," after the latter had denounced Krog for engaging in "the dirty, loathsome activity that the upper class's parlor radicals are carrying out under the guise of being socialists."[90] But neither had the final word. The debate over Trotsky continued into the next year, although not with the same urgency as when Trotsky was still in the country. The very issue of *Arbeiderbladet* with Tranmæl's response to Krog also carried the headline "Trotsky is on his way to Mexico."

Before he left Trotsky did have the opportunity to witness the outcome of the break-in at Wexhall. Those responsible went on trial in the Court of Appeals (*lagmannsretten*) for Buskerud province on Wednesday, December 9, in Drammen. The court met in the building that also served as the music hall for the town's symphony orchestra, Harmonien. The six defendants had often been described sympathetically as "the boys" by those interested in downplaying their action, although the oldest was forty-two and the youngest twenty-three.[91] They stood accused of having sought to gain illegal entry, use of false documentation, unlawful utilization of official documents, and attempted illegal exercise of official authority. In addition, Per Imerslund, having now returned from France after fleeing abroad, was separately charged with stealing documents, while the hapless driver of the getaway car similarly faced additional charges—for drunk driving and attempted auto insurance swindle.[92] Because of the seriousness of the crimes, the "boys" confronted the possibility of spending several years in jail.

The defendants did not deny their deeds since all except Imerslund had been apprehended on the night of the break-in. They sought instead to justify themselves by maintaining that they had acted against Trotsky's illegal politics only after officials had refused to heed National Union's warnings.[93] A more prominent figure, Johan B. Hjort, similarly made no attempt to disguise NS involvement. He testified that his subordinate, Thomas Neumann, was responsible for planning the operation.[94] Since several of the accused also pointed to Neumann's role, it seems strange that he avoided becoming a defendant.[95] Equally curious was the court's failure to charge any NS member with having illegally tapped the telephone at Wexhall.

Considerable discussion took place during the first two days of the trial about whether the most celebrated person involved, Lev Trotsky, would testify. *Arbeiderbladet*, reflecting the official position of wanting to provide him with as little notice as possible, maintained that it was "doubtful" he would appear.[96] But defense attorney Albert Wiesener had good reason to have Trotsky in court, hoping to implicate him in "illegal" political activity that would justify the NS members' actions. Wiesener therefore petitioned to have Trotsky give evidence. The court, led by Senior Judge (*lagmann*) Finn Nygaard, sided with Wiesener but issued precise restrictions that carefully protected the government's interests. Nygaard decreed that Trotsky would testify behind closed doors and that no record of what he said would be made public. The court specifically declared that this was done for the benefit of the Department of Justice "in consideration of the state's relationship to a foreign power."[97]

The scene was thereupon set for yet another dramatic appearance by the socialist revolutionary leader. Naturally, he aroused great interest, with a large number of curious onlookers having gathered outside Harmonien. But, as before, the authorities had made careful preparations to ensure as little notoriety as possible. When Trotsky arrived by car a few minutes after eleven on the morning of December 11, the courtroom was cleared of all spectators. Only attorneys, court officials, the jury, and the defendants were allowed to remain. The building swarmed inside and outside with members of the State Police and the regular Drammen police, making certain that unauthorized persons did not gain admission. The witness himself was accompanied by several State Police agents. The vehicle proceeded all the way up to the front entrance, where Trotsky was whisked inside so quickly that the photographers were unable to get even a hurried picture of him.[98]

Because of the absence of a stenographic record, there is no exact account of what he stated as a witness. Trotsky himself reconstructed his testimony soon after he returned to Sundby, and this version was published in his *Les Crimes de Staline* (Paris, 1937), which appeared soon after he settled in Mexico.[99] Although not fully accurate,* his reconstruction, in its broad outline, has been corroborated. Albert Wiesener, the by-no-means-friendly defense attorney, wrote admiringly almost forty years later concerning Trotsky's tremendous ability to express himself, which had left his

---

* His understanding of the Norwegian jury system, for example, left a great deal to be desired.

listeners "filled . . . almost as if possessed." Not only did he answer Wiesener's inquiries in detail, but he was given full opportunity to hold forth about what mattered the most for him: to attack Stalin for the lies that the Soviet government was propagating, to deny he had violated his asylum, and to denounce how he had been treated since the start of his internment.[100]

He began his bravado performance almost immediately, at about 11:30 a.m., continuing until 1:00 p.m. Then, after a brief half-hour's pause, he continued well into the afternoon.[101] He was on the witness stand for a total of some four hours, speaking forcefully in German that was translated as he progressed. However, as he fully understood, shown by his vow to "open doors and windows" when later given the opportunity,[102] his words had no impact outside the courtroom. Nor did his testimony affect the trial's outcome.

Judgment against the accused was delivered on Tuesday, December 15. All were found guilty. As the ringleader, Didrik Rye Heyerdahl received a sentence of 120 days in jail. Four other defendants, including Imerslund, were sentenced to sixty days, while the driver received a ninety-day sentence. However, the first five defendants had their sentences suspended. Only the driver, also convicted of having caused an accident while driving drunk and attempted auto insurance swindle, was required to serve his sentence.

Considering the gravity of the indictments, the court's decision was noteworthy. It evidently considered drunk driving and insurance fraud more serious than falsely impersonating the police, illegal use of official documents, burglary, and illegally altering an automobile's license plates. It is furthermore worth noting that Imerslund did not receive more than the minimum sentence, despite having burglarized Wexhall on his own and thereafter fleeing abroad to avoid arrest. As justification, the court pointed out that none of the defendants had a prior conviction. Also, their action was judged to have been motivated solely by their desire to prove that "the 17th witness" in the case, Trotsky, had violated his residence permit or was guilty of other "punishable offenses."[103]

As *Dagbladet* correctly pointed out, the judgment was unquestionably politically motivated. The court could not have avoided being influenced by the government and the Labor Party's abrupt change in the Trotsky affair, with the victim of the burglary being deprived of his liberty and placed in detention while the perpetrators avoided jail.[104]

Arbeiderbladet's immediate response to the verdicts was heated and indignant. It described the decision as a scandal, a blot on Norwegian jurisprudence.[105] By the next day, however, the paper's tone had changed. Tranmæl now at least partially condoned the mild sentences, describing the defendants as "dissolute youngsters" who had been used as tools by "stronger forces" within NS.[106] Clearly, the party wished to put the burglary behind it as soon as possible. With the election over and with NS no longer a political threat, there was no chance that the Justice Department would keep the issue alive by appealing to the Supreme Court.

Because its outcome had not been as successful as the Labor Party had hoped, Prime Minister Nygaardsvold tended to be pessimistic following the election, believing that when the Storting convened after the New Year, the bourgeois majority might very well sweep his government out of office.[107] In order to try to prevent this, the need to eliminate Trotsky's asylum as a political issue remained great, if not as urgent, as it had been before the election.[108]

At the same time Trotsky's followers sought to find a new country for their leader, fearful that if they did not succeed, he might simply be handed over to the Soviet Union. A two-pronged endeavor therefore took place in the aftermath of the election, with the Nygaardsvold government and Trotsky's adherents for once having a common interest, but for different reasons. They largely pursued their goals independently and with, not surprisingly, little trust on either side.

The government, using its international connections, proceeded rapidly. A member of the diplomatic corps, Sigurd Bentzon, received instructions to discuss options for disposing of Trotsky while on a visit to Turkey in the first half of November. The Turkish foreign minister, Tevfik Aras, declared himself certain that Mexico would accept him. Somewhat condescendingly, Aras added that he would not be surprised if Mexico would get "a certain amount of pride" in admitting Trotsky because it would thereby gain prominence in the civilized world, which no doubt would "flatter the Mexicans."[109] Subsequently, acting on this lead, the Foreign Ministry established contact with Mexico concerning the question of asylum, with the Norwegian and Mexican legations in Paris serving as important conduits for the exchange of diplomatic messages.[110]

Trotsky, too, had reached the conclusion that his deteriorating situation made it urgent for him to leave, and he instructed Rosenthal as early as November 22 to examine the possibility of gaining admission to "another country." But Trotsky was pessimistic about his chances. He believed there was a real possibility that the government, following an administrative rather than a judicial procedure, might simply expel him to Russia once his residence permit expired. He based his gloomy calculation on the threatening tone of Trygve Lie's ultimatum of November 11.[111]

Trotsky's followers responded energetically to his worsening predicament. With all doors locked in Europe, his French comrades appealed for help from their counterparts on the other side of the Atlantic in the American Committee for the Defense of Leon Trotsky (ACDLT).[112] While there was no chance for him to be admitted to the United States, they were in a better position to establish contacts in Mexico, under the very liberal and nationalistic government of Lazaro Cardenas. Furthermore, in Mexico Trotsky enjoyed the support of the highly influential, if notoriously quixotic and flamboyant artist, Diego Rivera, who was internationally known for his Marxist radicalism as well as his art. Although he later returned to the communist fold, Rivera initially backed the underdog Trotsky in his battle with Stalin. Because of his cultural influence and the radical, at times anti-capitalist atmosphere in Mexico City, in which Rivera was a major force, he enjoyed many connections on the highest levels, including the president himself. When Rivera engaged himself in the effort, unknown initially to Trotsky, there was good reason to believe it would succeed.

By December 2 Rosenthal was forwarding information about Mexico to Trotsky.[113] Also on the second, *Arbeiderbladet* referred to reports that labor leaders in Mexico had applied for a residence permit for Trotsky.[114] The process leading to departure therefore continued to gain momentum. On December 9 several new developments made the journey to Mexico even more likely. In Oslo the country's honorary consul phoned the Foreign Ministry that his superiors in Stockholm had ordered him to relay the following message: the Mexican government had instructed its Swedish legation to provide Lev Trotsky with travel documents.[115] On the following day the honorary consul more formally notified the Foreign Ministry in writing that the Mexican minister in Stockholm, Dr. Jose Perez-Gil y Ortiz, had been authorized to issue a passport for Lev Trotsky. The minister furthermore requested information concerning Trotsky's departure date and the port at which he would arrive in Mexico.[116]

Also on December 9 *Arbeiderbladet* published the headline "Trotsky to Mexico." The paper reported that the Mexican Foreign Office had sent out a news release that Trotsky would be granted asylum once he formally applied for admission. Currently, Mexico had only received an appeal signed by Trotsky's supporters. However, in Norway the administration greeted the announcement with pleasure. Prime Minister Nygaardsvold expressed satisfaction when *Arbeiderbladet*'s journalist showed him a copy of the telegram from Mexico. He confirmed that his government would not extend Trotsky's residence permit once it expired.[117]

Acting on very limited and selective information from the government, Trotsky's followers similarly looked forward to his departure. Writing to Erwin Wolf on December 9, Walter Held declared that it was "most likely that our old friend will soon travel home to the great painter Rivera in the next week." Those who were to accompany Trotsky included van Heijenoort, Held, and possibly Held's companion, Synnøve. Held added that, not only would the Justice Department supply him with papers, but the Labor Party would pay for his journey. The party, he maintained, wanted to get him out of the country because he had witnessed the shameful treatment of Trotsky.[118]

While most individuals assumed that the exit journey would begin shortly, there remained one obstacle—Trotsky himself. He was not opposed in principle, but he intended to leave on his own terms. Therefore, before he applied for a visa he insisted on being allowed to consult with his friends—Konrad Knudsen, Håkon Meyer, and Walter Held.[119] He obviously did not trust the officials to make his travel arrangements.

His refusal to make a formal application to Mexican authorities, however, completely frustrated American Trotskyites who had worked so hard through Diego Rivera to obtain Cardenas's consent. But they received no reply to frantic appeals asking whether Trotsky had accepted Mexico's offer.[120]

Trygve Lie visited Hurum on December 13, accompanied by one of his Justice Department subordinates.[121] Jonas Lie and other high police officials were also present.* The meeting turned into a highly charged confrontation that became legendary. In the course of their conversation, the minister of justice raised the question of acceptance of Mexican asylum. Trotsky had no objection, but he vehemently made clear his suspicion of

---

* In his memoirs Trygve Lie makes no mention of Jonas Lie, no doubt because of the latter's infamous reputation as head of the police under Quisling during the occupation.

Norwegian authorities and demanded full control of his travels. He also gave voice to his bitter contempt for the government due to the way it had behaved since the end of August. Displaying his considerable literary knowledge, he referred to Ibsen's *An Enemy of the People,* comparing the treatment that he had received with the sad fate of Dr. Stockman, who was ostracized and hounded for telling the truth. Brushing aside Lie's contention that Ibsen could be interpreted in different ways, Trotsky maintained that the cabinet was equally as hypocritical as the local town officials in the play. The Labor government, he declared, had all of the vices but none of the virtues of a bourgeois administration.[122] Specifically, he emphasized his contempt for not only Lie but also the "Minister President in slippers," Nygaardsvold. In a famous prophesy, which turned out to be accurate, Trotsky predicted that, like the German Social Democrats, the Norwegian cabinet would soon be forced to flee into exile.[123]

The Nygaardsvold administration had no intention of allowing Trotsky to block its plan. Whether or not he was willing to leave was immaterial. Following a telephone conversation between Koht and Trygve Lie on December 11, orders were given to the Central Passport Office. Konstad responded by sending the requested personal information that was needed to prepare a joint passport for Lev and Natalia.[124]

Trotsky's followers had mixed feelings about his pending departure. Lev Sedov was primarily concerned about the perils his father might face once he moved. Prophetically, Lyova stated that danger in Mexico was greater than anywhere else. But somewhat resignedly he added that if it proved necessary for Trotsky to go, then he should do so as soon as possible.[125] The prospect that he might be handed over to the tender mercies of Stalin was obviously far more perilous.

On the same day that Sedov posted his letter in Paris, December 11, Held sent the first of two telegrams to New York. They by no means provided Max Shachtman (who headed the ACDLT) with the definitive answers he had been hoping for. In his initial message Held pointed out that Trotsky had no intention of submitting an application to Mexico until Norwegian authorities had accepted his conditions for departure. Two days later Held reported somewhat more positively that "Papa agrees in principle" to leave, and he thanked his American followers for their assistance. But, Held cautioned, there were difficulties with the Norwegians. Trotsky wanted to make his travel arrangements with persons whom he could trust.[126]

This likelihood was bleak. Meyer informed Trotsky already by December 12 that while he was ready to be of assistance, he was pessimistic. His repeated requests to meet with Trotsky had only resulted in the government becoming increasingly irritated with him.[127]

As before, however, insurmountable obstacles did not daunt persons who sought to provide aid. Held reported on December 9 that they were fighting continuously to gain direct contact with Trotsky. Held personally tried to use all of his connections in the Labor Party for this purpose, and he maintained that he had been promised permission by Trygve Lie to meet Trotsky once the latter had obtained his visa.[128]

This, however, was putting the cart before the horse as far as Trotsky was concerned. He intended to pressure the government until his terms were met. Although Lie later wrote that Trotsky had expressed little interest in going to Mexico during their dramatic confrontation on December 13,[129] this was not true. What he did demand was to meet unhindered with his supporters to plan his journey. Although Trotsky related that Lie was "staggered" by this request, he did not initially refuse. Instead, the sly minister of justice promised that he would consider the question and provide an answer within a short time.[130]

Lev clearly regarded control of arrangements for the journey as a "life and death matter."[131] With the assistance of people whom he considered reliable, he would "be able to secure an escort, and to assure the safety of my archives."[132] If this could be attained, he was in fact eager to leave: "The Mexican government's offer and the present state of affairs present an opportunity that must be taken advantage of immediately." But he did not intend to go into this "with my eyes closed." Nevertheless, because of the urgent need to embark, he informed Meyer that, while he wished to meet all three of his confidants, a visit by Meyer alone would be acceptable, in particular if he were accompanied by his wife. As Trotsky delicately put it, Mrs. Meyer could be of assistance in helping Natalia make a number of purchases in preparation for the trip.[133]

Lie did not provide the quick answer that Trotsky expected as early as Monday, December 14. Reminiscent of how the minister of justice had kept Trotsky in the dark, counting on a positive response, just before he was interned, Lie again skillfully used the same tactic. Trotsky complained to Meyer on December 17 that "valuable time is being lost," which made him fear that the Mexican offer might be "compromised." Nevertheless, he declared that he would "wait a few days" for an answer, not wanting to jeopardize the possibility of leaving. Trotsky added a threat, which he was sure Meyer would pass on. He was certain, said Lev, that the government did not wish to force him and Natalia to resort to the "extreme protest measures" they had employed in tsarist prisons, protest actions that rarely failed to affect public opinion.[134]

As this letter revealed, as late as the day before his residence permit expired, Trotsky still believed the government would yield, whereas it was stringing him along until it could act. Having been told by Lie on December 13 that Held, and possibly also Synnøve Rosendahl-Jensen, would join him on the voyage, Trotsky, strongly desirous of meeting anyone from the outside, argued that he needed to ascertain whether Held intended to remain in Mexico or return to Norway, and whether the government would allow him to come back. According to Trotsky, Lie openly admitted that the government wished to get rid of Held because of his activism. In response, Trotsky declared that while he had no objection to having Held accompany him, he would not assist in setting a trap for Held, who would have to be the one to make the decision. Hence the urgent need to talk with him.[135] Trotsky wrote personally to Synnøve on the seventeenth to inform her and Walter that the latter most likely would not be permitted to return. For this reason, a meeting with Held and, if possible, also with Synnøve, was absolutely necessary.[136]

Held in turn continued his fruitless attempt to visit Sundby. He wrote to Trotsky that Trygve Lie had invited him to a meeting on Saturday, December 19. Hopefully, said Held, a solution to how Trotsky would travel would then be arranged.[137] But Trotsky's young disciple was no more successful in receiving satisfaction from Lie than his mentor. Not until December 21 did the minister of justice deign to let Held know that he would not be allowed to help with travel preparations. This meant he now knew for the first time that he would not be able to accompany Trotsky. Quite pathetically, however, assuming Trotsky was still in Norway, Held dispatched a letter to Sundby, indicating a readiness to travel separately should Trotsky need his assistance in Mexico.[138]

As with Held, Lie waited until the last minute before he revealed the government's intent to Trotsky. On December 18 the latter finally received the reply he had been waiting for. It was unexpected. Lie first informed Trotsky that he would not be allowed to meet his designees unless the police could monitor their conversation, a condition that he rejected on the spot.[139] To his great surprise he next learned that Norwegian officials, without his cooperation, had secured a passport from the Mexican government. As he later wrote, "How this was done remains a mystery to this day."[140]

For his followers outside of Norway, the question of what would happen once Trotsky's residence permit expired still remained uncertain in mid-December. From Paris his son wrote rather resignedly on the fourteenth that, while he still lacked enthusiasm about "the Mexico matter," he awaited Trotsky's decision.[141] In New York Shachtman continued to be in a state of uncertainty. He again urgently telegraphed Puntervold on December 17, referring to an Associated Press dispatch claiming that Trotsky had "disdainfully" rejected Rivera's offer and intended to stay in Norway "indefinitely." This, said Shachtman, had "paralyzed our efforts," causing "incalculable damage," and he insisted on receiving a "detailed reply" within the hour.[142]

Shachtman remained uninformed. Held wrote to the ICL secretariat on December 14 that Trotsky wished to make the voyage on an English or American ship as a "free man," with a guarantee of secure transport for his baggage and with his own staff accompanying him. The government, however, continued to have the whip hand. Held reported that it intended to transport Trotsky on a Norwegian ship under police escort. Furthermore, Held maintained that Koht had threatened to send Trotsky to the Soviet Union if he refused to go to Mexico. Faced with this disastrous possibility, the only alternative, Held pointed out, was a three-week trip on a Norwegian vessel that would face the threat of attack "by the evil Joseph." Held had told Koht it would be more satisfactory if Trotsky's followers could make arrangements through their contacts in London and New York, but the foreign minister refused to make any concessions.[143]

Despite attempts by Trotsky's small group of sympathizers in Norway to stay informed, they were denied insight into the steps taken by the government to send the Trotskys on their way. In Stockholm Minister Johan Wollebæk forwarded to the Foreign Ministry on December 15 a joint passport for the couple, issued by the Mexican legation, even though it lacked Natalia's first name and both of their places of birth.[144] Two days later Wollebæk received an official notification from Dr. Perez-Gil y Ortiz that Lev Trotsky, his family members, and his secretaries would be admitted to Mexico as political refugees and would therefore not be required to fulfill

regular immigration requirements. The Mexican minister further stipulated that Lev and Natalia should be informed that they were expected to
respect his country's laws and not conduct "propaganda" in Mexico.[145]

With the acquisition of the Mexican government's formal approval, and
with the newly issued passport in hand, Norwegian officials were free to
send them out of the country. Trotsky's refusal to sign the passport[146] posed
no hindrance. When Trygve Lie next came to Sundby, on December 18,
he, in an ultimatum, simply informed Trotsky that he and Natalia would
depart the next day and that the government had made all arrangements.
Although he protested this high-handed action, Trotsky soon bowed to
the inevitable. Being desirous of escaping the restrictions under which he
lived, leaving for Mexico was the only way he could regain his freedom of
expression. But his indignation at the manner in which he had been outmaneuvered was reflected in his icy disdain as he refused to shake hands
with Lie when they parted.[147]

The cold contempt that Trotsky felt on the eve of his departure for not
only Lie but all leading members of the Labor Party stood in contrast to
the warm, positive atmosphere that had existed when he first met the
minister of justice, along with Tranmæl and Colbjørnsen, in the summer
of 1935. The sharp differences in their perspectives are readily apparent
in Trotsky's and Lie's later recollections. When Trotsky looked back on his
internment, he declared, "Never, anywhere in the course of my entire life
. . . was I persecuted with as much miserable cynicism as I was by the
Norwegian 'Socialist' government. For four months these ministers, dripping with democratic hypocrisy, gripped me in a stranglehold to prevent
me from protesting the greatest crime history may ever know."[148] Lie, on
the other hand, focused on what he considered to be Trotsky's greatest
weakness—his self-centeredness. Lie declared, "I have most likely never
met a person with greater knowledge and greater intelligence than Lev
Trotsky. But he was to a high degree arrogant and egocentric, which great
men often tend to become as they grow older."[149]

While Natalia, with aid from the guards, struggled during their final
hours at Sundby to pack their belongings, Lev wrote to persons close to
him. These included letters to special friends in France[150] and to Rosenthal,[151] who would soon embark on his fruitless journey to Norway.
Trotsky also wrote fondly to his former host, Konrad Knudsen, expressing
his warm feelings for "Tamada" and his family. Trotsky regretted not being
able to see him one last time, and he hoped the police would return the

precious radio Knudsen had provided, as well as a number of books. He assured his friend that he departed without any feelings of bitterness toward the Norwegian people. With respect to those in "higher politics," he had a different outlook, but he could not go into detail since he wanted his message to reach Wexhall.[152] In a later letter, written from the much freer atmosphere of Coyoacan, he declared that even if one recognized that the measures taken by the cabinet had been necessary, it was still impossible to understand why it had acted in such a brutal manner. Psychologically, he concluded, he could only "explain the attitude of the government . . . by the fact that it felt its acts against me [were] so unjust that it began to hate me." The last four months had been "physically equivalent to five years."[153]

To Lyova, Lev sent what he described as "my last letter from Europe," which proved to be portentous. He left his estate to his sons, which consisted entirely of future book earnings. Except for this, "I have nothing." Expressing the vain hope that Lyova would be reunited with Sergei, Trotsky asked Lyova to tell his brother that his parents had never forgotten him. Lev emotionally declared his love for his sons and expressed the same sentiment on behalf of the long-suffering Natalia, too tired to write.[154]

Before they left, they made their farewells to the staff—the guards and housekeepers. Several had spent part of their meager income to purchase a copy of Trotsky's autobiography and were pleased when he graciously provided them with personal dedications. Aagot Sæthre, the chambermaid, was happy to leave Sundby with a signed copy of *My Life*, although the author referred to his domicile as "Sundby Prison" (an inscription he made in other books as well).[155] As thanks for the maid's hard work, Natalia slipped 15 kroner into Aagot's hands as they said goodbye.[156] In return, the Trotskys took with them one final friendly reminder from the housekeepers. Aagot and Karoline Robert had already begun Christmas preparations before they received news that the Trotskys would be departing. Lev and Natalia therefore carried with them several boxes of freshly baked Norwegian Christmas cookies when they left.[157]

Unknown to any sympathizers and associates, Trotsky and Natalia began their journey on the *Ruth* out into the darkness of the Oslo Fjord on Saturday, December 19, 1936, accompanied only by Jonas Lie, the "reactionary" highranking police officer whom Lev disliked so intensely. The shroud of secrecy surrounding their journey was favored by everyone concerned. As an indication of the pervasive fear that Trotsky's enemies, in particular Stalin's agents, might attack the *Ruth* if its location became known, Trygve Lie, on the day of departure, wrote to the vessel's owner, Hagbart Waage, with assurances that the Justice Department would reimburse any loss or damage to the ship during its trip to Mexico.[158] Waage had agreed to transport three passengers—Lev, Natalia, and Jonas Lie—in return for a payment of $120.00 each, plus a special payment of $2000.00 as compensation for the need to reroute the vessel to Tampico from Port Arthur, Texas, its original destination.[159]

In order to keep their exodus secret, the staff at Sundby was instructed to carry out their duties as if the Trotskys were still present. Originally the guards and maids were informed that they would be required to remain for the next three weeks, by which time the Trotskys would have reached Mexico.[160] Harald Halvorsen II, the dispossessed owner's son, happened to be hunting at the farm when the three automobiles, with shuttered windows, pulled out of the courtyard. He received a strict warning not to reveal that the Trotskys had left.[161]

The staff stayed on until the secret of Lev and Natalia's exodus leaked out via Sweden.* Aagot Sæthre remembered having remained at Sundby until Christmas Eve, when the farm was vacated.[162] The Halvorsen family almost immediately regained possession. Harald Halvorsen II recalled having moved back in at Sundby by Christmas Day, which he spent, as usual, hunting, no longer having to concern himself about the watching eyes of the police.[163]

Trotsky's supporters in the meantime remained in the dark, still under the illusion that they might be able to influence how he and Natalia traveled. From both abroad and within Norway they vigorously attempted to make arrangements for Trotsky that were independent of the government.[164] One of their main arguments was that Natalia's health was too delicate to undergo a direct sea voyage from Norway to Mexico, a point of view that Trotsky had similarly asserted.[165] The ideal journey that Trotsky's "friends" sought to arrange was for Lev and Natalia to go to Mexico via Belgium, France (where Natalia would receive medical treatment), and the United States.[166]

---

* In Storsand news of the Trotskys' departure became known even before they had left, most likely because members of the local community were still able to purchase milk from the farm when the Trotskys were interned (Harald Halvorsen d.y. to the author, February 16, 2005).

The efforts made by the "friends" apparently succeeded. Transit visas were obtained from both the French and Belgian governments.[167] But as Rosenthal, Held, Meyer, and other followers and sympathizers were to learn shortly, all of their work had been wasted. From the time of his admission to Norway until the day he arrived in Mexico, the Nygaardsvold government maintained control of Trotsky's destiny.

It did not, however, succeed in concealing the journey. Three days after the *Ruth* pulled away from the dock at Fagerstrand, the conservative Stockholm daily, *Nya Dagligt Allehanda* (New Daily General News), citing a telegram from Mexico, broke the story that the Trotskys were on their way across the Atlantic.[168] With the secret out, the Oslo papers rushed the news into print on December 23. However, the alleged report from Mexico was simply a ruse by the Swedish paper to disguise its true source. No Mexican, not even the country's diplomatic representatives in Scandinavia, had any knowledge of when the Trotskys had left. It did not take long for sharpeyed reporters in Oslo to conclude that the true informant most likely was a Norwegian journalist who had broken his vow of secrecy, someone who no doubt was ideologically close to the views of the conservative Stockholm newspaper. The government immediately announced that it had launched an investigation to track down the culprit,[169] but the outcome was predictable. The guilty party was never found.

Not until after the newspapers printed the sensational news did his would-be helpers learn that Trotsky was at sea. Meyer, Held, and Puntervold were later that morning summoned to Foreign Minister Koht's office, where Lie informed them of what had occurred in the preceding days.[170] In their surprise, disappointment, and frustration there was nothing that Meyer and Held could do except draw up a letter, addressed to Koht, in which they summarized their outraged reaction to the government's secrecy, pointing out that they had been denied any knowledge of what was happening to Trotsky, despite Held's daily inquiries.[171] Puntervold, already in the process of breaking ties with his departed client, did not make a written response.

Trotsky's sympathizers in Norway failed, however, to receive a complete account of what had transpired. The government refused to divulge specific information about the ship. When Lyova was made aware of this, he immediately assumed that the *Ruth* might be heading to a different

destination. Writing later to his parents, he stressed that Trotsky's followers had suspected "the worst, that the ship is not going to Mexico
but [to] Leningrad." But upon receiving confirmation of his parents'
safe arrival, Lyova at last felt relief plus the satisfaction of writing to
them in his native Russian, no longer having to take Norwegian censorship into consideration.[172]

He obtained much of his information from Rosenthal, who had been
equally frustrated upon reaching Oslo on Christmas Eve, hoping to arrange
for Lev and Natalia to travel via Antwerp and France, only to learn that they
had already departed. With the limited facts available all he could do was to
write to Trotsky's American followers, urging them to use their contacts in
Mexico to ensure that the ship would be directed to a safe harbor.[173]

While Trotsky's friends regarded his exodus with anxiety, there were
others who were pleased with how his internment ended. These included
the Russian minister to Oslo. A source of possible friction between the
U.S.S.R. and his host nation, as well as a headache for himself, had been
eliminated. In gratitude, Jakoubowitch chose to send a (symbolically appropriate) bouquet of pink tulips to Trygve Lie, in recognition of having
handled Trotsky in a way that satisfied the interests of both the Nygaardsvold government and Stalin's dictatorship.[174]

Held and Meyer quite naturally reacted in a diametrically opposite manner. In their December 23 letter to Koht, with a copy to Lie, they stressed
that Trotsky, under protest, had been forced to accept an exodus that he
did not prefer.[175] Lie responded by declaring this view to be in error, but he
maintained that he had neither the opportunity nor the time to provide a
written reply, being only willing to meet with Meyer personally to discuss
the matter. But Lie did instruct a subordinate in the police office to send a
detailed rejoinder, which stated that not only had Trotsky made the voyage
of his own free will but that he had not issued any formal protest against
the travel arrangements. Furthermore, the official denied that the government was preventing Trotsky from having radio contact with the outside
world during the voyage.[176]

In his public statements Lie similarly sought to present the illusion that
the Trotskys had left willingly.[177] The justice minister obviously wanted to
give the impression that the right of asylum had been maintained up to
the time that Trotsky set off for Mexico and that his alleged voluntary departure meant that this in no way had been abrogated. This Jesuitical interpretation did not remain unchallenged, however. *Dagbladet* immediately

took issue in an editorial entitled "The Deportation." It pointed out the obvious—that Trotsky had been refused the right to remain in Norway and had been expelled by the government. Not only had he been *utvist* (expelled), he had been *utsendt* (banished) from Norway. The editorial went on to castigate the government for its violation of the right of asylum. Historically, the paper stated, it had not been often that a foreigner had been expelled from Norway because of his political beliefs. The last such case had been in 1850, when an associate of the early socialist radical, Marcus Thrane, had been deported by an archconservative government. At that time leading "parlor radicals"—outstanding writers such as Ibsen, Bjørnstjerne Bjørnson, and Aasmund Olavsson Vinje—had been among the protesters against the government's contravention of this basic human right. Today it was writers such as Helge Krog. *Dagbladet* declared its support for Krog's argument that the government had damaged the right of asylum to a greater degree by first admitting and then expelling Trotsky than would have been true if he had simply been denied entry. But the paper regretfully had to concede that this violation would not have any political consequences. The government and its party were advancing from victory to victory, first in elections and now in the praise they were receiving in the conservative press for having ousted Trotsky.[178]

Tidens Tegn, which usually did not have much good to say about the government, served as one example. It declared that, while the government had made an error in allowing Trotsky to live in Norway, it must be admitted that the cabinet did its best to correct this mistake by working to oust him. *Tidens Tegn* further insisted that the incident might serve as a warning to a small democratic nation to avoid similar divisions in the future.[179]

The attitude of the Labor Party leadership was very similar. Moreover, its negative opinion of Trotsky was heightened even more by, as noted, the December 22 publication of yet another critical article by Krog in *Dagbladet*, condemning the government for its conduct toward Trotsky. Tranmæl therefore had nothing complimentary to say about the latter on the day his departure became known. Trotsky was portrayed as a tragic figure who had become entirely negative in outlook because of his defeat at the hands of Stalin. His attempt to establish a Fourth International had succeeded only in sowing division within the international labor movement, and the paper expressed its belief that he would never again play a historic role in world affairs. The obvious conclusion that Tranmæl wanted his readers to draw was that Norway was much better off as a result of

Trotsky's exit.[180] Nor was Tranmæl willing to allow contrary opinions to be expressed about how Trotsky had left the country. When Håkon Meyer asked for space to provide a "detailed account,"[181] Tranmæl responded that this would open a floodgate of differing interpretations that would serve no "positive purpose."[182]

Not all Labor Party editors, however, shared this outlook. In Kristiansand Olav Scheflo maintained his defiant position. Although he described Trotsky's departure in neutral, factual terms, he made no effort to conform to Tranmæl's negative assessment. On the contrary, Scheflo repeated his contention that Trotsky was the greatest, most positive figure among leading personalities within the international labor movement. Scheflo concluded his December 23 editorial by expressing full honor to Mexico for being willing to provide refuge for Trotsky (thereby getting across his disapproval of the Nygaardsvold government's failure to uphold the right of asylum).[183]

In Mexico there was actually for a time some disquiet about the manner in which Trotsky had been dispatched. Wanting to avoid complications when Lev and Natalia left from Fagerstrand, Norwegian officials had kept the Mexicans, like everyone else, uninformed about what had transpired on the nineteenth. Not until two days later did Trygve Lie send a message to Stockholm with the request that Wollebæk should let Perez-Gil y Ortiz know that Trotsky and his wife had set off on the motor tanker *Ruth*. Making no mention of a police escort, the message declared that they were traveling alone, without secretaries, and were to be set ashore in Tampico. Furthermore, because they had departed on the nineteenth, it had not been possible to deliver the Mexican minister's letter of December 17 to Trotsky, containing the terms under which he was to be admitted to Mexico. This proved to be especially significant because the Mexican government had expected Trotsky to accept its conditions **before** he left Norway. Finally, Wollebæk asked approval for the *Ruth* to change course to a harbor nearer Port Arthur. The shipowner desired a disembarkation port to the north of Tampico, and suggested "Progresso" [sic].[184]

When Wollebæk met with Perez-Gil on the morning of December 22, the Mexican minister immediately ruled out Progreso as suitable. In addition, as Wollebæk diplomatically put it, the minister became "somewhat concerned" when he learned that his letter had not been submitted to

Trotsky. The Mexican minister's anxiety was understandable, considering the importance his government placed on Trotsky's acceptance of the terms in the letter prior to his departure.

Perez-Gil's attitude did not improve when Wollebæk asked whether his government had any objection to allowing the public to be informed about the journey. Undoubtedly fearful of disturbances by Mexican communists if it became known that Trotsky was on his way, the minister replied that he could immediately confirm his government's view that nothing should be publicized until Trotsky's arrival.[185] Already later that day, however, Perez-Gil learned from the Swedish press that there was no possibility of keeping the voyage hidden.

When the Foreign Ministry received news of Perez-Gil's concerns, Koht instructed Wollebæk to provide a satisfactory explanation for why it had not been possible to present the Mexican terms to Trotsky.[186] Living up to the characterization of a diplomat as "an honest man, sent abroad to lie for his country," when Wollebæk again met with Perez-Gil on the afternoon of December 23, he informed his counterpart with a straight face that Trotsky had not been deported but was traveling to Mexico "of his own free will." As explanation for why the letter had not been submitted to him, Wollebæk maintained that it had not reached the Justice Department until the nineteenth, too late to be delivered to Sundby since the department's contact with Trotsky (Jonas Lie) had already left. Furthermore, since Trotsky was described as living quite isolated, "far out in the countryside," there was no telephone where he could be reached—a statement that the guards at Sundby would have found amusing.

Clearly revealing concern, Perez-Gil asked if it might not be possible to send a radio telegram to the *Ruth*, communicating with Trotsky in this manner. Wollebæk promised to submit this to his superiors but already expressed reservations, declaring that such a message might compromise the secret of which ship Trotsky was traveling on. Wollebæk also took the opportunity of returning to the question of the *Ruth*'s destination. Both the Norwegian government and the shipping firm preferred Progreso. If this was unacceptable, then the Mexican government was asked to designate a harbor that lay further to the north of Tampico.[187]

The minister forwarded this request and, much more importantly, the news that Trotsky was on his way without having received the requirement that he must "completely refrain from all propaganda in Mexico involving his political-social convictions."[188] Norwegian diplomats experienced some unease during the next several days, fearful that the Mexicans might refuse Trotsky entry. However, there was but small chance that would occur. The Cardenas government had already publicly announced that it would grant him asylum. To retreat now on a technical provision that, as it turned out, the Mexican administration would not rigorously enforce, would have been regarded as a serious setback. During his remaining four years, Trotsky enjoyed more freedom in Mexico than he experienced in Norway, even during the fourteen months he spent at Wexhall.

The Mexican government not only refrained from objecting to having been kept ignorant about his departure but at the end of the month declared its indifference to which port he could arrive at.[189] In the end, however, the latter question proved to be of no significance. The *Ruth*'s owner, Hagbart Waage, informed Trygve Lie that his ship would proceed to its original Mexican destination.[190] The public, however, remained in the dark concerning where Trotsky would land. Indeed, the Labor Party deliberately provided misinformation, with *Arbeiderbladet* stating on January 4 that the *Ruth* was proceeding to "Puerto Obrego[n] in Tabasco," where Trotsky allegedly would stay until a permanent residence had been decided on.[191]

While these questions played out in diplomatic circles, the person most directly affected traveled in a cocoon of uncertainty, continuing to be shut out from insight into events and decisions that were determining his fate. When he and Natalia were ushered on board the *Ruth*, they made no effort to resist. Nevertheless, by their demeanor it was obvious that they regarded the journey as taking place "under duress"—something that Trotsky had previously made plain.[192]

The crew received them "with curiosity but not the slightest animosity." The first question to be settled was their cabin. Trotsky wrote shortly afterward that the government had originally intended to have him and Natalia stay "in the semi-dark infirmary with its three cots and no table,"* but the elderly shipowner, Waage, intervened, kindly letting them use his "comfortable cabin," which allowed Trotsky to write during the voyage.[193]

---

* Jonas Lie disputed this after Trotsky was dead. According to Lie, Trotsky's claim was but one of several examples of how he falsely attempted to gain sympathy by belittling his treatment in Norway. In reality, said Lie, the *Ruth* only had three vacant sleeping quarters: the shipowner's cabin, the infirmary, and the pilot's cabin. It was, of course, obvious, maintained Lie, that the Trotskys were allowed to select the owner's cabin, while he made do in the small pilot's cabin.

Casting off from the dock at Fagerstrand, the vessel began a voyage that would last twenty-two days. Except for a ballast of 1200 tons of sea water,[194] its only cargo were two human beings, to be dropped off somewhere on the Mexican coast. As was generally normal for that time of year, the weather was quite rough during the first few days as the ship crossed the North Sea, with the wind at gale strength, at times reaching the velocity of a small storm.[195] Natalia predictably stayed in her cabin, not able to take any meals. Trotsky, however, thrived as usual while at sea and showed no symptoms of seasickness. Fortunately, the winds became calmer even before the ship had completed its passage through the English Channel. On Tuesday, December 22, Natalia made her first appearance at the captain's table, where she, Lev, Captain Rolf Lundberg, and Jonas Lie formed a foursome. And for the remainder of the voyage, the weather remained "splendid."[196]

Except for dining together Trotsky did not seek Lie's company. Their relationship, while polite on the surface, continued to be one of mutual distrust. Lev spent most of his time engaged in his favorite pursuits, reading and writing. He gave every indication of having accepted his upcoming exile. He read several additional books on Mexico, showing special interest in President Cardenas's conflict with foreign oil companies. He repeatedly let it be known that he was enjoying himself,[197] a feeling unquestionably heightened by the knowledge that with each day he was nearer Mexico and further from his "prison" in Hurum. Unlike the difficulties that accompanied his undiagnosed malady during much of the fall and winter, his health was good during the voyage. This allowed him to write his negative assessment of his internment as well as his critical account of the Moscow trial,[198] buoyed by the knowledge that his views would reach his intended readers.

The relationship between Lev and Natalia and members of the crew was excellent. Trotsky always had the ability to establish good rapport with ordinary people, and the officers and crew of the Ruth were no exception. He and Natalia were treated as passengers, not prisoners. He later wrote that Captain Lundberg and his men "treated us very graciously and accorded us a great deal of attention."[199] Even the unsympathetic Lie conceded that Trotsky always behaved tactfully and with consideration. For example, he made no effort to go up on the bridge until after he had received the captain's express invitation.[200] The crew fully accepted him. He had his shaggy mane of gray hair carefully cut by the third mate.[201] At the height of the holiday season, on Christmas Eve, Lev and Natalia were invited to join the celebration, but he did not agree until after inquiring whether their presence would inconvenience the festivities. They were promptly informed that the crew very much wanted them to attend, which they did. They joined in the merriment, which included the ship's orchestra performing a Russian melody and Trotsky trying his hand at playing a saw, which he gave up only after having been instructed to shake his knee in rhythm.[202]

At the stroke of the new year, 1937, the *Ruth* fired two cannon shots and sounded its siren, followed by the crew singing the Norwegian national anthem. Everyone on board wished each other "happy new year." But there was one new year's greeting that Trotsky greatly resented. Jonas Lie, the "fascist police officer accompanying me,"[203] received a telegram from his superiors, Minister of Justice Trygve Lie and State Police Chief Askvig, wishing him every success in the new year. Jonas Lie, seeing this as confirmation of his mission's importance, informed Trotsky of the greeting with great satisfaction.[204] The latter's reaction was very different. Writing later to followers in Norway, Trotsky declared that he remembered that "this minister of justice was several years ago a member of the Third International and in this way my comrade. I cannot conceal that at this idea I spat in the Atlantic ocean [sic]."[205] Trygve Lie, Trotsky wrote, could just as well have included greetings from Yagoda, the head of the NKVD, and Vyshinsky, the chief prosecutor during the Moscow trial.[206]

Contrary to what Norwegian officials were maintaining, Trotsky could not access the ship's radio to send out telegrams. One of Jonas Lie's main tasks was to prevent this, which Trotsky made no attempt to circumvent. He was allowed to receive ordinary telegrams after they first had been screened by Lie, but he was not permitted to read messages that discouraged him from entering Mexico, nor could he answer numerous questions from journalists.[207]

Jonas Lie's primary responsibility was to make certain that Trotsky was permanently put ashore, thereby eliminating any possibility of a return to Norway. On January 2, the *Ruth* received in code a message to proceed to Tampico. Further instructions would follow.[208] Trotsky remained uninformed about his destination, but he knew that Lie and the captain were using the wireless, no doubt making plans for his landing. As the ship entered the Gulf of Mexico on January 6, having skirted the Florida Keys, he correctly deduced that Tampico would be his port of entry, not Veracruz, as he had guessed as recently as just a few days before. The water temperature in the gulf was eighty degrees, and he and Natalia experienced "stifling" conditions in their cabin,[209] in an age when air conditioning was but a futuristic fancy.

The heat and humidity no doubt played a part in causing the relationship between Trotsky and Lie to reach a critical boiling point. With the *Ruth* rapidly approaching its destination, Lie began to prepare for Trotsky's disembarkation. Therefore, on January 6, three days before arrival, Lie decided to return two pistols that had been confiscated when Trotsky was interned, plus ammunition. More importantly, Lie requested that Trotsky and Natalia sign their joint passport, issued by the Mexican legation in Stockholm. Trotsky immediately signed a receipt for the pistols, but he refused in no uncertain terms to provide signatures for the detested passport. Instead, he made "the most violent accusations against the Norwegian government" for having obtained it without his approval. He made it clear that he would not sign until he had an absolute guarantee that his followers would meet him on his arrival. Not wanting Lev and Natalia strolling about on the *Ruth* armed with pistols, Lie tore up the receipt in front of Trotsky and retook possession of the weapons, as well as the unsigned passport.[210]

Since his first priority was to ensure Trotsky's departure from the ship, Lie wanted this to take place as smoothly as possible. He therefore took Trotsky's demand into account and telegraphed the Norwegian consul in Tampico, asking him to inform Mexican officials that Trotsky required "Diego Rivera or other friends" to meet him. This generated no response, but on the eighth Lie received a transmission from Trygve Lie and Waage with a mixed message. On the one hand, it contained news that George Novack, the secretary of the ACDLT, had arrived in Mexico to provide security for Trotsky, thereby satisfying at least in part his insistence to be met by friends. However, the telegram also instructed Jonas Lie how to proceed in case Trotsky refused to leave the *Ruth*. In that case he was to be forcibly "brought ashore" with the assistance of the captain, which meant that crew members would make certain that he disembarked.

Acting accordingly, the police official began careful preparations to have Trotsky, if necessary, physically ejected. His luggage was marked and made ready to be moved ashore. Lie also asked to have several crew members "ready for assistance." In case of trouble he intended to have Trotsky (1) confirm before witnesses that he was aware of the government's refusal to renew his residence permit and (2) acknowledge his intent to violate the government's decision (by attempting to remain on board a vessel flying the Norwegian flag).

Following instructions from the Norwegian consul in Tampico, the *Ruth* reduced its progress to half speed during its final twelve hours so that it would arrive early on the morning of January 9. This took place at 7:00 a.m., when the pilot came on board to guide the ship. No sooner had the anchor been dropped when Mexican military and police, heavily armed and led by General Jose Beltrán, swarmed on board, indicating that the Cardenas government had left nothing to chance as far as security was concerned. But also accompanying this armed group were three persons whom Lev and Natalia were very pleased to see: Max Shachtman, George Novack, and Frida Kahlo, Diego Rivera's wife.

Reassured by their presence, Trotsky, to Jonas Lie's relief, offered no difficulties. However, prolonged bureaucratic procedures had to be completed with the head immigration official. Lie provided Trotsky with the controversial passport, which he accepted without comment. In the course of later negotiations, Lie, having made sure that the general had no objections, handed over the previously disputed pistols to Trotsky, who accepted them without reservation. He thereby indicated his willingness to go ashore.

Events did not, however, go entirely according to plan. While Lie was still engaged in discussions with officials, yet another outside group invaded the ship. It consisted of impatient journalists, who demanded an interview with the celebrated exile. Lie had no desire to have this take place on board because any controversial statements by Trotsky could be interpreted as having been made while he technically was still under Norwegian jurisdiction. However, Lie was forced to cease his objections because General Beltrán, whose men now really controlled the *Ruth*, let it be known, albeit diplomatically, that he favored a news conference on the vessel since many of the newsmen had traveled a long distance, including one from New York and another from Paris, and there supposedly were no facilities ashore for an interview.

Not wishing to create an incident, Lie allowed it to proceed. Seeking to reassure his superiors, he reported, however, that it had been rather short and that Trotsky had expressed himself moderately. Furthermore, at Beltrán's request, Trotsky asked the journalists to have their bylines show that the news conference took place in Tampico, rather than on board a Norwegian ship. Following the departure of the journalists, the final preparations were made for Lev and Natalia to go ashore. A highly relieved Jonas Lie could in his report—completed on January 10 while the *Ruth* was on its way to Port Arthur—inform his superiors that the Trotskys at last had cut their connection with Norway when they disembarked at 2:00 p.m. the previous afternoon, accompanied by their entourage.[211]

Bureaucrats in Oslo thereupon began to terminate their involvement in the affairs of the unwanted exiles. Konstad, still refusing to include a polite closing salutation in his messages to Trotsky, quite happily forwarded to Mexico City the letters that had arrived after his departure, mainly from Sedov and Rosenthal, as well as a separate mailing of newspapers and periodicals.[212] Officials could also start to tally up the expenses the Trotskys had incurred. The amount during the Depression-ridden '30s was not insignificant. The fare for transporting the trio of Jonas Lie, Trotsky, and Natalia to Mexico came to $2,360 ($37,910 in 2012 value), plus a minor separate bill of 189,60 kroner ($1086; 6104 kroner—2012 value) for the *Ruth*'s incidental expenses while at Tampico.[213] The fact that the Norwegian state paid the entire amount gave lie to the claim that the Trotskys had traveled of their own free will. Had this been true, they obviously would have covered some, if not all, of their expenses.

Not unexpectedly, their internment at Sundby cost even more. It came to 23,311 kroner ($133,467; 750,500 kroner—2012 value), almost twice the total expense of sending them on the *Ruth* to Tampico, estimated at 12,000 kroner ($68,703; 386,341 kroner—2012, value). This did not include the salaries of the State Police guards, which would have been paid even if they had not been stationed at Sundby.[214]

Although the Trotskys had left the *Ruth*, the debate over their Norwegian exile continued, in particular since the government could no longer censor Trotsky. Awaiting him in Tampico on the afternoon of January 9 were additional journalists, wanting their stories, which he willingly provided.[215]

When Jonas Lie reported that Trotsky, in his initial interview, had expressed himself moderately, this was not merely Lie's attempt to downplay his failure to prevent the news conference but also a reflection of Lie's experience, having previously heard Trotsky make far more intemperate comments. In Tampico Trotsky rather judiciously explained his bad treatment as being due to "the external diplomatic and economic pressure" that the Norwegian government had been subjected to. He nevertheless did complain that the two provisional decrees had deprived him of "the right to challenge my detractors and those who slandered me," not only in Norway but in other countries. Nor had he been permitted to gather evidence to refute the claims "of my detractors." Even during the voyage he had been refused use of the ship's radio to answer inquiries from American newspapers—a point that he raised rather unfairly on a number of occasions. He did not acknowledge the need to keep the *Ruth*'s location secret, something that was definitely in his interest.

His somewhat low-key statement was also made with the Mexican government in mind. He did not wish to create a furor at the time of his arrival but thanked his new host for its "kindness" in granting him asylum, contrasting its generosity with the "inflexible attitude" of Norway, which had made it difficult for him to obtain a visa to other countries.[216] With a wide spectrum of reporters assembled in Tampico, his comments created considerable attention due to the large number of readers he now could reach. Among the journalists was Frank L. Kluckhorn of the *New York Times*, who immediately cabled his home office. Although his story focused mainly on Trotsky's refutation of Stalin's accusations, plus his insistence on having the controversy settled by an impartial commission, Kluckhorn also noted Trotsky's disparagement of his Norwegian internment.[217] This immediately caught the attention of Norway's minister in Washington, D.C., Wilhelm Morgenstierne, who cabled the Foreign Ministry on January 12 that Trotsky's "misleading" press statement in Tampico had received prominent mention in the *New York Times* and that other American newspapers had contained similar "one sided" accounts. The diplomat nevertheless recommended there should be no response because this would simply result in an undesirable newspaper dispute with Trotsky.[218]

Within Norway, however, there was no need for restraint, and the press immediately seized on Trotsky's criticism of his former host country. *Tidens Tegn* headlined that Trotsky, on his arrival, had leveled an "embittered attack against the Norwegian government."[219] Among Labor Party newspapers Scheflo's *Sørlandet* as usual remained an exception when it came to Trotsky. It reported positively that "Trotsky received a friendly reception in Mexico" and emphasized how its government had placed both a plane and a train at his disposal for travel to Mexico City.[220]

In contrast, *Arbeiderbladet* was true to form. In a sarcastic editorial Tranmæl contended that Trotsky was behaving disgracefully toward his previous asylum country, which had generously provided him with refuge. And despite having engaged in forbidden political activity, forcing the government to intern him, he had been housed at one of Norway's "most beautiful" locations, where he was allowed to continue his "political-literary work," although compelled to stop his "party political propaganda." Making no mention of Norwegian officials, it was his "Mexican and American friends," said Tranmæl, who had secured exile for him in Mexico, something neither he nor his immediate family were especially interested in. Tranmæl went so far as to state that if it had been left up to him, Trotsky would have preferred "imprisonment in Hurum rather than freedom in Mexico." But because of his friends' intervention, he could not decline the Mexican offer and had therefore "traveled of his own free will to his new asylum." Consequently, he had nothing to complain about.[221]

Quite predictably, Held responded the next day, requesting to have published an article repudiating the Labor Party viewpoint.[222] Being no more interested in a debate in *Arbeiderbladet* than Morgenstierne had been internationally, Tranmæl rejected Held's account in the same way that he previously had turned down Meyer. But as Tranmæl anticipated, the last word was not said. Helge Krog, having access to the "bourgeois" columns of *Dagbladet*, proceeded to write yet another critique denouncing the Labor Party and its government. Although he incorporated many of Held's arguments—the latter having given Krog a copy of his article—as always, Krog's invective was far more biting, incisive, and humorous.

Provocatively entitled "The Monument of Shame," it appeared on January 26. Krog directed much of his attack against Tranmæl, who was described as the government's "henchman," someone who had changed editorial opinion about Trotsky from week to week, sometimes from day to day. Furthermore, Krog charged him with being unethical, refusing to accept evidence contrary to what he published. Even after Trotsky had been "expedited out of the country," said Krog, the government and Tranmæl had continued this nefarious practice. Alluding to Held (not mentioned by name), Krog pointed out that *Arbeiderbladet* had been unwilling to print truthful information about Trotsky's experiences during his final days in Norway.

He declared that Trotsky had accepted with joy the offer of asylum from Mexico because it allowed him to escape "imprisonment in Norway." But he had wished to travel as a "free man," not as a prisoner. He had therefore refused to apply for a visa unless this condition was accepted, insisting as well on discussing his situation with persons whom he could trust. The government, however, would allow no such meeting unless it occurred under police supervision. Since it was in the government's interest to get

Trotsky out of the country as quickly as possible, it had acted without his knowledge or approval in obtaining a Mexican visa. Trotsky's departure, Krog maintained, therefore assumed the character of a deportation, taking place in a manner that might be common in a "fascist dictatorship" but which was "highly unworthy and improper" for a socialist government. Trotsky had protested against the government's arrangements, said Krog, **not** because he was unwilling to leave but because he did not want to be "shipped" to Mexico like a piece of baggage.

Krog next described how officials had kept Trotsky's departure secret, giving his friends, who were frantically working to secure transit visas, the false impression that he would not leave until some time in January. Finally, when the news became known, *Arbeiderbladet* made the false assertion that Trotsky had really been unwilling to leave, supposedly preferring imprisonment in Hurum to freedom in Mexico. Krog seized on the obvious inconsistency in this claim. Members of the Labor government had previously denied that Trotsky had been expelled or deported. When it now maintained that he had *not* (Krog's emphasis) really wished to go to Mexico, how could he then have traveled there without having been deported or expelled? Krog instead concluded that until the time he arrived in Mexico, Trotsky had been the Norwegian government's prisoner, under the supervision of its "fascist henchman," Jonas Lie.

With reference to Tranmæl's denunciation of Trotsky's negative comments from Mexico, Krog asked rhetorically whether one should laugh or cry. He emphasized that officials had kept Trotsky imprisoned for four months, not allowing him to defend himself from a "flood of accusations" coming not only from Stalin and his Norwegian cohorts, from Norwegian Nazis and the conservative press, but also from the Labor government and *Arbeiderbladet*. When Trotsky finally had the opportunity, in a more chivalrous and freer nation, to tear the gag from his mouth and express his feelings and opinions, then Tranmæl, commented Krog ironically, expected Trotsky to remain silent and not belittle the government, his "oppressors and prison guards." Krog concluded that when faced with this hypocritical attitude, one could only cry.

On the other hand, one had to laugh in reaction to Tranmæl's argument that Trotsky should have expressed thanks for his stay in Norway. Krog asked sarcastically whether the first thought that came to Tranmæl's mind, when *he* emerged from jail (in 1925) after having been imprisoned for his political convictions, was to thank his hosts, the reactionary authorities, for having provided him with a "solid, inexpensive shelter?" The writer then went on to poke fun at the current, allegedly nonreactionary, socialist government for having so generously made available "one of the most beautiful places we have" for Trotsky's internment.

Using Held's arguments from the draft that *Arbeiderbladet* had refused, Krog refuted point by point Tranmæl's assertion that Trotsky had been allowed to work while interned. Finally, when wrapping up his article, Krog made clear the meaning of his title. He pointed out that he had written earlier that if "urgent appeals from socialists in all countries" to free Trotsky were not heeded, the affair would become a "monument of shame" in Norwegian history and in the history of the international labor movement.* Now, because of its actions, the Labor government was responsible for the "monument of shame"'s erection. It was permanent, immovable. In its iniquity the government had treated Trotsky even worse than what Hitler or Stalin could have hoped for.

Krog concluded by declaring that he was downcast by this outcome, which was sad and dangerous. He did not gain malicious pleasure from the praise that the "reactionary and fascist press" showered upon the Labor government when it, after four months of ill treatment, "quitted itself with its great revolutionary guest."[223]

Tranmæl proved to be no more willing to respond to Krog than he had to Held.[224] Having received a copy of Krog's article, Trotsky, on the other hand, was warmly appreciative, declaring "The Monument of Shame" to be "marvelous." He praised Krog for his temperament, devotion to truth, and outstanding writing style.[225]

Lev and Natalia quickly settled down in Mexico. Writing later in the year to Meyer, Trotsky expressed pleasure over living "quite undisturbed." He could "quite openly . . . carry on the struggle" against the falsehoods of the Moscow trials, with the Cardenas government doing "everything possible to make our stay easier."[226] While he did not say so explicitly, his new place of exile was much more favorable than what he had experienced in Norway. But not all bonds were cut with his previous host country. As Krog's article showed, Norway was not yet finished with the effects of Trotsky's asylum. Following his departure there continued to be reverberations that impacted many of the key players on all sides of the political battle lines.

---

* Krog was referring to the previously mentioned second of his series of two articles in *Dagbladet*, on December 16, 1936, which denounced the Nygaardsvold government and the Labor Party.

9 Ongoing Controversy

> Minister of Justice Lie declared [in the meeting of] the Student
> Association that there were few future possibilities for a Trotskyite
> movement in Norway. . . . Concerns for our future can the Minister
> of Justice safely let us take care of ourselves. We are, on the contrary,
> the only trend within the labor movement that has a future.
> —Editorial, *Oktober*, no. 1 (April 1937)

AFTER TROTSKY MOVED INTO DIEGO RIVERA and Frida Kahlo's
Blue House in the exclusive district of Coyoacan in Mexico City, he quickly
discovered that troubles from his previous exile were by no means over.
The most immediate difficulty he faced concerned his contentious relationship with his attorney, Puntervold.

This was surprising because his followers had assumed that his ties with
Puntervold would be severed satisfactorily.[1] Indeed, they were of the opinion
that since the attorney had been paid to conduct a court case that had not
been held, he should at least refund part of his advance. As Lev Sedov put it,
this was something that an "honorable attorney" would do.[2] But Puntervold
proved to be anything but honorable, at least from a Trotskyite perspective.
Once he learned of Trotsky's arrival in Mexico, Puntervold requested transfer of 2500 kroner to his bank account. He rather vaguely indicated that the
sum was needed to obtain evidence in his ongoing lawsuits.[3]

Upon receipt of this cable, Trotsky instantly recognized that his funds
were in jeopardy. On the next day, January 12, he telegraphed his bank
in Oslo, Christiania Bank og Kreditkasse, to transfer his account to the
American Express office in Mexico City. But this move was unsuccessful.
Puntervold had already frozen more than half of Trotsky's account, 2800
kroner ($16,037; 90,146 kroner—2012 value).[4] Informing Trotsky of this

unfortunate development on January 15, Walter Held recommended that the Norwegian Attorneys Association should mediate the question of attorney fees. With no opportunity to follow day-by-day developments in Oslo, Trotsky telegraphed that he wished to have the association settle the matter and that he was revoking Puntervold's power of attorney.[5]

When news of Puntervold's action was published in afternoon newspaper editions on January 14, Held immediately contacted Andreas Støylen. He had been Held's first choice to represent Trotsky during his internment, but after due reflection Støylen had turned down the proposal. It was he who now suggested that the Attorneys Association resolve the dispute, assuring Held that it would reach an impartial decision. Held reported to Trotsky that if the disagreement were settled in a regular trial, not only would the outcome be more in doubt but legal expenses would be far greater.[6]

However, on the very next day, January 16, Held had to send another piece of bad news to Mexico. The tax office in Norderhov County (according to Held, inspired by Puntervold) had laid claim to the balance of Trotsky's account. Unlike the conflict with Puntervold, which Held planned to handle with the advice of Støylen, the tax matter required the direct attention of a skilled attorney. Not surprisingly, Held recommended Støylen, describing him as not only someone who resisted the temptations of the bottle (unlike Puntervold) but also as unassuming and honorable, willing to serve in return for but a modest fee.[7]

The Attorneys Association recommended binding arbitration, which Held advised Trotsky to agree to, as well as to authorize him to act on Trotsky's behalf.[8] Trotsky's son, however, provided a more somber assessment, raising the question of whether it was wise to have the conflict decided by members of the legal profession. They might be biased in favor of Puntervold, who had many friends among Oslo attorneys.[9] Held replied that, while he understood Lyova's concern, he was observing due diligence in close consultation with Støylen.[10]

Held had his way. As requested, Trotsky cabled separate authorizations for Held to represent him in the Puntervold case, while Støylen would act in the tax dispute.[11] Although he could not be directly involved, Trotsky followed the attorney fee dispute closely and provided information for Held's use. Trotsky maintained that not only had Puntervold been of little assistance but he had in many ways been a detriment. He had delayed the start of the libel case, thereby giving the government the opportunity to forbid it. He also had not adequately understood the Moscow show trial, had visited Trotsky only five or six times at Sundby, and had been of no use in conducting negotiations for the voyage to Mexico. Trotsky declared that he had nevertheless been willing to write off the amount he had previously paid, but he had never expected Puntervold's "brutal" seizure of his assets. He had therefore landed in Mexico without even a "sou."[12]

Held delivered his initial brief on February 17 in which Puntervold was severely criticized. Although he had been engaged at the end of August 1936, he had not filed the libel suit papers until October 6, while constantly demanding more money. Unable to find another attorney, and because of Trotsky's desperate situation, Held declared that there had been no alternative except to retain Puntervold. The latter received several payments in the fall of 1936, totaling 4692 kroner ($27,523; 154,836 kroner—2012 value). But he had done little to deserve this. He had only met with Trotsky at Sundby a total of seven or eight times. Alluding to Puntervold's alcohol problem, Held, citing Trotsky, declared that the attorney during his visits had been unable to remember anything from previous conversations. Held further insisted that Puntervold had not been involved in any work disproving the Moscow trial. Instead, Held claimed that he had done almost all the work for Trotsky at the attorney's office, including translations and correspondence with foreign supporters. Consequently, he requested that (1) Puntervold should immediately surrender his (somewhat reduced) claim against Trotsky's frozen assets of 2350 kroner ($13,449; 75,659 kroner—2012 value); and (2) that the attorney repay 2000 kroner ($11,446; 64,390 kroner—2012 value).[13]

In contrast to Held, Puntervold initially did not want fellow lawyers, familiar with his personal life, to sit in judgment of his ethics. He had to be reminded that the Attorney Association's bylaws required its members to submit to binding arbitration. It was not until May 11, almost three months after Held had presented his initial arguments, that he and Puntervold signed a formal agreement, committing them to accept the decision of the Oslo district (*krets*) of the association.[14] But due to its late start the case could not proceed until after summer vacation.

On August 4, however, the situation changed entirely with Puntervold's death, exactly one month short of his fifty-eighth birthday. He left behind not only a grieving widow and several children but also a large debt. But prior to his decease he had sent a fifty-page response to Held's brief. Although Held counterattacked energetically with a new set of arguments,[15] he recognized that sympathy would now be with Puntervold's heirs.[16] He therefore suggested a settlement whereby Puntervold's widow would surrender her claim in return for Trotsky ceasing to seek partial return of his payments.[17]

Held's attempt got nowhere, forcing him to reinstate his brief.[18] After a suitable delay in the best tradition of the legal profession, the arbitration board reached its conclusion on November 24. In its summary the committee provided a more detailed, and balanced, assessment of Puntervold's services than Held. This included his examination of the material from the Moscow show trial that he had used for his filings in the libel actions, the work he conducted in appealing the government's provisional decrees, his effort to gain the release of the manuscripts of *The Revolution Betrayed*, his work (rather exaggerated) in the tax case involving Norderhov County, and his research for rebutting the arguments of an English attorney who supported the first Moscow trial. Not least, the board cited various conferences that Puntervold had arranged or attended, including meetings with officials in the Central Passport Office, the Justice Department, the attorney general's office, the prime minister's office, and the Foreign Ministry. Puntervold had also spent time answering press inquiries, having discussions with Trotsky's French attorney and Trotsky's doctor, and (contrary to what Trotsky asserted) doing some work in connection with admission to Mexico. All this took time, and attorneys measure their time very carefully, a factor that Held had failed entirely to recognize.

As a result, the Attorneys Association's Oslo district concluded that Puntervold's salary should be valued at 5000 *kroner* (which happened to be the sum that he originally had requested when taking the case [$26,069; 146,667 kroner—2012 value]). Although two members of the board felt that the salary estimate might be too high, they did not believe this merited a separate dissent.

The decision was therefore unanimous. As is frequently the outcome in arbitration cases, neither side gained fully what it wanted, but Puntervold's estate was very definitely the winner. With the attorney originally having demanded 2350 kroner, plus retention of everything he previously had been paid, the arbitration unit awarded his widow 1094.14 kroner ($5,705; 32,095 kroner—2012 value), while Held's request for restitution was denied.[19]

Although the judgment might not have been quite so negative had Puntervold been alive, it is most unlikely that the process under any circumstances could have resulted in Trotsky's favor. The dispute was arbitrated by Puntervold's peers, while Trotsky was an outsider, a foreigner and a Jew whose revolutionary politics was regarded negatively by the great majority of Norwegian attorneys and who was in disfavor with the country's political establishment (socialist and nonsocialist alike). The outcome could actually have been worse for Trotsky. He at least did not have to pay the entire amount that Puntervold initially had sought.

Trotsky did not at all view the arbitration result charitably.[20] The attorney for Puntervold's estate was forced to write twice, appealing for him to make payment because Mrs. Puntervold greatly needed the money.[21] Lev did not have to do so, being out of the reach of Norwegian authorities. But, as previously shown, he had an ingrained sense of integrity in meeting his obligations, even when he considered himself wronged. Mrs. Puntervold eventually did receive the results of her late husband's final major legal exertion. The outstanding amount was forwarded to the Michael Puntervold estate by one of Trotsky's secretaries on May 30, 1938.[22]

While the dispute involving Puntervold's salary proceeded convolutedly, Trotsky's tax dispute was unfolding on a parallel track. But whereas the open break with Puntervold did not take place until after Trotsky arrived in Mexico, there had earlier been indications that he might face tax difficulties. At the very beginning of his internment, even before he left Wexhall, officials from Norderhov County contacted Konrad Knudsen, seeking information about Trotsky's tax obligations, the value of his assets, and his income. Possibly due to the serious difficulties Trotsky was then experiencing, Knudsen did not bring the matter to his attention. Instead, based on his knowledge of Trotsky's affairs, Knudsen responded by declaring publicly that Trotsky had no assets, and that his sole income during the six months he had resided in Norway in 1935 was the 500-kroner advance he had received from his publisher, Tiden norsk Forlag. Since the tax authorities did not immediately react, it appeared as if Trotsky would not be required to make a payment, a conclusion that the Labor Party press noted in apparent agreement.[23]

On the contrary, the tax officials were by no means satisfied, and in late September 1936 they made another inquiry. This time Puntervold, as Trotsky's counsel, sought to evade the matter by maintaining that his client needed more time to provide an explanation, while assuring Trotsky that the question was of little importance. Norderhov's tax office clearly felt differently, demanding a detailed account of Trotsky's income in 1935, plus the value of his estate as of January 1, 1936. The office set two deadlines, which Puntervold failed to meet,[24] providing support for Trotsky's later claim that he had been illserved by his attorney in the tax dispute. However, Trotsky could not claim total ignorance because he had received a German translation of the tax office's letter,[25] but he doggedly remained convinced that he owed no taxes.

As a result, without his being aware of the consequences, Trotsky was on a collision course with the tax office, with the legal advantage entirely on the side of the officials. This became apparent in January 1937, when the county, following Puntervold's example, put a lien on Trotsky's bank account, claiming that he owed no less than 4657.50 kroner ($26,644; 149,949 kroner—2012 value) in taxes, plus costs and interest.[26]

Even before Trotsky's authorization had been received, Held immediately engaged Støylen, who wasted no time beginning his work.[27] But when the news reached Mexico, Trotsky became as upset over his tax difficulties as he was about Puntervold's action. He complained bitterly that the claim was unjustified. Not only had he been unable to earn an income while interned, but he had been compelled to expend two and a half times more at Sundby than what he paid for the very good room and board he and Natalia had enjoyed at Wexhall. He also pointed out that, while his whereabouts was well known in Norway, county officials had never contacted him about paying taxes before his internment. Furthermore, he maintained that Puntervold had told him that he did not owe taxes due to lack of assets and because he covered his expenses with the "very moderate income" which he, a foreigner, received from abroad. He insisted that he had already paid taxes on such earnings from France, the United States, and Great Britain. Moreover, he had provided full disclosure to Puntervold. If the latter had failed to inform Norderhov County, then it was his fault.[28]

Trotsky, however, received a cold shower when Støylen, in early March, provided a crash course in Norwegian tax regulations. The attorney pointed out that under Norwegian law all residents were obligated to pay tax on one's assets and income, based on their value as of January 1 of each year. Taxes were paid in part to the state, in part to the county in which one resided. These requirements applied also to foreigners permanently domiciled in Norway, and Støylen concluded that Trotsky "without a doubt" had established permanent residence. Therefore, the attorney conceded that the best he could hope to achieve was a "major reduction" in the tax obligation. In order to accomplish this, he requested detailed information. He wanted an account of all of Trotsky's income in 1935, earnings in foreign countries, and the value of his assets as of January 1, 1936. Any taxes that Trotsky had paid abroad would be deducted from his income. Deductions would also include Trotsky's professional expenses.[29]

In his response Trotsky's exasperation remained undiminished. He declared that he had earlier provided Puntervold with everything Støylen asked for. Specifically, Trotsky pointed out that he had no assets except his "clothes and books." The income from foreign countries had already been taxed. In 1935 he and his wife only had at their disposal a total of about 500 kroner a month, which they used to cover expenses. Their son received a monthly payment of 170 kroner for his work in Paris, while Trotsky's typist, Mrs. Dahl, was paid 120–150 kroner per month. He added angrily that the tax authorities needed to take into consideration that the government had "unconstitutionally" interned him for four months, preventing him from conducting literary activity.[30]

On the basis of this information, which was not as extensive as he could have wished because of Trotsky's failure to itemize earnings from foreign publishers except a royalty payment from Doubleday Doran & Co., Støylen drew up an estimate of Trotsky's income for 1935, which he set at 5400 kroner ($32,472; 182,769 kroner—2012 value). However, the attorney indicated that he needed a more detailed statement of Trotsky's earnings.[31]

Although Trotsky later did provide additional data, it was still not complete. Furthermore, the tax dispute proved to be as protracted as the conflict over Puntervold's fees. Summer came and went with no resolution in sight. However, Støylen, on the basis of the information Trotsky had sent, now estimated that Trotsky's income for 1935 could not have been more than 6000 kroner ($36,080; 203,077 kroner—2012 value).[32] Although Norderhov County insisted that it had been considerably higher,[33] in the end a break occurred. As Held put it, "the opposition" finally proposed that Trotsky agree to a settlement to bring the dispute to a conclusion. Støylen urged acceptance in order to prevent further delay.[34]

Trotsky continued to argue against having to pay any tax at all. But he finally indicated that if Støylen judged it inadvisable "to fight against the dishonest attitude" of Norderhov County, then he accepted that he "must make payment."[35] For his part, Støylen, in his last letter to his client in mid-November, explained that he had conducted negotiations with Norderhov County in order to avoid a formal trial, whose outcome was most uncertain.

As a result, he had succeeded in persuading the county to accept a settle-ment of 1650 kroner ($8,599; 48,400 kroner—2012 value). To make his point that this result was reasonable, Støylen reminded Trotsky that tax officials had originally demanded 4657.50 kroner, plus interest.[36] Further-more, Støylen only charged Trotsky an attorney's fee of 250 kroner ($1,303 in 2012 value), thereby living up to Held's positive portrayal of him.[37]

As a result of the unfreezing of the account, after all deductions had been made, there remained only 897.55 kroner. Because Held had been promised twenty percent of the final amount, he now subtracted 179.50 kroner "for my work and expenses in both cases," since the Puntervold dis-pute was also close to completion. This meant that Trotsky only received a residual sum of 718.05 kroner ($3,742; 21,063 kroner—2012 value), which Held dutifully forwarded as a check.[38]

While this outcome did not meet Trotsky's expectations, it could have been much worse. Støylen unquestionably represented his client capably. Not only could Norderhov County have obtained full satisfaction in court, but Trotsky could have been required to pay taxes to the state. Nor were any tax liens levied by Norderhov County against his income for 1936, which was considerate in light of his internment. But, as is true in most income tax disputes, the loser remained dissatisfied. Moreover, Trotsky was convinced that the tax claim was simply part of a greater plot that the government had orchestrated against him.

Although the fiscal disputes in Norway annoyed him, Trotsky was fo-cused primarily on renewing his battle with Stalin, which had been so abruptly interrupted by his internment. As before, he was determined to disprove the Kremlin's false accusations from the first Moscow trial. However, two weeks after his arrival in Mexico, he faced a new series of equally bogus charges. These were from Stalin's second major show trial of the 1930s, whose occurrence Trotsky had anticipated. On January 23, 1937, seventeen defendants stood before the kangaroo court in Moscow. Among them were several Old Bolsheviks, the most prominent being Yuri Pyatakov, Karl Radek, and Grigori Sokolnikov. They did not have quite the stature of the main victims of the first trial, but all three were well known. Sokolnikov had held a number of diplomatic assignments, including that of Soviet ambassador to London; Radek, a highly colorful personal-ity, had served in several capacities, among them as the Soviet Union's most important press spokesman; while Pyatakov, as deputy commissar of heavy industry, was recognized as a major economic expert, the driving force in implementing Stalin's rapid industrialization program. But once more the key defendant, Lev Trotsky, was not in court. All of the accused were charged with participating in the alleged conspiracy that he was orchestrating from abroad, resulting in sabotage and acts of terrorism in the Soviet Union. Trotsky, described as having met Rudolf Hess, Hitler's second in command, was said to be plotting with Germany and Japan in order to come to power. With the defeat of the Soviet Union, Germany would receive Ukraine, while the Japanese would be rewarded with strategic territories on the Pacific coast. Trotsky, as the new head of government, would then begin the restoration of capitalism in what remained of the U.S.S.R.[39]

Again the courtroom proceedings were carefully staged, with the witnesses having been coached by their NKVD handlers. News of the trial created an international sensation. The immediate reaction in most Norwegian papers was disbelief, as forcefully expressed in *Fremtiden*. It wrote that when one reads the confessions of Old Bolsheviks who had helped create the Soviet Union—that they secretly had agreed to surrender Russian territory to Germany and Japan while daily dynamiting factories and carrying out murder attempts—then the only logical conclusion was to characterize the entire process as "total nonsense."[40]

What especially aroused great interest in Norway was Pyatakov's testimony. Undaunted by the failure of their phony claim in the first trial—that Trotsky and his son had hatched murderous plots in a Copenhagen hotel that had been demolished fifteen years earlier—the prosecution in the second trial made use of an even more absurd story. The hapless Pyatakov was forced to declare that, while on a special mission for the Soviet government in Berlin, he had secretly flown to Norway on or about December 12, 1935, in order to meet Trotsky. Upon landing in Oslo, Pyatakov said he was immediately whisked away in a waiting automobile, and after a drive to a suburb lasting only half an hour, he entered "a small house that was furnished quite nicely." Here he met Trotsky, and during the next two hours they had a wide-ranging discussion in which Trotsky urged his Russian followers to pursue their "destructive activity" in preparation for seizing power with the aid of anti-Soviet forces.[41] Pyatakov provided no details about what supposedly occurred afterwards, including his return to Berlin.

Skepticism was immediately aroused. The possibility that Pyatakov might have conspired with Trotsky did not seem very likely. Although

Pyatakov had initially been against Stalin in the early '20s, he has been described as "among the first to abandon Trotsky."[42] Not unexpectedly, the latter at once issued a denial from Mexico.[43] His host, Konrad Knudsen, similarly dismissed the story as "fictitious." He insisted that Trotsky had been in no condition to accept visitors, being very weak after having recently returned from the hospital at the time Pyatakov supposedly had shown up. Furthermore, said Knudsen, Trotsky had never met with **any Russians** at Wexhall.[44]

So many critical questions were raised in the Norwegian press that the issue had international repercussions, forcing the Kremlin to respond. On January 26 the Soviet legation in Oslo contacted the Foreign Ministry, requesting answers to two questions: (1) Were there regular passenger flights between Oslo and neighboring countries (Sweden, Denmark, and Germany) during the winter months of December, January, and February? (2) If regular passenger flights did not occur, were Norwegian airports nevertheless open for landings and departures to and from the above-mentioned countries?

Since Kjeller, a military airfield, was the only airport in the Oslo area at the time, but located some distance east of the city near the small town of Lillestrøm, the Foreign Ministry forwarded the inquiry to the Defense Department. The Russians received their answers already by the next day. The details were not exactly what they wanted: (1) There were **no** scheduled passenger flights between Oslo and neighboring countries; and (2) although it was possible to land at Kjeller during the entire year, nevertheless, because it was a military airport, it was not held open for regular civilian air traffic. Furthermore, landings during the winter were affected by weather conditions, and the arrival of planes was very sporadic. And because of frequent snowstorms, planes touching down at Kjeller had to have **ski landing gear**.[45]

In Moscow the prosecutor, Andrei Vyshinsky, attempted the best he could to turn this information to his advantage. Recalling the unfortunate Pyatakov to the stand on the afternoon of January 27 to repeat his story of having been in Oslo, Vyshinsky inserted into the trial record that the Soviet legation had confirmed that Kjeller airport accepted aircraft during the entire year and that it was possible for planes to land and take off during the winter.[46]

This maneuver failed to have the desired effect; the Soviet claim was quickly disproven. *Arbeiderbladet* interviewed the head of the airport, Director Gulliksen, who insisted that no plane from Germany had landed at his field in December 1935.[47] This was later verified by Koht's Foreign Ministry. Through the Norwegian legation in Berlin, the German government confirmed that no plane had flown to Norway during the entire month of December 1935. In Oslo the Defense Department corroborated that there had been only one landing at Kjeller during December. This was a Norwegian plane with two passengers, which had flown in from Stockholm on December 21. It had remained on the ground until January 5 (thereby allowing the crew to recover sufficiently from any New Year's revelry they might have indulged in). Except for this single flight, no plane arriving from a foreign destination had been on the ground longer than twenty minutes between September 19, 1935, and May 1, 1936. Koht thereby concluded that it was impossible for Pyatakov to have flown to Kjeller in 1935–36, either in December or in any other month.[48]

Long before Pyatakov's alleged flight had been assessed, it was obvious that the story would not hold. Trotsky quickly realized this. Already on January 27 he drew up a list of thirteen questions (an appropriate number, considering Pyatakov's turncoat status) that he demanded Pyatakov answer before the trial was over. These were very specific, requiring him to provide much more concrete information about his supposed trip than the vague statements he had made in court.[49] Shortly afterwards, Knudsen sent a telegram to Vyshinsky, informing him that he, as Trotsky's host, could confirm that no conversation had taken place "between Trotsky and Pyatakov."[50] But such endeavors to force the Russians to accept the truth had no chance of success, as Trotsky knew perfectly well, although the idealistic Knudsen may have thought that his intervention could achieve positive results. The issue was quickly put to rest on January 30, the day after Knudsen sent his cable, when the court handed down its verdict. Pyatakov, along with twelve other defendants, received the death sentence.[51]* They were quickly dispatched in the usual manner—shot by the NKVD. Stalin thereby again revealed his steely resolve to allow no one to survive who could pose a potential threat to his dictatorial control and who in this instance might disprove the lies of Vyshinsky's prosecution.

In the case of Pyatakov's alleged journey, however, the hollowness of his coerced testimony was unmistakable to objective observers. Not only was it impossible for him to have traveled from Kjeller to Wexhall in only half an hour, but the statement by the airport director showed conclusively that

---

* Although Radek and Sokolnikov were among the four who did not formally receive the ultimate penalty, in reality they did. Both died in one of Stalin's hideous camps in 1939.

no flight had occurred. Nevertheless, there remained special interests who wished to sustain the myth that a conference between Trotsky and Pyatakov had indeed taken place. Using rather dubious logic, *Tidens Tegn* informed its readers in February 1937 that since Trotsky had received visitors in February 1936, this was adequate proof that he could have met Pyatakov during the previous December.[52] By early March 1937 the paper had concocted the hypothesis that Pyatakov's plane had landed not at Kjeller but on a snow-covered lake, Øyangen, located close to the Knudsen cabin, where Trotsky and Natalia had stayed for several days before Christmas. The paper even discovered a purported eyewitness who claimed he had seen the plane arrive.[53]

The Norwegian communists as usual accepted all of Moscow's accusations.[54] *Arbeideren* therefore enthusiastically agreed that Pyatakov's plane had come "from the south and landed on Øyangen." But even they realized that this version was weaker than the original myth of Pyatakov having flown to an airport near Oslo. Therefore, rather than provide evidence in support of their story, the communists insisted that the burden of proof rested with those who doubted that Pyatakov had deplaned at Øyangen in order to attend his clandestine meeting.[55]

This did not prove too difficult. The purported landing by a German pilot on a frozen lake in mid-winter in a heavily forested area that contained hundreds of snow-covered lakes might appeal to the conspiratorially minded, but it could not stand up to critical scrutiny. How had the pilot supposedly succeeded in finding the one lake that lay closest to the Knudsen cabin? Furthermore, the new fable completely contradicted Pyatakov's original story. Instead of meeting Trotsky in a comfortably furnished small villa a short distance from the airport, the tryst now allegedly had taken place on a different date in a spartan cabin on a tree-covered mountaintop that could only be reached by horse sled and skis. Knudsen effectively demolished *Tiden Tegn*'s fictional journalism.[56]

For Trotsky, however, what mattered most was the chance to destroy Stalin's credibility internationally. Now free of restrictions, he believed he was in a position to do so. He instructed Walter Held to secure affidavits from Norwegians who could discredit Moscow's claims. This included not only evidence to disprove Pyatakov's "alleged flight" but everything that had to do with Trotsky's stay in Norway.[57]

This material was for the investigative commission that Trotsky had been pushing for since the first Moscow trial. But, as he had experienced in Norway, it continued to be impossible to find an international socialist organization willing to sponsor such an inquiry, knowing it would immediately arouse a storm of denigration not only from the Kremlin but from communists worldwide. Nevertheless, Trotsky pressed ahead, maintaining that it was "utopian to wait for an ideal commission, above all attack and reproach."[58] As a result, the Preliminary Commission of Inquiry into the Charges Made Against Leon Trotsky in the Moscow Trials was created by the Trotskyite American Committee for the Defense of Leon Trotsky. Although the Preliminary Commission of Inquiry came to be known popularly as the Dewey Commission after its head, the eminent philosopher John Dewey,[59] who was not a follower of Trotsky, the fact that it had grown out of a Trotskyite group could not help but cast doubt on its objectivity.

Held busied himself with gathering the proof that Trotsky requested, which proved to be more laborious than anticipated. Støylen, as Trotsky's attorney, contacted airport director Gulliksen, asking him to provide an affidavit to reaffirm his statement that Pyatakov could not have landed at his airfield. But Gulliksen's superiors in the Defense Department refused permission.[60] Nevertheless, he did confirm the accuracy of his interview with *Arbeiderbladet*, which was exactly what Trotsky's supporters wished. Held could therefore report on March 12 that notarized translations of the Gulliksen interview, as well as copies of his letters to Støylen, had been forwarded to "the American committee."[61]

Trotsky placed special importance on notarized statements by the Knudsen family because of his close association with them. Although it proved time consuming to obtain English translations of affidavits from Konrad, Hilda, Hjørdis, and Borgar, this eventually was accomplished.[62] Erling Falk also provided an affidavit that refuted the Kremlin's claim about Trotsky's alleged conspiratorial activity in Copenhagen in 1932.[63]

The bulk of the Dewey Commission's work was conducted by a five-person subcommission headed by Dewey himself, which met at Trotsky's residence in Coyoacan from April 10 to April 17, 1937.[64] The location was undoubtedly chosen for security reasons. However, the fact that a more neutral site could not be utilized once more gave the impression that the commission was acting partisanly.

This was unfortunate because the testimony and affidavits formed a large body of evidence that conclusively proved Trotsky's innocence. Falk's affidavit showed that Trotsky's address in Denmark had been kept secret from all who spoke with him in order to protect his security, thereby precluding Russian conspirators from having met him at their leisure.[65]

Foreign visitors to Wexhall testified that the distance from Oslo to Heradsbygda disproved the claim that Pyatakov could have arrived after a short
drive of only half an hour.⁶⁶ Their testimony was buttressed by a road map,
plus director Gulliksen's statement about the absence of foreign planes at
Kjeller during the time of Pyatakov's mythical journey.⁶⁷

The Knudsen affidavits provided especially weighty evidence. Konrad, Hilda, and Hjørdis stated that a member of their family had always
been together with the Trotskys except for the brief period when Lev was
hospitalized. His only mode of travel when he left Wexhall had been as a
passenger in Knudsen's car. They further pointed out that no one could
have arrived at Wexhall without this being noticed, nor could Lev and
Natalia make arrangements for visitors by telephone since, in an age when
telephones were controlled by operators, they did not speak Norwegian.
And while it was revealed that Trotsky had met with Czechs, Germans,
Englishmen, and Americans, he never had received a Russian, and no visitors had arrived at all in December 1935, the time of Pyatakov's alleged
trip. As for the few days that Lev and Natalia had spent at their cabin, the
Knudsens showed convincingly that its location was little known, making
it impossible for foreigners to find their way there.⁶⁸ Borgar, in his separate
statement, testified that Trotsky, since he did not know how to ski, had stayed
entirely inside the cabin at Ringkollen, and it would have been impossible
for anyone to have met him without Borgar's knowledge. In an affidavit forwarded from Belgium, Erwin Wolf similarly declared that nearby Øyangen
had been covered with sixty to seventy centimeters of snow, and there had
been "not the slightest sign of a plane."⁶⁹ Trotsky himself completely demolished the story of Pyatakov's alleged trip with the telling observation that if
a German plane had flown to Norway, it would have needed wheels to take
off from Tempelhof, but ski landing gear to touch down on Øyangen's snow-
covered surface (incorrectly described by Trotsky as a "frozen fjord"). And if
a plane had landed on the lake, Pyatakov could only have traveled by horse
and sleigh, not by car, as he had claimed.⁷⁰

The evidence gathered by the Dewey Commission was impressive; it
was eventually published in two volumes. Trotsky was elated when the full
commission exonerated him in late 1937. He regarded its conclusion not
only as a personal vindication but, equally important, as a decisive blow
against Stalin: "a terrible verdict" against "the rulers of a great country."⁷¹

Ever the intellectual rationalist, Trotsky failed to recognize that political
opinion is not formed solely, or even primarily, by objective truth but rather

by a host of irrational attitudes that include self-interest, bias, preconceptions, ideology, distorted perceptions, and power. Trotsky's standing at the time was too weak, and he was generally regarded too negatively, for favorable conclusions about him to receive a positive reaction in world opinion. As Robert Conquest has put it, one might have thought the Pyatakov "debacle alone would have discredited the whole trial in foreign eyes. Anyone who may have hoped so found that Stalin's ideas about political gullibility were even better based than had first appeared."[72]

The Dewey Commission's judgment consequently did not have the effect that Trotsky had hoped for. Morgenstierne, the Norwegian minister to Washington, instead provided a more realistic assessment when he reported to Oslo: "In view of the commission's composition, this result was generally expected, and the conclusion therefore arouses little surprise here."[73] In Norway preconceived attitudes similarly remained unchanged. Although *Dagbladet* provided broad coverage of the commission's conclusion, *Arbeiderbladet*'s account consisted of five extremely small lines, carefully hidden away in the depths of the paper.[74]

Arbeiderbladet's lack of objectivity was not due merely to the controversy that Trotsky had previously generated. His ideological influence, referred to by opponents as "Trotskyism" (*trotskismen*), became an even more divisive question within the party than it had been before he left for Mexico. Not surprisingly, Olav Scheflo was embroiled in this controversy from its very beginning. His bitter rival was his former good friend, Jakob Friis, an ideologue who could find no wrong with the Soviet Union and who strongly supported Stalin's popular front tactics of the mid-1930s.

Friis was the state archivist in Kristiansand, and he also wrote foreign affairs commentary for *Sørlandet*. He was a veteran member of the labor movement. Always on its left wing, he had been an active communist in the late '20s and early '30s. By 1935, however, he rejoined the Labor Party, becoming its chairman in Kristiansand with Scheflo's active support. But during the fall of the next year, their friendship turned to enmity. Although they had divergent views on popular-front movements in France and Spain, they first and foremost disagreed bitterly about Trotsky. Friis had nothing but contempt for him and his politics. In yet another of his anti-Trotsky articles, published in *Arbeiderbladet* on December 29, 1936, he accused Scheflo of encouraging opposition to the government within party youth organizations in the Kristiansand area. In return, Scheflo vehemently charged Friis with being "dishonest and malicious." Their disagreement thereby became public.[75]

At issue were resolutions passed by two youth groups in the Kristiansand area in opposition to Trotsky's imprisonment. They favored full asylum rights for antifascist refugees, including freedom of expression. But Friis refused to submit their views to a party meeting in Kristiansand, arguing that this would result in a resolution that was critical of the government. The youth groups then turned to Scheflo, who declared himself willing to participate in a special meeting about the issue. It took place in late December, and although Scheflo was not present at first, he later joined the debate—of course, favoring the youth groups' viewpoint. Such a resolution was passed.[76]

The Labor Party in Kristiansand thereupon split, with Scheflo and Friis leading warring factions. The rivalry was intense, in particular because the two blocs were fairly evenly divided, with Scheflo enjoying a small majority. Nevertheless, it proved necessary for his supporters to mobilize each time the local party committee (*representantskap*) met in order to prevent Friis's backers from ousting Scheflo as editor of *Sørlandet*.[77]

In Oslo the leadership sought to eliminate this disunity by sending Trygve Lie to arrange a settlement. On January 17, at a large party meeting, Lie spoke about Trotsky and the right of asylum, followed by a long discussion. In the end an apparent compromise was worked out, with a resolution being passed that declared that no one was guilty of organizing factional division in Kristiansand.[78] In reality, however, this was a repudiation of Friis since he had charged Scheflo with engaging in just this kind of activity.

For the time being the latter had the upper hand since the Labor Party did not want to reject one of its best-known figures. But Friis was never one to abandon his position for the sake of harmony. He and Scheflo constantly collided at party meetings because of their different viewpoints concerning the Moscow trials, the role of the P.O.U.M. in the Spanish Civil War, and Trotsky. Friis resigned as local party chairman in March, and Scheflo editorially warmly welcomed his successor. Friis thereupon ceased writing for the paper.[79] However, he remained active in politics on both the local and national levels.[80]

The Labor Party leadership was therefore faced during 1937 with two factions that refused to be quiescent. On the one hand, there was the small but vocal group of critics centered around Meyer, Scheflo, and Knudsen—supported by persons outside the party—who continued to fault the government because of its treatment of Trotsky, and who, in particular in the person of Meyer, was equally critical of the party's recent change to more moderate politics. The second faction, fiercely opposed to the first, included Friis and his backers, plus a similarly minded group in the southwest coastal town of Stavanger. Sometimes referred to jointly as the "popular front" faction, it favored the Soviet Union's policies. Its members obviously detested Trotsky and what they regarded as Trotskyite politics.[81]

Such disunity was greeted with pleasure by the party's nonsocialist opposition. *Tidens Tegn*, for example, early in 1937 raised the absurd possibility that Scheflo might rejoin the Communist Party because he and the communists both opposed certain moderate policies of the Labor leadership. Seeking to make this bogus issue as plausible as possible, *Tidens Tegn* added that Scheflo enjoyed considerable support within the Labor Party, as evidenced by Meyer's equally critical point of view.[82]

Scheflo soon disabused anyone naive enough to think so by launching a biting attack against a leading communist, Christian Hilt, who had just published a brochure defending the second show trial. His entire publication, Scheflo editorialized, consisted of lies. He furthermore took the opportunity to denounce Friis indirectly, pointing to certain unnamed "fellow [Labor] party members" who had warmly endorsed Hilt's scurrilous tract.[83]

Others among Trotsky's defenders similarly attempted to discredit those who gave credence to the trial. In February eight well-known left-wing authors, including three who had previously voiced sympathy for Trotsky—Helge Krog, Sigurd Hoel, and Arnulf Øverland—issued an open letter denouncing Lion Feuchtwanger, a prominent German author in exile who had whitewashed the show trials. The letter condemned the recently completed show trial of Radek, Pyatakov, and Sokolnikov, accusing Feuchtwanger of defending "judicial murder." The authors specifically referred to the falsity of Pyatakov's alleged confession, pointing out that he could never have met with Trotsky.[84]

Although only a minority of the writers had ties to Trotsky, his backers sought to attract as much publicity for the letter as possible. Held informed Trotsky that he had sent copies to all German exile periodicals, to Scandinavian newspapers, and to the *Manchester Guardian*.[85] Held further emphasized that Krog, Hoel, and Øverland had played a part in gaining the Nobel Peace Prize for Ossietzky in 1935, defending him from Knut

Hamsun's attacks.*[86] Trotsky in turn asked Held to convey his heartiest best wishes to the eight authors for their "very good letter."[87]

The pro-Trotsky faction did not restrict itself just to polemics against defenders of Stalin's show trials, as Trygve Lie discovered when he attempted to justify the government's handling of Trotsky at a meeting of the Norwegian Student Association on Saturday, February 20. A number of Trotsky's defenders were on hand. Although Held, with the threat of deportation hanging over his head, kept quiet, he thoroughly enjoyed the fireworks that erupted. Krog spoke up immediately after Lie, declaring that although Hambro had previously held the record for political dishonesty and unreliability in Norway, he was now facing a strong challenge from the Minister of Justice. Konrad Knudsen followed with a detailed factual repudiation of what Lie had stated. He rejected as a falsehood in particular the allegation that Trotsky really had preferred to remain a prisoner in Norway rather than go to Mexico. Held described the audience as being "shocked" by Knudsen's stern denunciation, but he nevertheless received a warm ovation because of his moving admiration for Trotsky. Thereafter, said Held, the "Nazi attorney" Albert Wiesener was the first to attempt to justify "Stalin's and Trygve Lie's case." The minister of justice himself was not about to be silenced and defended his point of view vigorously, but Meyer, seconded by Kjell Ottesen, sharply and effectively repudiated Lie point by point.[88]

Lie was not without additional defenders, including Trond Hegna, the current leader of Mot Dag, plus a "Stalinist" attorney. The debate in the Student Association, which Knudsen and his friend Terje Morseth described as being the most contentious they could ever remember, continued into the early morning, not ending until 1:30 a.m. Knudsen and Held were both satisfied, with Held maintaining that most of the audience had "provided great support for us."[89]

The confrontation was commented on broadly in the press. The Labor Party paper in Stavanger, *Iste Mai* (May 1), condemned Krog for having unleashed "a downpour of insults against the Justice Minister and his party," with Knudsen not lagging far behind. Meyer also was censured for allegedly saying that Lie's presentation had been "disgraceful," causing him to

---

* Carl von Ossietzky, an internationally renowned pacifist, was jailed by Hitler. He was not allowed to come to Oslo to receive the Peace Prize and died while still imprisoned in 1938. Hamsun, one of Norway's major authors who was well known for his pro-German sympathies, attacked Ossietzky for being a traitor to his country.

feel "ashamed [to be] a member of the party." The paper reported that Lie, on the other hand, regarded the unexpected hostility he received as evidence of the likely "start of a Trotskyite group."[90]

Not surprisingly, Lie's critics experienced repercussions. The justice minister was highly upset and on the following day threatened Knudsen with exclusion from the party. But to expel a newly elected member of parliament who enjoyed significant goodwill in his province, at a time when the Storting had not finished its deliberations about Trotsky, could have had significant ramifications. Lie therefore had to content himself with snubbing Knudsen.[91]

Meyer was in a more exposed position and received considerably stronger criticism. The chairman of the Oslo Workers Association demanded to know why Meyer allegedly had declared he was ashamed to belong to the Labor Party and why he had publicly announced that he had been threatened with expulsion because of his attitude concerning Trotsky.[92] Meyer refused to reply. He instead sent the association's board of directors a statement that he had submitted to *Arbeiderbladet* (which refused to publish it). He declared, as he had in the debate, that Trygve Lie's handling of the Trotsky affair had damaged the Labor Party's international reputation. His viewpoint, said Meyer, had only been strengthened by Lie's attempt to defend himself at the meeting.[93]

Meyer's defiant attitude did not affect his position within the Workers Association, where he continued to serve as its representative on the Oslo Labor Party's Central Committee (*representantskap*) until the German occupation.[94] But for a time during 1937 he was hard pressed, facing a far more dangerous antagonist than the association's chairman. In May Martin Tranmæl launched a direct frontal assault against not only Trotskyism but anyone in Norway who had defended Trotsky. Obviously, Meyer would be one of the main targets of Tranmæl's wrath.

The reason for the crackdown had been alluded to by Trygve Lie at the contentious Student Association meeting—concern that a Trotskyite group might be established. As long as Trotsky had been in the country, this had not been possible due to his pledge of noninvolvement in Norwegian politics. But now, with Trotsky enjoying the balmier climate of Mexico, this was no longer a hindrance. On the contrary, he favored such a step. Consequently, in April 1937 an openly Trotskyite group came into being, centered around a small monthly paper, *Oktober*, named appropriately in honor of the revolution that Lenin and Trotsky had led. It was edited by Jeanette Olsen, a veteran member of the labor movement. Although Meyer and Scheflo did not belong, they could not avoid being identified with it.

In its first issue the paper headlined a quote from Scheflo in which he bitingly condemned Stalin for branding everyone who opposed him as "Trotskyites."[95] The inference was clear—in Norway the Labor Party leadership was equally guilty of this offense. With reference to the now infamous Student Association meeting, Olsen also took the minister of justice to task, derisively challenging Lie's claim that a Trotskyite organization had no chance of success. Reactionaries, she maintained, had used the same argument when socialism first appeared in Norway. She brashly argued that, on the contrary, Trotskyism was the only part of the labor movement that had a future.[96] Olsen had thereby thrown down the gauntlet, a challenge that Tranmæl could not ignore.

He fired the first shot across the bow of the rising threat of Trotskyism when *Arbeiderbladet* on May 7 printed Trond Hegna's review of the proceedings of the second show trial, recently published by the Norwegian Communist Party. As a leading supporter of the Soviet Union in the Labor Party, Hegna accepted the conclusion that the defendants were guilty. He was not willing, however, to go as far as Friis and other defenders of Stalin and assume that leading Old Bolsheviks had conspired with "the fascist world powers." But they most likely, Hegna maintained, had engaged in anti-Stalinist activity and had confessed to atone for past misdeeds and to strengthen the communist cause. He credulously concluded that their admissions of guilt were voluntary, not the result of coercion.[97]

Having prepared the ground, Tranmæl followed five days later with a damning editorial. Attacking Trotsky and his followers for dividing the international labor movement, he described Trotskyism as a "poison plant." In Spain, where the people were fighting heroically against Franco and his mercenaries, Trotskyites and anarchists in Catalonia had stabbed the popular front in the back. In France and in other countries, Trotskyites were working to undermine attempts at political unity. Tranmæl to some degree even held Trotskyites responsible for misdeeds in the Soviet Union. Although he admitted that he previously had taken the strongest stand against the show trials, refusing to believe that Old Bolsheviks had become "traitors and provocateurs," he now asked whether they nevertheless might have developed dubious ties and made mistakes. He thereby, at least by inference, gave some credence to Stalin's accusations.

Within Norway *Arbeiderbladet's* editor claimed that there was no threat of the degenerative Trotskyite sect gaining influence. Nevertheless, he warned that certain members of the labor movement might not know where to draw the line separating the Labor Party from Trotskyism. One example was Scheflo, whose positive outlook toward Trotskyites and anarchists in Catalonia could only be explained by his admiration for Trotsky. Tranmæl specifically warned Scheflo to reconsider in time to avoid serious consequences. Tranmæl was even more withering toward Meyer, accusing him of leading the "intellectual circle" that acted as Trotsky's armed retainers in attacking the Labor Party and its government. Tranmæl went so far as to charge Meyer and his associates with creating an independent position outside the party, with their own organization and publication. This revealed a real danger of "backsliding" into Trotskyism.[98]

Walter Held, reporting to Trotsky the next day, maintained that Tranmæl's "shameless campaign" had been triggered by the first two numbers of *Oktober*. Held indignantly felt that Tranmæl wished to deprive his targets of their livelihoods, which would be especially severe for "old, sick Scheflo."[99]

The latter clearly recognized the exposed position he was in, but it would have been unnatural for him to recant. In a carefully worded response he avoided confrontation by devoting most space to attacking Norwegian communists for spreading lies and distortions about him because of his opposition to Stalin. While he did not regard Tranmæl's criticism as "satisfactory," he nevertheless described the latter's editorial as having been "relatively objective." But Scheflo did defend his support for the P.O.U.M. and openly stated his sympathy for Trotsky. And in repudiation of Tranmæl's critique that he was in danger of sliding into Trotskyism, *Sørlandet's* editor firmly declared that his political sympathies had never tempted him to engage in factionalism.[100] He thereby made it plain he should not be viewed as a Trotskyite.

Held chose to interpret Scheflo's statement more positively, stating that while Scheflo had expressed himself diplomatically, he had succeeded in equating Tranmæl's outlook with that of the communists. Furthermore, Held wrote Trotsky that Scheflo was firm in his solidarity "with you and the Spanish revolution." Held was further encouraged by *Tidens Tegn,* which asserted that "the spirit of Trotskyism" was now beginning to spread also in Norway.[101]

He based his optimism on the belief that Scheflo and Meyer's personal sympathies meant that they fully agreed with Trotsky, which they did not. Nevertheless, Held had reason to feel encouraged. Shortly afterwards, Tranmæl's arch faultfinder, Helge Krog, delivered yet another broadside.

Although brief in contrast with his previous commentaries, what made this article unusual was the publicity it provided for the new Trotskyite movement in Norway. Even if he did not openly proclaim himself a member, Krog nevertheless sympathized so strongly that it is no exaggeration to conclude that at this time he could be regarded as such. And while he had no political following, his support was significant because of his celebrity status in intellectual circles. Trotsky, when reading the article,[102] unquestionably felt he had gained a dedicated follower.

Krog declared that persecution not only produced protests but also sympathy for the persecuted. Before the government had interned and muzzled Trotsky, there had been no Trotskyite organization in Norway. Now, however, Krog pointed out, such a group had come into being, led by Jeanette Olsen. She had recently issued a small pamphlet, a translation of a radio address relayed by Trotsky to some 6600 listeners in New York. Being free in Mexico, he intended to disprove Moscow's accusations in testimony to the Dewey Commission (whose hearings were upcoming). Krog praised the fact that Trotsky, living in a society that was "less fearful and more broadminded than ours," could now refute all the absurd charges in the show trials, and he encouraged his readers to buy Olsen's pamphlet.[103]

The controversy heightened even more when Meyer answered Tranmæl's editorial in a response that, unlike Scheflo's, was highly undiplomatic. He accused Tranmæl of making vague accusations, refusing to discuss specific issues. Meyer denied that two of the socialist endeavors he was associated with, the Socialist Cultural Front and *Kamp og kultur* (Struggle and Culture), could in any way be considered Trotskyite. Instead, he sarcastically compared Tranmæl to Stalin, calling everything Trotskyism that was in opposition to *Arbeiderbladet*'s viewpoint. Meyer did not deny that he disagreed with the government's current reform policy. He also openly declared that he did not regret his defense of Trotsky's right of asylum and his opposition to how Trotsky had been dealt with. As for his part in the Student Association meeting, Meyer maintained that he, unlike the minister of justice, had simply presented the truth. Meyer concluded with a challenge, insisting that since neither he nor Scheflo had sought to organize a Trotskyite faction, there ought to be room for free expression in the Labor Party so that it could develop to the fullest.[104]

Tranmæl could not allow such criticism to remain unanswered and attached his refutation after Meyer's lengthy reply. Since there was no possibility of reconciliation, he clearly intended to isolate Meyer for having separated himself from the mainstream of the Labor Party. Tranmæl charged that not only had *Kamp og kultur* engaged in "a slimy attack" against *Arbeiderbladet's* weekly magazine, it had published an article by Meyer that falsely gave the impression that Ossietzky could have been rescued from his Nazi jailers if only Koht, as both foreign minister and member of the Nobel Peace Prize Committee, had acted more decisively. Similarly, Meyer stood accused of helping create the Socialist Cultural Front without consulting the party leadership. With regard to Meyer's support for Trotsky, Tranmæl charged him with being closely associated with backstabbing "parlor radicals" (alluding to Meyer's family ties with Krog) during the debate in the Student Association. Furthermore, Tranmæl insisted, Meyer had admitted that he shared a basic Trotskyite trait: opposition to the "positive" politics conducted by all active socialist parties in Europe, who were implementing welfare reforms. While Tranmæl would not go so far as to characterize Meyer as a member of the Fourth International, he nevertheless was contributing to uncertainty and passivity within the working class, which Trotskyism speculated in.[105]

Nor did Tranmæl let up editorially against Scheflo. He and Meyer were lumped together, serving to illustrate a couple of negative examples within the labor movement that deserved special attention. In an editorial on May 29, most of Tranmæl's fire was directed toward Scheflo. While he and others who admired Trotsky might deny they were Trotskyites, they nevertheless were being steadily drawn down the slippery slope toward Trotskyism.[106]

Tranmæl's determination to prevent Trotskyite contamination colored ever more his opinion of events within the Soviet Union. In an editorial published on June 14, the day after the purge of leading Red Army officers, Tranmæl sent out mixed signals. He declared it was clear that an "extensive opposition movement" had been organized in Russia that did not hesitate to carry out "antisocial" or even "traitorous" actions. He went so far as to maintain that "systematic sabotage" had undoubtedly been conducted by Trotsky's backers, whom he also found guilty of collaborating with agents of foreign powers. Nevertheless, the editor qualified his condemnation by declaring that a feeling of "uncertainty and horror" still remained about whether those who had been purged were guilty.[107]

Three days later Tranmæl went even further, providing justification, or at the least tolerance, for Stalin's methods. He insisted that it was not enough to condemn what was happening in the Soviet Union; one had also to attempt to "*understand*" (*Arbeiderbladet's* emphasis) the forces that were in collision in Russia. Tranmæl accused the opposition supporting Trotsky, plus groups he cooperated with, of being responsible for negative developments in the U.S.S.R. Tranmæl now accepted the guilt of the executed officers, declaring that they were part of an elite class that had ties to the discredited tsarist regime. And while this group was described as having a different outlook from those around Trotsky and Zinoviev, all of the opposition forces had sought to establish a common front against Stalin. They were therefore, said Tranmæl, not revolutionary but rather counter-revolutionary. Although he still deplored Stalin's methods as "revolting," he maintained that they were typical of dictatorships in general, in other words not unique for the communist despot.

Arbeiderbladet's editor concluded by discrediting Scheflo's defense of Trotsky. Referring to "violent attacks" against Stalin in *Sørlandet*, Tranmæl mockingly commented that the paper placed Stalin in the same league as Ivan the Terrible and Philip II, with his being "accused of wanting to replace the dictatorship of the proletariat with his personal despotism." Tranmæl described this view, which Scheflo and Trotsky shared, as being "highly superficial and emotional."* He argued that if Trotsky were to replace Stalin, the methods employed by the Soviet government would not change but might even become worse.[108]

Although he felt beleaguered, Scheflo stuck to his guns. He was careful to print *Arbeiderbladet*'s viewpoint in *Sørlandet*, thereby giving the party leadership no grounds for expulsion, but he refused to compromise concerning two major points attacked by Tranmæl: (1) Scheflo's support for the P.O.U.M. in Spain and (2) his condemnation of Stalin's brutality and lies during the show trials. While Scheflo printed *Arbeiderbladet*'s criticism of the P.O.U.M., on July 10 he also expressed agreement with the paper's call for an inquiry into the persecution of Andres Nin's party. If such an investigation were held, Scheflo wrote, it would undoubtedly reveal that the Spanish section of the Comintern was responsible for the "horrible events" that had resulted in the bloody suppression of the P.O.U.M.[109]

The cagey editor managed to combine his denunciations of Stalin's practices with support for Meyer. The latter had disclosed in May that a book he

---

* Time would show Scheflo's view of Stalin to have been more accurate than that of Tranmæl in 1937, something the old party leader, who lived to experience the post-Stalin period in Russian history, could not fail to recognize.

was editing, *Behind the Moscow Trials* (*Bak Moskva Prosessene*), would soon appear. It contained articles by Scheflo, Knudsen, and several prominent international socialists. However, Meyer was its main contributor, as well as the driving force behind its publication. Furthermore, the book's key articles dealt with a topic that its title did not reveal—Lev Trotsky's Norwegian exile. The first third of the volume devoted itself solely to this subject, while several later articles on the show trials also made reference to Trotsky. To a considerable degree, Trotsky, not Stalin, was therefore the book's main focus. *Behind the Moscow Trials* was not only negative toward Stalin but also quite critical of how Trotsky had been treated. However, its polemics were not extreme, in particular because Meyer wisely did not include Krog's writings.

Not surprisingly, its publication received very favorable publicity in *Sørlandet*. Scheflo gave the assignment of reviewing the book to his young protégé, Per Monsen, thereby avoiding direct responsibility for the superlatives that it received. Monsen also provided support for Scheflo's controversial view of Spanish politics, having earlier covered the Civil War from Spain for both *Sørlandet* and *Arbeiderbladet*.[110] To further emphasize the relevance of *Behind the Moscow Trials*, Monsen included for comparison a second book within his review with a diametrically opposite point of view, Trond Hegna's *The Soviet Union, Stalin and the Generals* (*Sovjet, Stalin og generalene*).

Monsen pointed out that most of Hegna's publication provided a positive assessment of Soviet progress, with discussion of the Moscow trials limited to 31 of 112 pages. By using this organizational approach, said Monsen, the author skillfully created admiration for Stalin's leadership. And while Hegna did clearly state that the show trials did not provide specific evidence linking the defendants with German and Japanese fascism, he rationalized Stalin's methods, insisting that democratic niceties could not be observed when the Soviet Union was facing enemies on all sides while endeavoring to sustain the workers' revolution. Monsen attacked such "cynical reasoning," asking how socialism was helped, even if the Soviet Union became the world's most powerful state, if its political system was based on the murder of party comrades. He pointed out, quite correctly, that the purges were not limited just to the major show trials but involved the execution of thousands of dedicated party members and civil servants.

The review's content clearly showed Scheflo's tactical influence. Monsen made only passing reference to the parts of *Behind the Moscow Trials* dealing with Trotsky's experience in Norway. Instead, he focused almost all of his attention on the criticism of the show trials by foreign socialists. In this way his condemnation of Stalin's methods took on an international character, indicating subtly that Scheflo and Meyer's critical views did not represent just a small faction within the Labor Party that was in conflict with its leadership. Similarly, in support of Scheflo's positive outlook toward the P.O.U.M, Monsen showed how the book's articles provided evidence that Soviet practices had spread to other nations, as shown by mass arrests in Spain. The reviewer used this condemnation of communist procedure to criticize party leaders in Norway, stating that in addition to Russia and Spain, in other countries also, if on a more minor scale, socialists who did not agree with their party's general policy "are branded as criminals and semi-fascists." This tendency, said Monsen, could be "fatal for the labor movement." It stifled all revolutionary thought. If democracy within the labor movement were destroyed, the movement's revolutionary force would also be demolished.[111] This conclusion was, of course, identical to Scheflo and Meyer's position.

Their stand naturally endeared them to Trotsky, who regarded the two, plus Knudsen, as his most important allies in Norway.* When Trotsky received a copy of *Behind the Moscow Trials*, he declared that he intended to thank Meyer personally. He furthermore expressed appreciation for "old Scheflo," who despite his "paralyzing illness . . . is fighting so bravely." This, said Lev, could only deepen his and Natalia's devotion to their "courageous friend."[112]

Jakob Friis also appreciated *Behind the Moscow Trials* but for an entirely different reason. He believed it provided him with a perfect opportunity to inflict a political deathblow against his rivals, Scheflo and Meyer, already weakened by Tranmæl's onslaught. As his weapon he wrote yet another brochure, *Trotskyism: A Poison Plant* (*Trotskismen. En giftplante*).[113] As its title indicated, Friis sought to give the impression that he solidly agreed with the Labor Party leadership, plagiarizing Tranmæl's anti-Trotskyite editorial of May 12, in which he called Trotsky's movement a poison plant. Friis accused Scheflo and Meyer not only of factional activity but maintained that they were planning a new party. *Behind the Moscow Trials*, Friis argued, was intended to be its platform.[114] His goal was clear: to have Meyer and Scheflo expelled from the Labor Party.

Encouraged by Tranmæl's recent change in attitude toward Stalin, Friis went to extremes. He uncritically accepted as "evidence" Moscow's

---

* Trotsky's high regard for Scheflo did not extend to the latter's admiration for the P.O.U.M. and its leader, Andres Nin, who was regarded as a renegade after he broke with Trotsky.

accusations against Trotsky, and he maintained that Scheflo and Meyer had full knowledge of Trotsky's conspiratorial activity, including his alleged collaboration with fascist states.[115] Friis thereby insisted that his two opponents, especially his rival Scheflo, had become full-fledged Trotskyites. Friis sought to show how isolated Scheflo was by maintaining that only one Norwegian newspaper, *Sørlandet*, had defended the "criminal insanity" of the Barcelona uprising (of May 1937), in which the P.O.U.M. had been heavily involved. This in turn had created "anxiety" within the Labor Party's leadership, which now realized that Trotskyism had not departed with Trotsky to Mexico. Friis quoted with approval Tranmæl's warning that "Trotskyism both as an idea and a movement is a poison plant."[116] At the end of his brochure, Friis left his readers in no doubt that Scheflo and Meyer had to be ousted. Trotskyism, he wrote, needed to be dealt with in the same way as any evil: "one eradicates it."[117]

On this occasion, unlike previously, the party leadership did not reprimand Friis when he accused Trotsky's defenders of factionalism, although he could have been charged with the same offense. The brochures that he issued in 1937 were not published under the Labor Party's imprimatur but by the Communist Party's press. The Labor Party's Central Committee did consider this breach of party discipline serious enough to bring it up for discussion but chose to take no action.[118] This was in contrast to Meyer's *Behind the Moscow Trials*, which was published by a nonsocialist press, Tanum, only after having been rejected by Labor Party publishers. But while Friis received no reproof and was allowed to voice his views in *Arbeiderbladet*, he nevertheless did not gain the satisfaction of seeing Scheflo and Meyer ousted. Above all, Tranmæl wished to maintain party unity. His goal was to isolate and limit Scheflo and Meyer's influence, not to expel them.

There is no doubt, however, that for much of 1937 the party's leaders were concerned that the contagion of Trotskyism might spread, with the greatest threat coming from Meyer and Scheflo. Their fire therefore remained largely focused on this duo. However, as the issue began to fade, Scheflo, because of his loyal backing of the government's reform policy and since he heeded the warning against factionalism, retained his editorship. Meyer, on the other hand, consistently more critical of the party's policies as well as voicing intellectual disapproval of its mainstream publications, was perceived as needing to have his wings clipped even more. At the height of Tranmæl's campaign against "Trotskyism," the party therefore moved against two of Meyer's major bastions, the Socialist Cultural Front and its organ, *Kamp og kultur*. The periodical was denied funding in July 1937 and consequently was forced to cease publication. Later in the year, in September, the leadership arranged a discussion among party intellectuals that resulted in the Cultural Front's being co-opted. It was replaced by a new, party-true organization, the Socialist Cultural League (*Sosialistisk Kulturlag*) at the beginning of 1938.[119]

The Labor Party's campaign concluded in January 1938 when the party's National Committee formally condemned Trotskyism. Anyone considered a Trotskyite could henceforth be expelled. As the driving force behind this effort, Tranmæl, as always, was motivated by pragmatic considerations. The challenge posed by the possible spread of Trotskyism, in particular from the "Scheflo-Meyer group," had caused him, in order to compromise them, not merely to attack their alleged tendency toward "Trotskyism" but also to adopt a more positive view of Stalin's politics. This outlook was further influenced by ongoing negotiations in 1937 with the communists about some kind of a future union. When these ended in failure in late 1937/early 1938, and with any possible threat to party unity by Scheflo and Meyer having been effectively eliminated, Tranmæl immediately adopted a more critical tone toward Moscow. Most notably, from then on he consistently rejected the validity of the show trials.[120]

The hostility of the mainstream Labor Party press toward Trotskyism in 1937 was influenced during the first half of that year by yet another political factor that for a time proved significant. Although Trotsky had been ousted before the Storting convened, the cabinet still had to face an inquiry into how his exile had been managed, in particular its use of provisional decrees. The prime minister did not regard the upcoming parliamentary session with full confidence, having earlier, as noted, feared that repercussions from the Trotsky affair might lead to the fall of his government.

Following the king's speech from the throne, the Storting began its traditional debate in February, with its main focus on the past election. Although the tone was often strident, it quickly became apparent that the government was not threatened since the Agrarian Party signaled its continued cooperation.[121] Nor did the Trotsky question receive major attention. The government informed the Storting that the Justice Department would provide a full report about the Trotsky affair. When Hambro doubted whether it would contain a complete account of the exchange of diplomatic notes with the Soviet Union, Koht assured him that this would be included.[122] The report, officially authored by Trygve Lie, was presented immediately. It skillfully provided a sparse factual narrative, encompassing slightly more than five pages, of Trotsky's entire stay in Norway, from the time he sought asylum to when he went ashore in Tampico. It included also five appendices of reports and legal testimony used to justify his internment, plus the exchange of notes with the U.S.S.R.[123] The release of this information succeeded in placing Trotsky on the back burner, with the Storting being assured that it would have the opportunity of later returning to the issue. Koht, in a self-congratulatory manner, went so far as to declare that Norway had maintained its honor, even if this had involved the risk of offending "a foreign state." Somewhat bombastically, he insisted that everyone who valued "our freedom and independence" should be pleased with the way in which the matter had been resolved.[124]

Only one representative, Christian Stray of the Liberals, raised a really critical question. Referring to Pyatakov's alleged visit, he declared that it should be officially determined whether this really had occurred or whether the death sentences in Moscow had been levied "on a false basis." Furthermore, he wished to know whether relations with the Soviet Union had become less friendly because of failure to enforce Trotsky's original asylum terms.[125] Koht easily parried the question about diplomatic relations, providing his stock answer that the subject had been settled satisfactorily. As for Pyatakov's flight, however, he sought to postpone this difficulty by evasively stating that he had not yet obtained all "factual information" that he needed to make a determination, but he conceded that this would be "useful" for the government to have, and "perhaps" also the Storting.[126]

Trotsky's supporters attempted afterwards to force Koht to issue a formal conclusion, in particular since Vyshinsky's **entire** case rested on the defendants' oral testimony. Støylen, as Trotsky's attorney, requested Koht to provide him with the result of the investigation as soon as it was known, but the foreign minister did not answer.[127] Scheflo similarly sought to apply pressure in two articles, on March 3 and March 8. He stated that so much time had elapsed since the Storting debate that it was permissible to ask when Koht's finding might be released. Scheflo pointed out that this information would be invaluable for the Dewey Commission, which had just begun its work in the United States.[128]

His critical attitude diminished any influence he might have. Ole Colbjørnsen had earlier stated openly in parliament that the Labor Party leadership would not be responsible for "personal statements and articles by Mr. Scheflo and Mr. Håkon Meyer," and others whose "divergent opinions" differed from the party's official position.[129] Koht's internal investigation was never made public. As before, his main concern was to maintain good relations with the Soviet Union.

The Storting's deliberations about Trotsky had only been postponed, however, not concluded. Furthermore, one of his strongest champions, Konrad Knudsen, was now a member and could be expected to express his criticism with greater effect. He informed Trotsky that the subject was being discussed and he believed more than half of the Labor Party's delegation "were dissatisfied with the government . . . in this case."[130] The question had been submitted to the Storting's Protocol Committee, which procedurally would forward its conclusion to the parliament's lower chamber, the Odelsting.* But the process was slow, not completed until June.

The committee of five nonsocialist and four Labor Party representatives issued its report on the eighth. As expected, it split into two factions. The nonsocialist majority concluded that there had been no reason to allow someone as controversial as Trotsky into the country. Furthermore, it was inexplicable why the parliament had not been consulted, in particular since it was in session at the time. But the bourgeois representatives limited their criticism largely to this. They chauvinistically chose not to examine the use of the provisional decrees, stating that it was not necessary to determine whether they were valid because they had been applied only against Trotsky (a foreigner) in an emergency situation. Similarly, the majority declared that it would not present any additional criticism because the government had succeeded "under very great difficulties" in "removing Trotsky from the country," thereby admitting its error of granting him entry.

The Labor representatives, as expected, found the government blameless, insisting that it had adhered to the right of asylum that was standard in many countries and had acted in a humanitarian manner because Trotsky and his wife had both been ill when they sought admittance. However, the majority and the minority did agree that the provisional decrees were so far-reaching that it was obvious such measures should

---

* Although unicameral, the Storting until 2009 divided into two sections following each election, an upper chamber called the Lagting, containing one-fourth of the representatives and a lower chamber, the Odelsting, with three-fourths of the representatives.

be used only "under extraordinary conditions in which there is no doubt that the country's security absolutely requires it."[131] The entire committee thereby signaled its recognition that the government had acted in the national interest.

Certainly there was nothing in the report that Trotsky's supporters could consider encouraging. Held wrote angrily to Krog on the next day that he did not know which of the two findings was most "shameless," that of the majority or of the minority.[132] There still existed within the Labor Party, however, some concern that the question might have negative consequences. Therefore, prior to the Odelsting debate, *Arbeiderbladet* published an article by Jakob Friis, Trotsky's most vehement critic, that appealed to "honest bourgeois democrats" in the Storting not to be led astray by "impudent political swindlers" who merely used democratic arguments to mask their selfish interests.[133]

Friis's transparent ploy to divide the nonsocialist majority, the Liberals and Agrarians from the Conservatives, did not prove necessary. The debate was conducted in a low-key manner. Although the Conservatives had originally considered using the Trotsky affair to pass a motion of no confidence, as revealed by their representatives during the Protocol Committee's early deliberations,[134] the other nonsocialist parties refused to consider this. Furthermore, as the committee's report had shown, the government's position had been strengthened by its successful expulsion of Trotsky, preventing the opposition from exploiting the discontent that his continued presence would have created. The fact that the dispute had international implications also tended to dampen the debate.

The result was that the Odelsting completed its deliberations in a single day, June 21. The opposition maintained a low profile. Only a limited number of representatives took part in the debate, with Labor Party speakers being in the majority, including two cabinet ministers, Lie and Nygaardsvold. Especially noteworthy was the lack of participation by the Agrarian Party. Only one member, the Protocol Committee's chairman, added his name to the speakers' list, and he did so largely to rebut what he regarded as erroneous comments about his committee.[135]

Heaviest criticism of the government focused on the fact that it had granted Trotsky permission to enter Norway. The cabinet's critics maintained that he truly had not deserved asylum because of his previous political activity, which included urging the overthrow of the Norwegian system of government.[136] The cabinet's use of provisional decrees also came in for its share of disapproval, in particular from the Conservatives. Doubts were raised about the legality of denying Trotsky access to the court system; whether his internment constituted extralegal punishment; and the arbitrary, nonjudicial, manner in which the government had acted against him.[137] Nonsocialist representatives also repudiated the Labor Party's claim that they had unfairly used Trotsky as an issue in the recent election. Mowinckel in particular did not disguise his partisanship, declaring that he would have been "extremely stupid" not to have exploited "such an excellent card."[138]

Many of the arguments presented by Labor Party spokesmen were simply repeats of what had been stated over and over again in the press. Norway, it was maintained, had an obligation to provide asylum for political refugees, and Trotsky had especially deserved admission because of illness.[139] Lie furthermore cited as precedent that the Mowinckel government had also granted Trotsky an entry permit and argued tellingly that the Storting had been in session but offered no formal objection when he came to Norway. The minister of justice similarly asserted his conviction that the provisional decrees would have been found constitutional if they had been submitted to a Norwegian court[140] (which no longer was necessary after Trotsky had dropped his suit). As before, the official Labor Party line was that Trotsky was responsible for the treatment he had received. He had violated his asylum and refused to accept more stringent limitations. The government had thereby faced an emergency. If it had not interned Trotsky, this would have led to "international difficulties."[141] Prime Minister Nygaardsvold succinctly summarized his view of the dilemma when he intimated that if Norway had not been "a small country against a large [one]," then the outcome would have been very different.[142] When Scheflo read this, he understandably regarded it as vindication. Sørlandet's headline the next day underlined Nygaardsvold's inference that Trotsky's stay "had created difficulties . . . because Norway is a little country."[143]

For Held, this grudging admission was no consolation. Most speakers who faulted the government did not extend their sympathies to Trotsky. Even Konrad Knudsen did not fully live up to expectations. Held in particular had looked forward to his presentation.[144] The newly elected representative did act as anticipated in one sense. He made no attempt to hide his admiration for Trotsky. But at the same time, Knudsen made it clear that he now was a team player. He praised the government for its reform policies while castigating the opposition, especially the Conservatives, for having attempted to use Trotsky as a scare tactic in the election. Knudsen also took pains to emphasize that he was not a Trotskyite, insisting, "I too am a political opponent of Trotsky."[145]

Although he began his address, one of the longest in the debate, by praising the government for fulfilling its duty as a democratic state by granting asylum to political refugees, he deviated from the official position by declaring that Trotsky had not violated his residence permit but had "acted in good faith." Trotsky had not regarded its terms as a prohibition against commentary about current politics. To sustain his point, Knudsen brought up the embarrassing incident in July 1935 when Trotsky, in a newspaper interview, had expressed himself freely on a number of international topics, and no one at the time had considered this to be wrong. Although Knudsen did not reveal the paper's name, everyone who was politically aware knew immediately it was *Arbeiderbladet* and that those who had arranged the interview were none other than Tranmæl, Lie, and Colbjørnsen. This showed, maintained Knudsen, that "other things" were responsible for the actions against Trotsky. Specifically, "international conditions had changed significantly" in the next year. And while Knudsen declared understanding for the difficult position the government had been in, it could have handled the situation differently. He praised Trotsky as "a great person" in the struggle to create a new socialist society, declaring that Norway should have acted as Mexico now was doing, being willing to house someone who, "despite all disagreements with him, remains nevertheless one of the greatest personalities of our time."[146]

Contrary to his earlier claim that Trotsky enjoyed considerable support within Labor's parliamentary delegation, only one other member, Olav Vegheim, openly voiced agreement with Knudsen. What mattered in the Trotsky affair, Vegheim declared, was the political change that took place between 1935 and 1936, including the "witch trial in Moscow," which had given the bourgeois parties the opportunity to exploit the question of Trotsky's asylum in the election. Similarly, in defense of freedom of speech, Vegheim agreed with Knudsen that Trotsky had acted in good faith.[147]

The government, wanting to have the affair over as quickly as possible, saw no need to create additional controversy by censuring its own representatives. And Vegheim, like Knudsen, enjoyed considerable popularity in his home district.* So Knudsen, unlike Scheflo and Meyer, received no

---

* Vegheim was an important political figure in Telemark province, serving not only in the Storting, but also as editor of *Telemark Arbeiderblad* (Telemark's Labor Newspaper).

reprimand. On the contrary, cooption was clearly an advantage, in particular since Knudsen had not challenged the government directly. *Arbeiderbladet*'s editorial reaction was therefore entirely positive, describing his address as "a warmly felt speech for Trotsky . . . presented on a high level that gained sympathy and respect for Knudsen."[148]

The editorial bore the headline "The Trotsky Case's Final Act." Politically, this was true. The nonsocialist parties had no reason to make their disagreement more obvious. There was no longer political capital to be gained from Trotsky's exile by any of the parties, socialist and nonsocialist alike. The Agrarian Party's Andreas Maastad, chairman of the Protocol Committee, summarized this viewpoint when he declared that he had no intention of scolding the government. It deserved honor for its "resolute action," allowing the country to escape "from this rather difficult situation."[149] The debate in the Odelsting ended without a vote of no confidence. Instead, the Protocol Committee's conclusion was accepted by both the majority and the minority. The Nygaardsvold government, as Knudsen observed, could "sit securely."[150] As a national issue, the Trotsky affair had reached its conclusion. Only among partisans on the left were there still some final political reverberations.

With Trotsky's departure from Norway, there no longer remained any impediment to the formation of a Trotskyite organization. In his first letter to Trotsky in Mexico, Held wrote confidently that a "Norwegian section" of the movement would be established "so that your stay here will nevertheless bear fruit for the . . . labor movement."[151] As has been seen, the Labor Party reacted with concern to the possibility that this might occur.

In order to realize his goal, Held sought during the early months of 1937 "to collect people who belonged to, or leaned towards, the Trotskyist position."[152] This resulted in a meeting, called by Held, where it was decided to start *Oktober*. The fact that Helge Krog and Sigurd Hoel were in attendance is of special interest.[153] Together with Arnulf Øverland they made up the widely known "radical trio" (*radikale trekløver*) that exercised considerable influence among leftist intellectuals during this turbulent decade.[154] All three had earlier exhibited sympathy for Trotsky. Øverland had visited him during his stay at Stangnesholmen in 1936 and shared his passionate opposition to the Moscow trials. This caused Øverland to cease his affiliation with communism in 1937, but he never became associated with

Trotskyism. Krog, on the other hand (as noted), was directly involved with the Trotskyite cause at the time that *Oktober* came into being.

Of the trio, Hoel occupied a somewhat vague middle-ground position. He was unquestionably interested in Trotsky's ideas and what he stood for. Along with Øverland and Krog, Hoel was well versed in Marxist theory, with all three having formerly belonged to Mot Dag. On several previous occasions Hoel had shown solidarity with Trotsky's plight and expressly repudiated Stalin's false accusations against him. This is significant because, as Per Thomas Andersen has stated, "Scarcely any other [Norwegian] author had greater influence during the interwar period than Sigurd Hoel."[155] Not only did he gain a reputation for being on the cutting edge of modern fiction as an author, but he held or had held a number of culturally important positions. These included being an editor or critic at *Mot Dag* (1921–1924), *Social-Demokraten* (later *Arbeiderbladet* [1918–1931]), and *Dagbladet* (1932–1936). He furthermore was employed by Norway's leading publishing house, Gyldendal, where he served as a literary consultant and editor of its highly influential "Yellow Series."[156] It is therefore rather remarkable that someone of Hoel's stature was part of the small group of Trotskyites that launched *Oktober*.

Nils Kåre Dahl, who was present at the meeting, recalled that the Moscow trials' deceitfulness provided major momentum for starting the paper, but the "men of letters," Krog and Hoel, also hoped that it would serve as a counterweight to *Veien frem* (The Road Forward), the procommunist magazine edited by the well-known author, Nordahl Grieg.[157] If so, then their expectations were unfulfilled. With its limited resources, *Oktober* restricted itself primarily to political issues. Krog's involvement with the Trotskyites continued—but at a distance since he often lived outside of Oslo. Hoel, on the other hand, eventually retreated to being a detached observer.[158]

Others who took part in the group included *Oktober*'s editor, Jeanette Olsen; her son Sverre Olsen; Brynjulf Jensen, the paper's assistant editor (*redaksjonssekretær*); and Knudsen's friend, Terje Morseth. The latter, an engineer, evidently provided office space for *Oktober* since he shared its address. The site also served as a cover for Held, where he received correspondence from abroad.[159]

Most persons affiliated with the paper used pseudonyms in their articles, not wishing to be identified with a publication that criticized a government that enjoyed overwhelming working-class support. *Oktober*'s masthead similarly reflected this preference for anonymity, stating that it was "edited by a committee."[160] But because she was one of the few persons who clearly stood out due to her post as "responsible editor," Jeanette Olsen became the figure most commonly associated with Norwegian Trotsky-ism during the late 1930s. As such, she was regarded within the labor movement as an outsider. This, however, had not always been true. With a working-class background as a seamstress, she originally rose to promi-nence within the Labor Party's women's movement, serving as a member of its national Women's Association (*kvinneforbund*) from 1911 to 1913. However, like her husband, Aksel Olsen, she later embarked on a career in journalism, first serving as editor of *Haugesunds Folkeblad* (Haugesund's Peoples Newspaper) on the southwest coast and thereafter as business manager (*forretningsfører*) of *Nordlys* (Northern Lights) in Tromsø, North Norway's largest town. Having joined Tranmæl's radical faction as early as 1911, she reached her greatest prominence in the years 1918 to 1923, when she was a member of the Labor Party's National Committee while serving on the Tromsø town council.

Olsen tended always to be on the radical edge of the labor movement, identifying fully with the plight of the workers in a rapidly expanding in-dustrial society. As someone who followed her heart, not surprisingly she was part of the large minority who chose to join the newly formed Com-munist Party in 1923, serving as its women's secretary (*kvinnesekretær*) and on its Central Committee. From 1925 to 1928 she was also editor of *Gnisten* (The Spark), the magazine for communist women.[161]

The year 1928 proved to be critical for her when her husband, with whom she had seven children, died. Also, her initial communist member-ship ended when she resigned in protest against the party's unwillingness to support the first Labor government in 1928. But although Olsen re-joined the Labor Party, her cooperation with communists within the trade union movement later led her to return to their fold only a short time before the first Moscow show trial. However, her outraged response to this tragic event turned her into a Trotskyite. In protest she wrote an article entitled "The Shots That Fell," published in *Arbeiderbladet* on August 31, which condemned a trial that had resulted in the execution of several of Lenin's closest associates.[162]

The communists immediately expelled her. Having burned her bridges with the Labor Party, her only alternative was to join the Trotskyites, how-ever fledgling they might be when their leader was interned. Her brochure, defending Trotsky and asking Norwegian workers to demand fair treatment for him, appeared in November 1936.[163] With her background in journalism, her defiant, unafraid character, and her strong sympathy for Trotsky, she was the obvious candidate for the post of editor.

Oktober was launched confidently in April 1937, with 1500 copies distributed widely in order to garner maximum attention.[164] In its first editorial Olsen proclaimed the credo for "our new paper." She pointed out that the question of whether or not Trotskyism existed in Norway had been raised frequently, with the communists demanding expulsion from the Labor Party of anyone who defended Trotsky's right of asylum or who condemned the Moscow trials. Olsen now boldly announced that, yes, there were Trotskyites who deplored not only the Labor government's unfair treatment of Trotsky and Stalin's injustice—attitudes that all honest socialists should share—but who also accepted Trotsky's viewpoint. First and foremost, they agreed with the necessity to build a "fourth international." The need for this was clear, said Olsen, with the Second International (the Labor and Socialist International) and the Communist International being responsible for the labor movement's defeats in recent years. While Hitler and Mussolini supported Franco with all their might, the Second International issued paper protests, costing the lives of Spanish workers. The Third International was even more destructive due to its lack of morality, with its politics based on intrigues, lies, and provocations.

Although the paper left no doubt about where it stood, it did not, however, intend "to start a new party" at this time, admitting that "we shall not hide that we are still small in numbers." Instead, *Oktober* had been established in defense against "all the attacks and slanders directed against us." The editorial urged that "we and everyone in agreement with us" should remain members of large labor groups such as the Labor Party, its youth organization, L.O., and the Workers Athletic Organization in order to protect the Trotskyite viewpoint.[165] *Oktober* thereby signaled its intent to accomplish exactly what Tranmæl feared—to act as a "poison plant" (to use his term), conspiring to spread its influence within the labor movement, rather than openly challenging the Labor Party by forming its own party.

The new venture faced difficult hurdles. *Oktober*'s future prospects lacked a significant component—adequate funding. The paper cost 15 øre and came out, at best, once a month or, for those willing to take the risk, 1.50 kroner for a year's subscription. Its editor, who was forced to resume work as a seamstress to support herself, only had enough time and energy to meet with persons interested in the paper for two hours once a week.[166]

The membership of the "Norwegian section of the Fourth International that is in the process of formation," as described by Synnøve Rosendahl-Jensen, was limited. It consisted "of six active persons and with perhaps the same number of sympathizers." Specifically, they included Nils Kåre Dahl and his wife, Morseth, Jeanette Olsen, Sverre Olsen, and Jensen. When Synnøve herself and Held were added, they totaled eight. No mention was made of Krog and Hoel, but they most likely were considered sympathizers, as were Scheflo and Meyer. Synnøve moreover added optimistically that they had formed a study circle to discuss the Soviet Union, attended by some "twenty very serious persons."[167]

Oktober's startup received little attention. *Arbeiderbladet* ignored it completely, but the Trotskyites were convinced that they would force Tranmæl to respond following *Oktober*'s next number, in May, because, as Synnøve put it, "we are violent in our attacks against the socialist government."[168] As has been seen, Tranmæl did react strongly, publishing his "poison plant" editorial on May 12, but he concentrated on warning Scheflo and Meyer against going too far in their support of Trotsky. As for the newly established Trotskyite group, Tranmæl never referred to it by name, declaring offhandedly that "such a destructive divisive sectarian movement" posed "no real danger" in Norway.[169]

His focus on Scheflo and Meyer rather than the fledgling Trotskyite section had its intended effect. At a time when Tranmæl's accusations against them had reached a crescendo, the two could ill afford to add to their difficulties by becoming involved in a venture that was fully dedicated to Trotsky. As evidence of their concern, Held complained that he had attempted during the past two weeks to establish a Norwegian "investigative commission" to assess the Soviet accusations against Trotsky, but Scheflo and Meyer had been unwilling to take part, allegedly because they would be regarded as too partisan. Nor would anyone else join such a committee, Held added woefully, because they were all under the influence of "the bureaucracy," the Trotskyite code word for the Nygaardsvold administration.[170]

In far-off Mexico Trotsky could do nothing except offer general encouragement to his Norwegian followers, few as they might be.[171] In response to greetings from the *Oktober* group on the anniversary of the Bolshevik Revolution,[172] he declared "your little *Oktober*" was immensely more important "than the great dailies of the Second and Third Internationals," and he wished them "the best revolutionary success."[173]

Those associated with the "little *Oktober*" recognized from the beginning that their success depended on gaining support within the Labor Party since almost all members of the labor movement belonged to the party. This explains why Tranmæl's attack against Trotskyism and his denunciation of Scheflo and Meyer aroused considerable anxiety. In *Oktober*'s next number the question was raised: "Will we be expelled from the Norwegian Labor Party?"[174] This query referred first and foremost to Scheflo, Meyer, and their immediate circles, who were regarded as current or potential sympathizers. Although there may also have been a few hidden Trotskyites in various Labor Party organizations, only Nils Kåre Dahl was clearly identifiable, and even he used a pseudonym when writing articles for *Oktober*.[175]*

In addition to articles by Jeanette Olsen and her son Sverre, writings by Scheflo and Meyer also appeared under their names, which explains *Oktober*'s solicitude for them. Scheflo's articles, however, were largely lifted from *Sørlandet*. Meyer, on the other hand, wrote directly for the paper. His publications included articles and commentaries on political issues. The *Oktober* group obviously regarded him as a friend. When Meyer in the spring of 1938 vigorously denounced the show trials at a meeting of the Oslo Workers Association, enthusiasm among the Trotskyites was great. They clearly expected him to make "the last decisive leap" to their side in the immediate future.[176]

Although he undoubtedly considered this possibility due to his feelings of sympathy, admiration, and friendship for Trotsky, there were too many obstacles, theoretical and practical, that stood in the way. While he felt alienated from the Labor government's politics, Meyer was equally critical of the fanaticism that Trotskyism displayed. He disapproved of Trotsky's failure to take into consideration the reality of power politics in international affairs. This resulted in the Fourth International's adopting the tactic of seeking to turn every opportunity into a revolutionary uprising—a practice, said Meyer, that gave Trotsky's movement a certain "anarchistic character."[177]

Even more significant, however, were the poor prospects for the Trotskyites in Norway, faced with a wall of silence in their one-sided battle against the overwhelming prestige of the Labor Party and its government.

---

* Although he was threatened with expulsion from the Labor Party, Dahl was protected because of his strong position within his trade union, the Oslo Stone Mason's Association (*Stein, jord og sementarbeideres forening*).

Had Meyer committed himself to their cause, it would have meant ostracism from the labor movement, sharing Jeanette Olsen's fate, which he was fully aware of.

The Labor Party furthermore strengthened its position to an even greater degree as a result of the town and county council elections of October 1937, the last nationwide elections before the German occupation. The party increased its representation in every province, gaining 43.4 percent of the popular vote, in comparison to 40.9 percent in the previous local elections of 1934. In contrast, the Conservative Party, the second largest, only slightly upped its percentage nationally from 12 percent to 14 percent. In Oslo, Labor tightened its grip on the absolute majority it enjoyed in the city council.[178] The Labor Party's string of successes during the 1930s also contributed significantly to increasing its membership. It reached 100,000 for the first time in 1934, and by 1939 the total had grown to 170,000.[179]

Oktober nevertheless attempted to fight this powerful force. In its sixth number, published fittingly enough in October, the editors called for support of their struggle against the government, termed "the agents of reaction in our own camp," as well as for its fight against the criminal methods of Stalin and his Comintern.[180] The same issue also contained an article that argued that a "left opposition" had begun to form within the Labor Party (in other words, a group of Trotskyite sympathizers). This faction would inevitably become part of the Fourth International.[181]

However, rather than finding their way to the Fourth International, members of the "left opposition" that *Oktober* counted on were in the process of joining the Labor and Socialist International through their membership in the Labor Party. After approving the party's resignation from the London Bureau, Labor's national conference in 1936 had authorized the National Committee to investigate other forums of international cooperation,[182] which meant affiliation with the Labor and Socialist International. In earlier times Scheflo and Meyer would have been in the forefront of opposition. But now, accused of having Trotskyite tendencies, they were in no position to add to their difficulties by speaking out against the upcoming change. As Held, obviously disappointed, tersely reported to Trotsky in late November 1937: "Håkon Meyer is also for it [membership]. Scheflo keeps silent."[183] In the following year the Labor Party formally joined the Labor and Socialist International.[184]

Oktober, on the other hand, remained largely on the sidelines in 1938. It continued to attack Stalin's regime for having betrayed the workers' movement and to denounce the Labor government for its cooperation with bourgeois interests.[185] Held, however, maintained a brave facade in his correspondence with Trotsky. In part this was due to his usual optimism, but in addition he wished to protect his status within the movement. Events obviously had not gone well of late in Norway, not only politically but also as far as Trotsky's finances were concerned. Held therefore wrote on a positive note: "The little periodical *Oktober* is still coming out regularly and has captured a good position." In reaction to Stalin's third major show trial, with Alexei Rykov and Nikolai Bukharin as its chief victims, in which the defendants, as previously, were accused of conspiring with Trotsky, Held boasted that "the comrades" in *Oktober* "have produced a free special edition of 3000 copies" condemning the proceedings. This publication was sent to various trade unions, factories, and other working-class locations.[186]

What preoccupied Trotsky most at this time, however, was the formal establishment of the Fourth International, which he had sought to realize since 1933. In preparation, by mid-April 1938 he had completed the draft of "The Death Agony of Capitalism and the Tasks of the Fourth International," generally called "The Transitional Program." Here he theorized how the Fourth International would serve as the vanguard of the proletarian masses, aiding them to bridge current protests by workers against the capitalist system with the successful execution of revolution. This bridge, wrote Trotsky, would include a system of "transitional demands" emanating from present conditions that would inevitably lead "to one final conclusion: the conquest of power by the proletariat." The objective of the Fourth International was "not in reforming capitalism but in its overthrow."[187]

"The Transitional Program" was submitted to the sections for discussion in preparation for the International's founding meeting, which took place in France on September 3, 1938. It proved to be anticlimactic, in particular considering the exertions that Trotsky had earlier made. Had the Fourth International been established in 1934, its chances might have been better. But in 1938, weakened by Stalin's persistent campaign of terror and intimidation as well as the popularity enjoyed by the Soviet Union in left-wing circles because of its pose as the enemy of fascism, the International, at its inception, was largely a shell.

Not only was Trotsky unable to attend, but three key figures within his movement were also absent, all dead as a result of Stalinist machinations. His greatest personal loss was his son, Lev Sedov. At the age of 32, Lyova died under highly suspicious circumstances after undergoing an operation in Paris. Soviet operatives had most likely been involved since they had infiltrated his network. His right-hand man, Mark Zborowski, was one such agent, having received the assignment to join the secretariat in Paris. The second loss was Rudolf Klement, Lyova's successor as the ICL's international secretary, who disappeared in July 1938 while preparing the start of the International. His mutilated body, minus its head, was found in the Seine. Still another of Trotsky's secretaries, his most important helper in Norway, Erwin Wolf, had been arrested in Spain the year before due to communist influence. He was never heard from again.

Formation of the Fourth International was limited to one day, due to fear that NKVD agents might try to gain entry. It took place on the outskirts of Paris at the villa of one of Trotsky's staunchest friends, Alfred Rosmer. The "Transitional Program" was adopted as the organization's preliminary blueprint. Present were twenty-one delegates, representing eleven countries. Almost all were European. Since there was no possibility for anyone from the Soviet Union to be present due to Stalin's iron dictatorship, the Russian delegate—none other than Mark Zborowski—acted on behalf of the Russian exile community.[188] No one from Norway attended, although the Norwegian "Bolshevik-Leninist Group" was listed among the organizations that were "regularly affiliated" with the Fourth International.[189]

As a theoretical guide for how the workers would conquer capitalist society through a pattern of ever-accelerating demands that led inevitably to a successful proletarian revolution, the "Transitional Program," in the abstract, appeared to be quite logical. However, what Trotsky lacked was a mass organization to implement his ambitious goal. At the time the Fourth International was proclaimed, it is estimated that the small groups and parties that worldwide pledged their allegiance to his cause at the most only had approximately eight to ten thousand members.[190]

In Norway *Oktober* changed its masthead to read "Organ for the Fourth International." The small cluster of persons involved with the paper exerted themselves strenuously to bring out a double number, fourteen pages in length, featuring the "Transitional Program" in Norwegian. Its publication, Held stated with pride, was "truly an achievement."[191] But as before, the major hurdle for *Oktober* was its small size, which prevented it from gaining attention. No other publications were willing to spread its message.

Oktober's effort to bring out the "Transitional Program" badly drained the paper's limited resources. This was the last issue that Jeanette Olsen published in 1938. From its start, *Oktober* had been entirely dependent on its limited readership plus contributions from Trotskyites and their sympathizers. Whereas the Labor Party press, due to its mass circulation, was filled with advertisements, the only ads in *Oktober* were for Trotskyite literature, first and foremost Trotsky's writings.[192]

By the end of the 1930s, the paper's bare-bones resources were drying up.[193] Whereas in its initial year, 1937, seven issues were printed, only five appeared in 1938. In the next year the total declined to three. *Oktober*'s final number, in September 1939, rather pathetically was a last gasp effort to survive by expanding its coverage. It now proclaimed itself the "Scandinavian Organ for the Fourth International," with as much space devoted to Denmark as to Norway.[194]

This effort too did not bear fruit. Jeanette Olsen became ill in the fall, thereby eliminating any possibility that *Oktober* might survive. Its demise was in keeping with the times, marking the end of any attempt at organized Trotskyite activity in the country. With World War II having broken out, only seven months remained before Norway was invaded and occupied. Those who followed or supported Trotsky would soon be scattered in different directions, political and/or geographic. He himself had less than a year to live before yet another Soviet agent, having successfully infiltrated his security cordon, sank an ice axe into his skull, thereby delivering a further debilitating blow to the international movement he had sought to organize.

Comprehensive Assessment

In Norwegian history, the Trotsky affair remains
a wound that will not heal.
—Haakon Lie, *Martin Tranmæl*, Vol. 2: *Veiviseren*

THE CONTROVERSY OVER TROTSKY'S EXILE in Norway reached
its height during the second half of 1936. Although it began with the NS
break-in at Wexhall, this in itself would not have been particularly significant had the incident been restricted only to the effort by Quisling's party
to create publicity. With the start of Stalin's major show trials, however, in
which Trotsky stood accused of organizing terrorist activity against the
hierarchy of the Russian Communist Party, followed by already anticipated Soviet diplomatic pressure against the Norwegian government for
providing Trotsky with refuge, the dispute assumed an entirely different
character. The Nygaardsvold government now came to the conclusion that
it could not afford to risk antagonizing its mighty neighbor to the east.*
As the prime minister alluded to in the Storting after Trotsky had been
dispatched to Mexico, Norway's situation would have been different if it
were not a small country. In 1936 it had a population of slightly less than
2,900,000, whereas the Soviet Union numbered close to 162,000,000. Mili-
tarily the disparity was even greater. Stalin in 1936 had the largest armed
force in Europe at his disposal. In contrast Norway had a poorly equipped
peacetime army theoretically numbering 30,000, a navy of largely outdated
ships, and hardly any air force.[1] Moreover, prevailing Norwegian political opinion assumed that strategically and diplomatically it was in the

---

* Although Norway in 1936 had no contiguous border with the Soviet Union, only a small
  strip of Finnish territory separated the two countries.

country's best interest to maintain good relations with Stalin's government. There was also the factor of ideological affinity with the Soviet Union. Although the ruling Labor Party had broken its ties with the Comintern more than a decade earlier, there still remained a considerable residue of goodwill among its members toward the Soviet state and its socialist experiment. And internationally the U.S.S.R. added to its popularity among socialists in the mid-30s by portraying itself as the champion of collective security against the danger of fascism, led by a resurgent Germany under Hitler.

Compounding the difficulty faced by the Labor government, it had to deal with the fact that Trotsky's asylum became a major issue in the election of 1936. Had the government stood alone, protecting his right to defend himself against Soviet accusations, it would have been isolated, denounced not only externally in the Russian media but also by all other Norwegian political parties for allegedly compromising the country's security. As it was, despite Trotsky's internment, charges ranging from serious to irresponsible were levied against the Nygaardsvold administration during the election campaign. From a pragmatic point of view, the cabinet's possible course of action seemed to be quite limited, restricted to silencing Trotsky's appeal to international opinion. It thereby attempted to reduce as much as possible the controversy as an election issue, while at the same time eliminating it as a source of contention with the Russian government. But although this was done, no responsible official attempted to justify Trotsky's internment and the government's refusal to allow him access to the courts by accepting at face value the ludicrous charges that Stalin's subordinates and supporters were making against him. Nor was any serious consideration given to the possibility of simply handing him over to the tender mercies of the Soviet dictator.

The only apparent option for the government was to send Trotsky out of the country as soon as his residence permit expired. However, to an even greater degree than had been true before his arrival, no democratic nation in Europe was willing to accept him. The world continued to be "the planet without a visa" for him. Only distant Mexico, far removed from a continent that already was being drawn into the maelstrom of violence that inexorably led to World War II, and with no diplomatic ties with the Soviet Union, had a government that agreed to grant him asylum (although its communist party was more dangerous to Trotsky's safety than the Norwegian communists). His move to Coyoacan, as it turned out, did secure him a few extra months of life, albeit in the long run he could not escape Stalin's reach. Had he been in Norway when the Germans invaded in April 1940, he most likely would have been trapped. He would have been prevented from escaping to either Sweden or Finland because neither country was in a position to allow him entry. Following his capture by the Germans, with the Nazi-Soviet nonaggression pact still in effect, Hitler most likely would have happily delivered Trotsky to Stalin. In this scenario Trotsky's end would have been even more sordid and gruesome than the fate that befell him in Mexico.

The Nygaardsvold cabinet's strategy of dealing with Trotsky proved to be successful from a political perspective. Contrary to what opponents of the Labor Party had hoped, the dispute concerning his exile did not have a major impact on the outcome of the 1936 election, from which the Nygaardsvold administration emerged in a strengthened position. And in the following weeks, before the newly elected parliament had an opportunity to debate how Trotsky's exile had been handled, the government quickly implemented on its own terms the manner in which he was transported out of the country. With Trotsky in Mexico, the issue proved to be largely settled—in internal politics and in Norway's diplomatic relations with the Soviet Union. Nygaardsvold no longer had to worry about whether his cabinet's very existence might be in jeopardy due to the way in which it had managed the Trotsky affair.

The difficulties that the Labor Party and its government faced during his stay, however, were to a considerable degree self-inflicted. The cabinet's decision to allow him into the country was based not solely on the abstract desire to uphold the right of asylum. This was equally a political decision, reflecting to a considerable degree the sympathy that existed within the Labor Party for the Bolshevik Revolution of 1917 and the creation of the Soviet Union, to whose success Trotsky had contributed significantly. The revolutionary Russian events of 1917–1921 were still vivid in the minds of Norwegian socialists, having occurred less than two decades before Trotsky settled at Wexhall. Many leading members of the Norwegian labor movement had been part of delegations that went to Moscow, almost as if on a pilgrimage, when the Labor Party belonged to the Communist International. These included persons of importance during Trotsky's exile such as Martin Tranmæl, Olav Scheflo, Trygve Lie, Håkon Meyer, Oscar Torp, Jeanette Olsen, Erling Falk, and Jakob Friis. And while the Labor

Party's ideological standpoint had changed significantly by 1935, it could not be denied that, at least theoretically, its leaders had shared the same revolutionary perspective as Lenin and Trotsky in the early 1920s, a Marxist outlook that Trotsky still championed when he received permission to enter Norway.

However, as a reform-minded minority government, dependent on nonsocialist backing to stay in office, the Nygaardsvold administration could not afford to antagonize the bourgeois parties needlessly. The terms of Trotsky's admission were therefore made quite stringent, in particular the provision that he could not engage in political activity or agitation against a country that was "friendly" toward Norway. But at the time he established his residence outside of Hønefoss, the government at first made no effort to enforce this requirement strictly, although prominent members of the Labor Party, both inside and outside the cabinet, were aware of Trotsky's attempt to establish a Fourth International to challenge Stalin's hegemony over the communist movement. They assumed that Trotsky's uphill battle would remain insignificant, restricted to scattered small parties, fringe groups, and individuals outside the mainstream of major socialist organizations. Nor was Trotsky in a position to exercise strong leadership over his limited number of followers, confined as he was to operating out of two rooms in a house in rural Norway that he shared with a number of other persons, while having at his disposal the services of only one secretary and a typist.

The Labor Party's belief that Trotsky's exile would be low-key failed to take into account Stalin's paranoid ruthlessness—his determination to eliminate anyone who potentially could oppose his grip on the U.S.S.R. and the communist movement. Although the purges that destroyed millions of lives in the 1930s were mainly directed inwardly against Soviet citizens, indicating that they would have occurred even if Trotsky had not been living outside the country, nevertheless he became the central figure in the show trials on which they were based. Examined from Stalin's twisted perspective, the possible threat from Trotsky appeared real, despite the small, fragmented nature of his organization. Stalin could recall that Lenin's Bolsheviks had similarly been largely crushed during the tsarist reaction that followed the failed Revolution of 1905, with the party's membership greatly reduced and its main leaders forced to live in precarious foreign exile. As the supposed mastermind who allegedly was organizing plots from abroad, Trotsky therefore was fallaciously indicted in the show trials with directing the effort to murder Russian leaders, eliminate communism, and destroy the Soviet Union. When conducting this mendacious campaign of charging Trotsky with being a terrorist, Stalin very effectively (1) directed international attention away from the terror campaign that he himself was executing in the Soviet Union during the purges and (2) increased Trotsky's negative reputation among those who already regarded him with suspicion or distaste, thereby creating even greater difficulty for him to gain a hearing or support. It also made foreign governments more unwilling to grant him asylum.

Even before it was confronted with the Soviet diplomatic initiative after Trotsky had vigorously attempted to rebuke the fabricated accusations of the first Moscow trial, the Nygaardsvold government adroitly limited his access to the media, followed quickly by internment, justifying these steps with the argument that he had violated his asylum by engaging in activity against a "friendly minded" state with which Norway wished to maintain good relations. When using this rationalization the government was not at all concerned with the literal truth but only with finding a solution to a difficult problem. The same was true with the cabinet's decision to prevent him from bringing cases before Norwegian courts when he sought to overcome the censorship that had been clamped down on him.

While the Nygaardsvold administration was subjected to severe criticism during the election for having admitted Trotsky, the majority of newspapers, not just the Labor Party press, supported the decision to confine him to Sundby. This prevailing view, which ranged across the entire political spectrum from the communists to National Union, met with little opposition except from a small minority of persons who had only limited means of voicing their opinions. They were either independent-minded members of the Labor Party or radical left-wing intellectuals. What bound them together was their strong feeling of sympathy for Trotsky, their clear perception of the perversity of Stalin's show trials, and their negative reaction to the duplicity of the Labor Party's defense of the government's actions, personified by the party line expressed in Tranmæl's *Arbeiderbladet*.

This did not mean that they alone understood that the treatment of Trotsky was morally wrong. Haakon Lie, the Labor Party's long-serving Secretary and major election strategist from 1945 to 1969, who on his 100th birthday in 2005 was feted by the party's National Committee, expressed in his memoirs the feeling of frustration felt by party loyalists during the Trotsky affair. Lie recounted how they fought on behalf of Trotsky until "the government knocked our legs from under us" by interning him. But their fidelity to their party compelled them, in particular in an election year, to remain silent about this "act of tyranny" ("*overgrep*").[2] This reaction was understandable from a practical point of view. What mattered most was strengthening Labor's control of government, not consideration of the unfair treatment received by an exile who no longer was welcome. The Nygaardsvold cabinet's action was equally expedient. It was not willing to risk facing antagonism from the Soviet Union or potential voter loss to nonsocialist parties. Furthermore, its options were limited, as even some of its detractors recognized. In the Storting, Knudsen expressed understanding for the dilemma that the government had been in but insisted nevertheless that it should have dealt more fairly with Trotsky.[3]

To have followed the advice of critics and handled Trotsky more leniently, while unquestionably a more difficult option, was not entirely beyond realization, however, when other political considerations are taken into account. Russian foreign policy in the mid-1930s stressed collective security against the threat of fascism and cooperation among peace-loving nations.[4] For the Soviet Union to have adopted a threatening posture toward Norway, or even badgered its government protractedly, would have been in direct contravention of the Stalin regime's diplomatic position and hard to sustain. Mexico experienced no significant difficulties in foreign relations or in domestic politics as a result of granting Trotsky an asylum that allowed him more freedom than he had experienced in Norway **before** he was interned. And in national politics what mattered most to Norwegian voters in 1936, despite the best efforts of the bourgeois opposition, were not issues such as the Trotsky affair but rather how effectively the government had dealt with the problems of the Great Depression. As the outcome showed, the electorate gave Nygaardsvold and his cabinet a vote of confidence. It is not likely that this successful result would have been weakened significantly had the government, despite attacks from the other parties, continued its original asylum policy toward Trotsky, with possibly some modifications. Trotsky himself had recognized the exposed position the government was in and showed willingness to negotiate a possible revision of his asylum terms, only to be easily outmaneuvered by Trygve Lie's stratagems.

In following the approach that it took, the Nygaardsvold administration based its actions on what it perceived to be realistic self-interest, of benefit to both the Labor Party and the country. But morally the cabinet's silencing of Trotsky and locking him up in "Norway's first concentration camp" was hard to defend. None of the leading officials within the government admitted, not even privately as far as is known, any misgivings or regrets over how Trotsky had been treated. Nevertheless, there did exist among some within the Labor Party, as well as among radical leftists outside the party, the conviction that the outcome should have been different, which it could have been if, as Helge Krog put it, Norwegian society under Johan Nygaardsvold's leadership had been "less fearful and more broad-minded."[5] Instead, the cabinet followed the prime minister and acted expediently, as governments are wont to do. But while the Nygaardsvold administration successfully carried out what later has been termed "damage control," Trotsky's asylum has not been regarded as a particularly proud episode. As Haakon Lie has said, "In Norwegian history, the Trotsky affair remains a wound that will not heal."[6]

Epilogue

RAMON MERCADER'S SUCCESS IN INFILTRATING Trotsky's security apparatus, enabling him to strike his deadly blow on August 20, 1940, is well known. The widowed Natalia Sedova, originally stranded because of the Second World War, remained largely in Mexico until shortly before her death. Suffering from ill health, she moved to Paris for medical treatment in December 1960. Here, in the city where she had met Trotsky, she passed away on January 23, 1962, at the age of 79. Natalia's ashes, together with Lev's, are buried in the garden of the home they shared in Coyoacan. It has been turned into a museum in memory of Lev Trotsky. Its director is Lev and Natalia's grandson, known to them as Seva, who, in honor of his famous forefather, now bears the name of Esteban Volkov Bronstein.

As a boy, Seva witnessed nothing but tragedy. Following his mother's suicide he lived in Paris with his uncle Lyova and Jeanne Martin, Molinier's former wife. But in February 1938, suffering from appendicitis, Lyova, on the advice of Mark Zborowski, entered a hospital run by Russian émigrés. He did not emerge alive, most likely having been poisoned by NKVD agents. Seva now became the object of dispute between Jeanne, who wished to keep him, and his grandparents, who wanted him to live with them. This bitter conflict was resolved only in 1939, when as a young teenager he was brought to Mexico. Having begun to readjust to yet another strange country, in the next year the person who meant most to Seva was once again torn from his life.

Among the many expressions of sympathy that Natalia and Lev had earlier received when Lyova died was one from Norway, signed by Håkon Meyer on behalf of not only himself but also several of Trotsky's other "Norwegian friends"—the "radical trio" of authors Helge Krog, Sigurd

Hoel, and Arnulf Øverland; Dr. Carl Müller, who had so conscientiously treated his former patient; and editor Olav Scheflo.[1]

The latter held out in his bastion, *Sørlandet's* editorial office, until September 1939, when he moved to Lillehammer, where he hoped that a more moderate inland climate would improve his declining health. The ravages of his chronic arthritic condition had led to a permanent curvature of his spine, and he was at times plagued by psoriasis. Moreover, as an ominous portent, he had developed a bad heart while still in his early forties.[2] Scheflo experienced little peace during his last years. On the day he began his retirement, World War II erupted. When Norway was invaded by Hitler, he fled with his family to Sweden. In Stockholm he had the opportunity to meet two old friends for the last time, Helge Krog and Erling Falk.[3] The latter was a tragic figure. He had suffered on and off from an unknown malady since 1935, and politically he had lost all influence when his former followers in Mot Dag merged with the Labor Party. He died shortly after his reunion with Scheflo. Krog stayed on in Sweden for the duration of the war, where he was a central figure in the Norwegian exile colony as a writer, editor and speaker.[4] In contrast to his former comrades, Hoel and Øverland, who with time became more conservative (especially the latter), Krog maintained his position as a leftist gadfly during the postwar era.[5] He denounced in particular business interests that had profited from the German occupation. His health, however, continued to deteriorate. Increasingly despondent, experiencing repeated hospitalizations, he made several attempts at suicide before succeeding at the age of seventy-three in 1962.[6]

Unlike Krog, Scheflo chose to return to Norway in August 1940. But by the spring of 1941 his irregular heart rhythm caused him to faint frequently. He was admitted to the National Hospital in Oslo, where he remained for two years. Unfortunately, intelligence about his involvement in anti-German planning while at the hospital reached the Gestapo. The resistance movement learned of plans to arrest him and moved Scheflo, hoping to arrange transport to Sweden. But he died from a new heart attack on June 25, 1943, shortly before his sixtieth birthday.[7]

Prior to his death he was reconciled with Jakob Friis. However, as Friis stood by the hospital room door, ready to leave, there came a final comment from Scheflo's bed: "But nevertheless, Jakob, I was right!"[8] Friis remained equally stubborn in his convictions. He was elected to the first postwar Storting that met in 1945. He was always on the left wing of the Labor Party's parliamentary delegation, not infrequently assuming positions that differed from those of the government led by Einar Gerhardsen. Although Friis did not vote against Norway's entry into NATO, he originally favored an alternative Scandinavian defense alliance, and he at times was highly critical of the United States during the Cold War. In 1952 he edited the first number of *Orientering* (Orientation), a journal representing dissenting views by Labor Party members, who in particular were hostile to the government's foreign policy.* Having served two terms, his parliamentary career came to an end in the following year.

As opposed to Scheflo, Håkon Meyer, the second of Trotsky's major defenders in Norway, joined the pro-German side during the occupation. From his perspective, however, he sought to remain true to his socialist ideals. Following the invasion he believed it was necessary, at least for the time being, to reach an accommodation with the victorious Germans in order to protect the interests of the workers. Meyer became the leading figure in the Trade Union Opposition of 1940 (plagiarizing Tranmæl's Trade Union Opposition of 1911), formed in June in disagreement with the official leaders of the labor movement. However, when Meyer in August entered into negotiations with Quisling, who enjoyed Hitler's favor, the Trade Union Opposition of 1940 began to fall apart due to the unpopularity of Quisling's treasonous activity. One of the first to disavow Meyer was his former devoted follower, Kjell Ottesen,[9] who earlier had served Trotsky in a number of capacities.

As "the major defector from the labor movement to NS," Meyer formally joined Quisling's party in December 1940. In the following year he became the "commissarial leader" of the Association of Norwegian Counties (Norsk Kommuneforbund) within the NS-controlled Interior Department, a position that he held for one year, until September 1942. Anticipating the outcome of the war, he maintained a low profile from 1943 until the end of the occupation.[10] He was arrested in 1945. From Ila Prison, previously the major German concentration camp in Norway, he sent a letter to his former close friend, Johan Nygaardsvold, insisting that his actions during the war had been based on his pacifist convictions and that many members of NS were naive idealists who had been betrayed by the Germans.[11] The prime minister did not respond. Meyer received a sentence of ten years at forced labor in 1946. He was released three years

---

* In 1961 *Orientering* succeeded where *Oktober* had failed. As a result of the split within the Labor Party, those associated with *Orientering* formed the Socialist People's Party, the forerunner of the present Socialist Left Party.

later and moved to Sweden, where he resided for the rest of his long life until his death in 1989 at the age of 93.

Leif Ragnvald Konstad, the former head of the Central Passport Office, who had served as Trotsky's censor during his internment, was also among those under arrest in 1945. Always regarded with hostility by the labor movement before the war due to his known right-wing convictions, Konstad openly came out in support of Quisling when he joined NS following Hitler's invasion. When the entire Supreme Court resigned in protest against the German administration's refusal to allow judicial review of its decrees, Konstad was one of the new "justices" appointed to the court by the NS minister of justice in late December 1940. In the postwar series of treason trials (*landssvikprosessen*), the district court that sentenced Konstad to a prison term of eight years of forced labor concluded that participation in the "commissarial Supreme Court" was a serious criminal offense.[12]

Another official similarly detested by Trotsky during his internment, Jonas Lie, held an even more important position during the occupation. A skillful intriguer, he maneuvered to join the winning side during the chaotic days following the invasion. He first cast his lot with the Norwegian government when it sought to resist. He refused an offer by Quisling, after his coup in April 1940, to join his short-lived "national government." Lie instead took part in military activity against the Germans. He was taken captive but allowed to return to Oslo. Due to his earlier police service in the Saar under the League of Nations, where he maintained an anti-French position during the plebiscite of 1935, Lie had already acquired a positive reputation within Nazi police circles that now benefited him.[13]

During the summer of 1940 Josef Terboven, whom Hitler had appointed as his highest administrator (*Reichskommissar*) in Norway, attempted to place Lie in charge of NS, having quickly concluded that Quisling's unpopularity3 and political incompetence made him an unsuitable Nazi ally. But Hitler, who had invaded Norway with no understanding of the country's politics and culture, gave his support to Quisling. Although the latter did not formally become the head of a puppet government until 1942, his party dominated the interim Commissarial Council (*Kommissariske Statsråd*) that Terboven appointed, with Hitler's approval, in September 1940. Jonas Lie made his peace with Quisling and, thanks to German backing, was appointed police minister. In addition to heading the police, he also played a major role in recruiting Norwegians for service in the German military, himself taking part in operations in the Soviet Union and Yugoslavia as an SS officer. Considered the Norwegian equivalent of Heinrich Himmler, he became, after Quisling, the most hated man in the country, known to opponents of Nazi rule as "Judas Lie." At the end of the war, facing an inevitable death sentence, he ensconced himself with two other high NS officials at a farm outside of Oslo. Determined first to resist, then to commit suicide, Lie died from a combination of excess alcohol consumption, morphine, fever, stress, lack of sleep, and a weakened heart.[14]

Martin Tranmæl, whom Trotsky regarded with such great distaste prior to, during, and after his internment, continued to wield significant influence in politics for many years. At the time of the German attack, he escaped northward, accompanying the Nygaardsvold government as an advisor. When further military resistance was impossible and the ministers, along with the royal family, decided to establish a government in exile in London, Tranmæl chose to move to Sweden. Unlike most refugees who returned home by the end of the summer of 1940, including future prime minister Gerhardsen, Tranmæl felt compelled to remain in Sweden because of his anti-Nazi past. He would undoubtedly have been immediately arrested had he gone back to Norway. Among his assistants was Scheflo's son, Inge Scheflo; their common desire to resist the German occupiers wiped out past differences between the Scheflo family and Tranmæl. The latter served as the Labor Party's chief representative in Sweden from his position in L. O.'s Stockholm secretariat. He followed closely developments taking place in his homeland during the occupation, as new refugees involved in resistance activity found safety in Sweden when conditions became too dangerous for them in Norway. As the war turned in favor of the Allies, Swedish restrictions on Tranmæl's public activity lessened. He used his great speaking ability in countless speeches on behalf of his country's cause, addressing Swedish and Norwegian audiences. Among Swedes his influence was especially strong within the labor movement, including government circles.

Returning to Norway in 1945 at age sixty-five, Tranmæl resumed his positions as a member of the Labor Party's Central Committee and editor of *Arbeiderbladet*. He plunged immediately into politics, where the Labor Party enjoyed a significant advantage because, unlike the nonsocialist parties, it had remained active during the occupation—in occupied Norway, in London, and not least in Sweden. Tranmæl exercised major influence in the decision to have his protégé, Gerhardsen, assume the post of prime minister in 1945, replacing Nygaardsvold. Gerhardsen became Norway's leading political figure for the next twenty years, serving as prime minister for most of this period, with but two interruptions.

Tranmæl chose to retire as editor in 1949, but he still continued to write for *Arbeiderbladet* until his early 80s. He remained part of the inner circle in the Labor Party. He finally stepped down from the Central Committee in 1963, a position he had held since 1918. In the next year he also resigned from the Nobel Peace Prize Committee, on which he had served since 1938 (interrupted by World War II). In failing health during his last two years, he died on July 1, 1967, at the age of 88. The author recalls vividly the banner displayed that day on Youngstorget, the square outside party headquarters. It read simply: "Martin Tranmæl is dead." A milestone in the history of the Labor Party, the major force in twentieth-century Norwegian politics, had passed.

Johan Nygaardsvold, who ultimately determined Trotsky's treatment during the stormy months of his internment, had not achieved quite the veneration of either Tranmæl or Gerhardsen at the time of his death. The happiest period in Nygaardsvold's career was as head of the prewar Labor government, when social reforms were enacted and Norway began to recover from the worst effects of the Depression. With the German invasion he became an embattled leader whose administration sought for two months to sustain a losing military campaign, followed by flight to England. Nygaardsvold remained prime minister for the duration of the war but as head of a coalition government that included representatives from the nonsocialist parties. To some extent he rather unfairly became the scapegoat for the country's military unpreparedness in the fight against the Germans. To make the argument that Norway could have withstood the most powerful armed force in Europe in 1940, at a time when the Germans overran with ease larger countries such as France and Poland, reflects the political opportunism and/or myopic nationalistic particularism of his detractors. Despite criticism, Nygaardsvold performed well during the war years, eventually establishing a good working relationship with the resistance leadership that initially had regarded him with some hostility. However, at the end of the war, his government resigned in June 1945. Nygaardsvold still enjoyed strong support within his party's parliamentary delegation, but he was unacceptable to the bourgeois parties. Furthermore, Labor's leadership, under Tranmæl's influence, wished to begin the postwar political period unencumbered by the disparagement that the party undoubtedly would have received if Nygaardsvold had remained its standard bearer. Gerhardsen therefore succeeded Nygaardsvold, who served one final term in parliament before retiring from active politics. A special investigatory commission, Undersøkelseskommisjonen av 1945, concluded that Nygaardsvold shared some responsibility for the country's weak military in 1940 but that he had served ably during the war. This sentiment was shared by the Storting, which voted him a special "honorary salary" (*æreslønn*) following his resignation as prime minister. Nygaardsvold defended himself vigorously against his critics, declaring in his unpublished memoirs that he awaited history's judgment with "a pure and calm conscience."[15] Born in the same year as Tranmæl, he died on March 13, 1952, at age seventy-two.

When Nygaardsvold returned to Norway in 1945, his cabinet did not include the figure who had dominated the Labor government's prewar foreign policy. Halvdan Koht during the '30s not only was supreme in diplomatic affairs but exercised significant influence on cultural issues, in particular as a leading proponent of language reform. In April 1940, at the time of the German assault, he, alongside King Haakon VII, demonstrated strong resolve not to surrender, although he understood that this decision could mean being forced to flee, never to see Norway again. Koht remembered then Trotsky's prophesy, made to Trygve Lie when he learned that he would be expelled from Norway: "In a few years you and the others in the government will be political refugees, without home and fatherland, just as I am now."[16]

When the cabinet went into exile, Koht's position quickly declined. His former policy of neutrality came under fire for having underestimated the danger from Germany, and he was accused of not heeding warnings of the pending invasion. His authoritarian manner had also irritated fellow ministers, and he was further weakened by his decision to set up his office outside of London, in isolation from the rest of the government. Although Nygaardsvold at first resisted pressure to remove Koht, in the end he had no choice, in particular because of the foreign minister's deteriorating relations with their British hosts. Among other issues Koht's desire to maintain good ties with the Russians did not sit well in England at a time when Stalin was slavishly adhering to his pact with Hitler. Although Trygve Lie did not officially succeed Koht until the following February, the latter had already left office in November 1940.

Koht chose to spend the rest of the war in the United States, where he resumed his writing and research as a historian. At the conclusion of the conflict, the controversy surrounding him continued, but his request to have his role as foreign minister subjected to a court of impeachment (*rik-srett*) was turned down by the Storting. He returned to his position at the University of Oslo, and his status as the leading figure in Norwegian historiography during the twentieth century was only enhanced in the later years of his life. Although blind at the end, Koht continued to publish up to the time of his death, which came in 1965 after he had reached the age of ninety-two.

Unlike Koht, his successor more skillfully maintained close relations with Norway's allies during the war. Trygve Lie's position within the cabinet had already been strengthened considerably by the time the conflict began, compared with his standing as its junior member when Trotsky arrived in Norway. On October 1, 1939, Lie took over as minister of trade and supply (*Handels- og Forsyningsminister*), a vitally important post after the outbreak of World War II. Following the government's move to London and the ouster of Koht, Lie quickly implemented an active policy of friendship and cooperation with the British, which he expanded to include the Russians and Americans after their involvement in the war. Lie's diplomatic skill unquestionably strengthened Norway's position in the Allied alliance. He and Minister of Defense Oscar Torp, a future prime minister, were the two most dynamic members of the government during wartime. However, unlike previously when they were confidants, Lie's relationship with Nygaardsvold deteriorated in London. The prime minister felt that he could no longer fully trust his foreign minister.

Following the conclusion of the war, Lie and Torp were the only members of the wartime cabinet to make the transition to Gerhardsen's brief national unity government. After the parliamentary election of the fall of 1945, which gave the Labor Party an absolute majority, Lie continued as foreign minister in Gerhardsen's second government. However, he soon gained a far more prestigious position, thanks in part to the care with which he had cultivated his diplomatic contacts during the war. He was the only candidate for the post of secretary general of the United Nations who was acceptable to both the United States and the Soviet Union. As a compromise choice he became the first head of the new international body in 1946.

Although a number of important UN initiatives occurred during his tenure—including the creation of Israel, Indonesian independence, and an end to fighting in Kashmir—Lie's effectiveness was lessened significantly when the U.S.S.R. became unalterably hostile toward him due to the UN's support of the American position at the outbreak of the Korean War. Although his term was extended in 1950 (without Soviet recognition), two years later, when extremists in the United States during the McCarthy period exhibited their traditional phobia against the world organization, denouncing the UN for allegedly harboring communists among its American staff members, Lie felt that his position had been undermined to the point that he had to resign.

At first it was difficult to fit him into Norwegian politics after he left the world stage. Torp, having succeeded Gerhardsen as prime minister, was not interested in having Lie as a member of his government. Eventually he was appointed provincial governor (*fylkesmann*) of Oslo and Akershus in 1955. During Gerhardsen's third ministry, however, Lie's international contacts brought him back into active politics in 1959, when he received the mission, with the rank of "Ambassador on Special Assignment" (*ambassadør med særoppdrag*), to promote foreign investment in Norway. Gerhardsen was pleased with the results that Lie achieved, declaring that he had done "a good and useful job."[17] This became the springboard for Lie's later appointment as minister of industry in 1963. He served in both this cabinet and in Gerhardsen's final government, which ended in 1965. But his health was declining. He was switched to the post of minister of trade in 1964, but colleagues observed that "he had become old" and that, suffering from impaired hearing, at times his questions and comments were entirely irrelevant.[18] Having sustained a massive heart attack, Trygve Lie passed away in 1968 at the age of seventy-two.

Whereas the major Norwegian figures who had an impact on Trotsky's exile all died of natural causes, the opposite was generally true for his foreign assistants who had worked on his behalf during his stay in the country. Of Trotsky's secretaries only one, Jan Frankel, did not experience a violent death. After he left Norway to avoid deportation, he remained in his native Czechoslovakia until summoned to Mexico to serve once again on Trotsky's staff. Arriving in February 1937, he made a major contribution to work involving the Dewey Commission, but he left for the United States by October, in part because of personal differences with Trotsky. In the United States Frankel briefly was active in the Trotskyite movement, but he sided with the minority, opposed to Trotsky's viewpoint, when the Socialist

Workers Party split in 1940. Shortly afterwards, disillusioned with politics, Frankel abandoned completely his involvement in political affairs.

Jean van Heijenoort, whose stay in Norway, though briefer than Frankel's, had been more dramatic, experienced a pattern that was similar to that of his Czech counterpart, but on a higher level. He did not remain long in France after his expulsion from Norway because, as Trotsky's longest-serving secretary, he was needed in Mexico. He stayed with Trotsky in Coyoacan until the fall of 1939, when, feeling the need for change, he came to the United States, initially intending to remain only for a few months. However, with the outbreak of World War II, the Fourth International's secretariat was moved to New York, and van Heijenoort became its international secretary. He corresponded regularly with Trotsky about conditions within the divided American Trotskyite movement. Following Trotsky's assassination van Heijenoort continued as international secretary for the duration of the war but became disenchanted with the Socialist Workers Party, from which he was expelled in 1947. In the following year he began a new life, returning to the study of his favorite subject, mathematics. This led him to a distinguished academic career in mathematics and logic at New York University, Columbia University, and Brandeis University. His writings also included the topic of his past association with Trotskyism, and he played an important part in securing collections of Trotsky's papers for Harvard. Like his revered former leader, van Heijenoort was murdered in Mexico but not at the hands of a communist agent. Instead, a jealous wife fired the fatal bullets that ended his life at age seventy-three in 1986.[19]

Erwin Wolf, who served longest as Trotsky's secretary in Norway and who was forcibly deported along with van Heijenoort in August 1936, rejoined the International Secretariat in Paris in the fall. Despite having received considerable attention because of his activity on behalf of the secretariat, Wolf nevertheless was sent to Spain in 1937 in order to reorganize the Trotskyite group. He did not travel alone. Hjørdis Knudsen had wished for a long time to leave the narrow confines of Hønefoss. Now she had the opportunity and joined her lover, permanently she believed, in Brussels, from which they left for Spain.

However, what should have been the happiest time in their lives turned into a nightmare for the young couple. In Barcelona they witnessed their friends and contacts within both the small Trotskyite faction and the P.O.U.M. systematically subjected to terror by the communist-controlled police, being rounded up, tortured, and jailed. Erwin and Hjørdis hoped to avoid a similar fate. They had come to Spain in the guise of being journalists. They joined the local journalist association in Barcelona, registered with the authorities, fraternized with newsmen at their favorite coffee house, and submitted their writings for censorship. But all proved to be in vain. Communist agents had gained knowledge of Wolf's Trotskyite association. They proceeded to play cat and mouse with him. He was arrested at the end of July but released the next day, informed that the incident had been a case of mistaken identity. Wolf and Hjørdis hurriedly prepared to leave for France as soon as possible. They had no difficulty getting exit permits, but on the evening of July 31, having arranged a last meeting with a contact who had served them as a clearinghouse for sending and receiving uncensored foreign correspondence but who most likely was an NKVD agent, Erwin disappeared. Hjørdis searched desperately for him during the next week, going from prison to prison, seeing everywhere pleading faces of imprisoned comrades who warned her to escape. She was able to trace Erwin to a prison in Valencia, the Republican capital during the Civil War, but there the trail went cold.[20]

Erwin Wolf never emerged from his second imprisonment. His Stalinist captors executed him, undoubtedly after having subjected him to severe torture to get as much information as possible about the Trotskyite organization. Rumors, although unlikely, suggested that he might even have been sent to the Soviet Union for this purpose.[21] But all that is certain is that his jailers had no intention of allowing him to live.

Hjørdis barely avoided a similar fate. The police came twice to her boardinghouse to arrest her. However, she escaped by seeking refuge with the Norwegian consul in Barcelona. He also personally escorted her to the harbor and made arrangements for her to leave on a ship bound for Marseilles. Had this good Samaritan not been present when she was examined by the police, who checked the papers of everyone boarding the vessel, Hjørdis was "absolutely certain I would have been arrested and placed in jail."[22]

Once in France she did everything in her power to alert attention to Wolf's plight. Her family in Norway forwarded her letter, through Held, to Trotsky. Both Norwegian and Czech officials were asked to intercede on Erwin's behalf, but their efforts in Spain had no results. Hjørdis herself traveled to Prague, only to have the Spanish embassy accuse her of being an agent provocateur, sent by Trotsky to stir up hostility against the Republic.[23] From Mexico Trotsky assured her that everything was being done to get officials in Spain and Czechoslovakia to intercede and that

Trotskyites in the United States were exerting themselves to persuade "important bourgeois" sympathizers to use their influence.[24] More pessimistically, however, Lev wrote to Hjørdis' father, "We are hoping for the best in Erwin's case but we must also be prepared for the worst."[25]

In Norway, Jeanette Olsen's *Oktober* of course reported Wolf's arrest.[26] However, it proved difficult to have the tragic event publicized in major newspapers. Held and Meyer sought for an entire week to get *Arbeiderbladet* to tell its readers about what had happened to Wolf. Only when Held turned to *Dagbladet* did the story first appear in a leading paper, which prompted *Tidens Tegn* and *Aftenposten* to publish articles, including interviews with the Knudsen family. Finally, said Held, *Arbeiderbladet* felt compelled to print a brief article about Wolf.[27] *Arbeideren*, the communist organ in Oslo, on the other hand, made light of the issue. It not only attacked the Knudsens for having "run to the Franco press" but alleged that Wolf had staged his disappearance in order to harm the Spanish government, or that he secretly had gone off to carry out some kind of a "shady assignment."[28]

Wolf's unknown fate was a severe shock for the Knudsen family, but their lives eventually resumed a degree of normalcy. Konrad Knudsen, busy with his parliamentary responsibilities and party activity, took an apartment in Oslo. His family, however, stayed behind in Buskerud. They moved from Wexhall to a "nice house" with "a big garden full of flowers" that lay closer to Hønefoss. His wife Hilda kept busy running the store that Hjørdis had previously managed.[29] Hjørdis, however, had great difficulty overcoming the loss of Erwin and her recollection of the terror she had experienced in Spain. It proved impossible for her to settle down in Hønefoss after what had happened, confiding to Natalia Sedova that she would only feel alive "when I first can set my feet outside of this town."[30]

During World War II Konrad Knudsen escaped to Sweden together with his family. Here they were reunited with Walter Held, who similarly had come to Stockholm together with Synnøve and their young son. Rather than risk being taken captive should the Germans invade Sweden, Knudsen decided to chance traveling to the United States by escaping through the Soviet Union. Having obtained the required transit visas for the journey, the Knudsens traveled without hindrance south through Russia to the Black Sea, where they embarked for Istanbul and the United States.

For the remainder of the war, Knudsen employed his talents as a journalist in the United States and Canada on behalf of the Norwegian cause. He resumed his seat in the Storting following the German surrender. He served three additional terms in parliament in the years 1945–1957, with his career in national politics coming to an end at the age of sixty-seven. He died two years later.

When Walter Held bid farewell to the Knudsens in Sweden, he believed he would soon follow them to the United States. His departure from Scandinavia had been long in coming. Already in his very first letter after he belatedly received news of Trotsky's expulsion, he displayed his eagerness to leave Norway, asking, "Do you need me in Mexico?" If so, Held eagerly declared, he would be on "the first Norwegian boat" that left for that country.[31] Within a short time, however, he learned from the Trotskyite network that van Heijenoort and Frankel, more seasoned members of the movement, had been delegated to serve Trotsky. Declaring that he did not want to impose himself, Held wrote next that he would nevertheless come "with thousand fold joy" should his leader decide he could be useful. Everything Norwegian, said Held, had become "unbearably distasteful" for him. If he was not needed in Coyoacan, he suggested that he be permitted to go to New York, in whose "favorable political environment" he could edit a theoretical journal, thereby allowing Trotskyite intellectual activity to continue in the event of a war in Europe.[32]

Although he responded diplomatically, Trotsky did nothing to encourage Held to leave Europe. He suggested that the best possibility for Held was to move to Brussels, where he could serve as a correspondent for various publications. It was clear that Trotsky did not want Held either in Mexico or in the Trotskyite community in New York. He did hold out the possibility that Held might come to New York in the future but only if conditions worsened due to fascism or the danger of war.[33] This was a major setback for Held. Despite Walter's long association with the movement, Trotsky did not feel Held to be competent to work directly under him. Held's inability to influence the depressing developments that Trotsky had experienced in Norway in a more positive direction most likely contributed to this, as well as did his partisan involvement in strident disputes within the French organization and among German Trotskyite exiles.[34]

Despite his declared dissatisfaction with things Norwegian, brought on by his failure to breach the fortress of Labor Party domination in politics, Held chose to remain except for brief trips to other countries on the continent. In part this was because he was settling down. Walter's earnings as a language teacher, Synnøve proudly informed Natalia in 1937, were "almost as much as mine."[35]

By the end of the following year, however, Held felt the threat from Germany was becoming alarming. Hitler had bloodlessly taken over Austria and the Sudetendland and was in the process of swallowing what remained of Czechoslovakia. On a personal level Synnøve was nearing the end of her pregnancy. Held therefore appealed for assistance so that he might be able to leave with his loved ones in time. Trotsky's response was not encouraging. In Mexico the government was tightening restrictions to the point where it was very difficult for him to secure entry for deserving comrades. He did write to Trotskyites in the United States on Held's behalf, and he hoped they would do everything possible. However, he concluded pessimistically, "The door is too small and the pressure from all parts of Europe is too great."[36]

In Held's case the pessimism was justified. He was still stuck in Norway when World War II broke out. His prospects for leaving were dim. The American consul, having earlier held out hope, now informed him that he was not in line to receive a coveted visa. Again Held wrote to Trotsky, asking for assistance from a prominent American Trotskyite. Held was not, however, entirely glum. He proudly announced that he was now the father of a baby boy. Their little family had spent the summer of 1939 in the countryside, close to where Helge Krog was vacationing. During this time Held had worked on translating a novel by Krog's close friend, Sigurd Hoel, described by Held as "also being close to us." As for the worldwide prospects of Trotskyism, Held remained confident as usual, maintaining that the Soviet government's willingness to enter into a nonaggression pact with Hitler had "given Stalinism its deathblow internationally."[37]

Held wasted no time in fleeing to Sweden as soon as the German invasion of Norway took place. From Stockholm he reestablished contact by mail with Trotsky's staff in Coyoacan, from whom he received some financial support. He continued to publish articles on behalf of the cause, but he deplored the fact that Hitler's military successes had resulted in the loss of "our whole European organization," and he complained about the split in the American Trotskyite movement at this critical time as a result of Shachtman's break with Trotsky.*[38]

Walter did not, however, feel secure in neutral Sweden, being fearful that the Germans would soon overrun it as well. His goal of escaping to the United States improved when he was granted Norwegian citizenship

---

* Shachtman reacted strongly against Trotsky's support of the Soviet Union's aggressive expansion in 1939, in particular Stalin's invasion of Finland.

through the country's legation in Stockholm. This smoothed the way for him to obtain the longed-for American visas that he had been seeking since 1938. But his efforts to embark with his family by ship from either Gothenburg or Petsamo, Finland, were all in vain. This left him with the sole alternative of traveling through the Soviet Union. Friends in Stockholm warned him against this, due to the obvious danger that he would be in as a prominent Trotskyite, and stressed what had happened to Erwin Wolf and other followers of Trotsky who had been exterminated by Stalin's minions.

Held, however, remained convinced that, risky though it might be, escape through Russia was preferable to being trapped in Sweden should Hitler attack. Receipt of confirmation that the Knudsen family had arrived safely in the United States, even though Hjørdis, as Wolf's companion, had been the target of communist arrest in Spain, decided the issue. Having earlier obtained the required Soviet transit visas with no difficulty (which in itself should have been a warning), Held left Stockholm by plane for Moscow together with Synnøve and little Ivar Roland, two years old, ironically on May 17, 1941, Norway's independence day. Held believed that he had taken all necessary precautions. He left behind a memorandum, to be published in a Swedish radical paper in case he did not arrive as scheduled in Istanbul. Having purchased his tickets from Cooks, he was armed not only with American and Russian visas but also with visas for Turkey, Syria, Palestine, and India, indicating that he intended to reach the United States via a roundabout route from India, rather than traveling through the perilous Mediterranean, then a heavily fought-over theater of war.[39]

The fears of Held's friends were realized. He was arrested, separated from his family, and subjected to interrogation. Although the Norwegian government in London formally became an ally of the Soviet Union in the summer of 1941, following the start of Hitler's Russian offensive, inquiries by officials concerning Held were rebuffed. The last information about him while he was still alive came from inmates who had been imprisoned with him in Saratov. Thereafter there was only silence. Not until after the Stalin era did Soviet officials confirm that Heinz Epe (alias Walter Held), Synnøve Rosendahl-Jensen, and little Ivar Roland Epe had all perished as a result of the atrocious conditions that existed in Russian prisons during the Great Patriotic War.[40]

Walter Held's tragic end before having reached his thirty-second birthday, compounded by the fates of his companion and their young son, can also be regarded symbolically as the death of Trotskyism in Norway. There would be no revival following World War II. Individual former Trotskyites might live on, but there was no organized activity. As Nils Kåre Dahl recalled in 1989, "After the war I found that most of my old comrades were useless for political work."[41] Jeanette Olsen, in poor health, did not pass away until 1959, twenty years after the last issue of *Oktober*. In the postwar period of recovery and gradual increase in prosperity under the Labor Party's commanding leadership, with attention directed toward the future, the question of Trotsky's exile in Norway and the ideas that he and his close followers lived and died for were no longer subjects of political debate. Instead, separated by the divide of World War II, the Trotsky affair became simply a dramatic episode to look back on as the 1930s more and more assumed the character of a chapter in Norwegian history and in the history of international socialism.

Appendix
Frequently Mentioned Norwegian Newspapers

Newspapers included in this list are often referred to in the book. Each entry includes a brief description of the publication's political orientation. Unless shown differently, the papers were published daily in Oslo (except on Sunday, when no newspapers appeared).

ABC: The Fatherland League's weekly. It revealed the organization's strong nationalist and antisocialist viewpoint. The paper was opposed to Trotsky's exile in Norway. It tended to be pro-German in outlook but not fascist in ideology.

Aftenposten (The Evening Post): A leading newspaper that strongly supported the Conservative Party. It argued forcefully in favor of Trotsky's expulsion. In general it commented favorably on Hitler's successes in 1935–36.

Arbeiderbladet (The Labor Paper): The Labor Party's major newspaper, edited by Martin Tranmæl. It set the tone for the party's official position throughout the country. Under Tranmæl it backed the Nygaardsvold government's policy toward Trotsky.

Arbeideren (The Worker): The chief spokesman for the Communist Party. The paper adhered to the shifting policies of the party leadership, who in turn followed the viewpoint of the Soviet government. Except for one short interval, it was entirely antagonistic toward Trotsky's exile in Norway.

Dagbladet (The Daily Paper): This publication represented the more radical wing of the Liberal Party. It was at times critical of Trotsky but printed articles by his defenders after he was interned that vehemently attacked the government.

Fremtiden (The Future): The Labor Party's main newspaper in Buskerud province, located in the town of Drammen. As opposed to *Arbeiderbladet*, it showed more understanding for Trotsky during his internment, which was not surprising because Konrad Knudsen was the paper's local editor in Hønefoss.

Fritt Folk (Free People): National Union's national newspaper, established in March 1936, replacing the weekly *Nasjonal Samling* (National Union). It reflected the anticommunist and anti-Semitic attitude toward Trotsky expressed by the party leader, Vidkun Quisling.

Nationen (The Nation): Although regarded as spokesman for the Agrarian Party, the paper was owned by the Farmers Association. Its independent-minded editor, Thorvald Aadahl, was more conservative than the majority of the Agrarian leadership. He was sympathetic toward Germany and one of Trotsky's most bitter critics.

Oktober (October): The only Trotskyite publication in Norway, it appeared infrequently as a monthly in the years 1937–1939, following Trotsky's departure to Mexico. The paper was edited by Jeanette Olsen, who had long been prominent in the labor movement. Her admiration for Trotsky drastically reduced her influence among socialists and communists alike.

Sørlandet (Southern Norway): Edited by Olav Scheflo, the Kristiansand daily served as the Labor Party's leading news outlet in this region. However, because its editor had been the key champion in bringing Trotsky to Norway, *Sørlandet* became Trotsky's strongest press advocate after the latter's internment. But Scheflo was always careful not to create a situation that would lead to a break with the party.

Tidens Tegn (Sign of the Times): As a political and cultural source for more conservative members of Oslo's intellectual elite, this paper exercised considerable influence during the 1930s, even though it was associated with the politically insignificant Independent People's Party. It was antisocialist and generally positive toward Hitler but distanced itself from Quisling in 1936. The paper was hostile toward Trotsky.

Notes

Prologue

1. "Rapport fra statspolitifullmektig Jonas Lie i anledning av *ledsagelse av Leo Trotsky og frue fra Norge til Mexico,* ifølge Justisministrens ordre," January 10, 1937, box 2, Trotsky-saken, Politikontoret, Justisdepartementets arkiv, Riksarkivet, Oslo. Hereafter cited as Trotsky-saken, Ra.

2. L. Trotsky, Storsand, to Lev Sedov, Paris, December 18, 1936, ibid.

3. L. Trotsky, Storsand, to Alexis Bardin, Paris, December 18, 1936, ibid.

4. J. Lie, *I "fred" og ufred,* 145.

5. L. Trotsky, "On the Atlantic, December 28, 1936," *Writings, 1936–37,* 39.

6. "Rapport fra statspolitifullmektig Jonas Lie i anledning av *ledsagelse av Leo Trotsky og frue fra Norge til Mexico,* ifølge Justisministrens ordre," January 10, 1937, box 2, Trotsky-saken, Ra.

7. L. Trotsky, Storsand, to Dr. Carl Müller, Oslo, December 18, 1936, ibid.

8. L. Trotsky, "On the Atlantic," *Writings, 1936–37,* 40.

9. Krog, *Meninger,* 61.

10. L. Trotsky, Storsand, to Håkon Meyer, Oslo, December 16, 1936, Håkon Meyer samlingen, Arbeiderbevegelsens arkiv og bibliotek (the Labor Movement's Archive and Library), Oslo, hereafter cited as Aa.

11. Held, Oslo, to Trotsky, n.p., December 21, 1936, doc #1935, Folder G 137, Exile Papers of Lev Trotskii, Houghton Library, Harvard University. This collection hereafter cited as Exile Papers, Hd.

12. Held, Oslo, to Trotsky, n.p., December 28, 1936, doc #1936, Folder G 137, ibid.

13. Rosenthal, Paris, to Trotsky, n.p., December 28, 1936, doc #4332, Folder F 113, ibid.

14. Meyer and Held, Oslo, to Foreign Minister Halvdan Koht, Oslo, December 23, 1936, box 3, Trotsky-saken, Ra.

15. J. V. [Jacob Vidnes], "Pressemøte," December 18, 1936, Journalnr. 19278, 1936, Utenriksdepartementets arkiv [Foreign Ministry archive], Oslo, hereafter cited as UDa.

16. "Trotski avreist til Mexico," *Arbeiderbladet,* December 23, 1936.

17. Meyer and Held, Oslo, to Foreign Minister Koht, Oslo, December 23, 1936, box 3, Trotsky-saken, Ra.

18. J. Lie, *I "fred" og ufred,* 145.

19. Harald Halvorsen d.y., tape-recorded interview with Aagot Sæthre, November 7, 1992. Sæthre was a member of the staff who served at Sundby during Trotsky's stay.

20. L. Trotsky, *Writings, 1935–36,* 486.

21. J. Lie, *I "fred" og ufred,* 144.

22. Box 2, Trotsky-saken, Ra.

23. L. Trotsky [Storsand], to Rosenthal [Paris], December 18, 1936, *Writings, 1935–36,* 501.

24. L. Trotsky, "On the Atlantic," December 28, 1936, *Writings, 1936–37,* 40.

25. Natalia and Leon Trotsky, Storsand, to Konrad Knudsen, n.p., n.d. [probably December 18, 1936], box 2, Trotsky-saken, Ra.

26. Ibid.

27. L. Trotsky, "On the Atlantic," December 28, 1936, *Writings, 1936–37*, 41.

28. "Leo Trotzky til Oslo idag," *Arbeiderbladet*, June 18, 1935.

29. "Trotski vil være i ro," ibid., June 19, 1935.

30. "En samtale med Trotski," ibid., July 26, 1935.

31. L. Trotsky, Hønefoss, to Olav Scheflo, Kristiansand, June 26, 1935, doc. #10022, Folder N 197, Exile Papers, Hd.

32. Laqueur, *Stalin*, 46.

33. Service, *Stalin*, 283.

34. Robert Service, his most recent English biographer, who is by no means uncritical, maintains that Trotsky as a literary stylist was equaled only by Winston Churchill among contemporary political figures. See *Trotsky*, 399.

35. Segal, *Leon Trotsky*, 337.

36. Ibid., 351.

1: Early Attempts to Gain Asylum in Scandinavia

1. Van Heijenoort, *Trotsky in Exile*, 9.

2. Serge and Trotsky, *Life and Death*, 164.

3. L. Trotsky, *My Life*, 572–73. For a more detailed study of Trotsky's effort to secure residence in Norway in 1929, see Høidal, "Unwelcome Exile," 32–45.

4. Ibid., 33.

5. Ibid., 33–34.

6. Pressemeddelelse nr. 62, April 17, 1929, Journalnr. 15708, 1929, UDa.

7. Høidal, "Unwelcome Exile," 35.

8. Ibid., 36.

9. "Tragedien," *Arbeiderbladet*, April 19, 1929.

10. Høidal, "Unwelcome Exile," 37.

11. Ibid.

12. Ibid., 39.

13. Storting debate, April 22, 1929, in Norway, Kongeriget Norges Otteogsyttiende Ordentlige Stortings Forhandlinger, 1929, syvende del, A (Oslo, 1929), 1210.

14. Unsigned press release, Prinkipo, March 19, 1930, doc. #15742, Folder US 223, Exile Papers, Hd.

15. "Trotski," *Arbeiderbladet*, March 21, 1930.

16. Evang, for Det Norske Studentersamfund, Oslo, to Trotsky, Prinkipo, November 15, 1930, doc. #906, Folder N 196, Exile Papers, Hd.

17. Scheflo, Oslo, to Trotsky, Prinkipo, November 13, 1930, doc. #4677, ibid.

18. Evang, for Det Norske Studentersamfund, Oslo, to Trotsky, Prinkipo, November 15, 1930, doc. #906, ibid.

19. Trotsky, Prinkipo, to Det Norske Studentersamfund, Oslo, December 2, 1930, doc. #9418, ibid.

20. Evang, Oslo, to Trotsky, Prinkipo, January 10, 1931, doc. #909, ibid.

21. "Trotski," *Norges Handels- & Sjøfartstidende*, January 6, 1931; "Trotsky og den norske regjering," *Middagsavisen*, January 7, 1931; "Er vi sikre på å bli kvitt Trotski igjen?" *Oslo Aftenavis*, January 7, 1931; "La ham bli hvor han er," *Aftenposten*, January 7, 1931.

22. "Trotski," *Dagbladet*, January 7, 1931.

23. Evang, Oslo, to Trotsky, Prinkipo, January 10, 1931, doc. #909, Folder N 196, Exile Papers, Hd.

24. Ibid.

25. Justisdepartementet to Centralpasskontoret, January 8, 1931, Journalnr. 00430, 1931, UDa.

26. Trotsky, Prinkipo, to Evang, Oslo, January 17, 1931, doc. #7741, Folder N 196, Exile Papers, Hd.

27. Evang, Oslo, to Trotsky, Prinkipo, February 18, 1931, doc. #914, ibid.

28. Bille Larsen, *Mod strømmen*, 146–47.

29. L. Trotsky, *Writings: Supplement, 1929–33*, 148.

30. Deutscher, *Prophet Outcast*, 183; R. Payne, *Life and Death*, 342.

31. Bille Larsen, *Mod strømmen*, 148–49; Deutscher, *Prophet Outcast*, 183–84; R. Payne, *Life and Death*, 342–44.

32. Bille Larsen, *Mod strømmen*, 153.

33. Deutscher, *Prophet Outcast*, 185.

34. Bille Larsen, *Mod strømmen*, 153–55.

35. Ibid., 150.

36. Ibid.

37. Molinier, Paris, to Det Norske Studentersamfund, Oslo, November 15, 1932, doc. #15071, Folder F 106, Exile Papers, Hd.

38. Det Norske Studentersamfund, Oslo, to Molinier, Paris, November 18, 1932, doc. #15174, Folder N 196, Exile Papers, Hd.

39. "Intet Trotsky-besøk i Norge," *Aftenposten*, November 28, 1932.

40. "A Bolshevik-Leninist Declaration on Comrade Trotsky's Journey," *Biulleten Oppozitsii*, no. 32 (December 1932), unsigned article in L. Trotsky, *Writings, 1932*, 336.

41. Bille Larsen, *Mod strømmen*, 150–51.

42. Ibid., 155.

43. C. V. Lange, Oslo, to Trotsky, n.p., August 3, 1933, doc. #2599, Folder N 196, Exile Papers, Hd.

44. Trotsky, n.p., to C. V. Lange, Oslo, October 2, 1933, doc. #8796, Folder N 74, ibid.

45. Kristian Gleditsch, Oslo, to Trotsky, Paris, December 11, 1933, doc. #1435, Folder N 196, ibid.

46. Gleditsch, Oslo, to Trotsky, Paris, December 31, 1933, doc. #1436, ibid.

47. Gleditsch, Oslo, to Pierre Naville, Paris, January 1, 1934, doc. #14651, ibid.

48. Trotsky [Barbizon, France], to "dear comrade" [Gleditsch], [Oslo], January 9, 1934, doc. #9419, ibid.

49. Gleditsch, Oslo, to Trotsky, n.p., January 14, 1934, doc. #1437, ibid.

50. Gleditsch, Oslo, to Trotsky, n.p., March 7, 1934, doc. #1438, ibid.

51. Trotsky, n.p., to Det Norske Studentersamfund, Oslo, March 19, 1934, doc. #9420, ibid.

52. Van Heijenoort, *Trotsky in Exile*, 59.

2: Arrival in Norway

1. L. Trotsky, "In Socialist Norway," *Writings, 1936–37*, 22.

2. L. Trotsky, *Diary in Exile*, 107.

3. Ibid., 108.

4. Ibid., 41.

5. Held [Oslo] to Durand [Lev Sedov], [Paris], March 27, 1935, Walter Held folder, Aa.

6. Lorenz, "Vår kamerat i Oslo," 153.

7. Broué, *Trotsky*, 806.

8. Held, Oslo, to Helge Krog, n.p., November 29, 1938, Helge Krog samlingen, MS folio 3956:8a, Håndskriftavdelingen, Nasjonalbiblioteket, Oslo, hereafter cited as HA-NB.

9. L. Trotsky, diary entry of May 8, 1935, *Diary in Exile*, 107.

10. L. Trotsky, *Writings: Supplement, 1934–40*, 584; Norway, Justis- og Politidepartmentet, "St. med. Nr. 19: "Om Leo Trotsky opholdstillatelse, internering og reise fra landet," Kongeriket Norges seksogåttiende Ordentlige Stortingsforhandlinger 1937, Annen del b, February 18, 1937.

11. Lorenz, "Vår kamerat i Oslo," 154.

12. Held, Oslo, to Krog, n.p., November 29, 1938, Helge Krogs samling, MS folio 3956:8a, HA-NB.

13. L. Trotsky, *Diary in Exile*, 138.

14. Ibid., 136.

15. Ibid., 136, 138.

16. Ibid., 138.

17. Ibid., 138–39.

18. Telegram from "Leo Sedoff" [Trotsky], Paris, to Minister of Justice [Trygve Lie], Oslo, June 11, 1935, box 1, Trotsky-saken, Ra.

19. L. Trotsky, Paris, to Scheflo, n.p., June 11, 1935, doc. #10021, folder N 197, Exile Papers, Hd.

20. Telegram from "Leo Sedoff" [Trotsky], Paris, to Prime Minister [Johan Nygaardsvold], Oslo, June 12, 1935, ibid.

21. L. Trotsky, *Diary in Exile*, 118–19.

22. Held, Oslo, to Krog, n.p., November 29, 1938, Helge Krogs samling, MS folio 3956:8a, HA-NB.

23. T. Lie, *Oslo-Moskva-London*, 66; Strandberg, "Fra gjest til fange."

24. T. Lie, *Oslo-Moskva-London*, 67.

25. Held, Oslo, to Krog, n.p., November 29, 1938, Helge Krogs samling, MS folio 3956:8a, HA-NB.

26. L. Trotsky, *Diary in Exile*, 140.

27. Ibid., 141.

28. H[alvard] H. Backe, for the Royal Norwegian Legation, Paris, to the Central Passport Office, Oslo, June 13, 1935, journalnr. 08590, 1935, UDa.

29. Copy of telegram from the Central Passport Office, Oslo, to Leon Sedoff [Trotsky], Paris, June 12, 1935, box 1, no. 1, Trotsky-saken, Ra.

30. Van Heijenoort, *Trotsky in Exile*, 79.

31. L. Trotsky, *Diary in Exile*, 142; H[alvard] Bachke, for the Royal Norwegian Legation, Paris, to the Central Passport Office, Oslo, June 13, 1935, journalnr. 08590, 1935, UDa.

32. L. Trotsky, *Diary in Exile*.

33. "Tattler" [Axel Kielland], "Trotsky og hans frue til Oslo idag," *Dagbladet*, June 18, 1935.

34. "Trotski kom igår til Oslo sammen med sin hustru og to sekretærer," *Tidens Tegn*, June 19, 1935.

35. Ibid.; Ustvedt, *Verdensrevolusjonen på Hønefoss*, 14.

36. Ustvedt, Verdensrevolusjonen på Hønefoss.

37. "Opholdstillatelse i Norge for 6 måneder. Statsråd Lie uttaler sig,"*Arbeiderbladet*, June 18, 1935.

38. Ustvedt, *Verdensrevolusjonen på Hønefoss*, 16.

39. L. Trotsky, *Diary in Exile*, 137. The entry dates in this section of the diary are incorrect, due either to errors made by the author himself or by the translator. The diary entry for June 17, for example, indicates that he had been in Norway for two days, whereas he did not arrive until June 18. Similarly, the entry for June 20 states that his permanent residence had been decided on, whereas in reality he was still living in Jevnaker, without any knowledge of where he would move to.

40. Ibid., 145.

41. "Opholdstillatelse i Norge for 6 måneder." Statsråd Lie uttaler sig," *Arbeiderbladet*, June 18, 1935.

42. "Trotski vil være i ro," *Arbeiderbladet*, June 19, 1935.

43. "Trotsky foreløbig utenfor Oslo," *Dagbladet*, June 18, 1935; "Trotski kom igår til Oslo sammen med sin hustru og to sekretærer," *Tidens Tegn*, June 19, 1935.

44. Egge, *Kirov-gåten*, 254–57, 258.

45. L. Trotsky, *Diary in Exile*, 130.

46. Ibid., 129.

47. Dagbladet, June 18, 1935.

48. "Trotsky kom igår til Oslo sammen med sin hustru og to sekretærer," *Tidens Tegn*, June 19, 1935.

49. "Trotski vil være i ro," *Arbeiderbladet*, June 19, 1936.

50. Patenaude, *Trotsky*, 78.

51. T. Lie, *Oslo-Moskva-London*, 65.

52. Ustvedt, *Verdensrevolusjonen på Hønefoss*, 52.

53. N. K. Dahl, "With Trotsky in Norway," 34.

54. Lorenz, "Vår kamerat i Oslo," 150.

55. Ibid., 150, 159 n8.

56. Ibid., 151, 156.

57. Author's interview with Dagmar Loe, Oslo, June 28, 1994.

58. Author's interview with Haakon Lie at his home in Oslo, July 6, 1994.

59. "Trotsky," *Aftenposten*, June 19, 1935.

60. "Trotski," *Arbeiderbladet*, June 19, 1935.

61. "Bøddelen er kommet inn i landet," *Vestopland*, June 20, 1935.

62. "En farlig mann," *Østlendingen*, June 20, 1935.

63. "Asylretten," *Arbeiderbladet*, June 24, 1935.

64. "Den kontrarevolusjonære Trotsky som Det norske Arbeiderpartis gjest," *Arbeideren*, June 21, 1935.

65. "Trotsky i Norge," *Sørlandet*, June 22, 1935.

66. "Trotsky proklameres som D.N.A.s kampfelle," *Arbeidet*, June 24, 1935.

67. "Trotski som redningens engel for Arbeiderpartiet," *Nasjonal Samling*, June 20, 1935.

68. "Asylretten," *Arbeiderbladet*, June 24, 1935.

69. "Opholdstillatelse i Norge for 6 måneder. Statsråd Lie uttaler sig," *Arbeiderbladet*, June 18, 1935.

70. "Vil Hambro interpellere?" *Arbeiderbladet*, June 19, 1935.

71. "Trotski," *Arbeiderbladet*, June 19, 1935.

72. "Trotski i korridoren," *Tidens Tegn*, June 19, 1935.

73. Storting proceedings, June 22, 1935, Kongeriket Norges Fireogåttiende Ordentlige Stortigsforhandlinger 1935, Syvende del B, Stortingstidende, Forhandlinger i Stortinget, 1540. Hereafter cited as Stortingsforhandlinger 1935.

74. Ibid., 1540–41.

75. Ibid., 1541.

76. "Asylretten," *Arbeiderbladet*, June 24, 1935.

77. L. Trotsky, *Diary in Exile*, 142–143.

78. L. Trotsky, "In 'Socialist' Norway," *Writings, 1936–37*, 21; Broué, *Trotsky*, 808.

79. Jean van Heijenoort stated in his memoirs that arrangements for the Trotskys' living accommodations "had been made through Scheflo, who was a friend of the Knudsens." Van Heijenoort, *Trotsky in Exile*, 81.

80. "Ringerike er vakkert og herlig, sier Trotsky," *Fremtiden*, June 24, 1935.

81. Trotsky, Hønefoss, to Scheflo, n.p., June 26, 1935, doc. #10022, folder N 197, Exile Papers, Hd.

82. L. Trotsky, diary entry of July 13, 1935, *Diary in Exile*, 154.

3: The Norwegian Labor Movement and Its Relationship to Trotsky

1. H. Lie, *Martin Tranmæl*, 1: 15.

2. Ibid.

3. B. G. Olsen, *Tranmæl og hans menn*, 283–84.

4. E. Bull, "Olav Scheflo," 321.

5. Brunvand, "Redaktøren og anti-Stalinisten," 23–24.

6. E. Bull, "Olav Scheflo," 322.

7. Krog, *Litteratur, kristendom, politikk*, 287.

8. Ibid.

9. Maurseth, *Gjennom kriser til makt*, 34.

10. Ibid., 100.

11. Ibid., 156.

12. B. G. Olsen, *Tranmæl og hans menn*, 153.

13. The question of whether demands made by the Comintern were responsible for the Labor Party's eventual break with Moscow, or whether it was originally triggered as a result of the internal dispute between the factions led by Tranmæl and Scheflo, has been the source of some dispute among Norwegian historians. However, the opening of Kremlin archives gives credence to the interpretation that the Comintern's demands for conformity were the major reason for why the rupture took place. See Egge, "Hvorfor ble Arbeiderpartiet splittet i 1923?" For opposing viewpoints, see Bjørgum, "En kommentar til Åsmund Egge," and Olstad, "Tradisjon og fornyelse," in *Historisk Tidskrift*, 83, no. 2 (2004), as well as Egge's response.

14. Friis, *Trotskismen*, 9; Deutscher, *Prophet Unarmed*, 28; Gilberg, *Soviet Communist Party*, 35–36.

15. Gilberg, *Soviet Communist Party*, 37; H. Lie, *Loftsrydding*, 118–20.
16. Maurseth, *Gjennom kriser til makt*, 298.
17. H. Lie, *Loftsrydding*, 136.
18. Maurseth, *Gjennom kriser til makt*, 252.
19. H. Lie, *Loftsrydding*, 140.
20. Lorenz, *Arbeiderbevegelsens historie*, 1: 172; H. Lie, ibid., 155; Keilhau, *I vår egen tid*, 424.
21. Lorenz, *Arbeiderbevegelsens historie*, 1: 175–76.
22. Ibid., 178–79.
23. Maurseth, *Gjennom kriser til makt*, 449; H. Lie, *Loftsrydding*, 179–80.
24. H. Lie, *Loftsrydding*, 181.
25. Berntsen, *I malstrømmen*, 265.
26. Ibid., 272; H. Lie, *Martin Tranmæl*, 1: 408.
27. B. G. Olsen, *Tranmæl og hans menn*, 232–34.
28. E. Bull, *Arbeiderklassen i norsk historie*, 309.
29. Ibid., 312.
30. Ibid., 313.
31. H. Lie, *Loftsrydding*, 237.
32. Pryser, *Klassen og nasjonen*, 15.
33. Maurseth, "Hva betydde regjeringsskiftet i 1935," 18–19.
34. H. Lie, *Loftsrydding*, 238.
35. Skaufjord, "Venstreopposisjonen," 35–36.
36. T. Bull, *Mot Dag og Erling Falk*, 226–27.
37. H. Lie, *Martin Tranmæl*, 2: 88–89; Skaufjord, "Venstreopposisjonen," 84–85.
38. Skaufjord, "Venstreopposisjon," 81.
39. Maurseth, *Gjennom kriser til makt*, 276.
40. Skaufjord, "Venstreopposisjonen," 82–83.
41. Zachariassen, *På forpost*, 441, 442–43.
42. Pryser, *Klassen og nasjonen*, 154.
43. Lorenz, *Arbeiderbevegelsens historie*, 2: 17; Pryser, ibid.,78–79.
44. Pryser, *Klassen og nasjonen*, 154.
45. Skaufjord, "Venstreopposisjon," 95; Pryser, ibid., 79.
46. H. Lie, *Loftsrydding*, 415.
47. Ibid., 241–42.
48. Maurseth, *Gjennom kriser til makt*, 577.
49. Radio speech of October 5, 1936, quoted in H. F. Dahl, *Norge mellom krigene*, 67.
50. "Nygaardsvold-regjeringen," *Tidsskrift for arbeiderbevegelsens historie* 11, no. 1 (1986), 59.
51. Berntsen, *I malstrømmen*, 212.
52. Ibid., 283–84.
53. Hirsti, *Gubben*, 155.
54. Pryser, *Klassen og nasjonen*, 73–74.
55. Maurseth, *Gjennom kriser til makt*, 578.
56. E. Bull, *Arbeiderklassen i norsk historie*, 325; Zachariassen, *Fra Marcus Thrane til Martin Tranmæl*, 337.
57. Zachariasen, *Fra Marcus Thrane til Martin Tranmæl*, 335.
58. E. Bull, *Arbeiderklassen i norsk historie*, 325–26.

59. Danielsen, *Norge–Sovjetunionen*, 192; H. Lie, *Loftsrydding*, 411.

60. Berntsen, *I malstrømmen*, 409.

61. H. Lie, *Loftsrydding*, 411.

62. H. Lie, *Martin Tranmæl*, 2: 139–48; H. Lie, *Loftsrydding*, 408–14.

63. Hansen, "NKP og regjeringen 1935—36," 64.

64. Pryser, *Klassen og nasjonen*, 90.

65. "Dagsorden for Det norske Arbeiderpartis 30te ordinære landsmøte i Folkets hus, Oslo, 22., 23., og 24 mai 1936," Arbeiderbevegelsens arkiv, Oslo; Det norske Arbeiderparti, *Protokoll over forhandlingene på det 30. landsmøte*, 133.

66. Pryser, *Klassen og nasjonen*, 89.

67. L. Trotsky, "In 'Socialist' Norway," *Writings, 1936–37*, 22. As a matter of fact, Trotsky in the early 1920s appears to have felt that the Comintern, under Zinoviev's leadership, had not been forceful enough in dealing with the Labor Party prior to its break with Moscow in 1923. See Egge, *Komintern og krisen*, 111–12.

68. Lorenz, *Arbeiderbevegelsens historie*, 1: 195.

69. Ibid., 176.

70. Lorenz, *Willy Brandt in Norwegen*, 146.

71. Skaufjord, "Venstreopposisjonen," 102.

72. Pryser, *Klassen og nasjonen*, 193.

73. Lorenz, *Willy Brandt in Norwegen*, 146–47.

74. L. Trotsky, *Writings, 1933–34*, 50–51.

75. "Dagsorden for Det norske Arbeiderpartis 30te ordinære landsmøte," 34.

76. L. Trotsky to Jacob Walcher, August 26, 1933, in *Writings: Supplement, 1929–1933*, 282.

77. L. Trotsky, *Writings 1933–34*, 349n82.

78. Lorenz, *Willy Brandt in Norwegen*, 89.

79. Ibid., 90; Lorenz, "Willy Brandt, regjeringen Nygaardsvold," 74.

80. L. Trotsky, *Writings: Supplement, 1929–33*, 346.

81. Ibid., 346–47.

82. Ibid., 351.

83. Ibid., 205.

84. Lorenz, *Willy Brandt in Norwegen*, 148.

85. Broué, *Trotsky*, 379.

86. Lorenz, "Willy Brandt i Norge," 115.

87. Lorenz, *Willy Brandt in Norwegen*, 150–51.

88. Ibid., 151–52.

89. Glotzer, *Trotsky*, 195.

90. Ibid., 198; Lorenz, *Willy Brandt in Norwegen*, 152–53; L. Trotsky, *Writings: Supplement, 1934–40*, 896n438.

91. Lorenz, *Willy Brandt in Norwegen*, 153–54.

92. Lorenz, "Vår kamerat i Oslo," 151.

93. Lorenz, *Willy Brandt in Norwegen*, 154.

94. Lorenz, "Willy Brandt i Norge," 127.

95. Ibid., 116.

96. Ibid., 155.

97. Ibid., 155–56.

98. L. Trotsky, *Writings, 1933–34*, 267.

99. Ibid.
100. Ibid., 538.
101. Ibid., 905n508.
102. L. Trotsky, *Writings, 1934–35*, 111.
103. Ibid., 232.
104. Ibid., 233.
105. Ibid., 234.
106. Lorenz, "Willy Brandt i Norge," 125.
107. Lorenz, *Willy Brandt in Norwegen*, 156.
108. L. Trotsky, *Writings: Supplement, 1934–1940*, 580.
109. Ibid.
110. Ibid.
111. Held, Oslo, to the International Communist League's Secretariat [Paris], July 15, 1935, doc. #14753, folder G 125, Exile Papers, Hd.
112. Lorenz, *Willy Brandt in Norwegen*, 156–57.
113. L. Trotsky, *Writings, 1934–35*, 273.
114. Ibid., 187.
115. "Dagsorden for Det norske Arbeiderpartis 30te ordinære landsmøte," 35.
116. Ibid.
117. Pryser, *Klassen og nasjonen*, 193.
118. A. Fenner Brockway, Secretary of the International Bureau for Revolutionary Socialist Unity, London, to the Executive Committee of the Norwegian Labor Party, Oslo, October 14, 1935, included in Brockway's memo to Erling Falk, Oslo, December 19, 1935, Erling Falk korrespondanse, 1935–36 folder, Mot Dag box 8, Mot Dag Arkivet, Aa.
119. The Norwegian Labor Party, Oslo, to the International Bureau for Revolutionary Socialist Unity, London, November 22, 1935, in ibid.
120. Danielsen, *Norge–Sovjetunionen*, 182.
121. L. Trotsky, *Writings, 1934–35*, 259.
122. L. Trotsky, May 9, 1935, *Diary in Exile*, 113.
123. "Dagsorden for Det norske Arbeiderpartis 30te ordinære landsmøte," 171–74.
124. Berntsen, *I malstrømmen*, 372–73.
125. Ibid., 373.

4: Life at Wexhall

1. Statsarkivet i Kongsberg to the author, July 14, 2000.
2. Commission of Inquiry into the Charges Made against Leon Trotsky in the Moscow Trials, 181. Hereafter cited as Commission of Inquiry.
3. L. Trotsky, "In 'Socialist' Norway," *Writings, 1936–37*, 22.
4. Halvor Hegtun, "Under samme tak som Trotskij," *Aftenposten*, February 18, 1989.
5. "En samtale med Trotski," *Arbeiderbladet*, July 26, 1935.
6. Preliminary Commission of Inquiry, Commission of Inquiry into the Charges Made against Leon Trotsky in the Moscow Trials, 207. Hereafter cited as Preliminary Commission.
7. Hegtun, "Under samme tak som Trotskij," *Aftenposten*, February 18, 1989; Anita Feferman, notes of interview with Gunvor Wraamann, September 6, 1989, Anita Feferman

Collection, Hoover Institution, Stanford University; "Innbruddet på Wexhall," *Fremtiden*, December 10, 1936.

8. Preliminary Commission, 212.

9. L. Trotsky, "In 'Socialist' Norway," *Writings, 1936–37*, 22; H. Lie, *Loftsrydding*, 273.

10. Hegtun, "Under samme tak som Trotskij," *Aftenposten*, February 18, 1989.

11. Haffner, *Stortinget og statsrådet*, 1: 401–2.

12. L. Trotsky, *Diary in Exile*, 209.

13. Haffner, *Stortinget og statsrådet*, 1: 401–2. Norby, *Storting og regjering*, 391.

14. L. Trotsky, "In 'Socialist' Norway," *Writings, 1936–37*, 21.

15. Hegtun, "Under samme tak som Trotskij," *Aftenposten*, February 18, 1989.

16. L. Trotsky, "In 'Socialist' Norway," *Writings, 1936–37*, 21.

17. L. Trotsky, diary entry, June 26, 1935, *Diary in Exile*, 146.

18. J. Lie, *I "fred" og ufred*, 131.

19. Elisabeth Dahl, Oslo, to Trotsky, n.p. , July 24, 1935, doc. #731, folder N 196, Exile Papers, Hd; Trotsky, Hønefoss, to Elisabeth Dahl [Oslo], July 26, 1935, doc. #7657, folder N 196, Exile Papers, Hd; Van Heijenoort, *Trotsky in Exile*, 81–82.

20. L. Trotsky, diary entry, September 8, 1935, *Diary in Exile*, 159.

21. Louis Marx, Oslo, to Trotsky [Hønefoss], July 15, 1935, doc. #3003, folder US 223, Exile Papers, Hd; Paramount Pictures, Oslo office, to Konrad Knudsen, Hønefoss, August 16, 1935, doc. #15216, folder N 196, Exile Papers, Hd.

22. L. Trotsky, diary entry, July 1, 1935, *Diary in Exile*, 152.

23. Eivind Mehle, "Liv og død og Trotski," *Nasjonal Samling*, July 25, 1935.

24. Strandberg, "Fra gjest til fange," 19–20; L. Trotsky, diary entry, July 30, 1935, *Diary in Exile*, 154–55.

25. L. Trotsky, diary entry, July 13, 1935, *Diary in Exile*, 152–53. For Trotsky's critical attitude toward Scandinavian socialism, see also Kan, "Les petits pays."

26. Norway, Kongeriket Norges Seksogåttiende Ordentlige Stortingsforhandlinger 1937, sjette del b., Innstillinger og beslutninger, Innst. O.IV.B. (1937), 2. Hereafter cited as Stortingsforhandlinger 1937, sjette del b., Innstillinger og beslutninger, Innst. O.IV.B. (1937).

27. L. Trotsky, diary entry, July 30, 1935, *Diary in Exile*, 154.

28. "En samtale med Trotski," *Arbeiderbladet*, July 26, 1935.

29. Ibid. Isaac Deutscher incorrectly states that the interview left "the readers in no doubt that the Minister of Justice himself had been instrumental in making the benefit of Trotsky's views available to them." Deutscher, *Prophet Outcast*, 294. As indicated above, Colbjørnsen, not Lie, wrote the article, in which the Minister of Justice was not referred to by name.

30. Ibid. The interview with Trotsky in *Arbeiderbladet* was reprinted verbatim four days later in *Sørlandet*, Scheflo's Kristiansand newspaper.

31. Leo Trotzki, "Wer verfeldigt die USSR und wer hilft Hitler?" *Unser Wort*, early September 1935.

32. Strandberg, "Fra gjest til fange," 27.

33. "Ole Colbjørnsen som linedanser," *Nasjonal Samling*, November 21, 1935.

34. L. Trotsky, diary entry, June 24, 1935, *Diary in Exile*, 145.

35. Diary entry, June 26, 1935, ibid., 146–47.

36. Diary entry, July 1, 1935, ibid., 151.

37. Diary entry, July 13, 1935, ibid, 152.

38. "En samtale med Trotski," *Arbeiderbladet*, July 26, 1935.

39. Broué, *Trotsky*, 811; L. Trotsky, diary entry, September 8, 1935, *Diary in Exile*, 159.

40. Trotsky, Oslo, to Held [Oslo], September 18, 1935, doc. #8501, Folder G 137, Exile Papers, Hd.

41. Author's visit to Skoger, July 10, 1994.

42. Nils Kåre Dahl, rough draft of unpublished memoir, Aa.

43. Mildred Gordon, et al., Nils Kåre Dahl interview, December 27, 1983, 2, 10, Nils Kåre Dahl samling, Aa.

44. L. Trotsky, Oslo, to Held [Oslo], September 18, 1935, doc. #8501, Folder G 137, Exile Papers, Hd.

45. Trotsky, n.p., to Carl Müller [Oslo], September 10, 1935, doc. #9316, Folder N 196, ibid.

46. Müller, Oslo, to Knudsen, Hønefoss, August 23, 1935, doc. #3445, ibid.

47. Trotsky, Oslo, to the Knudsen family [Hønefoss], October 6, 1935, doc. #8694, Folder N 197, ibid.

48. "Trotsky innlagt på Ullevål. Opdaget av en besøkende igår," *Dagbladet*, October 9, 1935.

49. Trotski, *Mitt liv*, 9.

50. "Trotsky innlagt på Ullevål. Opdaget av en besøkende igår." *Dagbladet*, November 9, 1935.

51. "Bedraget i fredens navn. Av Trotskijs meriter," *Nasjonal Samling*, October 17, 1935.

52. Müller, Oslo, to *Aftenposten*'s editor, Oslo, n.d., doc. #15208, Folder N 196, Exile Papers, Hd.

53. "Overlæge Carl Müller gir Aftenposten det glatte lag," *Arbeiderbladet*, October 23, 1935.

54. Preliminary Commission, 222.

55. Commission of Inquiry, 178, 183–84.

56. Ibid., 184.

57. Serge and Sedova Trotsky, *Life and Death*, 197–98.

58. L. Trotsky, Coyoacan, to Held, Oslo, March 28, 1937, doc. #10968, Folder N 196, Exile Papers, Hd.

59. Gordon et al., Nils Kåre Dahl interview, December 27, 1983, 6, Aa.

60. Preliminary Commission, 222.

61. Gordon et al., Nils Kåre Dahl interview, December 27, 1983, 20, Aa.

62. Deutscher, *Prophet Outcast*, 296.

63. Erwin Wolf, Hønefoss, to Müller, Oslo, March 15, 1936, doc. #12116, Folder N 197, Exile Papers, Hd.

64. Van Heijenoort, *Trotsky in Exile*, 81.

65. H. H. Bachke, Norwegian legation in Paris, to the Central Passport Office, Oslo, October 17, 1935, Journalnr. 15626, 1935, UDa.

66. Van Heijenoort, *Trotsky in Exile*, 79, 82.

67. Isaac Deutscher incorrectly states that Trygve Lie, "to appease his police," ordered the expulsion of Frankel. Deutscher, *Prophet Outcast*, 325.

68. Van Heijenoort, *Trotsky in Exile*, 82.

69. Broué, *Trotsky*, 809.

70. Norway, Justis- og Politidepartementet, St. med. nr. 19, *Stortingsforhandlinger 1937*, annen del b., February 18, 1937, 2.

71. Broué, *Trotsky*, 809.

72. Wolf, Hønefoss, to Lev Sedov [Paris], January 14, 1936, doc. #13140, Folder C 86, Exile Papers, Hd.

73. Fjeld, Oslo, to Trotsky, Hønefoss, June 25, 1935, with attachment, doc. #1018, Folder N 197, ibid.

74. Trotsky, Hønefoss, to Tiden norsk Forlag, Oslo, June 29, 1935, doc. #10571, ibid.

75. Trotsky, Hønefoss, to Tiden norsk Forlag, Oslo, July 11, 1935, doc. #10572, ibid.

76. For the most recent biography of Krog, see Vold, *Helge Krog*.

77. Trotsky, Hønefoss, to Tiden norsk Forlag, Oslo, July 18, 1935, doc. #10573, Folder N 197, Exile Papers, Hd.

78. Pryser, *Klassen og nasjonen*, 201.

79. Trotsky, Hønefoss, to Tiden norsk Forlag, Oslo, July 30, 1935, doc. #10574, Folder N 197, Exile Papers, Hd.

80. [Frankel], Hønefoss, to Tiden norsk Forlag, Oslo, August 1, 1935, doc. #1244, ibid.; Erik Kay, for Tiden norsk Forlag, Oslo, to Trotsky, Hønefoss, August 2, 1935, doc. #5507, ibid.

81. Wolf, Hønefoss, to Held, Oslo, November 19, 1935, doc. #11496, Folder G 137, ibid.

82. Fjeld, Oslo, to Trotsky, Hønefoss, June 25, 1935, doc. #1018, with attachment, Folder N 197, Exile Papers, Hd.

83. Trotsky, Hønefoss, to Tiden norsk Forlag, July 18, 1935, doc. #10573, ibid.

84. Trotski, *Mitt liv*, 7.

85. Ibid., 8–9.

86. "Trotzki—18. Juni–18. Desember?" *Adresseavisen*, November 29, 1935.

87. Finn Moe, "Trotski," *Arbeiderbladet*, December 5, 1935.

88. Eriksen, "Leo Trotskijs internering og deportasjon," 10.

89. Fjeld, Oslo, to Trotsky, Hønefoss, June 25, 1935, doc. #1018, with attachment, Folder N 197, Exile Papers, Hd.

90. Trotsky, Hønefoss, to Tiden norsk Forlag, Oslo, June 29, 1935, doc. #10571, ibid.

91. Trotsky, Hønefoss, to Tiden norsk Forlag, Oslo, July 18, 1935, doc. #10573, ibid.

92. Fjeld, Oslo, to [Wolf, Hønefoss], April 22, 1936, doc. #1023, ibid.

93. Ibid.

94. L. Trotsky, diary entry, April 4, 1935, *Diary in Exile*, 66; Deutscher, *Prophet Outcast*, 267.

95. "Trotski skal ikke reise," *Arbeiderbladet*, March 20, 1936.

96. Walter Held, "Lenins ungdom," ibid.

97. Wolf, Hønefoss, to Held, Oslo, November 19, 1935, doc. #11496, Folder G 137, Exile Papers, Hd.; Held, Oslo, to Trotsky [Hønefoss], January 9, 1936, doc. #1922, Folder G 137, Exile Papers, Hd.

98. Trotsky, Hønefoss, to Fjeld, Oslo, June 2, 1936, doc. # 10576, Folder N 197, ibid.

99. Deutscher, *Prophet Outcast*, 298.

100. Volkogonov, *Trotsky*, 429.

101. Thatcher, *Trotsky*, 194.

102. L. Trotsky, *Revolution Betrayed*, 94.

103. Ibid., 105.

104. Ibid., 278.

105. Ibid., 285.

106. Ibid., 284.

107. Volkogonov, *Trotsky*, 370.

108. L. Trotsky, "In 'Socialist' Norway," *Writings, 1936–37*, 22–23.

109. Deutscher, *Prophet Outcast*, 321.

110. L. Trotsky, "In 'Socialist' Norway," *Writings, 1936–37*, 22.

111. Held, Oslo, to Wolf [Hønefoss], January 3, 193[6], doc. #6435, Folder G 137, ibid. The letter is misdated 1935.

112. Held, Oslo, to Wolf [Hønefoss], November 18, [1935], doc. #6433, ibid.

113. Skaufjord, "Venstreopposisjonen," 175.

114. Scheflo, Kristiansand, to Trotsky [Hønefoss], July 9, 1935, doc. #4679, Folder N 197, Exile Papers, Hd.

115. Trotsky, Hønefoss, to Scheflo, n.p., July 19, 1935, doc. #10023, ibid.; Trotsky, Hønefoss, to Scheflo, n.p., September 2, 1935, doc. #10024, ibid.

116. Sverre Opsal, Kristiansand, to Trotsky [Hønefoss], doc. #4681, ibid.

117. Trotsky [Hønefoss], to Anton Ciliga, n.p., January 2, 1936, in L. Trotsky, *Writings: Supplement 1934–40*, 633–34.

118. Held, Oslo, to Trotsky [Hønefoss], September 11, 1935, doc. #1920, Folder G 137, Exile Papers, Hd.

119. Trotsky [Hønefoss], to Held [Oslo], September 14, 1935, doc. #8500, ibid.

120. Den norske Creditbank, Oslo, to Natalia Sedova, c/o Konrad Knudsen, Hønefoss, November 6, 1935, doc. 3638, Folder N 197, ibid.; Den norske Creditbank, Oslo, to Natalia Sedova, c/o Konrad Knudsen, Hønefoss, December 9, 1935, doc. #3639, Folder N 197, ibid.

121. Scheflo, Kristiansand, to Knudsen, n.p., December 10, 1935, doc. #15373, ibid.

122. Trotsky, Hønefoss, to Scheflo, Kristiansand, December 12, 1935, doc. 10025, ibid.

123. Quoted in Held, Oslo, to Wolf [Hønefoss], January 10, 1936, doc. #6437, Folder G 137, ibid.

124. L. Trotsky, *Writings: Supplement, 1934–40*, 919.

125. Trotsky [Hønefoss], to Held [Oslo], September 2, 1935, doc. # 8499, Folder G 137, Exile Papers, Hd.

126. L. Trotsky, *Writings, 1935–36*, 122.

127. Held, Oslo, to Wolf [Hønefoss], January 3, 1936, doc. #6435, Folder G 137, Exile Papers, Hd.

128. L. Trotsky, *Writings: Supplement, 1934–40*, 919.

129. Trotsky [Hønefoss], to Frankel, n.p., December 24, 1935, ibid., 630.

130. Trotsky [Hønefoss], to Scheflo [Kristiansand], December 23, 1935, ibid., 632.

131. Scheflo, Kristiansand, to Trotsky, n.p., doc. #4678, Folder N 197, Exile Papers, Hd. Scheflo's letter is incorrectly dated January 30, 1935, and is listed as such in the Houghton Library's collection. However, its contents indicate that it was written not at the beginning but at the end of 1935. The error can be explained by the fact that Scheflo dated his letter in the Norwegian manner: "30-1-35." In doing so, he most likely omitted a two, which would have made the correct date 30-12-35, enabling Trotsky to receive the letter at Wexhall before the New Year's holiday. As evidence of this, Trotsky quoted extensively from Scheflo's letter when he wrote to Anton Ciliga on January 2, 1936. See L. Trotsky, *Writings: Supplement, 1934–40*, 633–34.

358 Notes to Pages 95–100

132. Scheflo, [December 30, 1935], ibid.

133. Trotsky, Hønefoss, to Scheflo, n.p., January 3, 1936, doc. #10027, Folder N 197, Exile Papers, Hd.

134. Held, Oslo, to Trotsky [Hønefoss], January 16, 1936, doc. #1923, Folder G 137, ibid.

135. Held, Oslo, to Wolf [Hønefoss], January 21, 1936, doc. #6439, ibid.

136. L. Trotsky, *Writings, 1935–36*, 245.

137. *Ny Dag*, December 19, 1935, quoted in Held, Oslo, to Wolf [Hønefoss], January 10, 1936, doc. #6437, Folder G 137, Exile Papers, Hd.

138. Held to Wolf, ibid.

139. Held, Oslo, to Wolf [Hønefoss], January 3, 1936, doc. #6435, ibid.

140. Held, Oslo, to Wolf [Hønefoss], January 30, 1936, doc. #6440, ibid.

141. Mot Dag, "Protokoll for Mot Dags sekretariat," sekretariatsmøte 27.3.36, boks 0002, Serie Aa—Møtebøker, styrende organer, Møtebok, sekretariatet og styremøter 1935–1936, Aa.

142. L. Trotsky, *Writings, 1935–36*, 331.

143. Trotsky [Hønefoss] to the International Secretariat [Paris], June 26, 1935, doc. #8007; July 11, 1935, doc. #8008, Folder FI 36, Exile Papers, Hd.

144. "Für die Vierte Internationale!" *Unser Wort*, No. 8, early August 1935.

145. Wolf, Hønefoss, to Lev Sedov [Paris], January 14, 1936, doc. #13140, Folder C 86, Exile Papers, Hd.

146. Trotsky [Hønefoss] to the International Secretariat [Paris], June 26, 1935, doc. #8007; July 11, 1935, doc. #8008; August 27, 1935; doc. #8015; Folder FI 36, ibid.

147. Trotsky [Hønefoss] to the International Secretariat [Paris], July 11, 1935, doc. #8008, ibid.

148. Ibid.

149. L. Trotsky, diary entry, July 30, 1935, *Diary in Exile*, 155.

150. Trotsky [Hønefoss] to Lev Sedov [Paris], December 27, 1935, quoted in Deutscher, *Prophet Outcast*, 296–97. Excerpts from the letter are also printed in L. Trotsky, *Writings, 1935–36*, 220.

151. Deutscher, *Prophet Outcast*, 297.

152. Preliminary Commission, 208.

153. Commission of Inquiry, 182–83.

154. Preliminary Commission, 208–9; Trotsky, Coyoacan, to Held [Oslo], February 17, 1937, doc. # 8511, Folder G 137, Exile Papers, Hd.

155. Konrad Knudsen, Storting debate of June 21, 1937, Stortingsforhandlinger 1937, Syvende del B, Stortingstidende, Forhandlinger i Stortinget, Bind B, 381.

156. Trotsky, Prinkipo, to Maurice Paz [Paris], April 20, 1929, quoted in Van Heijenoort, *Trotsky in Exile*, 23.

157. Ibid., 24.

158. Ibid., 1.

159. Ibid., 71.

160. Ibid., 84.

161. Abraham John Muste, "Report on European Trip," Copenhagen, July 7, 1936, doc. #17054, Folder US 271, Exile Papers, Hd.

162. Max Shachtman, "Statement on the Visit of R. Molinier and LeRicard to H[ønefoss], July 15–16, 1936," Hønefoss, July 21, 1936, doc. #17246, Folder US 275, ibid.

163. Quoted in Reed and Jakobson, "Trotsky Papers," 366.

164. L. Trotsky, *Writings, 1935-36*, 535n262.

165. Abraham John Muste, Oslo, to Tranmæl, Oslo, July 5, 1936, doc. #15119, Folder US 196, Exile Papers, Hd.

166. Trotsky [Hønefoss] to James Cannon and Max Shachtman, n.p., September 4, 1935, in L. Trotsky, *Writings: Supplement, 1934-40*, 603.

167. Ibid., 922n611.

168. Muste, "Report on European Trip," Copenhagen, July 7, 1936, doc. #17054, Folder US 271, Exile Papers, Hd.

169. L. Trotsky, *Writings: Supplement, 1934-40*, 17.

170. Muste, "Report on European Trip," Copenhagen, July 7, 1936, doc. #17054, Folder US 271, Exile Papers, Hd.

171. Max Shachtman, Hønefoss, to the International Secretariat of the International Communist League, Paris, July 13, 1936, doc. #15413, Folder US 275, ibid.

172. Muste, "My Experience," 147.

173. Van Heijenoort, *Trotsky in Exile*, 82-83.

174. Trotsky [Hønefoss] to Henricus Sneevliet [Amsterdam], November 5, 1935, in L. Trotsky, *Writings: Supplement, 1934-40*, 622.

175. Held, Oslo, to Trotsky [Hønefoss], September 11, 1935, doc. #1920, Folder G 137, Exile Papers, Hd.

176. Trotsky [Hønefoss] to Henricus Sneevliet [Amsterdam], November 5, 1935, in L. Trotsky, *Writings: Supplement, 1934-40*, 622; Van Heijenoort, *Trotsky in Exile*, 83.

177. "Et farlig brevkort," *Sørlandet*, December 16, 1935; "Trotskys medhjelper Fred Seller [sic] opfordrer til mord på STALIN," *Arbeideren*, December 13, 1935.

178. The Norwegian translation of the postcard varied slightly when published in several newspapers. However, the meaning was clear. See "Trotskys medhjelper Fred Seller [sic] opfordrer til mord på STALIN," *Arbeideren*, December 13, 1935; "Ny bakvaskelse av Trotski," *Arbeiderbladet*, December 18, 1935.

179. *Arbeideren*, December 13, 1935.

180. "Et farlig brevkort," *Sørlandet*, December 16, 1935.

181. "Ny bakvaskelse av Trotski," *Arbeiderbladet*, December 18, 1935.

182. "Trotsky får ytteligere et halvt års opholdstillatelse i Norge," *Tidens Tegn*, December 16, 1935.

183. Trotsky [Hønefoss] to Scheflo [Kristiansand], December 24, 1935, in L. Trotsky, *Writings: Supplement, 1934-40*, 631-32.

184. Trotsky [Hønefoss] to the International Secretariat of the International Communist League [Paris], December 15, 1935, in L. Trotsky, *Writings, 1935-36*, 219.

185. Norway, Justis- og Politidepartementet, St. med. nr. 19, Stortingsforhandlinger 1937, annen del b., February 18, 1937, 1.

186. "Blir Trotski i Norge for godt?" *Aftenposten*, August 28, 1935.

187. "Trotzki—18. juni-18. desember," *Adresseavisen*, November 29, 1935.

188. Trotsky, Hønefoss, to Trygve Lie, Oslo, doc. #9423, Folder N 197, Exile Papers, Hd.

189. Norway, Justis- og Politidepartementet, St. med. nr. 19, Stortingsforhandlinger 1937, annen del b, February 18, 1937, 2.

190. Trotsky, Hønefoss, to Trygve Lie, Oslo, June 16, 1936, doc. #8888, Folder N 197, Exile Papers, Hd.

191. Held, Oslo, to Wolf [Hønefoss], January 20, 1936, doc. #6438, Folder G 137, ibid.

192. "Trotski på linje med Fe-laget mot Stakanov-bevegelsen," *Arbeideren,* January 20, 1936.

193. Held, Oslo, to Wolf [Hønefoss], January 21, 1936, doc. #6439, Folder G 137, Exile Papers, Hd.

194. "'Arbeideren' og Trotski," *Arbeiderbladet,* February 5, 1936.

195. "Trotski," *Arbeideren,* February 7, 1936.

196. L. Trotsky, *Writings, 1935–36,* 540n298; [Olav Scheflo], "Angrepene på Trotsky," *Sørlandet,* February 7, 1936.

197. L. Trotsky, ibid.

198. Trotsky [Hønefoss] to Scheflo [Kristiansand], January 30, 1936, in ibid., 255.

199. Trotsky [Hønefoss] to James Cannon [n.p.], January 28, 1936, in L. Trotsky, *Writings: Supplement, 1934–40,* 643.

200. Trotsky, statement to the Associated Press, February 8, 1936, L. Trotsky, *Writings, 1935–36,* 263.

201. [Scheflo], "Angrepene på Trotsky," *Sørlandet,* February 7, 1936.

202. Held, Oslo, to Trotsky [Hønefoss], July 3, 1936, doc. #1927, Folder G 137, Exile Papers, Hd.

203. Ibid.

204. Ibid.

205. Colton, *Leon Blum,* 134.

206. Ibid., 154–55.

207. Ibid., 154.

208. Broué, *Trotsky,* 815; ibid., 153.

209. Shirer, *Collapse of the Third Republic,* 295.

210. Colton, *Leon Blum,* 155.

211. Leon Trotsky, "The French Revolution Has Begun," *Nation,* July 4, 1936.

212. Ibid.

213. Leo Trotzki, "Wer verteidigt die USSR und wer hilft Hitler?" *Unser Wort,* early September 1935. English translation in L. Trotsky, *Writings, 1935–36,* 58–64.

214. Leo Trotzki, "Wer verteidigt die USSR und wer hilft Hitler?" *Unser Wort,* early September 1935.

215. T. Lie, *Oslo-Moskva-London,* 69.

216. Rougthvedt, *Med penn og pistol,* 113.

217. Box 1, Trotsky-saken, Ra.

218. "Trotsky og Stalin har inngått hemmelig samarbeide," *Fritt Folk,* June 24, 1936.

219. Norway, Justis- og Politidepartementet, St. med. Nr. 19, Stortingsforhandlinger 1937, annen del b., February 18, 1937, 2.

220. Muste, "Report on European trip," Copenhagen, July 7, 1936, doc. #17054, Folder US 271, Exile Papers, Hd.

221. Trotsky [Hønefoss] to the ICL Secretariat, Paris, July 11, 1935, doc. #8008, Folder FI 36, ibid.

222. Trotsky [Hønefoss] to the ICL Secretariat [Paris], April 11, 1936, doc. #8039, ibid.

223. Trotsky [Hønefoss] to the ICL Secretariat [Paris], June 18, 1936, in L. Trotsky, *Writings: Supplement, 1934–40,* 687.

224. Trotsky [Hønefoss] to the Dutch section of the ICL, July 15, 1936, in L. Trotsky, *Writings, 1935–36,* 363.

225. Trotsky [Hønefoss] to A. J. Muste, n.p., July 17, 1936, in L. Trotsky, *Writings: Supplement, 1934–40*, 701.

226. Trotsky [Hønefoss] to the Central Committee of the Dutch section [Amsterdam], July 15, 1936, in L. Trotsky, *Writings, 1935–36*, 367.

227. Ibid., 366; Trotsky [Hønefoss] to Muste, n.p. July 17, 1936, in L. Trotsky, *Writings: Supplement, 1934–40*, 700–701.

228. Trotsky [Hønefoss] to the Central Committee of the Dutch section, n.p., July 15, 1936, in L. Trotsky, *Writings, 1935–36*, 364–67.

229. Trotsky [Hønefoss] to the Dutch section [Amsterdam], June 16, 1936, in L. Trotsky, *Writings: Supplement, 1934–40*, 690; Trotsky [Hønefoss] to Max Shachtman, n.p., July 7, 1936, in L. Trotsky, *Writings: Supplement, 1934–40*, 697.

230. Trotsky [Hønefoss] to the Dutch section [Amsterdam], July 16, 1936, in L. Trotsky, *Writings, 1935–36*, 376.

231. Ibid., 503n1.

232. Trotsky [Hønefoss] to Shachtman, n.p., July 7, 1936, in L. Trotsky, *Writings: Supplement, 1934–40*, 696. Trotsky incorrectly referred to August rather than July as the month that had been tiring for him. The editors of this volume of Trotsky's collected writing have noted this error. See 928n656.

233. Meyer, Oslo, to Trotsky [Hønefoss], June 11, 1936, doc. #3068, Folder N 123, Exile Papers, Hd.

234. Trotsky, Hønefoss, to Meyer, Oslo, June 15, 1936, Håkon Meyers samling, Aa.

235. Meyer, Oslo, to Trotsky [Hønefoss], June 23, 1936, doc. #3070, Folder N 123, Exile Papers, Hd.

236. Held, Oslo, to Trotsky [Hønefoss], June 25, 1936, doc. #1926, Folder G 137, ibid.

237. Trotsky, Oslo, to Scheflo [Kristiansand], July 28, 1936, doc. #8507, ibid. Houghton Library at Harvard has catalogued this letter as being written by Trotsky to Walter Held, rather than to Scheflo. However, the letter's content indicates that this is incorrect. Trotsky asks if the recipient's daughter could assist in making arrangements for his visit. This, of course, rules out Held, who did not have a daughter. Most significantly, there is a handwritten notation at the bottom of the letter, indicating it was sent "to Scheflo[,] Kristiansand."

238. Scheflo, Kristiansand, to Knudsen [Hønefoss], July 29, 1936, doc. #15374, Folder N 197, Exile Papers, Hd.

239. Høidal, *Quisling. En studie i landssvik*, 152.

240. Ibid., 158, 174.

241. Høidal, *Quisling: Study in Treason*, 200.

242. "Trotskys forbindelse med Gjøvikoverfallet," *Fritt Folk*, May 27, 1936.

243. "Når blir Trotsky norsk borger?," ibid., June 11, 1936.

244. "Trotsky," ibid., July 16, 1936.

245. "Trotskis rolle i Breda-sammensvergelsen," ibid., July 18, 1936.

246. Held, Oslo, to Trotsky [Hønefoss], June 25, 1936, doc. #1926, Folder G 137, Exile Papers, Hd.

5: From Vacation to House Arrest

1. Emberland and Rougthvedt, *Det ariske idol*, 262–63.

2. "Heyerdahls uskyldige vandrefugler," *Fremtiden*, August 27, 1936. This article refers

only to a "Dr. Löffler," while National Union's *Fritt Folk*, a less reliable source, provided more detail, stating incorrectly that Löffler's first name was Arthur and that he came from Vienna. "Trotsky flytter i hast revolusjonsredet til Kristiansand," *Fritt Folk*, August 7, 1936.

3. Broué, *Trotsky*, 1068.

4. "Heyerdahls uskyldige vandrefugler," *Fremtiden*, August 27, 1936.

5. "Trotsky forfulgt under sin Sørlandstur," *Aftenposten*, morning ed., August 7, 1936.

6. "Trotski ferierer på øy ved Kristiansand," *Sørlandet*, August 7, 1936; Knudsen, *Jeg var Quislings sekretær*, 59.

7. Knudsen, *Jeg var Quislings sekretær*, 60–61. Although Harald Franklin Knudsen's book provides the most detailed description of Trotsky's trip to Kristiansand, his account should be used with great caution, and only in conjunction with contemporary newspaper articles, because of exaggerations, inaccuracies and distortions.

8. L. Trotsky, "In 'Socialist' Norway," *Writings, 1936–37*, 23.

9. "Trotsky drikker kaffee hos Scheflo!," *Fremtiden*, August 7, 1936; Inge Scheflo, "Sommer med Trotski," *Aktuell*, no. 15, April 14, 1956.

10. "Knudsen og Trotski forfulgt av NS bil," *Fremtiden*, August 7, 1936.

11. Ibid.; "Trotsky flytter i hast revolusjonsredet til Kristiansand," *Fritt Folk*, August 7, 1936; "Trotski forfølges," *Arbeiderbladet*, August 7, 1936.

12. Knudsen, *Jeg var Quislings sekretær*, 61–62.

13. "Trotski drikker kaffee hos Scheflo," *Fremtiden*, August 7, 1936.

14. L. Trotsky, "In 'Socialist' Norway," *Writings, 1936–37*, 23.

15. Sverre Opsal, Kristiansand, to Oddvar Høidal, San Diego, December 5, 1994, author's personal collection; "Trotskij på ferie i Per Johnsens hus i Randesund," *Sørlandet*, October 12, 1974.

16. Author interview with Dagmar Loe, Oslo, June 18, 1999.

17. "Hun var husholderske for Trotsky," *Sørlandet*, July 25, 1967; Inge Scheflo, "Sommer med Trotski, *Aktuell*, no. 15, April 14, 1956.

18. "Trotskij på ferie i Per Johnsens hus i Randesund," *Sørlandet*, October 12, 1974.

19. Telephone interview with Dagmar Loe, Risør, June 28, 1994.

20. Inge Scheflo, "På nært hold," 36.

21. Author's copies of photographs from Dagmar Loe's private collection.

22. Author interview with Dagmar Loe, Oslo, June 18, 1999.

23. "Gangsterne og dens [sic] forsvarere," *Sørlandet*, August 8, 1936.

24. Ibid.

25. Author interviews with Dagmar Loe, Oslo, June 18 and June 21, 1999.

26. Torsten Bygdal, "Trotskij i Norge," transcript of a program in Sveriges Radio, March 16, 1967, Ms. fol. 3956: 8e, HA-NB, Oslo; Inge Scheflo, "Sommer med Trotski," *Aktuell*, no. 15, April 14, 1956; "Hun var husholderske for Trotsky," *Sørlandet*, July 25, 1967.

27. Although generally reliable, the collected *Writings of Leon Trotsky* does contain a number of errors. These could have been eliminated if, for example, the sections covering Trotsky's Norwegian exile had been proofread by someone with adequate language skills. Had this been done, not only would Reidar Sveen's name not have been misspelled as Reider Swen, but his correct title, Chief of Investigations in the Oslo police department, would have been noted, not "chief of Oslo police." Most unique, Sveen's Norwegian title of "*opdagelseschef*" (1930s usage) is described as being the "small island where he [Trotsky] was vacationing" in August 1936. See L. Trotsky, *Writings, 1935–36*, 15, 386, 549n385, 572.

28. "Driver Trotsky revolusjonær konspirasjon fra Norderhov?," *Aftenposten*, morning ed., August 7, 1936; "Innbrudsgangstere i retten," *Arbeiderbladet*, August 20, 1936.

29. "Nazibanden setter rekord i råskap," *Fremtiden*, December 11, 1936.

30. "Provokasjon mot Arbeiderpartiet," ibid., August 7, 1936.

31. "Nazi-gangsterne beså Knudsens hjem i forrige uke, ibid.; "Nazibanden setter rekord i råskap," ibid., December 11, 1936.

32. "NS-gangsterne optrer frekt i lagmannsretten," ibid., December 9, 1936.

33. "Brukte nazistene 'stråmenn' efter Hønefoss INNBRUDDET," *Arbeiderbladet*, August 26, 1936.

34. "Nazipøbel bryter sig inn hos Trotski," *Fremtiden*, August 6, 1936; "Brukte nazistene 'stråmenn' efter Hønefoss INNBRUDDET," ibid.

35. "Innbruddet på Wexhall," *Fremtiden*, December 10, 1936; "Spionene innom Knudsen," *Arbeiderbladet*, August 27, 1936.

36. "Brukte nazistene 'stråmenn' efter Hønefoss INNBRUDDET," *Arbeiderbladet*, August 26, 1936; "Innbruddet på Wexhall," *Fremtiden*, December 10, 1936.

37. "Nazipøbel bryter sig inn hos Trotski," *Fremtiden*, August 6, 1936.

38. Knut Skistad, Statsarkivet i Kongsberg, to the author, San Diego, March 22, 2001, author's personal collection.

39. Ibid.

40. "Innbruddet på Wexhall," *Fremtiden*, December 10, 1936; "Innbrudsgjengen holder ikke godt sammen," *Arbeiderbladet*, December 10, 1936.

41. "Resultatsløst 'efter-innbrudd' gjennem Trotskis vindu," *Arbeiderbladet*, December 10, 1936.

42. "Nazipøbel bryter sig inn hos Trotski," *Fremtiden*, August 6, 1936; "Innbruddet på Wexhall," *Fremtiden*, December 10, 1936.

43. "Innbruddet hos Trotski," *Sørlandet*, August 7, 1936.

44. "Politimester Urbyes merkelig optreden," *Fremtiden*, August 6, 1936.

45. "Nazipøbel bryter sig inn hos Trotski," ibid.

46. "En meget alvorlig sak! sier riksadvokat SUND," *Arbeiderbladet*, August 6, 1936.

47. "Tiltale mot nazi-gangsterne," *Arbeiderbladet*, August 8, 1936.

48. "Provokasjon mot Arbeiderpartiet," *Fremtiden*, August 7, 1936; "Trotskys forhold anmeldt," *Fritt Folk*, August 7, 1936.

49. "Trotskys forhold anmeldt," *Fritt Folk*, August 7, 1936.

50. "Innbruddet hos Trotsky," *Sørlandet*, August 7, 1936.

51. "Trotski avsløret!" *Fritt Folk,* August 7, 1936.

52. "Trotsky forbereder Sovjets i Frankrike," *Fritt Folk,* August 8, 1936. As the headline of this article and that cited in the previous footnote show, *Fritt Folk* was not particularly consistent in its spelling of Trotsky's name.

53. "TIMES gir TROTSKI skylden for bolsjevikorgiene i Madrid og Barcelona," *Fritt Folk*, August 8, 1936.

54. "Fellende bevis mot TROTSKY og regjeringen" *Fritt Folk*, August 10, 1936; "Ut med Trotsky." *Fritt Folk*, August 10, 1936.

55. "Åpning av valgkampen," *Arbeiderbladet*, August 8, 1936.

56. "Trotski," *Arbeiderbladet*, August 13, 1936.

57. "Innbruddet var arrangert av nazi-lederne," *Arbeiderbladet*, August 8, 1936.

58. "Generalens dattersønn," *Sørlandet*, August 12, 1936.

59. "Oslo-arbeiderne protesterer mot gangster-politikerne," *Arbeiderbladet*, August 8, 1936.

60. "Trotski-affæren," *Arbeideren*, August 7, 1936.

61. "Vil der nu bli ryddet op?," *Arbeideren*, August 10, 1936.

62. Untitled editorial, *Nationen*, August 8, 1936.

63. "Hr. Trotsky og køpenickiaden," *Aftenposten*, morning ed., August 8, 1936.

64. "Opnår Trotsky det han vil?" *Aftenposten*, morning ed., August 13, 1936.

65. "Straffbar politikk," *Dagbladet*, August 7, 1936.

66. "Beviser og selvtekt," *Tidens Tegn*, August 8, 1936.

67. "Leo Trotzky," *ABC*, August 13, 1936.

68. Untitled editorial, *Nationen*, August 11, 1936; "Asylrett," *Dagbladet*, August 13, 1936; "Beviser og selvtekt," *Tidens Tegn*, August 8, 1936; "Leo Trotzky," ibid.

69. "Innbruddet var arrangert," *Arbeiderbladet*, August 8, 1936; "Alvorlig siktelse reist mot N.S. folkene for Trotsky besøket," *Aftenposten*, morning ed., August 10, 1936.

70. "Alvorlig siktelse reist mot N.S. folkene for Trotsky besøket," *Aftenposten*, morning ed., August 10, 1936; "De norske nazister samarbeidet med Gestapo," *Arbeiderbladet*, August 10, 1936.

71. "De norske nazister samarbeidet med Gestapo," ibid.

72. "Trotski-ranet et ledd i Gestapos internasjonale terror?," *Arbeiderbladet*, August 11, 1936.

73. "Advokat Hjort fremlegger sine beviser mot Trotski," *Tidens Tegn*, August 13, 1936.

74. "Trotzky," *ABC*, August 13, 1936; "Advokat Hjort forsøker å bortforklare det norsk-tyske samarbeid," *Tidens Tegn*, August 12, 1936; "Opnår Trotski det han vil?" *Aftenposten*, morning ed., August 13, 1936.

75. "De norske nazister samarbeider med Gestapo," *Arbeiderbladet*, August 10, 1936.

76. "Advokat Hjort søker å bortforklare det norsk-tyske samarbeid," *Tidens Tegn*, August 12, 1936.

77. Ibid.; "Forgjeves forsøk på å bortforklare samarbeidet med Gestapo," *Arbeiderbladet*, August 12, 1936.

78. "Bare verdiløse papirer blev funnet hos Trotski," *Arbeiderbladet*, August 13, 1936.

79. Ibid.

80. Ibid.

81. "De norske nazister samarbeider med Gestapo," *Arbeiderbladet*, August 10, 1936. Held's description of the situation in Spain, while largely correct, nevertheless did not provide a full explanation. Andres Nin, the leader of the Trotskyite Communist Left organization, broke with Trotsky when Nin agreed to have his followers become part of a new party, the Workers Party of National Unification (POUM) in 1935. However, a few members of the Communist Left in Madrid and Barcelona refused to accept this change and "retained their own miniscule Trotskyist organization, which they called 'The Bolshevist-Leninist Section.'" See S. Payne, *Spanish Revolution*, 170.

82. "Et varsel fra valgkampen," *Arbeiderbladet*, August 11, 1936.

83. "Politiet kikker nazi-lederne etter i sømmene," *Arbeiderbladet*, August 14, 1936. Trotsky incorrectly described his interview with Sveen as having occurred on August 13. L. Trotsky, "In 'Socialist' Norway," *Writings, 1936–37*, 24.

84. "Trotski har gitt opdagelseschefen en helt uttømmende forklaring," *Tidens Tegn*, August 15, 1936.

85. [Reidar Sveen], "Rapport fra Opdagelseschefen i Oslo," appendix 1 to Norway,

Justis- og Politidepartementet, St. med. nr. 19, Stortingsforhandlinger 1937, annen del b., February 18, 1937, 7–8.

86. "Trotski har gitt opdagelssechefen en helt uttømmende forklaring," *Tidens Tegn*, August 15, 1936.

87. Reidar Sveen, Oslo, to Trotsky, Hønefoss, August 19, 1936, doc. #5442, Folder N 197, Exile Papers, Hd.

88. Martin Bolstad, Moscow, to the Norwegian Foreign Ministry, August 13, 1936, Journalnr. 12398, 1936, UDa.

89. Quoted in "Sovjet har ALDRI besværet sig over Trotskis opholdstillatelse," *Arbeiderbladet*, August 15, 1936. See also "Zinovieff to Face Capital Charge," *Daily Telegraph*, August 15, 1936.

90. Volkogonov, *Trotsky*, 376.

91. Tucker, *Stalin in Power*, 368. Tucker's emphasis.

92. "Trotski påviser at anklagene fra Moskva er OPKONSTRUERT," *Arbeiderbladet*, August 21, 1936.

93. L. Trotsky, "In 'Socialist' Norway," *Writings, 1936–37*, 25.

94. Broué, *Trotsky*, 826.

95. "En erklæring fra Trotsky," *Sørlandet*, August 15, 1936.

96. Ibid.

97. L. Trotsky, "Beskyldningene mangler konkret innhold," *Arbeiderbladet*, August 25, 1936; "Trotski vil stilles for en norsk domstol," *Tidens Tegn*, August 25, 1936.

98. "Trotsky i slett selskap," *Aftenposten*, evening ed., August 18, 1936; "Den ubudne gjest," *Tidens Tegn*, August 17, 1936; "Prosessen i Moskva," *Nationen*, August 24, 1936; "Trotzky," *ABC*, August 20, 1936.

99. "Skrekk," *Dagbladet*, August 22, 1936.

100. "Trotsky har drevet storstilet oprørsagitasjon mot Stalin fra Hønefoss," *Fritt Folk*, August 14, 1936; "Trotsky og Stalin samspiller om Spania!" *Fritt Folk*, August 14, 1936.

101. "Fellende tilståelse under Trotsky-prosessen i Moskva," *Fritt Folk*, August 20, 1936.

102. "Djevelen på Hønefoss, *Dagbladet*, August 22, 1936.

103. "Trotski," *Arbeideren*, August 17, 1936.

104. Olaf Nikolai Hals, "Til Russland med Trotsky," *Fritt Folk*, August 21, 1936.

105. "Trotski," *Arbeideren*, August 17, 1936.

106. Ibid.

107. "Sovjet har ALDRI besværet sig om Trotskis opholdstillatelse," *Arbeiderbladet*, August 15, 1936.

108. Skaufjord, "Venstreopposisjonen," 28–29.

109. "Uventet støtte, *Arbeiderbladet*, August 15, 1936.

110. "STALIN gir fascistene en håndsrekning," *Fremtiden*, August 15, 1936.

111. "På vakt," *Arbeiderbladet*, August 17, 1936.

112. Untitled editorial, ibid., August 19, 1936.

113. Untitled editorial, ibid., August 20, 1936.

114. Untitled editorial, ibid., August 21, 1936.

115. Trotsky, Hønefoss, to Reidar Sveen, Oslo, August 19, 1936, box 2, Trotsky-saken, Ra.

116. L. Trotsky, *Writings, 1935–36*, 389.

117. "Trotski gir opdagelsessjefen nye oplysninger om sin virksomhet i Norge," *Tidens Tegn*, August 21, 1936.

118. Trotsky, Hønefoss, to Reidar Sveen, Oslo, August 19, 1936, Box 2, Trotsky-saken, Ra.

119. Ibid.

120. Ibid.

121. Tucker, *Stalin in Power*, 368. In his writings Trotsky referred to the Soviet secret police by their former initials, GPU.

122. "Trotski i samarbeid med Tysklands hemmelige politi," *Dagbladet*, August 20, 1936.

123. "Attentatet på Kirov var arrangert for å ramme opposisjonen, hevder Trotski," *Dagbladet*, August 21, 1936. See also "Trotski påviser at anklagene fra Moskva var OP-KONSTRUERT," *Arbeiderbladet*, August 21, 1936. *Arbeiderbladet*'s account of the press conference, however, was somewhat more general and, to a degree, milder and more vague than *Dagbladet*'s, indicating restraint due to the need for *Arbeiderbladet* to take into consideration the delicate position in which the Labor government found itself as a result of this escalating, contentious dispute.

124. Held, "Rundschreibung," Hønefoss, August 22, 1936, doc. #14753, folder G 125, Exile Papers, Hd.

125. Trotsky [Hønefoss] to "The Prague Committee," August 23, 1936, in L. Trotsky, *Writings, 1935–36*, 407–8.

126. "Har Julian-[sic]Berman vært i Oslo?," *Dagbladet*, August 20, 1936.

127. "Trotski vil stilles for en norsk domstol," *Tidens Tegn*, August 25, 1936; "Bes-kyldningene mangler konkret innhold. En erklæring fra Trotski," *Arbeiderbladet*, August 25, 1936.

128. "Trotski vil stilles for en norsk domstol," *Tidens Tegn*, August 25, 1936; "Besky-ldningene mangler konkret innhold. En erklæring fra Trotski," *Arbeiderbladet*, August 25, 1936.

129. L. Trotsky, "Svar til hr. Johan Scharffenberg,"*Arbeiderbladet*, August 25, 1936.

130. "16 dødsdommer i Moskva," ibid., August 24, 1936.

131. Untitled editorial, ibid.

132. Ibid.

133. "De 16 dødsdømte er henrettet," *Dagbladet*, August 25, 1936.

134. Ibid.

135. "Ofre for sitt eget system," *Aftenposten*, morning ed., August 26, 1936.

136. Bille Larsen, *Mod strømmen*, 186.

137. Photocopies of correspondence from Leon Trotsky's Papers, Harvard University Folder, Box 9, Albert Glotzer Papers, Hoover Institution Archives, Stanford University.

138. L. Trotsky, *Writings, 1935–36*, 407. See also L. Trotsky, *Writings, 1935–36*, 90.

139. Norway, Justis- og Politidepartementet, St. med. nr. 19, Stortingsforhandlinger 1937, annen del b, February 18, 1937, bilag 4, 12.

140. Van Heijenoort, *Trotsky in Exile*, 89.

141. Ibid.

142. Held, Oslo, to Trotsky et al. [Hønefoss], August 25, 1936, doc. #1929, Folder G 137, Exile Papers, Hd.

143. Eugen Johannessen and Arnfinn Vik, for the Oslo Labor Party, to the Labor Party's local political and trade union organizations in Oslo, August 6, 1936, Oslo Ar-

beidersamfund Diverse 1936 folder, Oslo Arbeidersamfund Korrespondanse 1936–1937 folder; Oslo Arbeidersamfunds arkiv, Aa.

144. H. Lie, *Martin Tranmæl*, 2: 160.

145. "De 16 dødsdømte er henrettet," *Dagbladet*, August 25, 1936.

146. "Misbruk av asyl," *Aftenposten*, morning ed., August 24, 1936.

147. Norrøne, "Arbeiderpartiet og Stortingsvalget i 1936."

148. "Et varsel fra valgkampen," *Arbeiderbladet*, August 11, 1936.

149. H. Lie, *Martin Tranmæl*, 2: 160.

150. "Trotski-materialet går til stats- og riksadvokat," *Arbeiderbladet*, August 15, 1936.

151. "Justisminister Lie om Trotski-sakene," ibid., August 18, 1936.

152. Norway, Justis- og Politidepartmentet, St. med. nr. 19, Stortingsforhandlinger 1937, annen del b., February 18, 1937, 2.

153. "Vil siktelsen bli utvidet?," *Arbeiderbladet*, August 19, 1936.

154. "Hvad vil regjeringen gjøre med Trotski?" *Tidens Tegn*, August 20, 1936.

155. "Trotskis opholdstillatelse." *Arbeiderbladet*, August 24, 1936.

156. Eriksen, "Leo Trotskijs internering og deportasjon," 20; "Trotskis opholdstillatelse," ibid.

157. "Bare verdiløse papirer blev funnet hos Trotski," *Arbeiderbladet*, August 13, 1936.

158. Johannes Halvorsen, for Centralpasskontoret, to Justisdepartementet, August 25, 1936, Box 1, Trotsky-saken, Ra.

159. Norway, Justis- og Politidepartementet, St. med. nr. 19, Stortingsforhandlinger 1937, annen del b., February 18, 1937, 3; "Wer war iloyal?" statement by Jean van Heijenoort and Erwin Wolf, Copenhagen, August 30, 1936, doc. #17369, folder FI 86, Exile Papers, Hd.

160. "Erklæring," Wexhall, the .... August 1936, Box 1, Trotsky-saken, Ra.

161. "TROTSKI SKAL BLI I NORGE," *Dagbladet*, August 26, 1936.

162. Trotsky, Hønefoss, to Scheflo [Kristiansand], August 27, 1936, doc. #10031, Folder N 197, Exile Papers, Hd. Later, however, Trotsky corrected this, referring to Halvorsen not by name but simply as "a functionary" of the Central Passport Office. See L. Trotsky, "In 'Socialist' Norway," *Writings, 1936–37*, 27–28.

163. "Trotski stillet under opsikt og censur av statspolitiet," *Tidens Tegn*, August 27, 1936.

164. "Centralpasskontoret konstaterer," *Arbeiderbladet*, August 26, 1936; Strandberg, "Fra gjest til fange," 81–82.

165. "Overtredelsene," *Sørlandet*, August 26, 1936.

166. Broué, *Trotsky*, 825.

6: The End of Asylum

1. "Et besøk hos statspolitiet som holder vakt over Trotski," *Tidens Tegn*, August 28, 1936. The article incorrectly states that the visit occurred on August 26, rather than on August 27.

2. Ibid.

3. Trotsky, Hønefoss, to Scheflo [Kristiansand], August 27, 1936, doc. #10031, folder N 197, Exile Papers, Hd.

4. Ibid.

5. Trotsky [Hønefoss] to Trygve Lie [Oslo], August 26, 1936, in L. Trotsky, *Writings, 1935–36*, 422.

6. Ibid., 423.

7. Ibid., 423–24.

8. Trotsky, Hønefoss, to Scheflo [Kristiansand], August 27, 1936, doc. #10031, Folder N 197, Exile Papers, Hd.

9. "Wer war iloyal?" joint statement by van Heijenoort and Wolf, Copenhagen, August 30, 1936, doc. #17369, folder FI 86, ibid.

10. Ibid.

11. "Trotski prosederer," *Arbeiderbladet*, August 27, 1936.

12. Ibid.

13. "Justisminister Lie svarer på Trotskis prosedyre," ibid.

14. "Erklæring," Wexhall, ..., August 1936, box 1, Trotsky-saken, Ra.

15. "En samtale med Trotski," *Arbeiderbladet*, July 26, 1935.

16. "Ole Colbjørnsen bekrefter fremstillingen," *Arbeiderbladet*, August 27, 1936.

17. "Wer war iloyal?" joint statement by van Heijenoort and Wolf, Copenhagen, August 30, 1936, doc. #17369, Folder FI 86, Exile Papers, Hd.

18. L. Trotsky, *Writings, 1935–36*, 553, fn. 418.

19. "Trotski skriver åpent brev til justisministeren," *Fremtiden*, September 10, 1936.

20. J. Ræder, Norwegian Legation, The Hague, to the Foreign Ministry, September 4, 1936, Journalnr. 13502, 1936, UDa.

21. "Bolsjevikene i Russland er utryddet, erklærer Trotski," *Tønsbergs Blad*, September 1, 1936.

22. H.F., untitled report, initialed by Trygve Lie [Oslo], September 5, 1936, box 1, Trotsky-saken, Ra.

23. "Innbrudsgangstere I RETTEN," *Arbeiderbladet*, August 20, 1936.

24. "Brukte nazistene 'stråmenn' efter Hønefoss INNBRUDDET," ibid., August 26, 1936.

25. "Spionene innom hos Knudsen og bad om melk," ibid., August 27, 1936.

26. "Trotsky innrømmer at han har drevet politisk virksomhet," *Aftenposten*, evening ed., August 28, 1936.

27. "Trotski innrømmer å ha drevet aktuell politikk," *Dagbladet*, August 28, 1936.

28. "Trotski innrømmer at han har drevet politisk virksomhet," *Aftenposten*, evening ed., August 28, 1936.

29. "Ekstraktgjenpart av rettsboken for Oslo forhørsrett nr. 2224–1936 forsåvidt angår rettsmøte den 28. august 1936," Box 1, Trotsky-saken, Ra.

30. "Timelang vidneforklaring av Trotski i gangstersaken," *Arbeiderbladet*, August 28, 1936.

31. "Trotsky innrømmer at han har drevet politisk virksomhet," *Aftenposten*, evening ed., August 28, 1936. In this instance, contemporary newspaper coverage of Trotsky's testimony in the court of inquiry is more complete than that in official documents provided by the Justice Department and the Foreign Ministry.

32. "Trotski innrømmer å ha drevet aktuell politikk," *Dagbladet*, August 28, 1936.

33. "Trotski innrømmer at han har drevet politisk virksomhet," *Aftenposten*, evening ed., August 28, 1936.

34. Ibid.

35. "Timelang vidneforklaring av Trotski i gangstersaken," *Arbeiderbladet*, August 28, 1936.

36. "Trotski kjenner ingen norske tilhengere," *Arbeiderbladet*, August 28, 1936.

37. "Utdrag av Oslo forhørsretts protokoll aug. 1936," Journalnr. 13242, 1936, UDa.

38. "Trotski kjenner ingen norske tilhengere," *Arbeiderbladet*, August 28, 1936; "Trotski innrømmer å ha drevet aktuell politikk," *Dagbladet*, August 28, 1936.

39. "Trotski kjenner ingen norske tilhengere," Arbeiderbladet, August 28, 1936; "Trotski innrømmer å ha drevet aktuell politikk," Dagbladet, August 28, 1936.

40. "Trotsky innrømmer å ha drevet aktuell politikk," Dagbladet, August 28, 1936; "Trotsky innrømmer at han har drevet politisk virksomhet," *Aftenposten*, evening ed., August 28, 1936.

41. "Trotski i Justisdepartement," *Arbeiderbladet*, August 28, 1936; "Trotski hos statsråd Lie," *Dagbladet*, August 28, 1936; "Trotsky til alvorlig konferanse i Justisdepartementet," *Aftenposten*, August 28, 1936.

42. *Dagbladet*, August 28, 1936; *Aftenposten*, August 28, 1936.

43. Meyer, "Ved Leo Trotskys avreise," 43; T. Lie, *Oslo-Moskva-London*, 72.

44. Meyer, "Ved Leo Trotskys avreise," 43; Meyer, Oslo, to Helge Krog [Oslo], December 1, 1936, MS fol. 3956:8a, HA-NB. Meyer maintained in his letter to Krog that Scheflo had presented the government's terms to Trotsky while driving him to Oslo to appear as a witness in the court of inquiry on August 28, 1936. This assertion is most likely in error, considering the fact that Trotsky already was under police guard, and all Oslo newspapers reported that the State Police had chauffeured Trotsky to Oslo.

45. "Erklæring," Oslo, ... August 1936, box 1, Trotsky-saken, Ra.

46. "Blir Trotski fange på en norsk festning?" *Dagbladet*, August 29, 1936.

47. T. Lie, *Oslo-Moskva-London*, 72–73; Meyer, "Ved Leo Trotskys avreise," 43. Isaac Deutscher's dramatic account of Trotsky's meeting with Trygve Lie on August 28, 1936, unfortunately is not documented adequately. See Deutscher, *Prophet Outcast*, 340–42.

48. L. Trotsky, "In 'Socialist' Norway," *Writings, 1936–37*, 29.

49. Ibid., 30.

50. T. Lie, *Oslo-Moskva-London*, 73.

51. Ibid.

52. "Blir Trotski fange på en norsk festning?" *Dagbladet*, August 29, 1936.

53. "Wer war iloyal?" joint statement by van Heijenoort and Wolf, Copenhagen, August 30, 1936, doc. #17369, Folder FI 86, Exile Papers, Hd.

54. "Pressemeddelelse fra Justisdepartementet," August 28, 1936, box 1, Trotsky-saken, Ra.

55. L. Trotsky, "In 'Socialist' Norway," *Writings, 1936–37*, 29.

56. Ola Apenes, interview with Trotsky, Coyoacan, October 19, 1937, in L. Trotsky, *Writings, 1936–37*, 510.

57. "Wer war iloyal?" joint statement by van Heijenoort and Wolf, Copenhagen, August 30, 1936, doc. #17369, Folder FI 86, Exile Papers, Hd.

58. Ibid.

59. "Trotski har vært illojal og må ta følgene," *Arbeiderbladet*, August 29, 1936.

60. "Blir Trotski fange på en norsk festning?" *Dagbladet*, August 29, 1936; van Heijenoort, *Trotsky in Exile*, 89. Van Heijenoort's autobiographical recollection of the chronology of events that he experienced in Norway in August 1936 is not always reliable. For

example, he stated that he traveled directly from Wexhall to the main police station in Oslo on August 28, whereas this did not take place until the following day, with Wolf and van Heijenoort both staying overnight in the Hønefoss police station. They corroborated this in their joint statement, "Wer war iloyal?," Copenhagen, August 30, 1936, doc. #17369, Folder FI 86, Exile Papers, Hd.

61. Van Heijenoort, ibid., 89.

62. "Wer war iloyal?" joint statement by van Heijenoort and Wolf, Copenhagen, August 30, 1936, doc. #17369, Folder FI 86, Exile Papers, Hd.

63. "Blir Trotski fange på en norsk festning?" *Dagbladet*, August 29, 1936.

64. "Wer was iloyal?" joint statement by van Heijenoort and Wolf, Copenhagen, August 30, 1936, doc. # 17369, Folder FI 86, Exile Papers, Hd; Nils Kåre Dahl, rough draft of unpublished memoir, 10, Aa.

65. Norway, Justis- og Politidepartementet, St. med. nr. 19, Stortingsforhandlinger 1937, annen del b, February 18, 1937, 3–4.

66. "Blir Trotski fange på en norsk festning?" *Dagbladet*, August 29, 1936.

67. Van Heijenoort, *Trotsky in Exile*, 90.

68. Ibid.

69. Erwin Wolf, on board the *Algarve*, to the editorial staff of *Politiken*, Copenhagen, September 1, 1936, doc. #15623, Folder C 74, Exile Papers, Hd.

70. Van Heijenoort, *Trotsky in Exile*, 90.

71. Ibid.

72. Ibid., 90–91.

73. Alf Hassel, Brussels, to the Norwegian Foreign Ministry, Oslo, September 5, 1936, Journalnr. 13597, 1936, UDa.

74. Ibid.

75. Van Heijenoort, *Trotsky in Exile*, 90.

76. Jean van Heijenoort and Erwin Wolf, "Declaration," [Paris], September 5, 1936, doc. #17315, Folder F 120, Exile Papers, Hd.

77. Trotsky, Hønefoss, to Attorney General Haakon Sund, Oslo, August 29, 1936, box 1, Trotsky-saken, Ra.

78. Haakon Sund, Oslo, to Trotsky, Hønefoss, August 29, 1936, doc. #5441, folder N 196, Exile Papers, Hd.

79. Andreas Urbye, Moscow, to the Norwegian Foreign Ministry, August 27, 1936, Journalnr. 13180, 1936, UDa.

80. "De foraktelige beskyttere av fascisten Trotski," *Izvestia*, August 28, 1936, Norwegian transl., Journalnr. 13600, 1936, Uda.

81. Ibid.

82. "Terroristen Trotski under det Norske Arbeiderpartis vinger," *Pravda*, August 28, 1936, Norwegian transl., Journalnr. 13600, 1936, UDa.

83. "Trotsky is Interned in Norway: He Rejected Revolutionary Curb," *New York Times*, August 28, 1936.

84. I. S. Jakoubowitch, Oslo, to Vice Commissar for Foreign Affairs N. N. Krestinsky [Moscow], September 9, 1936, in Holtsmark, ed., *Norge og Sovjetunionen*, doc. #185, p. 247. With reference to Holtmark's documentary collection in this and subsequent footnotes, the abbreviation p. is used in order to distinguish clearly page numbers from document numbers.

85. I. S. Jakoubowitch, Oslo, telegram to the U.S.S.R. Foreign Ministry, August 29, 1936, in ibid., doc. #183, p. 244.

86. Jakoubowitch, Oslo, to Vice Commissar for Foreign Affairs N. N. Krestinsky, [Moscow], September 9, 1936, in ibid., doc. #185, p. 248.

87. Jakoubowitch, Oslo, telegram to the U.S.S.R. Foreign Ministry, August 29, 1936, in ibid., doc. #183, pp. 244–45.

88. Olaf Alfred Tostrup, note entitled "Affæren Trotzky," August 31, 1936, Journalnr. 13242, 1936, UDa.

89. "Meddelelse avgitt til den norske regjering av kamerat Jakoubowitch, Sovjetsam-veldets befullmektige representant i Norge," *Izvestia*, August 30, 1936, Norwegian transl., Journalnr. 13501, 1936, UDa; "Soviet Note to Norway on Trotsky," *Moscow Daily News*, August 30, 1936, Journalnr. 13599, 1936, UDa.

90. Olaf Alfred Tostrup, note entitled "Affæren Trotzky," August 31, 1936, Journalnr. 13242, 1936, UDa.

91. "Meddelelse avgitt til den norske regjering av kamerat Jakoubowitch, Sovjetsam-veldets befullmektigede representant i Norge," *Izvestia*, August 30, 1936, Norwegian transl., Journalnr. 13501, 1936, UDa.

92. Jakoubowitch, Oslo, to Vice Commissar for Foreign Affairs N. N. Krestinsky [Moscow], September 9, 1936, in Holtsmark, *Norge og Sovjetunionen*, doc. #185, p. 248.

93. F[rede] C[astberg], "P.M. Traktaten av 27/15. desember 1860 og spørsmålet om utlevering av Trotzky," G 17 F3/29, Journalnr. 13242, 1936, UDa.

94. Jakoubowitch, Oslo, telegram to the U.S.S.R. Foreign Ministry, August 29, 1936, in Holtsmark, *Norge og Sovjetunionen*, doc. #183, p. 244.

95. Halvdan Koht, "Notat," August 29, 1936, appendix 1 to a letter from the Foreign Ministry to the Ministry of Justice, signed O[laf] Tostrup, December 1, 1936, box 1, Trotsky-saken, Ra.

96. Jakoubowitch, Oslo, telegram to the U.S.S.R. Foreign Ministry, August 29, 1936, in Holtsmark, *Norge og Sovjetunionen*, doc. #183, p. 245.

97. "Koht: Norge vil holde oppe ayslrettens prinsipp," *Arbeiderbladet*, August 31, 1936.

98. "The Case of Leon Trotzky," *Washington Post*, September 1, 1936.

99. "Vanskeligheter," *Dagbladet*, August 31, 1936.

100. F[rede] C[astberg], "P.M. Den russiske henvendelse angående Trotzky," August 31, 1936, Journalnr. 13242, 1936, UDa.

101. Ibid.

102. "Provisorisk anordning om tillegg til fremmedlovgivningen," August 31, 1936, box 1, Trotsky-saken, Ra.

103. "Henvendelsen fra Sovjet," *Arbeiderbladet*, August 31, 1936.

104. See, for example, the draft by L[udwig] A[ubert], "Aide-mémoire," entitled "Det omredigerte utkast. Beholdes i Doss.," September 2, 1936, Journalnr. unreadable, 1936, UDa.

105. Jakoubowitch, Oslo, to Vice Commissar for Foreign Affairs N. N. Krestinsky [Moscow], September 9, 1936, in Holtsmark, *Norge og Sovjetunionen*, doc. #185, p. 248.

106. The Norwegian Foreign Ministry's *aide-mémoire* to the Soviet mission in Norway, September 3, 1936, in ibid., doc. #184, 245–47. This document was also published in Norway, Justis- og Politidepartementet, St. med. nr. 19, Stortingforhandlinger 1937, annen del b., February 19, 1937, bilag (appendix) 6, 13–14.

107. Ibid. Most previous writers have refused to accept the government's assertion that it took action against Trotsky before the Soviet Union applied pressure concerning his asylum. See Danielsen, *Norge–Sovjetunionen*, 188; Strandberg, "Fra gjest til fange,"

108; Eriksen, "Leo Trotskijs internering og deportasjon," 116–19. Instead, these and other authors believe that the Norwegian government's treatment of Trotsky was the result of Soviet arm-twisting prior to August 29. This conclusion has been based on their assumption that the Russians first contacted Norwegian authorities verbally and then later presented a formal, written inquiry. This view, however, fails to take into account that the Soviet representative had returned to Oslo from vacation as late as August 28, two days after Trotsky had been placed under house arrest and on the same day that he and Natalia were interned. Not until the **following day** did Jakoubowitch have his meetings with Lie and Koht. Furthermore, as this study has shown, the diplomat restricted himself **entirely** to making an oral presentation when he first raised the matter. The date of his contact does not mean, however, that Norwegian treatment of Trotsky was uninfluenced by Soviet considerations. As has also been shown, by the beginning of the Moscow trial of the Old Bolsheviks, Norwegian authorities fully anticipated that the question of Trotsky's exile would become a critical issue with the Russians, and they began to take steps to deal with this problem.

108. The Norwegian government's *aide-mémoire* to the Soviet mission in Norway, September 3, 1936, in Holtsmark, *Norge og Sovjetunionen*, doc. #184, p. 246.

109. Jakoubowitch, Oslo, to Vice Commissar N. N. Krestinsky [Moscow], September 9, 1936, in ibid., doc. #185, p. 248.

110. Ibid.

111. Urbye, Moscow, to the Norwegian Foreign Ministry, September 5, 1936, Journalnr. 14042, 1936, UDa.

112. Urbye, Moscow, to the Norwegian Foreign Ministry, September 9, 1936, Journalnr. 14041, ibid.

113. Ibid.

114. Jakoubowitch, Soviet Legation, Oslo, to [Ludvig] Aubert, Foreign Ministry, Oslo, September 10, 1936, box 1, Trotsky-saken, Ra.

115. Urbye, Moscow, to the Norwegian Foreign Ministry, September 16, 1936, Journalnr. 14471, 1936, UDa.

116. Koht, note of discussion with Foreign Minister M. M. Litvinov, September 25, 1936, in Holtsmark, *Norge og Sovjetunionen*, doc. #189, p. 251.

117. Quoted in Tucker, *Stalin in Power*, 372.

118. A number of such reports and newspaper articles are found in box 2, Trotsky-saken, Ra.

119. L. Trotsky, "In 'Socialist' Norway," *Writings, 1936–37*, 30.

120. Broué, *Trotsky*, 830; Deutscher, *Prophet Outcast*, 338.

121. "Koht om Sovjet-samveldets note," *Arbeiderbladet*, September 3, 1936.

122. "Halvdan Koht forteller om sin reise i Nord-Norge," ibid., September 15, 1936.

123. Zachariassen, *Trygve Lie*, 17.

124. Danielsen, *Norge—Sovjetunionen*, 190.

125. This viewpoint is reflected in the attitude of the editors of Trotsky's collected writings. They state that Lie "was responsible for arresting Trotsky and holding him incommunicado so that he could not defend himself against the Moscow trial slanders." See L. Trotsky, *Writings, 1936–37*, 515–16n6.

126. Haakon Lie, interview with the author, Oslo, July 6, 1994.

127. Berntsen, *I malstrømmen*, 426; Hirsti, *Gubben*, 155.

128. "Halvdan Koht forteller om sin reise i Nord-Norge," *Arbeiderbladet*, September 15, 1936.

129. Lahlum, *Haakon Lie*, 116.

130. Gabrielsen, *Martin Tranmæl ser tilbake*, 133.

131. T. Lie, *Oslo-Moskva-London*, 75.

132. Untitled editorial, *Arbeiderbladet*, August 28, 1936.

133. "Hvorlenge [sic] skal Trotski trekke den norske offentlighet efter nesen?" *Arbeideren*, August 28, 1936.

134. *Fritt Folk*, August 28, 1936.

135. Konrad Knudsen, "Trotskis internering," *Fremtiden*, August 29, 1936.

136. Editorial comment following ibid.

137. "Trotskys internering. Av Konrad Knudsen," *Sørlandet*, September 3, 1936.

138. Protest resolution by Oslo Lokale Samorganisasjon, September 11, 1936, in Holtsmark, *Norge og Sovjetunionen*, doc. #187, p. 250.

139. "Skal engelske og amerikanske advokater ta seg av Trotskis sak?" *Tidens Tegn*, September 1, 1936.

140. H. Lie, *Loftsrydding*, 274.

141. "Henvendelsen fra Sovjet," *Arbeiderbladet*, August 31, 1936.

142. "Vanskeligheter," *Dagbladet*, August 31, 1936.

143. "Hvad nu med Trotsky?" *Aftenposten*, August 31, 1936.

144. Arnold Ræstad, "Trotski og asylretten," *Dagbladet*, August 31, 1936.

145. [Thorvald Aadahl], untitled editorial, *Nationen*, September 2, 1936.

146. "Norsk godtroenhet," *Fritt Folk*, September 2, 1936.

147. Untitled editorial, *Arbeiderbladet*, September 2, 1936.

148. "Trotsky og valgkampen," *Aftenposten*, September 2, 1936.

149. Untitled editorial, *Arbeiderbladet*, September 3, 1936.

150. Jakoubowitch, Oslo, to N. N. Krestinsky [Moscow], September 9, 1936, in Holtsmark, *Norge og Sovjetunionen*, doc. #185, p. 249.

151. Norway, Justis- og Politidepartementet, St. med. nr. 19, Stortingsforhandlinger 1937, Annen del b, February 18, 1937, 4.

152. Håkon Meyer, Oslo, to Helge Krog, Schweigårdsholm, December 1, 1936, Håkon Meyers samling, Aa; Meyer, *Bak Moskva Prosessene*, 26.

153. Trotsky, end of August 1936, to unknown recipient, in L. Trotsky, *Writings: Supplement, 1934–40*, 711.

154. "Wer war iloyal?" joint statement by van Heijenoort and Wolf, Copenhagen, August 30, 1936, doc. #17369, Folder FI 86, Exile Papers, Hd.

155. Untitled editorial, *Arbeiderbladet*, September 3, 1936.

156. Heinz Epe [Walter Held], Oslo, to Trotsky, Hønefoss, September 1, 1936, doc. #1930, Folder G 137, Exile Papers, Hd.

157. Telegram from Michael Puntervold, Oslo, to Trotsky, Hønefoss, August 31, 1936, doc. #4184, Folder N 198, ibid.

158. Justice Department, initialed T[rygve] L[ie], to Chefen for utrykningspolitiet, September 1, 1936, "nytt oppholdssted for Trotsky," Box 1, Journalnr. 3944, 1936, Trotsky-saken, Ra.

159. Walter Held [Oslo] to Lev Sedov [Paris], early September 1936, Box 358, Series 231, Boris I. Nicolaevsky Collection, Hoover Institution, Stanford University. Hereafter cited as Nicolaevsky Collection, Stan.

160. Pressemeddelese fra Justisdepartementet, September 2, 1936, Box 1, Trotsky-saken, Ra.

161. Halvor Hegtun, "Under samme tak som Trotskij," *Aftenposten,* September 6, 1989.

162. "Trotskis nye bolig," *Tidens Tegn,* September 3, 1936.

163. Held, Oslo, to Rudolf Klement, Paris, September 2 [sic], 1936, folder #88, Box 369, Series 231, Nicolaevsky Collection, Stan. Held dated the letter incorrectly since it was written on the day after Trotsky's move to Sundby, which was September 3.

164. Hegtun, "Under samme tak som Trotskij," *Aftenposten,* September 6, 1989.

7: Internment at Sundby

1. Harald Halvorsen d.y., Århus, Denmark, to the author, San Diego, CA, September 12, 2003.

2. Ibid.; "Et stykke verdenshistorie i Hurum: Sundby Gård på Storsand," *Røyken og Hurums Avis,* August 12, 1987.

3. Author interview with Harald Halvorsen II, Sundby, June 16, 1999; J. Lie, *I "fred" og ufred,* 132.

4. Harald Halvorsen d.y., Århus, Denmark, to the author, San Diego, CA, September 12, 2003; pictures of Sundby in 1936 immediately following Trotsky's departure, Harald Halvorsen d.y.'s archive, Sundby; J. Lie, *I "fred" og ufred,* 133.

5. "Et stykke verdenshistorie i Hurum: Sundby Gård på Storsand," *Røyken og Hurums Avis,* August 12, 1987.

6. Author interview with Harald Halvorsen II, Sundby, June 16, 1999.

7. Tine Faltin, "Revolusjonsheltens NORSKE FENGSEL," *Dagbladet,* July 22, 1995.

8. "Lov om rekvisjonsrett for politi av 1933, 19. mai, nr. 8, " provided by Tarjei Lie, Oslo, to the author, Oslo, July 7, 1999; "TROTSKIS NYE BOLIG i Hurum," *Tidens Tegn,* September 3, 1936.

9. Trygve Lie later maintained that Sundby, when not occupied by the Trotskys, "otherwise was empty." See T. Lie, *Oslo-Moskva-London,* 75.

10. Harald Halvorsen d.y., tape-recorded interview with Aagot Sæthre, November 7, 1992, Harald Halvorsen d.y.'s archive, Sundby; Tine Faltin, "Revolusjonshelten NORSKE FENGSEL," *Dagbladet,* July 22, 1995; Anders Franck, TROTSKIJ "JO, JO HAN BODDE HÄR. ÄN SEN?" *Göteborgs-Posten,* June 25, 1995.

11. Bernhard Askvig, Utrykningspolitiet, to Justis- og Politidepartementets Politikontor, February 10, 1937, box 3, Trotsky-saken, Ra. The Halvorsens were awarded 501 kroner for "wear and tear."

12. Harald Halvorsen d.y., Århus, Denmark, to the author, San Diego, CA, September 12, 2003; author interview with Harald Halvorsen II, Sundby, June 16, 1999; J. Lie, *I "fred" og ufred,* 133; L. Trotsky, "In 'Socialist' Norway," *Writings, 1936–37,* 34; Laila Strand, "Jeg var Trotskys husholderske," *Drammens Tidende, Buskerud Blad,* July 12, 1985.

13. Harald Halvorsen d.y., Århus, Denmark, to the author, ibid; author interview with Harald Halvorsen II, Sundby, June 16, 1999; pictures of Karoline Robert, Aagot Sæthre, and the police guard, Harald Halvorsen d.y.'s archive, Sundby.

14. Laila Strand, "Jeg var Trotskys husholderske," *Drammens Tidende, Buskerud Blad,* July 12, 1985.

15. Harald Halvorsen d.y., tape-recorded interview with Aagot Sæthre, November 7, 1992, Harald Halvorsen d.y.'s archive, Sundby.

16. Author interview with Edith Johansen, June 16, 1999, Storsand.

17. Harald Halvorsen d.y., Århus, Denmark, to the author, San Diego, CA, September 12, 2003.

18. Author interview with Harald Halvorsen II, Sundby, June 16, 1999,

19. Krog, *Meninger*, 50.

20. Harald Halvorsen d.y., tape-recorded interview with Aagot Sæthre, November 7, 1992, Harald Halvorsen d.y.'s archive, Sundby.

21. Trotsky, Storsand, to Lev Sedov [Paris], September 29, 1936, doc. #10165, folder Fam 8, Exile Papers, Hd; Konrad Knudsen, Hønefoss, to Natalia Sedova and Trotsky [Storsand], September 21, 1936, doc. #2360, Folder N 197, Exile Papers, Hd.

22. Harald Halvorsen d.y., Århus, Denmark, to the author, San Diego, CA, September 12, 2003; author interview with Harald Halvorsen II, Sundby, June 16, 1999; Tine Faltin, "Revolusjonsheltens NORSKE FENGSEL," *Dagbladet*, July 22, 1995.

23. Trotsky [Storsand] to Puntervold [Oslo], October 26, 1936, appendix 2 of Leif Ragnvald Konstad, Central Passport Office, to Trygve Lie, Justice Department, October 28, 1936, box 2, Trotsky-saken, Ra.

24. Konrad Knudsen, Hønefoss, to Natalia Sedova and Lev Trotsky, Storsand, October 23, 1936, doc. # 2361, Folder N 197, Exile Papers, Hd; Knudsen, Hønefoss, to Trotsky, Storsand, November 2, 1936, doc. # 2362, Folder N 197, Exile Papers, Hd; L. Trotsky, "In 'Socialist' Norway," *Writings, 1936–37*, 32–33; J. Lie, *I "fred" og ufred*, 133.

25. J. Lie, *I "fred" og ufred*, 133.

26. Held, [Oslo] to Sedov [Paris], November 9, 1936, Folder #92, box 358, Series 231, Nicolaevsky Collection, Stan.; Laila Strand, "Jeg var Trotskys husholderske," *Drammens Tidende, Buskerud Blad*, July 12, 1985.

27. Konrad Knudsen, Hønefoss, to Trotsky [Storsand], September 21, 1936, doc. #2360, Folder N 197, Exile Papers, Hd.

28. Trotsky [Storsand] to Lev Sedov, Paris, October 3, 1936, doc. # 10168, Folder Fam 3, ibid.

29. J. Lie, *I "fred" og ufred*, 135.

30. Konrad Knudsen, Hønefoss, to Trotsky [Storsand], September 21, 1936, doc. #2360, Folder N 197, Exile Papers, Hd.

31. L. Trotsky, "In 'Socialist' Norway," *Writings, 1936–37*, 31–32.

32. Trotsky [Storsand] to Konrad Knudsen, Hønefoss, October 23, 1936, box. 2, Trotsky-saken, Ra.

33. Held, Oslo, to Martin Tranmæl, Oslo, January 12, 1937, Walter Held folder, Aa.

34. L. Trotsky, "In 'Socialist' Norway," *Writings, 1936–37*, 35.

35. Laila Strand, "Jeg var Trotskys husholderske," *Drammens Tidende, Buskerud Blad*, July 12, 1985; Harald Halvorsen d.y., tape-recorded interview with Aagot Sæthre, November 7, 1992, Harald Halvorsen d.y.'s archive, Sundby.

36. Strand, "Jeg var Trotskys husholderske," *Drammens Tidende, Buskerud Blad*, July 12, 1985·

37. Preliminary Commission, 38.

38. Rosenthal [Oslo] to Trotsky [Storsand], September 18, 1936, doc. #4316, Folder F 113, Exile Papers, Hd; Rosenthal, *Avocat de Trotsky*, 159–62.

39. Held [Oslo] to Sedov [Paris], November 9, 1936, Folder #92, box 358, Series, 231, Nicolaevsky Collection, Stan.

40. Trotsky [Storsand] to Sedov, Paris, [September 1936], doc. #10166, Folder Fam 3, Exile Papers, Hd.

41. Puntervold, Oslo, to Trotsky [Storsand], September 23, 1936, doc. #4188, Folder N 198, Exile Papers, Hd.

42. Trotsky [Storsand] to Puntervold [Oslo], October 26, 1936, appendix 2 of Leif Rangvald Konstad, Central Passport Office, to Trygve Lie, Department of Justice, October 28, 1936, box 2, Trotsky-saken, Ra.

43. Halvdan Koht, Foreign Ministry, to Central Passport Office, October 7, 1936, Journalnr. 15097, 1936, UDa.

44. Olaf Broch, Oslo, to Konstad, Central Passport Office, October 30, 1936, box 2, Trotsky-saken, Ra.

45. Leif Rangvald Konstad, Central Passport Office, to Trygve Lie, Department of Justice, November 2, 1936, box 3, Trotsky-saken, Ra.

46. Trotsky [Storsand] to Puntervold [Oslo], October 26, 1936, appendix 2 of Konstad, Central Passport Office, to Trygve Lie, Department of Justice, October 28, 1936, box 2, Trotsky-saken, Ra.

47. Trotsky [Storsand] to Lev Sedov, Paris, September 5, 1936. doc. # 10163, Folder Fam 3, Exile Papers, Hd.

48. L. Trotsky, "In 'Socialist' Norway," *Writings, 1936–37*, 33.

49. Konstad [Central Passport Office] to Puntervold, Oslo, November 6, 1936, with copy of Konstad [Central Passport Office] to State Police Chief Askvig, Oslo, November 6, 1936, doc. #14878, Folder N 197, Exile Papers, Hd; Trotsky [Storsand] to Rosenthal [Paris], October 9, 1936, in L. Trotsky, *Writings, 1935–36*, 435–36.

50. Konstad to Askvig, November 6, 1936, doc. #14878, Folder N 197, Exile Papers, Hd.

51. L. Trotsky, "In 'Socialist' Norway," *Writings, 1936–37*, 34.

52. Charles Yale Harrison, Oslo, to [Halvdan Koht], Foreign Ministry, September 18, 1936, Journalnr. 14352, 1936, UDa.

53. Koht, Foreign Ministry, to [Kornelius Bergsvik], acting head of the Justice Department, September 18, 1936, Journalnr. 14352, 1936, ibid.

54. Kornelius Bergsvik, Justice Department, to Foreign Ministry, September 19, 1936, Journalnr. l4450, 1936, ibid.

55. "Ny klage over Centralpasskontoret," *Arbeiderbladet*, September 23, 1936.

56. Ibid.

57. Held [Oslo] to Lev Sedov [Paris], September 11, 1936, Folder #82, box 358, Series 231, Nicolaevsky Collection, Stan.

58. The protest letters and telegrams are located in box 2, Trotsky-saken, Ra.

59. H. H. Bachke, Paris, to Foreign Ministry, Oslo, September 5, 1936, Journalnr. 13636, 1936, UDa.

60. Strandberg, "Fra gjest til fange," 114; Brouckere, "De politiske flyktninger og rettighetene deres."

61. Håkon Meyer, Oslo, to Trotsky [Storsand], October 24, 1936, doc. #3073, Folder N 197, Exile Papers, Hd.

62. Strandberg, "Fra gjest til fange," 114.

63. J. Olsen, *Trotski*.

64. Krog, *Meninger*, 51.

65. Lorenz, "Vår kamerat i Oslo," 156.

66. Held [Oslo] to Lev Sedov [Paris], September 11, 1936, Folder # 83, box 358, Series 231, Nicolaevsky Collection, Stan.; Held, Oslo, to "my dear friend" [possibly Jean van Heijenoort] [n.p.], November 2, 1936, Folder # 91, box 358, Series 231, Nicolaevsky Collection, Stan.

67. Håkon Meyer, Oslo, to Prime Minister Johan Nygaardsvold, Oslo, September 9, 1936, appendix 1 of Håkon Meyer, Oslo, to Helge Krog, Schweigårdsholm, December 1, 1936, Håkon Meyers samling, Aa.

68. Johan Nygaardsvold, Oslo, to Håkon Meyer [Oslo], n.d., 1936, appendix 2 of Håkon Meyer to Helge Krog, ibid.

69. Knudsen, Hønefoss, to Håkon Meyer, Oslo, September 15, 1936, part of appendix 6, ibid.

70. Knudsen, Hønefoss, to Trotsky and Natalia Sedova [Storsand], September 21, 1936, doc. # 2360, Folder N 197, Exile Papers, Hd.

71. Håkon Meyer, Oslo, to Konrad Knudsen, Hønefoss, September 11, 1936, part of appendix 6 of Håkon Meyer, Oslo, to Helge Krog, Schweigårdsholm, December 1, 1936, Håkon Meyers samling, Aa.

72. Konrad Knudsen, Hønefoss, to Meyer, Oslo, September 15, 1936, part of appendix 6, ibid.

73. Meyer, Oslo, to Krog, Schweigårdsholm, ibid.

74. Meyer, Oslo, to Trygve Lie, Justice Department, September 30, 1936, appendix 3 of Meyer, Oslo, to Krog, Schweigårdsholm, December 1, 1936, Håkon Meyers samling, Aa.

75. Trotsky [Storsand] to Meyer [Oslo], October 17, 1936, in L. Trotsky, *Writings: Supplement, 1934–40,* 723.

76. Trotsky [Storsand] to Meyer [Oslo], October 22, 1936, ibid., 724.

77. Trotsky [Storsand] to Puntervold [Oslo], November 26, 1936, ibid.

78. Meyer, Oslo, to Oscar Torp, Oslo, October 7, 1936, appendix 6 of Meyer, Oslo, to Krog, Schweigårdsholm, December 1, 1936, Håkon Meyers samling, Aa.

79. Meyer, Oslo, to Krog, Schweigårdsholm, December 1, 1936, Håkon Meyers samling, Aa.

80. Meyer, Oslo, to Trotsky [Storsand], October 20, 1936, doc. # 3072, Folder N 197, Exile Papers, Hd.

81. Meyer, Oslo, to Trotsky [Storsand], October 24, 1936, doc. # 3073, ibid.

82. Meyer, Oslo, to Oslo Arbeidersamfund, September 10, 1936, appendix 5 in Meyer, Oslo, to Krog, Schweigårdsholm, December 1, 1936, Håkon Meyers samling, Aa; Meyer, Oslo, to Oslo Arbeidersamfund, September 10, 1936, Korrespondanse 1936 folder, Korresp. 1936–37 box, Oslo Arbeidersamfund, Aa .

83. Meyer [Oslo] to Norsk Rikskringkastning, Foredragsutvalget, October 24, 1936, part of appendix 14 in Meyer, Oslo, to Krog, Schweigårdsholm, December 1, 1936, Håkon Meyers samling, Aa.

84. Olav Midthun, for Norsk Rikskringkasting, to Meyer, Oslo, November 9, 1936, part of appendix 14, ibid.

85. G. O., "Trekk av fagorganisasjonens historie. Litt om foregangsmennene. Michael Puntervold," *Fri fagbevegelse* 48, no. 3 (1955); "Michael Puntervold. Arbeiderpartiets stortingskandidat for Aker," *Agitatoren* 3, no. 41 (August 10, 1909); www.norgeslexi.com/arbeiderlexi.

86. T. Lie, *Oslo-Moskva-London*, 47.

87. Larsen, "En uforbederlig optimist," 117.

88. Held, Oslo, to Lev Sedov [Paris], September 26, 1936, box 358, Folder # 84, Series 231, Nicolaevsky Collection, Stan.

89. Boman-Larsen, *Roald Amundsen*, 528.

90. Held, Oslo, to Sedov [Paris], September 11, 1936, folder # 82, box 358, Series 231, Nicolaevsky Collection, Stan.

91. Held, Oslo, to Trotsky [Storsand], October 9, 1936, doc. #1932, Folder G 137, Exile Papers, Hd.

92. Erling Falk, Tønsberg, to Lev Sedov, Paris, November 21, 1936, box 0001, Serie F—enkeltpersoner, Mot Dags arkiv, Aa.

93. Puntervold, untitled and undated legal declaration, doc. # 17398, Folder N 197, Exile Papers, Hd. The statement unquestionably was drawn up during the first days of September. Parts of it were quoted in "Advokat Puntervold begrunder hvorfor Trotski må anlegge injuriesak," *Tidens Tegn*, September 4, 1936.

94. "Trotskis søksmål," *Arbeiderbladet*, September 3, 1936.

95. Ibid.

96. Trotsky [Storsand] to Lev Sedov, Paris, September 5, 1936, doc. # 10163, Folder Fam 3, Exile Papers, Hd.

97. Lev Sedov, Paris, to Trotsky [Storsand], September 12, 1936, doc. # 4851, Folder Fam 7, ibid.

98. Lev Sedov, Paris, to Trotsky [Storsand], September 12, 1936, doc. # 4851, ibid.; Trotsky [Storsand] to Lev Sedov [Paris], September 17, 1936, doc. # 10192, Folder Fam 3, ibid.

99. Puntervold, Oslo, to Trotsky [Storsand], September 9, 1936, doc. # 4186, Folder N 198, ibid.; Puntervold [Oslo], to Lev Sedov, Paris, October 20, 1936, doc. # 12992, ibid.

100. Bjarne Komdahl, Oslo, to Trotsky [Storsand], September 18, 1936, doc. # 4187, ibid. Komdahl was Puntervold's law partner.

101. Trotsky [Storsand] to Puntervold [Oslo], September 15, 1936, Håkon Meyers samling, Aa.

102. Puntervold, Oslo, to Trotsky, Storsand, October 6, 1936, doc. # 4189, Folder N 198, Exile Papers, Hd.

103. Ibid.

104. Held, Oslo, to Trotsky [Storsand], October 7, 1936, Folder # 87, box 358, Series 231, Nicolaevsky Collection, Stan.

105. Meyer [Oslo] to Krog [Schweigårdsholm], December 1, 1936, Håkon Meyers samling, Aa.

106. Held, Oslo, to Trotsky [Storsand], October 7, 1936, Folder # 87, box 358, Series 231, Nicolaevsky Collection, Stan.

107. Ibid.

108. Held, Oslo, to Trotsky [Storsand], October 9, 1936, doc. # 1932, Folder G 137, Exile Papers, Hd. In this letter Held erroneously stated that Puntervold had not submitted his preliminary complaint to the Conciliation Board until October 8, whereas the correct date was October 6, 1936.

109. Puntervold, Oslo, to Trotsky, Storsand, October 17, 1936, doc. # 4194, Folder N 198, ibid.

110. Puntervold, Oslo, to Trotsky, Storsand, October 23, 1936, doc. # 4195, ibid.

111. Ibid.

112. General message from Trotsky to his followers, late August 1936, in L. Trotsky, *Writings: Supplement, 1934–40,* 712.

113. Trotsky [Storsand] to Lev Sedov[Paris], October 12, 1936, ibid., 716–22.

114. Bille Larsen, *Mod strømmen,* 185.

115. Trotsky [Storsand] to Lev Sedov [Paris], October 12, 1936, in L. Trotsky, *Writings: Supplement, 1934–40,* 721.

116. Preliminary Commission, 516.

117. Trotsky [Storsand] to Lev Sedov [Paris], October 3, 1936, in L. Trotsky, *Writings, 1935–36,* 438–39.

118. Keller [Jan Frankel], Prague, to Trotsky [Storsand], September 22, 1936, doc. #1255, Folder C 80, Exile Papers, Hd; L. Trotsky, *Writings, 1935–36,* 554n429.

119. Rosenthal, *Avocat de Trotsky,* 160; Broué, *Trotsky,* 835.

120. Bille Larsen, *Mod strømmen,* 187–88.

121. Ibid, 189–90.

122. Broué, *Trotsky,* 835.

123. Held [Oslo] to Durand [Sedov], [Paris], September 26, 1936, Folder # 84, box 358, Series 231, Nicolaevsky Collection, Stan.

124. Puntervold [Oslo] to the International Federation of Trade Unions [Amsterdam], October 22, 1936, with copies to the Labor and Socialist International, the International Bureau of Revolutionary Socialist Parties, and the International Secretariat for the Fourth International, in L. Trotsky, *Writings, 1935–36,* 441–42.

125. Trotsky [Storsand] to Rosenthal [Paris], October 22, 1936, ibid., 436–37.

126. Puntervold [Oslo] to League of Nations, Geneva, October 22, 1936, ibid., 443.

127. "Trotski-saken kontra Moskva innbragt for Folkeforbundet," *Tidens Tegn,* November 25, 1936.

128. See L. Trotsky, *Writings, 1935–36,* 556n439.

129. Sedov, Paris, to Erwin Wolf, n.p., September 9, 1936, Folder # 56, box 368, Series 231, Nicolaevsky Collection, Stan.

130. Rosenthal [Paris] to Trotsky [Storsand], October 21, 1936, doc. # 4319, Folder F 113, Exile Papers, Hd.

131. Sedov, Paris, to Trotsky [Storsand], October 26, 1936, doc. # 4858, Folder Fam 7, ibid.

132. Appendix, ibid.

133. Rosenthal, *Avocat de Trotsky,* 160.

134. Reed and Jacobson, "Trotsky Papers," 368.

135. Sedov, Paris, to Trotsky [Storsand], October 26, 1936, doc. #4858, Folder Fam 7, Exile Papers, Hd.

136. Trotsky [Storsand] to Sedov [Paris], October 21, 1936, doc. #10174, Folder Fam 3, ibid.

137. Appendix to Sedov, Paris, to Trotsky [Storsand], October 26, 1936, doc. #4858, Folder Fam 7, ibid.

138. Broué, *Trotsky,* 837.

139. Ibid.

140. Rosenthal, Paris, to Trotsky [Storsand], October 24, 1936, doc. #4320, Folder F 113, Exile Papers, Hd.

141. Urbye, Moscow, to the Foreign Ministry, Oslo, September 23, 1936, Journalnr. 14845, 1936, UDa.

142. Ludvig Aubert, for the Foreign Ministry, to Trygve Lie, Department of Justice,

Oslo, October 3, 1936, box 3, Trotsky-saken, Ra.

143. Alf Hassel, Norwegian Legation, Brussels, to Foreign Ministry, November 6, 1936, Journalnr. 17081, UDa; "Trotski har direkte stimulert oprørsbevegelsen i Belgia," *Tidens Tegn*, September 23, 1936.

144. J. Ræder, Norwegian Legation, The Hague, to the Foreign Ministry, September 23, 1936, Journalnr. 14720, 1936, UDa.

145. Haakon Sund, Oslo, to the Justice Department, October 7, 1936; Trygve Lie, Oslo, to the Foreign Ministry, October 13, 1936, Journalnr. 4697, 1936, UDa.

146. Koht, Norwegian Foreign Ministry, to the Norwegian Legation, Brussels, October 17, 1936, Journalnr. 15741, 1936, UDa; Alf Hassel, Brussels, to the Foreign Ministry, Oslo, October 22, 1936, Journalnr. 16369, UDa.

147. "Trotski har direkte stimulert oprørsbevegelsen i Belgia," *Tidens Tegn*, September 23, 1936.

148. Michael Puntervold, "Trotski og Belgia," *Tidens Tegn*, September 25, 1936. An English translation of the press release, published in *Aftenposten* on September 24, 1936, is found in L. Trotsky, *Writings, 1935–36*, 432–33.

149. Alf Hassel, Norwegian Legation, Brussels, to the Foreign Ministry, November 6, 1936, Journalnr. 17081, 1936, UDa.

150. Trotsky [Storsand] to Sedov, Paris, September 5, 1936, doc. #10163, Folder Fam 3, Exile Papers, Hd.

151. Fjeld, Oslo, to Trotsky, Storsand, September 18, 1936, doc. #1025, Folder N 197, ibid.

152. Fjeld, Oslo, to Trotsky, Storsand, October 6, 1936, doc. #1026, ibid.

153. Trotski, *Mitt liv*.

154. Trotsky [Storsand] to Sedov, Paris, September 5, 1936, doc. #10163, Folder Fam 3, Exile Papers, Hd.

155. Trotsky [Storsand] to Sara Weber [n.p.], September 10, 1936, in L. Trotsky, *Writings: Supplement, 1934–40* 714–15.

156. Service, *Trotsky*, 406–7, 467–68.

157. Trotsky [Storsand] to Sara Weber [n.p.], September 10, 1936, in L. Trotsky, *Writings: Supplement, 1934–40*, 715.

158. Ibid., 714.

159. Trotsky [Storsand] to Sedov [Paris], September 28, 1936, doc. #10164, Folder Fam 3, Exile Papers, Hd.

160. Sedov, Paris, to Trotsky [Storsand], September 25, 1936, doc. #4853, ibid.

161. Trotsky, Coyoacan, to Held [Oslo], February 3, 1937, doc. #8509, Folder G 137, ibid.

162. Trotsky [Coyoacan] to Jan Frankel [n.p.], February 3, 1938, L. Trotsky, *Writings: Supplement, 1934–40*, 753. 163. Trotsky [Coyoacan] to Jan Frankel [n.p.], February 7, 1938, ibid., 757.

164. Christiania Bank og Kreditkasse, Oslo, to Trotsky via Central Passport Office, October 20, 1936, doc. #566, Folder N 197, Exile Papers, Hd.

165. Norderhov tax office, Hønefoss, to Puntervold, Oslo, October 14, 1936, with an addendum from Puntervold to Trotsky of October 16, 1936, doc. #4193, Folder N 198, ibid.

166. Johan Scharffenberg, "Ytringsfrihet for politiske flyktninger," *Arbeiderbladet*, September 4, 1936.

167. "En selvbestaltet fangevokter," *Tidens Tegn*, September 23, 1936.

168. "Den uskyldige fisker—Eller en fisker i rørt vann?" *Tidens Tegn*, September 23, 1936.

169. "Et uheldig inngrep i Trotskis internerings-bestemmelser," *Tidens Tegn*, September 23, 1936.

170. Ibid.

171. J. Br.—e., "Trotski som norsk statsfange og revolusjonene," *Nationen*, September 28, 1936.

172. "Nye dødsvarsler fra Stalin," *Tidens Tegn*, October 13, 1936.

173. Waldemar Brøgger, "Rettsikkerhet," *Tidens Tegn*, September 2, 1936.

174. Copy of [Haakon Sund] to the Justice Department, October 16, 1936, box 1, Trotsky-saken, Ra.

175. J. Br. - e., "Trotski som norsk statsfange og revolusjonene," *Nationen*, September 28, 1936.

176. "Regjeringens kostbare gjest," *Aftenposten*, October 8, 1936; Norway, Justis- og Politidepartementet, St. med. nr. 19, Stortingsforhandlinger 1937, annen del b., February 18, 1937, 5.

177. "Regjeringens kostbare gjest," *Aftenposten*, October 8, 1936.

178. "Revolusjonenes rådgiver," *Tidens Tegn*, September 25, 1936.

179. "Trotski," *Arbeiderbladet*, October 8, 1936.

180. "Trotski," *Arbeiderbladet*, October 17, 1936.

181. "Hvis ikke Trotski frigis, går det over justisministerens lik," *Tidens Tegn*, October 8, 1936.

182. "Trotski—siste chanse," *Fremtiden*, October 10, 1936.

183. "To anklager," *Morgenbladet*, October 9, 1936.

184. "Trotski," *Arbeiderbladet*, October 8, 1936.

185. Held, Oslo, to Sedov [Paris], October 10, 1936, Folder #89, box 358, Series 231, Nicolaevsky Collection, Stan.

186. Naville, Paris, to Puntervold, Oslo, October 10, 1936, doc. #15133, Folder F 198, Exile Papers, Hd.

187. Puntervold [Oslo], press release, n.d., doc. #17401, Folder N 198, ibid.

188. F. Werring, Paris, to Foreign Ministry, October 16, 1936, Journalnr. 15986, 1936, UDa.

189. Two handwritten initialed comments on ibid., one by H[alvdan] K[oht].

190. "Justisdepartementet går erend [sic] for trotskistene," *Tidens Tegn*, October 13, 1936.

191. "Hvad var det Trotski arbeidet for mens han satt på Hønefoss?" *Tidens Tegn*, October 14, 1936.

192. "Landsulykken Trotski," *Nationen*, October 14, 1936.

193. "Trotski har fremdeles forbindelse med 4. internasjonale," *Tidens Tegn*, October 15, 1936.

194. "De siste Trotski-skremsler dementeres," *Arbeiderbladet*, October 16, 1936.

195. "Hullet i Trotskis internering," *Tidens Tegn*, October 16, 1936.

196. "Trotski," *Arbeiderbladet*, October 17, 1936.

197. "Tidens Tegn Naville-intervju," *Arbeiderbladet*, October 20, 1936.

198. "En skamplett på norsk presse," *Fremtiden*, December 2, 1936.

199. Ibid.

200. Bertheus Eilewsen, for Gratangen Skipperforening, to Foreign Ministry, September 23, 1936, Journalnr. 15484, 1936, UDa.

201. "Trotsky-affæren har fått handelspolitiske følger for Norge," Aftenposten, September 30, 1936.

202. Norges Rederforbund, "P.M.," September 30, 1936, delivered by the association's president, Fr. Odfjell, and its administrative director, W. Klaveness, to utenriksråd Olaf Alfred Tostrup, Journalnr. 15005, 1936, UDa.

203. O[laf] T[ostrup], "Notat," October 3, 1936, Journalnr. 15276, 1936, UDa.

204. Eriksen, "Leo Trotskijs internering og deportasjon," 32.

205. "Trotsky-affæren ødela forhandlingene om sildesalg til Russland," Aftenposten, October 13, 1936; "Flere alworlige følger av Trotsky-affæren," Aftenposten, October 14, 1936.

206. "Den dyre gjest," Morgenbladet, October 19, 1936.

207. L[udvig] A[ubert], "P.M. Trotzky-saken. Vanskeligheter for norske skib med hensyn til befraktninger for Sovjet-Samveldet," October 16, 1936, Journalnr. 15949, 1936, UDa.

208. H[alvdan] K[oht], "Notat," October 17, 1936, Journalnr. 04960, 1936, UDa.

209. Fr. Odfjell, for Norges Rederforbund, countersigned W. Klaveness, December 14, 1936, Journalnr. 19230, 1936, UDa.

210. Statistisk sentralbyrå to the author, email, September 4, 2003.

211. Norway, Statistisk sentralbyrå, Utenrikshandel, Tabell 18.11, "Innførsel og utførsel, etter viktige land." http://www.ssb.no/emner/historisk_statistikk/tabeller/18-18-11.txt.

212. Knudsen, Hønefoss, to Trotsky [Storsand], September 21, 1936, doc. #2360, Folder N 197, Exile Papers, Hd.

213. Copy of NS flyer, "Norge for Trotsky," 1936 parliamentary election, courtesy of Harald Halvorsen d.y., Sundby gård, Storsand.

214. Hansen, "NKP og regjeringen 1935—36," 64–65.

215. "La valgvinden feie," Nationen, October 17, 1936.

216. "Stem den ned!" Aftenposten, October 19, 1936.

217. H. Lie, Martin Tranmæl, 2: 162.

218. Knudsen [Hønefoss] to Natalia and L[ev] D[avidovich Trotsky], [Storsand], October 23, 1936, doc. #2361, Folder N 197, Exile Papers, Hd.

219. Trotsky [Storsand] to Knudsen, Hønefoss, October 23, 1936, appended copy in Konstad, Central Passport Office, to Trygve Lie, Department of Justice, October 28, 1936, box 2, Trotsky-saken, Ra.

220. Trotsky [Storsand] to Puntervold [Oslo], October 26, 1936, appended copy in ibid.

221. "Trotskis injuriesøksmål," Arbeiderbladet, September 4, 1936.

222. Annæus Schjødt, "Injuriesaker av storpolitisk innhold," Dagbladet, September 10, 1936.

223. Puntervold, Oslo, to Trotsky, Storsand, October 10, 1936, doc. #4190, Folder N 198, Exile Papers, Hd.

224. Trotsky [Storsand] to Sedov [Paris], October 21, 1936, doc. #10174, Folder Fam 3, ibid.

225. "TROTSKI NEKTES SAKSANLEGG," Dagbladet, October 29, 1936.

226. T. Lie, Oslo—Moskva—London, 76.

227. Norway, Kongeriket Norges Seksogåttiende Ordentlige Stortingsforhandlinger

1937, sjette del b., Innstillinger og bestlutninger, Innst. O. IV B. (1937), 4–6.

228. Ibid., 6.

229. Trygve Lie, countersigned Jørgen Scheel, Department of Justice, to the chief judge, Oslo Municipal Court, October 29, 1936, box 2, Trotsky-saken, Ra.

230. "Trotskis sak," *Arbeiderbladet*, October 29, 1936.

231. Ihle, "Den norske arbeiderbevegelse," 15.

232. "Trotskys injuriesak stanset!" *Aftenposten*, October 29, 1936.

233. Eriksen, "Leo Trotskijs internering og deportasjon," 34.

234. "TROTSKIS ADVOKAT: Regjeringens 'anordning' er grunnlovsstridig!" *Dagbladet*, October 29, 1936.

235. See box 358, Series 231, Nicolaevsky Collection, Stan.

236. Held, Oslo, to "my dear friend" [most likely Jean van Heijenoort], [Paris], November 2, 1936, Folder #91, ibid.

8: Adios Noruega

1. Håkon, Ingerid, Karin, and Eli Meyer, Oslo, to Trotsky [Storsand], November 7, 1936, doc. #3074, Folder N 197, Exile Papers, Hd.

2. Sedov, Paris, to Natalia Sedova [Storsand], December 3, 1936, doc. #13265, Folder Fam 8, ibid.

3. Trotsky [Storsand] to Puntervold [Oslo], November 26, 1936, in L. Trotsky, *Writings: Supplement, 1934–40,* 726.

4. Trotsky [Storsand] to Rosenthal [Paris], December 10, 1936, in L. Trotsky, *Writings, 1935–36,* 454.

5. Sedov, Paris, to Friedrich Adler, Brussels, November 8, 1936, doc. #13154, Folder G 9, Exile Papers, Hd.

6. Conquest, *Great Terror*, 140–41, 142.

7. Sedov, Paris, to Natalia Sedova and Trotsky [Storsand], November 22, 1936, doc. #4862, Folder Fam 7, Exile Papers, Hd.

8. Trotsky [Storsand] to Puntervold [Oslo], November 26, 1936, in L. Trotsky, *Writings: Supplement, 1934–40,* 724–25.

9. Sedov, Paris, to Puntervold [Oslo], December 11, 1936, doc. #13217, Folder N 9, Exile Papers, Hd.

10. Trotsky [Storsand] to Puntervold [Oslo], November 26, 1936, in L. Trotsky, *Writings: Supplement, 1934–40,* 725–26.

11. Sedov, Paris, to Adler, Brussels, November 8, 1936, doc. #13154, Folder G 9, Exile Papers, Hd.

12. Reed and Jacobson, "Trotsky Papers," 369.

13. Trotsky [Storsand] to Sedov [Paris], November 10, 1936, doc. #10180, Folder Fam 3, ibid.

14. Ibid.

15. Trotsky [Storsand] to Meyer [Oslo], November 10, 1936, Håkon Meyers samling, Aa.

16. Reed and Jacobson, "Trotsky Papers," 371.

17. Trotsky [Storsand] to Sedov [Paris], November 13, 1936, doc. #10182, Folder Fam 3, Exile Papers, Hd.

18. Sedov, Paris, to Trotsky [Storsand], November 22, 1936, doc. #4862, Folder Fam 7, ibid.

19. Sedov, Paris, to Trotsky [Storsand], December 14, 1936, doc. #4864, ibid.

20. Trotsky [Storsand] to Sedov [Paris], December 12, 1936, doc. #10189, Folder Fam. 3, ibid.

21. Sedov, Paris, to Natalia Sedova [Storsand], December 3, 1936, doc. #13265, Folder Fam 8, ibid.

22. Trotsky [Storsand] to Sedov [Paris], December 2, 1936, in L. Trotsky, *Writings: Supplement, 1934–40*, 727.

23. Sedov, Paris, to Trotsky [Storsand], December 14, 1936, doc. #4864, Folder Fam 7, Exile Papers, Hd.

24. Rosenthal, Paris, to Trotsky [Storsand], November 6, 1936, doc. #4321, Folder F 113, ibid.

25. Held [Oslo] to Sedov [Paris], November 10, 1936, Folder 93, box 358, Series 231, Nicolaevsky Collection, Stan.

26. Trotsky [Storsand] to Sedov [Paris], November 8, 1936, doc. #10179, Folder Fam 3, Exile Papers, Hd.

27. L. Trotsky, *Writings, 1936–37*, 534n161.

28. Held [Oslo] to Sedov [Paris], November 19, 1936, Folder 93, box 358, Series 231, Nicolaevsky Collection, Stan.

29. Trygve Lie, countersigned Jørgen Scheel, Oslo, to Puntervold [Oslo], November 11, 1936, typed copy; appended to Puntervold, Oslo, to Meyer, Oslo, November 14, 1936, appendix 13, Meyer, Oslo, to Krog, Schweigårdsholm, December 1, 1936, Håkon Meyers samling, Aa.

30. Trotsky [Storsand] to Rosenthal [Paris], November 22, 1936, doc. #9813, Folder F 113, Exile Papers, Hd.

31. Natalia Sedova [Storsand] to Rosenthal [Paris], November 23, 1936, quoted in Rosenthal, *Avocat de Trotsky*, 177–78.

32. Puntervold, Oslo, to Oslo byrett, November 13, 1936, German translation, doc. #15278, Folder N 198, Exile Papers, Hd.

33. Puntervold, Oslo, to Judge Johs. Koefoed, Oslo byrett, November 20, 1936, German translation, doc. #15279, ibid.

34. Puntervold, Oslo, to Oslo byrett, November 13, 1936, German translation, doc. #15278, ibid.

35. Justis- og Politidepartementet to Oslo byrett, December 7, 1936, box 2, Trotsky-saken, Ra.

36. Diego Rivera [Mexico City] to the Nygaardsvold government, November 17, 1936, box 2, Trotsky-saken, Ra.

37. Norman Thomas, New York, to Minister Wilhelm Morgenstierne, Washington, D. C., November 30, 1936, Journalnr. 19015, 1936, UDa.

38. Sedov, Paris, to Trotsky [Storsand], November 3, 1936, doc. #4859, Folder Fam 7, Exile Papers, Hd.

39. Ibid.

40. Rosenthal, Paris, to Trotsky [Storsand], November 6, 1936, doc. #4321, Folder F 113, ibid.

41. Rosenthal, Paris, to Trotsky [Storsand], November 17, 1936, doc. #4324, ibid.; Sedov, Paris, to Natalia Sedova and Trotsky [Storsand], November 22, 1936, doc. #4862, Folder Fam 7, ibid.

42. Trotsky [Storsand] to Rosenthal [Paris], November 13, 1936, in L. Trotsky, *Writings, 1935–36*, 450; Sedov, Paris, to Natalia Sedova [Storsand], December 3, 1936, doc. #13265, Folder Fam 8, ibid.

43. Rosenthal, Paris, to Trotsky [Storsand], November 7, 1936, doc. #4322, Folder F 113, ibid.

44. Trotsky [Storsand] to Victor Basch [Paris], December 3, 1936, in L. Trotsky, *Writings, 1935–36*, 453.

45. H. H. Bachke, Paris, to the Foreign Ministry, December 8, 1936, Journalnr. 18870, 1936, UDa.

46. Puntervold, Oslo, to Victor Basch, Paris, December 10, 1936, doc. #15273, Folder N 198, Exile Papers, Hd.

47. Sedov, Paris, to Trotsky [Storsand], December 16, 1936, doc. #4865, Folder Fam 7, ibid.

48. Trotsky [Storsand] to Rosenthal [Paris], December 10, 1936, in L. Trotsky, *Writings, 1935–36*, 454.

49. Meyer, Brussels, to Oslo Arbeidersamfunds styre, November 2, 1936, korrespondanse 1936 folder, Korresp. 1936–37 box, Oslo Arbeidersamfund, Aa.

50. Meyer, Oslo, to Brockway, London, November 7, 1936, Håkon Meyers samling, Aa.

51. Brockway, London, to Meyer, Oslo, November 23, 1936, ibid.

52. Brockway, London, to Nygaardsvold, Oslo, November 23, 1936, copy appended to Brockway, London, to Trygve Lie, Oslo, November 23, 1936, box 2, Trotsky-saken, Ra.

53. Meyer, Oslo, to Trygve Lie, Oslo, November 9, 1936, appendix 8 of Meyer, Oslo, to Helge Krog, Schweigårdsholm, December 1, 1936, Håkon Meyers samling, Aa.

54. Nygaardsvold, Oslo, to Meyer, Oslo, November 13, 1936, appendix 10 to Meyer, Oslo, to Krog, ibid.

55. Meyer, Oslo, to Adler, Brussels, November 16, 1936, Håkon Meyers samling, ibid.

56. Meyer, Oslo, to Nygaardsvold, Oslo, November 24, 1936, appendix 11 of Meyer, Oslo, to Krog, Schweigårdsholm, December 1, 1936, ibid.

57. Meyer, Oslo, to Trotsky, Storsand, December 12, 1936, Håkon Meyers samling, ibid.

58. Held, Oslo, to Sedov [Paris], November 15, 1936, Folder #94, box 358, Series 231, Nicolaevsky Collection, Stan.

59. "La Trotskys sak bli undersøkt av en internasjonal kommisjon," *Sørlandet*, December 14, 1936.

60. Falk, Tønsberg, to Sedov, Paris, November 21, 1936, 1936–11–21 folder, box 8, Mot Dag arkivet, Aa.

61. J. Olsen, *Trotski*, 30–31.

62. Held, Oslo, to Trotsky [Storsand], n.d. (fall 1936, most likely in November), doc. #1933, Folder G 137, Exile Papers, Hd.

63. Held, Oslo, to Sedov [Paris], November 9, 1936, Folder 92, box 358, Series 231, Nicolaevsky Collection, Stan.

64. www.aviana.com/per/braatoy/braato04.htm.

65. Trygve Braatøy, "Trotski," *Dagbladet*, November 7, 1936.

66. "Trotski," *Arbeiderbladet*, November 10, 1936.

67. Synnøve Rosendahl-Jensen, Oslo, to Trotsky [Storsand], November 19, 1936, doc. #1891, Folder N 196, Exile Papers, Hd.

68. Jakob Friis, "'Bakunisten' Trotski," *Arbeiderbladet*, November 11, 1936.

69. Håkon Meyer, "Friis—Scharffenberg—Trotski," Arbeiderbladet, November 17, 1936.

70. Meyer, Oslo, to Scheflo, Oslo, November 11, 1936, Håkon Meyers samling, Aa.

71. Håkon Meyer, "Friis—Scharffenberg—Trotski," *Arbeiderbladet*, November 17, 1936.

72. Walter Held, "Trotski og Hitler," *Arbeiderbladet*, November 20, 1936.

73. "Trotski-saken," *Arbeiderbladet*, November 21, 1936.

74. Johan Scharffenberg, "Asylretten og Trotski. Svar til Håkon Meyer," *Arbeiderbladet*, November 23, 1936.

75. "Trotsky-saken," *Sørlandet*, November 23, 1936.

76. Walter Held, "Trotski. Replikk til Jakob Friis," *Arbeiderbladet*, November 24, 1936.

77. Jakob Friis, "Trotski. Sluttord til Walter Held," *Arbeiderbladet*, November 28, 1936.

78. Håkon Meyer, "Jakob Friis og trotskismen," ibid.

79. Oslo Arbeidersamfund, Oslo, to Trygve Lie, Oslo, November 23, 1936, Korrespondanse 1936 folder, Korresp. 1936–37 box, Oslo Arbeidersamfund, Aa.

80. Held, Oslo, to Sedov [Paris], December 5, 1936, Folder 99, box 358, Series 231, Nicolaevsky Collection, Stan.

81. Held, Oslo, to the Oslo Workers Association's board of directors, November 30, 1936, Korrespondanse 1936 folder, Korresp. 1936–37 box, Oslo Arbeidersamfund, Aa.

82. Held, Oslo, to Sedov [Paris], December 5, 1936, Folder 99, box 358, Series 231, Nicolaevsky Collection, Stan.; Meyer, Oslo, to Krog, Schweigårdsholm, December 1, 1936, Håkon Meyers samling, Aa.

83. *Sørlandet*, December 14, 1936.

84. Helge Krog [Schweigårdsholm] to Meyer, Oslo, December 30, 1936, Håkon Meyers samling, Aa; Held, Oslo, to Trotsky [Storsand], n.d. (most likely in November 1936), doc. #1933, Folder G 137, Exile Papers, Hd; Meyer, Oslo, to Helge Krog, Schweigårdsholm, December 1, 1936, Håkon Meyers samling, Aa;

85. Helge Krog, "Trotski og arbeiderregjeringen. To artikler av Helge Krog," *Dagbladet*, December 14 and December 16, 1936.

86. Trygve Lie, note entitled "'Trotski og arbeiderregjeringen' av Helge Krog," December 15, 1936, box 1, Trotsky-saken, Ra.

87. J. L. Mowinckel, Jr., "Trotski, regjeringen og Helge Krog," *Dagbladet*, December 17, 1936.

88. Helge Krog, "Svar til Arbeiderbladet," *Dagbladet*, December 22, 1936.

89. "Trotski," *Arbeiderbladet*, December 23, 1936.

90. Martin Eide, "Den redigerende makt," www.nored.no.

91. Domsutskrift, lagmannsretten, Buskerud lagsogn, sak nr. 124/1936, December 15, 1936, box 2, Trotsky-saken, Ra.

92. Ibid.

93. "Nazigangsterne optrer frekt i lagmannsretten," *Fremtiden*, December 9, 1936. 94. "Trotskis egen forklaring grunnlag for interneringen," *Arbeiderbladet*, December 10, 1936.

95. "Resultatløst 'efter-innbrudd' gjennem Trotskis vindu," ibid.; "Nazibanden setter rekord i råskap," *Fremtiden*, December 11, 1936.

96. "Innbruddsgjengen fra Wexhal [sic] for lagmannsrett i Drammen," *Arbeiderbladet*, December 9, 1936.

97. "Trotski for lukkede døre idag," *Fremtiden*, December 11, 1936.

98. Ibid.

99. For the English translation, see L. Trotsky, *Writings, 1935–36*, 455–85.

100. Albert Wiesener, "Trotskij terrorist—men også ridder," *Aftenposten*, evening ed., December 11, 1974.

101. "Trotski som vidne i Drammen," *Arbeiderbladet*, December 11, 1936; Wiesener, ibid.

102. L. Trotsky, *Writings, 1935–36*, 455.

103. "Domsutskrift," lagmannsretten, Buskerud lagsogn, sak nr. 124/1936, December 15, 1936, box 2, Trotsky-saken, Ra.

104. "Mild dom," *Dagbladet*, December 16, 1936.

105. "Betinget dom for nazi-gangsterne ved lagmannsrett," *Arbeiderbladet*, December 15, 1936.

106. "Dommen," *Arbeiderbladet*, December 16, 1936.

107. Koht, *Rikspolitisk dagbok*, 78.

108. Pryser, *Klassen og nasjonen*, 199.

109. Sigurd Bentzon, Athens, to Norwegian Foreign Ministry, November 14, 1936, Journalnr. 17762, 1936, UDa.

110. T. Lie, *Oslo-Moskva-London*, 78.

111. Trotsky [Storsand] to Rosenthal [Paris], November 22, 1936, doc. # 9813, Folder F 113, Exile Papers, Hd.

112. Broué, *Trotsky*, 839.

113. Rosenthal, Paris, to Trotsky [Storsand], December 2, 1936, doc. #4327, Folder F 113, Exile Papers, Hd.

114. "Det søkes nytt opholdssted for Leo Trotski," *Arbeiderbladet*, December 2, 1936.

115. Note entitled "Trotski," December 9, 1936, with an added handwritten comment by HK [Halvdan Koht], December 10, 1936, Journalnr. 19100, 1936, UDa.

116. Th. L. Torall, Oslo, to Foreign Ministry, December 10, 1936, Journalnr. 19110, 1936, UDa.

117. "Trotski til Mexico," *Arbeiderbladet*, December 9, 1936.

118. Held [Oslo] to Erwin Wolf [n.p.], December 9, 1936, Walter Held folder, Aa.

119. L. Trotsky, "On the Atlantic," *Writings, 1936–37*, 39.

120. Shachtman, New York, to Puntervold, Oslo, three telegrams dated December 8, 11, and 13, doc. #15429, Folder US 275, Exile Papers, Hd.

121. T. Lie, *Oslo-Moskva-London*, 77.

122. L. Trotsky, "On the Atlantic," *Writings, 1936–1937*, 38.

123. T. Lie, *Oslo-Moskva-London*, 77–78; L. Trotsky, "On the Atlantic," ibid., 39.

124. Konstad, Oslo, to Ministry of Foreign Affairs, December 11, 1936, Journalnr. 18905, 1936, UDa.

125. Sedov, Paris, to Held [Oslo], December 11, 1936, Folder # 8, box 365, Series 231, Nicolaevsky Collection, Stan.

126. Held [Oslo] to Sedov [Paris], handwritten telegraph responses of December 11 and 13 to Shachtman's three telegrams of December 8, 11, and 13, Folder 103, box 358, ibid.

127. Meyer, Oslo, to Trotsky, Storsand, December 12, 1936, Håkon Meyers samling, Aa.

128. Held, Oslo, to Sedov [Paris], December 9, 1936, Folder 101, box 358, Series 231, Nicolaevsky Collection, Stan.

129. T. Lie, *Oslo-Moskva-London*, 77.

130. L. Trotsky, "On the Atlantic," *Writings, 1936–37*, 39; Trotsky [Storsand] to Meyer [Oslo], December 16, 1936, in L. Trotsky, *Writings, 1935–36*, 486.

131. Trotsky [Storsand] to Meyer [Oslo], December 16, 1936, in L. Trotsky, *Writings, 1935–36*, 486.

132. L. Trotsky, "On the Atlantic," *Writings, 1936–37*, 39.

133. Trotsky [Storsand] to Meyer [Oslo], December 16, 1936, in L. Trotsky, *Writings, 1935–36*, 486–87.

134. Trotsky [Storsand] to Meyer [Oslo], December 17, 1936, ibid., 488.

135. Trotsky, Coyoacan, to Held [Oslo], February 4, 1937, doc. #8510, Folder G 137, Exile Papers, Hd.

136. Trotsky [Storsand] to Synnøve Rosendahl-Jensen [Oslo], December 17, 1936, Walter Held folder, Aa.

137. Held [Oslo] to Trotsky [Storsand], December 18, 1936, doc. #1934, Folder G 137, Exile Papers, Hd.

138. Held, Oslo, to Trotsky [Storsand], December 21, 1936, doc.#1935, ibid.

139. Held and Meyer, Oslo, to Halvdan Koht, Oslo, December 23, 1936, Håkon Meyers samling, Aa.

140. L. Trotsky, "On the Atlantic," *Writings, 1936–37*, 39.

141. Sedov, Paris, to Trotsky [Storsand], December 14, 1936, doc. #4864, Folder Fam 7, Exile Papers, Hd.

142. Shachtman, New York, to Puntervold, Oslo, December 17, 1936, doc. #15430, Folder US 275, ibid.

143. Held, Oslo, to "dear friends," Paris, December 14, 1936, Folder 104, box 358, Series 231, Nicolaevsky Collection, Stan.

144. Johan Wollebæk, Stockholm, to Foreign Ministry, December 15, 1936, Journalnr. 19140, 1936, UDa.

145. Minister Jose Perez-Gil y Ortiz, Stockholm, to Minister Johan H. Wollebæk, Stockholm, December 17, 1936, translated copy in Swedish forwarded to the Norwegian Foreign Ministry, Journalnr. 19268, 1936, UDa.

146. T. Lie, *Oslo-Moskva-London*, 78.

147. L. Trotsky, "On the Atlantic," *Writings, 1936–37*, 40.

148. L. Trotsky, "In 'Socialist' Norway," ibid., 36.

149. T. Lie, *Oslo-Moskva-London*, 78.

150. Trotsky and Natalia Sedova [Storsand] to Alexis Bardin [n.p.], December 18, 1936, box 2, Trotsky-saken, Ra, copy, Norwegian translation.

151. Trotsky [Storsand] to Rosenthal [Paris], December 18, 1936, in Rosenthal, *Avocat de Trotsky*, 181–82.

152. Trotsky [Storsand] to Knudsen [Hønefoss], December 18, 1936, box 2, Trotsky-saken, Ra, copy, Norwegian translation.

153. Trotsky, Coyoacan, to Knudsen [Hønefoss], January 20, 1937, doc. #8696, Folder N 197, Exile Papers, Hd.

154. Trotsky [Storsand] to Lev Sedov [Paris], December 18, 1936, box 2, Trotsky-saken, Ra, copy, Norwegian translation.

155. Harald Halvorsen d.y., taped interview with Aagot Sæthre, November 7, 1992; Bernhard Hjelmervik, Skånsvik, to "lensmanen i Hurum," August 29, 1984, Harald Halvorsen d.y. collection, Sundby.

156. Laila Strand, "Jeg var Trotskys husholderske," *Drammens Tidende, Buskerud Blad,* July 12, 1985.

157. Harald Halvorsen d.y., taped interview with Aagot Sæthre, November 7, 1992; Tine Faltin, "Revolusjonsheltens norske fengsel," *Dagbladet,* July 22, 1995.

158. Trygve Lie, Oslo, to Hagbart Waage, Oslo, December 19, 1936, box 3, Trotsky-saken, Ra.

159. Norway, Justis- og Politidepartementet, St. med. nr. 19, Stortingsforhandlinger 1937, annen del b, February 18, 1937, 5–6.

160. Harald Halvorsen d.y., taped interview with Aagot Sæthre, November 7, 1992.

161. Author interview with Harald Halvorsen II, Sundby, June 16, 1999.

162. Laila Strand, "Jeg var Trotskys husholderske," *Drammens Tidende, Buskerud Blad,* July 12, 1985.

163. Author interview with Harald Halvorsen II, Sundby, June 16, 1999.

164. Rosenthal, Paris, to Trotsky [Storsand], December 18, 1936, doc. #4330, Folder F113, Exile Papers, Hd; Held [Oslo] to Trotsky [Storsand], December 21, 1936, doc. #1935, Folder G 137, Exile Papers, Hd.

165. Held [Oslo] to Trotsky [Storsand], December 21, 1936, ibid.; Trotsky, Storsand, to Sedov, addressed as Yvonne Carillon [Paris], December 17, 1936, doc. #10187, Folder Fam 3, ibid.

166. Meyer [Oslo] to Friedrich Adler, Brussels, December 22, 1936, Håkon Meyers samling, Aa.

167. Telegram from Held, Oslo, to Shachtman [New York], December 22, 1936, doc. #6430, Folder G 137, Exile Papers, Hd; Adler, Brussels, to Meyer, Oslo, January 7, 1937, Håkon Meyers samling, Aa.

168. "Trotski avreist til Mexico," *Arbeiderbladet,* December 23, 1936.

169. "Oslo-journalist bryter taushetsløfte til utenriksdepartementet," *Fremtiden,* December 24, 1936.

170. Meyer, *Bak Moskva Prosessene,* 49.

171. Meyer and Held, Oslo, to Koht, Oslo, December 23, 1936, with a copy from Meyer to Trygve Lie, same date, Håkon Meyers samling, Aa.

172. Sedov [Paris] to Trotsky and Natalia Sedova [Coyoacan], February 1, 1937, doc. #4871, Folder Fam 7, Exile Papers, Hd.

173. Rosenthal, Oslo, to Trotsky [n.p.], December 28, 1936, doc. #4332, Folder F 113, ibid.

174. Gabrielsen, *Martin Tranmæl ser tilbake,* 132–33.

175. Meyer and Held, Oslo, to Koht, Oslo, December 23, 1936, with a copy from Meyer to Trygve Lie, same date, Håkon Meyers samling, Aa.

176. Unknown official, Justice Department's Police Office, Oslo, to Meyer [Oslo], n.d., box 3, Trotsky-saken, Ra.

177. "Trotski avreist til Mexico," *Arbeiderbladet,* December 23, 1936.

178. "Utvisningen," *Dagbladet,* December 23, 1936.

179. "Farvel," *Tidens Tegn,* December 23, 1936.

180. "Trotski," *Arbeiderbladet,* December 23, 1936.

181. Meyer, Oslo, to Tranmæl, Oslo, December 24, 1936, Håkon Meyers samling, Aa.

182. Tranmæl, Oslo, to Meyer, Oslo, December 28, 1936, ibid.

183. "Trotsky til Mexico," *Sørlandet,"* December 23, 1936.

184. Confidential message from Trygve Lie, cosigned Jørgen Scheel, to the Norwegian legation, Stockholm, December 21, 1936, Journalnr. 19386, 1936, UDa.

185. Wollebæk, Stockholm, confidential report to the Foreign Ministry, December 22, 1936, Journalnr. 19583, 1936, UDa.

186. Koht, confidential message to the Norwegian legation, Stockholm, December 22, 1936, Journalnr. 19386, 1936, UDa. The message was phoned to Wollebæk on the next day.

187. Wollebæk, Stockholm, to Foreign Ministry, Oslo, December 23, 1936, Journalnr. 19619, 1936, UDa.

188. Dr. Jose Perez-Gil y Ortiz, Stockholm, to Wollebæk, Stockholm, December 25, 1936, Journalnr. 19619, 1936, UDa.

189. Koht, Oslo, to Trygve Lie, Oslo, December 31, 1936, Journalnr. 19926, 1936, UDa.

190. Hagbart Waage, Oslo, to Trygve Lie, Oslo, January 4, 1936 [sic, 1937], Journalnr. 00275, 1937, UDa.

191. "Trotski til Mexico 9. januar," *Arbeiderbladet*, January 4, 1937.

192. Jonas Lie, "Rapport fra statspolitifullmektig Jonas Lie i anledning av *ledsagelse av Leo Trotsky og frue fra Norge til Mexico*, ifølge Justisministerens ordre," January 10, 1937, box 2, Trotsky-saken, Ra. Hereafter cited as "Rapport."

193. L. Trotsky, "On the Atlantic," *Writings, 1936–37*, 40–41.

194. Ibid., 85.

195. Jonas Lie, "Rapport," January 10, 1937, box 2, Trotsky-saken, Ra.

196. J. Lie, *I "fred" og ufred*, 145–46.

197. Jonas Lie, "Rapport," January 10, 1937, box 2, Trotsky-saken, Ra.

198. L. Trotsky, *Writings, 1936–37*, 94.

199. Ibid., 85.

200. Jonas Lie, "Rapport," January 10, 1937, box 2, Trotsky-saken, Ra.

201. J. Lie, *I "fred" og ufred*, illustration opposite p. 152.

202. Jonas Lie, "Rapport," January 10, 1937, box 2, Trotsky-saken, Ra; Jonas Lie, ibid., 147–148.

203. L. Trotsky, *Writings, 1936–37*, 56.

204. Trotsky [Coyoacan] to Held [Oslo], May 21, 1937, doc. #8517, Folder G 137, Exile Papers, Hd.

205. Trotsky, Coyoacan, to the editors of *Oktober*, December 19, 1937, doc. #7945–4, Folder N 196, ibid.

206. L. Trotsky, *Writings, 1936–37*, 56.

207. Jonas Lie, "Rapport," January 10, 1937, box 2, Trotsky-saken, Ra; L. Trotsky, *Writings, 1936–37*, 85–86.

208. Jonas Lie, ibid.

209. L. Trotsky, *Writings, 1936–37*, 75.

210. Jonas Lie, "Rapport," January 10, 1937, box 2, Trotsky-saken, Ra.

211. Ibid.

212. Konstad, Oslo, to Trotsky, Mexico City, January 15, 1937, doc. #3650, Folder N 197, Exile Papers, Hd.

213. Waage, Oslo, to the Justice Department, February 17, 1937, box 3, Trotsky-saken, Ra.

214. Justis- og Politidepartementet, St. med. nr. 19, Stortingsforhandlinger 1937, annen del b., February 18, 1937, 5–6.

215. Jonas Lie, "Rapport," January 10, 1937, box 2, Trotsky-saken, Ra.

216. L. Trotsky, *Writings, 1936–37*, 85–86.

217. Frank L. Kluckhorn, "Trotsky in Mexico Asks Trial by Impartial Body," *New York Times*, January 10, 1937.

218. Wilhelm Morgenstierne, Washington, D.C., to Foreign Ministry, January 12, 1937, Journalnr. 00615, 1937, UDa.

219. "Trotski innleder ankomsten til Mexico med forbitret angrep på den norske regjering," *Tidens Tegn*, January 11, 1937.

220. *Sørlandet*, January 11, 1936.

221. "Takk for vertskapet," *Arbeiderbladet*, January 11, 1937.

222. Held, Oslo, to Tranmæl, Oslo, January 12, 1937, Håkon Meyers samling, Aa.

223. Helge Krog, "Skamstøtten," *Dagbladet*, January 26, 1937.

224. Held, Oslo, to Sedov [Paris], February 13, 1937, Folder 114, box 358, Series 231, Nicolaevsky Collection, Stan.

225. Held [Oslo] to Krog [n.p.], March 18, 1937, Walter Held folder, Aa.

226. Trotsky, Coyoacan, to Meyer [Oslo], August 10, 1937, Håkon Meyers samling, ibid.

9: Ongoing Controversy

1. Held, Oslo, to Sedov [Paris], December 5, 1936, Folder 99, box 358, Series 231, Nicolaevsky Collection, Stan.

2. Sedov [Paris] to Held [Oslo], December 28, 1936, Folder 11, box 365, ibid.

3. Puntervold, Oslo, to Trotsky, Mexico, January 11, 1937, doc. #4202, Folder N 198, Exile Papers, Hd.

4. Christiania Bank og Kreditkasse, Oslo, to Trotsky, Mexico City, January 13, 1937, doc. #567, Folder N 196, ibid.

5. Trotsky [Coyoacan] to "Advokatverein," Oslo, n.d., doc. #7298, Folder N 198, ibid.

6. Held, Oslo, to Trotsky [Coyoacan], January 15, 1937, doc. #1938, Folder G 137, ibid.

7. Held, Oslo, to Trotsky [Coyoacan], January 16, 1937, doc. #1939, ibid.

8. Held, Oslo, to Trotsky [Coyoacan], January 18, 1937, doc. #1940, ibid.

9. Sedov, Paris, to Held [Oslo], January 19, 1937, doc. #13173, ibid.

10. Held, Oslo, to Sedov [Paris], January 23, 1937, Folder 109, box 358, Series 231, Nicolaevsky Collection, Stan.

11. Trotsky, Coyoacan, to Støylen, Oslo, February 2, 1937, doc. #10534, Folder N 137, Exile Papers, Hd; Trotsky [Coyoacan] to Held, Oslo, February 2, 1937, doc. #8508, Folder G 137, Exile Papers, Hd.

12. Trotsky, Coyoacan, to Held [Oslo], February 3, 1937, doc. #8509, Folder G 137, ibid.

13. Held, Oslo, to the Norwegian Attorneys Association's Secretariat, Oslo, February 17, 1937, German trans., Folder 36, box 375, Series 231, Nicolaevsky Collection, Stan.

14. "Voldgiftsavtale" between Michael Puntervold and Heinz Epe [Walter Held], Oslo, May 11, 1937, witnessed by Rolf Christophersen, General Secretary of the Norwegian Attorneys Association, attachment to Held, Oslo, to Trotsky [Coyoacan], May 20, 1937, doc. #1949, Folder G 137, Exile Papers, Hd.

15. Held, Oslo, to Trotsky [Coyoacan], September 4, 1937, doc. #1950, ibid.

16. Held [Oslo] to Sedov [Paris], September 30, 1937, Folder 128, box 358, Series 231, Nicolaevsky Collection, Stan.

17. Held, Oslo, to Trotsky [Coyoacan], September 4, 1937, doc. #1950, Folder G 137, Exile Papers, Hd.

18. Held, Oslo, to Trotsky [Coyoacan], October 13, 1937, doc. #1951, ibid.

19. H. J. Grundt, Birger Eriksrud, Sven Arntzen, Einar Grette, Einard Sunde, Einar Løchen, Finn H. Strøm, Fr. H. Winsnes, Finn Arnesen, "Volgiftskjennelse i Sak: Leo Trotsky mot advokat Michael Puntervold," Oslo, November 24, 1937, doc. #15752, Folder N 198, ibid.

20. Trotsky [Coyoacan] to Held [Oslo], December 19, 1937, doc. #8521, Folder G 137, ibid.

21. Ragnar Christophersen, Oslo, to Trotsky, Coyoacan, January 21, 1938, doc. #1990, Folder N 198, ibid.; Ragnar Christophersen, Oslo, to Trotsky, Coyoacan, April 4, 1938, doc. #1991, Folder N 198, ibid.

22. Joe Hansen, Coyoacan, to the law firm of Holm og Rode, Oslo, May 30, 1938, doc. #11500, ibid.

23. "Trotskis mulige skatteforhold," *Arbeiderbladet*, September 3, 1936.

24. Norderhov tax office, Hønefoss, to Puntervold, Oslo, October 14, 1936, doc. #4193, Folder N 198, Exile Papers, Hd.

25. Norderhov tax office, Hønefoss, to Puntervold, Oslo, German translation, November 12, 1936, doc. #15173, ibid.

26. Christiania Bank og Kreditkasse, Oslo, to Trotsky, Mexico City, January 20, 1937, doc. #568, Folder N 196, ibid.

27. Held, Oslo, to Trotsky [Coyoacan], January 18, 1937, doc. #1940, Folder G 137, ibid.

28. Trotsky, Coyoacan, to Held [Oslo], February 3, 1937, doc. #8509, ibid.

29. Støylen, Oslo, to Trotsky, Coyoacan, March 1, 1937, doc. #5408, Folder N 197, ibid.

30. Trotsky, Coyoacan, to Støylen, Oslo, March 19, 1937, doc. #10535, Folder N 139, ibid.

31. Støylen, Oslo, to Trotsky, Coyoacan, April 30, 1937, doc. #5409, Folder N 197, ibid.

32. Støylen, Oslo, to Trotsky, Coyoacan, October 23, 1937, doc. #5410, ibid.

33. Ibid.

34. Held, Oslo, to Trotsky [Coyoacan], October 31, 1937, doc. #1953, Folder G 137, ibid.

35. Trotsky, Coyoacan, to Held [Oslo], November 11, 1937, doc. #8520, ibid.

36. Støylen, Oslo, to Trotsky, Coyoacan, November 17, 1937, doc. #5411, Folder N 197, ibid.

37. Held, Oslo, to Trotsky [Coyoacan], November 16, 1937, doc. #1954, Folder G 137, ibid.

38. Held, Oslo, to Trotsky [Coyoacan], November 18, 1937, doc. #1955, ibid.

39. "Fantastiske 'tilståelser' i Moskva," *Arbeiderbladet*, January 25, 1937; Tucker, *Stalin in Power*, 394–96.

40. "Prosessen i Moskva," *Fremtiden*, January 26, 1937.

41. Andreas Urbye, Moscow, "Prosessen mot Pjatakov, Radek, Sokolnikov m.fl.," confidential report to the Foreign Ministry, January 26, 1937, Journalnr. 01894, 1937, UDa.

42. Volkogonov, *Trotsky*, 283. See also Service, *Trotsky*, 372.

43. "Trotski protesterer," *Arbeiderbladet*, January 25, 1937.

44. "En opdiktet konferanse," ibid.

45. Halvdan Koht, "Om politisk arbeid mot Sovjet-Samveldet av Leo Trotsky medan han var i Noreg 18. juni 1935—19. desember 1936," confidential report, n.d., UDa. The foreign minister's report, written some time during the first half of 1937, most likely in May or June, was later published in Koht, *Rikspolitisk dagbok*, 62–66.

46. Andreas Urbye, Moscow, "Pjatakovs flyvning til Oslo," to the Foreign Ministry, January 31, 1937, Journalnr. 02347, 1937, UDa.

47. "Pjatakov's underlige reise til Kjeller," *Arbeiderbladet*, January 29, 1937.

48. Koht, "Om politisk arbeid mot Sovjet-Samveldet av Leo Trotsky medan har var i Noreg 18. juni 1935—19. desember 1936," confidential report, n.d., UDa.

49. L. Trotsky, "Pyatakov's Phantom Flight to Oslo," *Writings, 1936–37*, 154–156.

50. Held, Oslo, to Sedov [Paris], January 29, 1937, Folder 111, box 358, Series 231, Nicolaevsky Collection, Stan. Knudsen's telegram is quoted in English in Preliminary Commission, 564.

51. Conquest, *Great Terror*, 182–83.

52. Trotsky [Coyoacan], to Harold Isaacs [n.p.], February 20, 1937, in L. Trotsky, *Writings, 1936–37*, 210.

53. Held, Oslo, to Sedov [Paris], Folder 117, box 358, Series 231, Nicolaevsky Collection, Stan; Bøe, "Norges Kommunistiske Parti," 49.

54. "Rettsaken i Moskva," *Arbeideren*, January 26, 1937; "Pjatakovs reise til Norge," *Arbeideren*, January 26, 1937.

55. Bøe, "Norges Kommunistiske Parti," 49.

56. Knudsen [n.p.], to Trotsky [Coyoacan], March 9, 1937, doc. #2356, Folder N 197, Exile Papers, Hd.

57. Trotsky, Coyoacan, to Held [Oslo], February 17, 1937, doc. #8511, Folder G 137, ibid.

58. Trotsky [Coyoacan] to Susan La Follette [n.p.], March 15, 1937, in L. Trotsky, *Writings, 1936–37*, 237.

59. George Novack, "Introduction," Preliminary Commission, vii.

60. Held, Oslo, to Trotsky [Coyoacan], March 9, 1937, doc. #1943, Folder G 137, Exile Papers, Hd.

61. Held, Oslo, to Sedov [Paris], March 12, 1937, Folder 117, box 358, Series 231, Nicolaevsky Collection, Stan.

62. Held, Oslo, to Wolf [n.p.], March 18, 1937, doc. #14779, Folder G 137, Exile Papers, Hd.

63. Preliminary Commission, 143; Held, Oslo, to Wolf [n.p.], March 18, 1937, doc. #14779, ibid.

64. Patenaude, *Trotsky*, 38–49; Noack, "Introduction," Preliminary Commission, vii.

65. Preliminary Commission, 143.

66. Commission of Inquiry, 181.

67. Ibid., 184–85.

68. Preliminary Commission, 211; Commission of Inquiry, 182.

69. Commission of Inquiry, 183–84.

70. Preliminary Commission, 223.

71. Trotsky [Coyoacan], telegram to the Dewey Commission [New York], Decem-

ber 13, 1937, in L. Trotsky, *Writings of Leon Trotsky, 1937–38*, 72.

72. Conquest, *Great Terror*, 152

73. Wilhelm Morgenstierne, Washington, D.C., to Foreign Ministry, December 14, 1937, Journalnr. 23295, 1937, UDa.

74. Held, Oslo, to Trotsky [Coyoacan], January 3, 1938, doc. #1957, Folder G 137, Exile Papers, Hd.

75. Sverre Opsal, note, n.d., Dagmar Loe, private collection, Oslo.

76. "Friis og asylretten," *Arbeiderbladet*, January 4, 1937.

77. Brunvand, "Redaktøren og anti-Stalinisten," 29–30.

78. Sverre Opsal, note, n.d., Dagmar Loe, private collection, Oslo.

79. Ibid.

80. Skaufjord, "Venstreopposisjonen," 55.

81. Ibid., 142–43.

82. "Går Scheflo over til kommunistpartiet igjen?" *Tidens Tegn*, January 5, 1937.

83. Scheflo, "Stalinistenes løgnpropaganda," *Sørlandet*, January 22, 1937.

84. Nini Roll Anker, Lars Berg, Sigurd Hoel, Helge Krog, Gunnar Reiss-Andersen, Axel Sandemose, Nils Collet Vogt, Arnulf Øverland [n.p.], "To the writer, Lion Feuchtwanger" [n.p.], February 1937, doc. #13751, Folder N 196, Exile Papers, Hd.

85. Held, Oslo, to Trotsky [Coyoacan], February 12, 1937, doc. #1941, Folder G 137, ibid.

86. Held, Oslo, to Sedov [Paris], February 13, 1937, Folder 114, Box 358, Series 231, Nicolaevsky Collection, Stan.

87. Held [Oslo] to Krog [n.p.], March 18, 1937, Walter Held folder, Aa.

88. Held [Oslo] to Trotsky [Coyoacan], February 22, 1937, doc. #1942, Folder G 137, Exile Papers, Hd; Knudsen [n.p.], to Trotsky [Coyoacan], March 9, [1937], doc. #2356, Folder 197, Exile Papers, Hd.

89. Held [Oslo] to Trotsky [Coyoacan], February 22, 1937, doc. #1942, Folder G 137, Exile Papers, Hd; Knudsen [n.p.], to Trotsky [Coyoacan], March 9, [1937], doc. #2356, Folder 197, Exile Papers, Hd.

90. Skaufjord, "Venstreopposisjonen," 167.

91. Knudsen [n.p.], to Trotsky [Coyoacan], March 9, 1937, doc. #2356, Folder N 197, Exile Papers, Hd.

92. John Johansen, Oslo, to Meyer, Oslo, February 27, 1937, Håkon Meyers samling, Aa.

93. Meyer, Oslo, to Oslo Arbeidersamfunds styre, Oslo, March 2, 1937, ibid.

94. Skaufjord, "Venstreopposisjonen," 104.

95. "Scheflo svarer Stalin," *Oktober*, no. 1 (April 1937).

96. Jeanette Olsen, "Vår avis," ibid.

97. Trond Hegna, "Moskvaprosessen enda en gang," *Arbeiderbladet*, May 7, 1937.

98. "En giftplante," *Arbeiderbladet*, May 12, 1937.

99. Held, Oslo, to Trotsky [Coyoacan], May 13, 1937, doc. #1948, Folder G 137, Exile Papers, Hd.

100. Scheflo, "En nødvendig redegjørelse," *Arbeiderbladet*, May 19, 1937.

101. Held, Oslo, to Trotsky [Coyoacan], May 20, 1937, doc. #1949, Folder G 137, Exile Papers, Hd.

102. Held, Oslo, to Trotsky [Coyoacan], May 24, 1937; "Ich setze mein Leben ein. Von Helge Krog." Doc. #16979, Folder N 197, ibid.

103. "Jeg innestår med mitt liv!" *Dagbladet*, May 24, 1937.

104. Meyer, "Svar til Arbeiderbladet," *Arbeiderbladet*, May 26, 1937.

105. Ibid.

106. Editorial, *Arbeiderbladet*, May 29, 1937.

107. "Oprenskningen i Sovjet," *Arbeiderbladet*, June 14, 1937.

108. Untitled editorial, *Arbeiderbladet*, June 17, 1937.

109. "P.O.U.M." *Sørlandet*, July 10, 1937.

110. Held [Oslo] to Trotsky [Coyoacan], March 2, 1937, Folder #119, Box 358, Series 231, Nicolaevsky Collection, Stan.

111. Per Monsen, "To bøker om Moskvaprosessene. Og to artikler," *Sørlandet*, July 13, 1937.

112. Trotsky [Coyoacan] to Held, Oslo, August 10, 1937, doc. #8518, Folder G 137, Exile Papers, Hd.

113. Friis. *Trotskismen.*

114. Ibid., 3.

115. Ibid., 19.

116. Ibid., 27–28.

117. Ibid., 32.

118. Skaufjord, "Venstreopposisjonen," 45, 158.

119. Pryser, *Klassen og nasjonen*, 157–158.

120. Ibid., 204–5.

121. "Arbeiderregjeringen går styrket ut av trontaledebatten," *1ste Mai*, February 22, 1937.

122. Storting debate, February 19, 1937, Norway, Kongeriket Norges Seksogåttiende Ordentlige Stortings Forhandlinger 1937, syvende del A, Stortingstidende, Forhandlinger i Stortinget, Trontale- og finansdebatt, 70–71. Hereafter cited as Stortingsforhandlinger 1937.

123. Norway, Justis- og Politidepartmentet, St. med. nr. 19, February 18, 1937, "Om Leo Trotskys opholdstillatelse, internering og reise fra landet," Stortingsforhandlinger 1937, annen del B.

124. Storting debate, February 20, 1937, Stortingsforhandlinger 1937, 162.

125. Storting debate, February 23, 1937, ibid., 203–4.

126. Storting debate, ibid., 204.

127. Held, Oslo, to Trotsky [Coyoacan], March 9, 1937, doc. #1943, Folder G 137, Exile Papers, Hd.

128. "Piatakovs flyvetur," *Sørlandet*, March 3, 1937; "Piatakovs reise," *Sørlandet*, March 8, 1937.

129. Storting debate, February 22, 1937, Stortingsforhandlinger 1937, 193.

130. Knudsen [n.p.], to Trotsky [Coyoacan], March 9, 1937, doc. #2356, Folder N 197, Exile Papers, Hd.

131. Stortingsforhandlinger 1937, sjette del B, Innstillinger og beslutninger, Innst. O. IVB. (1937), "Innstilling fra protokollkomitéen angående regjeringsprotokollenes gjennemgåelse," I. Provisoriske anordninger, 10–11.

132. Held, Oslo, to Krog [n.p.], June 10, 1937, Walter Held folder, Aa.

133. Friis, "Trotski-saken og borgerpartiene," *Arbeiderbladet*, June 15, 1937.

134. Stortingsforhandlinger 1937, Åttende del, Stortingstidende, I, Forhandlinger i Odelstinget, Moss, 384–385. Hereafter cited as Stortingsforhandlinger 1937, Forhandlinger i Odelstinget.

135. Stortingsforhandlinger 1937, Forhandlinger i Odelstinget, Maastad, 398–400.

136. Ibid., Undrum, 375; Mowinckel, 401; Hambro, 394–96.

137. Ibid., Undrum, 374–75, Hambro, 395–96.

138. Ibid., Mowinckel, 402.

139. Ibid., Lie, 387; Moss, 385.

140. Ibid., Lie, 388, 386.

141. Ibid., Johannesen, 378.

142. Ibid., Nygaardsvold, 401.

143. "Odelstinget diskuterer Trotsky-saken," *Sørlandet*, June 22, 1937.

144. Held, Oslo, to Krog [n.p.], June 10, 1937, Walter Held folder, Aa.

145. Stortingsforhandlinger 1937, Forhandlinger i Odelstinget, Knudsen, 382.

146. Ibid, Knudsen, 379–83.

147. Ibid., Vegheim, 392–93.

148. "Trotski-sakens siste akt," *Arbeiderbladet*, June 22, 1937.

149. Stortingsforhandlinger 1937, Forhandlinger i Odelstinget, Maastad, 399.

150. Ibid., Knudsen, 382.

151. Held, Oslo, to Trotsky [n.p.], December 28, 1936, doc. #1936, Folder G 137, Exile Papers, Hd.

152. Nils Kåre Dahl, "With Trotsky in Norway," 39.

153. Nils Kåre Dahl [n.p.], to Meyer, Simrishamn, Sweden, March 26, 1979, Håkon Meyers samling, Aa.

154. Andersen, *Norsk Litteraturhistorie*, 400.

155. Ibid., 399.

156. Ibid., 399–400.

157. Dahl [n.p.], to Meyer, Simrishamn, Sweden, March 26, 1979, Håkon Meyers samling, Aa.

158. It should be noted that one study on left-wing opposition within the Labor Party, Terje Skaufjord's unpublished thesis, not only refers to Hoel as the initiative taker in the establishment of *Oktober* but also as one of its writers. As his source, Skaufjord cites an oral interview with Nils Kåre Dahl on June 22, 1977. See Skaufjord, "Venstreopposisjonen," 162 and 240n127. However, although Dahl in later correspondence and writings mentions that Hoel was present when the decision was made to set up the paper, the latter is never described as the person primarily responsible for its creation. One should not exclude the possibility that Dahl, in the interview, may have sought to enhance the importance of Norwegian Trotskyism by including Hoel among its adherents. And while Hoel could have authored articles published in *Oktober* since many of its contributors wrote under assumed names, this, in my opinion, is not likely. It would have been extremely difficult to prevent Hoel's participation from becoming known in left-wing political circles during the 1930s.

159. Held, Oslo, to Trotsky [n.p.], December 28, 1936, doc. #1936, Folder G 137, Exile Papers, Hd; *Oktober*, no. 1 (April 1937).

160. *Oktober*, no. 1 (April 1937).

161. Lorenz, *Det er ingen sak å få partiet lite*, 294; Lorenz, "Jeanette Olsen."

162. Lorenz, *Arbeiderbevegelsens historie*, 1: 192; Pryser, *Klassen og nasjonen*, 203.

163. J. Olsen, *Trotsky*.

164. Rosendahl-Jensen, Oslo, to Natalia Sedova [Coyoacan], [April ? 1937], doc. #13432, Folder N 137, Exile Papers, Hd.

165. "Vår nye avis," *Oktober*, no. 1 (April 1937).

166. *Oktober*, no. 1 (January 1938); *Oktober*, no. 2 (February 1938).

167. Rosendahl-Jensen, Oslo, to Natalia Sedova [Coyoacan], [April ? 1937], doc.

#13432, Folder N 137, Exile Papers, Hd.

168. Ibid.

169. "En giftplante," *Arbeiderbladet*, May 12, 1937.

170. Held, Oslo, to Trotsky [Coyoacan], May 13, 1937, doc. #1948, Folder G 137, Exile Papers, Hd.

171. Trotsky [Coyoacan] to Held, Oslo, May 21, 1937, doc. #8517, ibid.

172. Editors of "Kotober" [sic], Oslo, to Trotsky, Coyoacan, November 6, 1937, doc. #3663, Folder N 196, ibid.

173. Trotsky, Coyoacan, to the editors of *Oktober* [Oslo], December 19, 1937, doc. #7945, ibid.

174. Skaufjord, "Venstreopposisjonen," 163–64.

175. "Interview with Nils Kåre Dahl in London on 27th December 1983," Aa.

176. Skaufjord, "Venstreopposisjonen," 173.

177. Meyer, "Svar til 'Arbeiderbladet,'" *Arbeiderbladet*, May 26, 1937.

178. Pryser, *Klassen og nasjonen*, 61; "OSLO-SEIEREN," *Arbeiderbladet*, October 10, 1937.

179. Pryser, *Klassen og nasjonen*, 63.

180. "Abonner på OKTOBER," *Oktober*, no. 6 (October 1937).

181. "Arbeiderbladet og sannheten," ibid.

182. Pryser, *Klassen og nasjonen*, 194.

183. Held, Oslo, to Trotsky [Coyoacan], November 30, 1937, doc. #1956, Folder G 137, Exile Papers, Hd.

184. Pryser, *Klassen og nasjonen*, 194.

185. Trotsky, "Det er på tide å gå til en internasjonal kamp mot Stalinismen;" "Arbeiderregjeringen tramper på fagkongressens beslutninger;" *Oktober*, no. 1 (January 1938).

186. Held, Oslo, to Trotsky [Coyoacan], March 8, 1938, doc. #1959, Folder G 137, Exile Papers, Hd.

187. Alexander, *International Trotskyism*, 8.

188. Patenaude, *Trotsky*, 204; Volkogonov, *Trotsky*, 400–401.

189. Alexander, *International Trotskyism*, 270.

190. Volkogonov, *Trotsky*, 403.

191. Held, Oslo, to Krog [n.p.], November 29, 1938, Helge Krogs samling, MS folio 3956: 8a, HA-NB.

192. *Oktober*, no. 6 (October 1937); *Oktober*, no. 2 (February 1938).

193. Dahl [n.p.], to Meyer, Simrishamn, Sweden, March 26, 1979, Håkon Meyers samling, Aa.

194. Skaufjord, "Venstreopposisjonen," 239n118.

Comprehensive Assessment

1. Kersaudy, *Norway 1940*, 10–11.

2. H. Lie, *Loftsrydding*, 274.

3. Stortingsforhandlinger 1937, Forhandlinger i Odelstinget, Knudsen, 382.

4. Roberts, "Maxim Litvinov," 2: 354.

5. "Jeg innestår med mitt liv," *Dagbladet*, May 24, 1937.

6. H. Lie, *Martin Tranmæl*, 2: 163.

Epilogue

1. Meyer, Oslo, to Trotsky, Coyoacan, February 21, 1938, doc. #3076, Folder N 196, Exile Papers, Hd.

2. Scheflo, "På nært hold," 44.

3. Dagmar Loe, interview with the author, Oslo, June 18, 1999.

4. Vold, *Helge Krog*, 268–69.

5. Nilsen, "Myten om kulturradikalismen," 18.

6. Vold, *Helge Krog*, 383.

7. Dagmar Loe, interview with the author, Oslo, June 21, 1999; Scheflo, "På nært hold," 45–46.

8. Sverre Opsal, "Hundre år siden Olav Scheflo ble født," *Sørlandet*, September 7, 1983.

9. Aagesen, "Fagopposisjonen av 1940," 426.

10. Sørensen, "Håkon Meyer," 268.

11. Meyer, Ila landsfengsel, Bærum, to Nygaardsvold, Oslo, June 1, 1945, Korrespondanse 1945, Box 1–0001, Serie 1-Diverse, Johan Nygaardsvolds arkiv, Aa.

12. Norway, Justis- og politidepartementet, *Om landssvikoppgjøret*, 127.

13. Rougthvedt, *Med penn og pistol*, 156.

14. Ibid., 353; Rødder, "Min ære er troskap," 222.

15. "Manuskripter og utskrifter fra erindringer og dagbøker," Box 0005, Serie 1—Diverse, Johan Nygaardsvolds arkiv, Aa.

16. Koht, *Frå skanse til skanse*, 47.

17. Gerhardsen, *I medgang og motgang*, 169.

18. Haugland, *Dagbok frå Kongens råd*, 216.

19. Feferman, *Politics, Logic and Love*, 362.

20. Hjørdis Knudsen, Marseilles, to Konrad and Hilda Knudsen [n.p.], August 13, 1937, German translation forwarded by Held to Trotsky, n.d., doc. #14874, Folder N 197, Exile Papers, Hd.

21. Broué, *Trotsky*, 875.

22. Hjørdis Knudsen, Marseilles, to Konrad and Hilda Knudsen [n.p.], August 13, 1937, German translation forwarded by Held to Trotsky, n.d., doc. #14874, Folder N 197, Exile Papers, Hd.

23. Hjørdis Knudsen, Hønefoss, to Trotsky [Coyoacan], June 20, 1938, doc. #2358, ibid.

24. Trotsky, Coyoacan, to Hjørdis Knudsen [n.p.], October 2, 1937, doc. #8691, ibid.

25. Trotsky, Coyoacan, to Konrad Knudsen [n.p.], October 2, 1937, doc. #8697, ibid.

26. "Ervin Wolf, Trotskis sekretær på Hønefoss, kidnapped av stalinistene i Spania," *Oktober*, no. 6 (October 1937).

27. Held, Oslo, to Trotsky [Coyoacan], October 13, 1937, doc. #1951, Folder G 137, Exile Papers, Hd.

28. "Hvad gjorde dr. Wolf, Trotskis sekretær, i Valencia?" *Arbeideren*, October 13, 1937.

29. Hilda Knudsen, Hønefoss, to Trotsky and Natalia Sedova [Coyoacan], May 1, 1937, doc. #2355, Folder N 197, Exile Papers, Hd.

30. Hjørdis Knudsen, Hønefoss, to Natalia Sedova [Coyoacan], July 2, 1938, doc. #13443, ibid.

31. Held, Oslo, to Trotsky [n.p.], December 28, 1936, doc. #1936, Folder G 137, ibid.

32. Held, Oslo, to Trotsky [Coyoacan], January 15, 1937, doc. #1938, ibid.

33. Trotsky, Coyoacan, to Held [Oslo], February 4, 1937, doc. #8510, ibid.

34. Held, Oslo, to Trotsky [Coyoacan], September 4, 1937, doc. #1950, ibid.

35. Synnøve Rosendahl-Jensen, Oslo, to Natalia Sedova [Coyoacan], n.d. (1937), doc. #13432, Folder N 137, ibid.

36. Trotsky, Coyoacan, to Held [Oslo], January 9, 1939, doc. #8523, Folder G 137, ibid.

37. Held, Oslo, to Trotsky [Coyoacan], September 1, 1939, doc. #1963, ibid.

38. Held, Stockholm, to Trotsky's staff [Coyoacan], July 1, 1940, doc. #1964, ibid.

39. "Walter Held File: VI. Held's statement."

40. "Heinz Epe forhørt av selveste Beria," *Arbeiderbladet*, October 10, 1957.

41. N. K. Dahl, "With Trotsky in Norway," 42.

Bibliography

I. Archives

Foreign Ministry Archive (Utenriksdepartementets arkiv), Oslo
  Journaler 1929, 1931, 1935, 1936, 1937
Hoover Institution, Stanford University
  Albert Glotzer Papers
  Anita Feferman Collection
  Boris I. Nicolaevsky Collection
Houghton Library, Harvard College Library, Harvard University
  Leon Trotsky Exile Papers
Labor Movement's Archive and Library (Arbeiderbevegelsens arkiv og bibliotek), Oslo
  "Dagsorden for Det norske Arbeiderpartis 30de ordinære landsmøte"
  Håkon Meyers samling
  Johan Nygaardsvolds arkiv
  Mot Dags arkiv
  Nils Kåre Dahls samling
  Oslo Arbeidersamfunds arkiv
  Walter Held-mappen
National Archives (Riksarkivet), Oslo
  Trotsky-saken, Politikontoret, Justisdepartementets arkiv
National Library (Nasjonalbiblioteket), Oslo
  Helge Krogs samling, Håndskriftsavdelingen
  Torsten Bygdal: "Trotskij i Norge." Avskrift av et program i Sveriges Radio,
    March 16, 1967, Håndskriftsavdelingen

II. Published Documents and Official Publications

Commission of Inquiry into the Charges Made against Leon Trotsky in the Moscow Trials.
  *Not Guilty: Report of the Commission of Inquiry into the Charges Made against Leon
  Trotsky in the Moscow Trials.* London: Martin Secker and Warburg, 1938.
Det norske Arbeiderparti: *Protokoll over forhandlingene på det 30. Ordinære landsmøte 22–
  24 mai 1936.* Edited by Alfred Aakermann. Oslo: Arbeidernes Aktietrykkeri, 1937.
Holtsmark, Sven G., ed. *Norge og Sovjetunion 1917–1955. En utenrikspolitisk Dokumentas-
  jon.* Oslo: J. W. Cappelens forlag, 1995.
Koht, Halvdan. *Rikspolitisk dagbok 1933–1940.* Edited by Steinar Kjærheim. Oslo: Tiden
  norsk Forlag,1985.
Norway, Justis- og Politidepartementet. *Om landssvikoppgjøret.* Oslo: Justis- og politidepartementet, 1962.

Norway, Justis- og Politidepartementet, St. med. nr. 19 (1937): "Om Leo Trotskys opholdstillatelse, internering og reise fra landet."

Norway, Kongeriket Norges Fireogåttiende Stortingsforhandlinger 1935, syvende del B, Stortingstidende, Forhandlinger i Stortinget.

Norway, Kongeriket Norges Otteogsyttiende Ordentlige Stortingsforhandlinger 1929, syvende del A, Stortingstidende, Forhandlinger i Stortinget.

Norway, Kongeriket Norges Seksogåttienede Ordentlige Stortingsforhandlinger 1937, annen del b, February 18, 1937.

Norway, Kongeriket Norges Seksogåttiende Ordentlige Stortingsforhandlinger 1937, syvende del A, Stortingstidende, Forhandlinger i Stortinget, Trontale- og finansdebatt.

Norway, Kongeriket Norges Seksogåttiende Ordentlige Stortingsforhandlinger 1937, syvende del B, Stortingstidende, Forhandlinger i Stortinget, bind B.

Norway, Kongeriket Norges Seksogåttiende Ordentlige Stortingsforhandlinger 1937, Sjette del b., Innstillinger og beslutninger, Innst. O.IV.B. (1937).

Norway, Kongeriket Norges Seksogåttiende Ordentlige Stortingsforhandlinger 1937, åttende del, Stortingstidende, I, Forhandlinger i Odelstinget.

Norway, Statistisk sentralbyrå, Utenrikshandel, tabell 18.11, "Innførsel og utførsel, etter viktige land." http://www.ss.no/emner/historisk_statistikk/tabeller/18-18-11.txt

Preliminary Commission of Inquiry, Commission of Inquiry into the Charges Made against Leon Trotsky in the Moscow Trials. *The Case of Leon Trotsky: Report of Hearings on the Charges Made against Him in the Moscow Trials.* New York: Merit Publishers, 1968.

Trotsky, Leon. *Trotsky's Diary in Exile, 1935.* 2nd ed. Translated by Elena Zarudnaya. Cambridge, MA: Harvard University Press, 1976.

———. *Writings of Leon Trotsky, 1932.* Edited by George Breitman and Sarah Lovell. New York: 1973.

———. *Writings of Leon Trotsky, 1933–34.* Edited by George Breitman and Bev Scott. New York: Pathfinder Press, 1972.

———. *Writings of Leon Trotsky, 1934–35.* Edited by George Breitman and Bev Scott. New York: Pathfinder Press, 1970.

———. *Writings of Leon Trotsky, 1935–36.* 2nd ed. Edited by Naomi Allen and George Breitman. New York: Pathfinder Press, 1977.

———. *Writings of Leon Trotsky, 1936–37.* 2nd ed. Edited by Naomi Allen and George Breitman. New York: Pathfinder Press, 1978.

———. *Writings of Leon Trotsky: Supplement, 1929–33.* Edited by George Breitman. New York: Pathfinder Press, 1979.

———. *Writings of Leon Trotsky: Supplement, 1934–40.* Edited by George Breitman. New York: Pathfinder Press, 1979.

III. Oral Interviews

Harald Halvorsen II
Edith Johansen
Haakon Lie
Dagmar Loe
Aagot Sæthre (tape recording)

IV. Newspapers

ABC
Adresseavisen
Aftenposten
Arbeiderbladet
Arbeideren
Arbeidet
Dagbladet
Drammens Tidende, Buskerud Blad
Fremtiden
Fritt Folk
1ste Mai
Middagsavisen
Morgenbladet
Nasjonal Samling
Nationen
New York Times
Norges Handels- & Sjøfartstidende
Oktober
Oslo Aftenavis
Sørlandet
Tidens Tegn
Tønsbergs Blad
Vestopland
Washington Post
Østlendingen

V. Theses

Bøe, Jan Bjarne. "Norges Kommunistiske Parti 1932–1939. En studie i partiets ideologiske og praktisk-politiske reaksjon på fascismen." Hovedfagsoppgave i historie, University of Bergen, Spring 1972.

Eriksen, Are. "Leo Trotskijs internering og deportasjon." Særoppgave i historie grunnfag, University of Oslo, Spring 1978.

Hansen, Erling. "NKP og regjeringen 1935–1936. En studie av holdningen til statsmakten, regjeringen og den dertil knyttede taktikk." Hovedfagsoppgave i historie, University of Oslo, Spring 1976.

Ihle, Øyvind. "Den norske arbeiderbevegelse og Moskvaprosessene." Hovedfagsoppgave i historie, University of Oslo, Fall 1964.

Larsen, Lars A. Døvle. "'En uforbederlig optimist.' *Social-Demokraten*s rikspolitiske linje i Olav Scheflos redaktørtid 1918–1921." Hovedfagsoppgave i historie, University of Oslo, Fall 1996.

Norrøne, Odd Sverre. "Arbeiderpartiet og Stortingsvalget i 1936." Hovedfagsoppgave i historie, University of Oslo, Spring 1978.

Skaufjord, Terje. "Venstreopposisjonen i Det norske Arbeiderparti 1933–1940."

Hovedfagsoppgave i historie, University of Oslo, Fall 1977.

Strandberg, Roar. "Fra gjest til fange. Leo Trotskijs opphold i Norge 1935-36." Hovedfagsoppgave i historie, University of Oslo, Fall 1970.

VI. Books and Articles

Aagesen, Knut. "Fagopposisjonen av 1940." In *1940—Fra nøytral til okkupert*, edited by Helge Paulsen. Studier i norsk samtidshistorie series. Oslo: Universitetsforlaget, 1969.

Alexander, Robert J. *International Trotskyism, 1925-1985: A Documented Analysis of the Movement*. Durham, NC: Duke University Press, 1991.

Andersen, Per Thomas. *Norsk Litteraturhistorie*. Oslo: Universitetsforlaget, 2001.

Berntsen, Harald. *I malstrømmen. Johan Nygaardsvold 1879-1952*. Oslo: Aschehoug, 1991.

Bille Larsen, Steen. *Mod strømmen. Den kommunistiske "højre" og "venstre" opposition i 30-ernes Danmark*. Copenhagen: Selskabet til forskning i arbejderbevægelsens historie, 1986.

Bjørgum, Jorunn. "En kommentar til Åsmund Egge." *Historisk Tidsskrift* (Norway) 83, no. 2 (2004).

Boman-Larsen, Tor. *Roald Amundsen. En biografi*. Oslo: J. W. Cappelens forlag, 1995.

Brouckere, Louis de. "De politiske flyktninger og rettighetene deres." *Kamp og kultur* no. 8, October 1936. Reprinted in *Bak Moskva Prosessene*, edited by Håkon Meyer, 29-32. Oslo: Johan Grundt Tanum, 1937.

Broué, Pierre. *Trotsky*. Paris: Fayard, 1988.

Brunvand, Olav. "Redaktøren og anti-Stalinisten." In *Olav Scheflo som politiker og mennsekse*, edited by Inge Scheflo. Oslo: Tiden norsk Forlag, 1974.

Bull, Edvard. *Arbeiderklassen i norsk historie*. 2nd ed. Oslo: Tiden norsk Forlag, 1948.

———. "Olav Scheflo." *Norsk biografisk leksikon*. Vol. 12. Oslo: Aschehoug, 1954.

Bull, Trygve. *Mot Dag og Erling Falk*. 3rd ed. Oslo: Cappelen, 1968.

Colton, Joel. *Leon Blum: Humanist in Politics*. New York: Alfred A. Knopf, 1966.

Conquest, Robert. *The Great Terror: A Reassessment*. New York: Oxford University Press, 1990.

Dahl, Hans Fredrik. *Norge mellom krigene. Det norske samfunnet i krise og konflikt, 1918-1940*. Oslo: Pax forlag, 1971.

Dahl, Nils Kåre. "With Trotsky in Norway." *Revolutionary History* 2, no. 2 (Summer 1989).

Danielsen, Egil. *Norge-Sovjetunionen. Norges utenrikspolitikk overfor Sovjetunionen, 1917-1940*. Oslo: Universitetsforlaget, 1964.

Deutscher, Isaac. *The Prophet Outcast: Trotsky, 1929-1940*. New York: Vintage Russian Library, 1965.

———. *The Prophet Unarmed: Trotsky, 1921-1929*. New York: Vintage Books, 1965.

Egge, Åsmund. "Hvorfor ble Arbeiderpartiet splittet i 1923?" *Historisk Tidsskrift* (Norway) 82, no. 3 (2003).

———. *Kirov-gåten. Mordet som utløste Stalins terror*. Oslo: Unipub, 2009.

———. *Komintern og krisen i Det norske Arbeiderparti*. Oslo: Universitetsforlaget, 1995.

———. "Tilsvar til Jorunn Bjørgum og Finn Olstad." *Historisk Tidsskrift* (Norway) 2 (2004).

Eide, Martin. "Den redigerende makt." www.nored.no.

Emberland, Terje, and Bernt Rougthvedt. *Det ariske idol. Forfatteren, eventyreren og nazisten Per Imerslund*. Oslo: Aschehoug, 2004.

Feferman, Anita Burdman. *Politics, Logic and Love: The Life of Jean van Heijenoort*. Boston: Jones & Bartlett, 1993.

Friis, Jakob. *Trotskismen. En giftplante*. Oslo: Internasjonalt Arbeiderforlag, 1937.

Gabrielsen, Bjørn. *Martin Tranmæl ser tilbake*. Oslo: Tiden norsk Forlag, 1959.

Gerhardsen, Einar: *I medgang og motgang. Erindringer 1955–65*. Oslo: Tiden norsk Forlag, 1972.

Gilberg, Trond. *The Soviet Communist Party and Scandinavian Communism: The Norwegian Case*. Oslo: Universitetsforlaget, 1973.

Glotzer, Albert. *Trotsky: Memoir and Critique*. Buffalo, NY: Prometheus Books, 1989.

Haffner, Vilhelm, ed. *Stortinget og statsrådet 1915–1945*. Vol. 1, *Biografier*. Oslo: Stortinget, 1949.

Haugland, Jens. *Dagbok frå Kongens råd*. Oslo: Det norske Samlaget, 1986.

Hirsti, Reidar. *Gubben. Johan Nygaardsvold—mannen og epoken*. Oslo: Gyldendal norsk Forlag, 1982.

Høidal, Oddvar K. "Hjort, Quisling, and Nasjonal Samling's Disintegration." *Scandinavian Studies* 4 (1975).

———. *Quisling. En studie i landssvik*. 2nd ed. Oslo: 2002.

———. *Quisling: A Study in Treason*. Oslo: Norwegian University Press, 1989. Distributed worldwide outside of Scandinavia by Oxford University Press.

———. *Trotskij i Norge. Et sår som aldri gror*. Oslo: Spartacus forlag, 2009.

———. "The Unwelcome Exile. Leon Trotsky's Failure to Receive Asylum in Norway, 1929." *Scandinavian Studies* 52, no. 1 (1980): 32–45.

Kan, Alexander. "Les petites pays dans la vision historique et politique de Trotsky." *Cahiers Leon Trotsky*, no. 48 (July 1992).

Keilhau, Wilhelm. *I vår egen tid*. Vol. 11 of *Det norske folks liv og historie*. Oslo: Aschehoug, 1938.

Kersaudy, François. *Norway 1940*. New York: St. Martin's Press, 1987.

Knudsen, Harald Franklin. *Jeg var Quislings sekretær*. Copenhagen: self published, 1951.

Koht, Halvdan. *Frå skanse til skanse. Minne frå krigsmånadene i Noreg*. Oslo: Tiden, 1947.

Krog, Helge. *Litteratur, kristendom, politikk*. Oslo: Aschehoug, 1947.

———. *Meninger om religion og politikk*. 2nd ed. Edited by Hans Heiberg. Oslo: Aschehoug, 1971.

Lahlum, Hans Olav. *Haakon Lie. Historien, mytene og mennesket*. Oslo: Cappelen Damm, 2009.

Laqueur, Walter. *Stalin: The Glasnost Revelations*. London: Unwin Hyman, 1990.

Lie, Haakon. *Loftsrydding*. Oslo: Tiden, 1980.

———. *Martin Tranmæl*. Vol. 1: *Et bål av vilje*. Oslo: Tiden norsk Forlag, 1988. Vol. 2: *Veiviseren*. Oslo: Tiden norsk Forlag, 1991.

Lie, Jonas. *I "fred" og ufred*. Oslo: Steenske forlag, 1940.

Lie, Trygve. *Oslo-Moskva-London*. Oslo: Tiden norsk Forlag, 1968.

Lorenz, Einhart. *Arbeiderbevegelsens historie. En innføring. Norsk sosialisme i internasjonalt perspektiv*. Vol. 1: *1789–1930*. Oslo: Pax forlag, 1972. Vol. 2: *1930–1973*. Oslo: Pax forlag, 1974.

———. *Det er ingen sak å få partiet lite. NKP 1923–1931*. Oslo: Pax forlag, 1983.

———. "Jeanette Olsen." www.leksikon.org/art.php?n=1948.

———, ed. "Nygaardsvold-regjeringen." *Tidsskrift for arbeiderbevegelsens historie* 1 (1986).

———. "'Vår kamerat i Oslo.' Om Heinz Epe / Walter Held og hans bidrag til å få Trotskij til

Norge." *Tidsskrift for arbeiderbevegelsens historie* 11, no. 1 (1986).

———. "Willy Brandt i Norge." *Arbeiderhistorie 1987. Årbok for arbeiderbevegelsens Arkiv og Bibliotek*. Oslo: Arbeiderbevegelsens Arkiv og Bibliotek, 1987.

———. *Willy Brandt in Norwegen. Die Jahre des Exils 1933 bis 1940*. Kiel: Neuer Malik Verlag, 1989.

———. "Willy Brandt, regjeringen Nygaardsvold og bruddet med Erling Falk." *Tidsskrift for arbeiderbevegelsens historie* 10, no. 2 (1985).

Maurseth, Per. *Gjennom kriser til makt, 1920–1935*. Vol. 3 of *Arbeiderbevegelsens historie i Norge*, edited by Arne Kokkvoll and Jakob Sverdrup. Oslo: Tiden norsk Forlag, 1987.

———. "Hva betydde regjeringsskiftet i 1935 for utviklingen av demokratiet i Norge?" *Tidsskrift for arbeiderbevegelsens historie* 11, no. 1 (1986).

Meyer, Håkon, ed. *Bak Moskva Prosessene: Artikler av norske og utenlandske sosialister*. Oslo: Johan Grundt Tanum, 1937.

———. "Ved Leo Trotskys avreise." In *Bak Moskva Prosessene*, edited by Håkon Meyer. Oslo: Johan Grundt Tanum, 1937.

Muste, Abraham John. "My Experience in the Labor and Radical Struggles of the Thirties." In *As We Saw the Thirties: Essays on Social and Political Movements of a Decade*, edited by Rita James Simon. Urbana: University of Illinois Press, 1967.

Nilsen, Håvard Friis. "Myten om kulturradikalismen." *Prosa* 6, no. 6 (2011).

Norby, Trond, ed. *Storting og regjering, 1945–1985*. Oslo: Kunnskapsforlaget, 1985.

Olsen, Bjørn Gunnar. *Tranmæl og hans menn*. Oslo: Aschehoug, 1991.

Olsen, Jeanette. *Trotski. Arbeiderklassens fiende?* Oslo: privately published, 1936.

Olstad, Finn: "Tradisjon og fornyelse. Tilsvar til Åsmund Egge." *Historisk Tidsskrift* (Norway) 83, no. 2 (2004).

Patenaude, Bertrand M. *Trotsky: Downfall of a Revolutionary*. New York: HarperCollins, 2009.

Payne, Robert. *The Life and Death of Trotsky*. New York: McGraw-Hill, 1977.

Payne, Stanley. *The Spanish Revolution: A Study of the Social and Political Tension That Culminated in the Civil War in Spain*. Revolutions in the Modern World Series, edited by Jack P. Green (New York: W. W. Norton, 1970.

Pryser, Tore. *Klassen og nasjonen, 1935–1946*. Vol. 4 of *Arbeiderbevegelsens historie i Norge*, edited by Arne Kokkvoll and Jakob Sverdrup. Oslo: Tiden norsk Forlag, 1988.

Reed, Dale, and Michael Jacobson. "Trotsky Papers at the Hoover Institution. One Chapter of an Archival Mystery Story." *American Historical Review* 92, no. 2 (April 1987).

Roberts, Henry L. "Maxim Litvinov." In *The Diplomats, 1919–1939*, edited by Gordon A. Craig and Felix Gilbert. Vol. 2: *The Thirties*. New York: Atheneum, 1965.

Rosenthal, Gerard. *Avocat de Trotsky*. Paris: R. Laffont, 1975.

Rougthvedt, Bernt. *Med penn og pistol. En biografi om politiminister Jonas Lie*. Oslo: Cappelen Damm, 2010.

Rødder, Sverre. *"Min ære er troskap." Om politiminister Jonas Lie*. Oslo: Aschehoug, 1990.

Scheflo, Inge, ed. *Olav Scheflo som politiker og menneske*. Oslo: Tiden norsk Forlag,1974.

———. "På nært hold." In *Olav Scheflo som politiker og menneske*, edited by Inge Scheflo. Oslo: Tiden norsk Forlag, 1974.

Segal, Ronald. *Leon Trotsky: A Biography*. New York: Pantheon Books, 1979.

Serge, Victor, and Natalia Sedova Trotsky. *The Life and Death of Leon Trotsky*. Translated by Arnold J. Pomerans. London: Wildwood House, 1975.

Service, Robert. *Stalin: A Biography*. Cambridge, MA: Harvard University Press, 2005.

———. *Trotsky: A Biography*. Cambridge, MA: Harvard University Press, 2009.

Shirer, William L. *The Collapse of the Third Republic: An Inquiry into the Fall of France in 1940*. New York: Simon and Schuster, 1969.

Sørensen, Øystein. "Håkon Meyer." In *Norsk krigshistorisk leksikon*, edited by H. F. Dahl et al. Oslo: J. W. Cappelens forlag, 1995.

Thatcher, Ian D. *Trotsky*. Routledge Historical Biographies Series, edited by Robert Pearce. London: Routledge, 2003.

Trotski, Leo. *Mitt liv. Forsøk på en selvbiografi*. Translated by Helge Krog. Oslo: Tiden norsk Forlag, 1935.

———. *Mitt liv. Försök til en självbiografi*. Translated by Bertil Hansson. Stockholm: Natur och Kultur, 1937

Trotsky, Leon. *My Life: An Attempt at an Autobiography*. New York: Charles Scribner's Sons, 1930.

———. *The Revolution Betrayed: What Is the Soviet Union and Where Is It Going?* Translated by Max Eastman. Garden City, NY: Doubleday, Doran, 1937.

Tucker, Robert C. *Stalin in Power: The Revolution from Above, 1928-1941*. New York: W. W. Norton, 1990.

Ustvedt, Yngvar. *Verdensrevolusjonen på Hønefoss. En beretning om Leo Trotskijs opphold i Norge*. Oslo: Gyldendal norsk Forlag, 1974.

Van Heijenoort, Jean. *With Trotsky in Exile: From Prinkipo to Coyoacan*. Cambridge, MA: Harvard University Press, 1978.

Vold, Helge. *Helge Krog, 1889-1962. En biografi*. Oslo: Z-forlag, 2011.

Volkogonov, Dmitri. *Trotsky: The Eternal Revolutionary*. New York: Free Press, 1996.

"The Walter Held File." *Revolutionary History* 1, no. 4 (Winter 1988-1989).

Zachariassen, Aksel. *Fra Marcus Thrane til Martin Tranmæl*. Oslo: Arbeidernes Opplysningsforbund, 1962.

———. *På forpost. Oslo Arbeidersamfund, 1864-1964*. Oslo: Oslo Arbeidersamfund, 1964.

———. *Trygve Lie*. Oslo: Det norske Arbeiderparti, 1969.

Index

against, 102–3, 135–36; and Diego
Rivera, 252; and economic policies
of, 52, 80, 105, 212; and relations with
Norway, 169, 177, 219-20; and show
trials, 129–33, 135–38, 140, 143, 157,
168, 170, 174–76, 181, 183–84, 200,
203, 207, 212–13, 225–26, 229–30, 234,
236, 267, 278–79, 283–84, 290, 292–93,
295, 299–300, 303, 308–9, 311–12, 314,
316, 319, 322–23
Stauning, Thorvald, 21
Støstad, Sverre, 15
Støylen, Andreas, 277, 281–83, 288, 304
Stray, Christian, 304
Sund, Haakon, 121, 140, 167–68, 200, 208,
212
Sunde, Arne, 18–19
Sveen, Reidar, 118, 127–29, 134, 140–41,
165

Tarov, Arben, 94–96, 105–6
Terboven, Josef, 329
Thatcher, Ian D., 90
Thomas, Norman, 234
Thrane, Marcus, 263
Tomski, Mikhail, 141
Torp, Oscar, 14, 57, 197–98, 236–37, 321,
333–34
Tranmæl, Martin, 76, 146, 181–82; and
dispute with Trotsky before his arrival
in Norway, 64–66, 68–69, 70–73; as
editor of *Arbeiderbladet*, 37–40, 59,
88, 144, 155–56, 172–73, 178–79, 184,
240–42, 245–48, 251, 263–64, 272–75,
323; and Fourth International, 309,
311–14; and Labor Party, 45–55, 61–62,
95, 199, 221, 294–99, 301–3, 321; and
meeting with Trotsky at Wexhall, July
19, 1935, 78–79, 81, 156–58, 161, 258,
308; and Soviet show trials, 132–33,
136–37, 176, 298–99; and World War
II, 328, 330–32
Trotsky, Lev: and admission to Norway,
14–19, 20–21, 22–24, 25–44; anti-Semitism, object of, 39–40, 81, 113, 131,
214, 216, 220, 280; as "Crux," 97–98;
in Denmark, 19–22; and disputes with

Tranmæl 64–65, 68, 70–73; and expulsion from Norway, 3–7, 251–66; and
failure to found Fourth International
while in Norway, 98, 110–12; finances
of, 4, 28, 85, 87, 94, 186, 188, 202, 204,
209–13, 232, 260, 271; first marriage
of, 11; and France, 9, 20, 22, 24, 25–26,
27–28, 43, 63, 71, 77, 89, 109, 162, 242,
245; and foreign visitors to Wexhall, 42,
98, 99–103, 112, 127, 134, 158, 284–85,
287, 289; health of, 4, 10, 17, 22, 28–29,
33, 36, 81–85, 102–3, 110, 114, 191,
229, 233, 267, 305, 307; and journey
to Mexico, 266–71; stay at Knudsen's
Ringkollen cabin, 84–85; and national
election of 1936, 211–23; and Norderhov *kommune* tax dispute, 280–83; and
Puntervold salary dispute, 276–80; and
relations with U.S.S.R., 5–6, 8–10, 19,
21, 27, 29, 36, 50, 61–62, 77, 80, 87–88,
91, 94, 96, 106, 114, 130, 133–34,
135–36, 142, 161, 176, 186, 201, 212,
217–20, 226, 241, 243, 247, 285–86,
289; and *The Revolution Betrayed*,
90–92, 112, 192, 210–11, 230–31, 279;
and safety concerns, 6–7, 14–15, 28,
30, 186, 252, 254–55, 259–60, 320; in
Turkey, 5, 9, 13, 43, 99, 242, 245; and
vacation in southern Norway, 115–18;
and Wexhall burglary, 116, 118–28,
158–62, 248–51
Trotsky, Natalia Sedova, 11, 22, 74–77, 81–
82, 84, 86, 91, 100, 103, 112, 115, 145,
149, 151, 222, 287, 289, 301, 337–38;
departure from Norway, 3–7, 254–60,
266–71; in France, 11, 25; and internment in Norway, 143–44, 156, 163–65,
167, 173–74, 183–86, 189–92, 209, 212,
228, 232–34, 262, 264; in Mexico, 275,
281–82, 326; in Norway, 7–8, 17, 27–34,
42–43; and relations with U.S.S.R.,
33–34, 93–94, 117–18

Ullevål Hospital, 83–85, 87, 102
Urbye, Andreas, 168, 174–76, 207
Urbye, Robert A., 120–22, 124–25, 165

www.ingramcontent.com/pod-product-compliance
Lightning Source LLC
Chambersburg PA
CBHW030253100426
42812CB00002B/421